An Admiral's Yarn

Naval War College
Historical Monograph Series
No. 14

The historical monographs in this series are book-length studies of the history of naval warfare, edited historical documents, conference proceedings, and bibliographies that are based wholly or in part on source materials in the Historical Collection of the Naval War College. Financial support for research projects, conference support, and printing is provided by the Naval War College Foundation.

Our cover photograph is of Admiral Harris Laning, U.S. Navy, commanding the Battle Force, U.S. Fleet, standing at the stern of his flagship, the battleship *California*. Steaming astern in column open order are the *New York* (nearest), *Oklahoma*, and two of the *New Mexico* class. Cover designed and prepared by Patrick F. Rossoni.

Photographs kindly provided by Dr. Evelyn Cherpak of the Naval War College Naval Historical Collection, reproduced by Thomas W. Cookingham of the Naval War College Photography Department, and prepared for publication by Patrick F. Rossoni of the Naval War College Graphic Arts Division.

Where required, assistance in identifying subjects in photographs was graciously provided by Frank Uhlig, Jr., Editor Emeritus, Naval War College Press; Dr. John B. Hattendorf, Ernest J. King Professor of Maritime History at the Naval War College; Dr. Thomas C. Hone, Industrial College of the Armed Forces; and Robert M. Cembrola, Curator, Naval War College Museum.

The editors of the Naval War College Press also thank Gina Vieira, Jeremiah Lenihan, and Samuel Johnson of the publications department at the College for their diligence and patience in typing this monograph through its many phases of editing.

Finally, the editors express their special gratitude to all the members of the Naval War College Foundation, whose generosity made possible the publication of *An Admiral's Yarn*. Captain Elizabeth Wylie, U.S. Navy (Retired), Executive Director of the Foundation, was a constant source of encouragement in this project.

An Admiral's Yarn

by

Harris Laning

Admiral, United States Navy, Retired

With an Introduction

by

Mark Russell Shulman

Edited

by

Mark Russell Shulman

and the

Naval War College Press Staff

Naval War College Press
Newport, Rhode Island
1999

Library of Congress Cataloging-in-Publication Data

Laning, Harris, 1873-1941
    An Admiral's Yarn / by Harris Laning; with an introduction by Mark Russell Shulman ; edited by Mark Russell Shulman and the Naval War College Press Staff.
    p.   cm.—(Naval War College historical monograph series ; no. 14)
    ISBN 1-884733-12-3
    1. Laning, Harris, 1873-1941. 2. Admirals—United States Biography. 3. United States. Navy—Officers Biography.
I. Shulman, Mark R. II. Naval War College (U.S.) III. Title. IV. Series: U.S. Naval War College historical monograph series ; no. 14.
    V63.L36A3 1999
    359'.0092—dc21
    [B]   99-30641
                                                                               CIP

Printed in the United States of America

Dedicated to my wife—
Charming companion, devoted pal, and staunch supporter
in my adventure

Midshipman Harris Laning, USN, U.S. Naval Academy, Annapolis, Maryland, class of 1895.

Contents

Foreword by Vice Admiral A. K. Cebrowski		ix
Introduction by Mark Russell Shulman		xi
I	Boyhood	1
II	Leaving Home	7
III	I Join the Navy and Take a Cruise	15
IV	At the Naval Academy	21
V	At Sea as a Middy	29
VI	Middy Days in Puget Sound	35
VII	Middy Days in Southern California	43
VIII	In the *Oregon*	49
IX	The Woods Again	61
X	Still in Wood	71
XI	Off to War in a Monitor	79
XII	In Manila Bay	85
XIII	Insurrection in the Philippines	95
XIV	Around Luzon in a Gunboat	103
XV	More Gunboating	111
XVI	In the *Monadnock* Again	119
XVII	Ordered Home	127
XVIII	Annapolis Once More	135
XIX	In the *Dolphin*	143
XX	A Painful Interlude	149
XXI	More of the *Dolphin*	153
XXII	A New Shooting Game	163
XXIII	Another Season with Small Arms	171
XXIV	In a Battleship Once More	177
XXV	A Trip Around the World	183
XXVI	A New Type of Work	191
XXVII	The Olympic Games	195

Contents

XXVIII	In Destroyers	207
XXIX	Commanding a Destroyer Flotilla	217
XXX	War	223
XXXI	The First Transatlantic Flight	235
XXXII	London and Paris	245
XXXIII	Destroyers after the War	253
XXXIV	Naval War College Student	261
XXXV	A Vacation in the Oregon Woods	265
XXXVI	On the War College Staff	273
XXXVII	Commanding a Battleship	283
XXXVIII	We Visit the Antipodes	289
XXXIX	We Return to the U.S.A.	299
XL	Shore Duty Again	305
XLI	At Sea as a Rear Admiral	311
XLII	A Cruise to Europe	317
XLIII	President of the War College	327
XLIV	Interlude at Sea	337
XLV	Vice Admiral	343
XLVI	In Heavy Cruisers	351
XLVII	We Change Oceans	361
XLVIII	Four-Star Admiral	371
XLIX	A Transcontinental Cruise	379
L	Commanding a Naval District and Navy Yard	387
LI	The Naval Home	393
	USS *Laning* history	395
	Appendix I	397
	Opening address delivered before the Naval War College staff and classes of 1931 on 2 July 1930.	
	Appendix II	403
	Revised version (in May 1933) of Laning's thesis written while a student ten years earlier, "The Naval Battle."	
	Endnotes	449

Foreword

Established in 1975, the Historical Monograph Series serves the specific purpose of publishing research that is based upon sources found in the Naval Historical Collection of the Naval War College. Hence, the College not only encourages scholarly examination of its remarkable archival holdings but provides a medium to display valuable historical work done for the benefit of a much larger audience of interested scholars and readers.

Admiral Harris Laning was President of the Naval War College from 1930 to 1933, and quite naturally his papers, including the manuscript of his memoirs, were archived in the Naval Historical Collection of the College. They had lain there for decades until Dr. Mark Shulman, a historian of considerable distinction, provided us with this opportunity to study and enjoy *An Admiral's Yarn,* the memoirs of Admiral Laning.

Had these recollections been in essence *merely* a "yarn" or the reminiscences of a distinguished naval officer and former head of this institution, the criteria for publication in this series would not have been met. In fact, though, Admiral Laning's career coincided exactly with the rise of the United States Navy from a small and technologically obsolete service to the world's largest and, in most respects, most advanced naval organization. His leadership of the Naval War College occurred when many of the ideas about the conduct of naval warfare received detailed attention from a great number of men who would implement those ideas a dozen years later.

While no single person can encompass every aspect of an era—even within the confines of a single profession—and no educational institution can adequately address all the requirements that its graduates subsequently will need, in *An Admiral's Yarn,* we are offered a glimpse of the experiences and thinking of a man who served in and eventually guided the United States Navy in a lifetime marked by enormous change. We observe his own awareness, sometimes approaching disbelief, of the transformations he had witnessed and his responsibility to grow, to abandon familiar ways, and to lead his service into an exciting albeit confusing future.

Dr. Shulman and the editors of the Naval War College Press have produced a highly readable and enjoyable volume in our Historical Monograph Series. Working from a typescript kept in the College's archive, they have corrected, annotated, and edited the text for today's readers. (Historians are invited, of course, to consult Admiral Laning's papers at the Naval War College.) It is my pleasure to offer *An Admiral's Yarn* for the edification and enjoyment of anyone

An Admiral's Yarn

who wishes to understand how to live though change with professional dedication and good humor.

A. K. CEBROWSKI
Vice Admiral, U.S. Navy
President, Naval War College

Introduction

by

Mark Russell Shulman

HARRIS LANING SERVED as an officer in the United States Navy from 1891 to 1937. As well as anyone, he represents the men who built up the service into the world's greatest maritime fighting force. Born in 1873, when the old Navy's fighting effectiveness was at its nadir, he joined the service during the "era of the battleship." Captain Alfred Thayer Mahan had recently published his *The Influence of Sea Power upon History, 1660–1783*, and the U.S. Navy had begun to modernize and professionalize itself, constructing its first steel battleships to replace those warships remaining from the Civil War era. The Navy from which Laning eventually retired in 1937 was arguably the world's greatest, boasting fifteen dreadnoughts that cruised alongside aircraft carriers and fleet submarines. With the exception of the carriers and submarines, Laning served in every type of fighting ship: frigate, monitor, gunboat, destroyer, cruiser, and battleship. Admiral Laning's final cruise, as commander of the Battle Force, U.S. Fleet, culminated his long and distinguished service in the United States Navy.

Laning epitomizes the finest of a generation of naval leaders who viewed "Neptune [as] God, Mahan his prophet, and the United States Navy [as] the only true Church."[1] While Mahan never detailed specifics for effecting his geopolitical theories, his blue-water doctrine delineated and even circumscribed American naval thought in the several decades preceding World War Two. For much of his career, Laning, who had earned a reputation in some naval circles as a premier tactician, devised the tactical methods by which the Navy planned to implement blue-water strategy. This Mahanian philosophy called for control of

---

Mark Russell Shulman studied at Yale (BA), Oxford (M.St.), and the University of California at Berkeley (Ph.D.), and Columbia University, School of Law (J.D.). He has served as an Olin Fellow at Yale's International Security Program and as a Bradley Fellow at the National Strategy Information Center. He has also taught history and international affairs at Yale, Columbia University's School of International and Public Affairs, and at the United States Air War College. He is the author of *Navalism and the Emergence of American Sea Power, 1882–1893* (1995) and co-editor of *The Laws of War: Constraints on Warfare in the Western World* (1994). Dr. Shulman has also written numerous articles and book chapters on military history and national security affairs.

An Admiral's Yarn

the seas by fleets of battleships—in distinct contrast to the Navy's earlier system of sea denial, which combined cruisers for commerce-raiding with monitors and fortresses for coastal defense. Mahan's notions of a decisive battle were axiomatic to the new American Navy after the 1890s, eradicating all support for the tradition of sea-denial. In theory at least, the battle fleet would obviate long wars and the destruction of life-bearing commerce.[2] True to Mahan's devotion to decisive gun battles, Laning and most leading naval officers of his generation viewed carriers and submarines as peripheral to U.S. strategic, operational, and tactical doctrine. By the time of Laning's death in 1941, however, this view had become antiquated.

Harris Laning was born into a well-respected, rural, southern Illinois family. His father was a banker and his grandfather a Congressman. Healthy, active, and well-connected, Harris secured a Congressional appointment to the Naval Academy in 1891. The previous November, his brother-in-law, John McAuley Palmer, had taken young Harris to the first Army-Navy football game, hoping to encourage the lad to enroll in Palmer's alma mater, West Point. The effort backfired, however, when Navy won (24–0). Laning began preparations for the Annapolis entrance exams. Nonetheless, he remained close to the Palmers, even in latter years, as he moved from station to station. In 1900 he married Mabel Clare Nixon, a Californian. The Lanings' daughter, Hester Marie, grew up primarily in her mother's care, residing generally at shore establishments along the eastern seaboard. She recalls that Laning found his family to be a constant source of joy and support.

Laning's dossier as a midshipman fits the typical profile, as noted by a social historian of the Navy, Peter Karsten. Approximately 65 percent of the officer candidates were from the business or professional classes, as was young Laning. He was of the white race of western European descent as were all midshipmen during that period. In addition to his experience at the Army-Navy game, his decision to join the service was influenced by a family member's profession as well as by his own readings of the various navy-oriented novels of the nineteenth century. Like 40 percent of his Annapolis classmates, Laning was a member of the Episcopalian Church. Some in his family preferred, as did the families of many of his classmates, that he join the priesthood of the Church rather than that of Neptune.[3]

Ethnocentricity and racial arrogance, which precluded understanding and acceptance of other cultures and standards, remained a hallmark of the pre-World War II Navy. These prejudices were reinforced by decades of inculcation that extended into the 1930s during Laning's tenure as president of the Naval War College. For instance, the pseudo-scientific racist lectures of Dr.

Introduction

Lathrop Stoddard, such as "Racial Aspiration as the Foundation of National Policy," were presented to the staff and students at Newport throughout the 1930s.[4] Thus, in comparison to the more innovative professions that were emerging or changing in the late nineteenth century, the Navy suffered from such a homogeneous background among its officers that the scope of critical thinking and creativity was limited. Some historians contend that it was this focus that permitted American strategists to disregard the threat of a Japanese attack in 1941.[5] The interface between this background and the occasionally repressive Mahanian doctrine gave birth to a group disparagingly labeled "The Gun Club." Yet it was to this group that the nation delegated its first lines of defense. And throughout Laning's career, this line generally deterred enemy aggression.

Although known to some as "the greatest tactician in the United States fleet in recent years, perhaps in this century," Laning fought in neither of the declared wars in which the United States engaged during his career.[6] His active and dangerous service was in the various "Progressive Era" constabulary conflicts in the Philippines, China, and Mexico. Within this framework Laning achieved notable success, and within this context he wrote his autobiography.

The genre of naval officers' memoirs was well established when Laning began his writing in 1937. Many naval leaders had profited from their published memoirs; major commercial houses such as Harper's and D. Appleton frequently printed and reprinted these lucrative books.[7] Laning's completed work, however, has remained unpublished for over half a century, although not for lack of historical or even literary value; it is replete with both. Rather, the timing of his career and World War Two obscured the work's significance. Hence, while Laning finished a polished manuscript shortly before his death, he was not able to see it through to publication, and a decade passed before his widow compiled the typescript that was eventually entered into the Naval War College archives. There it lay for several more decades, available, but examined only by a handful of naval scholars.[8]

In the decades following his death, publications on World War II proliferated, obscuring the service careers of the prewar era. Hence, Laning's career came to be seen essentially as that of a peace-time leader of a force oriented for war. During the First World War he played a crucial role in organizing personnel—fashioning the shaft for the Navy's spear.[9] A leader of men and a superb organizer, Laning frequently did his best work behind the scenes. For example, during the First World War, as acting Chief of the Bureau of Navigation (which was then responsible for personnel matters), Laning helped facilitate the extraordinarily rapid expansion of personnel from 60,000 to

An Admiral's Yarn

500,000 within one and a half years. In the two decades that followed, Laning and his cohorts trained the succeeding war-time leaders, built many of their ships, and laid the groundwork for much of the strategy and tactics of the Second World War. Nonetheless, few of the officers of Laning's generation published memoirs, because, as scapegoats for the tragedy at Pearl Harbor, they had fallen into disrepute despite their crucial roles in preparing the generation that won the war at sea. Consequently, Laning's neglected account of the Navy he helped to build, and the life he lived, make *An Admiral's Yarn* a unique historical chronicle.

During his three tours at the Naval War College, Laning outlined a theory of tactics upon which the Navy relied for decades.[10] Fleet Admiral Chester Nimitz later lauded the tactical education he received at the college in 1921-1922, declaring that "the courses were so thorough that, after the start of World War II, nothing that happened in the Pacific was strange or unexpected."[11] Laning's layout of the "Naval Battle" detailed four phases of an operation: approach, deployment, engagement, and follow-up. This outline presented tacticians with the paradigm within which to focus their efforts.

Laning himself concentrated on the follow-up, making it clear that the key to all tactics "lies in that phase."[12] With the focus of "follow-up," and echoing his sometime mentor, William S. Sims, Laning emphasized the importance of fire control and the need to retain position in the line. Emphasizing the importance of a lesson brought home during the Battle of Jutland, Laning noted that ships in a confused order are more valuable to concentrated and devastating gunfire.[13] As did most of his contemporaries, Laning continued to focus his intellectual energy on battle-fleet tactics throughout the 1920s—a period during which even the War College digressed from its priority on history and strategy, shifting to emphasis on engagement. Within its paradigm, this emphasis on daylight gunfire was highly successful. Indeed, the U.S. Navy set the international standards by which other fleets were judged, using such novel tools as the Ford instrument and the Royce clock.[14]

In the early 1930s, at approximately the time he attained flag rank, Laning gained a broader vision and awareness of the value of historical inquiry to the study of strategy. Thus, during his tour as president of the War College, he developed a deeper strategic vision that complemented his long-standing and highly respected tactical views. These new perspectives, as we shall see, grudgingly acknowledged a place for non-Mahanian craft, although always within the context of a line of battle. With his personal development, Laning strengthened and persistently shaped the nation's defense. His tale is the eloquent and personal record of these efforts.

Introduction

The literary merit of *An Admiral's Yarn*, and that of several other naval memoirs, enhances understanding of the evolving world view of American naval officers in the emerging century. Much of the discourse appears to support Robert Jordan's conclusion that "American notions of the proper way to organize force in international society are outgrowths of British thought."[15] By the late nineteenth century, the new American Navy had come to emulate much of the Royal Navy, not only in tonnage and type of ship but also in personal attitudes.[16] Inherent in Laning's memoirs and those of his peers is an assumed moral, and especially cultural, superiority that echoes much British imperial literature.

Written before the Japanese Pacific onslaught of 1941–1942, *An Admiral's Yarn* presents a confident and competent imperialistic outlook. Three literary techniques that are typical of this era's naval memoirs provide narrative texture and insights into the specific brand of American brashness: self-effacing heroism, cosmopolitan parochialism, and objective absolution.

Laning's literary self-effacement is apparent early in the story. While in his first command, in command of the captured Spanish gunboat, *Panay*, during the Philippine-American war (1899), Ensign Laning consistently endured the physical duress of heat, fatigue, and danger.

> Small and cramped as our ships were, no one could leave them without danger of being killed or captured, and we were ever facing catastrophe when we moved about in those dangerous waters. We lived through all those troubles only to encounter a more trying and dangerous one, when we met a typhoon as we stood down the China Sea returning to Manila.[17]

Fighting the storm for three days left Laning exhausted. As his narrative continues, he temporarily abandons the first person to applaud his own heroics. "Then the Captain made a rousing speech toasting the officers and men of the *Panay* for their wonderful achievement."[18] When Laning attempted to rise, he found that he could not move. "The doctor rushed to me and although he found me clear as a bell mentally, I was paralyzed from head to foot from sheer physical exhaustion."[19] Apparently the doctor validated that Laning in fact could not move, thus rendering Laning's description of his struggles more objective, credible, and sympathetic.

An Admiral's Yarn contributes a temperate affirmation of America's uniquely admirable qualities: moral rectitude, industriousness, and Christian mission. In a career that spanned nearly half a century, Laning observed many cultures, peoples, and customs which, while frequently entertaining and even delighting him, also left him convinced of the special and even "fittest" nature of American

An Admiral's Yarn

culture. This affirmation is apparent during the narration of his first voyage abroad, which included an extended visit to the then-Republic of Hawaii.[20]

In Hawaii, Ensign Laning encountered a culture that he chose to judge by the standards of his own society. He selected entertainment based on indigenous criteria, but failed to appreciate the geniality and artistry of a culture so unlike his own. He noted that he attended "an old-time Hawaiian hula dance, which in those days decidedly lacked refinement."[21] He left early, without friendly discourse with anyone, and observed that "what the outcome of an ancient hula was supposed to be, I can only guess, but it evidently was to offer the dancers to the guests."[22]

Laning continues: "A week or two went by before Dan [an American civilian friend] and I were invited to another party. This one was to be a luau, or native feast, attended by the leading Hawaiians of Honolulu—a very fine affair of its kind and Dan and I were the only white people invited. . . ."[23] Leading citizens were those who had most thoroughly adapted to American ways—"[a]ll spoke English perfectly and dressed in the height of American fashion."[24] Unfortunately, Laning's appetite was lost when he tasted a snail. He failed to enjoy the luau despite the fact that "after two or three hours [the guests] moved to a large lanai where native musicians had assembled and [they] danced in the usual formal European way."[25] But "that form of dancing did not continue long. The musicians, having imbibed freely of swipes [rum], ceased playing waltzes and two steps—and from then on there were only native airs that gradually became more and more temperamental and seductive."[26]

Once again, Laning and his friend left early, and indignant. Although logic suggests that one might well expect alcohol and sensuality to be found at a native luau, Laning was piqued. Such moral rigidity questions the measures of his tolerance and the extent to which this trait may have been reflected in the young officer's relationships with his crew. It also could be proposed that this puritanism supported the proclivity of Laning's generation to ignore the capabilities and power of non-Anglo-Saxons. The cultural superiority they felt may have blinded them to the power of insurgency or, in this case, the possibility of warfare waged without the goal of engaging in a decisive battle.

Interestingly, however, the journal that Ensign Laning kept during his first visit to Guam is generally less judgmental than his later autobiography. For instance, he commented on the fine appearance of the native women and concluded, "they are very bashful and seeing strangers usually run away." Laning found these people to be thoroughly decent. Concluding a long journal entry, he commented, "I am very glad to have seen Guam."[27] Perhaps the autobiography's moralizing reflects more of the retired admiral's somewhat rigid *persona* than do the contemporary perceptions in the diary of the impressionable ensign on his first tour of the Pacific.

Quite naturally, an autobiographer will present explanations to his advantage for the blemishes on his record. Laning explained one such occurrence, which obviously weighed heavily on his pride. In 1934, while Commander Cruisers, Scouting Force, U.S. Fleet, Laning raised his three-star flag in the new cruiser *Chicago*.[28] One foggy morning his flagship collided with a steamer. Although the *Chicago* was not seriously damaged, two officers died. "The next day, front pages of newspapers the country over were devoted to the thrilling yarn."[29] Although Laning, as the flag officer, was merely a passenger on the *Chicago*, he obviously felt the need to exculpate himself and his command. Shortly thereafter, a Navy Court of Inquiry met to assign responsibility for this embarrassing incident.

Laning's journal iterates the court's findings to be certain that the outcome is perfectly clear. He first observes, "As was to be expected, the court placed the entire blame on the freighter." He notes further, "the blame for the collision was officially placed on the freighter." For the third time on one page, he comments that "it should be a comfort to Americans to know that in the case of the *Chicago* collision, the courts placed the entire blame on the freighter."[30] It was a comfort conspicuously shared by the author. Here Laning uses ostensibly unassailable court findings to repudiate blame. His balance between objective (or impersonal) writing and his personal reflections marks the texture of this autobiography.

Laning's career of writing and action also sheds light on the history of early U.S. naval aviation and submarine warfare. In many instances he acknowledges the increasing importance of aircraft to naval warfare. Paradoxically, his career represents a study in how the Navy continued to rely on surface ships, a policy that was detrimental to its capacity to engage in the type of war for which the Japanese were prepared by late 1941. It is not that Harris Laning dismissed air, or even sub-surface, power or denied them a place in strategic doctrine. But his hesitancy to grasp their significance and his affinity for battleships leave insufficient his support for the claim in *An Admiral's Yarn* that "it mattered not to the Navy what type or types of craft—surface, sub-surface, or air—might dominate the war, only that the United States be better prepared to use them than anyone else."[31] More farsighted naval aviation enthusiasts such as Bradley Fiske and William Moffett, and the more aggressive of the submarine commanders, were forced to fight for decades for grudging support from "The Gun Club."

Aircraft and torpedo design did catch up with the enthusiasm of farsighted naval officers, but only in the late 1930s. With hindsight, we see that many

An Admiral's Yarn

officers could have done a great deal more to recognize the potential of air and undersea power. As early as 1916, Fiske had called for support of naval aviation, saying "the torpedo plane under favorable conditions would make the $20,000 airplane a worthy match for a $20,000,000 battleship."[32] But until the close of World War One, Laning and most other officers ignored air power. After all, his previous military service—in the imperial wars of 1898–1915—had been in gunboats and battleships that had never faced a serious threat from the air. During the following era, Laning took time to adjust to post-1914 tactics, and this included the dimensions of submarine and air warfare.[33]

It was only during his tenure as chief of staff to the Commander, Destroyer Force, in 1919, that Laning advanced his first formal consideration of air power. Laning's post had been created in 1913 by the ever-innovative William Sowden Sims to help ensure that "the torpedo fleet could be made an enormous board game . . . for trying out all kinds of maneuvers at small expense. There is a lot to be learned . . . by study combined with actual maneuvers."[34] By 1919 this gaming included tactics to defend the fleet against aerial and submarine attack. To this end the Chief of Staff, Destroyer Force, was among those compelled to consider the new and developing threats as they related to surface ships. In planning the defense of the line, Laning was at his most creative.

Air power after the war still had not an irrefutable capability to destroy warships—a capacity moot even after 1921 when General William "Billy" Mitchell's army bombers sank the captured German battleship *Ostfriesland*. For the most part, "the U.S. Navy took the view that carrier-borne aircraft would be useful principally in scouting for the main battle fleet. [Only] a few renegade thinkers had more expansive ideas of what is now called a power-projection role against targets ashore."[35] However, the literature promised a threat limited only by the speed with which the ideas could be translated into reality. Many air theorists at this point were predicting extraordinary growth in the potential for air forces to decide military outcomes. Laning, like most of his peers, reacted cautiously, with limited speculation on these forecasts: "either submarines or aircraft, or a combination with or without surface craft, may to a great extent upset the old order."[36]

Laning's initial evaluation of air power while Chief of Staff, Destroyer Force, involved designing and effecting the provision of support for the first successful transatlantic flights—the Navy-Curtiss seaplanes (NCs). Consequently, he framed his perspective of air power as it related to surface ships in 1919, when the bombs were light and battleships were still regarded as unassailable from the air. Accordingly, his strategic vision restricted air power to only an ancillary role.

Introduction

Chapter XXXI of his *Admiral's Yarn*, which discusses this time during his career, does not mention the potential of air power for military purposes.

Chapter XXXVI recounts Laning's service on the Naval War College staff and gives a clue as to how he was able to continue to underestimate the significance of air and submarine power. He viewed them as merely tactical threats to the battle line and implicitly assumed that only actions involving opposing battle lines could be "major naval battles." His observation that "[a]t the time the World War ended, neither submarines nor aircraft had taken part in a major naval battle, so no one knew much about their use" embodies Laning's Mahanian orientation.[37] So thoroughly did he reject notions of sea power that did not include decisive fleet operations that he was blinded to the significant achievements of the *guerre de course* of the German U-boats. For Laning, the German war against shipping was not a "major naval battle" meriting examination for its implications for future naval warfare.[38] "Changes in tactics . . . were very great [but the] fundamental principles of fighting that centuries of war had proved to be immutable were of course the same as ever."[39] Laning viewed submarines, and by extension, airplanes, as cause for concern only for their effect upon this traditional form of fleet action.

Historian Paul Kennedy has suggested that the pervasiveness of the Mahanian lessons of history allowed naval officers to ignore other interpretations of the past and of strategy. "Successful admirals made their reputations in gunnery practices and fleet maneuvers, not in their knowledge of Thucydides, Clausewitz or other works of broad military history."[40] This focus fostered in Laning an absence of long-range vision and his conviction that long-standing fundamental principles of fighting were immutable. And yet, Kennedy notes, "There was, for example, *nothing* in the actual strategical circumstances of 1917–18 which conformed with the assumptions of the U.S. Navy prior to 1914."[41] But American admirals, including Laning, saw the naval war as a departure from the norm rather than as a harbinger of change.

The events of the 1920s did little to encourage Laning to revise further his opinions. The Washington Naval Conference codified this approach and severely limited the nascent development of carriers, while restricting only the quantitative growth of battleships. Consistently acknowledging a mostly defensive role for air power in naval war, Laning found himself protesting against an over-reliance upon airplanes. In contrast to Mitchell—a visionary who frequently ignored contemporary reality—Laning considered strategic situations for what they were at the time, demonstrating little imagination for what they could become.

An Admiral's Yarn

In a statement that he gave to a newspaper in 1923, Laning granted that airplanes were useful for scouting, skirmishing, and sometimes even bombing surface craft, but only under ideal circumstances.[42] The headline, however, accurately characterized the breadth of his opinions: "Captain Laning Ridicules Air Enthusiasts." The article opened, "Distinguished aviation enthusiasts are jeopardizing the national defense by theories that shake the faith of the country in the Navy." In this statement, Laning appeared to conflate the Navy and battleships and further cloud the reality of the Navy's mission, which was to *assure* the nation of its security, not merely to *reassure* the nation.

Mahanian philosophy appears to have limited Laning's perspective. "Planes," the article summarized with dangerous finality, "cannot dominate battleships."[43] Although Laning's argument was easily tenable in 1923, it would have been insightful for the Navy to be investigating what the effects of aircraft would be upon sea power in the forthcoming years. Since 1921, the Japanese navy had included three carriers.[44] By 1929, even after the United States had commissioned three carriers, many officers remained steadfast in their belief that air power posed little threat to sea power. And, despite the startling events in the year's war game (Fleet Problem IX), wherein American naval aviators "destroyed" the locks and land defenses of the Panama Canal, doctrine continued to lag behind the reality of deployment. For instance, the 1929 Naval War College *International Law Situations* casebook regarded aircraft as practical only for scouting, defending capital ships, or possibly for attacking merchant shipping.[45]

A few years later, during his tenure as president of the Naval War College, Laning's perspective had broadened through earnest interaction with war games and the college's study of history, strategy, and tactics. Indeed, in *An Admiral's Yarn*, he remarks on how much he learned during his tour. Unfortunately, the students did not profit as much as Laning, for they failed to respond positively to his new exhortations for imaginative approaches to naval warfare.[46]

In the 1929 war game, while Laning was serving as Commander Battleship Division Two of the Scouting Fleet at the behest of the fleet's commander, William V. Pratt, the *Saratoga* launched a surprise attack on the Panama Canal. The flat-top's air wing "destroyed" the defending aircraft on the ground as well as two of the canal's critical locks.[47] Shortly thereafter, Laning, as president of the War College (from 1930 to 1933), made several statements that strongly supported air power as a potential, albeit limited, offensive weapon. In so doing, Laning acknowledged the achievements of air power without speculating on its future. Three years later, as a referee, Laning observed a similar but larger air attack, this

Introduction

time on Pearl Harbor. Despite the precedent of Fleet Problem IX, this surprise attack also proved successful.

Thus it was only when he reached flag rank that Laning's strategic perspective broadened to include airplanes for power projection rather than strictly for the defense of capital ships. In testimony before the House Naval Affairs Committee in January 1932, Rear Admiral William A. Moffett, Chief of the Bureau of Aeronautics, included a supporting comment by Laning.[48] Laning's statement, which premised a situation of forward war against a continental power, was designed to emphasize the importance of constructing new aircraft carriers. Calling for more "Flying Deck Cruisers," he gave them a tough task: "Even with the present allowed tonnage for air carriers, we cannot hope to be as strong in the critical war areas as other countries can make themselves with shore based aircraft."[49] The statement implied the Navy's assumption of a forward maritime war strategy against the enemy's territory by expecting the carrier-based planes to engage those based on land.[50]

A year later, however, concluding his study and his presidency at the Naval War College, Laning again consigned air power to an ancillary role in battle, primarily for the protection of battleships from land-based aircraft. Even at this point, he resisted ascribing to it the potential to be a weapon for taking decisive offensive action against ships. "Great as will be the influence of aircraft in the trend of a naval battle, it is apparent that to get full results, the aircraft must be closely coordinated with the efforts of other types [of craft]."[51] (It was only in 1933, after Laning's presidency, that the college examined seriously the "accuracy and efficiency of aerial bombing.")[52] Similarly, in the same paper, Laning relegated submarines to an auxiliary role in the battle force—this despite the extraordinary commerce-raiding successes that U-boats had in the First World War. Because of his Mahanian orientation and Allied success in that war, Laning rejected a commerce-raiding strategy.[53]

His next two tours, as Commander, Cruisers, Scouting Force, U.S. Fleet (1933–1935), and then especially as Commander, U.S. Battle Force (1935–1936), did little to de-emphasize the relative importance of large, powerful surface fleets for control of the seas. Laning did, however, learn to rely upon his aircraft for attacking ships and bases—but still the focus was on decisive gun battles. At the Naval War College, he had supervised game exercises which, by their nature, focused his attention on battles. Once he returned to the Scouting and then the Battle Force, Laning continued to concentrate on the importance of traditional surface battles. Rear Admiral Harris Laning remained a battleship enthusiast into his 1937 retirement. He died on 2 February 1941, ten months before Japan's attack on Pearl Harbor forced the Navy to rethink air

An Admiral's Yarn

power, and approximately a year before it would turn to the new-found twin-pronged Pacific warfare strategy, a *guerre de course* fought by submarines and a *guerre d'escadre* fought by carrier-borne aircraft.[54]

This rendering of *An Admiral's Yarn* contains an edited version of the typescript that Laning's widow assembled some years after his death. Patricia Goodrich and the Naval College Press staff have edited the text for style. I have provided editorial comments, a few figures, and some background in the endnotes. My work on this project was supported by a grant from the Naval War College Foundation. At the College, Ernest J. King Professor of Maritime History, John Hattendorf, and Head Archivist, Evelyn M. Cherpak, generously helped guide *An Admiral's Yarn* to press. We are most grateful for the enthusiastic support of Mrs. D. Sergeant Pepper (Hester Laning), who provided the typescript and gave permission to publish it, as well as for the personal papers and photographs of her father, Harris Laning.

I

Boyhood

IT IS A FAR CRY from the rolling prairie of Illinois to the rolling sea, and a still farther cry from rowing flat-bottomed boats on the Sangamon River[55] to commanding the Battle Force of the United States Fleet. Nevertheless, for those of us fortunate enough to be born in the United States, such far cries are not uncommon, though naturally each one is a story all its own. As the far cry in my case was full of amusement for me and has seemed even of interest to those who have heard stories of it, there may be others who might enjoy hearing about it too. For them I spin my yarn again.

The little town, Petersburg,[56] where I was born, differs some from other towns in the Middle West. It sprawls along the banks of the Sangamon, in its valley, and on the hills that border it. Because of its hills, Petersburg looks unlike most prairie towns, but the difference is mostly in appearances, for in its life and habits, it is much like the others. Still, its differences are sufficient to make those who were born there, ever love Petersburg.

In 1839 my father was born in that town at a time when it consisted of only seven log houses. By the time I was born there in 1873, it had become a very pretty town of nearly three thousand people and has remained about the same ever since.

Small though Petersburg was, like all Middle West towns, it was a place of intense and sound Americanism. My earliest recollections are of the political "rallies" held there by the several parties and of the responsibility in citizenship felt by every inhabitant. Not only was every political question studied carefully and voted on, but each person did his utmost to argue everyone else to his point

An Admiral's Yarn

of view. I learned early what was expected of each one of us in our democratic form of government and that the responsibility of each individual was to express his personal viewpoint at the polls so that the opinion of the majority might be learned and carried out. Perhaps young people of today are still as much impressed with the responsibility of citizenship as I was, and I hope they are, so that the splendid system of government developed for the United States may continue.

Although my earliest impressions were of the importance of exercising the individual responsibilities of citizenship, my life as a boy was typical of a boy's life in a small town. We did all the things other young Americans did—we played games with each other, fought with each other, got in and out of scraps together, argued for and against the political views we picked up from our fathers, and in general behaved as most American youngsters. During the winter months, our free time was given to coasting, skating, sledding, sleighing parties, and such winter pastimes. When weather permitted, we played marbles. When the weather became warmer, out came the balls and bats. Ball playing held sway throughout the summer, but occasionally we collected birds' eggs or Indian relics, made swimming holes to enjoy all season, and went fishing, gathering berries along the way. We spent much time scouring the country 'round about and knew the woods well, the springs of water, and all the secrets of the forest. Summer was a busy and joyous time, and like most boys we were always sorry when fall came and we were obliged to return to school.

But even school had its points of interest. There were games of football—not like today's game but a game in which all hands could play on one side or the other and only kicking the ball was allowed. We had "shinny,"[57] in which everyone took part. For that game we made ourselves heavy shinny clubs with a knot or a bent at the end for hitting the shinny puck, which was always a good-sized tin can that soon became a small, heavy lump that bruised or cut badly if it hit one of us. Then too, we had "duck on rock," "coo-sheepie," "cross tag," "old man," and a complicated form of "prisoner's base." In the fall we gathered and stored our winter's supply of nuts, all of which grew wild and plentiful—black walnuts, butternuts, hickory, and hazel nuts, also pecans. When frost came we gathered paw-paws and persimmons.

Taken all in all, the boys of my time and town had a joyous young life. As a side issue during the winter months, some of us collected postage stamps, cigarette pictures, and even buttons. There was so much to do that boys I knew never had time to get into mischief. Leading this wholesome life, we became strong and healthy, each of us imbued with the highest, natural principles and ideals, each with a realization that upon reaching "man's estate" at the age of

Boyhood

twenty-one, we, too, would become voters, our votes of as much importance in establishing the policies of the country as those of men of long experience.

Coming through our youth with impressions of that kind, we boys must have had as sound an early training as American lads can receive, and yet there was another very definite influence directly available to us in Petersburg, which, as far as I am personally concerned, was perhaps the greatest of all influences in my life.

That influence was Abraham Lincoln. Although Lincoln was assassinated eight years before I was born, during my boyhood days in our town, he was being given the truly great place that he was to occupy in the United States and in the world.

Abraham Lincoln is the outstanding example of what a "far cry" may bring to an American boy. His example particularly affected us boys, because he had lived his young manhood in the very place where we were living, which was intensely interesting to us and brought home the wisdom of preparing ourselves for great responsibilities should they occur. This has been a valuable influence throughout my life.

Unless familiar with the territory thereabouts, people do not generally associate the name of Abraham Lincoln with the town of Petersburg, yet Petersburg grew out of the Lincoln village of New Salem. It is even said to have been surveyed and laid out by Lincoln himself when the village of New Salem was moved down the river a mile or two and became Petersburg. My boyhood home was only a short distance from where Lincoln actually lived and worked. Consequently, we boys, who were endeavoring to learn about Lincoln as a youth, did not have far to go for the facts.

When the village was moved down the river, New Salem, as such, disappeared. As a boy I was told that some of the New Salem houses, all of logs, were torn down and transported to Petersburg to be set up again. Anyhow, there was no village of New Salem when I was a lad, although since then the village has been completely restored as a state park and is perhaps the most interesting of all the Lincoln memorials in our country today.

However, we boys fairly haunted the site of Lincoln's home, treasuring any relics of Lincoln we might find there and trying always to learn more of his young life, as there were people still living who had lived in or near New Salem and who had known him personally. There were many friends and acquaintances who were only one generation removed from actually living there with Lincoln and who could furnish true stories and tales about him.

During my boyhood, the site of New Salem had become pastureland with large trees which had probably been there since the days of Lincoln; part of the

An Admiral's Yarn

limestone foundation and remainder of the cellar of "Offutt's Store," where Lincoln worked, were still there. Also there remained a few of the earth foundations upon which the log house of the Lincolns had stood. Perhaps the most interesting of all was the old grist mill and the dam across the Sangamon River, at the foot of which was the old village. Although Lincoln probably never worked in that mill, we boys never tired of visiting it. We particularly liked to fish in the water below the dam, and when the water ran over it, we often caught good-sized strings of "croppies," that delectable fish found only in the Mississippi basin, as well as bass, sunfish, and pike.

Unfortunately the old mill and dam disappeared. As for the mill, I well remember the night it burned, for looking out of the window when the fire bells rang, I saw a considerable flare to the southwest and thought it was a farmhouse. When morning came, we learned that some tramps camping in the old mill had caused the fire, and there being no means for fighting it, the old landmark had quickly burned to the ground. I will ever remember my heartache when I learned that the "old mill," so revered by us all as the most important landmark of Lincoln's time in New Salem, was gone forever. (I understand that both the mill and the dam are being restored as part of New Salem Park.)[58]

There were, of course, other relics of Lincoln which we were constantly hunting—stones from his house foundation, the mill and dam and parts of rail fences which we considered great treasures, as "Old Abe" was often spoken of as the "rail splitter." We always thought the best of the rail fences must have been made by Lincoln.

Among the old houses moved from New Salem to Petersburg was one in which Lincoln had actually lived, and when it was later torn down, a woodworker in Petersburg, with considerable foresight, bought the logs—there being no doubt of their authenticity—and made what we called "Lincoln canes," one side of them bearing a carving of Lincoln's face. The carving was very clever and accurate, and he developed such a reputation that he had little difficulty selling his canes for five dollars each. When the carver needed money for a good time, he would sell a cane and then enjoy himself five dollars' worth!

The woodcarver did not confine his efforts to perpetuating Lincoln's features on canes, and his later work was of greater interest. As it happened, out of what was left of the basement of "Offutt's Store," two trees started to grow, with trunks of six or eight inches in diameter when I first saw them. Those trees held tremendous interest for us, because, although one was a sycamore and the other probably an oak, there seemed to be only one root. To us boys, the trees symbolized what Lincoln had done for the Union—binding the North and South together. Many visitors to the spot seemed to feel as we did.

The woodcarver too showed great interest in the trees and, to ensure their close relationship, made a splendid carving of Lincoln's face on the trunk of the sycamore tree, about eight or ten feet from the ground. Each spring thereafter, as the trees grew and changed, he made the necessary alterations in the face, thereby keeping the perfect likeness of Lincoln. What happened to the trees and the carved face during the last forty-five years since the woodcarver died I do not know, but I did not see a trace of them in the recently restored village of New Salem.

While all of us boys had our interests in Lincoln mementos, some of us developed a keenness for Lincoln lore and never tired of hearing the numerous stories about him. One of the points always being touched on by those who had known him in New Salem was his poverty and loneliness. Without parents to look out for him and help him, he had only that which he could provide for himself. It was very difficult for us to understand how Lincoln, born into poverty and without the benefit of parental guidance, accomplished greatness in the world. We thought seriously of preparing ourselves for great opportunities that might come our way and tried in every way to learn more about Lincoln lore of the neighborhood. At that time there were few books on his life as a young man, but numerous publications about what Lincoln did during the Civil War when he was President. Even in 1890, Henderson was still at work on his book of Lincoln, which dealt mostly with his political career and the Civil War—the most interesting phase of Lincoln's life.[59]

At that point, I received a book for Christmas called *Bluejackets of 61,* in which were accounts of the naval high spots of the Civil War, and through that book and another, titled *Sailor Life on Man of War and Merchant Vessel*, I developed a keen appetite for sea stories of all kinds but especially for naval history and naval yarn. I devoured Cooper's *Sea Tales, Midshipman Easy, Young American Abroad*, the *Yankee Middy* series, and such other sea tales and naval histories as were available.[60]

Thus there grew in me a great longing to be a naval officer and wear the navy uniform. Although I could not see such a life coming to me, I read about and was told by an uncle who graduated from the Naval Academy in 1870 what the mental requirements were at the Academy, and they seemed much too formidable for a boy of my ability.[61] Nevertheless, I fostered the longing, not mentioning it to anyone.

II

Leaving Home

I GRADUATED FROM THE PETERSBURG HIGH SCHOOL in 1890 at the age of sixteen. All during my last year there, I learned all I could about the schools of our country, especially where the boys wore uniforms and were under military training and discipline. There were many of them and selection was difficult, but those located on the Hudson River held special attraction for me. Then something happened that enabled me to make a decision—an old friend, Cadet John McAuley Palmer, came home from the U.S. Military Academy at West Point on his second class leave.[62]

John Palmer, who is now a brigadier general (retired) after a splendid career in the army, came to our house in Petersburg in the summer of 1890 to see my sister. They had been childhood sweethearts and eventually married after John's graduation. I was much impressed with John, but probably more so when I saw him in uniform. What he did and said was quite tops with me!

Like all West Pointers of that time, John did not think highly of the so-called "tin soldier schools," so when I spoke to him about going to a private military school, he was most disdainful. However, knowing my preference for ones on the Hudson River, and realizing that if I went East my sister might select a school there too, he took more interest in the matter and we decided upon Peekskill Military Academy, where I not only would be in a fine school but near enough to West Point to acquire an understanding of proper military life. Therefore, the following September found me entering that fine old school—the Peekskill Military Academy.

An Admiral's Yarn

Leaving home to go to a school a thousand miles away brought a great change in my life. While I had often been on trips to the larger mid-western cities, it had always been with my father. Entering the Academy was the beginning of life "on my own."

The change from boyhood homelife to military routine and discipline was a great one, but, happy as I had been in my early years, I was deeply interested and content at the Academy. Going East on the train, I met several other boys en route to Peekskill—some being "old boys" others "new"—but all friendly and willing to start me off the right way when we arrived at our destination.

No boy who goes to Peekskill Military Academy ever forgets it or loses his love for it, so in going there, I felt my choice a particularly fortunate one. I was assigned a room with another "new" boy from near New York City, whose father was an officer in what was then our largest condensed milk company, and Frank proved to be a fine, steady-minded roommate. We became great friends.

The Peekskill Military Academy is on a hill overlooking not only the village of Peekskill but also a considerable stretch of the Hudson River in its most picturesque spot. Frank and I had a room in what was known as the "upper tower" at the corner of the dormitory, which was shaped like an "L," and as this was above the top floor of the building, it had its own stairway; therefore, we had much more privacy and were somewhat segregated from the other cadets. Consequently, because of that and the beautiful views from the "upper tower," our rooms were most sought after and, until I entered that year, had always been reserved for "old boys." However, they abused this privilege, taking advantage of their isolation to smoke, have nightly feasts, and breaking other rules of the school, so a change was made in which Frank and I, joined by some other new boys, were assigned to the coveted tower. One boy was from New York City, one from Butte, Montana, and another from Anaconda, Montana. With boys of such widespread backgrounds, previously unacquainted, and all of them wishing to retain the delightful and highly prized rooms, we were careful about our conduct. However, some of the old boys did take advantage of our location to smoke, take unauthorized snoozes, even have feasts, but they usually avoided getting us into trouble. They being "old boys," we were rather in awe of them and did little to prevent their invasion.

One "old boy" I shall never forget hailed from a Dutch family in Pennsylvania. He had in his possession an old and very large Dutch pipe with a long, bent stem and high bowl. Berlinger was very proud of that pipe and took pride in making us boys think that he could not get along without smoking it. One day he filled it with tobacco and brought it to my room, supposedly for a smoke. Just as he lighted it, he jumped to his feet asking me to keep it going until

Leaving Home

he returned with a book he had forgotten. I was much flattered with the responsibility thrust upon me and began to draw hard on it. It was not the first time in my life that I had smoked a pipe, but one puff from this Dutch variety about knocked my head off and almost made me sick, so it took me some time to recover. Just as I was doing so, Berlinger returned. Although I was sitting up, the pipe was out, and when I asked what kind of tobacco he had put in it, he said "pure perique,"[63] and I noticed he did not relight it. I have not smoked pure perique since!

We did not depend entirely on "old boys" for excitement in the tower but occasionally had feasts of our own after receiving boxes from home. One we particularly enjoyed came to Frank each month filled with a great variety of delicious edibles, some of which were to be used with condensed milk, also enclosed. We all enjoyed the cakes and candies but found difficulty at first with the condensed milk—much too sticky and sweet, as made then, but the boy from Anaconda quickly took charge of the milk situation and devoured cans of it! Later, when I was at sea and the only milk available was the condensed variety, I could not use it.

The life at Peekskill was not all devoted to pleasure, for there was much serious work to be done in studies and drills in which we all made good progress. But when not engaged in those, there were many amusements, playing all the games for boys of our age—skating, coasting when ice and snow came, and roaming over the interesting hills when free. Saturdays were always enjoyable with its recreations, but especially so when we made excursions to numerous historical points around or near Peekskill. Mount Dunderbury, Bear Mountain, Iona Island, where the navy has a great ammunition depot,[64] and Anthony's Nose, a point famous during the Revolutionary War, were all to be seen from our windows but more interesting when visited—although to me, the Military Academy at West Point topped them all. Fortunately, my cadet friend there, whose interest in me led to my meeting many of his classmates, gave me considerable prestige among the boys at Peekskill, and I grasped every opportunity to go to West Point. In fact, for a time I thought that I would like to become a cadet. However, I remained true to my first love—the navy.

In November 1890 an event that affected my entire life thereafter came to pass. At that time I received from John Palmer an invitation to West Point on Thanksgiving Day to witness a football game between the Military and Naval academies—a rare treat indeed, as never before had either team been allowed to leave home base to play any game whatsoever.[65] That game was the start of what is now one of the most spectacular sporting events in our country—the Army-Navy Football Game! I do not remember that much attention was given

An Admiral's Yarn

to it in the newspapers, but there was much talk amongst the boys at Peekskill, as we knew something about West Point and most of us were supporters of the Military team. College football was not new in 1890, although it was practically so at the academies, and neither team knew much about the game nor did they seriously prepare for it, as there were no coaches—graduates or professionals—at that time.

At neither academy was there a regular football field, but a place was provided by roping off a section of the parade ground and marking out a field on it. A few chairs and temporary benches were placed along the sidelines for the spectators, who either stood up to watch the game or ran up and down the field to keep abreast of the play. At that first Army-Navy Game there were some temporary seats like circus stands along the center of the sidelines on one side of the West Point Cadets and some provided on the other side for Annapolis Cadets, since at that time and for several years after, only members of the team were allowed to leave the Academy for a game. Although the first game was played in the beautiful setting of West Point's Parade Ground, there was nothing of the great spectacle that Army-Navy games present today.

Cadet Palmer, being in his third year (second class) at the Point, took me with him to the seats of the "upper classmen" to watch the game, and I rooted for the Military Academy. It was the first game of college football that I had ever seen, but it did not take me long to realize that in the game they played, the Naval Academy team had much the better of it. I stuck to my guns in my choice of winner all during the game, but in spite of wanting the West Pointers to win, the Naval Academy came out on top, the score being 24-0.

One thing that especially interested and amused me was the way the navy team gave its signals, which were the commands used in the old "square-rigged" sailing ships, some of which were still in operation in the navy. Thus, when the navy had the ball, the team captain would shout "ready about," "station for stays," "haul taut, mainsail haul," "man the weather lifts and braces," "man clew garnets and buntlines," "all hands up anchor," "hoist away topsails," "man the cat," "heave 'round," "man the port battery," "shift pivot to starboard," etc. The West Point captain gave his signals entirely by numbers. However, later on, the West Point team added military commands to its signals. Thus, after calling the signal by number, the captain would add "company right wheel," "fours left," "forward double time," "charge bayonets," "commence firing," etc. Inasmuch as military commands were fairly well known to the Naval Cadets as well as to the spectators, and while amusing, they did not seem especially mysterious or efficacious and were given up later by both teams.

Leaving Home

Going back to Peekskill that night after the game, I thought long and hard about it and the idea came to me that there must be something especially wonderful about the training of the Annapolis team to make it superior to the mighty men at West Point. The following Sunday, when I wrote my father, telling him about the marvelous football game, I said that I would like to go to the Military Academy but much preferred Annapolis, not having any idea that something would come of it.

It so happened that about the time my father received my letter, the congressman from our district, William M. Springer, came to see Father at his office at the bank.[66] (By this time Father had founded the First National Bank of Petersburg, of which he was president until the time of his retirement.) Mr. Springer was an old and very close friend of my family, had been a leader in Congress for over eighteen years, and had known me from the time I was born. Hence, when Father read him my letter, he became greatly interested and said, "If Harris wants to go to Annapolis, I will see what I can do to send him there."

At that time, except for ten Presidential appointments a year, all appointments to the Naval Academy were made by Congressmen of various Congressional districts—each one being allowed to have one appointee as a Naval Cadet. The course at the Academy took six years to complete—four in Annapolis followed by two at sea as a Naval Cadet. Consequently, appointments from any one district were few and far between, so it was not surprising when word came later from Mr. Springer that our district had an appointee at the Academy who would not complete the course for about five years and there was little hope of a vacancy before I had passed the age limit for entrance. I was not too disappointed but rather surprised that Mr. Springer had thought of me at all.

Then occurred another coincidence of very great importance in my life, for on the next "semiannual exam," the appointee to the Naval Academy from our district "failed," and in March 1891, the Navy Department informed Congressman Springer that there was a vacancy at the Naval Academy for his district, and he at once thought of me. If I still wanted the appointment, I must telegraph him immediately. You can well imagine my excitement and joy, but I did not impart the news to anyone and there was no way to send a telegram until late afternoon after school hours—and how they dragged—but as soon as Release sounded, I ran down the hill to the telegraph office and sent a message to Mr. Springer saying, "You bet I want that appointment to the Naval Academy!"

It was not long after that I received my first communication from the Navy Department informing me that I had been nominated for appointment as Naval Cadet from the 13th Congressional District of Illinois and directing me to

An Admiral's Yarn

report to the Academy early in May (then less than two months away) for the examinations specified in a circular enclosed with the letter.

When I read that circular, I was truly awed, for not only did the mental requirements appear staggering to me, but also the physical qualifications seemed beyond those any boy might be expected to possess. It did not seem possible that I could meet them all, but I wanted to try—only I did not want anyone to know if I failed. It was decided that I should go at once to a Naval Academy "prep" school in Annapolis to prepare for the "exams" still six weeks away. The idea that I might fail in the "exams" made me particularly anxious that no one "at home," except my immediate family, know that I was taking them. But there was no way to keep the boys at Peekskill from knowing that I had left school, and why, but I did keep my Petersburg friends from learning of it by not changing my address. They continued to send letters to Peekskill for me, which my roommate, Frank, forwarded. My replies were also sent to him to post from Peekskill to be properly postmarked.

Having arranged for covering my trail, I was all set to leave Peekskill when my father arrived a few days later to take me to Annapolis. Leaving the Peekskill Military Academy, which I loved and where I had made so many good friends, was very hard indeed. I also had to give up my uniform of which I was so proud, as it was bad form to appear in a "tin soldier" outfit when taking "exams" for a national academy. However, I felt the loss of that uniform might not be for very long, as I was fully determined to return to Peekskill and finish my course in case I failed to become a Cadet.

The quaint, old city of Annapolis still remains very much as it was in 1891 when I arrived there. Many of its old buildings and houses have been rejuvenated, and while new ones have been built in both the city and the suburbs, the charm of Annapolis has not been spoiled. Although the capital of Maryland ever since it became a state, during my life, Annapolis had been famous not as a state capital but rather as the site of the U.S. Naval Academy.

When I went to Annapolis, the hotels were very old and small, and visitors did not often use them, preferring the homes of the delightful old families where paying guests were accepted and where they could enjoy true Maryland hospitality and entertainment. But even those charming old houses tended to follow Naval Academy dictates and traditions, and although most of them would take candidates for the Academy as guests, most candidates preferred to stay at the "prep school houses" for candidates. Thus, those preparing for the Academy were seldom in the life of either Annapolis or the Naval Academy.

In my own case, I entered Werntz' "prep school" as soon as I could, for with the exams only six weeks away, I had no time to waste. Professor Werntz, or

Leaving Home

"Bobby," as he was always called by candidates, had a particularly good record in preparing candidates, and as he had a large house, he took them in as boarders while coaching them. Candidates were not so numerous as they are now, because at that time it took six years to complete the course and Congressmen were allowed but one appointee at a time. Now, as well as the many Presidential and at-large appointments, Senators and Congressmen may have as many as five appointees at the Academy. The four-year course also increases the number of appointees.

Inasmuch as only a very few of the cadets that graduated then could be commissioned as ensigns in the navy, the entrance examinations and the course at the Naval Academy were made especially severe to ensure that only a few of the appointees would complete the course, and the candidates had to "bone" hard not only to enter but to stay there. We candidates had very little time to play or to get into mischief, and although a few who had been "prepping" for a long time might show a little "speed" on occasion, as a rule they all stuck close to the task ahead. It was not an easy one, for in order that we might have some understanding of what was expected of us in the mental examinations, Bobby would give us tests taken from former entrance "exams." To a new candidate they seemed staggering, especially as there was a time limit on all questions. Speed and accuracy in examinations were essential.

My first test as a candidate discouraged me, for while I might have attained a passing mark in most of the subjects had I been allowed sufficient time, I failed rather badly and this did not help my homesickness or loneliness one little bit! However, I wanted too much to become a Naval Cadet to give up, so I worked harder than ever to learn the newer, shorter, and better methods used at the Academy.

"Bobby" was not enthusiastic about my work and wrote to my father that as there was little likelihood of my passing the May examinations, it would be wise to have my appointment changed to take the September exams, which, if I studied with him in the interim, I might pass. However, when father wrote and asked what I thought about it, I told him I, at least, would try it in May. Then "Bobby" suggested to father that for a "consideration," he could put on more "steam" in my case, but my answer to that was that I was steaming as hard as I could and would go on as usual.

After two or three "test exams," I began to catch on, and by the time of the real exams, I felt I had a fair chance of passing them. In those days, candidates who failed in one or more subjects were allowed a re-exam immediately, and it was with great nervousness that we watched for the posting of the first marks. To

An Admiral's Yarn

my surprise and very great delight, I found I had passed in all subjects, so was left with only the physical tests—which I passed the next day.

After passing the entrance "exams" there were several steps for a candidate to take before becoming a Naval Cadet. First he had to register in the "big book" wherein were recorded his age and details regarding his parents and family, then he had to make a deposit of money necessary to pay the cost of his original outfit of clothes, after which came the usual oath to support the Constitution of the United States and to observe the country's laws and navy regulations.

While completing the preliminaries for entering the Academy, I immediately telegraphed my father, wrote letters to my relatives and friends, giving them the first information of my recent activities. One of the first letters was to my maternal grandmother who was very close to me all during my boyhood and who had tremendous interest in my future.

Grandmother was an Episcopalian, a pillar of the Church and well-versed in its doctrine and history. I always thought she might have missed her calling by not having been born a man and entered the ministry. Be that as it may, from the time of my earliest memory she seemed bent on my becoming a minister, and every Sunday I went to both Church and Sunday school. Under her guidance I learned a great deal about the Church but never told her that I did not intend to become a minister. When it was certain I was going to be a Naval Cadet, I wrote grandmother that I feared she would be very disappointed; she answered promptly saying that she had always hoped I would be a minister and ultimately a bishop, since our family had every other kind of representative, but she thought the next best thing was for me to be an officer in the United States Navy.

III

I Join the Navy and Take a Cruise

O N 19 MAY 1892, having completed the tests, I became a Naval Cadet.

The Naval Cadets of my time, like midshipmen of today, were grouped by classes as at colleges. However, at the Naval Academy, instead of being freshmen, sophomores, juniors, or seniors, we were named successively from the lowest as Fourth, Third, Second and First, the designations becoming effective each year on Graduation Day, usually the first Friday in June. Therefore, entering on 19 May, I did not become a Fourth Classman until all the classes moved up a notch at graduation time. Fourth and Third Classmen were known respectively as "plebes" and "youngsters," but before we attained that rating we were called "functions"—derived from the course in higher mathematics where "functions" could grow into something else!

The term "function" disappeared when new cadets began being admitted after graduation day. As might be surmised, the life of a "function" was none too gay, though we were kept constantly busy living it. As soon as we had taken the oath and been admitted, we had to draw our outfits (every article of regulation pattern) and establish ourselves in the *Santee*, an old sailing ship hulk.[67] In the *Santee*, each "function" had one small locker for his paraphernalia and was given a hammock to sleep in, but we lived on a large open deck known as the "berth" deck, which had to be kept shipshape at all times.

When a lad enters the Naval Academy, he retains practically none of his clothes or articles and must at once adopt the regulation outfit. It was quite a job to stencil one's name on each article in the place designated for it and to fold and

An Admiral's Yarn

stow them in the locker exactly the way the order prescribed and to take up a completely new and seagoing manner of living. But in addition to undergoing that very great change, we also had to take up Academy "routine" immediately.

"Functions" were far from prepossessing! As soon as we had drawn our outfits, having discarded every piece of our civilian attire, we donned the working clothes supplied us; because they would shrink when laundered, the suits issued to the fast-growing cadets were much too large. We must have looked grotesque in them! They hung on us like bags. The trousers and sleeves had to be rolled up, and in general we presented the poor bearing of young and very raw recruits.

To make our poor appearance worse, most "functions" had no knowledge at all of military methods or discipline and were both awkward and uncouth. Soon all of us became stiff in our muscles because of rigid schedules and drills which we started the morning after entering: setting-up drills, infantry drills, boat drills, and gymnasium drills! In addition, just across the pier from the *Santee* was the famous old sailing ship, USS *Constellation*,[68] used as a "practice ship" on which we were immediately put to learn the "square-rigger" seamanship then being taught at the Academy. Of all the trials and tribulations of that time, I think the most nerve-racking to us were our first attempts at going aloft on the *Constellation*'s 180–foot masts and endeavoring to learn the handling of sails. At first our holds nearly squeezed the tar out of the rigging, but later we enjoyed the new experience, although it took time and effort to reach that stage.

We "functions" had the *Santee* to ourselves, and under the guidance of the old sailors aboard soon learned the rudiments of living in the very crowded "between decks" of an old sailing ship. Among them, we were taught how to swing a hammock on the hooks assigned; but how to sleep in them was another matter as well as how to make them up and stow the hammocks rapidly when "all hands" were called in the morning. None of us took happily to hammock life at first, but with experience and especially after we had found comfort in them at sea, we decided they were worthwhile.

Although our quarters were in the old *Santee*, we neither drilled nor messed there and had to walk a quarter of a mile before reaching the mess hall or drilling grounds. Of course, the awkward, untrained, and uncouth "functions" were in no way fitted to join the old and very snappy cadets in anything, so we ate our meals by ourselves in a small room next to the main mess hall. We were marched up to this room at mealtimes and marched back to the *Santee* when we finished eating!

It rather surprised us to see how many of the then "plebes" would gather around us as we marched back to the ship and how they tried during the march

I Join the Navy

to make us realize our status and shortcomings. Naturally, being in ranks, "functions" could not talk back and would not have done so anyway, but we did as we were told and made every effort to brace up and appear military. However, even out of ranks, we would have been quite docile, as we believed the hazing given us was right and proper and good for us.

It was on the march back to the *Santee* after mess that many of us received the nicknames that have clung to us through life. My classmates, after seeing me in the new working clothes said I looked like a Chinaman and at once dubbed me "Ching," which even to this late day I remain to many of my classmates. To the upperclassmen I was never "Ching," but they gave me a nickname of their own. It was so typical of the way nicknames are derived that I must tell of it. When I entered the Academy, I was given some old working suits by a "bilger,"[69] and having had his name on the jumpers covered over with my own name, I proceeded to wear one of the suits to supper on about the third night at the Academy. As the suit had been made for a fellow not nearly as heavyset as I, it fit too snugly. That night after mess, many plebes followed us to the ship. When we broke ranks, one of them, with a loud guffaw said, "Mister, you look just like a bologna sausage and from now on you are 'Mr. Bologna Sausage'!" Being far too long a name for even upperclassmen to call a "plebe," my name was changed to "Mr. Bologna" and finally to "Bolog" when I became a "youngster."

The hazing we received as "functions" and "plebes" will ever be remembered by me. Then, as now, the general public was bitterly opposed to it in all forms, and the newspapers were vociferous in denouncing it and demanding reform. But as is so often the case in so-called news items, only one side of hazing was presented, the result being that it eventually became condemned. Thus although the conclusions of the public in regard to hazing at the Naval Academy were far from correct, the entire system was outlawed. Hazing in my days, however, was quite in vogue and a far cry from the "sheer brutality" accusations of the press. We "functions" felt it was much more sinned against, than it was sinning.

The hazing at some schools and colleges was brutal at that time but not at the Naval Academy, and the hazing we generally underwent was important training for our futures as officers in the navy, inspiring us to keenly appreciate and observe the high standards necessary to bring proper credit to our country. Woe betide a cadet who failed to live up to these standards, for not only was he ostracized by the other cadets but was often obliged to leave the Academy.

In 1891, hazing at the Academy was little more than fun and never really harmful. It is true that plebes were often directed to do things they disliked, but strict obedience to orders is a prime necessity in the naval service, and it did us plebes much good to learn that lesson. It was considered highly improper for an

An Admiral's Yarn

upperclassman to touch a plebe, either directly or indirectly—the reason being to make it clear that force should never be used to ensure obedience. In the case of hazing, it was never expected that obedience be exacted through physical injury or degradation. Thus, if an upperclassman told a plebe to drink a bottle of ink, he would grab an ink bottle, keep it tightly corked, pretend to drink it and then go into apparent convulsions. If the plebe put on a good show, he was liked for it. But if his act was poor, he was often called upon to improve it.

One day I was with a plebe when he was told to drink a bottle of ink. He pulled the cork and actually started to drink before the upperclassman could grab the bottle from him. What a rage the upperclassman went into, and how he berated the plebe for not having the guts to avoid a thing which might injure his health or be considered degrading. The plebe knew the rule but was so lacking in nerve that he feared to live up to it. So incensed were the upperclassmen over his weakness that they tried to make him fight to prove otherwise. This he refused to do and we wondered how one so lacking in nerve could serve as an officer in the navy; but that particular man was "bilged" in our plebe year.

There were many purposes in hazing at that time: to ensure a cadet's knowledge that all seagoing officers in either the navy or merchant marine service below the rank of captain were always referred to as Mister "so-and-so"; that plebes were addressed as "Mister"; that "Mister" was always used before the name of an upperclassman; and that to show proper respect to those above him, a plebe had to say "sir," after "yes" and "no" and end sentences with "sir." As well, when in the presence of upperclassmen, plebes always stood rigidly unless directed otherwise.

One of the most important aspects of the hazing was the continuous drive by all upperclassmen to bring plebes to a military bearing, position, manners, and attitude. When plebes overcame slouching and slovenliness and became "smart" appearing, the pressure of the upper classes lessened accordingly, and at the end of the year the plebes were well set up and remained that way.

Those starting a seagoing life had much to learn. To ensure that a plebe would be properly awed by a mistake he was observed to have made, a rather clever idea had been developed by the cadets which, as expressed in the jargon of the day, was: "Nothing makes a plebe level-headed as quickly as standing on it." Hence, for every mistake, a plebe was told to stand on his head a certain number of times, always against a wall or bulkhead so the position was not too difficult. Some upperclassmen of a nautical turn of mind would require plebes to get on top of their wardrobes and go through the motions of reefing topsails; others might require them to carry on drills armed with brooms, or propound ridiculous questions in seamanship or give a lecture on a designated subject,

I Join the Navy

political or otherwise. It developed rapidity, ingenuity, resourcefulness, and good nature—qualities essential to a naval officer's success.

Our change from being "functions" to "plebes" took place on graduation day, but our advancement to Fourth Classmen produced no change for or in us. Expressed in Academy parlance, "plebes are nothing and 'functions' are a damned sight less than nothing" (not to be measured either mathematically or otherwise). Nevertheless, graduation day marked a very great change in Naval Academy routine, for on the following day the "practice cruise," which lasted about three months, started. The new plebes then transferred to the practice ship together with the new youngsters and new First Classmen.

In my time at the Academy, entrance examinations were held in early May and again in September—hence "May plebes" and "September plebes." Within a class there was no feeling of distinction between the two—but among the upper classes there was considerable, because during the practice cruise they lived very closely with and worked hard over the "May plebes," whereas their indoctrination of "September plebes" could not start until October when the upperclassmen returned from leave and the winter routine started.

May plebes were the small part of any class, and in mine there were only nineteen out of a class that ultimately numbered eighty-six. Having so small a number during the exercise, the hazing was most thorough and constant, and May plebes were well-trained by September when the cruise ended.

My first cruise was on the USS *Constellation*, an old square-rigger, built in 1797 in the same building program as the USS *Constitution*, its sister ship. Old as the *Constellation* was, it was still one of the fastest, smartest, and best working full-rigged ships afloat. Even a three-month practice cruise in it gave a young fellow, especially a "plebe," a fine experience in what is spoken of today as "square-rig" seamanship.

The experiences were in concentrated form—a practice cruise is not merely going from one place to another but learning seamanship in all its various forms. Five days a week, from 8 a.m. until 5 p.m., the ship was handled by First Classmen who over and over again put it through each possible maneuver in order that those who would graduate the following June would learn them all. Hence, the underclassmen, youngsters, and plebes who handled the gear obtained as much actual seamanship experience in three months as an ordinary seaman would receive in years of cruising. Furthermore, in addition to the experience of working a sailing ship, all cadets were required to make an intense study of seamanship in all its forms and were examined orally at any time an officer of the ship requested it. Needless to say, all hands were busy during the cruise, but it was an exciting life and intensely interesting. On that cruise I was a

An Admiral's Yarn

"fore royal yardman" and of course soon learned to work aloft on even the highest yard, no matter what the weather might be. The constant work on the practice cruise tended not only to make us fairly good seamen but also developed us physically as perhaps no other training could. Outdoor life, fresh sea air, the constant use of every muscle in the body and plentiful wholesome food could not but build us up so that when the cruise ended we were about as hardy, husky, healthy, and tanned as boys could be.

One might think that days like ours left little time for hazing, but it never ceased as the plebes messed with other cadets, swung their hammocks alongside them, and lived and worked all day in their company—never for a moment away from the supervision of upperclassmen. Under the circumstances, plebes simply had to learn every phase of seamanship—and the hazing was generally of great benefit to them and at all times humorous. Frequently I was ordered by upperclassmen to supervise and run a concert which was called "Bologna's Band," wherein each plebe pretended to be a certain musical instrument; but more often I was told to sing a song, preferably "Life on the Ocean Wave," regardless of my being the world's worst singer—never able to carry a tune or stay on key. But in spite of my defects I was ordered to sing fifty verses, not one of which had ever been heard before. Needless to say I became quite adept at improvising rapidly and endlessly. Thus it taught me to think quickly.

Before the cruise was over, some of the upperclassmen said to me, "Mr. Bologna Sausage, we do not want a good plebe like you to bilge [I never disagreed with them on that point], so the savvy youngsters of our class are going to help you in your studies of next winter by making you learn some of the important things now." And start they did, by assigning certain cadets to teach me French, mathematics, history, English, etc., until all subjects of the plebe year were covered—a great help, especially in French, which I have never been able to master and would have "bilged" had it not been for my lessons at sea.

For me, the plebe cruise was all too short, for I enjoyed it and became intimate with my classmates but also developed friendly relations with upperclassmen who have remained true friends to this day.

IV

At the Naval Academy

UPON OUR RETURN FROM THE SUMMER practice cruise late in August, all upperclassmen went on leave, so there were only plebes at the Academy for the month of September. During that month without upperclassmen, the May plebes were the "cocks of the walk," while the September plebes, who were just entering, took on the purely plebe role of being "nothing." That month was the happiest of my plebe year—a condition that lasted only through September when the upperclassmen returned and both May and September plebes had to wait until graduation day in June to become youngsters.

Having had three months of especially hard training on the cruise, September found the May plebes differing little in appearance from upperclassmen. All had grown rapidly, developed in physique, manner, and military training, and in general had some conception of what a snappy naval cadet should be and do. Also, the sea knowledge gained on the cruise was helpful to us on the old *Santee*, where all plebes were quartered during September. We May plebes took great delight in greeting the new September members of our class.

By the time the upper classes returned from leave and the academic courses begun on October first, all plebes were sufficiently trained to participate with other classes in drills and become regular members of the "Cadet Battalion."

Except for the ever-continuous hazing and restricted privileges at the Academy that first year, the following three years were much the same. On weekdays reveille sounded at 6 a.m., when all cadets turned out immediately and doubled over their mattresses and bed clothes to ensure no chance of their

An Admiral's Yarn

turning in again. Rooms were inspected to see that orders were carried out. We then had thirty-five minutes to dress and arrive at breakfast formation, where we were again inspected individually to see that all were completely and properly dressed, clean, and neat! All formations were held out-of-doors when weather permitted. After the inspection, we marched into the "mess hall" where we took our permanent seats, arranged by companies. At each table every class was represented—first classmen at the head and foot and the other classes in grade order from each end, with plebes in the middle seats where their conduct at the table was easily observed by upperclassmen. No elbows on the table there, or slouching in one's seat, and no talking except when required by an upperclassman. Plebes were the last to be served and were never allowed a second helping of such delicacies as milk or dessert. But upperclassmen saw to it that we had plenty to eat, so we fared well.

By about 7:25 a.m. breakfast would be over, and all cadets would go to their rooms to sweep, dust, and make their beds. All rooms had exactly the same furniture. Under the gas jet in the center of the room was a study table, on either side of which was a straight-backed wooden chair used for study. On each side of the room was a single iron bed, a wardrobe, and a washstand with its fittings as well as a place for a broom and dustpan. Except for bookshelves, there was no other furniture. Each item had its place; even the bottle of ink had to be exactly in the center of the table, and no frills or displays of any kind were allowed. Wealth or social position meant nothing at all, and each cadet was measured and evaluated solely on what he himself did. Because of that, both the U.S. Navy and the Naval Academy have always been splendid examples of democracy at its best.[70]

Leaving their rooms in order, all cadets would be ready at 7:50 a.m. for the daily academic work, which was divided into three periods of two hours each; one hour of each period was devoted to study and one to recitation. Including the dinner hour, this part of our day lasted until 3:30 p.m. Then came a drill period until 5:30 p.m., and an hour for relaxation before supper formation at 6:30. From 7:30 until 9:30 p.m. we studied in our rooms, and from 9:30 until 9:55, when "tattoo" sounded, we had another period of recreation, remaining in quarters. At 10 p.m. "taps" was sounded, and all cadets had to be in bed.

On Saturdays the schedule ended at 12:30 p.m., and for the rest of the day and on Sundays, there was much less work. However, on Sunday morning we had rigid inspection of rooms and personnel before being obliged to go to church. We considered it a day of rest, although we could be out of the Academy grounds for only short periods in the afternoon and could never leave the city limits of Annapolis. There was little desire to leave the academic limits even on

At the Naval Academy

Saturday or Sunday, as Saturday afternoons were given to sports of all kinds and the evenings to hops,[71] while Sunday we devoted to letter writing, girling, or just resting, and evenings to a study period of two hours.

Busy though all cadets were, there was much fun, joy, and happiness at the Academy—though less perhaps for plebes with their many restrictions and only one dollar a month spending money! At almost no other school in our country does the word classmate have quite the meaning that it has at the Naval Academy. Throughout his life, the closest mark of friendship a naval officer can express is to say, "We were classmates at the Academy."

Plebe year passed quickly, strenuous though it was with both semiannual and annual examinations. Those who failed to make passing marks had to resign and were called "bilgers." However, it did not mean, in many cases, lack of intelligence or ability but rather failure to study in the proper way for the courses that had intentionally been made difficult. With marking very close, a large percentage of cadets failed their plebe year, each class losing about 60 percent of those who entered it.

The heartaches at both examinations, annual and semiannual, were universal among the cadets, for it was the great ambition of each one to graduate and become a naval officer, and it was distressing to every classmate when one of their number had to leave. There is little wonder that every cadet worked his hardest to remain at the Academy and obtain a commission.

Like all plebe years, ours passed just as did those subsequent, each being eight months of hard study, three months of cruise, and one month's leave. Naturally all cadets were too busy to give much thought or time to anything outside their duties and work. Nevertheless, such diversions as we had were much enjoyed. We made the most of sailing, swimming, sports, hops, and dates, and little time remained for mischief, though now and then a bit of it would crop out. There were a few cases of "frenching," such as when an individual would seek a few extra hours with his girl by climbing over the wall, or when perhaps a small gathering of cadets took a drink or two of an alcoholic beverage. But such breaches of discipline were rare, because being caught meant dismissal, and the risk was much too great for such little pleasure as might be derived. However, both my first and second-class years produced episodes worth relating.

In the nineties, the most conspicuous and largest building at the Naval Academy was the one used as "main quarters" by the cadets. It was a long building, four stories high, and over the center was a dome and clock tower, on top of which was a tall flagpole. The building being much the highest at the Academy, the clock could be seen not only from all over the Academy but from most of Annapolis. However, while the flag staff over it was visible from a

An Admiral's Yarn

considerable part of the surrounding country, it was never used officially. The national flag was always flown from a great flagpole that stood in the grounds. It was therefore a tremendous surprise to Annapolis as well as to the Academy to see at sunrise one morning a large skull and crossbones flag flying high over main quarters.

Great as the surprise was to see that private flag, far greater was the consternation of the Academy officials over its being there. A man was sent at once to haul it down, but he found he could not do it. The flag had not been run up on halliards but had been nailed at its very top. Later, a sailor was ordered to climb the mast, but when he attempted the feat, he found the pole too rotten to hold him, and ladders were of no help—so the flag remained for some hours, much to the excitement of the neighborhood.

Everyone took it for granted that the culprit would be apprehended and punished, but as every mark had been removed from the sheet of which the flag was made, and fingerprint identification was as yet unknown, the authorities never learned who was responsible for the trick, and it remains a secret to this day, as far as I know.

The other unusual episode of my Academy days was what we cadets called the "Asphyxiation of 'Frenchy'"—a rather ludicrous prank that, through newspaper accounts, took on a very serious aspect in the eyes of the public. To us cadets it was never more than a huge joke, but expanded as it was by the press, it became an attempted murder that had to be taken seriously.

In general, the facts were these:

"Frenchy" was the nickname the cadets had for a very efficient "officer in charge"[72] who, like any other officer in direct supervision of cadets, was a bit unpopular with those who did not observe the regulations very closely. Such cadets found great pleasure in "putting it over" on Frenchy and occasionally took advantage of his inability to smell, by smoking, which was entirely forbidden at the Academy. How Frenchy ascertained the presence of smoke that he could not smell, we never knew, but it was a fact that his reports were invariably correct and cadets were punished accordingly.

I suppose it was to play on the weakness of Frenchy's sense of smell, or to express someone's dislike for him, that one night an apparatus for generating sulfurated hydrogen was placed on the veranda outside his room. The rubber tube from which the gas emanated was shoved through his open window. The apparatus was one of a dozen or more used in our laboratory work. Although one machine could make only very little gas—all that was required for our experiments—and would generate that only when fresh acid was put in and the machine well shaken, nevertheless, the rotten egg smell, which even that small

At the Naval Academy

amount of gas generated, was very strong. In fact it was so much so that the machines were always kept out-of-doors on a porch of the laboratory where we would go to shake one if we needed gas! Apparently the lower half of Frenchy's window was up when the tube was thrust in, but it did not remain so. When he turned in that night he slammed the lower half down on the tube, without noticing it, before opening his window from the top. Thus the gas was cut off.

When Frenchy awakened the next morning, he saw the tube and machine, etc., and at once reported the entire matter to the Commandant of Cadets[73] who became greatly perturbed over the matter. His first step was to issue an order to the then second class to maintain during the hours of darkness a sentry post on the brick wall just outside the window of the room of the officer in charge. The order was based on the assumption that some member of that class must have committed the foul act, since only the second class, which occupied "old quarters," was allowed outside of the "new quarters" where the officer in charge and all other classes of cadets roomed. Making cadets do night duty as sentinels, when their time was fully occupied with studies and drills, was a great hardship, and the fact that it was then winter did not make the duty any more pleasant.

When the order was published, the second class was astounded, for despite the fact that the entire class was generally well informed whenever one of its members successfully pulled off a prank, in this instance, not one of them had even heard of the "smelling attack made on Frenchy" until the sentry post was ordered. Therefore, the class held a meeting to ascertain its responsibility, if any, for the escapade. They were quite willing to do the sentry duty if a member of the class were responsible, but did not want to suffer such severe punishment for the stunt of another class. The class meeting did not disclose any responsibility on the part of a second classman or any knowledge of the prank, and it was decided to send in a written statement to that effect, signed by each member of the class and addressed to the Commandant. That cleared all second classmen, and they were taken off post duty. Then the other classes followed the same course, which put the authorities in a greater-than-ever quandary, for not only were the daily papers making a tremendous ado about the inability of the Academy to find the culprit in what they called an attempted asphyxiation, but also it implied that one, or perhaps two, of the cadets who had declared innocence must have issued a false statement. This was too much for either the authorities or the cadets—the latter having an unwritten code that falsehood was utterly taboo.

Faced with such a scandalous situation, which the authorities could not solve, it was believed that only the cadets themselves would be able to fix the responsibility for the prank and determine which cadet had lied. Since the cadets

An Admiral's Yarn

were as bitter as the authorities over the possibility of there being a liar in the battalion, it was decided that the cadets themselves should investigate the matter.

Accordingly, a board of investigation made up of cadets was appointed, and it set to with a will to ascertain who the culprit might be. All classes were represented on the Board, and in order that its investigations might be conducted thoroughly and quickly, both the members of the Board and the witnesses called before it were excused from recitation during the hours of sitting. Although the Board worked its hardest and was backed strongly by all cadets, it failed utterly to obtain a single clue, and the authorities ordered it disbanded.

It is probable that the answer to the affair would never have been solved except for a death-bed confession many years later. It seems that at noon on the day of the attempted asphyxiation, the resignation of a cadet had been published, and early in the afternoon he was required to leave the Academy grounds. For some reason he was full of bitterness toward Frenchy and apparently wished to express his feelings, so at dusk, he slipped back into the Academy yard, and while the officers in charge and the cadets were at supper, he perpetrated the sulfuric acid prank. The culprit left Annapolis that evening to return home, so it is not surprising that he was not found. However, the publicity the affair was given and the discredit his act had brought to his classmates must have preyed heavily on his mind, for as he lay on his death bed years later, he confessed to the entire stunt. By so doing, he proved that, as always, the cadet code had not been violated by a lie.

To ensure oneself a place in the navy took constant hard study and work, and although the entrance examinations prevented all but the better prepared students from entering the Academy, only about one out of three succeeded in graduating.

The teaching system at the Naval Academy, which was somewhat different from most schools at the time, was designed to allow one instructor for each subject in a section composed of ten or twelve cadets. Lessons assigned were of such length that only a person with a fairly active and clear mind could learn them thoroughly in the half hour allotted for the study of each subject. We were called on each day to recite orally or in writing on the blackboard, and we were marked accordingly. At the end of each month there was an examination in each subject, and at the end of each half year there was another that covered the work of the entire half year. These exams were very thorough and had to be completed in a specified time. Since monthly marks were a combination of daily marks and monthly exams, and half-year marks were a combination of the

At the Naval Academy

monthly marks and half-year examinations, all counted very heavily and were a certain test of knowledge retained during the half year.

As a class approached its graduation, these members of the hierarchy became more important and were a source of constant influence that kept the other classes to the high standards and traditions of not only the Academy but the navy.

A few months prior to graduation, when the First Classmen were told to request assignments to ships at certain points in the Atlantic, Pacific, and Asiatic waters, small groups were formed so that friends would not be separated, and the Department, as far as possible, observed the grouping, and orders were carried out accordingly. My desire was to be assigned to the USS *Philadelphia*, the flagship of the Pacific Station, covering the eastern half of the Pacific Ocean.[74]

U.S. Naval Academy sloops and midshipmen, Annapolis, Maryland.

V

At Sea as a Middy

AT THE TIME I WAS GRADUATED from the Academy, we ceased being "Naval Cadets First Class" and officially became "Naval Cadets." However, except in official communications, we were seldom referred to by that title; we were midshipmen on our "middy cruise."

The change from being a first classman at the Academy to a middy at sea is tremendous. One passes from the highest estate in our great naval school to the lowest estate of an officer aboard ship—and instead of a practice cruise, we began a permanent life at sea in the navy. We all loved the excitement and experience.

In 1895, the United States was attempting to become a great naval power. The population of our country had so increased that it was rapidly changing from being a mere producer of food products and raw materials for the world to becoming an industrialized country with manufactured products to sell. As happens in the growth of all young countries, the United States was passing from an agricultural country to an industrialized one. While we were producers, the industrialized countries of the world sought food stuffs and raw materials from us to sustain their industrialized populations, hence there was little competition in our international trade. Accordingly, the United States did not need a very large navy to protect its commerce at that time. But as we moved from primarily agricultural to industrial, our country was forced to compete with other nations; thus, a larger navy became necessary to ensure our use of the trade routes across the sea. Change from one of the weaker naval powers to one of the greatest was gradual. Our navy grew only commensurate with the economic increase in, and the vitality of, our industries and world trade. Thus, when I became a "middy,"

An Admiral's Yarn

the navy was just starting its new role. Its wooden ships of sail were being replaced with steel and steam. Such ships that it had were neither numerous nor large, and only a few had any real quarters for midshipmen. Those provided were so poor that they were known in the navy as the "steerage."

Although it was the flagship of the Pacific Station, the *Philadelphia*, on which I started as a middy, would today be known as a small cruiser. The steerage was a compartment about thirty feet long by fourteen feet wide with banks along two of its sides and at one end—for ten people. There was a mess table, which, when set up for meals, occupied all of the center space. There were small lockers and drawers between the bunks and under them, and "Carlin boxes," in which we stored our clothes, were slung overhead between the beams; a washroom containing a washbasin and bathtub was at one end of the steerage. Other toilet facilities were in the bow of the ship, above seventy-five yards distant. To make matters worse, in the compartment there were coal hatches and chutes through which all coal for the bunkers below was passed. Consequently, our quarters were often filled with coal dust. We had only ten bunks in our steerage, and thirteen junior commissioned officers and middies lived there. The three for whom there were no bunks slept in hammocks swung over the center of the compartment; the hammocks had to be taken down so the mess table could be set up. In the present day, such quarters would not be allowed in the navy, but at that time, we midshipmen managed to get along and enjoyed ourselves immensely.

There were only eight "middies," six in the regular line of the navy and two in engineering, and no sooner had we settled on board than the training in our new duties began.[75]

One of the six "line" middies became assistant to the executive officer (who was charged with all administrative details of the ship); another became assistant to the navigator (who was responsible for the proper navigation of the ship); one was assigned as "mate of the deck," responsible for the upkeep, cleanliness and observance of the regulations in the men's quarters; and three were assigned to the gun division and placed on deck watch under the supervision of the officers of the deck (who were responsible for the ship and in carrying out details of the ship's routine while on watch). In the same manner, the two engineer "middies" were assigned understudy jobs in the engineering department. By rotating the duty assignments, all midshipmen were given thorough training in the regular duties they might be called upon to perform, but especially in their duties as "watch officers"—the supervision here by the older watch officers was both thorough and constant. Consequently, we referred to them as "wet nurse watches," and we still speak of these officers as having "wet-nursed" us in our middy days.

While the work was difficult, it was always interesting, but the great enjoyments of the steerage were found elsewhere. No sooner had we joined up than the *Philadelphia* was ordered to the Mare Island Navy Yard for overhaul and docking, and we were introduced to local life in a Navy Yard. We stood watch to see that the work on the ship was completed properly and promptly, and we had our free time for the social activities of the yard. There were tennis and baseball to play, picnics and small dances to attend, and the more formal luncheons and dinners. We of the steerage helped each other out, not only in clothes and equipment but in putting up as much of a "front" as we could with our limited means, outfits, and poor quarters. I cannot say our "front" was always faultless, but at best it was sufficient to "get by" among our understanding naval friends. The fact was well demonstrated to us one night when there was to be a dance at the Navy Yard. A newly commissioned ensign came on board for a few hours visit, having with him only the clothes he was wearing. When he learned of the dance scheduled for that night, he was particularly anxious to take a certain young lady to it, even though he was without the prescribed uniform evening dress. As he was courting the young lady and we were anxious to help him out, we agreed to outfit him in the proper uniform as best we could.

The young officer was very short, especially his legs. When we inspected all of the evening dress uniforms that would not be used that evening, we found that the only ones available were suited for much taller and longer-legged officers. However, we "decked" him out in the best we had—the shirt sleeves being much too long, the evening dress coat much too large, too long in the sleeves, and not only that, the tails nearly reached his ankles, while the trousers had to be turned up several times at the bottom. Although we did our best to take up the slack in the clothes, the young officer certainly did not have the natty appearance every naval officer aspires to. Nevertheless he escorted his girl to the dance and reported having a fine time without hearing any mention of his rather grotesque appearance, even by his best girl, whom he afterward married. Ultimately that officer became a very prominent admiral and, except at that dance, always maintained the "nattiest" appearance.

The United States Navy was then very different from what it is today. Except in the engineer force, practically all of the enlisted men were square-rigger men. Although all ships were then being built of steel and had steam engine motive power, they still followed the general arrangement of the old sailing ships. Turrets, except on the old monitors, were just coming into being on the battleships being built. Broadside guns were still the main battery guns of most

An Admiral's Yarn

ships, and though such guns were breech-loading and rifled, and were operated mechanically, the power used was still only manpower—just as it had been with the smoothbore muzzle-loaders. Each of the more modern ships was allowed one, or at most, two steam launches, but as they were of low power and were always breaking down, the main boating reliance was still on pulling boats. Admirals had twelve-oared barges and captains six-oared gigs, but all other officers and men used the sailing launches, cutters, whale boats, dinghies, and wherries. Getting supplies and personnel to and from shore in such boats was always a considerable task, even with the little steam launches towing.

The manner of living on board had not greatly changed from the old sailing ship days. Small boxes to hold natural ice furnished the only means of preserving even a few days' supply of fresh provisions, so that even a short time at sea put us on the old-time salt[76] and dry provisions that could be stored for months. New ships were being given small dynamos, generally run only at night, but as electric plants on shipboard were still very unreliable, oil lamps and candles were always kept ready and far too often had to be used. Consequently there was a "lamplighter," whose sole job was to keep them in readiness.

If the officers had enough clothes to last them between ports, their laundry could be sent ashore, but enlisted men did all of their laundry aboard ship, even their blue uniforms.

One of the interesting features of that time, which had been carried over from sailing ship days, was the tailoring and embroidering done by members of the crew. Each ship had several men who, in their spare time, made clothes for the others. They did fine work, turning out uniforms that were not only splendid fits and well made but also had fancy embroidery, stitching, and wonderful buttonholing. Somewhere in the ship, each tailor had a particular spot where he would set up his small, hand-powered sewing machine, and sit on his "ditty box"[77] while sewing. It was worthwhile to watch their deftness. In those days every sailor could sew fairly well, but it was the old seamen who excelled.

Thus, in the gay nineties, the enlisted men of the navy were still just old type sailormen, far different from today. The ships had not become greatly mechanized, and the deep-sea sailors, who were in great demand, could be found only on the waterfronts of our seaboard cities. As could be expected, these men were often of the poorer class, unreliable, generally foreigners who could not speak English or read and write, and were the very riff-raff of the sailorman's world. In those days there were no restrictions requiring citizenship for the men who enlisted in the navy, so our crews in the nineties contained many hard characters and almost no native-born Americans.[78]

At Sea as a Middy

Of course that situation has long since changed. The "old salt" sailor is no longer useful or wanted and has been replaced by young full-fledged citizens—and with the ships' vast and complicated masses of machinery today, we find the finest young men in our country seeking to join the navy. The first enlisted men of the navy today represent a cross section of the best from the high schools of the United States. They have the ability, energy, and resourcefulness to do their jobs well; they lead fine, clean lives and are the best of young Americans.

It is difficult today to appreciate the navy's personnel difficulties of forty or fifty years ago. Now, when half or even more of those in a ship's company go ashore "on liberty," they return from it on time—clean, sober, and immediately ready for even a complicated form of target practice. But it was not that way when I first took up sea life. All men entitled to go on liberty each day were listed on the "Liberty List" to be "checked out" as they left the ship. The time of their return and their condition noted when they returned on board was reported to the officer of the deck. All men who had been on "liberty" were lined up on the quarterdeck, inspected and mustered as each one stepped in front of the officer and walked forward. If the man was reasonably clean in appearance and could walk without staggering, he was marked C&S (clean and sober). Otherwise his marking was D&D (drunk and dirty), but few of the latter class would be in such condition as to require being locked up or put in irons. Then, too, there would be a few absentees, some of whom would end their debauches and get back to the ship within the ten days allowed before being declared a deserter; a good proportion, however, never returned to the ship at all.

Thus we never knew just what the crew status would be when we left port, and particularly when we departed from what the men called a "good liberty port." Even when we succeeded in filling vacancies, it would take quite a few days before the crew would again be in condition to do a man of war's work smartly.

It seems strange that the U.S. Navy was considered efficient at that time, but of course it was measured by the purposes and standards of the navy then. How different are things today, when the well-being of our country is so dependent on the ability of the navy to prevent control of the seas from falling into the hands of those who would stifle our seaborne trade.

Today, it takes fleets of many different and powerful ships working together as a team to ensure the protection of our rights, should there be countries that would deny us these rights. But it was not until after the turn of the century that our country needed this type of navy.

An Admiral's Yarn

In the nineties, the United States was not seeking to sell a vast supply of manufactured articles to the world. The U.S. trade at that time was mostly in food and raw materials that were sought by industrialized countries. Because sea routes were kept open by other countries, it was not necessary for our country to maintain vast fleets of great power to protect our interests. Ships that were necessary at that time were assigned stations such as the North Atlantic, the Pacific, the European, the Asiatic, the South Atlantic, etc., and, for the most part, went singly to ports within the area of the station to show the flag or to handle some local situation involving U.S. interests. The navy at that time was primarily for such purposes, and it was rather unusual for two or more naval ships to be together at sea or in port. Since, too, it was only necessary for ships to be ready for individual action at sea, at close range, or more often, in port, naval ships prepared for their requirements accordingly. Getting ready for sea operations at that time required considerably less preparation than did port operations, where the popularity of the United States was of utmost importance. The necessary drills and work aboard ship could be completed each day before noon, so that by afternoon almost everyone, except half of the ship's company on duty, could go ashore where the conviviality and sociability were of prime importance and where the use of liquor was thought to be essential in spreading good will. It is little wonder that at that time the older officers of the navy had developed quite a reputation for their drinking abilities; nor is it any wonder that on our middy cruise we found it well deserved.

Fortunately it did not continue, for as the purpose of our navy changed to more serious duties, heavy drinking decreased among both officers and enlisted men who were assigned to dangerous work with heavy explosives and high-powered machinery.

Operating under the guiding influences of that time, cruises had altogether different objectives than those of today, and my first cruise followed the objectives of the era. When the overhaul of the *Philadelphia* at the Mare Island Navy Yard was completed, we started on a cruise. At the time, peace and quiet prevailed in all foreign ports of the Pacific, so during my first cruise aboard the *Philadelphia* we visited U.S. west coast ports while keeping the ship ready and in training for such other duties as we might be called upon to perform. We went first to Puget Sound.

VI

Middy Days in Puget Sound

Although the "gold rush" and "pioneering days" of the Pacific Coast were part of the past during the nineties, there was, nevertheless, not only a marked newness to the life we found there but also a considerable difference in civic manners and enterprise. The western cities and towns were young, not beset with traditions, and were growing fast with men and women from all parts of our country and from all walks of life. They seemed to have a strong urge for pioneering and an eagerness to develop and exploit the vast resources of the great Northwest. While there were tremendous changes from the "gold rush" days, the towns were wide open in comparison to the East. The people were so wholesome and congenial that even then the future greatness of "the slope," as we affectionately spoke of it, was assured.

After leaving the Navy Yard and San Francisco Bay, we arrived at Port Angeles, Washington, situated on a small bay formed by a low sandy and rocky point called Ediz Hook—a projection from the mainland about midway along the south side of the Strait of Juan de Fuca. Standing eastward into the strait to reach Port Angeles, we passed into one of the world's greatest scenic splendors. The strait is not broad; on its north side lie the mountains of Canada's island, Vancouver, while far ahead rise the Coast Range mountains with the ever snowcapped peak of Mount Baker, apparently standing watch over the whole stupendous scene.

On a clear day, after seeing only broad expanses of ocean, one cannot but be overwhelmed by the majestic beauty of the Strait of Juan de Fuca—gazing upon snowcapped mountains and their descending terrain covered with great, green

An Admiral's Yarn

forests. Here and there were a few small fishermen's huts, but when we reached Port Angeles we found that several hundred acres of the forests had been cleared for a village there.

In 1895, Port Angeles seemed to be the "jumping-off place." Even though it was the only harbor completely protected from gales on the U.S. side of the strait, it was beautifully situated at the face of the great Mount Olympus and was in the very center of a splendid lumber and fishing area. We found Port Angeles and its people incredibly poor. There was no market there at all for what they produced and no means of transportation, except tiny steamers that occasionally made short stops. There were no roads to other towns, the nearest by land being sixty miles away. There were few trails leading from the village into the forests and mountains, but even horses and pack animals were very, very few. Today we can hardly conceive of Port Angeles as it was in 1895, but it served the USS *Philadelphia*'s purposes at that time, so we spent nearly two months there.

In 1924, when I was in command of the battleship *Pennsylvania*,[79] our division of battleships again took me to Port Angeles, then a thriving and fairly well-to-do city of over ten thousand people. When the Mayor came on board to pay his official call on the Admiral, I received him and his party at the gangway and noticed as they came on board that they looked hard at me and then started a whispered conversation. A few minutes later the Mayor said, "Captain, have you ever been in Port Angeles before?" and I replied "Yes, in 1895, when I was a midshipman on the *Philadelphia*." At that he grabbed both of my hands, saying, "I thought I recognized you. Don't you remember me? I am [H.M.] Fisher, one of the boys of the town who used to come over now and then to the steerage mess of the *Philadelphia* to get a square meal." I remembered him then, and we talked of the days when the *Philadelphia* came to Port Angeles and actually prevented the town from being "starved out," by buying and paying for products with the only money the village had seen for months.

Port Angeles was anything but a metropolis in 1895, but we loved the life there and soon everyone on the ship knew the townspeople. The ship bought the chickens, eggs, butter, meat, and vegetables that were being sold there, and the people did all in their power to make our stay pleasant, with small dances, fishing parties, and picnics. However, most of the time we drilled and drilled and drilled and drilled. We did boat drills, cutting-out drills, infantry and artillery drills on shore, gun drills on board, target practice on Ediz Hook with rifles and artillery pieces, trained our force on shore for camping out, practiced destroying ships with mines, and trained for everything and anything a ship of that day might be called upon to do. That stay in Port Angeles was a joyous time for everyone, both on the ship and ashore. A more healthful and pleasant experience, or one more beneficial to a naval ship in keeping prepared for its duties, can hardly be imagined.

The two outstanding features of Port Angeles at that time, and ever since, were its lumber and fishing. Surrounded by forests of fine timber, we thought then that some day the lumber industry would flourish and Port Angeles would become an important place.

There was one young officer in our mess who, unbeknownst to us, had inherited three or four thousand dollars. Apparently this information became known to one of Port Angeles' citizens, who had erected a small shingle mill. While superior shingles could be made cheaply, there was no market for them at that time and the little shingle mill remained idle. The owner talked our young officer into buying it, and the Port Angeles citizen then departed for Seattle, never to be heard from again—nor was the shingle mill, as far as I know.

While lumber has ever been the industrial backbone of Port Angeles, there is something else that makes the town famous too—a fish!—and strange to say, not from the salt waters around the port but from nearby Lake Crescent.

Back in the mountains some fourteen miles from Port Angeles, Lake Crescent's surrounding streams afford fine freshwater fishing. In 1895 it could be reached from Port Angeles only by pack animals over a cinder trail that wound its way over the rough and rugged foothills of the heavily forested Olympus. Therefore, a fishing trip to Lake Crescent was not an easy one; three days had to be devoted to the trip in order to have one day's fishing.

Rear Admiral Lester Beardslee, Commander of the U.S. Pacific Station, was an active fisherman. He loved fishing and always carried with him, when cruising, complete fishing paraphernalia, including many books on the subject. He was a "student of fish," and during our visit to Port Angeles he caught and classified and made known to the world the fish that made Lake Crescent famous.[80] That the Admiral was even able to reach Lake Crescent over this rough trail speaks well of his energy, physique, and love of the sport. (A few days after his trip, a few of us youngsters made the same trip and thoroughly realized what he had endured for one day's fishing in the lake.)

On the day of his fishing trip, after having fished from dawn until late afternoon and still not having caught a fish, the Admiral was sitting in the stern of his little boat, discouraged and about to order his guide to return to the landing, when suddenly there came a terrific "strike" on his line, which had drifted in the water and gradually sunk to the bottom. The Admiral galvanized into action. For how long or how hard he played that fish is not recorded, but ultimately he brought it in and found he had caught an unusually large trout, which not only had some amazing peculiarities but weighed about sixteen

An Admiral's Yarn

pounds. He had never heard, seen, or read of such a trout, and at once tried the same fishing tactics again. By dark that evening he had landed four more of the great fellows. Having had what he considered the greatest fishing day of his life, he returned to the ship with his catch, which completely mystified everyone who saw the fish. The Admiral immediately took steps to identify the fish, but in not one of his books on fish could he find a record of that kind. They were undoubtedly of the trout family but a different type than described in the books.

Having more fish than he could use in his mess, the Admiral distributed large pieces among the several officers' messes. On receiving its share, the steerage pronounced it the most delicious trout they had ever eaten.

Unable to classify the trout himself, Admiral Beardslee sent one to the University of California, requesting its Natural History Department to classify it. In a short time he was informed that while the fish undoubtedly belonged to the trout family, it had certain characteristics peculiar to itself, developed probably from some ordinary trout having been in the lake for generations, imprisoned there through terrestrial upheaval that had dammed up a stream. So confined and cut off for generations in water that could not be reached by other trout, the fish evidently had gradually developed along lines enforced upon it. The university gave the species a Latin name but also named it the "Beardslee Trout," by which it is still known.

What the "Beardslee Trout" did for Lake Crescent and Port Angeles you must see to appreciate. Port Angeles became the place from which to reach Lake Crescent, and Lake Crescent became a fisherman's "mecca," and therefore a renowned pleasure resort in an area full of beautiful lakes and mountains. Hotels and cottages were built as well as a macadam highway from Port Angeles. Later, the Olympic Highway, which runs along the south shore of the Strait of Juan de Fuca from Puget Sound to the sea, afforded direct access by automobile to Port Angeles from the whole Northwest. An auto ferry connects with Victoria in Canada on Vancouver Island, a railroad affords transportation to the east, and Puget Sound's large steamers touch there daily. Tourist travel to and from Lake Crescent and Port Angeles is heavy, and the lake is advertised all over the Northwest, even in nationally read magazines, as the home of the "Beardslee Trout." Enough are caught each season to retain its name and reputation.

In 1935, when I was in command of the Battle Force during its visit to the Port Angeles and Puget Sound area, I was amazed to see the changes that had been made by the industrial growth of the great Northwest. Also in port at that time were several British ships. They were maintained on the Pacific Coast by the Dominion of Canada, and the officers of the two navies met frequently in the ensuing social activities. One day in Seattle we were together on a yacht to

Middy Days in Puget Sound

watch some naval boat races held on Lake Washington. The captain of one of the Canadian ships and I, who were sitting together, noticed as we steamed along the shoreline many large signs of advertisement. One which caught my eye advertised Lake Crescent as the home of the "Beardslee Trout." Later, in Victoria, I met an old and very dear friend of Admiral Beardslee to whom the Admiral had not only written about his famous catch but had sent pictures of the fish. She recovered them from storage and sent them to me—greatly treasured to this day, I assure you.

We anchored at the British Naval Station just across the strait from Victoria—a charming little town called "Esquimalt," with a decided English background. But like our ports in that area, it was quite "wide open." There we made our first contact with a foreign naval ship, which was most interesting. The exchange of "national salutes" as the *Philadelphia* entered the Canadian port, the exchange of gun salutes between the two admirals, the numerous official calls between the officers, and the luncheons, dinners, and receptions given by each navy to honor the other, were all new experiences to us middies.

At all official affairs in those days there was considerable drinking, and the group from one ship would always try to outdrink a similar group from the other ship—especially to put them "under the table." It was an expensive habit, but we were sorry to leave after a few days with those delightful English officers.

After leaving Victoria we visited Port Townsend, Seattle, Tacoma, Olympia, Port Orchard, Everett, Bellingham, and finally Vancouver, B.C., each port being very attractive and interesting to us.

Our first stop, Port Townsend, presented us with quite a different picture from the other towns on Puget Sound, since not long before we arrived there had been a great boom to make it the greatest seaport of the Pacific Northwest. Port Townsend had many qualifications for such a status. It is beautifully situated and has a large, deep, and well-sheltered harbor with an excellent shoreline for piers and warehouses. It also is the Puget Sound port nearest and most accessible to the sea, and every ship that enters or leaves Puget Sound must pass close to the town. Under such circumstances it is little wonder that in visualizing the sea trade of the Northwest, many had the idea that Port Townsend was destined to become a great port, and thus the boom started. Heavy forests were cleared, streets were surveyed, business buildings and houses were started, and Port Townsend became a typical "boom town."

Unfortunately, for all its qualifications, Port Townsend—on the west side of the sound—did not have the means to handle cargoes, except by water; there were no rail facilities. To reach Port Townsend, railroads working eastward would be obliged to build many miles of track over rough country to pass

An Admiral's Yarn

around Puget Sound, which could not be bridged. Railroads, which became essential to handling freight to and from the great country, had no difficulty finding excellent harbors on the eastern side of the sound where the short additional water hauls for cargoes were as nothing compared with the freight shipment from Port Townsend.

It was truly a dead city when we first saw it. Underbrush had taken over the miles of prepared city blocks, buildings started in the boom days had been abandoned, and the citizens were depressed with financial difficulties. Visiting there brought acute sadness. In the years since then, however, Port Townsend has recovered to a marked extent owing to its excellent location, and it still remains a port of entry for Puget Sound shipping. It provides the quarantine and custom inspections, and one transcontinental railroad has a spur around the sound that reaches to Port Townsend and Port Angeles. Fine highways open the Olympic peninsula to auto traffic, and there is lumbering, fishing, and some farming in the cleared areas near the city—and, of course, it is still very beautiful.

Next we went to Seattle, where we found things very different, for even in 1895 it was very much alive, busy, and bustling. In the rivalry between the two cities on the sound to become the great seaport of the Northwest, even then Seattle was well in the lead. While still crude and rough as a city, the people were charming and showered us with hospitality. Seattle's fine harbor, beautiful hills, and transcontinental railroads, and the vast and productive northwest country it opened for trade via the sea assured its greatness.

There was intense rivalry between Tacoma (about thirty miles distant) and Seattle, two cities almost exactly alike in natural resources, beauty, charm of inhabitants, life, business, and accessibility to the resources of the vast country behind them. But probably because it was nearer the sea, Seattle became the great seaport of the Northwest, and the rivalry eventually ceased. In the nineties, however, there was some jealousy over the name of that magnificent peak, Mt. Rainier—so near both cities as to overshadow them. In Seattle it was always called Mt. Rainier, but it was "Mt. Tacoma" if you lived in Tacoma—and woe betide anyone who called it Mt. Rainier.

Our visits to other Puget Sound ports were less exciting than those to Seattle and Tacoma, for they were still small and undeveloped. At Port Angeles we had to spend much time in drilling and preparing our "landing force" of about two hundred and fifty men for exercises on shore, and at each of the ports we visited, we landed a force to give exhibition drills. These were gala days in the town, and nothing more exemplifies the conditions of that time than the closing of most local shops in order that "all hands" could watch the drill.

Middy Days in Puget Sound

 We later visited Port Orchard, where the Navy had acquired a tract of land on the shore for a Navy Yard. Our Admiral wished to see what progress was being made on a dry dock there. We were not much impressed by what we saw. Where there were dense forests in 1895, today stands not only one of our largest, busiest, and best-equipped Navy yards[81] but also the flourishing twin cities of Bremerton and Charleston.

 Our cruise in Puget Sound ended late in November when the *Philadelphia* went south to spend the winter in southern California ports. San Francisco was still the great metropolis of the West, and our stay of several weeks there was filled with the joys of living that even to this day are its greatest charm. After the Christmas holidays we were on our way to southern California.

VII

Middy Days in Southern California

WE WENT FIRST TO SANTA BARBARA, that delightful old town of Spanish descendants and their customs, where the residents lived the easy-going old Spanish way of life and to which visitors came from all over the East to enjoy.

Built along the sea, where mountains rise behind it, and blest with a sunny climate that seldom changes, Santa Barbara seemed to hold all the pleasures that one could desire, with its natural beauty and ease of living.

Our visit there was all too brief, but before we left we were introduced to horseback riding—a novel sport for sailors, which became most popular. No sooner would a liberty party reach shore then it would stampede to the livery stables. Very shortly, the principal street of the town, State Street, would become a race course for sailors on horseback. The street was not paved and made a good track for them; up and down rode our sailors at full gallop, waving their arms. But, strange to say, they never tumbled.

The *Philadelphia's* next stops were in Santa Monica, Redondo Beach, and San Pedro, that the Admiral might examine and report on the possibilities of a seaport for the growing city of Los Angeles. As I recall, although Los Angeles then had a population of only seventy thousand, it was growing fast, and while there was still no evidence of oil, only little indication of the tremendous productivity water would bring to the surrounding country, and no reason to believe that an enormous seaborne trade would develop there, the city was, nevertheless wanting of and demanding a harbor that would give it access to the sea.[82] Hence, among the three places we visited, there was great rivalry.

An Admiral's Yarn

At Santa Monica (off one of the finest of California beaches) we found, upon anchoring, no protection at all from the long Pacific swells that rolled and rolled for the next few days. Making the trip ashore would have been both difficult and dangerous, and we could see no reasonable way to build a suitable and sufficient breakwater there.

We steamed a few miles down the coast to Redondo Beach, another stretch lying on the northwest side of Cape Vicente [today the Palos Verde Peninsula]. The possibilities of a port there were a trifle better, since the area was somewhat protected by the Cape and San Pedro Hill from easterly and southeasterly gales and seas, but the long Pacific swells were ever rolling in, and the wallowing of the ship made life unbearable.

We then went around Cape Vicente to San Pedro Bay just east of Point Fermin, where we found some protection against the easterly, stormy weather. Even then, our Admiral realized it would be a tremendous task to build a port there and gave much thought to the weather before recommending San Pedro as a seaport for Los Angeles.

To see now the great San Pedro [Long Beach today] port, it is almost impossible to visualize what it was in 1896. Of breakwaters, piers, inner harbors, or storehouses there was barely a hint. The only shipping was the twice weekly steamers that ran up and down the coast of California, the occasional trips of the little boats to Catalina, a few sailing ships delivering lumber and reloading with hides, and several small fishing boats. There may have been a tugboat or two, but as a seaport, with its small, rickety pier, it had few advantages. A mile or so down the shore, where today rises the fine, modern city of Long Beach, there was only the long stretch of beautiful white sand.

Despite its undeveloped state, San Pedro had been connected with Los Angeles, some twenty-two miles distant, by a branch line of one of the transcontinental railroads. There were some fairly good dirt roads between the two cities, but taken as a whole, what is now one of the great seaports of the world seemed, in 1896, a desolate place.

Today, practically all the ships of the United States Fleet find safe and secure anchorage there, and a huge amount of overseas commerce is handled in that harbor.[83] Little did I think that I would ever see a great port and large cities there, much less that I would someday command the Battle Force of the U.S. Navy anchored in security in the magnificent harbor of the port of Los Angeles.

When our Admiral finished his inspection of San Pedro, we proceeded to San Diego Bay—then about the middle of January—and anchored midway between the boat landings of Coronado and San Diego, to remain for about three months.

Middy Days in Southern California

While there, we worked hard to maintain the ship in complete readiness for jobs that an independently operating cruiser might be called upon to do to protect the interests of the United States in a foreign country. To this end, we carried out a weekly schedule of drills that trained us for contingencies we believed might arise. In addition to gunnery work, we held landing force drills of all kinds, as well as fire, collision, and arms drills; we also devoted much time to training our landing force for indefinite stays on shore under conditions of war. A camp was then established on the then vacant North Island—now the site of the U.S. Fleet's great Naval Air Station. There the men were given target practice with field pieces, rifles, and revolvers. They were taught how to occupy and control areas in cities and countrysides, and were trained in the fighting techniques of Marines and soldiers.

Our training duties that winter did not consume all of our time, since five weekday mornings were devoted to drills on ship or shore, while Saturday mornings were "field days" spent scrubbing and cleaning the ship inside and out for inspections held on Sunday. At other times, the half of the ship's company not on watch was allowed shore leave, which was devoted to the enjoyments of southern California life; both residents and Eastern visitors were most hospitable and delightful. Since then, the lovely homes surrounded by wonderful flower gardens and the rarity of freezing temperatures have changed very little, and the introduction of electricity, gas, and water have brought many conveniences and comforts to the residents. The population has grown tremendously, and business activities, generally, have flourished.

During our stay in San Diego, the city was flooded with tourists who filled the famous old Coronado Hotel, which became the center of our contact with visitors.[84] Our Admiral made the Coronado Hotel, which is as famous today as it was fifty years ago, the shore abode for his family. Because the social activities of the visiting Easterners centered there, the hotel was frequently the mecca of us youngsters when on shore leave. Not only were we generally given delightful rooms, but we found there were several dances each week in the great ballroom. Thus, with the certainty, too, of good food, the Coronado Hotel appealed to us greatly.

Whenever there was a dance at the hotel, our Admiral ordered all junior officers not on duty to attend it in uniform, and we would all be on hand with the other guests when the dance started. We would meet the Admiral and his wife in one of the reception rooms, and they would lead our entry into the ballroom. That gave us a good start. The Admiral was an imposing figure in full uniform and his wife equally attractive and charming.

An Admiral's Yarn

Quite naturally our interests did not center entirely on the visitors to California. We also were attracted to the permanent residents across the bay in San Diego and members of the wardroom became acquainted with several very charming young ladies.

There was one group that particularly interested us. We saw a beautiful rowing barge putting across the bay, piloted entirely by young ladies. The barge was of somewhat different build and rig but looked much like the rowing shells used by the college crews. Instead of young men, however, it was crewed by girls in natty, attractive uniforms. Counting the coxswain, there were nine of them in the boat, and when they rowed around the ship, every youngster went on deck to have a look.

At first the crew seemed to take little interest in the ship or even us middies, but when we noted that they came close to the ship at about the same time each day and that it was up to us to do something about it, we invited them on board. To our delight they accepted, and we soon, after introductions, established friendly relationships.

That particular group of young ladies had organized a rowing club, taking the name of Zlacs, and it proved a lasting and popular one in San Diego.[85] Many of the original members were still Zlacs when I was stationed in San Diego thirty years later, but their daughters were the rowing members, and I was delighted when my own daughter became one of them.

When we left San Diego Bay in March, there began a life of gaiety that lasted for nearly three months as the ship went from port to port, following the same route taken by the Eastern visitors attending celebrations that were held during that season by several towns along the coast. The first was the famous Flower Carnival at Santa Barbara, where the festivals apparently originated. It was so beautiful and unique that visitors from far and wide came to see it. Since then other festivals of flowers have been held in California, but they differ from the carnival in Santa Barbara which was, at first, rather a social ebullition carried out by the individuals of the town for their personal pleasure and to show their flowers. Consequently, floats were very small, horse-drawn vehicles, and riding horses played a very important part in the displays which were bedecked with gorgeous flowers.

The Flower Carnival was a gala week of entertainment, but the crowning events were the Flower Parade and the Battle of Roses, for I think every carriage, coach, tally-ho, buggy, trap, and fancy cart—even one of the beautiful riding horses in Santa Barbara—were decorated with flowers and entered in the parade. The horses had beautiful saddles inlaid with silver coins, and silver appeared on the harnesses. The caballeros who rode them wore handsome old Spanish

Middy Days in Southern California

costumes embroidered in silver and gold. The charming young ladies in their flower-covered vehicles were exquisitely gowned in colors to match the flowers, many carrying parasols of roses.

The parade, after covering some distance, passed between what were called "the tribunes"—stands erected on both sides of State Street for a block or more. People not taking part in the parade sat in "the tribunes," each person with a basket of small bouquets. Those in the parade were similarly equipped, and as they passed between the tribunes, the "Battle of Roses" began with the tossing back and forth of the flowers. A beautiful sight indeed, and when it ended, that part of State Street was covered with a thick carpet of lovely flowers. The carnival ended that evening with a ball, a beautiful affair at which I met the young lady who was later to become my bride and life's companion.

We middies were sad to leave the following day for San Pedro. However, we were to be the guests of Los Angeles during "La Fiesta" there—another gala week of festivities ending with a flower parade and grand ball.

The ship's next stop was Port Orford, a small village which was then, as now, the port for San Luis Obispo. While there was no particular celebration there, we had a good time enjoying the hospitality of the residents who staged a grand ball before we left. The memory of it remains, for just before the refreshments were served, two men crossed the ballroom floor to the supper room carrying a full-sized galvanized washtub filled with ice and bottles of champagne.

Leaving Port Orford, we went to Monterey where a small anniversary celebration connected with the annexation of California was being held, and we were obliged to march in the parade.[86]

The old Del Monte Hotel was then in its prime and filled with the very same Eastern guests we had met in Coronado, Santa Barbara, and Los Angeles. Thus we had charming company when we went in carriages on the famous "Seventeen Mile Drive," or wandered through the hotel's enormous "Mystic Maze," or attended the hotel's numerous dances. We were loathe to leave, but Santa Cruz on the north side of Monterey Bay was holding its Water Carnival the following week, and the ship was ordered there.

When we reached Santa Cruz, my days as a middy in the *Philadelphia* ended.

For some time we had known that the new battleship *Oregon* was being completed in San Francisco, and that upon its commissioning the *Philadelphia*'s middies would be transferred to it.

Thus we were expecting the change, though for me, it came sooner than anticipated, since the very day we reached Santa Cruz, three of us received orders to proceed at once to the USS *Independence*,[87] the old receiving ship of the

An Admiral's Yarn

Mare Island Navy Yard, where we were to attend to shipping supplies to the *Oregon*.

There was not anything especially interesting in assembling those stores—putting them on freight barges and starting them to the *Oregon*—but we were kept busy doing it and only at night did we have an opportunity to renew our Navy Yard friendships.

Having completed our duty at Mare Island, we went to San Francisco and joined the *Oregon*.

VIII

In the **Oregon**

THE OREGON AND ITS SISTER SHIPS, *Indiana* and *Massachusetts*, were the first modern battleships of steel built by the United States.[88] Compared with those of today, they were small, displacing only ten thousand tons, and seemingly weak in offensive and defensive power. But they had heavy guns and armor and sufficient speed, and we believed them to be invincible at sea.

Though too young and inexperienced to grasp the full meaning of such a marked change in naval ships, we did realize that we had to progress and work harder to prepare ourselves to be efficient officers of the navy. The purpose of the battleships was to fight and destroy ships of every type, while cruisers were to protect the interests of our country in various ports and parts of the world and to control traffic on the seas.

This new battleship, the *Oregon*, posed difficulties for the navy. Inexperience in preparing a heavily gunned and armored ship for battle at sea raised problems never before encountered. The ship's designers and builders confronted equal problems in this new venture, striving for the impossible—to draw flawless plans and to construct perfect offensive and defensive equipment. The minds of many men, engaged for many months, worked on what to incorporate into the ship; and although it had been launched in October 1893, the *Oregon* was not ready to sail until June 1896. During those months we waited at the Union Iron Works in San Francisco where the ship was built.

We followed the general hours of work observed in the navy, though details were vastly different than those carried on in the *Philadelphia*. Our time off did

An Admiral's Yarn

not change materially, and we had many interesting experiences and much enjoyment during our stay in San Francisco.

Our transfer to the *Oregon* brought a very welcome improvement in our living conditions. While we were still in the steerage, even with more officers in our mess we were not obliged to eat, sleep, and live in the messroom. While the steerage of the *Oregon* would be considered utterly inadequate for even junior officers today, in 1896 it seemed splendid to us. The messroom, though of very peculiar shape because of the ship's armor, was large. Nearby were small rooms that contained not hammocks but two or three bunks for sleeping. We thought ourselves decidedly well off in the *Oregon*.

We found vast improvements such as the electric light plant which kept the ship's interior lighted at all times, the modern facilities that preserved food in a refrigerator room, the mechanical devices for turning turrets and handling heavy ammunition, the increased number of steam launches to help with boating, and a ventilating system that kept the air fairly fresh throughout the ship. Improved devices were of course essential in the great mechanical plants that our ships had become in 1896, but the older officers seemed to think we youngsters were getting soft. Thus arose the contemptuous remark—"In the old days we had wooden ships and iron men, but in the new navy we have iron ships and wooden men!" Having served in both types of ships with both types of men, however, I believe the manhood of the navy today is as great if not greater than the improvement in its ships.

Midshipmen keenly enjoyed the cosmopolitan San Francisco of the nineties, where we were received into the hospitality of the city and the social life. Some rather enjoyed the wide open nightlife and the delicious and inexpensive food found at most of the best bars. In fact, there were free delicacies for those engaged in drinking. The most attractive was Pop Sullivan's place. We came to know Pop Sullivan, who always welcomed us warmly and provided us "free lunch" with our liquor. To a midshipman who had just $88 per month for food, clothes, and all living expenses, Pop Sullivan's was a lifesaver and at once became a gathering place for beginning and ending an evening on shore.

When we felt "flush," we would drop into some well-known restaurant for a meal, the finest at that time, in our opinion, being the Palace Hotel Grill where for seventy-five cents one would be served a whole teal duck, fried potatoes, bread and butter, coffee, and a dessert. At many smaller restaurants, several course dinners with California wine were thirty-five cents. San Francisco is still famous for its good food but not at the prices we midshipmen paid.

Even in the late nineties, only gold and silver coins were used; paper money was not obtainable from the banks. I once tried to buy a pair of shoes with paper money, but the clerk would not accept it, and I had a difficult time changing it for gold.

Included in our principal amusements when on shore were the theaters, operas at the Tivoli, melodramas at Morosco's, regular plays at the Baldwin, and vaudeville at the Orpheum. Then, too, prizefighting was in its heyday in San Francisco—then the home of the great James J. Corbett, champion of the world. All the well-known fighters of the time gathered in San Francisco, and each week Woodward's Pavilion would advertise a number of important fights which we were eager to attend if we had the price.

Of all the fighters we saw there, the most important to us middies was Tom Sharkey, for at that time he was still in the navy and had been our shipmate and master-at-arms on the *Philadelphia*. We were thrown in with him every day and acquired great respect and friendship for him. He was a large and heavy-set man, afraid of nothing, and one who thoroughly enjoyed a real fistfight. He always looked every inch the sailor, especially because of the tattooing on his chest. Even now when I think of Tom Sharkey, I see him as he appeared in the prize ring, his fine body and great muscle development, with a full-rigged sailing ship tattooed on his massive chest. And how he did fight, never losing once during our time and generally winning by a "knockout." At one bout we saw him tackle a fine, tall, active fighter from another ship who was heavily backed to beat Sharkey. When the bell rang, they rushed at each other and went at it hammer and tongs, but forty-five seconds later, Sharkey's opponent lay unconscious in the ring, felled by one of Sharkey's terrific blows.

Between work on the ship and good times ashore, time flew for us in San Francisco, and finally we were able to take our new battleship to sea. The older officers had more confidence in her behavior afloat than we middies, noting the tremendous weight of guns, turrets and armor, but fortunately all went well.

Our first cruise was to Acapulco in Mexico, and I think that even the older officers were a bit awed. Many of them had acquired their sea experience on wooden ships largely under sail, and none had ever served in a heavy, massive ship like the *Oregon*. It required a week or more to reach Acapulco, and the captain and navigator, who stayed right on the bridge for all of that time, were thankful for a rest when we reached our designation.

Acapulco lies on a bay, and because of the high mountains and hills surrounding the city, it has the appearance of a huge, extinct volcano. The hills block breezes to the bay, and the beating down of the tropical sun makes the harbor so insufferably hot that our great steel ship was like a red-hot oven.

We anchored early in the morning and saw the flag of Admiral Beardslee hoisted on the *Philadelphia*. Soon, a signal came from the Admiral announcing

An Admiral's Yarn

that he would make an official inspection of the *Oregon* at ten o'clock that morning.

"Admiral's inspections" are complete and severe, for not only is a ship and its crew inspected thoroughly for cleanliness, appearance, and neatness, but its readiness for service is tested by drills for each and every one of the nearly innumerable activities of the ship. A thorough job of inspection often required two days of hard work, but because of the intense heat, Admiral Beardslee and his staff completed it in one day—and seemed pleased with the condition of the ship. Thus, our care and attention to training had borne fruit.

The details of our battle drill were new to Admiral Beardslee, hence, when we "cleared ship for action" and went to "general quarters," he found it difficult to find a satisfactory place to observe. All the activities of the ship were carried on from behind the armor of the casemates, armor belt, and turrets, and at one point, when the Admiral became lost, his aide rescued him and took him to the bridge and conning tower.

The drills seemed to go splendidly until the very last—held in the late afternoon—the "abandon ship" drill. If a catastrophe occurs and a disabled ship cannot remain afloat, all hands are expected to take to lifeboats in an effort to save as many lives as possible. Each lifeboat is to be equipped with specified articles and food.

When I reported to the *Oregon*, I was placed in charge of a cutter and took much pride in always having it perfectly equipped by personnel well trained in providing the necessary rifles, pistols, ammunition, food, and water. On the way south I had checked over every detail of my boat, so that at inspection time I was confident that the boat was ready in every way for abandoning ship. I was a rather cocky middy when my boat came to the ship's gangway for inspection. The inspection officer directed me to show him each one of the required articles, the last one being the boat's bucket, which I grabbed by its bale, holding it out for him to see. When he asked me to "shake it," I did so and alas, although brand new, the intense heat had dried the wood and the bucket flew apart. This left me a dazed and shocked middy. I felt that a fine inspection of my boat had been utterly wrecked by this mishap; fortunately the inspector took it as a joke on me—knowing it was a lesson I would never forget.

As soon as the inspection was finished, the Admiral returned to the *Philadelphia* and put to sea—evidently in a hurry to leave the terrific heat of Acapulco—and how we envied them as we were obliged to remain several days longer to complete some necessary machinery adjustments. The heat put such a burden on our new refrigerating system that it broke down completely and our cold storage, which held two months' supply of fresh meat and vegetables, became a hot box. Decay took place rapidly and we worried over getting rid of the spoiled meat which could not be dumped overboard while in port. Fortunately the repair work went so well that we were able to leave Acapulco sooner than expected. Once at sea, we emptied our refrigerators, and after a thorough cleansing, we felt quite shipshape again.

Our next stop was that wonderful body of water in lower California, Magdalena Bay. In all the world there is probably not a more perfect harbor, but because it is so distant from a populous area and entirely surrounded by desert country, with few natural resources, it is doubtful that it will ever become important for commerce. While its waters teem with fish and its surrounding mountains are beautiful, there is almost no vegetation or fresh water, and very few people could exist there in the nineties. Still, to those who go there in ships, Magdalena Bay has many attractions. We made the most of its possibilities in our training work, with splendid advantage to the ship and to ourselves.

Perhaps the most important aspect of our training was target practice. While the *Oregon's* guns and mountings had been tested by firing, it was not until we arrived in Magdalena Bay that we could approximate firing them under battle conditions or give the gun crews practice in marksmanship. The Magdalena training period became a vital one, especially for our gun crews.

As my station for battle was to command the forward port 8" turret, I was very busy in Magdalena Bay. Day after day I trained my crew in the details of loading, pointing, and firing those 8" guns. Of course, the crews of every turret and gun in the ship were trained in the same manner—but my own turret was all-important to me.

Naval gunnery at that time was quite different from that of today. The development of rapidity and accuracy in gunfire was given little attention, and although longer range and higher powered guns were being installed in the ships, every navy was still unversed in how they could be used to best advantage. Hence, the training focused on the handling of guns. Accuracy in pointing and aiming was particularly important, and, having taught our crews how to load and handle the guns, we believed their gunnery training was complete and that our ship was ready to test its ability by firing at a target. But our target practice was as crude and undeveloped as our other gunnery work, because our ship would be either at anchor or stopped dead in a perfectly smooth sea. Guns would always be fired individually and at ranges of about a thousand yards and, instead of testing the accuracy of the fire on an actual target, a marker was put out as an aiming point of a theoretical target. Whether or not a shot hit that theoretical target, which was supposed to be as large as a ship, was determined by means of observers with rakes—one on the ship to ascertain how many degrees a shot

An Admiral's Yarn

went to the right or left of the marker and another in a boat abreast the target at right angles to the line of fire, to note the distance if a shot was over or short of the marker.

Knowing what can be done in gunnery today, we can only marvel at the crudities of the nineties. Under target practice conditions at that time, we could not even measure how close our gunfire came to the target, because reports from the boat near the target and those from the ship were not in accord. To my mind, the object of the target practice was to hit the point of aim. So, when we began firing from my turret, I kept making such changes in sight-setting that I deemed necessary for accuracy. Hence, very shortly after my turret began firing, shells began falling near the target. I jumped with glee when the target was hit and demolished. Then I suffered a blow that I shall never forget, for not only did the executive officer and others of high rank berate me for carelessness, but even the captain called me to the bridge to tell me I had spoiled the day's firing by ruining the target. The desire to complete a target practice was always so great that any occurrence that caused delay was sure to bring condemnation—but I had not known that when the *Oregon* had begun its practice at Magdalena Bay. Today, thank heaven, we no longer fire at theoretical targets, and woe betide the gunnery officer who fails to make a hit.

Because our refrigerator plant broke down in the heat of Acapulco, we arrived in Magdalena Bay without fresh provisions, planning to look ashore for food. As soon as we dropped anchor, however, a small boat came alongside with a giant green sea turtle so common in lower California. Hungry for almost any kind of fresh meat, the officer of the deck at once began to bargain for it. It must have weighed at least one hundred and fifty pounds, and much to our surprise the fisherman offered it for fifty cents. That started quite a traffic in turtles.

Although we caught many other kinds of seafood, we still enjoyed the turtles and found many different ways to cook them—turtle soup, turtle steaks, croquettes, and stew were all popular. To meet our demand, the few men of the Magdalena Bay area made it their number one job to capture the turtles across the bay on the beach where they deposited their eggs and basked in the sun. The men would slip up on one, throw it on its back, and carry it to their boat to deliver to the *Oregon* (and as the demand grew), the price was raised to seventy-five cents). Then the thought came to us that our friends in San Francisco might enjoy some of these fine turtles. Many of the officers acquired some for that purpose, so before we sailed we built a pen out of the balcony on the port side of the superstructure to hold fifteen or more turtles. Each had its owner's name painted on its back, and once very four hours, by order of the officer of the deck, the fire hose was brought out to spray the turtles. They were a

In the Oregon

great deal of trouble, and the officers who owned them finally lost interest. They also realized the great difficulty in presenting them to their San Francisco friends, so the turtles were given, finally, to a huge market.

We arrived in San Francisco and went once more to the Union Iron Works for our final work. That done, the ship spent several days in speed trials and then anchored in San Francisco Bay. Just as we approached the Golden Gate on our return, the ship had a most extraordinary experience—one that is not soon forgotten.

As is so often the case during the early morning hours, a dense fog so completely obliterated the entrance to the bay that the captain decided to anchor in the clear atmosphere of Drake's Bay, a few miles north of the Golden Gate, until the fog lifted. Drake's Bay was beautiful that morning. The air was perfectly clear, and the mountains reflected their glory in the water, which did not have a ripple. Except for the very long, low swells that rolled in from the ocean, there seemed to be little movement of any kind. Heading into that low swell as the anchor was dropped, the ship seemed as steady as a church, and my friend "Stephen Victor" [probably Stephen Victor Graham] and I started walking up and down the port quarter deck in keen enjoyment, little reckoning what was about to happen.

Ships that anchor in a swell when there is not enough wind to keep the ship heading into the rollers gradually work around to a position broadside to the swells. The ship then rolls with the swells, and usually the amount of roll depends on the length of the swell. Therefore, no one gave notice when the *Oregon* was broadside to the slight swell that was running.

Now a rolling ship sets like a pendulum or swing, and we all know that by giving a swing little pushes in its downward motion, the total swing will be increased. By synchronizing the push or "run under" with the movement of the swing, its descending arc stretches larger and larger. This is also true for a ship as it rolls in the arc of the swells. The length of time for a ship's roll is known as a "period." The elapsed time between successive wave crests passing a fixed point is the "period" for the swells. It is very unusual for the two periods to be exactly the same length, and for that reason the two seldom synchronize. They may start out and stay fairly close together for a short time, but ultimately the two rolling factors begin to clash. While the two periods synchronize, swells gradually increase a ship's roll, but as the synchronization abates, the rolls of a ship slacken. Because synchronization is generally brief, sailors seldom worry over a ship's rolling. Quite naturally, no one on the *Oregon* worried when their ship got into the trough of the almost imperceptible swells and started to roll. But walking up and down the quarter deck, Stephen Victor and I began to note that the rolls

An Admiral's Yarn

were gradually increasing to what seemed greater than possible in such a small swell. Finally I said to Stephen, "If this roll increases, the ship's rail will go under." On the very next roll the water came to the edge of the deck, and with the one following, part of the quarter deck went under and we had to scramble to keep above water. We were then abreast of the after turret and realized that the next increase in the roll would hit it and dip the lifeboat under. The ship was then rolling so far to starboard that Stephen and I walked right up the side of the turret, got hold of the sight hoods on top, and clung there as the ship rolled the other way and the port lifeboats went under while the water came halfway up the side of the turret. That roll most have been well over 60° to one side, and it was very evident that if the rolls increased the ship would be on its beam ends. Fortunately quick action already taken by the officer of the deck saved the day, and we learned a never-to-be-forgotten lesson in good seamanship.

It happened that because the captain wanted the ship to enter Golden Gate as soon as the fog cleared, the anchor was no sooner down than the chain was "brought to," steam was put on the anchor engine and made ready to "heave in." The fact that that was done instead of merely dropping and securing the anchor, as is the usual procedure, is probably the only thing that prevented a terrible catastrophe. For no sooner did the officer of the deck observe the perfect synchronization of the periods of the sea and ship, than he rushed toward the anchor engine calling out, "Heave round," "Heave round." Although a ship at anchor will assume a position in the trough of the swells when there is no wind blowing, the anchor and chain that hold the ship will usually lie 90° from the direction the ship is headed and in the direction from which the sea is coming. Hence, as soon as the ship lying across a swell starts heaving in, the very first strain on the chain tends to draw the ship's head toward the swell. That is exactly what happened to the *Oregon*. The anchor engine started as soon as the order "heave in" was given and immediately there came a strain on the chain, the ship's head turned through a few degrees and the *Oregon* righted into the swells and was soon without any roll at all. However, the tremendous rolls the ship had suffered did considerable damage aboard, for every article that could move from side to side was dashed, as the ship rolled, and we heard crashes all during the excitement. To prevent a recurrence, the captain got the ship underway, and as the fog was disappearing, he stood on into San Francisco Bay where we thought our rolling troubles were over. Alas they were not.

In those days, the only deep-water channel leading to the Golden Gate from the sea was Bonita channel. It is near and parallel to high, mountainous cliffs until Point Bonita is reached, and then a turn of about 90° takes a ship straight through Golden Gate. Bonita channel is probably a mile or two long, and in

In the Oregon

standing through it a ship has the rolling Pacific swells right abeam. Then, because they come in over a large shoal called the "Potato Patch," the swells become much higher and steeper than in the open sea, although their period remains the same. Hence, as the *Oregon* stood down Bonita channel on a course that could not be changed without running the ship on the shoal or cliffs, the terrible rolling started once more, and even worse than before, as the steepness of the waves caused a sudden drop of the ship when it was already nearly on its beam ends. So terrific was the pounding and rolls in Bonita Channel that it seemed doubtful we could keep control of the ship until the turn at Bonita where the synchronization of the ship and waves would be broken.

The strain of those few moments was terrific. To keep from being thrown from side to side and badly injured, all hands clung to whatever was available. Yet while so clinging, the captain still had to use his utmost skill in seamanship to work the ship's head a degree or two one way or the other to meet the tremendous seas and prevent the wreck of our country's newest and finest battleship as well as the loss of eight or nine hundred lives.

Our captain never wavered under the strain, and at about the instant when I thought there was not a chance for us, he ordered "hard a-starboard," the helm was thrown over, and in a few seconds the ship began its turn around Point Bonita. Almost at once the roll and pounding stopped and the great *Oregon*, without any visible damage, stood majestically into San Francisco Bay where it was anchored off the city.

It was fortunate for the *Oregon* and for the United States that there were not any newspaper reporters on board on that trip, for had there been, it is probable the great, new ship might have been condemned by the press as unseaworthy. Newspapers, in fact, paid little attention to out visit, and only meager accounts of the terrible rollings of the ship were ever published, allowing the steps to correct this tendency to be taken in a quiet, methodical way. Doing that was not difficult, as the principal thing, of course, was to make a slight change in the ship's rolling period so that it would not be quite so near the elapsed time between the crests of the Pacific swells. One of the first steps in accomplishing this was to provide the *Oregon* with what are known as "bilge keels." The idea was not new even then, for when great steel battleships for heavy fighting at sea became our country's policy, bilge keels were decided upon as a means to reduce the ship's roll and provide a better gun platform. The keels were merely very long, fin-like protuberances attached to a ship's bottom well below the waterline at the turn of the bilge. Being at about right angles to the hull's surface and extending over half the length of a ship, the resistance of the keels would naturally slow and reduce a ship's roll, tending to produce steadiness. There was not a dry dock on the Pacific

An Admiral's Yarn

Coast large enough to take our ship immediately, but very shortly the dock that we had seen being built in the woods of Puget Sound at Port Orchard was completed, and the *Oregon* was ordered there to have the bilge keels installed.

In the spring of 1897 the *Oregon* arrived at what is now Puget Sound Navy Yard. We found the Yard little changed from what we middies had seen when there on the *Philadelphia* a year and a half before. It was still a place out in the forest where a dry dock had been built, with only a few work ships and a pumping plant for the dock. We shuddered at the mere thought of putting our huge magnificent battleship in such a dock, and I fear we youngsters were a bit skeptical over what might happen when we did so. But orders were orders and the work to be done was essential, so on we went with the docking.

Compared to dry docks today, the first one in Puget Sound was a small affair. It was only large enough to take a ship of about the *Oregon's* size, 10,000 tons. Even for that size ship, a high tide was necessary to ensure enough water on the dock's sill to float the ship over it. Therefore, docking was chosen for the time of the highest tide during the lunar month, taking utmost precaution to ensure the water would be high enough to meet the draft requirements.

On a Sunday morning when the time of high water would be between ten and eleven o'clock, the ship was moored close to the entrance headed into the dock to be prepared to enter without delay at high water slack. Mooring in that position was a simple matter, since when the dock was built, a large pier had been constructed extending out from the south side of the dock's entrance, and a row of pile bollards had been driven along the north side of the approach parallel to the pier. By moving the ship between the pier and row of bollards, it was ready to be pulled into the dock the instant the tide reached its greatest elevation.

Unfortunately, the strength and direction of the wind can cause unpredictability in the tides. A strong wind blowing up or down a long stretch of tidal water causes the depth of a tide to become greater or less than predicted. The wind in Puget Sound that morning was against the inward tidal current. Therefore, the rise of the tide at the dock was too low to permit the ship to pass over the sill. For that reason it was decided to postpone the docking until the next high water, which would be about eleven o'clock that night. To await the tide, the ship was moored alongside the pier at the dock's entrance where crowds of excursionists from Seattle could see it.

I had the twelve to four watch on the forecastle that afternoon, and when I came on duty, the officer of the deck warned me that the tide would drop considerably and I was to be sure to slack off the mooring lines to the pier if they became taut as the ship went down with the tide. That I might keep a more careful watch on the lines, I stood on one of them as they continued to be slack

In the Oregon

until about two o'clock. Then, with the pier lined with people looking down on the ship, it suddenly rolled far to starboard, and the lines became as taut as iron bars. I immediately slacked them, off but as the strain left, the ship merely rolled over a little farther and stayed there.

It was painfully evident that the *Oregon* was hard and fast aground, resting heavily on the port side of its keel. The chart had shown a much greater depth of water at the pier area during extreme low tide than even the *Oregon* would draw. We were at a loss to account for what had happened. Our first reaction was to take soundings all along the pier and port side of the ship, but to our amazement every sounding showed fifteen or twenty feet more water than the *Oregon* was drawing. We used the mooring lines and all available tugs in our attempt to pull the ship off, but it simply would not budge. We then inspected the double bottoms and found that for a length of about seventy feet, the outer skin and frames of the ship were badly "dished in" where the *Oregon* was touching. Nothing could be done during the falling tide, and as there were not any breaks in the hull, the captain decided to let the ship rest until high tide floated it again. At high tide that night there was sufficient depth of water on the dock's sill, and midnight found our battleship safely in the dock.

Of course the damage to the *Oregon* was considerable, and all of the outer hull frames and plates at the turn of the port bilge had to be removed. Although there could be no doubt of the ship having rested heavily on something, we were still unable to locate the trouble. Starting at daylight the next morning, we took soundings all over the approach to the dock, but never once did we get a showing of insufficient water. Even in the lowest of the waters there, the *Oregon* could float. Nevertheless, an obstruction of some sort was there. Finally the captain laid a network of lines between the pier and bollards and had a sounding taken of every square foot of the bottom. After a long time, a diver was sent down and he found a line of piles sticking up from the bottom. It was upon these piles that the ship had come to rest its great weight when the tide fell. After investigation we learned that when the dock was constructed, the piles had been used as a support for the coffer dam, and they had not been removed when the dock was completed. Thus our new navy learned a never-to-be-forgotten lesson.

Work was started at once on the bilge keels and to repair the hull. We midshipmen took little part in it, however, for we soon left the ship for Annapolis to take our final examinations at the Naval Academy. While the examinations covered the higher theoretical book courses, they also covered the practical side of naval work that we had gathered on our middy cruise. The exams were very comprehensive and our marks were averaged with those in the

An Admiral's Yarn

Academy course. The tests were vitally important to us because they determined our standing in the lineal list of the navy. All during our middy cruise we had prepared for them, and after our return to Annapolis we were allowed a couple of weeks to study for the examinations.

It was enjoyable for the remaining thirty-one or two classmates to meet again and swap yarns about our cruises. It was also a relief to end our competitive work as students and learn our place on the list of commissioned officers of the U.S. Navy. We new ensigns were then ordered home on a month's leave to await out assignments to various navy ships.

Before leaving the Washington area, I decided to interview the Detail Officer in the Navy Department to learn where I might be ordered. Having had two years in the Pacific, I had made written application for assignment to the Atlantic Station but thought a personal request might improve my chances.

The Detail Officer receives requests from many officers, and he must consider the various duties that each position will require. His role is a difficult one, and he often becomes very unpopular. I received a cordial reception, and with every assurance of being sent to a ship in the Atlantic, I went on leave in a happy frame of mind.

Imagine my shock, after being home for about ten days, to receive orders to the USS *Marion*, an old wooden square-rigged sailing ship with auxiliary steam power, then in Honolulu.[89] While the jolt of being ordered to another three years' cruise on the Pacific was considerable, the greatest displeasure for me came from being assigned to one of the oldest "wooden tubs" in the navy. My recent training had been in the newest and finest of steel ships, and I felt the blow very keenly. But there was not a thing I could do about it, so I pocketed my pride and went to Honolulu to join the *Marion*.

IX

The Woods Again

WHILE HAWAII IN 1897 was not the Hawaii of today, nor that of ten and more years prior, it was still a kingdom that observed nearly all the old native customs. When I reached there it had become the Republic of Hawaii, and the old element was losing some of its power to representatives of the white race.[90] New ways of life and government were gradually usurping the old, although the population at the time was still preponderantly native and the islands only a foreign country to which the *Marion* had been sent to protect United States interests, if necessary. The islands were, even then, strongly for annexation, so all the *Marion* had to do was show the flag!

When I arrived, the ship was in the small harbor of Honolulu, moored at the end of the "Man O' War" Row. To moor in the row, a ship had to drop anchor in the middle of the harbor and then, with lines leading from its stern to some old boilers on the coral reef, be hauled into position. A telephone line from the city would be installed via the reef.

In such a small harbor the boating problems were simple, and although the ship was only a five-minute pull from the landing, our own boats were seldom used for transportation to shore, as we were constantly surrounded by those manned by natives eager for regular customers. In addition to this regular work, when a passenger steamer entered port, the "boat boys" would swim alongside it and dive for pennies and other coins that passengers would throw into the water. If ever a coin escaped them, I did not hear of it. Their boats, which accommodated two or three passengers, were well-kept, fine-pulling boats,

An Admiral's Yarn

beautifully painted, with each name displayed on the stern, inside and out. The boat service was perfect, except on three occasions when a boat boy got drunk.

One evening shortly after I arrived, my shipmate, "Brit" England,[91] and I were going off to the ship for dinner. We went down to the boat landing and, as usual, it was surrounded by boat boys. Among them was "Sam," who was Brit's particular boy. On the way over to the ship, "Brit" said to him, "What would you do if I gave you an extra quarter?" "Oh," said he, "I'd get drunk." We asked how that could be done on a quarter and Sam assured us it was easy if he drank "swipes." That was a very strong and cheap form of rum distilled from a by-product of refined sugar. "Well," said Brit, "Here's the quarter, and when I return ashore in about an hour you had better be good and drunk." "All right, I will," said Sam. After we had our dinner, Brit and I found that Sam had sent my boat to the ship to take us ashore, but there was no sign of Sam, even though he was the only one who knew that we wanted a boat at that particular time. Rather surprised, we immediately, upon landing, inquired of the boat boys about Sam. Almost as one man they replied, "In his boat drunk, like he said." Sure enough, there Sam lay, as thoroughly drunk as he could be.

Living in our ship with its excellent telephone and boat service to Honolulu, we used our free time to enjoy Hawaii. The *Marion*, of course, followed the usual navy routine of calling "all hands" at five o'clock, cleaning ship, and polishing the "bright work" until nine-thirty. The weekly routine of drills or inspections was carried out until eleven-thirty, when the "watch" on duty took over the ship's work until the next morning, allowing those not on duty to go ashore.

Honolulu was not the large, sprawling city that it is now. Its people, numbering about thirty thousand, were clustered rather near the harbor and the business section of the city, the outlying areas being devoted mostly to agricultural activities.[92]

There were few rail or trolley cars, practically all transportation being by foot or horseback, by bicycles, or by carts and carriages over unpaved streets and country roads that led to the numerous homes and villages 'round about. The center of tourist activity was the old Royal Hawaiian Hotel near the town and, as now, near the Waikiki Beach where the swimming was delightful.

Waikiki has changed much since 1897 when it was just a great, long stretch of sand some distance inside the reef over which the Pacific swells rolled or broke before coming up on the beach. The only structures one could see along the beach were bathhouses, all else being open country covered with rice and taro fields, with palm trees growing here and there. At the eastern end the old mountain crater, "Diamond Head," rose majestically, and at the other end of the beach was the Honolulu harbor. In the background were the beautiful

The Woods Again

mountains of Oahu. The warm, balmy air, the delightful tropical temperature of the water, and the delicious languor in lying on the beach amid such beautiful surroundings entranced everyone. Waikiki became a great social gathering place. While the beautiful Hawaiian moonlight turned it into a veritable fairyland during the full moon, the Royal Hawaiian band played in nearby Rapiolani Park. How romantic it all was.

However, not all of our free time was devoted to Waikiki, moonlight, Hawaiian music, and romance, for there were other places to visit which were perfectly fascinating. When we could afford a horse and buggy, we drove to the places of glorious beauty which today remain the great scenic attractions, although now with paved roads leading to them and automobiles whisking along too quickly for one to fully appreciate the beauty of the surrounding country. In 1897 it took an entire day to drive up Tantalus, the highest mountain on the island of Oahu; a half-day for a trip to the Pali;[93] an afternoon to visit the "Punch Bowl" (the old extinct volcano now inside the city limits) or the outlying plantations or beautiful valleys where waterfalls were everywhere.

Such pleasures were quite routine for visitors to Honolulu, but occasionally there were other events to enjoy, and I was especially fortunate in having my friend Dan from San Francisco to experience them with me. Dan, who was about my age, was the son of a San Francisco banker and seemed to have about everything a young man could wish for—good looks, money, free time, and the happy, winsome ways of his charming ancestors—perhaps too attractive for his own good. In any event, his father thought it best for him to leave San Francisco, go to Hawaii, and take charge of a coffee plantation which his father had given him. Dan came to the Island of Hawaii all right, but he seemed to prefer Honolulu life to that on a plantation and took quarters at the Royal Hawaiian Hotel. He remained there, where he at once established close intimacy with the leading families of the city, whatever race or nationality. Wanting companionship when he arrived, he got in touch with me, and I offered what hospitality was available, based mostly on the attractions of the islands that I have mentioned. But there were some attractions that were peculiar to the Hawaiians and not usually open to visitors, so when Dan was invited to those rare parties, he generally took me along.

One night we were asked to an old-time Hawaiian hula dance, which in those days decidedly lacked refinement. (And because of their lewdness were finally regulated under the laws of the Republic.) The hulas of today retain many of the less lascivious motions and actions of the old ones. Their interpretations are considerably different and far more beautiful to watch.

An Admiral's Yarn

Under the circumstances, the old hula in 1897 had to be a very secret affair and was difficult to plan. It so happened that this hula could be arranged because of a rising and already prominent young lecturer, Burton Holmes, who was visiting Hawaii for the first time, seeking material for a lecture.[94] Quite naturally, he sought to learn about the old Hawaiian customs, the most famous of all being the hula dance.

Wishing to see only the authentic, true Hawaiian hula, Mr. Holmes got in touch with the former king's old master who agreed, I suppose for a "considerable consideration," to arrange for a hula such as the king himself would have given. As he did not dare to stage it in the city, it was given in a native's house far up the mountain, which in reality was a very large lanai, not unlike a dancing pavilion.

Those of us attending the hula met at a hotel where I expected to see a fairly large group of guests, but to my amazement there were only four in the party: Burton Holmes and his secretary, Dan, and I. Waiting for us outside the hotel was a mysterious looking light-weight bus driven by an elderly native and drawn by a lively team of horses. Into that we piled and were rapidly driven up the mountain over a narrow and tortuous road to the place where the dance was to be held. So far as seclusion went, it seemed ideally isolated. We saw neither lights nor people during the last half hour of our drive, and all remained dark until we found the lanai, which, though perfectly dark from the outside, was well-lighted within. Entering, we found about twenty or more Hawaiians ready for the hula, about half of whom were musicians and the rest dancers—young Hawaiian girls of the ages between fourteen and eighteen. The musicians had an unusual array of instruments, mostly made out of large, highly polished gourds on which they could beat time to their chanting for the dance. The dancing girls wore only grass skirts, to their knees, and flowers in their hair, leis around their necks, and small decorations around their ankles added to their costumes.

Hawaiian girls of the age of those dancers are beautiful women. They have not yet begun to get enormously fat as they generally do after the age of twenty; they have not become as sun-burned as the older natives; they are graceful and splendidly proportioned and have lovely features and complexions. With the dancers standing in a row behind the musicians, who sat on the floor in a large semicircle, the group made a wonderful picture.

We four guests were seated well in front of the musicians, and when the dance was ready to start, immediately a door opened behind us and in came two huge native men lugging a large tub. When they placed it on the floor in front of Burton Holmes, I said to Dan, who was sitting next to me, "What in the world is all that tub of booze for?" It was filled with bottles of gin and beer. "Don't worry,

The Woods Again

the beer is for the guests and the gin is for the natives." At that instant, the men in charge of the liquor began opening bottles and pouring gin in ordinary water tumblers. Then, to my surprise, each native present—musicians, dancers, chanters, or whoever—was handed a glass and proceeded to down the contents, gin neat, without batting an eye.

With that formality over and with the gin taking hold, the musicians at once started the music while the dancers moved out in front of them, and the dance was on. The first part of the hula was not unlike the lovely hulas of today, and except for the absence of clothes, it was not suggestive and was really beautiful to watch.

However, as the dancing continued, both musicians and dancers gradually increased their fervor, though whether from physical emotions aroused by the dance or from the additional glasses of gin each one took from time to time, I cannot say. In any event, the dancers and musicians grew wilder and wilder, and the girls, seemingly overwhelmed, became more and more lewd and suggestive in their dancing. Each one of them seemed to select one of the guests to dance to, and when her chosen one failed to respond, she would redouble her lasciviousness.

What the outcome of an ancient hula was supposed to be, I can only guess, but it evidently was to offer the dancers to the guests. At this point we decided we had better go home. However, the girls clung to us and we had a difficult time drawing away so that we could enter the bus for the drive back to Honolulu.

A week or two went by before Dan and I were invited to another party. This one was to be a luau, or native feast, attended by the leading Hawaiians of Honolulu—a very fine affair of its kind, and Dan and I were the only white people invited, so I was keen to accept.

On the day of the feast we engaged a horse and buggy and eventually found our way to the place where it was to be held. The older members of families were holding the luau, and they welcomed us royally. All spoke English perfectly and dressed in the height of American fashion. They had grown up together in the days of the kingdom and liked renewing their friendships at an old-time luau circle in the atmosphere of old Hawaii. But none of the guests were our age, and instead of sitting on the ground in a semicircle, we were seated at a temporary table laid with up-to-date silver and china.

A servant passed a bowl of water and towel around the table so that the guests could wash their fingers before dipping into the poi. The table was laden with calabashes and native foods, the most conspicuous being bowls of poi, a product of taro root, which, when cooked, is much like our oatmeal. There were dishes

An Admiral's Yarn

of sliced raw fish and snails, great platters of cut chicken rolled in tea leaves and cooked over very hot stones, quantities of cooked yams, and many delicacies of the island. It was a great display that included several varieties of fruit. I was much interested when my neighbor at the table described each one, adding that, being a foreigner, I should not be tempted to taste all the dishes. In fact, when I sipped a glass of liquor, I was warned that it was swipes and very strong; but the native women all took a full tumbler and had their glasses refilled once.

Eating poi is an art, using either two or three fingers dipped in the poi, stirred around a bit, and then quickly put in the mouth. I ate little of it, as I did not care for the fermented taste, although I am told that it is an excellent and nourishing food. I was doing very well with the chicken and yams when Dan sang out from across the table, "Harrie, I'll eat a snail with you," and I promptly reached for one, much against the advice of my neighbor. I realized I had made a sad mistake, thinking it would be similar to a raw oyster and slide down easily—but not the snail. It was like a piece of leather that could not be chewed or swallowed and had a most unpleasant taste. I worked on it for a long time with everyone at the table watching me. Although there were no uncomfortable results, I lost my appetite completely.

The other guests, however, found much pleasure in eating heavily and drinking quantities of swipes, and after two or three hours moved to a large lanai where native musicians had assembled, and we danced in the usual formal European way. That form of dancing did not continue long. The musicians, having imbibed freely of swipes, ceased playing waltzes and two step—and from then on there were only native airs that gradually became more and more temperamental and seductive. Our hostesses were more familiar with the native dances and enjoyed them, even though their dress in fashionable European clothes appeared rather ludicrous. Although assured that the party was just beginning, Dan and I decided it was time to go home.

While we officers found many personal enjoyments in Honolulu, none of us were disappointed when after three months the orders came for the *Marion* to return to Mare Island to be taken out of commission; it was a very old wooden ship that had to be shelved. We worked on it for some time to strengthen the knees and frames in the bilges before taking our chances at sea. Before we left Honolulu, the captain announced that we would proceed under sail, using the engines only for leaving and entering port. That meant a much longer trip for us; instead of about ten days under steam, it would be three times longer, because under sail the prevailing winds would be dead against us on the direct course. Therefore we would have to go north to a much higher latitude than San Francisco before we would find a favorable wind to take us to the Golden Gate.

The Woods Again

No one would have thought much of such a sea trip had the ship been just starting on a cruise with a full supply of sea stores, but having been away for so long, our stores were very low, and for some months we had been living almost entirely on fresh supplies obtained daily from shore. Our problem was to subsist without carrying a lot of sea stores and to make the fresh supplies last a month or more at sea without cold storage facilities.

Although I had no responsibility in the matter, I was keenly interested in how the food problem could be solved—and, as a matter of fact, it was a rather simple one.

At that time, manufactured ice was still little used, even in the United States, but was the only kind available in Honolulu. A large ice plant had been built there and it had served us well during our stay, although our ice boxes could hold only a day's supply. The large blocks of ice weighed about three hundred pounds, and when delivered, each cake was well wrapped in gunnysacking. When the ice was ordered for the trip to San Francisco, it was arranged to have butter, fresh meat, fowl, etc., suspended in the ice tanks and frozen into the cakes, thereby being available each day. But the problem of storing such quantities of ice remained. A large wooden bin was built on the gun deck, and several wagonloads of sawdust were packed around the large blocks of ice, properly tagged, and the bin then covered with tarpaulins.

I was surprised at the success of that cold storage, as we had fresh food during our entire trip to San Francisco, which took about three weeks. The trip was very monotonous, as we did not sight a single sail. The breezes were generally steady and favorable, but there was little to do, so we rather enjoyed shortening sail and reefing top sails each evening before sunset and then slaking out the reefs and making sail again at dawn.

The distance we covered was about three thousand miles or more, and it took us just twenty-one days to reach "soundings" off Golden Gate. The weather was fine and clear until the last two days when we encountered a dense fog which held until we crossed the bar to enter the bay. This was a clever bit of navigation, without celestial observations and when nothing could be seen or even heard; it was long before the days of radio or listening devices, and a ship depended on the depth of the water and character of the bottom to fix its position. Because of this, surveys and charts of coastal waters are very complete and accurate, showing not only the exact location of every landmark, navigational mark, shoal, and channel but also the depth of water at every point on the chart and exactly the kind of bottom to be found there.

Having a chart of that type and lead lines or sounding machines that bring up a sample of the bottom on every sounding, and knowing the course and speed of

An Admiral's Yarn

the ship over the bottom, the navigator is able to determine the ship's position. He does this by first drawing a line on a transparent piece of paper to represent the course of the ship. Then, using the exact scale of the chart and the speed of the ship to determine the distance run between the soundings, he marks along the course line on his transparent paper each depth obtained and the kind of bottom found. Then, keeping his rulers on the chart in the direction of the ship's course and moving them along together with markings he has made on the transparent paper, he finally locates a line on the chart where his line of plotted soundings agrees exactly with the soundings and bottoms found on the chart. Having established that, he has fixed the ship's position, with this position as a starting point and continuing to use his soundings, bottoms, and the runs between, he follows the chart to enter the harbor.

Using this method in the fog, the *Marion* was led right up to the channel entrance buoy. As the visibility improved, we stood on into San Francisco Bay, and the next day went to the Navy Yard and at once started on the work of decommissioning.

Long before the nineties, the United States organized the Weather Bureau.[95] It was not quite the efficient Bureau of today, for there were no radios for reporting weather conditions at sea or from remote places, and only a few places had telegraphic reports. However limited, the Weather Bureau made excellent forecasts for that time, each day telegraphing weather data to key points from which the forecasts were published. Every Navy Yard was sent the forecasts and, as received, copies were sent at once to each ship present. Hence, each day at about 2 p.m. the Mare Island ships received a forecast.

One day, while I was officer of the deck, the regular afternoon weather report was delivered, which I read at once. It predicted generally clear weather with "northwesterly winds of gale force." Inasmuch as there was not anything unusual in that report, since it merely indicated we might expect the usual good weather with the strong winds so frequent on the California coast in winter, I did nothing more than send it directly to the executive officer, who happened to be in command that afternoon while the captain was ashore.

The executive officer, well known in the navy, had been on duty at the Naval Academy while I was a cadet there. He was quite popular, as the cadets often succeeded in "putting things over on him," but their being able to do so resulted in his being called "Wooden Dan." He was in command of the *Marion* the afternoon I received the weather report.[96]

At the time, the ship was securely moored to the wharf by numerous heavy lines, more than enough to hold it safely in a storm. Since the usual fair winter

The Woods Again

weather was to be expected, I made no attempt to put out more lines and continued to stand by watch in the usual way.

About five minutes after Wooden Dan received the weather report, he rushed up on the quarter deck, report in hand, and cried out, "Mr. Laning, there's a gale coming. What have you done to secure the ship better?" I replied that I had not done anything as the weather report was just the usual good winter weather, and as we were secured for much worse weather than even experienced at this yard, we should not put out any more lines. He looked at me in a disgusted manner and said, "You don't know much about northwesterly gales. Double the lines at once."

I broke out the watch and doubled the lines, much to the amazement of the old sailors in the crew. With that done, the ship was secured even for a hurricane, and I sent word to Wooden Dan, "All lines have been doubled." No sooner did he receive that report than he rushed up on deck again and said, "Those northwesterly gales are terrible. Put out all lines in the ship."

So once more we went to work and in about an hour, when we had put out every line in the ship, I reported the fact to Wooden Dan. Again he bounced up on deck and said "Those gales are terrible. Find more lines," and when I told him all were used, he said to put on the mooring chains then lying on the deck. With that he went below.

When the mooring chains were out, the *Marion* was secured to the wharf as never before, the lines and chains making an almost solid network between the ship and dock. I was standing on the gangway when Wooden Dan appeared again, and I at once started to point out the splendid job the men had done in securing the ship against any wind that ever blew, when suddenly he turned to me and said, "Northwest winds are terrible. Is there not something more you can do?" "Great Heavens," I said, "the only other protection I can think of is to let go an anchor." Then said Wooden Dan, "Let go the starboard anchor."

That order was too much for me, and I asked him not to do this, but he looked me in the eye and said, "You let that anchor go, young man, or I'll put you under suspension at once!" Whereupon I let go the starboard anchor.

By the time I secured the anchor chain and reported the fact to the executive officer, it was late in the afternoon. As he did not come on deck, I once more took station at the gangway to look over the lines. While I stood there pondering, the captain started up the gangway. Suddenly he stopped and began looking up and down over the moorings, seemingly unable to believe his eyes. Then he said, "What is the meaning of all these mooring chains and lines?" I told him of the afternoon weather report and that the executive officer had ordered the ship secured that way. "Well," said the captain, "you certainly did some job."

An Admiral's Yarn

As he started along the quarter deck for his cabin, I squealed out, "And, Captain, we have dropped the starboard anchor too!"

At that, the captain almost exploded and cried out. "Young man, what did you mean by letting go an anchor alongside a pier when the ship is secured as this ship is?" I replied that I had remonstrated with the executive officer but was told by him to drop anchor or go under suspension. With that the captain bolted for his cabin, calling out in a loud voice, "Orderly, orderly, tell the executive officer I want to see him in my cabin immediately."

I never learned what was said in that interview, but my imagination was very vivid, for in a few moments the executive appeared on deck and ordered me to get the anchor up at once and I did!

X

Still in Wood

ALONG WITH OUR ORDERS to put the *Marion* out of commission were orders to place the USS *Mohican* into commission. The change in ships was very welcome, for although the *Mohican* was another old wooden ship, an exact sister of the *Marion*, it had been under reconstruction for years and was completely rebuilt.[97] It was like moving to a new ship but just like our old one. However, the *Mohican* was to serve a far different purpose, for instead of doing "Pacific Station" duty as did the *Marion*, it was to be the training ship for the West Coast apprentices, making long cruises over the Pacific Ocean. It is no wonder that we looked forward to the change.

Fitting out the *Mohican* was routine uninteresting work. We retained as many as possible of the old *Marion*'s crew, saving sufficient space for the three hundred apprentices who were to come aboard for training.[98]

Our orders were for a circular cruise around the South Pacific Ocean over a route to Honolulu, Fanning Island, Samoa, Fiji, Australia, New Zealand, Chile, and then north along the coast of the Americas to San Francisco. A more interesting cruise could hardly be imagined.

Although the *Mohican* had been nearly entirely rebuilt, it had not been modernized. It still had only the old muzzle-loading guns of Civil War days and cramped quarters for both officers and men. While the officers had the usual small rooms in the wardroom, all enlisted men slept in hammocks, which had to be lashed and stored in the nettings on the spar deck every morning. Here and there throughout the ship were the usual old-time oil, standing lamps, but in the officers' rooms there were only candles. There were neither baths nor running

An Admiral's Yarn

water; the enlisted men always washed on deck from buckets, generally filled with salt water. Each officer's room had a tin water pitcher and basin, but for bathing, a small, shallow, round tub was placed in each room with a bucket of water in it. Since the floor space was tiny, there was not enough room for the tub unless the chair was removed. As soon as the officer had dried himself after a bath, he had to climb up on to his bunk while the little tub was moved out to provide floor space for dressing. All in all, no one lived very sumptuously in the *Mohican*, yet we were all well pleased to be there and starting on such a wonderful cruise.

Having completed our Navy Yard work, we dropped down to San Francisco to load our fuel and supplies before sailing. Our bunkers were already full of coal, but as we would have much steaming to do entering and leaving ports on such a long cruise, it was decided to take on a deck load also. To permit that, the waist broadside guns were run out and the ports closed tightly before bulkheads were erected all along the deck, inboard of the guns. Thus we created a space around and over the guns between the bulkheads and the ship's side that could be filled with coal to the level of the hammock nettings. It was a crude arrangement but the best we could do before taking on a deck load of coal.

While we were thus engaged, the newspapers printed the startling news that the USS *Maine* had been blown up in Havana Harbor. Unable to predict the ramifications of this, we continued coaling and preparations for sea.[99] Just before the hour set for our sailing, we received an order to depart on our cruise as scheduled but to await further orders when we arrived at Honolulu.

Our departure from San Francisco was the usual "get-away," but as we crossed the bar we found a heavy swell running, and that night we ran into a strong gale and heavy seas. Being an excellent sea boat, the ship stood the bad weather well enough, although it rolled and pitched so heavily that not only were all of the young apprentices seasick but our deck load of coal began to shift and knock down the bulkheads.

There was no great danger to the ship, however, and we thought little of it beyond the mess it caused, as it finally packed itself down again. Still there was danger to our seasick apprentices, for they dropped just any place and we did not know if any of them had been caught in the shifting coal. We therefore held a muster, a very difficult matter in the darkness of night when the boys were lying all over the ship, too sick to answer when their names were called. The muster took most of the night, and we accounted for every soul but one, a rather small boy named Ross. Consequently, all the next day we searched the ship high and low for Ross. When he was not found, we feared he had been caught under the coal, so be began to dig frantically trying to find him. How all the hands worked

Still in Wood

on that coal in the rolling, pitching ship, I do not know, but when all three hundred tons of it was moved and not a trace of Ross was found, we made another complete search of the ship for him. We were unsuccessful and had to enter in the log that Ross has been lost overboard during the night.

The bad weather continued for two or three days, and during all of it the apprentices remained too seasick to work. Wherever there was a clear space on deck, it was always full of seasick boys, and even when the sea had gone down and water no longer came over the forecastle, the deck remained covered with boys too ill to be disturbed.

It was while I was on watch looking over the forecastle on our third afternoon out that a small apprentice started up the forecastle ladder looking very dirty and pale. But as he seemed rather spry, I began watching him when suddenly I realized it was Ross. I could hardly believe my eyes, for there he was, alive and on board, so I called him to the bridge and asked where in the world he had been hiding during our search for him. Ross was greatly surprised that he had been missed, and still more that we thought he had fallen overboard. When I insisted on knowing where he had been, he said he could not tell exactly but would show us the place. A master-at-arms was sent with him, and it turned out to be a tiny, remote corner in the ship's bilges—a place that had been looked into repeatedly but in which Ross, who was then about the color of the bilge water itself, could not be seen. He seemed at a loss to know how he found the place but did remember being "awfully sick" and, thinking there would be less motion at the bottom of the ship, had squeezed himself into a tiny niche. When he recovered, he crawled out and followed daylight until he finally came out on deck where he soon began to feel better.

I was delighted to find Ross safe and sound and told the master-at-arms to take him to the galley for something to eat and then have him "wash up," put on clean clothes, and carry on. Toward the end of my watch I saw Ross again, apparently sneaking up on the forecastle where some twenty-five or thirty seasick boys were lying seemingly "dead to the world."

Ross looked them over in a superior sort of way. He then went to one, unrolled a good-sized piece of bacon rind stolen from the galley, to which he had tied a string, placed the bacon close under the nose of the sick boy, withdrew to the length of the string and sat down to watch. His victim suddenly jumped up, made a dash for the side of the ship and heaved up. Ross then began to look for another victim, but before he could locate one, I called him to the bridge for "look-out watch," made him toss the bacon overboard, and thus ended that bit of mischief.

An Admiral's Yarn

Finally the sea quieted down, the wind came out from the northeast, and we put on all sail. Soon our seasick boys became better and we made a fine trip to Honolulu.

But while the boys all went back to work with a will, Ross did not. He was always up to some mischief, loafed and shirked all the time, and was on report every day for some wilful disobedience of regulations. He was surly and insubordinate and such a nuisance that shortly after we arrived in Honolulu, the captain decided to discharge him as undesirable, even though he knew that was exactly what Ross wanted.

There is a naval regulation that undesirables cannot be discharged in a foreign port, and since Hawaii was not then a part of the United States, it was impossible to discharge Ross there. The captain told him that no more time could be wasted on him, but he would merely keep him on board until the opportunity arrived to send him home. In the meantime, Ross was told not to consider himself a member of the ship's company or work with it and to remain under a certain deck where he could sleep on a chest and have his meals brought to him, not associating with any of the boys.

Ross then appeared in fine feather as he moved his belongings to the chest and proceeded to live there. At first he seemed happy and proud as he saw the other boys at work and made fun of them, but when the tables were turned and they jeered at him, that was a different story, and he became sullen.

One day when I was on watch, Ross put on his best uniform and came around to "the mast" where men stood when they wished to present a grievance. When asked what he wanted, he said, "I want to see the captain and tell him I'll be good if he will take me off that chest." The captain really hurried to the deck when told that Ross wanted to see him. Little Ross stood there like a man, saluted the captain and said gravely, "Captain, if you will take me off the chest and let me go back to work, I promise that you will never have trouble with me again." He was at once restored to duty and for the remainder of my duty on the *Mohican*, little Ross was one of the best boys on board.

That stay in Honolulu was uneventful, and those who had friends there were soon again engulfed in the pleasures of Honolulu life. But although all seemed quiet on the surface, there was great unrest throughout the islands because of the question of annexation. Hawaii was frantically seeking it, but Congress, although in session, had not voted on it, and then, too, there was the growing possibility of the United States declaring war on Spain.

Under the circumstances, intense interest for news from the Coast was paramount, but there was no cable, and the only means of hearing was via the

Still in Wood

mail which steamers brought about twice a week. Both Americans and Hawaiians were very aroused.

After several weeks of waiting, still without news of war or annexation, one of the mail steamers brought orders for the *Mohican* to return to San Francisco, and we lost no time in starting. With bunkers full, we made the best speed possible, using sail to increase it whenever there was a fair wind. Even so, the trip took about seven days and it was May 3rd [1898] before we reached San Francisco bar. As we headed for the entrance buoy, the pilot stood to intercept us, and when within hailing distance, we heard that war had been declared on Spain the week before. Our Asiatic Fleet under Commodore [George] Dewey entered Manila Bay on May 1st and sank the entire Spanish fleet. After that news, the three hours it took us to reach San Francisco seemed endless, but when we finally anchored and confirmed the news, we were all agog as to what might happen to us on the old wooden *Mohican*, as it could not be used for war operations.

We immediately reported our arrival in San Francisco to the Navy Department, and the following morning we received telegraphic orders to proceed to the Mare Island Yard at once, where we waited impatiently for a few days to know our next assignment. To our amazement we received orders to disembark our apprentices and prepare for duty in the Pacific Islands. This was not very welcome news. We had expected the ship to be decommissioned at once and all of us sent East to ships in the fighting zone. So, when it appeared we were destined for other than was service, our disappointment knew no bounds.

Nor was the disappointment lessened as we noted the activities on more modern ships in the Navy Yard. Several years of rebuilding the *Baltimore* had just been completed, and she was hurriedly commissioned and then rushed to Honolulu to await further orders to proceed to the Philippines to join Dewey. The monitors *Monterey* and *Monadnock* came in to prepare for war service, as did other ships for hurried work, and officers of the yard were sent East to join ships there—while the *Oregon* was started around the Horn. But for us on the *Mohican*, nothing happened. We prepared the old ship for probable peaceful Pacific duty, while longing for active war service, but even our requests in writing for assignments in the Far East went unanswered.

A few days after the *Baltimore* departed for Honolulu, the Department received a cable from Dewey requesting ammunition be sent via the *Baltimore* to refill his magazines that were emptied at the battle of Manila Bay.

Because there was no cable to Honolulu and no way to intercept the *Baltimore*, the *Mohican* was ordered to take on the ammunition for Dewey and proceed at once to Honolulu with all speed.

An Admiral's Yarn

It was quite a problem to stow all that ammunition in the old *Mohican*, but we worked day and night, reduced our own supplies to a minimum, and in a few days started on our way. With a good wind behind us, filling our sails all the way and steaming at our best speed, we made Honolulu in less than a week. The transfer of ammunition was rushed to the *Baltimore* and it was soon on its way to Dewey.

Alone there in Honolulu, the *Mohican* prepared for war situations that might arise. None of us had hope of seeing active service, since the first mail steamer that came in brought word to each one who had applied for war duty that his request "had been placed on file." That irked me considerably, especially because I had also asked the Congressman[100] from my district to help me get Atlantic duty, and a letter from him in the same mail said he had written the Department but was told "We must keep experienced officers in Honolulu."

It was thus apparent that if I were to get into the war at all, I would have to find a way by myself, so I decided to write the Navy Department again. I pointed out that practically all of my experience at sea had been in modern ships, that I knew modern ordnance and had been turret officer on the *Oregon*, and that I knew nothing about the old muzzle-loading Civil War guns on the *Mohican*. Then I asked once more to be sent to war service and ended my letter by saying, "I do not want to spend the rest of my life explaining why I did not get into the war with Spain."

As was necessary with an official letter, I handed mine to the captain to forward it. He was furious when he read it and sent for me at once. When I appeared, he demanded to know what I meant by sending in such a letter. I explained that it was the only way I could be sent to the war and I would like to have it go to the Department. He just glared at me and said, "Young man, you will be court-martialled if you send in that letter," to which I replied, "I might as well be court-martialled as not get in that war." With that he yelled "Get out of my cabin," which I did.

For the next three or four weeks I was on "tenterhooks," for I knew the captain had sent the letter, although what he recommended for me, I did not know. All I could do was wait, helping as best I could to keep the *Mohican* ready to meet emergencies. But after the Battle of Manila Bay, Spain had no real fighting ships in the Pacific, and it did not seem possible that there would be trouble in Honolulu, a neutral port. Still, if there were Spanish sympathizers in Hawaii, they might attempt to seize our ship. Or, if there were Spanish merchant ships somewhere in the Pacific, they could be armed to attack us—so we made ready for those contingencies.

Still in Wood

The ship was moved so that its guns would cover the channel into the harbor, and we trained daily for firing on any ship that entered. Had a wooden ship with old-fashioned, muzzle-loading guns tried to come in, we probably could have stopped it. But, had steel ships with breech-loading rifles appeared, we could have been destroyed before even getting our guns within range. However, we were not deterred in our efforts. Our starboard battery, which covered the harbor entrance, was kept busy at all times. The ship's complement was divided into parts, each trained to operate the starboard battery; only the watch "off duty" was allowed ashore.

In such ways did we make ready for an attack from the sea and also from ships that entered the port, which our captain considered more probable, so we made greater preparations for that.

Not only were rifles, pistols, cutlasses, and pikes kept on deck, ready for instant use against "boarders," but the captain arranged for a "boiling water defense."

The boiling water defense was a new one on us! To provide it, the captain had the bottom blows [values and piping for expelling sludge] of our twelve Scotch boilers connected directly to the fire main. By merely opening the bottom valves of the boilers under steam, the pressure would drive the water and steam into the fire mains and out the fire hose. To permit the nozzles of the hoses to be handled while shooting out the hot water, they were covered with heavy burlap wrappings.

Our preparations for fighting made our spar deck a rare sight indeed. The entire starboard battery was kept case-loose, with the guns trained on the entrance channel ready for instant use. Easily available were the rifles, pistols, and cutlasses; and attached to each fireplug was a boiling water hose.

By drilling daily, we kept the ship in constant readiness, but when not on duty we enjoyed recreations and pleasures on shore—although the greatest excitement for everyone was the arrival of the steamers with mail which brought the only news we had of either the war or annexation, unless navy transports bound for Manila carried some mail for us. How we studied the war news and how we envied those being ordered to join Dewey in Manila Bay!

As the weeks went by, we gradually grew resigned to our fate but always hoped there might be a change for us. In the interim, I decided to buy a bicycle and enjoy riding, though always keeping an eye out for the arrival of mail, which became more and more important to me as the time approached for a reply to my last request for active service. Would the request bring war duty or an order to be court-martialled as the Captain predicted?

The answer came the very day I bought that bicycle. I had gone ashore after lunch, paid the $105 standard price for a new bicycle in Honolulu, and had

An Admiral's Yarn

ridden off on it to Waikiki for a swim. I was barely into the water when I saw a mail steamer nosing its way around Diamond Head. Anxious to learn what word, if any, it might be bringing to me, I rushed into my clothes, jumped on my bicycle, and hurried back to town.

The mail was on the *Mohican* when I reached it, and shortly thereafter the captain sent for me and handed me a paper to read. It was an order detaching me from the *Mohican* upon the arrival of the USS *Monadnock* on its way to Manila, directing me to report to that ship for duty.[101]

The captain was as mad as a hornet, for instead of a court-martial, which he had recommended for me, I was being sent to the war as I had requested. The Department had received my pleasing letter one day and issued my orders the next. Naturally I was overjoyed.

XI

Off to War in a Monitor

WHEN DEWEY DESTROYED THE SPANISH FLEET at Manila, the war changed for the United States. Until then, we had thought war would be almost entirely against the Spanish army in Cuba and against the Spanish navy in the Atlantic. But Dewey's victory so altered the picture that the Philippines took on great importance. By the Manila Bay battle, he had gained control of the sea, but the Spanish army still held the islands, even in the face of a then rising native insurrection. If we were to realize complete success in the war, we had not only to retain our control of the sea in the Philippines but to defeat the Spanish army there.

Our activities in the Pacific at once became intensified. The first step was to so increase the naval strength under Dewey that his superiority over any naval force that might be sent against him from Spain would be assured. As far as we knew, practically all the Spanish ships were then in Spain and under command of Admiral Cervera, and Admiral Cámara could be sent to fight Dewey.[102]

To prepare for such a naval threat, every suitable warship on our coast was hurriedly fitted out and dispatched to Manila. The first to go was the *Baltimore*, with the ammunition, followed soon by the cruiser *Charleston*. Then, as Dewey might require some really heavy fighting ships, it was decided to send him the two West Coast monitors, *Monterey* and *Monadnock*.

At the same time that the navy was preparing to retain command of the sea in the Philippines, the army was making ready to seize the islands and was moving troops to Manila Bay by transports as rapidly as possible. Hence, until the *Monadnock* left, Honolulu was a busy place, each transport having to stop there to replenish itself.

An Admiral's Yarn

I joined the *Monadnock* when it arrived, about ten days after I had received my orders. Up to that time, the warships and transports that touched at Honolulu hurried to be on their way, perhaps some of them leaving before being thoroughly prepared for duty in the war area. The *Monadnock*'s captain, however, did not take that chance. Having learned on the trip from San Francisco what the principal deficiencies of his monitor were for war service in the tropics, he determined to remedy them before leaving Honolulu. Consequently the *Monadnock* remained almost two weeks, working night and day to remedy defects.

Whether the delay was really advisable or not was a serious question. The ship was considerably improved for war service, but since Admiral Dewey could not be informed of the cause for the delay, he was greatly upset by our late arrival in Manila Bay, and our captain was terribly criticized for it.

Before leaving Honolulu, we knew that Cervera's squadron had crossed the Atlantic and reached Santiago de Cuba, to be bottled up there by [Rear] Admiral [William T.] Sampson's fleet. We knew of the military operations our country was undertaking in Cuba, not only toward capturing Santiago with Cervera's squadron hiding there, but also toward defeating the army that Spain had in Cuba. We also knew that the squadron in Spain under command of Admiral Cámara was being prepared for sea, but what we did not know was whether it was to cross the Atlantic to support Cervera, go to the Philippines to attack Dewey, or intercept the *Monadnock*. Such was the information as the *Monadnock* stood out in Honolulu.

Monitors like the *Monterey* and *Monadnock* were built solely for coastal defense purposes and were totally unsuited for deep-sea warfare; not only did every ocean swell roll right over their main decks, but their fuel supplies were far too small for long trips. At sea the main decks had always to be battened down and secured. The ships could engage in battle only in smooth water and only when comparatively little steaming would be required either before or after action. Since the monitors would be useful for defense purposes in the Philippine waters, our first major problem was to get them there even in the face of possible heavy enemy opposition.

Because their fuel supplies were too small to permit steaming from Honolulu to Guam or even from Guam to Manila against opposition, it was decided that the ships must be towed most of the way and refueled en route. A collier that could manage both was assigned to each monitor and was equipped with huge, specially made towing hawsers. For the *Monadnock*, the towing ship was the USS *Nero*, a commissioned collier purchased for that purpose.

Off to War in a Monitor

In addition to having its towing and fueling ship, the *Monadnock* carried not only all the coal it could stow in its bunkers but also as much of a deck load as could be put on board. The ship had a small deck over the superstructure, which was the only out-of-door space the personnel could use at sea, and that deck was filled with coal too. We rigged heavy rope netting entirely around each turret and filled it with bags of coal, hoping to use it before heavy seas could wash it overboard. So filled, the *Monadnock* had only fourteen inches freeboard when ready to sail, and more than ever looked like a heavily laden raft. To make the ship's appearance worse, each of the turrets stood out from a pile of coal and all personnel were black and dirty from coal dust when the monitor and collier stood out of Honolulu on the morning of July 13th, 1898.

As soon as the two ships were well clear of the channel, they stopped to rig the heavy towing gear, a trying and difficult bit of work in the swell that was running and which took until late afternoon to complete. Then, just as we were about to signal the *Nero* to start ahead with the tow, we saw the O. and O. steamship *Coptic* round Diamond Head and come at once toward us with unusual speed. We never learned why the *Coptic* did so, but it may have been that we looked exactly like a sinking warship.

The *Coptic* presented an unusual appearance, as the ship was dressed with flags from end to end and was flying a signal meaning "annexed." We immediately lowered a lifeboat which, under my charge, went to the *Coptic* for late newspapers and mail. The lifeboat was as messy a sight as could be imagined—both it and its occupants were grimy with coal dust and water-soaked with spray. It was difficult getting out of the boat and up the Jacob's ladder to the *Coptic's* deck, and by the time I clambered over the ship's rail, I couldn't have looked much like a naval officer. Not only was the *Coptic's* captain there to greet me, but all the passengers also, all talking at once about the war, about annexation, and about the great victory at Santiago just won by Sampson's fleet. Interesting as the news was, I could not stop to discuss it, but returned to the *Monadnock* with complete files of the latest San Francisco papers telling it all.

As soon as the boat could be hoisted, signal was made to the *Nero* to proceed towing. At last we were on our way to Dewey, leaving it for someone else to raise the United States flag over Hawaii.

Important though the annexation of Hawaii was, news of it meant very little to the *Monadnock* starting for the Philippines. What we needed most was information to indicate what we might expect on our way out, so it was indeed fortunate to have San Francisco newspapers with vitally important news items. Two of great interest to us were Sampson's destruction of the Spanish squadron

An Admiral's Yarn

at Santiago, which removed any threat from Cervera, and the bad news that Cámara's squadron had passed through the Suez Canal bound eastward.

This caused us great concern, for if his squadron had transited the Suez Canal a full week before the *Monadnock* left Honolulu, Cámara not only would reach Manila well before the *Monadnock* but might even defeat Dewey's fleet and attack the *Monadnock* before it could join up. We did not know the fighting strength Cámara might have, but no doubt Dewey's fleet would be superior with the addition of the monitors, so we hurried on, hoping to arrive before an engagement.

That passage to Manila was a nightmare. Speed was all-important, but even with the *Nero* up to its maximum towing speed, we found that we were making only 4½ knots instead of the 7½ we had counted on. Fortunately we could help some by using enough of our precious fuel to keep our engines turning over slowly, thereby overcoming our propeller drag—which we had planned to do in any event. Having adjusted ourselves to that fact, we soon learned as we neared the Philippines that we could not be sure of even 4½ knots if we were to have fuel enough for fighting. Not built for long trips in warm waters, the *Monadnock*'s machinery soon developed troubles that necessitated stopping for repairs that would take from a few hours to two days to complete—a very discouraging fact when speed was so vital.

Our speed provided anything but cheer, and there were other depressing things to keep our spirits low. The very first night out, heavy seas rolling over the forecastle washed overboard the eighteen tons of coal we had stowed around the forward turret—the supply for one day's steaming—and we also lost some of the coal from around the after turret! With our coal losses and poor speed, we were a depressed lot!

It took us exactly three weeks to reach Guam. Having the trade winds on our quarter, we rigged the bridge screens and made sails of our awnings to take advantage of it, but even with the wind and sea following us, we could never make over one hundred and ninety miles a day, and often much less.

During those three weeks our sufferings were great, for the ship was battened down to keep out the seas and almost no fresh air could enter except through the blowers to the fire rooms. Thus, the heat in the ship became intense and the air foul. In the steerage, where seven of us junior officers lived in a space of about ten feet by twenty feet, the temperature was usually 115°. One very smooth day we succeeded in luring a little fresh air into it and the temperature went down to 97° for a few hours, the lowest during our entire trip. Yet the seven of us had to eat, sleep, and live in that compartment, except when on watch on the superstructure, which for a week remained covered with coal.

We did not have refrigeration on the ship and were soon without fresh supplies, as the heat melted all the ice we had stowed aboard at Honolulu; the drinking water had a temperature of 100° and more, and we were obliged to resort to canned sea stores. Still, we gave little thought to our discomforts because we were on our way to fight for our country; we worked day and night to have the ship continuously ready for battle.

When we finally reached Guam, we found it had been captured by the USS *Charleston* and had the United States flag floating over it.[103] My, but it seemed good to be in a port, even such as Guam, to open the ship to fresh air, to eat fresh food, and to stretch our legs for a few hours on shore, and particularly to drink water under 90°, even though Guam had no ice. As pleasant as the change was, we could not stop for long. The *Monadnock* at once started repairs, the *Nero* came alongside, and we began coaling immediately. It took us two days to prepare our ship for the most dangerous part of our passage. Cámara could intercept us anywhere between Guam and Manila, so we had to be prepared at all times to fight his squadron as well as making all speed possible to Manila.

Cámara's squadron did not appear as we stood away from Guam, so the *Nero* again took us in tow and headed for a prearranged rendezvous six hundred miles due east of Cape Engaño where Admiral Dewey could communicate with us.

It was bright and early one Sunday morning when we sighted Cape Engaño, cast off the heavy towline, and headed west across the Gulf of Aparri at the northern end of Luzon. Being in the lee of the islands, the Gulf was as smooth as a millpond, an ideal condition for the *Monadnock* should we have the battle that everyone was expecting. But we did not see anything until we were just ready to round the northern point of Luzon and head to the southward for Manila Bay. Then on the horizon and about where were we heading, we saw three columns of smoke rising straight in the air and looking as though three large ships were steaming in column.

To us, that smoke meant but one thing—Cámara's squadron ready to attack us, and after our long, hard trip, we were delighted with the prospect, although we realized that with three powerful ships to our one, all the advantage would lie with Cámara. Nevertheless the *Monadnock* continued on its way toward the probable enemy, all hands feeling that in those waters, a monitor like ours might whip even three heavy Spanish ships. So sure were our men of a fight that they made all the preparations for battle; but the call for "general quarters" never sounded.

We never got much nearer to that smoke than when we first sighted it, as the ships responsible stood on to the northwest and finally disappeared over the horizon while the *Monadnock* headed for Manila, thus ending all chance of a

An Admiral's Yarn

battle. We learned later that the smoke came from three merchant ships bound from Manila to Hong Kong; but at the time our disappointment over missing a battle with the Spaniards was keenly felt. As the *Monadnock* stood down the west coast of Luzon, there was considerable sea which made heavy going for us. Just before dark that night we sighted a merchant ship flying the United States flag coming up on our starboard quarter. We endeavored to exchange calls with it, but after taking a good look at us, it continued, speedily, on its way.

At about noon the following day, while the sea was still heavy, and the *Monadnock* about thirty miles from the entrance to Manila Bay, we saw a man-of-war standing toward us at full speed dead ahead. We at once went to quarters, but as the ship neared we recognized our own USS *Baltimore*. It had been sent out full speed by Dewey when the merchant ship that passed us the evening before informed him of seeing an American man-of-war in a sinking condition.

While we were neither sinking nor in any danger of it, we were still glad to see a ship from Manila Bay, for the mere sight of it assured us that all was well with Dewey. But our happiness did not last long after reading a signal it flew that meant: "Hostilities have ceased." Then, as if that were not enough, a wig-wag message was received saying "Spanish army surrendered to Dewey before hostilities ceased. Our troops hold Manila. The war is over."

Our late arrival in manila was a terrible anticlimax for us. We were, of course, glad the war and our trip were over and we could return to peacetime living, but we felt we could never live down the stigma of having missed the war entirely.

XII

In Manila Bay

THE WAR WAS OVER and we were again at peacetime. Manila Bay and the surrounding area were fascinating, and after anchoring in smooth water at Cavite, we soon had awnings spread and the ship open to air. Natives in "bum" boats flocked around to sell us the local vegetables and fruits, and particularly "Filipino mangoes," the best in the world at the time. We also received fresh meats and ice from the refrigerating ships chartered by Dewey, which were known as "beef boats."

After six weeks at sea in a monitor, that change in living was delightful, but it was really only a small part of our total change, for Manila and Cavite were under the command of the army—and there were many pleasant contests between the army and the navy.

Our army in the Philippines numbered about fifteen thousand men, possibly less than Spain had in Manila, but the Spaniards surrendered—not so much because of the army, but because if they did not, Dewey's fleet stood ready to blast them out of Manila. However, it was to the United States forces that Manila surrendered. While a considerable army of Filipinos around the city were in insurrection against Spain, the insurrectionists took no part in the capture of Manila, and when the American troops entered the city, the Filipinos remained outside.

As Manila and Cavite were properly under our control shortly after the *Monadnock* arrived, we were soon allowed to visit. Each morning, one of the captured Spanish gunboats would leave the Cavite Navy Yard and stop near the *Olympia*, Dewey's flagship, to pick up a party from the fleet, take them to Manila,

An Admiral's Yarn

and return in the late afternoon. Thus, by taking advantage of this transportation, we could spend many off-duty hours in the interesting city.

Manila, just after the surrender, was little like the Manila of recent years. Today it is a modern American city, but then it was an ancient Spanish town. It was built around a large, old fort behind the heavy walls that enclosed the governor's palace and government buildings as well as the houses of important Spanish officials and businessmen. The walls were protected by a moat, and the area was known as the "Walled City"—truly representative of "Old Spain." Private business was not conducted there, so to see the "real" Manila, one remained in the large area outside. The strangest thing to me was to find nearly no Filipino stores in the business section; most of them were owned and operated by Spaniards or other Europeans. The less important and smaller shops were operated by Chinese or other Asiatics. The big hotel, the "Oriente," was typically Spanish in structure, built for the tropics and city limits. But as one wandered away from this district to the outskirts, only the reed and thatched huts of the natives were to be found.

There was enough sight-seeing to keep us amused for a while, but there was no social life at all, and it was not long before Manila grew monotonous. Some of us decided to organize the "Army and Navy Club," but even then we saw only officers of our service and then, too, there were restrictions on our wanderings—because of the Filipino insurrectionist army which had taken control outside, we had to remain inside our lines at Manila and Cavite.

The fifteen thousand U.S. troops in the Philippines as well as Dewey's fleet were barely sufficient to keep the armed Filipinos from taking over Manila and Cavite too.

For the first few months after Manila fell and the Spanish forces were being evacuated, the situation appeared fairly peaceful, though we knew the Filipino insurrectionists were claiming that the islands belonged to them rather than to the Americans. Pending the adoption of the treaty of peace with Spain, the Filipinos built up their army, ready to take over when the islands were handed to them. However, when the terms of the treaty were announced, Spain, of course, had ceded the islands to the United States. How our small military force could keep them safe for us was not apparent, and our country was not going to send more troops to the islands. The insurrection movement was confined chiefly to one tribe, the Tagalogs, which wanted to rule all others. It seemed to us that the majority of Filipinos wanted U.S. rule and protection, fearing the Tagalogs would control the islands to exploit the people for purely personal gain.

The Philippine situation became serious. Although the native group seeking control was only a small minority of one tribe, it was, unfortunately, an

In Manila Bay

organized and armed native that greatly out numbered the small force of the United States there. It is probable that, had it not been for our far-better equipped army and its artillery, the insurrectionists would have attempted to gain control as soon as Spain ceded the islands to us. A period of great tension arose during which the Americans did little to strengthen themselves against the increasingly ominous threat of the insurrectionists' efforts to gain strength and their apparent readiness to attack our troops to drive them out. With no reinforcements arriving from the U.S., there was little we could do to prevent the growth of the uprising. The army built and occupied a line of trenches completely around Manila, and at points north and south of the city where the entrenchments reached the bay, navy ships were anchored in position to support the army.

The defensive line around Manila was far from strong. Because of the size of the city, the line was perhaps twenty miles long, but we had only 15,000 troops to maintain it. The insurrectionists were said to number about 60,000 men and could make heavy attacks along our line should they so elect.

Because of its light draft and powerful guns, the *Monadnock* was detailed to support the army line near the Bay, south of Manila, at an old stone fort called "Malata." The line there was fairly strong, for in addition to Fort Malata, the Spanish had built a wall that extended inland some distance and could be held by comparatively small force if supported by a ship with guns to enfilade a frontal attack made on it. It was such a position, about seven hundred yards from Fort Malata, that the *Monadnock* took in the early winter of 1898. For nearly two months, little happened. Both the army and navy had been directed to avoid any act that might initiate trouble, so both attempted to carry on in a quiet manner, though being always ready to repel an attack. Supplies for the *Monadnock* were delivered by boat from the fleet, and each afternoon the dinghy would land three or four of us on the beach behind our lines just to stretch our legs a bit; but for the most part, we remained on board. Under such circumstances, life became monotonous. We were comfortable enough under our awnings with plenty of fresh food, but made much of any happening that was a trifle out of the ordinary. Hence, when a Filipino boat came down on us one night, it created a little excitement.

The officer of the deck was a young ensign, generally spoken of as "Dickey." He was very popular in the ship and was one who took his duties seriously.[104] For some reason, when he went on watch that night, he stuck his loaded revolver in his belt, although at that time there was no order for the officer of the deck to be armed. The usual lookout and sentries were at their several stations around the ship, the night was clear with bright starlight, and to Dickey, all seemed set for a

An Admiral's Yarn

pleasant watch in the beautiful tropical weather. As was the custom, Dickey spent most of his time walking back and forth on the quarterdeck, alert to every movement either on shore or around the Bay. Each half hour, he went entirely around the main deck, speaking to each sentry and lookout to check on their alertness. He found the watch being maintained faithfully and well. Some two hours after he had taken over, and while he was on the quarterdeck, Dickey heard the sentry on the forecastle cry out "Boat ahoy." Rushing to the forecastle, he saw a boat about seventy-five yards away approaching very slowly along the starboard side.

Dickey at once became suspicious and directed the lookout to hail the boat, which he did several times. But as the boat continued to move slowly, Dickey hailed the boat himself, calling "Boat ahoy." After no response, he finally ordered it to "halt." As the boat continued to move toward the ship, Dickey whipped out his revolver and fired a shot in the water near it. Still the boat did not stop or show any sign of life in it, and, as the deck watch had then gathered about him, Dickey ordered a couple of hands to take the dinghy and bring the boat to the ship. When the boat came under the ship's lights, it was found to be an empty Filipino canoe, dugout type, with an outrigger and a fishing net lying in the bottom. Apparently it was a poor fisherman's canoe broken adrift by the wind and tide. It was still secured alongside when all hands turned out the next morning, and it is probable that nothing more would have been heard of the boat incident had not Dickey been so "cocky" and pleased with himself over his actions. This stirred the other officers of his mess, so they began to plan a way to take him down a peg. To that end they evolved a scheme which, since I was the "captain's clerk," required my assistance.

I was much perturbed, as they wanted to use my office to give official appearance to their prank. I feared this might tend to compromise some interests of the captain, for which I was responsible. They then agreed to make the plan known to the captain who, to my surprise, allowed it to be carried out. He said to me, "I am rather put out with Dickey over the way he handled the matter, although it showed he was keen and alert, as I had given no orders for the officer of the deck to arm himself or to fire on an approaching boat. More than that," he added, "that one shot fired by Dickey might have started a Filipino uprising, as the present situation is so intense. I do not wish to punish him, as he is really an excellent officer, but it might be a good thing if the other officers could make him realize the danger of misapplied initiative. Tell the officers to go ahead with their prank, but they simply must not involve the admiral or me in any way." I was to keep him posted.

In Manila Bay

    The plotters were delighted and we all set about to put their plan into effect. The first step was to make Dickey write a report of his "Capture of a Filipino Vessel." Doing that proved easy, for when I said to him a day or two later, "Dickey, you recall, of course, Article ____ of the Navy Regulations, which requires a written report to be made of any vessels captured, so do not forget to hand it in to me." Dickey wrote a long letter giving every detail of his "Capture of one Filipino vessel," and while not describing the "vessel," he devoted his efforts to showing his own alert and efficient performance of duty which so closely followed the old adage, "Whoso tooteth not his own horn, the same shall not be tooted." Dickey dreamed of a promotion and became cockier than ever, even after reading a fake endorsement we had put on his letter, suggesting the court enquire into the capture. Why Dickey did not tumble to the joke when he saw that endorsement, we could not understand, for it had been prepared by the plotters and was so utterly unlike anything official that "fake" was apparent all the way through. Still, his hope of great glory was too keen to allow him to see any impropriety in it. His failure to recognize the absurdity of the endorsement caused the joke to go much further than the plotters ever intended and put them in the position of having to either continue with it or beat an ignominious retreat. Since the court must not have even a semblance of being official, it could not be carried on during working hours. It was therefore held at night as an after-dinner feature for the Wardroom Officers' Mess, but even that ridiculous procedure did not arouse Dickey's suspicion.

    After coffee, one evening, the self-appointed court members called for their swords while the other members of the mess moved from the table to chairs around the wardroom, and court opened. Dickey was told to take the seat next to the "recorder." It was unlike any court the navy had ever known. The senior member gravely began to read Dickey's letter to the court, putting particular emphasis on the most self-laudatory part. That reading was a histrionic masterpiece, I assure you, which should have brought the joke to a good end. However, Dickey still did not see anything wrong with the court, so it directed him to give a full verbal account of the capture. He was then asked what he, as a naval expert, considered the value of the Filipino vessel, and after thinking a moment, to our utter amazement replied, "About two thousand dollars." This valuation left the court gasping, but one member asked if he meant gold or "mex." "Two thousand gold," said Dickey without batting an eye. The court was more astounded than ever, as the little boat was about as worthless as a boat could be. Then he was questioned on the size of the boat—about which he seemed in doubt—but gave dimensions in figures almost double those of the captured vessel. The court followed along this line for half an hour, and Dickey at last had

An Admiral's Yarn

to admit it was only a small boat in poor condition and that perhaps he had overvalued it. Thus, apparently, he was beginning to feel some doubt as to the magnitude of his heroism. However, as Dickey still seemed very much in earnest, the court continued. To tell the truth, the proceedings were so ridiculously preposterous that the members wondered whether the "leg-pulling" was done by themselves or by Dickey!

Though the members were full of doubt, they decided on a new tack the following night and asked Dickey if it was customary for an officer of the deck to be armed and to fire on a passing ship when in an American port under conditions of peace. He answered in the negative and was then questioned on the political situation. Finally he admitted that it was so serious that a mere spark could easily explode it into a real war. He was growing a bit nervous but still did not belittle himself or his performance of duty, even when asked if he had turned the ship's searchlights on the boat. The court knew he had failed to do so, as it also knew he had neglected to have the lights tested.

With this evidence against him, Dickey began shifting from seat to seat along the table until, instead of being next to the recorder at one end, he was alongside the members at the other. The members then began shifting to the other side of the table, one seat at a time, and as Dickey continued to follow, they continued to move. I doubt if in all of naval history there is anything to equal the "run around" of that remarkable court, for it made two complete circuits before adjournment was announced to await action of the "convening authority." The recorder was directed to prepare the record for signing, since no other witnesses were to be called. When he realized all the work and time this involved, the recorder demanded to know who the victim of the joke was—Dickey or himself! It took much persuasion to convince the recorder that such an amusing and unusual court proceedings should be preserved in writing, but he finally agreed to cooperate. Although it took a week to complete, with signatures, etc., the record was then handed to the senior member of the court while Dickey was present. Then I was asked to deliver it to the captain and, in consequence, was hounded by Dickey to know what the captain would do about it. But I could not venture a hint. He feared the captain might send it to the commander in chief, and he watched the mail boats constantly. He was a good actor if he was "stringing us," because we were not quite sure of ourselves.

The next evening just before coffee was served, the captain's orderly, following instructions, hurried to the wardroom and without a word handed a huge envelope to the senior member of the court. Slowly he opened the envelope, glanced at the court record it contained and saying "Humph! Dickey's court," he uninterestedly stuck it back in the envelope, lighted a cigar, and began

In Manila Bay

his smoke over his coffee. Dickey nearly passed out. At last, the senior member again took up the record and, glancing slowly over its pages, suddenly said "Ah, here we are" and with that proceeded to read the endorsement to the record by the "convening authority," which I knew well, because I had typed it.

1. The convening authority desires this endorsement be read to Wardroom officers assembled at mess.

2. The convening authority wishes to express its appreciation of the zeal shown by Ensign _____ while officer of the deck at the time of the capture of the Philippine vessel. His bravery is clearly proven by his own testimony.

3. It is noted that although no details of the captured vessel were given by Ensign _____ in his written report, he did, while testifying as a naval expert, prove the vessel was only a very old, rotten canoe, the value of which he gradually reduced from two thousand dollars gold to twenty-five dollars "mex."

4. Certain facts were elicited from the ensign's report which the convening authority cannot ignore and are as follows:

First, That Ensign _____ armed himself with a loaded revolver before going on watch that night although he had no orders to do so.

Second, That Ensign _____ fired on a friendly vessel in time of peace, not having orders to do so.

Third, That by firing that shot, the ensign ignored the possibility of his starting a condition of war by firing on a Filipino vessel.

Fourth, The ensign failed to use a searchlight to determine the character of a suspicious vessel.

Fifth, That before shooting, the ensign had completely neglected to test the searchlights of the *Monadnock* when coming on duty.

These facts do not harmonize well with his testimony proving his zeal and bravery but indicate a laxity in the performance of duty by officers of the *Monadnock*, a laxity the "convening authority" does not concede. Since the actions of Ensign _____ on the night of the capture tend to reflect a certain amount of discredit on all of the *Monadnock's* officers, the "convening authority" deems it only right and proper that Ensign _____ furnish to the Wardroom Mess of the *Monadnock* six quarts of champagne properly chilled.

An Admiral's Yarn

There was, of course, great suspense while that endorsement was being read out, for only at the end, when we could see Dickey's reaction to it, would we know whether he would accept the joke or pass it back to the court. He showed various emotions, but finally broke into a broad smile of relief and pleasure. Almost at once he cried out, "Boy, boy! Bring on the champagne." It appeared almost at once, as all preparations for serving it had been prearranged, although it was not known whether the members of the court or Dickey would have to pay for it. Dickey elected himself the host!

We all remained at the table, talking the court over and drinking champagne for a considerable time, and when the last bottle was consumed and it was thought the party about ended, I said to Dickey, "When did you catch on to the fact that the court was a joke?" Looking around the table in wild-eyed amazement he said, "Joke! Joke! You don't mean the whole thing is a joke?" Then when we confirmed the fact, he looked solemn for a second and then called, "Boy! Boy! Bring on six more quarts." Thus ended the court.

Not every unusual event aboard the *Monadnock* had such a pleasant ending—there was one that caused us all sadness and regret. The Chief Petty Officer's mess had a drinking party which was kept very secret. No one except the mess members would ever have known of it except for the unfortunate fact that the day after it, the Chief Boatswain's Mate of the ship was found lying on the forecastle in a state of coma. He was at once carried to "sick bay," where the doctors quickly found that he had been drinking. But whether his condition was caused by that or not was not at once ascertained. However, instead of recovering, the man was sinking rapidly and was rushed ashore to the Naval Hospital where he died that night. Word of his alarming attack went through the ship like wildfire, but even the doctors were at a loss to determine whether it was caused by poison or excessive drinking. Soon the Chief Master at Arms was taken ill and, while in "sick bay" and badly frightened, divulged the fact that some alcohol had been stolen from the ship's supply and made into a punch of which they all drank freely.

At that time, because it was rather new to the world, the poisonous effects of wood alcohol were not known, and little attention had been paid when the alcohol supplied to naval ships was changed from grain to wood alcohol. Possibly the doctors knew about the deadly effects of the latter for which there was no known antidote, but not realizing anyone would steal or drink it, failed to caution those aboard ship. The Chief Master of Arms died, and the following day another of our Chief Petty Officers passed on.

The deaths of three leading enlisted men of the *Monadnock* from wood alcohol poisoning brought a wave of consternation in Dewey's fleet. Steps were

In Manila Bay

taken immediately to warn everyone in the fleet of the deadly effects of wood alcohol, for which there was no antidote, and to use caution against the fumes when applying shellac on inside doors.

Report was also made by cable to the Navy Department that it might inform all ships of the danger in the alcohol supplied them. We thought that having sent out such a warning, the Navy Department would continue to supply wood alcohol, but instead, it ordered all ships to rid themselves of wood alcohol at once and directed that thereafter they carry only grain alcohol. As far as I know, that order is still in effect.

Time dragged heavily from our arrival in August '98 until February 5, '99, on which day the great Filipino insurrection broke out. As far as we knew, there were no overt actions on our part that started it. Nevertheless, about two o'clock in the morning, February 5th, the insurrectionist army, in all its strength, suddenly began heavy attacks along the entire length of our defensive line around Manila.

XIII

Insurrection in the Philippines

WHY THE FILIPINOS ATTACKED when they should not have was ever a mystery to us. We firmly believed that every Filipino would benefit from U.S. rule and that the vast majority of them wanted that. We could only reason that not an act of commission by the United States but rather an act of omission caused the outbreak, i.e., because we could not immediately establish a civil government for them when Spain ceded the islands to us. I still believe that had the United States not omitted to promptly set up a government throughout the islands, the insurrection might not have occurred. However, that was nearly impossible for us. We had never before dealt with the problem of governing a large and populous area far across the sea. We were not prepared. Thus, at the outbreak of the insurrection, the only portion of the islands governed by us was the area around Manila Bay.

Apparently it was the absence of government at that time that prompted the Filipinos to establish one. The set-up was almost perfect, for except at Manila and Cavite close by, where our troops were, the only organized group on the islands was the one gathered around Manila, calling itself the "Filipino Army." It was a comparatively small, minority group of a local tribe, but it wanted to hold the reins and accumulate the spoils through governing the entire archipelago. They believed they were strong enough not only to defeat the small army we had in the islands but to establish a government of their own long before the United States could do anything about it. In the parlance of the time, "the psychological moment had arrived," so they struck.

It was said that the insurrectionists around Manila numbered nearly sixty thousand men, most of whom were equipped with rifles and plenty of

An Admiral's Yarn

ammunition. The remainder carried bolos, spears, and other native equipment. Holding the initiative and being in a position to select the points of attack, while our own small force was spread over the entire defensive line, the insurrectionists had us in the "jaybird seat." If such a movement could have ever succeeded, it should have been that day. Both sides realized this, and the fighting was desperate.

The *Monadnock's* position on the extreme right of the defensive line around Manila was a vital one. The terrain outside the line was dry and furnished such fine cover for the attacks that the insurrectionists close it for their major effort. If they could break through our defense there, they not only would have easy and quick access to the business and wealthy part of Manila for looting, but at the same time would outflank the defenders and have them at their mercy. For that reason, they concentrated their attack on that flank and on the *Monadnock*.

As signal officer of the *Monadnock*, and responsible for our communication with the army, I took station aloft where I had a wonderful view of the battle in the Fort Malata area. The insurrectionists had a good plan. They put the army line and the *Monadnock* under intense rifle fire, apparently to weaken or drive the defenders away, their intent being to seize the line. Therefore, from about 2 a.m. until early the following afternoon, we were besieged with a hail of Mauser bullets. The firing was incessant, so the noise of the battle continued steadily. But, although the army defenders were firing constantly, the *Monadnock* remained silent; the army had requested us not to open fire until they needed our support. It was not pleasant to be under such heavy fire and not reply to it, and it is possible the insurrectionists thought they had silenced the ship; since the time we had carried out a stern anchor and moored the ship so that it would be parallel to the beach when we "opened fire," they had not seen any activity on board. To haul the ship to its position necessitated using men to heave in on the exposed quarterdeck capstan. As we did that, the Filipinos concentrated their fire on the capstan. Strange to say, even with such a hail of bullets, only one man was wounded—a fireman who came up to get some fresh air. As he stepped on a deck, a bullet struck his kneecap, crippling him for life. Shortly after noon the volume of fire on the *Monadnock* decreased considerably. Nevertheless, we were kept under a constant stream of single bullets sufficiently accurate to be annoying. We could not see anyone firing the shots, but after careful watch we decided the most effective ones came from an old wreck lying on the beach just outside our defensive line. Making sure that insurrectionist sharpshooters were sniping at us from that wreck, we gained permission from the army to shell them with our 6-pdr. guns. It did not take long to rout the snipers, for when our little shells began to burst we saw some of them running, and later discovered the

Insurrection in the Philippines

bodies of others. The insurrectionists continued their heavy firing on our army's trenches, and when I saw they were massing their reserves in the wood, brush, and fields close behind their line of trenches, I sent a report at once to the army to warn them of an impending charge. They had just observed the concentration and requested us to open fire on it, which we did. Being all set up for it, we responded quickly with all our guns, 10-inch, 4-inch, 6-pdrs. and 3-pdrs. That heavy gunfire and the tremendous explosions of our 10-inch shells, coupled with the army's heavy, rapid fire, just as the Filipinos charged, was too much for them. The front of the charge barely reached our trenches when suddenly the entire charging line turned tail and ran. Our army rushed out of their trenches after them, and the *Monadnock* steamed along the beach while continuing its gunfire.

How far the insurrectionists on that Fort Malata front ran that day we never knew, but the army chased them about three miles to the village of Parañaque and then halted to dig in, not wanting to extend their defensive line to the breaking point. The *Monadnock* anchored off the village to continue its support, if necessary, but by dark that night, the great attack on Manila had not only utterly failed but our army had established a new defensive line around the city, two or three miles farther out.

The next several days were quiet. As we took stock of the battle, we felt we had inflicted a crushing defeat sufficient to stop the movement forever. However, we soon found we were wrong, for within a week the insurrectionists, not seeing the arrival of further troops or activity from us, again began to assemble outside our new defensive line. At first their slow movements were scarcely apparent to us, but before long troops and trenches began to appear, compelling the *Monadnock* to illuminate them with searchlights should their plan be to surprise attack us. For a while the searchlights kept the Filipinos fairly quiet at night, but as time passed they grew bolder and bolder. Finally they fired on the ship. This continued for several weeks and, although not incessant, it continued sporadically throughout the day and night.

Unpleasant as we found the firing, it was rather ineffective, for bullets hitting the ship did no damage at all and practically none hit personnel. We became so accustomed to their whizzing around that we paid little attention to them except when the firing became very heavy and in volleys, and we were obliged to seek protection. That condition held for several weeks before anyone was wounded. But one day, when the firing was light and we were sitting around the decks, a stray bullet came along where two men were talking. The bullet hit one of them in the jaw, passed through under his tongue, and brought up in his

An Admiral's Yarn

shoulder on the other side. It was not a particularly serious wound but enough to make us realize that real hits might be expected at any time.

During this period we remained generally inactive though occasionally, when the firing at us became unusually heavy, the ship would throw a few shells into the Filipino trenches and the buildings of Parañaque. The firing would then cease. But as we never made a hostile move, and as troop reinforcements were not arriving, the insurrectionists grew steadily bolder and more active. They not only fired on our trenches and the *Monadnock* continuously, but they started to attack and kill every American found outside our lines. We tried to "hold everything" until sufficient troops arrived to handle the situation, and when they finally did, our very weak lines were strengthened. The Filipinos continued a heavy fire all about the city and made every effort to establish their own government. Our first move against the insurrectionists was to the southward of Manila where the insurgent army was forming. The initiative for forcing matters was in our hands at last, so at a pre-established time, the army on our front advanced from the trenches and, with the *Monadnock* steaming along the shore and shelling just ahead of them, they drove the Filipinos back several miles more in what was called "the Battle of Parañaque."

Apparently in the belief that this southward attack would weaken our lines north of the city, the insurrectionists began to assemble a large army there and attack from that point. They did not succeed in breaking the line, yet the attempt was more than abortive—it resulted in the *Monadnock* being sent to support the line there and the army sending heavy reinforcements.

The area to the north of Manila was considerably more swampy than to the south and far more difficult for our army to attack, especially since the insurrectionists were well entrenched. Because of this swampy shoreline, they were unable to keep the *Monadnock* under fire while we waited for the army to attack. Also, the heavy swamp growth so hid the ship from shore that it attracted little attention. On the other hand, from our guns or from the bridge, we could not see the ground that we were expected to fire on or even see our army's position on shore. To send to or receive signals from the army, I had to climb high on the mast, and I found also from that position that I could see both our own and the insurgent lines beyond the low trees.

In those days, naval ships were not equipped for "indirect firing," and in order to inflict hits, we had to see the targets through our gunsights. Thus it appeared that the *Monadnock's* guns would be of little help in driving out the insurrectionists north of the city.

The first initiative was the army's. After a quick survey, it prepared an accurate map of the area showing the exact locations of the Filipino trenches and the

Monadnock, which was again moved head and stern in a fixed position. Then, having decided where they wanted our shells to fall, the army sent us messages giving the exact range and bearing from our guns and the spot they wanted our shells to strike. It then became the navy's problem to make them hit there!

Present day equipment can place an out-of-sight area under accurate gunfire, but this was not so in 1899. We had only the magnetic compasses used for steering from which to obtain direction, and no devices for transferring that direction to the guns—and gunsights were not designed to make hits at a particular range unless the target was visible to us. These were not the only difficulties, for while in the navy we ordinarily dealt only with magnetic directions, those given us by the army were always true directions. To shift from one to the other, we had to apply two correctives in azimuth—first the variation between the true north of the earth and the magnetic north as kept by a compass in the part of the world we were in at the time, and second, the deviation of the compass caused by the magnetism of the ship itself. With the gyrocompass we no longer have to compensate for these two errors. Getting true direction is easy now, but it was not that way forty years ago.

The azimuth corrections were quickly ascertained, but to lay the guns in a certain true direction given by the army was another problem. The only way we could meet that was to work from the true direction in which the ship was pointing (the true direction of our fore and aft line), and then train the guns through the proper number of degrees from the fore and aft lines to bring them to the correct true direction. Under today's conditions, pointing a ship's guns in the exact true direction desired requires only a few seconds, but at that time, it took a full day to accomplish it. With the guns pointed correctly in azimuth, our next problem was to point them above horizontal to the exact degree necessary to ensure that the shells would fall a given distance away. Today this is a simple matter, but not so in '99 when there was nothing to establish the horizontal or zero line—the angle of elevation from which the guns had to be measured. We were obliged to use a "gunner's quadrant," a device that when set on the gun itself would cause the pendulum to read 0° elevation when the gun was exactly horizontal. It would then show the number of degrees the gun moved through as its muzzle was elevated or depressed. This was a rather crude device for obtaining exact range, but it enabled us to lay the guns at the approximate angle of elevation necessary to hit the desired range.

It was fortunate that the ship was moored securely in position, for the slightest change in heading or heel would have necessitated complete alteration in the way the guns were laid. Being thus prepared, we were ready to do the navy's part when the army needed us. We arranged with them to do three trail shots, then to

An Admiral's Yarn

make the necessary corrections, and then to fire a designated number of single 10-inch shots. The explosion of the last shell was to be the signal for a general charge on the Filipino trenches. Out three trial shots were very deliberate, since after each one we had to await an army signal from the top of a church on shore informing us of exactly where our shot hit. Having made some corrections, the army then signaled us to "start string."

Not knowing just where the army wanted our shells to fall, I could not tell from my position high on the mast whether or not we were hitting "that" particular spot, but I could follow the shells with my eye and see them strike and explode close to the Filipino trenches. I think it was about the fifth shell of our string that raised unusual commotion as it threw up much debris. The army informed us later that the debris was the wreckage of the Filipino main artillery emplacement—the very object that the army had wanted destroyed. With the heavy artillery and rifle fire of the army and the terrific explosions of the *Monadnock's* 10-inch shells, the insurrection cracked, and cracked hard. From my perch on the mast I could see the entire Filipino line desert its trenches and run to the rear, pursued by our "dough boys." The firing became heavy and continued until, after capturing the village of Caloocan, the army stopped to consolidate its gains.

Those gains took them well beyond where naval ships could give support, and the natives suffered such defeat that their main army was badly damaged. However, the great victory at Caloocan was not without its cost to us—our army suffered severe losses in both men and officers. Killed in that fight was the very able and greatly beloved General Lawton.[105]

After the battle of Caloocan, the insurrection took a new turn. Numerous and heavy engagements continued to occur around Manila as the army carried on clean-up operations to destroy the large insurrectionist army north of the city. Under the pressure there and with the battle continuing southward, the army was kept busy, although it had the situation well in hand around Manila.

The islands at the time were populated by about seven million Filipinos who belonged to a large number of different tribes, each occupying certain areas on islands and each having its own language, customs, and religion. There was no common feeling or purpose among them, and each tribe wanted to fight with any other tribe they encountered. The Tagalogs were perhaps the strongest, the best-educated, and most politically minded of any, and it was they who first attempted to seize control. Without established government in the various areas, certain groups attempted to gain control, and it took the army and navy operating together to curtail this. To the navy fell the task of occupying the

Insurrection in the Philippines

larger towns, most of which were accessible by water, to prevent trade and assistance from reaching the rebel group.

There are hundreds of islands in the Philippine group, extending over an enormous area, and many of the islands are large. Therefore, covering the waters required many ships and especially several small ones of light draft, inland-water gunboats. The United States did not have gunboats of that type in the islands other than those taken from Spain. The sea-going ships of Dewey were available and their number slightly augmented by some from home, but they were generally too large and far too few to do all the reconnoitering and patrol work required of the navy.

Spain before us had faced the same problem, and so, while Dewey had destroyed their fleet of sea-going ships, there remained a considerable number of gunboats when the islands were ceded to us. Of no use to Spain, the gunboats were turned over when we took the islands and soon after transferred to Manila, where they were surrendered to Dewey.

Most of us had not heard about the gunboats, so when eighteen of them stood into Manila Bay, each flying its largest Spanish flag, we did not know what was up. The surprise was soon over as the gunboats steamed past our fleet into the Pasig River where they were moored in shallow water, their Spanish flags hauled down, and control of them given to Dewey. None of us expected those little gunboats to ever be of use to us. They were very old, sadly in need of repair, without equipment, and so covered surrounded by the silt of the Pasig River that they were considered junk. However, when suddenly faced with the necessity of establishing a naval force to cover the entire Philippine archipelago, the Admiral's eye turned longingly to those apparently worthless gunboats. He knew they were only junk according to our standards, but believed that by considerable patching up, they could be of use in the contingency. So each gunboat was assigned to a large ship. Each was to be taken out of the river, repaired, equipped, manned, and operated.

XIV

Around Luzon in a Gunboat

THE OLD SPANISH GUN-BOATS were of various types and sizes, and all were low in steaming power. Their displacement ran from about 30 tons to nearly 200, and their length from 50 to 120 feet, drawing about five to eight feet of water. They could not have been worth very much when new, and they were a sorry lot in their worn out and broken down old age. Still, all our young officers wanted duty in them and especially desired to have command of one.

Because I was the junior commissioned officer of the *Monadnock*, serving as Signal Officer and Captain's Clerk, it did not occur to me that the command of the *Monadnock's* gunboat might be given to me. I was therefore surprised and delighted one evening when the captain sent for me, told me the *Panay* had been assigned to our ship and that I would command it. He told me to get it out of the river and bring it to the ship to be patched up, equipped, and ready for three months of operation.[106]

To command a ship is the great ambition of every young naval officer, especially one on war duty. For those given command of the old gunboats, it mattered not at all that these ships were on their "last legs," weak, and not even seaworthy. They were commands and we were proud to get them.

It was scarcely daylight the next morning when our steam launch took me with a working party to the *Panay*—a discouraging sight deep in the mud of the Pasig River. Short of a wreck on the beach, it is difficult to conceive of worse looking ships than those old gunboats lying in the Pasig. Rusty and about to fall apart, they were filled with dirt. Bad as they were, we were an undismayed and

An Admiral's Yarn

set to with a will to getting the *Panay* out—which we accomplished at high tide that evening, using the *Monadnock's* launch as a tow.

For more than a week we worked hard on that ancient gunboat, uncovering all sorts of troubles and weaknesses. While discouraged at times, we ultimately effected sufficient repairs to permit the little ship to proceed under its own power. We painted it inside and out, stowed supplies and dry provisions to last a month, took on fuel and water, and with a crew of two officers and eighteen men, I reported "ready for sea." Gauged by the usual standards set for naval ships, my report "ready for sea" was overly optimistic. Except in emergencies, ships in the *Panay's* condition are not allowed at sea. However, I decided this was an emergency that required taking risks.

When I reported the *Panay* ready to Admiral Dewey, he ordered me to report at once to the captain of the USS *Wheeling*, one of our seagoing gunboats of over a thousand tons displacement, for a reconnaissance trip completely around the island of Luzon where the Tagalogs were fighting for control.[107] On such a mission we had to cover approximately a thousand miles of coast, investigate dozens of small towns and harbors, and do about six hundred miles of steaming in the open sea. It was a large order for the rickety little *Panay*, but we were glad to undertake it and started out with the *Wheeling* nearly at once.

While the *Wheeling* was well fitted out for cruising in most parts of the world, it was far from being well equipped for that particular bit of work. At the time, we knew almost nothing about the Philippines, and no one, even in Manila, could tell us much about the islands that would be of service to us. Few charts of the local waters had been drawn, even though the coasts and harbors of the islands were full of unmarked rocks, reefs, and shoals. The *Wheeling* was so poorly prepared for its task that it obtained the services of a so-called pilot, although we on the *Panay* did not even know that he was aboard. We had only one chart and almost no navigational instruments. Our chart was little help as it was just a general one for the northern half of Luzon, based on some rather rough surveys made in 1797. It carried the notations "incomplete," "inaccurate" and "not to be relied on." Fortunately for us, our runs between the little harbors were always short and made by daylight, keeping lookouts aloft where they could see shoal spots and rocks through the clear water. We remained just long enough in each harbor to learn about existing conditions there, but every port showed hostility when the ship appeared. In some of them, insurgent troops were lined up ready to fight or seize anyone attempting to land, while in others, insurrectionist flags were hoisted over the towns. In no case did native boats come to the ship either to barter or ascertain our purpose, but in a few ports groups of natives opened fire on us as soon as it was dark. We sometimes replied to their firing, but as our mission was one of peace and merely to learn what the native feeling toward us might be, we fought only when necessary to protect ourselves.

That reconnaissance was a month long, and when it was finished, we reported that every coastal village on the island of Luzon was in the hands of a hostile native group. The information was, of course, invaluable to our high command, and though visiting the ports was interesting and at times exciting, there was little pleasure in doing so. In that land of plenty, with its fresh fruits and vegetables, our only food was from cans in our storeroom. Small and cramped as our ships were, no one could leave them without danger of being killed or captured, and we were ever facing catastrophe when we moved about in those dangerous waters. We lived through all those troubles only to encounter a more trying and dangerous one, when we met a typhoon as we stood down the China Sea returning to Manila.

In Far Eastern waters, tropical storms are known as typhoons, and the one we encountered was of hurricane force, which would have meant trouble for any ship. But for the tiny *Panay*, with little steaming power and many serious defects in hull and machinery, that storm was just too fierce. I have been through innumerable storms at sea, in all parts of the world, but the nightmare of that China Sea experience, in command of the *Panay*, stands out as the worst in my memory.

There is little difference in the responsibilities of commanding officers, be the ship large or small, strong in structure or weak, seaworthy or not. No matter what it may be or what it encounters, it is up to him to bring it and its personnel through safely. There is no greater stigma for a seafaring man than to have it said of him that "he lost his ship." So although the *Panay* had a length of only 97 feet, a displacement of only 147 tons, only a small crew and, even when new, was for use only in inland waters, bringing it through that storm in the China sea safely meant as much to me personally as it would have to bring a great new battleship through.

The *Panay* had no barometer, but the weather looked perfect when we steamed out of the Gulf of Aparri at the northern end of Luzon, and we had no hint of the dangers ahead. Just before we passed into the China Sea, the *Wheeling* stopped, transferred its so-called pilot to the *Panay*, and directed us to make the best of our way to Manila. Then it proceeded at high speed, leaving the *Panay* behind.

I never did understand just why that pilot was sent to the *Panay*, unless he was supposed to compensate for the lack of charts and provide us with the barometer, which was of new design and caused much comment and admiration. It was a fine barometer, developed by the weather predictors for the

An Admiral's Yarn

Philippines, perhaps the most expert in the world for typhoon warnings. It was an aneroid with a huge dial so marked that a mere reading would give us a weather prognostication for the next twenty-four hours or more. When the pilot came to me with the barometer in his hand and said, "Barometer fall, fall, fall. Ship find harbor quick," and I did not immediately change course, he took on a most lugubrious air, gave a shrug to his shoulders, and in a loud sepulchrous voice cried out "*Panay* go down, down, down." Then after repeating the warning several times, he betook himself to place under a table secured to the deck and lashed himself to its legs. It was a most emphatic gesture of resignation. I did not head for a harbor. Inexperienced in typhoons and anxious to get back to Manila, I headed the ship farther out to sea and stood on down the coast.

There are numerous forerunners to tropical storms. Usually a long swell starts before there is any visible indication of a high wind, and just before sundown that day, we ran into such a swell. But although it was unusually high, the *Panay* took it so nicely that I decided to go on through it. At about nine o'clock the sky darkened and the wind increased rapidly, roughing up the swells and causing them to break over the ship, which gave us a terrific pounding. We could not make headway against the wind and sea, and we were in danger of being swamped if we continued, so I, at last, eased off toward shore hoping to make Lingayen Gulf.

We had a good deal of luck that dark, black night, for in spite of our fear that every sea that came along would surely swamp us, we managed to meet each one and go over rather than under it. The motion was terrible. The *Panay* seemed to stand first on one end and then on the other, then it would suddenly throw itself from bean end to beam end. Anything not tightly secured, including men, were thrown about like corks. Yet somehow we managed to keep the little ship afloat, and when daylight showed us to be in sight of the high point on the western side of Lingayen Gulf, we eased off to round it and seek protection.

It helped matters greatly to have something of a lee from the Point, for by the time we had reached it, the hurricane had grown to full strength. Only by steaming at maximum power and keeping as close to the land as we dared could we work our way down Lingayen Gulf. But shortly before dark we reached a little cove in the southwest corner and dropped our anchor close to the USS *Concord*.[108]

That night was a wild one. The wind blowing off shore could not raise much of a sea where we were, nevertheless it was of such force that we were obliged to steam toward our anchor all night and most of the next day to keep from dragging. Standing watch in the rain that came down in torrents was not a joyful

Around Luzon in a Gunboat

task, hence we felt greatly relieved on the second evening when both wind and rain eased.

By the following morning the weather had moderated to such an extent that it seemed the storm was over, but I went over the USS *Concord* to talk over weather conditions with the captain. His barometer had begun to rise from its very low, and the wind seemed moderate and the clouds were breaking. He agreed with me that I should start for Manila lest they worry there over the *Panay's* safety. So at about eight o'clock that morning we got underway for Manila.

The weather seemed fairly good that day, and as the pilot's barometer continued to rise for a couple of hours, we felt our troubles were over. However, they were not far away. As we rounded into the China Sea, we found the huge swells running as darkness approached, and the wind increased rapidly. By nine o'clock that night, not only was the hurricane again blowing full force, but the seas and motion of the ship were worse than ever. The sky was black, the rain came down in torrents, and we could see nothing at all in the inky darkness. I thought our situation was bad enough our first night in the storm, but it was much worse that second night. I thought of turning back to Lingayen Gulf but did not dare attempt turning the *Panay* in such a sea. I doubted we could keep afloat with the huge seas following us and breaking over the ship, and in the black darkness there was no chance at all of finding a harbor on that unlighted and hostile coast. We had to keep on. As it was impossible to maintain hold on anything for long, I lashed myself to a stanchion by the wheel to watch and advise the helmsman on meeting each wave and on the course he should try to hold to keep us off the shore. In that condition and with every hatch battened down, the pumps going hard, and all hands bailing, the long, dreadful night passed.

With the daylight, we were amazed to find ourselves still afloat, for the seas were still mountains high, lashed to fury by the terrific wind. The sky was black with clouds, and although the rain had ceased, the air was too full of flying spray for us to see much. On the crest of a wave we saw ourselves about to drop into a deep abyss of water, and when we dropped we found ourselves surrounded by walls of water far higher than our masts. Every minute we expected the little ship to be engulfed.

About three hours after daybreak the wind seemed to ease a bit and the seas, though as tremendous as ever, became a little more regular and did not break as badly. At least we found we could see through the flying spume. But even then we were not hopeful of saving the ship, for on our lee, and not far distant, we could see terrific seas breaking on the mountainous and rocky shores of Luzon.

An Admiral's Yarn

Meanwhile we still had to meet every great roller just right to keep from being swamped.

To make matters worse, every man on board was near exhaustion and collapse. We had not eaten food since noon the day before, and the seas rolling over us had drowned the galley fires. There was not even a cup of coffee to be had. Fortunately the ship's cook was a game old seaman, and although the terrible motion continued, he finally succeeded, about noon, in getting the fire going again. By skillfully lashing a kettle over the galley range, he succeeded in making a little coffee, which, together with some canned corned beef and soggy hard tack, was our first food in twenty-four hours.

Meager though it was, it revived hope in us, even though we had to work hard to keep off that dangerous lee shore and keep the ship from being swamped. I began to feel that if the wind did not increase, and if the old *Panay* and its worn out machinery would only hold together, we might survive, but my outlook was not optimistic.

As we went over one of the huge seas late that morning, and while it was still "touch and go" with us, we picked up a ship ahead of us, fighting its way through the storm toward us. We could see it only now and then when both ships were on the crests of waves, but we made it out to be the *Wheeling*, seeking to locate and rescue us from the storm. Although we knew the *Wheeling* could do little to help if disaster hit us, it did boost our morale greatly to see it. When it succeeded in rounding to our lee and blowing three blasts on its whistle, we felt much encouraged, although it was plain to see that the *Wheeling* was having nearly as difficult a time as the *Panay*.

Both ships battled on, the crew of the *Wheeling* doing its best to buck us up. They gathered aft, clinging to the rail and rigging, and every time they saw the *Panay* on top of a roller, they gave us a tremendous cheer. Each time the *Panay* fell into a trough in the sea, the watchers on the *Wheeling* thought we had surely gone under for good, so when we bobbed up again, they would go wild with joy.

Fortunately the wind abated and by about three in the afternoon both ships were making much better weather of it. We were then off the entrance to Subic Bay, and I was expecting to seek shelter there when the captain of the *Wheeling* [Commander William T. Burwell] sent orders for us to try to make Mariveles Bay, about twenty miles farther along. Completely worn out, as we all were on the *Panay*, the thought of trying to drive the little ship twenty miles more in such a sea seemed appalling, but drive we did, and just as the sun went down we made Mariveles Bay and anchored.

Around Luzon in a Gunboat

The relief we felt in having successfully brought our ship through such a storm buoyed us all up immensely, and although I looked worn and my eyes completely red, I at once put on a fresh uniform and went over to the *Wheeling* to report. All hands were on the quarterdeck to greet me, and as the captain led me into his cabin, I heard him direct the orderly to tell all officers to assemble in his cabin at once. They were congratulating me heavily for having brought the *Panay* safely through that storm, when I heard champagne corks pop and saw glasses passed to each officer. Then the captain made a rousing speech toasting the officers and men of the *Panay* for their wonderful achievement.

It was all very exciting and pleasant, and though almost dead with fatigue and hunger, I drank my glass of wine sitting in the captain's easy chair. Then a peculiar thing happened. Although the champagne seemed to have no effect on me while sitting down, when it came time for me to leave I could not move and had to tell the captain of my difficulty. The doctor rushed to me and although he found me as clear as a bell mentally, I was paralyzed from head to foot from sheer physical exhaustion.

I was carried back to the *Panay*, given a little food and tucked into bed where I slept for over twelve hours—orders being given on both ships for all possible quietude until I wakened. When I did so, I felt fine, and shortly after, the two ships went on to Manila.

Thus ended my trip around Luzon in a gunboat, but strange to say, it was not the end of the storm. The typhoon continued for three days and rain came down in such torrents that when a man was out in it, he involuntarily started the motions of swimming. Everything not secured was washed down into Manila Bay, which soon became a sea of muddy water covered with wrecked houses, floating trees, and all manner of debris. The Manila newspapers reported a "three-day cloud burst." At any rate, the official record of the rainfall for seventy-two hours was fifty-two inches—which is some rain.

XV

More Gunboating

As soon as the great storm was over, the *Panay* went to the Cavite Navy Yard for a week of repairs and immediately afterward was sent with another small gunboat, the *Mindoro,* to patrol Verde Island Passage, Balayan and Batangas Bays, and adjacent waters to prevent arms and supplies from reaching the very large insurrectionist forces assembling about thirty miles north of Manila in the vicinity of Lake Taal and Batangas.

That service was of much importance because, by bartering stolen hemp, copra, and other island products for rifles and ammunition, the insurgents were strengthening their military power greatly, even though they were a minority group. Our orders were to stop all waterborne traffic engaged in bartering and either destroy the seized vessels or take them to Manila with their cargoes. Such orders seemed rather piratical, but we were obliged to take drastic measures because the insurrectionists were not only operating as bandits but were killing every American in sight. However, until they began shooting our men, we took great care to send ashore every person from a seized ship before destroying the vessel, and we did not fire on the many insurrectionists gathered in troops on the shore.

I have often wondered whether our leniency toward the insurrectionists was not a mistake, since they attributed our not firing on them to fear and weakness on our part and were thereby greatly encouraged, and their sense of power attracted many natives who hastened to join them.

Though we did not kill anyone, the *Panay* and *Mindoro* were very busy, and during the first few days of our patrol we made many seizures in both Balayan and Batangas bays. Practically all that we confiscated, however, were bancas [109] leaving insurrectionist ports after having discharged their cargoes. All were sailing craft, the only type of boat that the natives possessed. Each carried passengers in addition to their crews, and each carried food stuffs, always numerous bags of rice, fresh fruits and vegetables, coconuts, chickens, occasionally a pig, and many bolos.[110] On boats other than bancas, we found shipments of cloth, cigarettes, crockery, sewing materials, etc., designated for a native store. Our task was to destroy the natives' means of getting supplies to the insurrectionist army, though rarely did we capture those supplies.

From the moment we arrived in the area, it was a war of wits between the natives and ourselves—the advantage laying mostly with the natives. The area was much too large for two slow gunboats to police effectively—we could not navigate during darkness in those dangerous channels, unknown to us but very familiar to the natives who did their running at night when we generally had to be at anchor. However, they never knew quite where we would appear at early dawn, and it was at that time of the day that we made most of our captures.

Each seized craft had to be destroyed, and the many useful articles found on them, particularly fresh foodstuffs that we could eat, soon gave an unusual appearance to our gunboats. Our crews quickly became outfitted with bolos and huge native hats large enough to keep off both sun and rain. We looked like pirates and our decks had the appearance of well-stocked farmyards. Bunches of bananas hung in the rigging, and in midship bins we had oranges, raw sugar in molds wrapped in palm leaves, coconuts, numerous small fruits, and yams. Under cover we had many large sacks of rice, and in the very eyes of the ship we had a well-stocked chicken coop and a pen with a pig in it. While we were well supplied with fresh food, our fresh-water tanks held only six hundred gallons, upon which we had to depend not only for drinking, cooking, and washing but for feeding the ship's boilers.

The water problem was significant, for we did not have a distilling plant and could operate for only a few days before having to replenish our supply. Good fresh water was very plentiful on shore but too dangerous to obtain, so we depended on the rain. Fortunately there are many rain showers every day in the Philippines, and we rigged a system of canvas gutters on our awnings to catch the rainfall. By skimping, we managed to have enough.

All in all, we were doing fairly well on our patrol, and although we made few captures of any value, we gradually succeeded in destroying most of the native shipping that carried arms and supplies to the insurrectionists. Now and then there was a bit of excitement, especially one day when some of the seized Filipinos launched at us with bolos and dirks,[111] but we managed to overpower

More Gunboating

them before much damage was done. Another time, we seized a banca with fifteen or twenty young men passengers who were in such a state of excitement that I knew something must be wrong. All were in ragged native clothing except for one whom they treated as the leader. He acted in a very suspicious manner, gathering several large sacks of rice around him, sitting on the top of one. When we attempted to examine them, he objected strenuously. Hidden in the sacks we found, a uniform, coat, and pants worn by insurrectionist officers, a pair of shoulder straps, a pocket compass, whistle, and most important of all, his commission as first lieutenant in the Philippine army, signed by Emilio Aguinaldo, and a paper directing that he be recognized by the Filipinos as Aguinaldo's representative.[112] Evidently the lieutenant had been out recruiting and was taking his "catch" to Batangas to join the army.

As we read the papers, the group became even more excited and began to beg for mercy, though of course we had no intention of maltreating them. My only desire was to keep them away from the insurrectionist army, so we took them about twenty miles to a little island where we put them ashore. They seemed much surprised at the action, but I rather think they felt it was from fear on our part rather than kindness.

After keeping out of Batangas Bay all of one day, I decided to slip in during darkness one night so that at dawn we would be off the town where the insurrectionist-based army was. Whether I fooled the natives or they simply had bad luck, I do not know, but just as it grew light, I found a good-sized, schooner-rigged banca near the *Panay*, trying to get to a landing that the insurrectionists had in a bayou. Of course we seized the banca, and to our amazement found it full of fine, live, fat steers crowded into the schooner. I considered it quite a catch and at once took it in tow to safer waters. Then arose the problem of what to do with the prize. I had either to take it to Manila intact or else destroy it, and killing thirty big, fat steers was a somewhat unusual task, even for sailors. I considered the matter for an hour or so and then, having sent the crew of the schooner ashore in their boat, I put two men on the schooner and set out for Manila to divide the steers among Dewey's fleet, which had been without fresh meat for several weeks.

For a man-of-war, the little *Panay* must have presented an amazing appearance at that time, with its chicken coops, pigpen, bunches of bananas, coconuts, yams, etc., on its deck, and some twenty-five live steers trailing behind in its tow. But we thought little of that as we gauged ourselves on results. We stood out of Batangas Bay and headed up the coast for Manila in beautiful weather. After several hours and shortly after midday, we rounded Cape Santiago

An Admiral's Yarn

to pass into the China Sea when suddenly, in the quiet afternoon, came a loud hail from our lookout aloft, "Horse, ho."

As far as any of us knew, never before had the lookout of a man-of-war passed such an outlandish hail, and being somewhat concerned anyway with the bucolic appearance of my command, I thought the "lookout" might be playing a joke. I therefore hailed him and demanded to know what he thought he was doing by passing such a ridiculous hail. But instead of assuming an apologetic attitude, he cried out loudly, "Captain, there is a horse swimming out there, broad off our starboard bow, and I didn't know how else to report it."

I at once headed the *Panay* toward the horse and stopped the ship, whereupon the horse began to circle round and round it as fast as it could swim, while we chased after it with a lowered lifeboat. For a few minutes there was an exciting race between boat and horse, but while the boat could easily overtake the horse, the bowman, in his attempt to grab the horse's mane or forelock, caused it to start off wildly in a reverse direction around the ship. It looked for a time that the horse might prevent our saving him, but when the resourceful sailors could not catch him by the head, they grabbed his tail, and while holding it tightly, the boat was worked up alongside the horse. They caught his mane and towed him, bows on, to the ship, where he was promptly swung into the grips of the lifeboat and hoisted on board with the boat falls.

We looked the horse over, found him to be a beautiful little native stallion, almost jet black, and we fell in love with him at once. Deciding to keep him if we could get him to Manila, the men began building a stall for him.

We had gone only a short distance, much excited over having added a fine horse to our barnyard collection, when the lookout once more passed a loud hail, "Horse, ho." Not to be caught napping again, I promptly called out "Where away horse?" "Two points on the starboard bow," reported the lookout. Sure enough, there was another horse swimming wildly. From our experience with the first horse, we knew exactly what method of rescue to take with the second one, and it was not to long before he too was on board—a beautiful little, dark, sorrel stallion. They were such fine horses, we wondered how they came to be adrift in the China Sea, several miles off shore. Then we saw, stretched along the large white beach at cape Santiago, clearly visible through our glasses, an insurrectionist cavalry regiment busily engaged in cleaning its horses. Evidently the ones we caught had gone beyond their depth and were swept out to sea by the strong current.

Once more starting for Manila, but losing the protection of land as we stood into the China Sea, we soon encountered a considerable trade wind swell. It was not too much for the *Panay* to buck, even laden as it was, but it soon proved difficult for the schooner with the steers. Old and not built to stand heavy seas or being towed into one, the vessel began to open its seams. I could see our men pumping frantically, trying to keep ahead of the water, but before long they hailed the *Panay* and reported that the schooner would surely sink if we continued to buck the sea. There was nothing to do but head back, and with great reluctance we did so, finally reaching a safe anchorage in Balayan Bay, long after dark, where the *Panay* took the schooner alongside and worked all night to keep it afloat.

Daybreak found us in a worse-than-ever fix, for in addition to the pigs, chickens, and horses that we had on the *Panay*, we had our twenty-five live steers on the sinking schooner. Thus, once again the valuable steers became a problem. We could not care for them, and even if we could have managed to land them, they would have been taken by the insurrectionists for whom they were originally intended. Under our orders, there remained only one thing to do—destroy the steers as well as the schooner.

As the steers had to be killed before we could destroy the schooner, we were obliged to find a humane way to do what we so abhorred. Fortunately, the way the steers had been loaded helped us greatly, for they were packed in tightly, standing on their feet, alternately head to tail. The heads of half of them were to starboard and the other half to port, so by first shooting all on the one side, in the head, and then quickly moving across and shooting the others, all were killed within two minutes without a commotion. Then, after tricing up one of the carcasses to a boat davit to butcher for our own use, we destroyed the schooner.

It was a great relief to get rid of those steers, which of course by that time had been suffering intensely from hunger and thirst. But we still had the one to be butchered, hanging at a davit, and I began to worry over that. However, worry is generally unnecessary when confronted with a job when sailors are around—I have learned from experience that always one is found who can handle a difficult situation. Hence, when I inquired of our crew if there was a butcher aboard, one old seaman agreed to tackle the steer. In less than an hour, the *Panay* was once more on its patrol task but with four beef quarters hanging in the rigging with the bananas.

That night, on falling in with the *Mindoro*, I relieved the strain on our rigging by sending two of the beef quarters to its crew—a considerable amount of fresh meat for a crew of eighteen. We had little worry about food, but we were concerned about our livestock, especially the two horses. We had captured enough rice to feed our cattle, and the horses seemed to enjoy it, but when it came to water, we found the horses drank so heavily of our small supply that if we continued to keep them on board we would soon not have any water for ourselves. We therefore sought to find a place where they could live until we again returned to Manila. We discovered a small island at the northern end of Verde Island Passage, which had both grass and water and but one empty native hut. We seized the island and put the horses ashore, taking a look at them every few days, but alas, when we started back to Manila we were in too great a rush to catch the animals—so, in spite of the pride we had expected to take in riding the horses around Manila, we were forced to leave them behind.

Our patrol duty went on as before, but by the time we had been out for nearly three weeks, there was little shipping left to be seized and our job became monotonous. Our one excitement, after meeting up with the *Mindoro*, was the gift, with the compliments of her captain, of a huge dressed pig, one of three they had captured a few days before.

We were all anxious to get back to Manila Bay where once again the *Panay* could assume the characteristics of a man-of-war. Also, the ship needed docking, painting, and numerous repairs, so as soon as we arrived we were ordered to the Cavite Yard to have the work done. While at the Yard the *Panay's* "mother ship," the *Monadnock*, was ordered to Cebu, and I was given orders to join it there with the *Panay* when our repairs were completed. I did not look forward to the run to Cebu, which was about three hundred miles through unknown waters filled with shoals. Because there were no navigational maps to be had, I bought a map of the islands which, while it showed the location of the principal towns, merely showed blue where there was water and nothing at all in the way of depths, dangers, or navigational marks. However, with our experience in navigating the unknown and dangerous waters, I felt we could get there if we knew where it was. We did so and found the *Monadnock* in port, expecting us.

We replenished our fuel, fresh water, and supplies, and with another similar gunboat, the *Calamianes* (always called "Calamity Ann"), were sent to stop traffic on the coast of Leyte and Samar. Up until that time, no attempts had been made to establish our control in those islands, and therefore, some fierce and bloodthirsty native groups had seized the various towns and were preying on the population. Of course there was little that gunboats could do to free the towns from bandits, but we did prevent the bandits from obtaining additional rifles and ammunition.

The arrival of the gunboats was a tremendous surprise to the insurrectionists, who, having seized all available hemp and other products, were busily engaged in shipping and bartering. Hence, the gunboats encountered much traffic, and for several days were busy destroying it. Since the natives would run their bancas ashore as soon as a gunboat was seen, remove their cargoes with great speed, and then abandon ship, we failed to capture rifles and ammunition. We did seize

More Gunboating

many fierce-looking bolos, some food, clothing, and occasionally a wooden rifle so expertly made that it exactly resembled the real article. For a while the natives bluffed us considerably with those wooden rifles, and by keeping near their grounded bancas in large and apparently well-armed groups, they caused us to do our destruction work by gunfire some distance away. However, we soon learned their "racket" and afterward used a small boat to take a party ashore to the grounded banca and burn it, being careful to avoid an attack of their horrible bolos.

On this trip, each gunboat captured a cargo steamer of about five hundred-ton capacity. Both were fine little ships that were used to carry hemp to Asiatic ports where they would trade it for ammunition. Unluckily, the steamers were empty when we took them, for having received word of our approach, they had been rushed to little piers in well-covered harbors and discharged of their cargo by the time we reached them. But even without cargoes, the ships were most important captures, since they were the principal means by which the Leyte and Samar insurrectionists were obtaining arms from Asia.

After finishing that expedition, the two gunboats were sent on a similar one around the Island of Bohol and along the north coast of Mindanao. Nothing of unusual interest occurred except toward the end of the trip when we were caught in a typhoon in the Mindanao Sea. Both gunboats endeavored to find refuge behind an island, in the center of which was a volcano, often active. We spent all of one day making a clockwise circuit of the island, trying to find a lee, but we never succeeded. The wind was shifting so rapidly that no matter which side of the island we reached there was always a gale blowing directly toward the shore. That condition was a result of our proximity to the center of the storm.

On our return to Cebu, we found that the *Monadnock* had just received a cable message from Admiral Dewey to be conveyed to the USS *Castine* at Zamboanga as soon as possible.[113] Although Zamboanga was in the Sulu Sea, two hundred miles away on the southern tip of Mindanao Island, I volunteered to deliver the message, and left the following morning. It was another trip into unknown waters, made especially difficult by the fact that on the way to Zamboanga I was to follow the Mindanao coast closely from Camiguin Island and destroy illicit traffic. Those orders added zest to the trip, and while several native vessels were seized, none carried munitions. In the Sulu Sea we saw its great display of water snakes and turtles; there were hundreds of them in sight on the surface at all times.

We delivered the dispatch to the USS *Castine*, and when I returned to Cebu my command ended, for while I had been four months in the *Panay*, the detail was limited, by order, to three. Of course I regretted having to give up my first

An Admiral's Yarn

command, but it had been a strenuous and trying experience, and it was advisable to rest a bit whether I wanted to or not.

XVI

In the *Monadnock* Again

IT WAS A GREAT TREAT to have the comforts of the *Monadnock* again, and I appreciated them. There were no clashes with insurrectionists, and it was safe to go ashore in Cebu, which was held by the army. On the ship it was cool, quiet, and pleasant. We received mail every week or two and were kept informed of important events by cable messages from Manila.

One of the most important events to us and to the army officers on shore was the approaching Army-Navy football game of 1899. We knew nothing about the teams, but had so many heated arguments over them that bets had to be made. The army files placed four hundred "dobie dollars" in a bag and dared the navy to cover them. We did, and by putting up all available cash and obligating every dollar we would receive in the next two months, we raised a few hundred dollars more than they did. We then shook the bag of money in the faces of the army until they raised additional money to cover ours. After that, we spent out time planning how we would spend our winnings. The *Monadnock* had orders to proceed to Hong Kong for docking and repairs after the game, and the nearly two thousand dobie dollars in the bag would ensure us a good time for the several weeks we were to be there. However, the army won, and we reached Hong Kong dead broke.

There was a little excitement before we left Cebu. A large British merchantman ran aground and I had to take a boat and working party to get it afloat. By putting tremendous strain on heavy kedge anchors that we planted, and by backing the engines full power at high tide, we succeeded in getting the ship off the reef. For the job which took us all day, we received a very curt

An Admiral's Yarn

"Thank You" from the captain, who I thought would provide food for my men for their hard work.

On another occasion, I was given six men and ordered to use the captain's launch, *Mercedes*, to hunt among the reefs and little islands north of Bobul to destroy all shipping found there. Because the *Mercedes* had only fifteen tons displacement and the crew was small, the three-day search had its dangers; not only was the area known to be a transshipping place and hideout for many insurrectionist groups and craft, but we were entirely unfamiliar with its very shallow waters and its narrow, intricate, and dangerous channels. To make matters more difficult, the islands and reefs were covered with heavy tropical growth, which prevented us from seeing more than two or three hundred yards in any direction, and we expected to be ambushed and attacked at any moment.

Evidently our entering these waters caught the natives unawares, and they assumed neither defensive nor offensive positions. We managed to avoid the shoals as we went through the tortuous channels, stopping frequently to investigate, seize, and often destroy the numerous native craft that we found. The papers of almost every one of them confirmed they were operating under insurrectionist control, in active trade. While we did not find firearms or ammunition to seize, we did appropriate many lots of war bolos, considerable materials that were used by the insurrectionists, and some large shipments of hemp and copra.

We caught one fair-sized schooner with a very large hemp shipment. As we approached, I noticed it was making considerable effort to keep its stern toward us, and as soon as we drew alongside, a fat Chinaman handed me a bamboo case containing the ship's papers. I took them out, and while unrolling them and looking over the schooner, I felt a peculiar tickling sensation on my hand that held the papers. Giving it a quick brush, I knocked off a sizeable object that plumped to the deck. It was a large centipede, about six inches long. Being brushed off so quickly, it did not have time, very fortunately, to sting me. Naturally I was furious, knowing that the centipede could have been there only by design. Then I wondered why it had been done, since the year-old papers had been issued by our own authorities in Manila, authorizing the schooner bearing the name painted on the stern to trade freely in the islands.

Of course, having such a permit to trade, the schooner seemed to be all right, and while weighing the situation in my mind, one of my men rushed to me saying, "Is it all right for this schooner to have on its bow a name in large letters that is different from the name on the stern?" Of course it was at least extraordinary, and when the fat Chinaman showed such great excitement over our discovery, I ordered a thorough search of the schooner.

In the Monadnock Again

For a considerable time we found nothing suspicious, and I had about decided the schooner could not be seized when another bamboo tube was found, cleverly hidden over a beam in the cabin. Inside that tube we found another complete set of ship's papers, but for a schooner with the name painted on the bow. Those papers had been issued by the insurrectionists some six months after those issued in Manila and showed that for several months the schooner had been engaged in insurrectionist traffic. Theirs was a clever ruse, for by showing the name of the stern and the American papers to Americans, and showing the name on the bow and insurrectionist papers to Filipinos, the schooner was ready for any contingency. Having discovered their trick, we were forced to burn the schooner and its large cargo of hemp.

When the *Mercedes* returned to the *Monadnock*, it was loaded with loot, especially weird-looking bolos of the Moro type, all very heavy and sharp as razors, which we gave away as souvenirs. During the next few, quiet days, the *Iris*, a combination collier and water ship, came in to supply the *Monadnock* with coal and water for our trip to Hong Kong.

We were eager for that visit, with its rest from war conditions, and looked forward to a little night freedom and the enjoyment we might find in the famous fleshpots of Hong Kong. But the prospects for pleasure were considerably dimmed by the loss of all our money, which had been bet money on the football game!

It was cold that winter, but we could visit back and forth with the British and American residents as well as with numerous foreign warships in the harbor. We could attend the races, but not bet on them, and there were even occasional dances. And, something quite out of the ordinary occurred. Ferdie lost his pants!

Ferdie (not his real name) was an ensign in the *Monadnock*. We were very fond of him, not only because of his ability as an officer but also because of his "happy go lucky" nature and disposition.[114] While on duty, Ferdie was very serious, but when off, particularly on shore, he would be so highly frivolous that we dubbed him "Festive Ferdie." He lived high, quickly spending every dollar he managed to get his hands on and often sponged a bit on the rest of us, even though he had no money for clothes. Because of these traits, the commissioned officers eventually refused to go ashore with him—and that was the state of affairs when we arrived in Hong Kong.

When in uniform, and especially while on the ship, Ferdie was a most courteous and punctilious gentlemen of the old school type and expected all naval officers to be the same. For that reason, Ferdie was quite upset over an incident that occurred on the *Iris* when that ship came alongside the *Monadnock* at Cebu.

An Admiral's Yarn

No sooner had the *Iris* secured than Ferdie went over to "call" on the officers and probably to acquire a few of the drinks usually served to visitors. To reach the wardroom, he had to go down a long, narrow passageway, so narrow in fact that two men of just ordinary size had to squeeze to pass each other. Just as Ferdie started down the passageway, a door at the other end of the wardroom opened and out came a large, rather obese, medical officer, lieutenant junior grade, one rank above Ferdie.[115]

Although each officer saw the other approaching, neither showed a sign of giving way. Ferdie, being a visiting officer, felt that mere courtesy gave him the right of way, while the junior lieutenant doctor felt that rank had its privileges. So they continued on, and when meeting, Ferdie told the doctor that he should give way to a visitor, while the doctor informed Ferdie that rank took precedence. When Ferdie backed out of the passageway, he called out, "You are no gentleman."

That incident so enraged Ferdie that he did not make his call; instead, he returned to the *Monadnock*, and complained bitterly of the lack of courtesy on the *Iris* and of what he called the insulting and ungentlemanly conduct of the doctor. The rest of us gave little thought to the occurrence, but it rankled and was not forgotten by Ferdie.

It was only a few weeks later that the *Monadnock* went to Hong Kong. Just before we left, Ferdie received a letter from home with an enclosed check for one hundred fifty dollars. As soon as we arrived in Hong Kong, he went ashore and bought fifty dollars worth of new clothes and decided to make a good liberty on the remaining hundred dollars. He based himself at the home of our consul in Hong Kong, who happened to be related to Ferdie.

For his night of liberty, Ferdie wanted company, but knowing his penchant for roughhousing when he had money, none of his messmates would join him. He therefore sought the ship's gunner, whose liberty tastes were similar. They went ashore together, Ferdie sending his suitcase to the consul's house, where he expected to overnight.

It was a bit early when they landed, so Ferdie and the gunner repaired to the bar of the Hong Kong Hotel where, for about an hour, they imbibed freely. They were a bit tight when about nine o'clock a large, obese man, also considerably in liquor, came in. Ferdie at once cried out, "My God! It's that damned doctor" and immediately went up to him and said, "You insulted me. You're no gentleman, and you've got to fight." The doctor was amazed, and in his confused state, Ferdie and the gunner were complete strangers to him. However, when Ferdie explained what had happened on the *Iris*, reiterated that the doctor was no

In the Monadnock Again

gentleman, and said he would have to fight, the doctor declared he was a gentleman, a Virginia gentleman, and in Virginia gentlemen fought!

Many details had to be arranged before the fight could be properly carried on, so the three of them decided to have a few drinks together while making the plans, which took about two hours to complete to the satisfaction of all. The doctor informed them that he was leaving for the United States on the mail steamer sailing at two o'clock the next day, so it was unanimously decided that the fight should take place that night and also that the gunner should act as second for both. They realized they could not fight in the Hong Kong Hotel or in the busy English part of the town, so a secluded spot must be found. On coming ashore, Ferdie had noticed a boatyard on the waterfront, and both he and the doctor thought that would be an ideal place for the fight.

Down to the boatyard they went, all fairly drunk by that time and locking arms to keep from falling. On the way, Ferdie happened to recall what a fighter he was, having won a hard fistfight while a cadet at Annapolis, and ever since had been considered a great scrapper—especially by himself. Thinking it over as they rolled down the street, Ferdie began to feel sorry for the doctor. Even though the doctor weighed about seventy-five pounds more than he did, Ferdie feared he might kill the doctor. So Ferdie suggested that the fight be six rounds, the first three of wrestling in which the heavy doctor would have great advantage, and the last three of fistfighting in which Ferdie excelled.

When they arrived at the boatyard, it seemed deserted. The place they selected for the fight was between boats where there was an arc light above the rough, cobblestoned ground. The three rounds of wrestling went off with both contestants fully dressed, the gunner acting as referee and second to both. As expected, the heavy doctor had considerably the better of it, and Ferdie, who was underneath on the cobblestones most of the time, by the end of the last round was much disheveled. Recalling that he was wearing his new suit of clothes and wishing to prevent further damage, Ferdie asked the referee to call "time" so he could remove his pants. That being done, Ferdie rolled them up carefully to keep his remaining cash from falling out of his pockets and placed them under a boat. Then the fight was resumed, this time with fists.

In the second round Ferdie suddenly launched a mighty swing, which he thought knocked the doctor far under a boat and probably killed him, so he started a search for the body, crawling under every boat, but not finding the doctor's body. He then began to look for his pants, and after he and the gunner had looked under every boat in the yard, they gave up the search.

By that time it was well after midnight and Ferdie and the gunner were in a predicament. Not only were they both very drunk, and Ferdie without his pants and money, but worse still, they were miles from the consul's house far up on the Peak, and had to go through the busiest part of town to reach it. Could the gunner have found one of Hong Kong's numerous chairs to carry Ferdie to the consul's, that problem would have been solved, but there were none at that time of night in that part of the city. By dodging from one door entrance to another and from shadow to shadow, clinging to each other, they finally reached the Hong Kong Hotel. There they found sedan chairs and Ferdie was escorted by the gunner to the consul's house. The maid, who was waiting up for him, did not at once recognize him, but after much explaining he was allowed to enter. The next morning, the Consul questioned the maid about Ferdie and she said, "Oh yes, the lieutenant came in all right, but he must have been riding very late as he was wearing his riding breeches." Ferdie was still without pants, and he was due back on the ship very soon, so the maid hurried a note to us on the ship, telling of his predicament and asking us to send him a pair of pants immediately. We did so and then waited to hear Ferdie's story when he came aboard.

Ferdie was much cut up over the loss of his pants and money, but he had greater worries over what had become of the doctor and expected to be arrested at any moment for killing him. Ferdie could stand the suspense no longer, and after lunch asked some of us to go ashore with him to find out the doctor's fate. The first thing we did was go to the steamer on which the doctor had expected to sail and find out if he was still alive and perhaps under medical care, badly battered and bruised. As we neared the boat, we saw the doctor leaning over the rail, looking clean, dapper, and carefree, without a mark on him. At the sight of him, Ferdie nearly collapsed and begged to be taken back to the ship and put to bed. Evidently he could stand the loss of his pants and money, but his loss of prestige in not having killed or marred the doctor in the fight was too much for him. He knew he was no longer "a great scrapper."

The *Monadnock* remained for several weeks in Hong Kong where, although ever full of interest, comfortable living, and pleasure, there were few incidents worth recounting. We saw all the points of interest, enjoyed the shops with their wonderful articles of Chinese handicraft, and were always cool and comfortable. For those reasons, we dreaded returning to the Philippines and once more engaging in hostilities.

It was therefore a pleasant and great surprise to me when a few days before the *Monadnock* was to sail orders arrived detaching me from it and directing me to report for duty on the *Isla de Cuba*, a Spanish ship which, sunk by Dewey at the Battle of Manila Bay, had been raised and sent to Hong Kong to be rebuilt.[116]

The work on it was nearing completion and the officers and crew were being assembled to commission the ship to be taken to Manila. I was delighted to go to

In the Monadnock Again

what had once been an old Spanish ship and would soon be an almost new one in the U.S. Navy. Also, I was pleased not to be returning to the Philippines immediately; the *Cuba* was not yet finished and would be in Hong Kong several months more.

XVII

Ordered Home

IT WAS NEARLY TWO MONTHS after the *Monadnock* left Hong Kong before the *Isla de Cuba* was commissioned, and during that time we officers of the *Cuba* had to live ashore. Doing so was delightful, and we found many interesting ways to enjoy life when not busy with our duties "fitting out" the ship.

All the officers took quarters at the Connaught Hotel where the very low prices afforded us all the comforts necessary, even at *our* pay. Adding to our easy living were the Chinese messmen, also waiting for the *Cuba*, who were assigned as our valets. Under such circumstances, we youngsters were living in a style we had never enjoyed before.

The boy detailed to me was named Ah Sing. He had been the personal servant of a Mr. Gillis, then President of the Hong Kong and Whampoa Dock Company, the great shipyard of Hong Kong that had the contract for rebuilding the *Cuba*. Ah Sing, like all man servants in China, had been very anxious to join the U.S. Navy, where the lowliest messman received pay of sixteen gold dollars a month, twice what he could earn in his native land. Of course we were delighted to enlist a reliable, energetic boy recommended by Mr. Gillis, although we had to turn down dozens of other applicants.

Assigned to look out for me, Ah Sing carried on just as he had for Mr. Gillis, for when a Chinaman first learns to do a job, he will continue the same routine forever after. He brushed my clothes and every morning arranged each piece so that I could jump into it quickly. Then, having everything ready, he would squat by my bed, very quietly, to watch for some indication that I was awakening.

An Admiral's Yarn

When this happened, Sing would say, "I catch coffee," and back he would come with a steaming cupful which I had to drink before getting out of bed. Ah sing seemed to think I should not move until I had my coffee, so I learned to wait for it, and when I had finished, he would say, "Bath ready." After that, Sing would hand me each garment in the order I was to put it on. During the day, Sing would anticipate my every move. Service of that kind was utterly unknown to me, and although I did not especially care for it, I felt I had to allow Sing to carry on—for the most part.

My street clothes were always immaculate and in perfect repair, cleaned, and pressed. One day I said to Sing, "You very good boy, always work, clean and press clothes, where you learn to be tailor?"

"Me no tailor," said Sing. "All time I take clothes to tailor man. He fix."

Then I said, "Tailor man no send me bill for work. You must not run up bills for me unless I tell you. I no got money to pay tailor man all the time."

"Oh, that all right" said Sing. "You no pay tailor man. He think clothes belong to Mr. Gillis."

In that way I became aware that Sing was actually carrying me on Mr. Gillis's credit, which he thought a clever thing to do. I finally straightened the matter out but had a difficult time convincing Sing that I did not do things that way.

About that time something happened to one of the higher officers of the *Cuba*, which left a lasting impression on me of the dangers of the alcohol in liquor. He was lovingly called "Blokie."[117] Able and efficient, Blokie never showed outward signs of overindulgence in liquor. Standing over six feet two, he looked the picture of health, and although we knew he was a steady drinker and that he consumed a quart or two of whiskey every day, we saw no evidence that it affected him. It was quite a surprise when we heard one day that "Blokie" was ill, in his room at the hotel, and that the doctor had told him that if he did not stop drinking, he would die.

That afternoon I went to see Blokie, expecting to find him in bed looking badly, but he was up and fully dressed when I went in and seemed in his usual bright and jovial mood. After I had been there a moment, Blokie said, "Let's have a drink," whereupon I refused, but he went to his locker, took out a couple of quarts of whiskey and some glasses and insisted that I have a drink with him. Then he said to me, "Laning, what do you think! The doctor told me yesterday that if I go on drinking whiskey it will kill me, but when I said it would kill me just as dead if I stopped drinking altogether, he advised me to taper off. Thus it was decided that I should take only four drinks a day, but I cannot restrain that long, so have hit on a scheme of dividing my drinks into quarters." With that Blokie filled his large glass to the brim, and with "Glad to see you aboard," drank it neat. I then decided it was time to leave and did so, realizing that even size and strength cannot stand up against alcohol. A few weeks later Blokie was invalided home where, shortly afterwards, he died.

For the most part, Hong Kong was mightily pleasant though not exciting. We finally commissioned the *Cuba* and expected to return to Manila in a month or six weeks when, to my surprise, a mail brought orders detaching me from the *Cuba* and directing me to proceed by mail steamer to Nagasaki, Japan, to report for duty on the USS *Remington*, which was then under orders to return to the United States. The orders meant that my cruise was over and I was delighted, especially because I was to be married as soon as I reached California.

Though the navy is full of romances, they all encounter difficulties and mine was no exception. I had met my fiancée while a middy on my first visit to Santa Barbara in 1895, and although we had danced together both there and in Los Angeles and our admiration for each other seemed mutual, we were too young to take ourselves seriously.[118] One afternoon in the late winter of 1897 when I was ashore in San Francisco, whom should I meet tripping down Kearney Street but the charming young lady from Santa Barbara. With her permission I accompanied her on her errands, after which we took a long car ride to the park and once more found ourselves at least a bit interested in each other.

It was about that time that the *Maine* was blown up in Havana and my ship, the *Mohican*, started on its extended training cruise with apprentices in the South Pacific. Having such a cruise ahead of me was of course a severe setback to a budding romance, for although we had not talked of love and marriage, we both feared what a long separation might do to us. But the blowing up of the *Maine* had greatly changed things, and although the *Mohican* had started on its long cruise, it was called off when we reached Honolulu. About four months later we returned to San Francisco where the lady of my heart was still attending the Mark Hopkins Institute of Art.

Because that term of the art school was about to close and my lady love about to return to Santa Barbara, and as the Spanish War was then on, we decided that because we were deeply in love we would become engaged before another unforeseen development could occur. Though we had known each other for nearly three years and had been devoted for months, the duration of our actual courtship was only a few weeks. We became engaged—and our troubles began. After seeing my fiancée on a train to go home and promising to follow ten days later in order to meet her family, the *Mohican* received orders to sail at once for Honolulu, carrying ammunition for Dewey. We wrote to each other every day, and the frequent mail steamers kept us in close touch, but it became very different when I was transferred to the *Monadnock* and sent to the Philippines.

An Admiral's Yarn

Even though we continued to write each day, mail became very irregular and infrequent, and at times did not get through at all. Not knowing whether our failure to receive letters from each other was due to a break in the mail service or a discontinuance of writing, our romance endured quite a strain.

For a matter of time, mail irregularity caused few misgivings, and several weeks or a month would go by without worry. However, there came a long period when not one letter from me reached Santa Barbara. After nearly three months of waiting and often reading in the San Francisco papers that mail was arriving from the Far East, my fiancée decided I had changed my mind and had stopped writing to her.

I still do not like to think of the strain our romance underwent at that time, and strange to say, I knew nothing of it until I began receiving letters from my fiancée stating that mail from me had not arrived for about three months and apparently our engagement was ended. I was greatly upset, because I had written every day and had posted the letters for every mail leaving for the States. Could the change in her letters mean that she herself was changing, or what? Then in the Manila papers I found the answer. It was the "bubonic plague."

In the United States we are fortunate to have infrequent contact with the bubonic plague and naturally have great dread of it. At the turn of the century, however, while the cities of the Far East feared and fought the disease, they never seemed to be entirely free of it, and one or two sporadic cases of plague would appear each day. The plague seldom became epidemic, because each case was promptly quarantined and treated, and every day the public health authorities issued a bulletin telling the location of each new case, specifying the area under quarantine. The situation seemed well in hand and little attention was paid to it beyond the health authorities in distant ports where cases were increasing to over a dozen a day—and only then were those cities severely quarantined.

Thus it was in '99 that plague cases in Manila increased so rapidly that our West Coast demanded a very strict quarantine against the Philippines, forbidding even mail from Manila to enter the United States.

For whatever reason, those of us serving in the Philippines had not heard of the quarantine. We of course were receiving our mail alright and continued writing and posting our letters as usual, not imagining that our mail for the United States was being held up. Fortunately for our peace of mind, just as we heard of the stoppage, the local papers also announced the release in San Francisco of the three months' mail held there because of the plague. So I knew my fiancée would soon cease to blame me.

It was over none too soon, for the interruption of letters had done great damage. Not only had my fiancée's family lost faith in me, but even my fiancée's

Ordered Home

faith had been taxed. Then, in one day's mail, the picture was changed, for in that one mail, tied in a huge bundle, were three months' of my daily letters. Needless to say, the arrival of those letters, showing the dates they were posted, brought our romance back to its even keel, and I decided it was the psychological moment to write my future father-in-law and ask for his blessing, which he promptly gave.

Thus stood our romance as my cruise neared its end. It was no wonder that I was overjoyed to have orders to join the homeward bound *Bennington*, for we were to be married as soon as I returned to the United States. I made the trip from Hong Kong to Nagasaki by mail steamer in a state of great excitement and was no less excited after joining the *Bennington*, which was filled with officers who were nearing the end of their tours of sea duty and going home.

It was on the mail steamer that I met a delightful person, a young man en route to Japan. His name was well known at home but meant nothing to me who had been separated from news in the United States for over two years. I therefore enjoyed him for his delightful and interesting self and not for his fame. When our steamer touched at Shanghai, we went ashore in the same tender and then returned to the ship together, displaying our purchases, etc., after a day of shopping. Finally my companion said to me, "My, this is a small world" and pulled from his pocket a small book. He said, "Well, I do a lot of writing, so I went to a shop to buy some stationery, quite a bit of it in fact, and the merchant gave me a 'cumshaw,' a little book just in from New York. Here it is. Would you like to read it?" Whereupon he handed me a copy of *Fables in Slang*, which had just been published.[119]

I took the book and with much enjoyment read it through that night, noting when I did, that it had been written by the author of *Artie*, another book that I had enjoyed. When I returned the book I thanked him for the pleasure it had given me and told him of my having read *Artie* by the same author. Then I said, "Would you mind telling me why you considered this such a small world when an up-to-date Chinese bookseller in Shanghai gave you a copy of it?" "Well," said my companion, "you see, I wrote the book." I was talking with George Ade.

It was a happy crowd on the homeward bound *Bennington,* and perhaps the happiest of all officers were Bill, Jack, and myself, as we three were going home to be married.[120]

Our trip through the beautiful Inland Sea of Japan to Yokohama where we were to fill with supplies for the long run to Honolulu seemed all too slow, and once in Yokohama we rushed to prepare the ship for carrying out its orders. Just as we were finishing, a sister ship to the *Bennington* anchored near us, also having on board a number of young officers homeward bound.

An Admiral's Yarn

Both gunboats were small and the run to Honolulu would be a severe test. The two skippers, in a discussion of the trip, decided to leave Yokohama together and make a race of the run to Honolulu. When we learned of the race, we were greatly excited. Although the *Bennington* was entirely ready to sail at once, those on board were quite willing to delay our departure for a few days that we might start with the *Yorktown* and, we hoped, leave it far behind.

It had been decided that the start of the race was to be about ten o'clock of a certain day, so the night before, the officers of the *Bennington* who were not on duty gathered at the Grand Hotel in Yokohama for a parting dinner. We finished and were sitting on the hotel veranda taking a final look over the night life of that fascinating city when suddenly into our midst walked a solemn young officer in uniform who informed us that the captain [Commander Conway Arnold] ordered us all to return to the ship immediately—orders by cable had just canceled the ship's return to the United States, directing it to proceed to Manila at once! We left at daybreak. No words of mine can do justice to the shock and disappointment when I learned that instead of going home we were returning to Manila and the insurrection. We hurriedly went back to the ship, hoping against hope the orders would be changed, but when daybreak came we were on our way to Manila.

We supposed that on reaching Manila we would immediately start operating once more against the insurgents, but although the *Bennington* eventually did, it was not until we officers due for home had been replaced by new arrivals. My orders to the *Monadnock* soon came, so after being due for home, there I was back on my old ship at Cavite.

Fortunately I did not remain there long. The *Solace*, then being used as the navy transport ship between Manila and San Francisco, arrived at Cavite, and after dispersing its personnel of young officers due for duty in the Philippines, we "homeward bounders" were ordered to it for the trip back to San Francisco. Only we did not sail for home. Just then the Boxer Rebellion in China broke, and the *Solace*[121] was filled with Marines to be taken to Tientsin to become part of the International Force marching to support the foreigners in Peking.

Again, Bill, Jack, and I were dreadfully disappointed, but taking part in the China Relief Expedition was preferable to fighting Filipinos, and we were not too unhappy. The *Solace* made all speed to Taku near Tientsin, discharged its Marines, and then awaited orders. All of us expected to be sent ashore but we were not, and after several days of waiting the *Solace* was ordered to Nagasaki to refuel before returning to Manila.

Nagasaki was a port of call for the army's homeward bound transports, and shortly after the *Solace* arrived, the largest and fastest transport, the *Hancock*, formerly the *Arizona* (the speed queen of the Atlantic), touched there. By then the commander in chief of the Asiatic Station [George C. Remey] had become weary of trying to get rid of those of us due for home and sent a cable message to our captain, directing him to send us via army transports or, if accommodations were not available, allow us to pay our own expenses on a mail steamer if we wished. This was agreeable to me and I made up my mind to get home somehow. With the orders in my hand, I went to the *Hancock* to seek passage but was informed by the captain that there was no space available. I was so discouraged. The *Hancock* would reach San Francisco ten days or more before any mail steamer could arrive there, so I decided to look up an old friend of mine, who was then the freight clerk of the *Hancock*, and see if he could find a place for me, even in a storeroom, where I could sleep for the trip home. My tale of woe impressed him deeply and he said, "Laning, there is a transom seat in my room which is less than a foot wide but over six feet long. Do you think you could manage to sleep on it?" I jumped at the chance, and with the Captain's permission, I sailed for home on the *Hancock*, the only one from the *Solace* to get passage, and even Bill and Jack had to return to Manila and suffer several more months delay. I was truly distressed over that.

My fiancée little knew what was taking place with me. I had told her of my cruise being over, of my start for home, the orders being changed, and that before I sailed I would cable her the name of the ship I was on, when I would reach San Francisco, and the earliest date she could set for the wedding. It was not a very satisfactory situation but the best we could do under the circumstances. We had said good-by for only ten days and I had been away for several months over a two-year period. We had reached the point where we had to be ready for eventualities.

As soon as I had established myself on the *Hancock* and just before the ship was to sail, I dashed ashore and sent my cable message "Arriving on *Hancock*. Wedding twenty-fourth." I had barely returned when the ship started, and when at last we were out of Nagasaki Harbor, I felt I was really on my way to be married.

But even then our way was not entirely smooth, for the *Hancock* was full of troops returning home, and on the way across the Pacific an epidemic of mumps developed among them. We little thought mumps would interfere with us on our quick trip across the ocean, but no sooner had we reached San Francisco than the ship was sent to a quarantine station behind Angel Island where health authorities interpreted the mumps as possible bubonic plague!

Of all the blows our romance had suffered, that quarantine seemed about the worst, for the 24th was only ten days away and the invitations had been mailed.

An Admiral's Yarn

We were told the quarantine would last for two weeks. For twenty-four hours there was great unhappiness and disappointment on the *Hancock*. Then the health authorities decided that since there had not been a case of mumps in the officers' quarters and that none of the officers had been exposed to it, they should be allowed to debark. We lost no time in going ashore and I was soon on my way to Santa Barbara where, on July 24th, 1900, we were married and started the happy life that has been ours ever since.

XVIII

Annapolis Once More

Having at last overcome the jinx that had for so long interfered with our wedding, we started on a honeymoon that took us to my old home in Petersburg to await orders. Where I might be sent from there I did not know, but shortly before leaving the Philippines, I had studied the places available for shore duty and, having in mind a temporary period away from strictly naval duties, submitted a request to be assigned to the Branch Hydrographic Office at Duluth, Minnesota. So, I expected to find orders to Duluth when I arrived in Petersburg.

My orders were not to Duluth but to the Naval Academy. The authorities there had reviewed the list of officers available for shore duty and requested that I be sent there as an instructor. I was greatly flattered and delighted to take my bride there but was not optimistic of my ability to instruct cadets, and I feared they would soon discover it.

To be an officer and instructor at Annapolis is altogether different from being there as a cadet, and while a bit apprehensive at first, I soon began to enjoy it. I was to instruct in the department of "English, History and Law," and because I had not specialized in those subjects, I was obliged to study hard to keep ahead of the cadets. There was great variety in what I was supposed to teach—English, including reading, writing, spelling, grammar, rhetoric, theme writing, etc; History, including U.S. history, ancient and modern world history, naval history, etc; and Law, including both military and international. It took nearly constant study to cover all the subjects, but I found time to enjoy most of the pleasures of Annapolis and the Naval Academy. On the social side there was always activity,

An Admiral's Yarn

although none of the officers had much money to spend. We clubbed together to give frequent dances in the gymnasium, when the only expenses would be for a bowl of lemonade. We had use of the many boats at the Academy for sailing parties and picnics; we watched the numerous cadet teams training for their games; we witnessed various drills and gathered at friends' quarters for parties; and we always went to the cadet hops.

Now and then something out of the ordinary would happen, such as my first examination for promotion, which had become due in July but was held in October after I settled in at the Academy. I studied hard for it and felt quite prepared when the orders came, but having heard of the thoroughness of the tests, I was rather in awe of them. With four of my classmates who also had just returned from the Philippines, I reported to the Naval Examining Board in Washington.

The members of that Board were "old sea dogs" who were well known to us, at least by name. Some of them had been our instructors at the Naval Academy and had written what we considered highbrow books on navigation, ordnance, etc. To prove ourselves worthy of promotion in the eyes of such men seemed a large order, and when I say we were shaking in our boots, I mean it.

The examination lasted from nine a.m. to four p.m. every day for a week. The members of the Board sat at desks facing the tables where we worked, and while each had charge of a particular subject, all members passed on the papers. The officer in charge of a subject would hand each one of us a slip with a question on it, which we answered in writing. No two of us were given the same question, and by thorough and separate examination, each candidate had to show the Board his fitness for promotion.

Not all the subjects were difficult for me, especially seamanship, navigation, and such, in which I had extensive experience while at sea. But there were other subjects, for instance, electrical engineering, steam engineering, ordnance and gunnery, which I had to study. Then, too, there was my "bête noir," French, for which I had no gift at all. Hence, when I saw the President of the Board as he looked at my French paper and heard him say to one of the other board members, "Laning's French is rich," I was more worried than ever as the end of the week approached.

Finally, just before the closing hour of the last day, the President suddenly announced, "The examinations are over. Turn in all papers." Then, with all of the Board members sitting there looking as solemn as owls, and without even glancing at the papers we had just turned in, we were directed to stand before the Board. As we did this, the President of the Board, the well-known [Rear] Admiral Asa Walker, jumped to his feet, extended his hand to each of us in turn

Annapolis Once More

and said, "Gentlemen, I congratulate you all in passing a fine examination." That of course was a great relief to us but we were not quite prepared for his next remark when he said, "The Board thought you fellows would never finish writing on this examination. You wore us all out waiting. Why, good heavens, with the fine work each of you did in the Philippines, the Board had decided to pass all of you on those records, long before you ever appeared before us!" A little later we received our commissions as lieutenants, junior grade.

Not long after, the first snow of winter arrived. My bride was from California, and while she had been in the snow in the mountains, she had never seen it falling, so this snowstorm was a new experience for her. Consequently, she hoped it would not happen at night when she might miss it. In any event, she asked the night watchman to keep her posted, no matter what time of night it might be.

We did not have long to wait. A little after two o'clock in the morning, while we were sound asleep, there was a terrific pounding on our door, and there was the watchman with the information that it was snowing. We looked out the window and sure enough snow was falling in huge, beautiful flakes. Of course my bride was terribly excited, and although it was well after two a.m., she insisted on dressing and going out into it. Of course I went too, and for over an hour we traveled the deserted streets of Annapolis, my wife marveling at the beauty of the snow, at the great flakes, and the depth it so quickly reached. She ate snow, washed my face in it, threw snowballs at me, and thoroughly enjoyed the new experience. So did I.

By morning, when I went to early recitations at seven-thirty, the snow was more than eight inches deep and still falling. When my classes were over and I started for home shortly after ten o'clock, who should I see on the Academy grounds but my bride and the wife of my dear friend and classmate, Jimmy Raby, also a Californian. They were throwing snowballs at the cadets as they marched and at anyone who came along. But as I looked at them, they suddenly stopped that bombardment and made for a figure coming from the superintendent's house. It was the superintendent himself, Captain Richard Wainwright of Spanish War fame.[122] Of course, I thought the brides would not dare attack him, but they did. I thought the end had come for me and I beat a hasty retreat, seeking back ways to reach home. When my wife appeared, she was in high spirits, her eyes dancing, and her rosy-cheeked face wreathed in smiles. I was not feeling quite that way myself and said, "Now you have done it, we might as well start packing our trunks, for the superintendent will surely have me sent to Guam."

An Admiral's Yarn

"My," she said in astonishment, "you are not worried about our snowballing Captain Wainwright are you? He liked it." Well, perhaps he did, as he told his wife about it and the very next day his orderly brought notes from Mrs. Wainwright asking the California brides and their husbands to dinner at the superintendent's house.

That first winter passed gloriously, and because I was then well settled in family life, I was much upset when orders came in the spring to report as watch and division officer for the summer cruise of the cadets. The ship for the cruise was a newly completed square-rigger sailing vessel especially built for training cadets and without engine power—I looked without favor toward the three months of strenuous teaching of seamanship on another windjammer.

That cruise in the *Chesapeake* gave me new experiences, for although the ship had only sails for motive power, every improvement devised from centuries of sailing ship experience had been embodied in it.[123] There were, of course, no changes in the arrangement of sails or rigging, so in respect to masts, yards, canvas, and gear, the *Chesapeake* was exactly like the old *Constellation* on which I had made my plebe cruise. But there the similarity to the old sailing ship ended. Built of steel instead of wood, the hull had been designed to give utmost speed. The ship had a "donkey boiler" that provided steam for the capstan, deck winches, little electric light plant, and even for certain galley cooking. There was more height between decks, better storerooms, larger and airier living spaces for officers and men, modern bathrooms and lavatories, and ever plentiful fresh water which we could distill on board. So, life on a modern sailing ship had its advantages.

The cruise that summer was north along the Atlantic Coast, stopping for weekends in a good port and then spending the five weekdays in old-time sailing work while making a roundabout passage to our next port. "Working ship" in the *Chesapeake* with its remarkable speed and easy handling was a joy to us, and the three months' cruise passed quickly, my wife always being in our weekend port to greet me when the ship arrived. But although I had at last found myself with "a sweetheart in every port," and liked it, I was glad when the cruise ended.

For our second winter in Annapolis we were assigned government quarters in the Yard. This had not been available to us when I reported for duty the first winter, and consequently we were obliged to live in a hotel in town. We came to know our new quarters as "the corrals"—two buildings where sixteen families lived in "flats." Compared with city apartments today, they had few attractions, but the rooms were rather large with high ceilings, French windows, and fireplaces, although sparsely furnished with heavy government furniture.

Annapolis Once More

We in Annapolis were fortunate in 1900 not to have what we now call the "servant problem." At that time, there were no industrial plants, and the numerous colored people in the area looked for employment with private families. One could hire a fine Maryland cook at the then-standard price of twelve dollars a month and a housemaid to do everything else for eight or ten dollars. As foodstuffs were cheap and plentiful, even the families of poorly paid naval officers could live well in Annapolis.

When we went into that flat, we were truly rookies in housekeeping; the lady of my house, although a splendid artist and musician, was utterly without housekeeping experience. However, having provided ourselves with both cook and maid, we went at it!

Our first meal was to be a luncheon, and preparing for it became our first problem when my wife told me that she had never put together a menu or purchased food. I had catered the mess aboard a ship, so I tried to help and suggested that she buy chops, whereupon she diligently wrote that down on her list and then inquired, "How many should I buy?" Counting ourselves as two, the cook and the maid as two, I told her that probably each would eat two chops, so she should buy eight. She wrote down seven, as she wanted only one.

The next morning, for the first time in her life, my wife went to the market, which she found filled with other wives buying their supplies. Since we were still classed as "brides" and just starting housekeeping, the others paused in their ordering to watch my wife do hers. This greatly confused her, so when the grocer asked what she would have, she gravely said, "Seven pounds of lamb chops." "Seven pounds did you say, Madam?" Sticking to her guns and knowing the others were watching, she repeated "Yes, seven pounds of lamb chops," adding in her confusion, "My husband is very fond of lamb chops." We have not cared particularly for lamb chops since!

After that we sought the advice of "Laura," our newly installed cook. Although still a young woman, Laura was not only an excellent cook but very experienced in housework, and was also perhaps the best-looking colored girl as well as the blackest in officers row. In face, figure, and activity, she was a real Amazon.

Toward the end of our first month with Laura, she came to us one day asking why two young people like ourselves living in a flat needed two servants to look out for us. She said, "Why does y'all keep that maid? I can cook and do everything she do, and better too, all for fourteen dollars. You just let that maid go!" We finally did, and thereafter Laura, who was not only the best cook along the line, was also quite the snappiest looking maid to admit guests to a house.

An Admiral's Yarn

Later, when winter was on us, Laura came to me and said, "What for you have that old nigger Josh to bring in the wood and coal?" I told her that he also took out the ashes, cleaned the walks of snow and ice, ran errands, and helped with the heavy work. This did not impress Laura's business calculations, for she argued, "Deed, Mr. Laning, you don't need Josh. After every meal of the cadets, these good-for-nothing mess hall boys going along the back alley stops at my kitchen door and bothers me. You jest get rid of Josh and I makes them boys do all that Josh does and more too." And she did.

With Laura taking over all the jobs so well, things went along smoothly, and we never gave housekeeping a thought until one day in February when she came to us holding a telegram in one hand while wiping away tears with the other and shaking with sobs. "My brother is daid. My brother is daid," she wailed. Doing our best to comfort her, we finally learned that her brother, one of several, had left home years before, joined a colored regiment and had been sent to the Philippines where he died. The telegram from the War Department notifying her of his death also asked if she wished his remains to be sent home at government expense or interred in the National Cemetery in the Philippines. The four hundred dollars allowed for transporting the remains to Annapolis would, in the latter case, be sent to her in cash.

Laura was in a quandary and asked my advice. Being reluctant to give it, I could only point out the advantages of burial in a well-kept National Cemetery over internment in the Annapolis colored one, and the great financial help to her family if the burial were in Manila. Otherwise, I left the decision to her.

What her decision was, Laura did not tell us at the time, and she carried on as usual, apparently not grieving. Then, to my great consternation, when I had to have breakfast at seven o'clock one morning before an early recitation, there was no Laura to prepare it nor was she there for a whole week after that. With full schedules every day and evening, our flat was soon in a most untidy condition. No mess hall boys appeared to clean the ice from our walks, handle the coal, ashes, and garbage, or run errands. We did not have time between engagements and my work to attend to house duties, and the situation grew worse as time went on. Every dish and cooking utensil was piled up in the kitchen sink waiting for Laura's return.

We were discussing the possibility of having to hire someone else when the door of our living room suddenly opened and the happy voice of Laura was saying "Here I is. I'se back" and there stood Laura, but such a Laura we had never dreamed of—a Junoesque Laura in a perfectly fitting black tailor-made suit with a large and most becoming widow's hat from which hung the heaviest display of "widow's weeds" I have ever seen. We gazed at her in speechless awe, for

Annapolis Once More

although her with teeth were gleaming out of a jet black face wreathed in smiles, she stood there in the most lavish display of mourning clothes we had ever beheld.

My wife and I little thought that anyone so magnificently garbed would want to work for us again, and probably Laura noticed the consternation on our faces as she quickly said, "These is fine clothes, all right, but I'll soon have 'em off and start work right away." What music to our ears!

Later Laura told us, "You know, Mr. Laning, I done just what you said. After you tole all those things about cemeteries, I decided to have my brother buried in Manila and the money sent to me, so I tole the War Department. Then I had to wait a long time, but at last my check came and I left for Baltimore to get me some clothes. First I goes to the best tailor and he fits me like the paper on the wall. Then I gets this hat and these here veils. Then having some money left, I just has a good time. Now my money is gone and I am ready to work."

I remarked that we were glad to have her back and she must be very proud of her clothes. "Yes, I is proud of them, Mr. Laning. I knows I'se got the bestest mourning ever in Annapolis and I sure had a good time in Baltimore, but" continued Laura, "do you know, Mr. Laning, I sometimes think I would rather have my brother back."

Shortly after, all was serene in our household, but we had more mess hall boys hanging around than ever!

At the end of that academic year, I was promoted to the rank of lieutenant and again became due for sea duty, but I could not ascertain where I might be sent. Probably it would be to one of the many new ships being added to our North Atlantic Squadron. However, in May [1902] I was ordered to the Torpedo Station at Newport, Rhode Island, for instruction in torpedoes. As torpedo work was highly professional and torpedoes were then becoming more and more important in naval warfare, I was delighted with the orders and soon became engrossed in that work.

However, I had completed only about two of the three months' arduous instruction course when I received a telegram to report for duty on the USS *Dolphin* immediately upon its arrival at Newport, and I went aboard the next day [23 July 1902].

From 1902 to 1905, Lieutenant (junior grade) Laning served as gunnery officer aboard the dispatch boat USS *Dolphin*, commanded by Lieutenant Commander John H. Gibbons. Based in Washington, DC, her main duty was to carry the Secretary of the Navy and other dignitaries for special occasions. This photograph, presumably taken in January 1905 during a cruise between Wilmington and Hampton Roads, shows Secretary of the Navy Paul Morton and Admiral of the Navy George Dewey. Laning is seated precariously on the rail.

XIX

In the *Dolphin*

IT WAS QUITE A SURPRISE to find myself an officer of the *Dolphin*.[124] Though built to be a gunboat, the ship had been fitted out in the manner of an official yacht for the use of high government officials in Washington. It had in fact been known as the President's yacht until the palatial *Mayflower* was placed at his service. The *Dolphin* was then turned over to the Secretary of the Navy to be used also for official trips with cabinet officers, senators, congressmen, and however the Secretary might direct. As the *Dolphin* generally remained at the Washington Navy Yard when not on a trip, sea duty on it was thought to be a great snap, and throughout the navy the officers on it were referred to as "Coburgers" (officers who, because of powerful political backing, had the softest and most desirable billets).

Being suddenly thrust into the "Coburger" class was a shock to me. The term originated in Great Britain where members of the "Saxe-Coburg" family were always given the easiest and most delightful jobs, and it had become a term of opprobrium when applied to officers in our service. I could not understand why it should be applied to me, for not only was I utterly unacquainted with even one high official in Washington, but I also did not want to enter the social life there. However, I soon learned that being ordered to the *Dolphin* was not subject to my wishes or influence but rather to my availability for the duty at a time when one of the ship's officers was hospitalized. I was the only married officer on the ship except for the captain.

If duty on the *Dolphin* was a snap or easy, I never found it out, for I avoided all social activities that I possibly could and spent most of my time working hard.

An Admiral's Yarn

When I joined, Mr. William Moody,[125] a bachelor, had just become Secretary of the Navy. Having a somewhat nautical mind and coming from the seagoing area of Massachusetts, he at once put the *Dolphin* on a hard schedule, not only using it frequently for his own official visits to our naval activities but also taking other cabinet officers and committees of Congress on their inspection trips. Through them I soon became acquainted with several national political leaders of the time, though if any of them developed a personal interest in me I never found out! It was interesting, however, to have the political bigwigs on board, and to talk with them, especially Senators Eugene Hale[126] and Boise Penrose,[127] Congressman "Uncle Joe" Cannon,[128] and other important personages, when they were relaxing on board and being natural!

It was during the summer of 1902 that the use of naval ships for official inspection trips became so popular. The *Dolphin* was under orders almost continuously, and the ship's officers, of whom there were only a few, were always busy preparing for any duty a gunboat might have while cruising with high dignitaries. The ship had only the captain, an executive officer, a medical and a pay officer, and three or four watch and division officers; the work was divided among them. Of these, the "watch officers" had the most to do, for in addition to one always being on watch, be it night or day, one acted as navigator, one was the chief engineer, and one (which happened to be me) had charge of the ship's battery and gun divisions. Thus, we not only had an average of from six to eight hours a day on watch but also devoted many hours a day to drills and other duties. However, we gave no thought at all to the amount of work on the *Dolphin*, and all were interested in doing their jobs well.

Consequently, I was greatly surprised over what Senator Boise Penrose said to me one night. I had the mid-watch (midnight to four a.m.), and at about half past one the senator came up on the bridge where I was alone. The night was balmy and beautiful, so he perched himself on a bridge seat, lighted a cigar, relaxed, and then suddenly said to me, "Young man, what are you doing up here on the bridge at this time of night? Don't you ever sleep?" "Yes," I said, "I sleep when I can, but this is my watch. You know, Senator, there are only three of us to stand the watches, and when underway, one of us is always on the bridge. This just happens to be my turn."

The senator simply sat there smoking, thinking, and looking around. Finally he said, "I certainly am learning a lot about the navy on this trip, and it is all so different from what I thought. You know, Lieutenant, when I came on board, I had the idea that our naval officers lived about the easiest and most delightful lives of anyone. I imagined that all you had to do was sit around a table in uniform with your sword in one hand and a highball in the other until a call

In the Dolphin

came, but I see I was all wrong. I find you officers never seem to rest or take a drink, but work all the time. Coming on deck after my breakfast this morning, I found you there drilling the crew at their guns and I watched during the entire forenoon. Then after lunch you were drilling them again, and when I came on the bridge to get some air just before dinner, there you were, looking out for the ship. Now I'm up here again, long after midnight, and here you are still on watch. I will have to change my mind completely about naval officers, swords, and highballs."

After that, Boise Penrose was one of the staunchest and most understanding supporters of our navy for as long as he lived.

Three nights later when I again had the mid-watch, Uncle Joe Cannon came on the bridge to smoke and get some fresh air before turning in. After sitting there a while, he said, "We had a mighty fine game of poker in the cabin tonight, but I didn't see any of you officers there. Why don't some of you come to the cabin after dinner and join our game? I know you would like it and so would we."

Perhaps we would have enjoyed playing poker with such important persons had we the time or could we have afforded it, but I merely said that in the navy we had to live by regulations and that all gambling on naval ships was forbidden.

Uncle Joe thought that over a minute and then said, "Well that may be a good regulation as regards gambling in general, but it is a fool one as far as poker is concerned, and if I am ever Secretary of the Navy, I will have that regulation changed."

The *Dolphin* did a great deal of cruising that summer, accompanying the Atlantic Fleet much of the time and visiting our East Coast ports and naval activities from Bar Harbor, Maine, to Key West, Florida. But as interesting as that summer was, it was also trying and brought home to me the difficulties a naval family endured when the ship moved from port to port too rapidly for a wife to follow. However, October saw the ship once more in Washington.

At that time, our navy was passing into a new phase. Larger ships had been added, and in the fall of that year we had about ten battleships, a number of cruisers, and torpedo boats in the Atlantic Squadron which assembled in November at Culebra Island, just east of Puerto Rico, for a period of training.

Although that squadron was the most powerful naval force our country had at the time, it was still being trained along the old lines—to protect United States interests in various ports of the world. This left little attention devoted to the great role of the navy—obtaining and maintaining control of the sea areas. As a matter of fact, it was while the ships were assembled at Culebra, years after Captain Mahan's *Influence of Sea Power upon History*[129] had made the real purpose

An Admiral's Yarn

of navies clear to the world, that Lieutenant Commander William S. Sims (later Admiral) planted the seed that grew into our present day navy.[130]

Sims had returned the preceding spring for a cruise of the Asiatic Station where he had learned (through a close friend in the British navy) about the remarkable shooting ability of the British ships that delivered many more hits in a given number of shots and fired many more shots in a given length of time than we were able to do in our navy. Sims invested his efforts to learn how the British did this and, after pondering it over, realized that our navy would be utterly wiped out if confronted with such superiority.

Ordered to Washington, Sims at once began a crusade to better our naval shooting skills. He did not have the enthusiastic support of naval officials but succeeded in reaching the President, Theodore Roosevelt, who recognized that the situation must be corrected at once. Roosevelt directed that an office, "Inspector of Target Practice," be established for the navy with Sims in charge and ordered him to elevate our navy's proficiency lest we suffer the consequences.

When the Atlantic squadron assembled at Culebra in the fall of 1902, Sims was Inspector of Target Practice for the navy, and the *Dolphin* was ordered to take him to Culebra to instruct the fleet in shooting. Because his ideas had not been well received by the high naval officials in Washington, Sims knew there would be great opposition among the higher officers in the fleet. This resistance did not issue from the absence of a desire to shoot better, but rather from a reactionary attitude, i.e., the additional work it would require, the criticism of the current training system that was implied by the introduction of a new and radically different method, and perhaps a hesitancy to question the idea voiced throughout the country that, being born American, our sailors, even without much training, could just naturally fight and shoot better than any other sailors.

Sims came to the *Dolphin* well realizing the opposition he would encounter, and in his quarters in the wardroom with the ship's officers, he proceeded to prove his case to us immediately after the ship left Washington. At first we too were a bit reactionary, but when Sims made it clear that to continue as we were was to invite "not honorable defeat for the U.S. Navy in war, but complete annihilation," we began to take notice as did the younger officers of the ships at Culebra after Sims had spent a day aboard each ship, explaining the situation. Hence, by the time the fleet left Culebra in December, I think nearly every officer junior to Sims was completely sold on his ideas, though many of the higher ranking officers would not permit themselves to be convinced. The navy was therefore rather divided into anti-Sims and pro-Sims groups, the latter in the vast majority, but the former with more rank.

In the Dolphin

I was thoroughly convinced that a great change in our navy's purpose and its training for it had occurred, and being in charge of gunnery on the *Dolphin*, I began to put the new ideas into effect as soon as the ship returned to Washington—as did other gunnery officers on ships throughout the navy. The new methods of training required altogether different equipment—equipment that seemed unnecessary on what was then considered a yacht rather than a fighting ship, but I went ahead with the preparations, confident that the same was being done on every fighting ship in the navy. In doing that, I reckoned without my boss, and when the captain [Lt. Commander George Stoney] came on deck one day and saw all the gear rigged and me busily trying to train our gun crew, he cried out, "Young man, what in the world are you doing?" When I told him that I was training our gun crews to shoot better, he said, "Stop it at once. You are trying to carry out the ideas of Sims and I do not like them," adding that he did not care about the ship's shooting, that all he wanted was a happy ship and instructed me to send all those funny contraptions ashore at once. To put it mildly, I was amazed at the captain's attitude, though as I learned later, it was not unusual. Similar opposition had often been encountered on other ships. However, I did not send my "funny contraptions" ashore but had them taken to the storeroom and continued the training work without them.

After the return from Culebra, we remained in Washington until the end of January when we received orders to prepare the ship for a long trip through the West Indies with the Secretary of the Navy and a party. This necessitated our going to the Norfolk Navy Yard for about a month to prepare the ship. After that, we started on the trip.

Our first port in the West Indies was Havana, where we arrived about the end of February 1903. Up to that time, not a great many of the high officials in our government had visited the capital of the new Republic of Cuba, so the visit of the *Dolphin* with high cabinet officers and other important government officials on board was an outstanding event. The Cuban government gave us a royal welcome, with receptions and a variety of interesting entertainments that lasted the several days we were there.

It was during the afternoon of the second day in port that an interesting incident occurred. I was officer of the deck at the time, responsible for the ship and for handling such emergencies as might arise. In connection with my responsibilities, I had studied up on weather dangers in Havana harbor and was consequently familiar with Havana's so-called "white squalls." Accompanied by terrific rains, they would arrive without warning and be of such force as to lash the harbor's surface into white foam (hence the name). Ships were warned of the dangers and prepared for them.

An Admiral's Yarn

It was shortly before four o'clock that day when a white squall hit the harbor with unusual suddenness. Up til then it had been one of the finest of Havana days. Then, when I looked north, out of the harbor entrance, I saw a small but very black cloud appear to form a few miles out. I had never seen a bleaker cloud or one that appeared so suddenly. As I looked in awe, I shouted an order to stand by to veer chain and let go the other anchor. But even as I did, the cloud grew with tremendous speed, and in an incredibly short time it had so completely covered the entire heavens with its dense blackness that night seemed upon us. Then, almost instantly, the rain and wind hit us and it was like a cloudburst and cyclone all in one. The wind caught the *Dolphin* broadside to with such force as to throw the ship so far over on its beam ends that I not only had great difficulty trying to reach the forward anchors but feared the ship might remain on its side. By the time I reached the forecastle, the ship was swinging round to the anchor and righting itself as the anchor continued to hold in the deep harbor mud, and we were soon head to wind and on an even keel. Knowing that the *Dolphin* was safe, I looked over the harbor as well as I could in the terrific wind and rain and saw weird sights. Every one of the little sailboats that had been carrying four or five passengers each across Havana harbor had capsized when the squall hit, and the passengers were frantically struggling in the water, crying for help. Fortunately the *Dolphin* had two boats secured at the lee boom and were still afloat when the ship righted. One of them was a pulling boat, the captain's gig, and I shouted to a boatswain's mate who was near me to get some volunteers into it and save everyone he could. At the same time I ordered our steam launch with its crew to go to the rescue also. How the men succeeded in climbing into the boats in that frightful storm or how they kept them afloat was a miracle, but they rescued everyone they could find in the water. It was a splendid job, and shortly after the squall ended they came alongside with their cargoes of half-drowned Cubans, about twenty-six in all. They were in pretty bad shape but were well taken care of by our doctors and crew before being put ashore.

I had not been overboard, or near drowning, but I was drenched to the skin and worn out from fighting the storm and its catastrophes.

It was some two hours after the squall had ceased before those of us on the ship could don dry clothes, and by that time I found myself still shaking and shivering from the exposure. Nevertheless, I continued with my duties all night, but the next day I noticed that I was feeling really ill all over, and my poor head was aching dreadfully. However, I thought it only a temporary condition, and at daylight the next morning the *Dolphin* got underway for Santiago.

XX

A Painful Interlude

As THE *DOLPHIN* STOOD ALONG the north coast of Cuba the following afternoon, I felt very ill. My head was bursting and my brain was in a most extraordinary muddle, but still, for some reason that I have never understood, I would not give up or consult the doctor but continued on with my regular watches, thinking my condition a temporary one.

This proved nearly disastrous, for while on duty, when a marked change of course to the southward was necessary through the old Bahama channel, I ordered the helm the wrong way and headed the ship toward the reef. Fortunately the navigator was on the bridge and, having noted what I had done, helped me to get the ship on the proper course. Then he said to me, "Laning, what is the matter with you? I have never known you to do anything like that before." I replied that I knew exactly what I wanted to do but my head was so woozy that I became confused. "Well!" said he, "You had better look out." Of course I tried to "look out" and managed to stand my next two watches, although as soon as I finished them, I climbed into my bed and stayed there. But the next night, as the ship stood into Santiago and all hands were called to bring the ship to anchor, I crawled out of bed and dressed. In some way I reached my station on the forecastle where I had change of the anchor gear, but felt too ill to stand, and I asked the boatswain's mate to help me to the punt. He did so and I collapsed, knowing nothing more until the anchor was down and secured and the boatswain's mate returned, shook me into consciousness and said, "Chain's secure, Sir. You had better report it." I told him I was too ill and he would have to help me to my room. I remembered nothing at all after that, but he told me

An Admiral's Yarn

afterward that he thought I was drunk, and since no one had seen him taking me to my room, he did not report it. The next morning I was called as usual, managed to dress somehow, and staggered into the wardroom where I collapsed into a chair. One of the doctors spied me and said, "Laning, you look sick." When he had taken my pulse and temperature, he rang for his assistants. I was so surprised when the sick-bay nurseman carried me to my room and put me in bed that I asked the doctors if I was really very ill. "Ill," they said, "Ill! Man, you have a temperature of nearly one hundred and five degrees."

That was a bad time for me with the doctors in constant attendance, taking temperature, marking red spots on my tummy, and giving me ice baths. Burning with fever, I could not understand what all the fuss was about, even when told that the *Dolphin* would make a rush run for Kingston, Jamaica—a new hospital had just opened, and I was to be left there. The Secretary of the Navy ordered the ship to take me there, and I was the first patient in the just completed Royal Naval Hospital. When I was being transferred by stretcher, with the Secretary and distinguished guests watching the procedure, I noticed considerable commotion at the gangway. I was told afterward that it was because the stretcher men carried me feet first over the side; in the navy, this means that the patient will never return.

It was a great relief to be out of my stuffy little room aboard ship and in a fine, large, airy room in the hospital. I was told this was at the personal request of "the first Lord of the American Admiralty," so I was given constant attention. However, I wanted so much to be with my ship and tour the West Indies as scheduled that I became very restless and took issue with the doctors about apparently everything. First, the bed was not comfortable, being just a thin mattress on ropes stretched across the frame. I begged for one without lumps and was put on a water mattress, which gurgled at every move, and I complained about that.

I continued to act so badly that the doctors became considerably alarmed, and when I fought against everything, the senior doctor decided to make me understand the situation. Accordingly, by the third evening in the hospital, and while I was in an especially fractious mood, Dr. Pollard, head of the hospital, took a chair near my bed and began a quiet little talk. Finally he said, "Laning, do you realize that you are a very bad patient. You fight us on everything and unless you stop it and work with us, you are not going to get well. You are a very sick man." Muddled though I was, the doctor's words had their effect, especially after he told me that I had a serious case of typhoid fever. Doctor Pollard was considered the outstanding fever expert in the British navy, and I owe my life to him and the wonderful care given me in the Royal Naval Hospital.

A Painful Interlude

It was a long hard pull while the fever ran its course, and I suffered greatly with fearful pains in my head and frequent hallucinations, some of which I could recall afterward. The worst periods were in the evenings when my temperature would be up and my nurse "Betty" was on duty.

In 1903, female nurses were not allowed in any naval activity, so all nurses were men. Those at the Royal Naval Hospital were the best available, and all were "Jamaican darkies," two of whom were assigned to my care. More faithful fellows there never were than "Brown" and "Betty," though it took me several days to understand them. Instead of a southern drawl with which I was familiar, they had of course acquired the words and intonations of the high-class British residents of Jamaica, which in a darkie sounded affected to me at first. Both of my nurses believed in voodoos and hoodoos, in dreams, witches, and weird things in general, but withal, they were splendid nurses.

Of the two, Betty appeared to be less intelligent than Brown, but I noticed that Betty always came on duty at six in the evening when I would be at my worst and that he would sit at the head of my bed, rubbing certain places on my head, which I did not like at first, but soon found made my headache easier and I could go to sleep. Thus I became very dependent on Betty and was so impressed with his ability that I reported it to the doctor as a form of treatment that might be developed to aid other fever cases. "Brown" did not have the same ability and apparently could not learn it, although he rubbed the exact spots and used the exact motions used by Betty. In talking with the doctor about it, he said, "Great heavens, man, did you think for a minute that we were unaware of Betty's ability in helping cases like yours? Of course we know about it and have known it for years." Then he added that Betty himself did not know how he did it. Doctors had worked with him for months trying to learn his methods, but only Betty could get results.

About ten days after I entered the hospital, and while at my worst, my wife arrived. She had been in Georgia on a visit, and, rushing to New York, she caught a little freight steamer coming to Kingston. I was too ill to appear enthusiastic over her arrival, but her nearness helped me greatly; gradually after that my fever went down, but it was weeks before it would remain down for twenty-four hours, and during that time I literally wasted away. Solid food of every kind was forbidden, and as only milk and barley water were allowed, and not much of either, I felt like a starving man after the fever left me, and I begged for food. My greatest longing was for Irish stew, though before my illness I had never thought much of it. But now it sounded "solid."

My convalescence was slow, and I thought I would never walk again. Strength finally came to my rescue, and I was allowed to be out in the beautiful grounds

An Admiral's Yarn

around the hospital where flowers and shrubs grew in profusion. Although I had lost forty-seven pounds and my clothes hung like bags on me, I was at last allowed to leave the hospital and join my wife at the Constant Springs Hotel, far up on the hills behind Kingston. We sailed home a week later.

The best steamers then available were those of the United Fruit Company, and our accommodations were on the *Admiral Farragut*, a rather new boat running to Boston. It carried about five hundred passengers in comfortable rooms on the upper deck, but its main purpose was transporting bananas—hence, seafaring men called them "banana boats." I found they were well named, for although the passengers were given excellent service and attention, they were "second fiddle" to the cargo of bananas which numbered about fifty thousand bunches.

As we struck some bad weather en route to Boston, I was often the only passenger in the dining room and I lived high and ate much!

When the ship entered Boston Harbor late one Sunday morning, I fully realized for how very little its passengers counted. We were told that because there was no way to cool off the banana holds, the ship would not be docked that night but would remain in the outer harbor until Monday so that the bananas would not spoil. Fortunately, a cool, fresh easterly wind brought relief by dark and the ship went in. The next day my wife and I went to West Point where we spent my month's "sick leave" with my brother-in-law John Palmer and his wife.

I grew stronger rapidly and by the latter part of June was able to return to the *Dolphin*, where I was not anxious to continue with Sims' method of shooting. By that time, I think, most officers were convinced it was the best and only way to train our navy to become the best shots in the world.

XXI

More of the **Dolphin**

A WONDERFUL WELCOME awaited me when I returned to the *Dolphin*, and I was soon again in charge of its guns and standing watch. I was a bit in doubt, at first, as to whether or not I would be allowed to work on the ship's shooting because of the captain's attitude toward it, but his tour of sea duty was coming to an end, and I was confident this would bring about a change.

In a few weeks the new captain [Lieutenant Commander John Gibbons] took over and, much to his apparent interest, found the ship with all its training gear rigged and the gun crews hard at work. He was a well-known bachelor in the navy and ideal for the command, but also known for not thinking highly of married naval officers, of whom I was now the only one on the ship. In fact, he said to me one day, "Laning, you probably know that I believe a naval officer married is a naval officer marred." Initially I was speechless with astonishment, but then said I had not asked for the duty and if he wanted to establish that policy on the *Dolphin*, to ask for my detachment. The talk thus ended and of course I expected my orders momentarily, but as time went on the captain seemed to be taking more and more interest in my gunnery work, and finally I ceased to think of the matter.

That summer on the *Dolphin* passed quickly, for not only were we busy improving our shooting, but we cruised almost continuously. A new Secretary of the Navy, Mr. Paul Morton, had been appointed, and he wanted to see the navy at work.[131] So, with the Congressional committees on their tours of inspection, we were kept busy until September when we went to the Brooklyn Navy Yard for repairs.

An Admiral's Yarn

When they were completed, we expected the *Dolphin* to return to Washington, but we were given orders to go directly to Pensacola, Florida, and New Orleans to pick up the Secretary of War and party and take them to Colón to inspect the work being done on the start of the Panama Canal. At that time, the canal was nearly in the stage of a project for which the preliminaries had just been completed by President Theodore Roosevelt. Through his farsighted energies, he had opened the way for the building of the canal by the United States. The project was at the forefront of national interest, and those of us attached to the *Dolphin* were greatly pleased with the opportunity to see the work being done as well as to be taking the Secretary of War, The Honorable William H. Taft, there.

We left New York one beautiful October morning, and for about twenty-four hours the weather remained perfect. It was still good when I took the deck for the four to eight watch the next morning, but when my relief came, he said, "With all this fine weather, the barometer is dropping as though the bottom has fallen out. I have reported to the captain each hour. It looks as though we are in for some bad weather."

At that time the ship was about opposite Cape Henry on a course to round Cape Hatteras, about seventy miles ahead. There was a long, rolling swell from the southeast but no wind at all, the water smooth, not a cloud in the sky, and the sunrise was beautiful. It seemed impossible for such perfect weather to become a full-fledged storm in a matter of minutes, and we thought we could round Cape Hatteras before real trouble started. However, the barometer continued to drop rapidly and clouds soon appeared in the sky in the southwest, while a breeze kicked up considerable sea. By eight o'clock the wind had reached gale force and the water was so rough that we were obliged to reduce our speed. Two hours later the *Dolphin* was in a tropical hurricane of terrific intensity.

There were no radios in those days, and ships at sea had no advance notice of storms except from their own barometer readings and the local weather conditions. Neither seemed to warrant the ships seeking shelter that day. We merely prepared the *Dolphin* for bad weather and continued trying to round Cape Hatteras. We did not accomplish it that day or even the next, as the southeast wind quickly grew into a hurricane and threw such tremendous breaking seas over us that the ship did not advance. We had to take the wind on our bow and make revolutions for seven knots speed in order to control the ship to meet the seas. But the great seas threw the ship first on one beam end and then on the other, and everything in the ship that could move was thrown about; even the men on deck did not escape injury. The heavy seas broke over us so fast that our "freeing ports" could not accommodate the water on deck and much of it

More of the Dolphin

forced its way below. Not only were all our steam pumps kept going, but the crew continued bailing out certain parts with buckets. Later on we learned that at Cape Hatteras the wind had attained a velocity of a hundred and twenty miles an hour.

For thirty-six hours we fought that storm with all our might, thinking every moment would be our last. When the sun went down on the second day, the wind and sea began to abate and we attempted working ourselves out of the dilemma that had given the ship and crew such a fearful beating. What a beating it was may be appreciated from the fact that though the ship bucked the wind and seas for thirty-six hours at a speed that should have advanced it some seven miles an hour, we found ourselves actually seventy miles farther back from where we had been when the storm struck us. Partly, I suppose, because the terrific wind had driven the Gulf Stream currents in shore to where we were.

It was about forty-eight hours after the expected time that we finally rounded Cape Hatteras and stood across the Gulf Stream into perfect weather. We may have thought ourselves foolish to continue going to sea in such a storm, but none of us wanted to give it up. One officer,[132] however, must have considered doing so for a long time, for he said to me when the storm was over, "Never again will I go through an experience like that, and just as soon as the ship reaches Pensacola, my resignation as a naval officer goes in by despatch."

Inasmuch as that officer was known to be financially well-fixed and had a splendid opening in business ready for him, I believed what he said, and after we anchored at Pensacola, I asked if he had resigned. His reply was "I cannot resign now and leave you fellows doing my work on this trip. That would not be fair. I will resign after the ship makes that trip to Panama." With that I let the matter drop until we were back in Washington where I asked once more if he was going to resign. This time he said, "No, I'll not resign now when winter is just starting and it is no time to start a job ashore. I'll wait until spring."

When spring came, he had given up the idea; he never resigned and rose to high rank in later years. Occasionally I see him and we often talk over the storm off Hatteras, but although neither he nor I will ever forget the horrors of such storms at sea, we certainly would never give up our sea life because of them.

Having taken most of the Secretary of War's party on board at Pensacola, the ship went to New Orleans to pick up the secretary himself. That visit was the first to New Orleans for many of us, and of course we were keen to see for ourselves if it was as fascinating and interesting as reported to be. Although our stay there was brief, we found the charms had not been exaggerated. We drove around the city looking at the lovely homes with beautiful grounds; we ate meals at Mme. Antonio's and other famous restaurants; we went to Szererac's for their

An Admiral's Yarn

well-known specialty, and met some of the city's prominent citizens—we were shown the true hospitality of old New Orleans. So pleased were we with our visit that we were loathe to leave, but as soon as Mr. Taft came on board we steamed away.

It is difficult for those who see the Panama Canal as it is now to visualize what it was in 1903 when we first saw it. Though the French had put a tremendous amount of work into it, what they had accomplished was a mere scratch on what had to be done—and even that had been absorbed by the tropical jungle that covered the workmen's quarters and shops. While the daily trains crossing the isthmus on the Panama Railroad kept the growth down on the mainline, one could see the miles of tracks and switches used by the French and also their dirt cars, engines, and derricks, now corroded with rust and disintegrating. The havoc and waste everywhere were appalling, and realizing what had to be faced in nature and in disease problems, it was hard to believe that even the United States could overcome it.

On our return to Washington we began to hear the news about "wireless telegraphy," then being developed by Marconi and others. We realized, if ever perfected, "wireless" would be of tremendous importance in seafaring life, but some were quite skeptical of the claims made for it at that time. Nevertheless, a wireless set was to be installed on the *Dolphin*.

It took a long time to complete the installation and still longer before the set would work satisfactorily. When I left the ship the wireless was still in the experimental stage, but as long as we were not far from other sending and receiving stations, we could get messages through when conditions were right. In that manner, use of radios in the navy began.

The winter of 1903–04 was a busy one, standing watches and training the crew for better shooting. We knew we were improving considerably in rapid and accurate firing, but our gun equipment was old and poor, and we felt we could not expect satisfactory results. However, our real purpose was to show that although the *Dolphin* was spoken of as a Coburger, it was a better shooting gunboat than others in its class.

When spring arrived, we were in Washington once more and facing two commitments: one to take a party up the James River for a thorough inspection of the many historical places located on or near its banks, and the other to exhibit our shooting ability by firing in the first competitive target practice ever held among all U.S. naval ships.

We spent about two weeks on the James River trip and enjoyed it to the utmost. At that time, not one of the old historical places had been modernized or restored, each being practically as it had been for years, occupied and cared for

More of the Dolphin

by the descendants of the original owners or local families. Under the circumstances, they were not quite the beautifully kept places that large money expenditures have since made them, but interesting and charming nevertheless, depicting as they did our country's earliest Colonial days, in the Revolution, and the Civil War. Jamestown Island, the site of old Jamestown, was quite bare, and Williamsburg, once the capital of the Virginia Colony, was somewhat dilapidated.

Fortunately many of the old houses and estates along the river were not greatly changed from what they had been, especially Westover, Upper and Lower Brandon, and Bermuda Hundred, to mention only a few.

We also visited the Civil War battlefields nearby and Yorktown, where we could follow our country's history for almost two centuries.

At the end of the James River trip, we fired the required target practice, and although the *Dolphin* did much better shooting than had seemed possible to us a year before, we still felt that with good gun equipment we could have done better. In that practice, each gun fired as many shots as it could in one minute, and the record for a gun was the number of hits made by it in that time. What counted was the actual hits per minute made in the target by a gunboat, and to obtain that goal we had worked first to develop rapidity in firing and second to develop accuracy.

Even on that first record practice, we were amazed at our shooting, for not only did we manage to fire three or four times as many shots as we had thought possible in the time allowed, but also we had made three or four times as many hits, which was most gratifying. That first record target practice therefore clearly proved to us on the *Dolphin* that Sims was on the right track, and never since has there been any question of it.

It took some weeks after June 30th, when the shooting year ended, before all the reports of the practices fired in different parts of the world could reach Washington, and as we were only hoping not to be shown up as the worst in gunboat shooting, we gave little thought to the result. You can therefore imagine our surprise one day when we received a letter from the Navy Department saying that in competing against the eighteen other gunboats in the U.S. Navy, the *Dolphin* had been awarded the shooting trophy for the gunboat class. The surprise and thrill to the *Dolphin* was equalled only by the amazement that it caused in the rest of the navy. It likewise surprised both Sims and his target practice officer, and when I saw Sims after the announcement, he said "Well, I'll be damned! To think of a Coburger ship doing that! Why, Laning, you are some good after all." From that day on Admiral Sims was ever my close and good friend.

An Admiral's Yarn

For the *Dolphin*, the summer, fall, and winter of 1904 were about the same as the two previous years. Once more the navy had been given a new Secretary, Charles J. Bonaparte,[133] who was to be shown around as were committees of Congress. The ship covered our Atlantic coast from end to end and also went to the West Indies. Later, in the spring of 1905, we took another important official party to inspect the Panama Canal—a repetition of previous trips and little to relate, though on all trips we continued our training in shooting, hoping to retain our trophy.

It was just before we were to fire our second record target practice that we made our second visit to the Panama Canal, about a year and a half after the first one. During the interval we had read much of the work being done to clear the jungles and of the new methods using vastly improved equipment; equally important were the changes made for bettering the health of Canal workers. However, we were not prepared to find that the Panama Railroad had become a modern and very busy one nor to see the splendid quarters provided for the Canal workers. Best of all, the mosquito problem had nearly been solved. Great as were the changes along the Canal, the greatest were within the prism itself, as the dense tropical growth had given way to fresh cuts through the hills that were teeming with workmen and huge excavating machines, while trains and scows carried earth and stone, clearing channels to the sea at both ends. We saw huge dams and locks being built at Gatun and Miraflores, and at last we could visualize the great ship canal across the Isthmus of Panama that was being built by the United States—a vast undertaking at tremendous cost.

Being practical seafaring men and not engineers, the problem of getting the ships in and out of the Canal impressed us mightily. Large, well-protected harbors were absolutely necessary at both ends and especially on the Atlantic side, where ships intending to transit the Canal had to be protected from the heavy seas and winds often experienced at Colón; during such times, shipping had to put to sea to be safe. Fortunately, the engineers realized this and requested the Canal Commission to permit the building of harbors. The request was finally granted, but not without heated arguments which lasted some time between the canal engineers and the commission.

To other than seagoing people, building the harbors seemed of small importance compared to building the canal. Fortunately, the engineers realized the necessity of the harbors and that construction of miles of breakwater would greatly simplify their work, allowing them to use the rock and stone taken from the canal to build the breakwater—solving the problem of what to do with the excavated material.

More of the Dolphin

The commission sent for the head engineer of the canal to question him on the advisability of the work, and when we reached Colón, that was the main subject discussed. When the commission asked the engineer how long it would take him to finish the harbor, if authorized to construct it, he replied, "We can finish that breakwater in less time than it takes the commission to make up its mind to build it," and with that, he left the hearing.

The work was soon authorized and begun. By the time the canal was finished, that harbor was ready too. Quite naturally, the wonderful harbor at Colón has proved to be one of the greatest assets of the canal and also has even greater value to our country because of its tremendous strategic importance to the United States Navy in its vital work of safeguarding our national interests.

Shortly after the *Dolphin* returned from the Panama trip, it went out to fire its second record target practice. We knew our standing at the top the first year had made the other gunboats work harder, but we had worked too, and every officer and man had given much time to gunnery training. Thus the interest in the practice was intense, and we had improved many of the defects in our worn-out guns. We believed we would shoot as well as any ship with our kind of ordnance equipment.

As I recall it, the *Dolphin* left Washington on a Monday to fire the practice, and we expected to take as many days for it as might be necessary for a good test. Although the ship had been away from Washington frequently that spring, there was no apparent reason for hurrying back. Even though we stood our watches as usual, our main interests were in shooting.

The first two days on the target range were fine ones. We checked up on the range, made a few practice runs and began our firing. We did splendidly the first few strings, and those of us at the guns were elated, but when we had finished about half the firing runs, there came a change in the weather, with heavy winds, rains, and squalls hitting us. Often we could hardly see the target, and high winds blew the spray from the rough sea over the crews and guns on the open deck.

Never before or since have I seen a ship fire a record target practice in such weather as the *Dolphin* did that afternoon, and as the rules for conducting practices directed that to be certain firing conditions were equal for all ships, record practice be held in good weather, I at once requested a postponement of further firing until the squalls were over. Although the captain knew the rules for practices as well as I did, he told me to go on with the firing because he wanted to return to Washington.

We tried to continue shooting, but it was soon evident that good firing was impossible under the conditions and that if we went on, the *Dolphin* would lose the trophy. The men had worked so hard to qualify as gunpointers, but it seemed the crews had no chance of winning the money prizes, which had been a great incentive to their training. Therefore, I again went to the bridge, and as the rules required me to do, requested the captain to order "cease firing" until the weather improved. He again refused and shouted loudly to me, "Do you think for a minute that I am going to devote another day to this practice? I certainly will not."

Knowing how much our good shooting meant to the ship and everyone on it, I begged him to reconsider, inviting his attention to the fact that because of his unwillingness to give a few days of his time to the firing, he would completely nullify the months and months of hard work done by his officers and crew to prepare his ship in its effort to again win the trophy. But my reminding him of this only increased his anger and he yelled, "You get off this bridge and go ahead with your shooting." I did so.

No words of mine can describe the anguish we endured during those remaining runs. After having worked a full year to prepare for them, we believed the fruits of our labor were being lost to us. Even so, we did not give up and still fought to make each shot good. But of course, we could not fire nearly as many shots or make nearly as many hits as we would have in good weather. Our training and skill entitled us to better treatment.

I was not at all happy doing my report of the target practice. Although we had not done badly, my heart wanted to prove we were really the very best shooters, and I hated to report the lowered score caused by the stormy weather. Perhaps I was galled also because no one but ourselves would know why we had not done better, since all ships were ordered to fire, for record, only in good weather. Hence, the poor scores made by the *Dolphin* would be attributed to its being a Coburger that did not work as hard or as successfully as other ships.

The reports of that year's practices were slow in reaching the Target Practice Office. Many of the ships on far distant stations did not fire until the end of the shooting year, and consequently, when they finished, it took a month or six weeks for the results to reach Washington.

Strange to say, when most of the reports were in, we found we had not done too badly, for the *Dolphin* still stood at the top. That fact encouraged us somewhat and we began to have hope. The captain's attitude changed a bit too when he saw that even under the handicap of firing in bad weather his ship had done well. But for the handicap that he himself had imposed, we probably would have been at the top again, and he told me frequently that he regretted not having taken my advice.

The reports drifted in slowly, and waiting to hear the result of the *Dolphin's* standing was a strain on everyone. Eighteen gunboats participated, and when

More of the Dolphin

seventeen had sent in their scores, the *Dolphin* was still ahead. but the eighteenth one had us worried; it had been the runner-up the year before, was known to be an excellent shooting ship, and had spent a full year of hard training in an effort to beat us. Knowing the race between the ships, Sims and his "Target Practice Office" became almost as interested in the outcome as we were. Sims also knew that the number of hits made by the *Dolphin* in even bad weather had been impressive proof of the value of his training methods.

I suspect he rather wanted us to win, because he seemed as disappointed as I was the day he telephoned to tell me that the last report was in and the *Dolphin* had lost the trophy by just a fraction of one point. Then he said, "Great God, Laning, if you people had not gone on firing in that bad weather, you would have again won the trophy hands down. You would have won it anyway had the ship made just one more hit in the practice."

Thus was the trophy lost by us, though we had done fairly well—remarkably so in a storm. Practically all of our gunpointers had qualified for pointer pay, and our gun crews had won a creditable number of prizes for excellence. We were commended highly for the shooting, and our records for the two years of shooting still put the *Dolphin* at the top. Nevertheless, we grieved deeply over losing that trophy, and I think the captain grieved too.

The summer of 1905 was another busy one as our ship continued to take out inspection parties, but during it, we had a new experience that was caused by the ending of the Russo-Japanese War. Few who were following the news believed the end was near, so the surprise was great when the move for peace made by President Theodore Roosevelt was met with quick response from both belligerents, and each rushed conferees to Washington to negotiate.

Summertime in Washington is much too hot for negotiating anything, especially peace. It became evident that the conference had to be held in a cooler place, so after careful consideration, Portsmouth, New Hampshire, was chosen. Then arose the problem of getting the two groups of conferees, who were gathering in Washington with all their aides and paraphernalia, established at Portsmouth to avoid their meeting before the actual conference. Since the members of the peace parties were the leading statesmen of their respective countries, they had to be taken to Portsmouth in a most official manner, so the two U.S. ships best equipped for the purpose were assigned the task.

The magnificent *Mayflower* (the President's yacht)[134] was directed to take the Russian delegation, and the *Dolphin* (the Secretary of the Navy's yacht) was directed to take the Japanese. The delegations were still not to contact each other, and they embarked on their respective ships on the same day, getting under way, singly, for Portsmouth. The run was uneventful, and we officers of the

An Admiral's Yarn

Dolphin found pleasure in meeting and conversing with the Japanese statesmen of whom we had read so much. We found them charming, courteous, affable, and intensely interested in both the United States and what they saw of its navy. We therefore were sorry to have them leave us at Portsmouth and establish themselves in hotels.

By that time my tour of sea duty was about over, and while I had not received word that I would be sent ashore, I had been attached to the *Dolphin* for over three years and had more than made up for the time lost while sick. Therefore, I was not surprised when toward the end of September orders came detaching me from the *Dolphin*, granting me one month's leave, and directing me to report for duty at the Naval Academy by the end of October.

I was sorry to leave the *Dolphin* where I was still the only married officer and where I had so many friends. On the day I left, after saying good-bye to my messmates, I went in to bid farewell to the captain who wished me all sorts of good things. Then, just as I was leaving, he looked at me and said, "Laning, I am sorry you are leaving the ship. You have done so much for it and for me by always being on the job. Do you remember when I first took command, I told you I considered a naval officer married, a naval officer marred? Well, I want to tell you now you've done much to make me change my mind."

A few months later we received an invitation to his wedding. I suspect he had been in love with his charming young lady all the time we were shipmates.

XXII

A New Shooting Game

IN MY ONE MONTH'S LEAVE before reporting to the Naval Academy, my wife and I went west, first to visit my family in Illinois and then to spend two weeks with her family in Santa Barbara. After our delightful vacation, we went to Annapolis where I reported for duty and was assigned to the Department of Applied Mathematics as an instructor.

It would be difficult to conceive greater consternation than mine when I found I was assigned to that office. Quite the most highbrow, it covered so many branches, and I had never been adept in any of them. By hard study I had completed them fairly well as a cadet, but since then I had used little of the knowledge gained and had not opened a textbook on any of the subjects. Yet, there I was, detailed to teach calculus, solid geometry, least squares, hydromechanics, and the like.

The situation seemed worse than when I was an instructor in English, history and law on my previous tour at the Academy. By resolute study I had been able to keep ahead of the cadets in those branches, but "applied math" was different. Cadets were not nearly as strong in "English, history, and law" as they were in mathematics. In fact, the essential for graduating from the Academy was to have a mathematical mind, and in each class there were always several geniuses who could properly appraise an instructor in mathematics.

Not wanting cadets to think for a minute that I was not as capable in mathematics as they were, I was forced to study every free moment to keep ahead of them. I succeeded, and then, when I had my subject well in hand, surprise orders transferred me to the Department of Ordnance and Gunnery.

An Admiral's Yarn

Teaching ordnance and gunnery is very different from teaching higher mathematics, for although mathematics enter into it, the former is truly a technical subject and a highly practical one. Under such circumstances, I was delighted to be made an instructor in that branch, and although I felt well qualified by virtue of my gunnery work at sea, I feared I was being transferred because of unsatisfactory work in "math."

Uneasy as to the cause of the transfer, I went to the superintendent's aide for information. He was greatly surprised at my asking, since he thought I knew all about it and said, "You know, Laning, Lieutenant B——,[135] who has just been ordered to sea, was not only captain of the Navy Rifle Team but also an instructor in ordnance and gunnery. He was responsible for training all cadets in small arms shooting and was in charge of the Academy rifle range and shooting galleries. Because the Navy Rifle Team is not part of the Academy but directly under the Inspector of Target Practice for the Navy, the Superintendent felt that Sims, not he, should name the successor. The superintendent got in touch with Sims by telephone and asked him to designate an officer. Sims asked for the names of the lieutenants at the Academy, and when the list was read to him, he said, 'Stop! Laning is the man.'" Hence, I was transferred to Ordnance and Gunnery to be captain of the Navy Rifle Team and to teach cadets both rifle and pistol shooting.

I was much relieved that I had not been fired from mathematics but had been chosen for another shooting job by the navy's head of target practice, even though I had little experience in small arms work. I therefore went at it with a will. Since I knew a good deal about ordnance and gunnery, instructing in that branch was not difficult, and I easily kept far ahead of the cadets. Teaching them to shoot rifles and pistols accurately, however, and leading the Navy Rifle Team were different matters entirely.

There was and still is a general idea in the United States that by virtue of being Americans we are somehow born to excel in certain things, especially shooting. I suppose the idea developed from the lurid tales of accurate shooting in our Indian and hunting days, wild West activities, and even early naval engagements. From my own reading, I had something of the same idea. Then too, I came from the Middle West, where every boy could shoot fairly well with a .22 caliber rifle and shotgun, which seemed to confirm this belief. I soon found that every man born an American is not a naturally good lawyer, doctor, businessman, ballplayer, artist, or whatnot.

In teaching cadets to shoot, I had to start from zero. Few of them had ever fired a rifle or pistol or knew anything about either weapon. They were only boys, most of them coming from cities and towns, and did not even know how

A New Shooting Game

to hold, load, or even sight a gun, so we began from scratch. Between recitation room and shooting duties, I had little free time. The former kept me busy from 8 a.m. until 3:30 p.m. each weekday, and the latter from 3:30 p.m. until dark. Besides that, I had to devote each night to study and research, and each Saturday and holidays to shooting in the gallery or on the range. Thus my work was never-ending, but interesting, and since it was with youngsters of fine understanding, great mentality, excellent physique, and perfect eyesight—all keen to learn shooting—we progressed rapidly.

As soon as the weather moderated in March, all shooting took place on the open range across the Severn River, but otherwise there was no change in my schedule. All drill periods were still devoted to teaching every cadet to shoot well, and all other daylight hours, except those on Sunday, were devoted to developing expert riflemen to represent the Academy in competitions. Selecting such a team was most important, and only by competing with known good "shots" could we gauge the efficiency of the navy's marksmanship. To that end, I was obliged to test the cadets' firing skills against the best shots in the country. Therefore, during the winter I invited three well-known rifle teams to come to the Academy for matches. One was a team of good average shooting ability, the National Guard of Maryland, one a team always above average, the National Guard of the District of Columbia, and the other best shooting regimental team in the United States at that time, the Seventy-first Regiment of New York. I knew there was little hope of winning all the matches against those teams, but at least they would prove a good yardstick to measure our shooting ability.

The matches proved to be just that, but they also showed us something else. The only match the cadets won was that with the fairly good team of the State of Maryland. When teamed against the shooting skills of the District and with the Seventy-first Regiment of New York, we were not good enough, and they both won easily.

It was evident that while probably sound in the rudiments of shooting, the navy had to learn the refinements if it were to excel. Therefore, at the end of the Academy shooting season, at the very time I had taken charge of the U.S. Rifle Team that was to compete in the National Matches, I was also obliged to begin learning the refinements of shooting. The Navy Rifle Team, of which I was captain in the summer, was not connected with the Naval Academy Rifle Team I had coached all winter. Cadets were neither available for it nor allowed on it; it was only for seagoing officers and enlisted men of the navy. As such men had few opportunities for small arms practice aside from their "great gun" work, it was something of an anomaly for sailors to compete with soldiers in military marksmanship, yet the Navy Rifle Team was for just that purpose—to compete

An Admiral's Yarn

with teams from the U.S. Infantry, Cavalry, Artillery, Marine Corps, and with National Guard teams from each state and territory. Quite an undertaking for the navy! Realizing that I new very little about expert rifle shooting, I was concerned about what would be the best way to teach the navy team. My predecessor had encountered that same problem, and the Navy Department had employed a professional to coach his team. Naturally I supposed a professional would also be allowed me, but Sims simply said, "No professional help. Coach the team yourself."

I new then I was "up against it" and in some way had to learn all about expert shooting to train the navy team. I had expected to train the team at the Naval Academy, and the candidates began to assemble there at the end of the cadet shooting season. When I found I had to do all the teaching and coaching myself, however, I knew the Academy range would not be suitable and that to learn expert rifle shooting, the practice range had to be of high quality. Therefore, I tried to arrange the training at Creedmoor, the magnificent range of the State of New York, where the finest rifle shots in the country did their practicing and where the New York State Rifle Team, which had always stood first in the national matches, did its training. Right there I struck a snag. The Navy Team had trained there the year before and had had some sort of row that ended with the New York authorities forbidding our team to use the Creedmoor range again. I was crushed. How we eventually managed to obtain permission to use the range again is too long a story to relate here, but by the first of July we were in camp at Creedmoor. At that time, the officer in charge of the range was the Inspector of Target Practice for the state of New York, Colonel Thurston, a martinet of the first order, but such a loved one that to every militiaman in New York, he was always affectionately called "Peggy." He was given to much boisterous bluster and talk, but behind it was knowledge, efficiency, ability, and above all, fairness. He was particularly famous for his profanity and could outdo even the hardiest of sailors; everyone stood in awe of him.

Not only was he in charge of the great Creedmoor range where all New York National Guardsmen were taught shooting, Peggy was captain of the New York State Rifle team. I cautioned our men to show utmost attention and respect to Peggy, but it may have been unnecessary, for every one of us was soon devoted to him and became greatly interested in his control at Creedmoor.

The navy team's devotion to Colonel Thurston soon became apparent to him, and he often called on our men to assist him, even though he could draw on the militia organizations for help. Consequently, I always had buglers and orderlies report to him whenever he came on the range. Dressed always in clean, white, working clothes and leggings, they stood out clearly from the hundreds of

A New Shooting Game

other men on the range who were dressed all in khaki. As they always kept just behind Peggy, it was not difficult for everyone on the range to know when the boss arrived. I was pleased when he asked our navy buglers to sound the firing and cease-firing calls and requested our orderlies to carry his verbal orders. He explained later that our men understood his orders and carried his messages exactly as given. Then he added that he knew only two languages, English and profane, and sailors always understood both.

What we learned at Creedmoor about small arms shooting was most valuable, although the experts who generously helped us were not very encouraging and warned that it took at least seven years to develop skills such as they had. I therefore did not expect the navy team to shine greatly at the National Matches—and it didn't! Nevertheless, the team scored better than the navy team of the year before and continued to stand in sixth place out of thirty-eight competing teams. But, of course, we were disappointed.

Perhaps the most important of the many things we learned at the matches concerned "team shooting." We realized there must be real teamwork in the National Match teams, but so far the only cooperation between team members was a brief discussion of shooting conditions between successive strings. The final score merely reflected the sum of the individual scores made by the twelve men.

It seemed that something vitally important was lacking, and although I had no idea just what to do about it, I felt that if the combined ability of the twelve navy men could be made available to each one of them while shooting, our team's score could be considerably increased—if not enough to win the match, perhaps enough to partly offset our lack of expertise. The National Matches of 1906 ended with that idea firmly planted in my mind.

When the matches were over, and as I bid good-bye to the various team captains, I was full of ideas and plans for improving the navy team. As usual, Peggy Thurston's New York State Team won the big match, and I congratulated him heartily as well as thanked him for what he had done for our team at Creedmoor, expressing the hope that he would authorize the navy team to train at Creedmoor the following year. I added that we had learned so much from him that even his New York team would have to look out for the navy team the next year. Peggy laughed heartily as he replied, "Of course your navy team can come to Creedmoor next year, and I do not doubt it will shoot better because of what you have learned here, but don't get the idea that a navy team will ever beat the New York State Team." Then he added, "Laning, if that ever happens, I quit rifle shooting then and there."

An Admiral's Yarn

Back in Annapolis, I devoted every moment to digesting what we had learned about rifle shooting and to applying the knowledge practically. Not content with what I had learned from actual firing, I bought every available book written on the subject of shooting, and by December, when the Academy shooting course began, I felt quite qualified to train our team in expert shooting. I still believed, however, that more teamwork was key to improvement and set myself to the task of developing it.

At this point, the big-gun shooting of naval ships gave me a clue, for, whether firing .30 caliber rifles or 14-inch guns, the problems are exactly the same; the means that determine the accuracy of guns fired by a team from a ship are the same as those that govern a rifle team. The navy used methods that made all the shots from a ship hit in practically the same place when fired at the same time, and I believed I could teach the rifle team to do the same.

It was easier to develop teamwork with ship's guns than with rifles. The sight readings of ship's guns could be adjusted mechanically, whereas the rifles could not be. For instance, on ships we could set the scales on all the sights to hit an object at five thousand yards. A similar adjustment on military rifles was not possible. All rifle sights were built exactly alike and merely screwed onto a gun. Each rifle required its sight to be set for each range of firing. For specified distances, the settings varied greatly between rifles. The sights of very few rifles could be set at a thousand when the range was a thousand yards. For some rifles, the correct range settings for this distance would be perhaps as high as twelve hundred yards and for others as low as eight hundred yards.

There were also wide lateral discrepancies. On a zero lateral setting, some rifles shot far to the right of the point at which they were aimed, while others shot far to the left. For that reason, team shooting with rifles was far more difficult than team shooting with a ship's guns. For team shooting with rifles, each one had to be given its own particular corrections for every range. To do this required the careful analysis of each rifle's shooting records.

I will not attempt to relate all that was done that winter to teach cadets how to shoot or to train the Naval Academy Rifle Team. The cadets liked shooting and many of them devoted every free moment to it, which enabled me to easily select candidates for their rifle team. The cadets advanced so rapidly in rifle shooting that, even though far less experienced than the riflemen they would have to compete with, I believed they would give excellent accounts of themselves in match shooting and decided it only fair to enter them—the Naval Academy Team—in the National Matches. I so recommended and their entry was authorized.

A New Shooting Game

While instruction in shooting a rifle was foremost, proficiency in pistol shooting was also very important. Naval officers always carried a pistol in combat, and both officers and men believed it essential to use this weapon with accuracy.

Trying to teach good pistol firing was a veritable nightmare, for although we had learned equally as much about it as rifle shooting, our navy men were getting poor results. So universally poor were the results, we came to the conclusion that navy men were poor shots with a pistol.

That they might qualify with both weapons, the members of the Navy Rifle Team continued practicing with pistols all during the 1906 summer at Creedmoor, and while on the pistol range met many of the crack shots of the country who were practicing there. It was noticed that nearly all of them used a Colt .38 revolver, apparently of the exact type used by the navy, but they made almost perfect scores. Our scores were poor, although some of our men seemed to do exactly as the crack shots did. Noting the unaccountability for the difference in scores, one of our men suggested to one of the crack shots that they exchange pistols and have a little match. This they did.

The result of that match was a revelation. The navy man made a perfect score, and the crack shot made a very poor one. After that there were several small matches with pistols exchanged, and in every case the man with the crack shot's pistol won.

Our men were convinced, of course, that there was something vitally wrong with our pistols. I hurried to my friend, Tom Anderton, of the Seventh Regiment of New York, who was one of the finest pistol shots in the country, to ask for an explanation. He said that the navy refused to use a standard "Navy Colt" and their problem stemmed from the size of the bore on the pistols they were using. He then asked me to come into the armory with him so that he could show me why the navy pistols would not shoot straight. The .38 caliber bullets completely filled the barrel of his pistol and took its rifling beautifully, while the same bullets dropped right through the barrels of navy pistols. Less accurate shooting weapons than those navy pistols could hardly be imagined.

What I had learned alarmed me greatly, for the navy was entirely equipped with them—every one of which was worthless. Delving into the matter with the Bureau that provided the pistols, we discovered that the specifications under which they were purchased called for barrels with a somewhat larger bore than .38 caliber pistols should have. No one could explain the error, but apparently the mistake was made in the first specification and carried on from there. Every .38 caliber pistol ever purchased for the United States Navy was defective—an astounding fact. This situation could not be tolerated, and the Bureau of

An Admiral's Yarn

Ordnance wanted to correct it at once, without having to wait until the new automatic pistols, then under consideration, could be developed and supplied.

I was directed to test various types of specially designed .38 caliber bullets to determine if, by merely changing the bullets, the pistols would shoot straight. That test went on for two months. Since there was no one else to do the shooting, all had to be done by cadets, and I chose the best shots among them. Each one selected was to fire hundreds of carefully aimed shots, and although some gave more accuracy than others, none gave anything near the standard of the .38 caliber ammunition fired from standard .38 Colt pistols. The tests confirmed the utter inaccuracy of the navy pistols and showed that our navy men were equal to most crack shots when using the standard Colt.

XXIII

Another Season with Small Arms

WHEN THE WEATHER PERMITTED, cadet shooting was transferred once more to the rifle range, where it soon became evident that the team would be greatly improved over last year, especially in team shooting. By the time the matches were to start, the Academy team had been making better scores than the expert visiting teams had made the year before. This of course was encouraging, and I began to feel that with a little luck, the Naval Academy might even beat the Seventy-first Regiment Team of New York.

Just then occurred an event of vast importance to me and mine. A few days before the cadet's first team match, the stork visited my house and left our daughter. Evidently other things were left too, because with her arrival came not only the luck I was looking for but also a happiness and contentment that has been ours ever since. Then, too, the Naval Academy Rifle Team immediately assumed our daughter for its mascot.

That she was a good mascot cannot be questioned, for when the team fired its first match of the year, with the State of Maryland's team, the cadets won overwhelmingly. Then, on the following Saturday they swamped the District of Columbia's team. On the third Saturday came the match with the crack team of the Seventy-first Regiment, many of whom were members of the New York State Team and thought to be invincible. In spite of that, and to the New York Team's enormous surprise and chagrin, not only did the Academy team win easily but almost man for man made better scores. Thus it took but one year to disprove the fallacy that the length of time required to make expert riflemen was close to "seven years."

An Admiral's Yarn

The match with the Seventy-first Regiment ended my direct responsibility for Naval Academy shooting instruction, for although the Academy team was to take part in the national matches, it was to do so under the supervision of the officer who had spent the spring understudying me while I assumed my duties as captain and coach of the Navy Rifle Team.

No sooner were the graduation exercises over than the candidates for the navy team began to assemble, and I looked them over with great interest, because the selection of them had been based on specifications that I had drawn up the previous winter. In addition to being sent better prepared candidates, I was infinitely better prepared to coach and train them. During the month of June, I was able to reduce the squad from about eighty fair shots to about thirty of the best shots available in the navy. Thus I had the material for the best rifle team the navy could turn out.

Just as they did the preceding year, the navy team went to Creedmoor around July first for two full months of training preparatory to the national match. We devoted the first month to individual firing, and by the end of it, I had selected the fifteen men best qualified for the team. Then it was time to weld them into the shooting team that I had in mind, but for which there was neither example nor precedent.

As I visualized it, team shooting had to be developed along two lines, one for slow fire shooting at fixed distances ranging from two hundred to a thousand yards, the other for skirmish runs in which, starting six hundred yards from the target, the team would run down the range to the two-hundred-yard mark, stopping at certain specified points to fire a given number of rounds. Because in the former the twelve men on a team shot by pairs in succession, and in the latter, all shot rapidly together during the few seconds at each stop, two quite different forms of teamwork were required, and both were essential if the navy was to overcome its handicaps in individual experience, knowledge, and ability. In its big-gun shooting, the navy had to employ both forms, and I intended to introduce them in team rifle shooting.

In naval gunnery, it is vital that the shots from every gun on the ship hit the same object simultaneously. My scheme was to have the very best shooters shoot first and then use their results to determine the exact data for making bull's-eye hits. Then, based on that data, give each succeeding shooter the exact sight readings to use to hit the bull's-eye. There was nothing particularly new or revolutionary in the idea, but the scheme was original in its intent to use all the precision and thoroughness of the United States Navy. It was also revolutionary for team shooting to have a team captain play a vital part, such as the navy captain would do, working out the correct data and passing it along.

Another Season with Small Arms

I doubt our scheme would have succeeded if tried by a team of other than navy men new to rifle shooting. For one thing, the experts of other teams simply could not be convinced that a team captain who was not actually shooting could be helpful to his men. The men preferred to get their own data, even though precious points might be lost to their team from the several shots it took to obtain it. They also believed that shooters were apt to make bull's-eyes on their very first shots, which were "sighting shots" not for record, and considered that to be bad luck. Their superstition against getting "bulls on sighting shots" prevented their acceptance of an innovation that would produce them. Thank the good Lord we sailors had no such superstition. We wanted to start with bull's-eyes and continue making them.

Although our "skirmish run shooting" worked on this same principle, there was a major difference in its application. On the run, the team members fired simultaneously rather than at an individual pace. The only way to apply the principle here was to ascertain what corrections, if any, should be made on one firing gun, referred to as the "master gun." The team was quickly directed to make exactly the same corrections on their guns. It was, of course, a considerable task to get all guns "standardized," but once done, with one command I could expect all guns to hit the mark simultaneously.

The members were chosen and we immediately began shooting as a team, continuously perfecting our system. Each weekday the team went through the entire national match course until it became merely a day's work. At first our goal was to have the best team score ever made in a national match, but as we scored higher every day, we correspondingly elevated our goal. Then we set for ourselves the task of scoring better at each distance than any match team had ever done before. This gave us a considerably higher objective, but by the end of the month we were surpassing it daily.

It might be thought that having attained such a high standard, we could be rather sure of winning the match, and although we had that hope, it was merely a hope, since we had no knowledge at all about the practice scores the expert teams were shooting.

Of the teams we thought dangerous, the one most feared was Peggy Thurston's New Yorkers, for they often watched us shoot and knew exactly how good our scores were. In particular, Peggy himself watched and often stood behind us buried in thought. The day of our last shooting at Creedmoor, we wound up shooting on the "Thousand-Yard Range," where Peggy approached and said, "Laning, you probably remember the little talk we had at the end of the national matches last year when I said that if ever a navy team beat the New York team I would at once quit rifle shooting. I'm sorry now that I made that remark

An Admiral's Yarn

and want to withdraw it. I don't want to quit rifle shooting just yet." Thereupon we shook hands and Peggy left, but I had the feeling he was quite impressed by the navy team's shooting.

The 1907 matches were held at Camp Perry on the wonderful range just completed by the State of Ohio. When we arrived there a few days before the matches, teams and individual shooters were pouring in from all over the country. Of rifle teams, I believe there were forty-eight and of other crack shots, several hundred—quite the greatest gathering ever in the Western Hemisphere, all quartered on the range in one vast camp.

At once there was a great deal of visiting between teams, and I was especially delighted to foregather once more with the Naval Academy team I had worked so hard to develop. It was by far the youngest team in age and shooting experience, but it made up for that with its tremendous will to win. I had brought the Academy's "standard Colt pistols" and was told the cadets were to enter both the pistol and the rifle matches.

One of the early visitors to the navy camp was the coach of the U.S. Infantry team, an outstanding military marksman whose books and treatises on the subject were considered authoritative. He commented on the many teams and expert shots attending the match and then expressed a hope that the five service teams would do well. Inasmuch as the Naval Academy team was a "service team," I said, "You mean six instead of five, do you not?" "No" he said, "I mean five. You are probably counting the Naval Academy team which no one takes seriously." He may have felt that way, but I could not agree with him.

A little later we talked of skirmish firing and after telling me how the Infantry team grouped its men by threes to dope out their sight corrections during a run, he said, "I am told you use a new and altogether different method for controlling the skirmish firing of the Navy team. As I could not possibly make use of it at this late date, would you mind explaining it to me?" Of course I did not mind, and he listened very carefully while I explained the method in detail. After thinking about it for a minute or two, he remarked, "Well, perhaps one has to use some scheme like that with the green shots of the navy team, but it certainly would not do for the experienced Infantry team." I could only smile!

The "national matches" were in reality two groups of matches, each lasting a week—first the matches of the National Rifle Association, and then the second, which were "national matches" conducted by the War Department for the National Board for the Promotion of Rifle Practice. The important matches of the first group were all individual matches, and while each one of them was important, the National Rifle Association Match was the "President's Match" to

Another Season with Small Arms

determine the best military marksman of the country, who would then be proclaimed as such by a letter from the President of the United States.

The real national matches were in the second group and consisted of the National Pistol Match, the National Individual Match, and the National Team Match. Of these, the last match was the one for which the navy teams and Naval Academy teams had been training.

Both navy teams entered all of the rifle matches, mostly for the practice to be obtained, and a few of the cadets entered the National Pistol Match. Under such circumstances there was utter amazement when the cadets won the President's Match, the National Pistol Match, and the National Individual Match. Then, all eyes turned to the National Team Match to see what the navy shooters would do in that.

The match was a hot one, the navy team standing at the top. In the skirmish run they made their usual excellent score, larger than ever before scored in the national match. However, our closest rival, the team from Massachusetts, made a phenomenal score on its run. As the match entered its final stage at the one-thousand-yard range, that team, famous for its long-range shooting, led us by twelve points.

At that time almost everyone at Camp Perry, except the navy, was conceding the match to Massachusetts. But the navy team, with true John Paul Jones spirit, was just beginning to fight, using its teamwork to the utmost, fighting for every possible point. Our first pair centered their first shots in the bull's-eye, making a splendid score and receiving perfect shooting data; the second and third pairs did equally well.

I could only believe that, with the scores made by our first three pairs, we were gaining on the Massachusetts team. But I was disappointed to learn that they had scored exactly the same as we had, and with the final stage half over, they still led by twelve points.

When our fourth team came to shoot, I said to them, "Our situation is desperate. I can put you two in the bull's-eye, but you will have to shoot better than you ever have before if you are going to win this match." "The pair" were "Captain Jack" Williams, a lieutenant, and Steve Doherty, an ensign, and almost together they said, "By God! We'll do it." They did, and by as fine a one-thousand-yard shooting as I have ever seen. Those two alone gained nine points on the Massachusetts' pair.

In the firing of the final pairs from each team, the match became the most hotly contested national match ever, and a tremendous gallery of spectators gathered behind the teams, who were shooting on nearly adjacent targets. When our fifth pair started to shoot, old Peggy, whose team was then out of the

An Admiral's Yarn

running, stood not far behind me. As I sat at my telescope, keeping close touch on the data for the team, the captain of the Massachusetts team joined Peggy, and I heard him say, "That navy team is shooting a lot better than it knows how! It is due for a blowup and my team will win." Then I heard Peggy say, "No, your team will not win but the navy's will." He then added, "I have been watching that bunch all summer, and once they are in the center of the bulls, as they are now, they will stay there. Your team may blow up, but the navy team won't." Dear old Peggy! The navy team did not blow up and the strength of team shooting was not to be denied. Our fifth pair gained three more points on the other team's pair, and as the sixth pairs started firing, the scores were a tie. Then teamwork again took its toll, this time against the best shots of Massachusetts, for our sixth pair gained three points and we won the match by that amount, to the great delight of the spectators. We had beaten the best previous team record by a large margin.

The navy shooters had come into their own. In one season we had accomplished what was theretofore unheard of—winning all four of the country's most important military matches: the President's Match, the National Pistol Match, the National Individual Match, and the National Team Match. In addition, the Naval Academy took sixth place in the Team Match, even beating the Marines and the U.S. Infantry Team that would not "take them seriously." Navy shooting and team shooting stood proved to the world. It was a fine time for me to give up the shooting game. I had received orders to sea, and I left to join my ship, leaving it to someone else to outdo our record.

XXIV

In a Battleship Once More

ABOUT A MONTH BEFORE the navy team left Creedmoor, I received a letter from Captain R.F. Nicholson,[136] then in charge of officer assignments in the Navy Department. He informed me that he had been selected to command the battleship *Nebraska,* about to be commissioned, and wished me to join the ship as navigating officer.[137] I was greatly surprised when I read that letter, because my acquaintance with Captain Nicholson was only a casual one, and I was much younger, less experienced, and far junior in rank to the officers usually assigned to navigating battleships. I lost no time in telling Captain Nicholson how honored and delighted I would be to serve under him in such a capacity and on so fine a ship. A week or two before the team left for Camp Perry, my orders came, effective after the national match.

The *Nebraska* was then at the Puget Sound Navy Yard, receiving its finishing touches, and as soon as I could close the affairs of the rifle team, I hurried there with my family—still hesitant to believe the honor and responsibility that I had been assigned. When I saw the ship I was even more impressed, for not only was it one of our newest and finest battleships, but also it was the largest naval ship I had ever seen or served on. Being only a lieutenant, thirty-four years old, and a commissioned officer for only ten years, I had my doubts, for not only was I to be responsible for the safe navigation of the ship, but also I was to be third in command under the captain. I would be responsible for the ship in such battle and war maneuvers that might be our lot, and it was up to me to prove myself equal to it.

Ten years had passed since my time in the USS *Oregon* at the Puget Sound Yard, and I was unprepared for the great changes there. The little gash in the

An Admiral's Yarn

woods for the first dry dock had become a huge, cleared space that boasted of a navy yard with many acres of improved land around it. Hills had been cut away and the ground leveled for another dry dock, and many shops for heavy equipment and buildings of all sorts had been added. The northern end of the yard was called Bremerton, a good-sized town, and at its southern end stood the village of Charleston. Everywhere there was great activity and bustle.

However, in spite of the almost unbelievable development, finding a place for my family to live was difficult. The building of residences could not keep pace with the rapid growth in population, and about the only shelter for newly arrived families was in the temporary houses and shacks left vacant by the workmen who had cleared off the area. Even most of those were occupied when the *Nebraska's* families reached there. The only empty building available was a dilapidated one, formerly a boarding house for about twenty lumberjacks, which had been abandoned as too crude and shaky for further use. Nevertheless, the higher officers of the *Nebraska*, having persuaded a woman to take charge and open the place, moved their families into it.

I will not attempt to describe the way we lived the next five or six months while the *Nebraska* was being completed, for no one would believe what we endured. The incessant chilly rains of a Puget Sound winter made it difficult for everyone aboard ship and ashore.

We officers were much better off than our families, for we lived aboard the ship during numerous "try-out" runs. Also, our days were full of work and our time aboard was considerably more than our time at home. I found myself particularly busy, not only brushing up on navigation but also supervising the electrical department of the ship, then a responsibility of the navigator.

That electrical department was not much like the old *Oregon's*, for in the years since she was built, electricity had advanced by such leaps and bounds that in the *Nebraska* it was used not only for light but for nearly all power except that of the main engines.

The *Nebraska's* electric plant was nearly equivalent to the light and power plant of a fair-sized city, and supervising it was no small task. Navigation was my primary duty, and the combination of duties kept me always busy, both in port and at sea.

My first and one of my most difficult problems had to do with the compasses of the ship. The magnetism in the tremendous mass of the steel hull, and particularly in the great superimposed turrets (one turret on top of another) close to the bridge, so affected the compasses that they pointed anywhere but to the north pole. In fact, the south pole of the compass used in steering was so attracted by the forward turret that no matter where the ship was heading, the

In a Battleship Once More

course shown by that compass was always south or only a very few degrees from it.

It took much time, ingenuity, and several trips to sea to correct the compasses to show true magnetic headings, and I spent many anxious hours until it was accomplished. Navigators should never cease to give thanks that gyroscopes, rather than magnetism, control compass directions today.

At last our compasses were right, our ship was completed, and we could start our "shakedown" cruise. The cruise was to Magdalena Bay in lower California where the weather always seemed perfect, and rain was almost unknown. We were delighted with the prospect. The executive officer and I, the only officers in our mess who had ever been there, were considered authorities on it, and we rhapsodized considerably over its suitability for training work, its perfect winter climate, its utter freedom from rain, and the wonderful hunting and fishing to be had there.

So much did we talk that the hunters amongst us outfitted themselves with shotguns and sporting rifles; all fishermen replenished their supplies and tackle; and the large seine [net] that was issued to the ship was gone over carefully and made flawless.

The usual winter rain of Puget Sound was falling when we started, and it followed us nearly all the way down the coast. The run to Magdalena seemed far from propitious to our rain-soaked crew, hence, as weather prognosticators for southern and lower California, the executive and I lost considerable prestige. We lost much more when almost as soon as the ship anchored in the bay the skies clouded over and rain came down in torrents. Worse still, the downpour continued for three days and prevented any training work. So much rain fell that the brown hills and desert land around the bay actually became quite green with verdure. Except that we were not quite as cold, we might as well have been in Puget Sound.

It was nearly a week before we could start our training work, and by the time the weather returned to normal for Magdalena Bay, anything the executive and I said about it was taken with a grain of salt, especially when all the carefully arranged hunting parties returned to the ship empty-handed. But in spite of that we continued with our fish stories, since the fishing parties always caught enough to supply the officer messes, though of course far from enough to provide a mess for the eight or nine hundred men of the crew.

As the executive and I continued our talk about fish and strongly urged using the seine to catch enough for the crew, many officers volunteered to take out seining parties and asked us where to go. We pored over the charts for likely places, and although the volunteer seiners tried all of them, not a fish did they

An Admiral's Yarn

catch. Before long, no one would volunteer for a seining party, but being sure there were plenty of fish to be had somewhere, the executive ordered officers, one-by-one, to organize and take out seining parties; although they seined everywhere, the fish evaded them. However, I continued talking about fish and suggesting this or that spot until there were no more spots to suggest. Then one day when the mess was at lunch, the executive loudly announced, "Laning, having talked more about fishing than anyone else, will take out a seining party today." Then turning to me, he said, "I expect you to bring back a boatload of fish for the crew."

Taken aback that the third ranking officer of the ship should be ordered to take out a seining party, and believing I was about to be shown up as a mere talky-talk fisherman, I shoved off with the party immediately after luncheon. Thinking that we could not be successful, no matter where we seined, we went to a place not far from the ship to make our try.

As it had proved the best place for fishing with lines, many seining parties had previously tried there without success. But it was easy to reach and to seine, so I decided I might as well be "shown up" there as anywhere else.

We made three hauls with the seine without getting a fish, then, being rather tired, we all went swimming. After enough time had elapsed for what would have been a day's work of seining, and I had recalled the party to the ship, someone suggested making "just one more haul." Having plenty of time, I told him to "go ahead." Everything was done as before, but when the party tried to haul the seine in, they could hardly pull the weight, it was so full of fish, hundreds and hundreds of pompano, therefore unknown to us in that locality. We had more than enough for the entire ship's company, but since we had not quite filled our boat, we decided to cast our seine again. While the next haul caught as many or even more fish than the preceding one, there was not a single pompano in it—every fish was Spanish mackerel, each weighing about three or four pounds. Amazed, we made another haul, but instead of pompano or mackerel, we caught a dozen or more huge sea bass and a five-foot tiger shark. Excited by then and wondering what would happen next, we made another try, which was the last for our seine; as we hauled, we watched a big sea lion tear its way out, ruining the net.

With our big boat full of fish and our seine ruined, we returned to the ship. I think all hands were on the rail to give us a big laugh at the expected empty boat. When we came alongside and pulled back the tarpaulin displaying our enormous catch, the laughs turned to wonder. Of course we had a great bit of "fisherman's luck," but just the same, I regained my prestige for fish stories and once more could "ad lib" to my heart's content on Magdalena fishing.

In a Battleship Once More

The remainder of our stay in the bay was more or less routine and unexciting, though we made great progress in our work, and by the time we started north, the *Nebraska* was in fine shape except for a few final adjustments for which we returned to the Puget Sound Yard. With these completed, we left to join the battleship fleet as it entered San Francisco Bay before its cruise around the world.[138]

"Cruising in formation" with battleships was then rather new to our navy, and no one in the *Nebraska* was experienced in doing it. Therefore, joining an experienced well-drilled fleet and standing into San Francisco Bay with it, while over a hundred thousand people watched, was a considerable strain on the navigator. However, we were not recognized as a "rookie" ship and from then on were accepted as a member of the fleet, enjoying the overwhelming hospitality of San Francisco for a week, then proceeding on to Seattle for a brief stay.

While the passage to Seattle was uneventful, it proved that the navy was advancing its preparations for the possibility of war. Up to that time, most of us had thought only in terms of the "Old Navy," wherein ships were expected to fight singly. But the commissioning of many ships that were to fight together in battle began a new era for the Navy, an era no longer of only individual ship skill in fighting but rather an era of "group skill." Our first step was to prepare our battleship group to function as a team in battle.

Although the "round the world" cruise of the battleships in 1908 was primarily to impress upon the world the tremendous sea power of the United States, the runs between ports provided a rare opportunity to prepare us to fight as a group in war, and doing that was the fleet's everyday job at sea. We drilled day and night, devoting each morning to battle drill and each afternoon to fleet maneuvers. It was the very beginning of the navy's teamwork, which has since progressed from teamwork in groups of battleships to teamwork in groups of different types of ships, to teamwork in all aspects of the entire United States Navy. Thus, this important world cruise shaped the navy's efficiency of today.

Having been introduced to an entirely new type of navy, we continued on to Seattle, where we received the usual great welcome and the overwhelming hospitality that we received in every port we visited. Then, leaving Seattle, we returned to San Francisco for the duration of the long cruise that would end at Hampton Roads, Virginia.

No sooner had we anchored off San Francisco than a signal came for me to report to the commander in chief [Robley D. Evans]. I did so at once, was handed a letter from the Melbourne Rifle Team challenging the fleet to a team rifle match in Melbourne and directing me to organize and captain a fleet team for that purpose. As navigator of the *Nebraska*, every day was a full day's work,

An Admiral's Yarn

and I thought I was finished with rifle shooting for all time. I was not greatly pleased with the order; nevertheless, I was obliged to organize a team. First I would have to comb sixteen battleships for riflemen and then train them into a team in the few days we would spend in port before reaching Melbourne. All in all, it was rather a large order, but difficult though it might be to carry out successfully, I was expected to do exactly that.

One might have thought I had trouble enough to last until the visit to Melbourne was over, but more problems arose almost immediately. When I started to assemble candidates for the team, several cases of scarlet fever developed in the *Nebraska*, and the ship was sent to Angel Island. It was placed in such strict quarantine that all rifle team matters had to be abandoned until we reached Honolulu. Even then I could not be certain of an opportunity to train my team, because the epidemic was so serious that the rest of the fleet departed before the fumigation of the *Nebraska* was completed. However, as soon as that was over, we managed to catch up with the fleet before it reached Honolulu.

XXV

A Trip Around the World

It was good to join up with the fleet and settle down once more to real naval work at sea. When people tour the world, they usually think more of the points to be visited then of the sea voyages between those destinations, but not so in the navy. While we enjoy the ports and especially the opportunities to represent the United States, the most important thing to the fleet in a world cruise is the training that is made possible. Our training goes on day and night.

Although every officer and man did a full day's work everyday, while the battleship fleet was at sea, I somehow felt that we navigators had rather more than our share. In addition to supervising the electrical department, we did all the navigation work and handled the ship in daily battle maneuvers.

Navigation work is about the same for a ship on its own as it is for one in a fleet. With the latter, however, there are added complications, due partly to continual maneuvering and the requirement that each ship indicate by signal its exact latitude and longitude three times every day, at 8 a.m., noon, and 8 p.m. Since every signaled position is noted and compared by each ship, the competition for accuracy is keen. Merely good navigation was not sufficient; ours had to be perfect—every instant.

Usually a navigator begins taking sights before dawn in order to insure a perfect "fix" prior to the 8 a.m. report. At nine o'clock he becomes officer of the deck for a two-hour drill in battle tactics, after which, at twelve by the clock (whether noon or not) he must again signal his position. While he has no direct responsibility from then until about four o'clock, the fleet generally maneuvers for two hours or more under the officer of the deck, and during that time the

An Admiral's Yarn

navigator keeps close watch on the ship and its course. Then, as the sun sets and the stars appear, the navigator tries to obtain new astronomical fixes for his 8 p.m. report. We thus became rather expert, both in navigation and in battleship tactics.

Although we were accorded the usual great welcome and hospitality at Honolulu, I could enjoy it but briefly, because I was obliged to assemble the rifle team candidates and test them on the rifle range.

Consequently, we started for the range as soon as the anchor went down. If we had not done so, we would not have reached there, because another case of scarlet fever was discovered and the ship was once more placed in quarantine and fumigated. As it turned out, the candidates did enough demonstration shooting for all but twenty-three to eliminate themselves before our start for Auckland. Among those retained were twelve members of my old navy and Naval Academy teams, out of whom a good ten-man team could be developed for the Melbourne match, even in the few days of practice. The eleven "green" riflemen were retained for emergencies, although it seemed improbable that I would use them.

We arrived in Auckland on a Sunday morning and were scarcely anchored when I was once more ordered, by signal, to report to the commander in chief immediately. When I did so, I found the aide de camp of the governor of New Zealand with him and was informed he would arrange for a rifle match between fifty men from the fleet and a like number from New Zealand.

As the proposal was utterly unexpected and involved a far larger number of good rifle shots than we had, even including the eleven "green" men, I had to confess that I did not know where to find fifty men who could shoot at all, much less be capable of representing the fleet in a match against fifty of New Zealand's best shots. Thereupon we compromised on twenty-five-man teams, ours composed of the twenty-three men on our squad plus two of the men whose shooting had not been satisfactory enough to warrant training. Then, with almost no training or practice for our team, we fired the match. Although our fifteen good shots did better shooting than the best fifteen on the New Zealand team, they could not make up for the poor shooting of our ten inexperienced men, so we lost the match. However, we had made a better showing than seemed possible with such a team, and I was not discouraged, knowing that among our fifteen good shots, I would have a strong ten-man team for Melbourne—our really important match.

After remaining in Auckland a week, the fleet proceeded to Sydney where we entered one of the world's most spectacularly beautiful harbors. We were given a tremendous ovation by the nearly one million Australians assembled to watch

A Trip Around the World

our entrance. Knowing that Sydney would be one of the highlights of the cruise, I wanted to enjoy it, but instead I had to rush to the rifle range to prepare the team for the match in Melbourne. We were then shocked by a challenge to a fifteen-man match by the Sydney rifle team—a challenge we felt forced to accept. Not having had an opportunity to train, I was somewhat skeptical of our ability, but we at once set to work to create a team. I had trained some of the men a year or two before, and with only three days practice, I was able to get such quick results that we won the match easily.

The extent of the Sydney team's surprise became apparent at a banquet hosted by the Minister of Defense for Australia the night after the match. Since I had never before been received as a guest of honor by a cabinet minister nor replied to one in a speech, much of that banquet was trying for me. But it had its compensation—the minister spoke of the unanticipated defeat of Australia's soldier marksmen by a group of American sailors. He said that knowing we had been beaten by New Zealanders, who were always beaten by Australians, they had not taken the U.S. Navy shooting seriously enough. Then he added, "But we will take you seriously in Melbourne, for in that match you will meet Australia's finest marksmen. We expect a very different outcome there."

By the time we left Sydney, I had determined the makeup of our ten-man team to fire against Australia's "best shots." Although these men had never fired together as a team, I felt certain they would uphold our navy's prestige in shooting. Immediately upon reaching Melbourne, we rushed to the range where we had four days of practice team shooting. It was fortunate that we had even that time, because the range at Melbourne is a difficult one and full of tricky conditions to be solved. Our knowledge of shooting proved sufficient to overcome them, and when the match started, we were not only ready to meet the problems of the range but also ready for real team shooting.

The match turned out to be a walkover for us, and we outshot the Australians from start to finish. Not only had we mastered the vagaries of their range, but we took only about half as much time to finish as they (who were so accustomed to shooting there) did, and our scores were invariably better at each distance. Perhaps the comment that pleased me most was made at a banquet that night by the Australian team captain who said, "We Australians little thought we could be taught anything about rifle shooting from sailors, but we learned differently today. Of course we hated to lose the match and be beaten so badly, but what we learned is worth it. Never before have we seen or heard of team rifle shooting such as we did today."

That match marked the end of our shooting season and, having foregone all the pleasures of ports ever since leaving San Francisco, the team held a big

An Admiral's Yarn

theater party that night to celebrate—and apparently did a thorough job! For that reason they were a seedy looking bunch the next morning when they "came to" sufficiently to start for the range of the Women's Rifle Club, where they were to fire a match with Australian ladies.

That match was in no sense a fleet team match but just a friendly little shoot between ladies and gentlemen, in which I did not participate. Our team was composed of just young officers of the fleet team who wanted the diversion of the first rifle match (that they had ever heard of) with women.

That match was utterly unlike any the officers had ever seen. It was fired at short range with special miniature rifles and other equipment provided by the ladies. It was an entirely new type of shooting. Instead of teammates firing together in their matches, each member of the "lady team" paired off with one of the opponents for shooting. That, of course, made the match rather a sociable affair and handicapped our young officers, since the members of the ladies team were young, good-looking girls with true Australian charm. Whether it was the manner of firing, the altogether different kind of shooting, the result of the night before, or all three, we never knew, but those Australian ladies so completely swamped the fleet's crack-shooting officers that the Australian papers could not help but comment on the gallantry of the Americans who one day outshot the best riflemen, only to allow the Australian ladies to outshoot them the next. Perhaps it was gallantry after all. I never knew!

The rifle team job ended, and I was at last able to enjoy the ports we visited. Our first, after Melbourne, was Albany in the southwest of Australia. From there we went to Manila, then to Yokohama before returning to Manila. The receptions at each place were wonderful, and we were shown many of the most interesting sights. That given at Yokohama was a stupendous affair. The Emperor and the Japanese people joined together, not only in hospitality but in showing us the attractions of their famous city. Few visitors see as much in a ten-day visit as we did. By Imperial command, the very best features of Japanese life were displayed in the palace grounds at the Emperor's garden party. Assembled from far and near, they were shown only by royal command, and thus we saw not only Yokohama and Tokyo at their best, but the finest in all of Japan.

After our visit to Japan, the fleet returned to Manila Bay for a month of target practice and similar training. I found Manila greatly changed from the days of the Empire, as the first few years of our occupation in the Philippines was called. The old Spanish buildings and walls were, of course, quite as they had been, but American-type buildings were everywhere now. An outer harbor had been constructed, the old Pasig River had been made usable for vastly increased shipping, and the Army and Navy Club, which I had helped to organize, had

A Trip Around the World

become the great service center of the islands. The changes were marked, and they greatly improved Manila as a city. Nevertheless, we were glad when our month's stay was over and we could proceed on our way.

The next run took us through the Strait of Malacca, past Singapore, to Colombo on the island of Ceylon. We were taken on trips to Kandy and other interesting parts of the island, but there was not as much official entertaining as in other ports, and we were glad to roam around and see something of Hindu life and activities.

Naturally, being near the equator, Colombo was too hot for comfort—so much so that we had not given a thought to Christmas, which was due in a few days. But once more, as sailors at sea always do at Christmas time, a proper celebration was arranged. Christmas parties are not especially difficult to prepare when trees, decorations, and presents are plentiful, but to plan one on the spur of the moment in the middle of the Indian Ocean is quite another matter. Of the essentials, the only one actually available to us was food for the dinner. A tree, Santa Claus' clothes, decorations, and presents had to be created from such material as we had on board, and a committee was appointed to provide them. Out of our lumber they made a tree trunk, limbs, branches, and twigs. And for the pine needles or leaves, they used straws and strips of paper dipped in green paint. Tree decorations were the brass rings and balls removed from all curtain rods, and for Santa Claus, they made whiskers out of rope fibre, a suit and cap out of red signal flag muslin trimmed with bands of absorbent cotton, and boots from black oilcloth wrappings. An empty coffee sack found in the galley served as his pack, and for presents, each officer ransacked his belongings for small mementos he had accumulated here and there.

The party was a huge success, and when the "beautiful tree" that was hidden behind curtains was revealed after dinner, a Santa Claus stood beside it with "snow" from a hatch above falling about him. There was great applause, and even in the Indian Ocean, close to the equator, we had a white Christmas never to be forgotten.

Our next stop was Suez, and while waiting to transit the Canal, we had time for a three-day visit to Cairo. As often attested to by others, Cairo was the most unusual and interesting of all the places we visited. Its centuries of history were recorded in the Pyramids of Giza, the Sphinx, the Roman Aqueduct, the old temples, and museums. Having visited each one singly, I spent my last few hours in Cairo on the hill of the Temple of Mohammed Ali from where I could see them all with the great Nile River and the desert beyond. It was indeed difficult to leave that fascinating spot and return to the ship.

An Admiral's Yarn

After transiting the canal, the fleet stopped at Port Said for a few days. The expectation was that the fleet would leave and then separate for visits to several Mediterranean ports, the *Nebraska* being assigned to Genoa. However, that order never did materialize because the great earthquake that destroyed Messina occurred[139] while we were in the Suez Canal. The only ships allowed to go to Italy were the relief ships sent to Messina. The *Nebraska* was diverted to Marseilles.

We enjoyed the opportunity to roam about and visit places of interest—although this freedom generated a temporary upset in our mess. No sooner did our negro mess attendants go on liberty than they were seized upon by French girls who held them captive until just before the ship sailed.

Leaving Marseilles, we went to Tangier for two days before crossing to Gibraltar where the fleet reassembled. Both places proved interesting, but by that time we were fed up with port visiting and talked only of the homeward trip to join our families waiting for us at Hampton Roads. We were a happy lot when the Rock of Gibraltar disappeared over the horizon, and happier still when we passed in review before President Theodore Roosevelt at the entrance to Chesapeake Bay at 10 a.m. on February 22nd, 1909, the exact instant set for our doing so in a schedule that had been made out for us more than a year before.

That review marked the end of the battleship cruise around the world, and we did not regret the fact. We had enjoyed a delightful experience and developed a wonderful battle team for the United States, but to us, the crowning event of the cruise was being with our families again. They filled every available space around Hampton Roads, Old Point Comfort, Newport News, Hampton, and even Norfolk, so our homecoming was a great event, and we made the most of it during the next week.

Although the family reunions culminated the cruise for officers and men, we were scheduled to attend a great celebration planned for the fleet by the officials of New York City. There can be no greater thrill for an American, who has been representing our country in foreign ports, than to witness the magnificent Statue of Liberty upon entering the greatest harbor of all at New York City. There were tears in my eyes and in my voice when I whispered to myself, "This is my own, my native land."

New York's celebration was rather different from the receptions given us elsewhere, inasmuch as it entailed none of the official stiffness of international courtesy. On the contrary, it was an outburst of cordiality and appreciation extended by a city of people to those who had served them in distant lands. These people, who spoke our language and whose every act and action we understood, reassured us, as nothing else could, that we were really home again.

A Trip Around the World

When New York's great welcome was over, the fleet disbanded and its ships were sent to navy yards for repair work and docking, etc., things that could not be accomplished at sea. It took several months for the work and many major improvements to be added before the ships were ready to continue routine cruises.

That next year was an important one to our ever-growing fleet—it was marked by many changes as the competitions in gunnery and engineering continued to bear fruit, causing armaments and engines to be improved. Battleships of the type used on the cruise around the world were fast becoming obsolete, for the super-imposed turret had long since been discredited as had the eight-inch guns, which were part of a ship's main battery. The day of "all big gun" battleships, often spoken of as "dreadnoughts," had arrived. The new ones were joining the fleet as were torpedo-boat destroyers, replacing the former torpedo boat, and even submarines were now being built. For the next year the fleet trained for battle.

We were a month in Cape Cod Bay for battleship torpedo practice before sailing for the southern drill grounds off the Virginia coast between Capes Henry and Hatteras. We did take time off, however, to attend the Hudson-Fulton celebration in New York on the 300th anniversary of Henry Hudson's discovery of the port. In the fall, we went to Cuba for several months training while based on Guantánamo Bay and the Gulf of Guacanayabo (this latter always spoken of in the fleet as "Hungry Gulf").

Guantánamo Bay, the site of our naval station in Cuba, was leased to the United States by the Republic of Cuba after the war with Spain and was developed into a splendid base for fleet training. Although there are no shops or storehouses, a great coaling plant was erected and athletic fields, tennis courts, baseball diamonds, and beaches made suitable for swimming were developed, making it almost ideal for the fleet's winter work.

The training took many forms; maneuvers at sea, gun and torpedo practice in Hungry Gulf, landing parties, regimental drills and encampments on the station's grounds, and continuous artillery, rifle, and pistol practice on the rifle range. These last were a most important part of our training, for although we had outgrown the idea of using battleships to protect American interests in foreign ports, we still devoted much time to training crews for that duty. Teaching accuracy with artillery, boat guns, rifles, and pistols was necessary, but there was a more important factor for developing riflemen—we had learned that the best shots were also the best pointers for a ship's big guns.

Although navigators are not supposed to be responsible for gunnery training, no sooner had we reached Guantánamo than I was put in charge of all range

An Admiral's Yarn

target practice and directed to supervise the shooting of the several thousand men sent each day to the range.

Though that was quite a task, I rather enjoyed it. Nevertheless, I was glad when after three months I resumed my regular duty of navigating the *Nebraska* during the Hungry Gulf and sea training that lasted until early spring. Having run what I thought was the full gamut of rifle shooting, I felt that I was finished with rifle ranges forever when the fleet started its northward trip.

Spring found the fleet once more on the southern drill grounds, firing its record target practices. About the time it was finished, I had been nearly three years in the *Nebraska*, and my cruise as navigating officer was nearing its finish.

As a young lieutenant commander, I had given little thought to my next assignment. Soon, however, orders arrived that directed me to take charge of Physical Training and Athletics at the Naval Academy, at the request of the commandant of midshipmen, Captain Charles A. Gove.

XXVI

A New Type of Work

RETURNING TO ANNAPOLIS THAT SUMMER, I found the Academy that I had known and loved almost entirely replaced by a new one. The only buildings left from my cadet days were the little watchman houses at the main gate, the "corrals" where my family had lived for two tours of duty and where my daughter was born, and several houses for officers in "Oklahoma," a newer area added to the Academy when I was a cadet. The name "naval cadet" had been officially changed to "midshipman," the two-year middy cruise had been abolished, and instead of having less than two hundred and fifty students as in my day, there were from twelve to fifteen hundred. Nor were we assigned to live in the "corrals," as before. Because of my new rank, we were given a fairly good-sized house, quite recently built.

Almost everything about the Academy was as new and strange to me as my new duty, which, as its name implied, did not require books, studies, or recitations. My primary task was to perfect the physique of the midshipmen and to supervise all of their athletic activities. I was also to run the Army-Navy football game, which had by then become one of the outstanding annual sports events of the United States. Never having given much thought to physical training—nor even having been athletically inclined--I found the work a complete change, but it was up to me to "make good."

Although by far the most important to the navy, physical training was one of my simpler tasks, because there were many assistants in the department, and each was an expert in his particular line, such as gymnastics, wrestling, boxing, swimming, etc. Also there were medical officers whose specialization in

An Admiral's Yarn

physique development insured that it was not overdone. All midshipmen were carefully instructed in each form of the prescribed course in physical training, one of which was the Swedish system, which measured their physical development. The system did not attempt to develop certain muscles but rather to increase the body's strength and agility sufficiently to meet any physical demand a naval officer might encounter. Anyone found under par was placed in the "weak squad" and required to carry out the system until results were satisfactory. Midshipmen were also obliged to be proficient with small arms and deft in boating of every kind as well as in swimming, boxing, wrestling, fencing, and dancing. All were encouraged to become adept in some form of athletic sport.

Although not as important to the navy as the physical development of its future officers, athletics attract great attention in the naval service, and every effort is made to perfect the midshipmen in the various sports. There were football and baseball teams when I entered the Academy, and later collegiate crew racing; but when I took charge of athletics there were many other teams too, such as basketball, swimming, gymnasium, boxing, wrestling, fencing, rifle, lacrosse, and tennis. Although I did not participate in the training, I had to provide coaches and equipment, arrange time for training, conduct all competitions, provide athletic fields, and so forth.

There were many "Academy teams," and a considerable number of midshipmen received athletic training through them, though of course the majority did not. We wanted every midshipman to participate in some form of sport, so I arranged for class teams in every sport, provided complete equipment, created and assigned playing fields, and laid out a full schedule of interclass events. Tennis courts were built to accommodate fifty or a hundred players. To encourage the midshipmen to enter some form of sport, one drill period each week was devoted to athletics.

Under the system we established, the Academy had two fine athletic years and won almost every competition, even including the Army-Navy football games, so I was well pleased, especially with the splendid physique of the men of our teams. However, during the second year I was in charge, a rather discouraging rule was established. Midshipmen with unsatisfactory marks in one or more studies for the month were prohibited from representing the Academy on an athletic team.

Although I was thoroughly in accord with the plan that every man in a "varsity team" should have a satisfactory scholastic standing, the rules established for the Naval Academy did not allow a midshipman the opportunity to redeem himself once his grades had slipped. Not only were unsatisfactory midshipmen

A New Type of Work

"bilged" from the Academy twice each year, but if a student's scholastic standing was considered below par for one month, he would lose his eligibility for varsity team participation.

Our troubles in athletics appeared at the end of October in my second year, when the marks for the month were posted, listing an unusual number of unsatisfactory grades. In particular, over one half of the first class was "unsat" in navigation because of the unusual and unexpected type of examination given. Since most of the football team came from that class and would be barred from playing, our team would be utterly ruined for the Army-Navy football game in November. Believing the rule, as applied to the Naval Academy, was wrong, and having experience in navigation, I decided to look over the examinations given the first class. I found that the questions were not at all on practical navigation but dealt almost entirely with the mathematical deductions of the abstruse formulae used in it. In other words, the so-called navigation examination was actually one in higher mathematics for which the midshipmen were not prepared.

Shocked by what I had learned, I hurried to the commandant, not only to protest the rule but more to right the wrong that had been made in trying to make our midshipmen highbrow mathematicians in nautical astronomy rather than teaching them the practical navigation so essential to every naval officer. Being a practical navigator, and knowing that the commandant was also, I suggested teaching practical navigation along the lines prescribed in Bowditch's book, a treatise prepared by the U.S. Navy Department and accepted the world over as the standard work on practical navigation.[140] Concerning the rules as applied to athletics, they were partially rescinded, giving the Naval Academy that year not only one of the best football teams it ever had but also unusual success in all its sports.

As can be surmised, it was a busy time for me, especially since I also had the rather extraneous task of building the first half of what continues to be the Academy's athletic stadium, now known as Thompson Field. Shortly after I was put in charge of athletics, I received a letter from Colonel Robert M. Thompson, a wealthy civilian alumnus of the Academy who for many years had been its athletic "angel."[141] In the letter he informed me that if I could raise a similar amount by subscription, he would donate ten thousand dollars toward a stand for spectators on our athletic field. His offer was accepted and I spent much of my first year in athletics raising our part of the money through the small subscriptions our graduates could afford to make. By the end of the year this was accomplished, and Colonel Thompson promptly sent his check. The work on a

An Admiral's Yarn

huge stand was started and then completed during my second year at the Academy, in time for the Army-Navy baseball game in May.

With the decision to organize and send a great United States team to Stockholm, Sweden, to compete in the Olympic Games to be held there that summer [1912], that spring became an exceptionally active period in American athletics.

Since we did not have midshipmen of outstanding ability in any of the many games that were scheduled, we gave little thought to any of them making the American team—although athletics had taken on greater importance for us, just as it had for everyone else.

One of the events scheduled was a match with military rifles between teams from the several more important countries, and I was interested, since the United States was entering a team in this competition. My interest was purely one of curiosity, and I was taken completely unawares one day when I received a letter from the president of the National Rifle Association, which sponsored the U.S. Rifle Team, urging me to take full charge of our team and be its captain. It was, of course, a great tribute to the navy's shooting and to me personally, and I at once placed the matter before the Navy Department. Orders were immediately issued that enabled me to prepare the team and take it to Stockholm.

While I was thinking over the problems confronting me with the Olympic Games, I was called to the commandant's [Commander George W. Logan] office and told to report to the superintendent of the Academy [Captain John H. Gibbons]. When I said to the commandant, "I wonder what I have been up to now," he laughed and replied, "I think he is going to ask you to become Head of the Department of Navigation when you return from the Olympic Games." Sure enough, he did. I warned him of some drastic changes I would want to make in teaching practical navigation to the midshipmen. The superintendent said, "That is exactly what I want and the department is yours when you return from Stockholm." I was most gratified and pleased.

Nevertheless, I was rather awed by the thought of becoming a member of the "Academic Board" of our great naval school, particularly because I was a grade lower than any other member and by far its youngest and least experienced.

XXVII

The Olympic Games

THAT THE UNITED STATES OLYMPIC TEAM might present the best it could offer in the many competitive games, great attention was given to selecting the team members. To this end, a long series of competitive "tryouts" was conducted in an effort that not only assured us of having the best team possible but also thoroughly fulfilled our country's democratic ideals.

The members of the rifle team that I was to captain were chosen by this method, hence, I was not responsible for the selection. That I might know their qualifications and lose no time in training the team, I attended the national "tryout" held on the U.S. Marine Corps range at Quantico, Virginia. When the team composition was determined, it was immediately turned over to me, and thereafter all responsibility for it was mine.

The men who made the team were the pick of the military marksmen of the Army, Navy, Marine Corps, and National Guards of the various states as well as civilian organizations. Although only eight men were scheduled to fire rifles, several extras were prepared to fill any vacancies that might occur before the team left the United States, and two alternates were also allowed for emergencies. Our squad of sixteen men was accompanied by Colonel William Libby of Princeton University (our adjutant) and Commander Neill McDonnell, Medical Corps, U.S. Navy (our doctor). The team had more riflemen than needed for the final tryout at Stockholm where the men who did not qualify would be let go. I now devoted all my energy to developing team shooting in the three weeks remaining before leaving for Stockholm.

An Admiral's Yarn

I knew that for the United States Rifle Team to win the greatest international match ever fired, not only should its individual members be the best shooters we could produce, but they must also be able to gain every point they could while shooting as a team. Except for three navy men who had been on my previous teams, not a man on the Olympic squad knew about, or believed in, team rifle shooting required for the match; so to win their hearty support, it was up to me to show them the value of it. Fortunately, one of the navy riflemen, Ensign C. [Carl] T. Osborne, had been "master gun" of the Navy Rifle Team when it won the national match. Because he had topped the field as an individual shot in the tryouts, there was no question that he would fill that role on the Olympic team; immediately the squad was assembled on the Naval Academy's range, I gathered our data for the Olympic shooting.

Although the targets for that shooting looked like our own from a distance, they actually were very different. They had a double bull's-eye about the size of ours, to provide a point of aim, but within it was a much smaller "invisible bull" into which shots had to hit to count as 5's. Also, distances for the match were in meters instead of in yards, and this made the shooting much more difficult than at the range we were accustomed to. For instance, when firing at six hundred yards in the United States, we had a bull's-eye twenty inches in diameter; but for the Olympic Games, the corresponding distance was six hundred meters (about 639 yards) and the "invisible bull" was only sixteen inches in diameter. It took real shooting skill to make the shots fired from a point 639 yards away strike within that circle, especially with the rifles, sights, and ammunition of that time.

For training the team, I had prepared an "Olympic range" at the Academy with targets and distances (in meters) just as they would be at Stockholm, and as soon as the team had assembled, we started work. With such splendid shots, getting the accurate data for the team shooting was rather easy, but I knew I would have some difficulty in convincing the country's best individual rifle shots that using it would greatly improve both individual and team scores. It was the old antagonisms of individual effort vs. team effort, and I had to win complete support for the team shooting idea at once if we were to perfect ourselves in it in the short time available to us.

Accordingly, as soon as the data was complete, I unexpectedly called the squad to the six-hundred-meter firing point one day, and after assigning each man a target, told them I would prove to them what team shooting could do. I then directed the "master gun," who knew exactly what was wanted, to fire shots to establish sight settings for the team. His allowed "sighting shots" put him "in the bull," and after he made some minor sight adjustments to center his hits in the center of the bull, he told me his sight readings. Based on them, I told each man

The Olympic Games

the sight setting for his rifle and directed him to fire one carefully aimed shot at his own target when I gave the order. Then, when the wind and light were the same as used by the "master gun," I gave the order to fire. To the complete amazement of the sixteen firing men (and to me too for that matter), fourteen fives and two fours were indicated on the targets.

That one demonstration sold the idea to the team, especially because the settings I had given to them were not at all what they would have used had they been firing as individuals. Then and there they announced their allegiance to team shooting, and in the week or so before starting for the games, the team became as nearly perfect in it as mere human beings could be.

The U.S. Olympic Team of 1912 went to the games in the chartered Atlantic liner *Finland* and lived on board for the duration. Of course it was expensive, but it kept problems to a minimum as well as representing the United State as a cohesive unit, something no country had done before. It was very worthwhile. All team members worked together to strive for perfection, and it was little wonder that every member of our fine team was imbued with "the will to win."

The trip across was intensely interesting, as each team member constantly tried to train at sea for his event, as best he could. The riflemen had a much easier time keeping fit than the athletes, but somehow all succeeded rather well and were quite ready for the games when the ship reached Stockholm.

The members of the team came from all over the United States, from large colleges and universities, small and remote ones, and even unheard of towns. They included full-blooded Indians, Hawaiians, and every nationality in our country.

At first the large university chaps rather "high-hatted" the others, although that soon wore off. One man, however, who particularly attracted my attention, was a splendid looking athlete who always wore a blue sweater with an enormous white Y on it. We assumed he was a Yale man, but strange to say, instead of mingling with the Yale men or other college groups, he associated with the rifle team entirely—so much so that at last we asked his reason for it. Thereupon he said, "I am not friendly with most of the other athletes. Seeing the Y on my sweater, they assume that I am from Yale, which I am not and don't want to be. I earned that letter at my own university, of which I am very proud, but many think I am pretending to be from Yale when I am not, so they high-hat me. I am a Mormon and won that Y at Brigham Young University, and I won't be high-hatted by Yale men or anyone else. Besides, there is another thing. These other fellows talk too much. I'm a high jumper and the other jumpers are always telling me how much higher they have jumped than I have. They talk of their five-feet nine-inch jumps, and when I tell them I can jump only five feet six

An Admiral's Yarn

inches, they sneer at me and I don't like it. Maybe they can jump to five-feet-nine now and then, and maybe they can't. I wouldn't know. But I do know one thing—I may not be in their class but I can always do my five-feet-six, and I'll do it at the games." He did exactly that and won the event.

Though chartered for the games, the *Finland* did not go directly to Stockholm but stopped at Antwerp to discharge a cargo, reaching Stockholm just before the track and field events opened in the stadium. Inasmuch as the shooting events were to be held before the stadium events, the rifle team could not wait for the ship but was obliged to leave it at Antwerp and hasten to Stockholm by rail and boat to be there in time for its matches. That trip took almost a day, as we encountered troubles upon reaching the German frontier. Our rifles and ammunition were held up, although they had supposedly been cleared for us by the U.S. State Department.

Immediately we established ourselves in Stockholm, donned shooting clothes, and rushed to the rifle range to learn as much as we could about conditions there and get in such practice as would be possible that afternoon and the next day before the matches started. We found many teams practicing and the range was sufficiently different from those we had used before, thus requiring careful study. The ground was not level, as on our ranges, and was surrounded by broken woods that produced peculiar wind currents; it was covered with the greenest grass we had even seen on a range. And because of the high latitude and low altitude of the sun, the light had a yellowish tinge that made everything look different. A day and a half of practice seemed all too little for mastering such a range, and since there was no time to lose, we went to work with a will. Our rather complete knowledge of shooting helped immeasurably.

At first we expected to show up poorly in comparison with the teams already there, but once we had obtained our data at one of the distances, our team shooting system became effective. From then on, our hopes and spirits rose.

Never before had any of us seen such a firing line. Instead of the teams dressed in like uniforms, each wore the uniform peculiar to his country—some of which seemed rather fantastic compared with our own khaki, "Rough Rider" outfits. Then too, directly behind each team stood the flag of the country represented. The long line appeared more like a gay bazaar than a firing line for the world's best military marksmen.

One vacant allocation became obvious when the line moved back to the six-hundred-meter distance, and curiosity was rampant about what country was missing. We were not uncertain for long, for scarcely had the firing started at the new distance when we heard a great honking of automobile horns behind us. Turning to look, we beheld a long cavalcade of open autos standing down the

The Olympic Games

range at high speed toward the vacant place on the line. The leading car bore a huge Russian national flag. In each car behind it were four men, two in the rear seat wearing green suits and alpine hats with a long cock feather sticking rakishly back on the left side, while the two in the front seat, in gaudy uniforms of some particular Russian regiment, were carrying the longest rifles I have ever seen.

As the cavalcade approached the firing line and the party disembarked, I thought we were about to be visited by a member of the Royal Family if not the Czar himself, but I soon found that I was mistaken. The Russian Rifle Team had arrived!

That team and its methods were eye-openers to us. The men in green were the shooters, the soldiers in uniform, their orderlies. As soon as the riflemen went to their firing points, their orderlies, with the rifles and ammunition, took stations directly behind them, handing the shooter his loaded rifle which, after each shot, would be handed back to the orderly who loaded and returned it to the riflemen when it came his turn to fire again.

Needless to say, the orderly performance was a new one to our men, who always did everything for themselves. However, though new to us, it was probably necessary to the Russians because of their peculiar rifles, which, fired with heavy bayonets fixed as their regulations required, were so long and heavy that merely aiming carefully and holding them between shots brought enough strain on firing muscles to ruin a man's accuracy. Although their team and equipment did not seem as business-like as ours, those Russians worried us considerably until we watched them shoot for some time and then realized that with all their folderols and show, they were not in our class. They were a long time attempting to hit the targets, and it was a much longer time before one hit the bull's-eye. When it did, all the other Russians stopped shooting long enough to congratulate and shake hands with the man who had fired the successful shot. As our team was then making bull's-eyes on nearly every shot, we ceased to worry about the Russians.

The next day was our one full practice day before the match, and we made the most of it, using our team system through the course and checking up carefully on every detail. When the day ended, we thought ourselves all set and ready—although perhaps the other teams did not think as highly of us, at least I know the British team did not.

For shooting, the U.S. Rifle Team wore a close approximation to the so-called "Rough Rider" uniform which, while not especially fetching to the eye, was an excellent one for the purpose and well known in Europe, because in his widely displayed pictures, President "Teddy" Roosevelt always wore one. We knew nothing of our uniform's prominence, however, until that last practice day when,

An Admiral's Yarn

having ceased firing for a delayed luncheon and a little rest, the captain of the British team approached me and said, "I say, old top, I see your Teddy Roosevelt is here with your team." As he was not, I asked what had given him that impression. "Why," he said, "if that is not Teddy Roosevelt dozing against that tree around the corner, who in the world is it?" When I looked to see, there was our big six-foot doctor [Commander Neill McDonnell], looking the perfect image of Theodore Roosevelt as a rough rider, even to the facial contour, brown mustache, and eyeglasses. I learned afterward that the doctor took considerable pride in his resemblance to Theodore Roosevelt. The British captain appeared greatly revived, for he turned to me and said, "I am glad of that, as I thought if he were with you, we might be beaten, but now there is only one team that worries me at all, the Swedes, and I am not greatly concerned about them."

For the United States Olympic Team, the games started the next morning with the Team Rifle Match. However, although specified as a "team match," and particularly designed as a test in team shooting, it was soon apparent that of all the teams participating, the only one shooting as a team, and not as a group of individuals, was our own. Shooting as a team we at once forged ahead, never wasting a point by having individuals establish their own sight settings. That, however, was not our only advantage, for instead of firing by pairs in succession as is usual in team matches, our four pairs (in each team) fired simultaneously, each on its own target, all under the control of the team captain. While on other teams, eight individuals struggled with their personal shooting problems, our team captain handled them all at one time, merely watching our "master gun" closely. When the firing conditions were right for the "master gun," I had only to order "commence firing" and our pairs would all shoot as rapidly as careful aiming permitted. Shooting in that manner, our team not only made better scores than the others but finished firing in less than half the time of the other teams.

It was little wonder the spectators massed to watch the United States Rifle Team at work, for as distances increased and the shooting became more difficult, the greater became our gains over other teams. One can gauge the quality of our shooting by what we did at 500 meters: out of 120 shots fired (15 per man), 118 were in the little bull's-eye, a truly remarkable performance, though not any more so than those we gave at the other distances. As was to be expected, and even in the face of the other teams shooting as good as they had ever shot, our team won the match by a wide margin.[142]

Although winning by such a large score once more emphasized the value of team shooting, I was particularly keen to see how it may have affected the scores of our individuals. To my surprise, not one man on any other team outshot a

The Olympic Games

single man on the United States Team. The highest score made by any one of them only tied the lowest made by a member of our team.

With the team match won, our great task had been accomplished. There were a few other rifle matches that we entered, although only one was with military rifles—that was an individual match. The others were the famous "running deer" team match for sports rifles and several "small bore" matches as well, none of which were familiar to our military marksmen. In fact, we knew so little about them that the only preparation we had given them was a hurried purchase of six "over-the-counter" sports rifles and six .22 caliber rifles before the *Finland* sailed from New York. Although neither rifle was the type or design considered suitable for the matches, and we had no experience with them, our men insisted on entering the matches.

It is interesting what Americans can do when they really try! As was to be expected, our men did well in the individual match with military rifles[143] and won points for the United States, but in the other matches, we surprised everyone, including ourselves. The first was the "running deer" team match in which four men fire at the silhouette of a deer while it apparently runs some fifty yards along the top of a target pit. The silhouette, which is made of paper, is divided into many parts, each assigned a value as a vital spot, the score for a team being the sum of the values of the hits made.

"Running deer" was not known in the United States, and our riflemen first encountered it on the afternoon allowed for practice. There at the running deer range they tried their luck. With sporting rifles they were not good at all, but with the military rifles so familiar to them they could do fairly well. So, based on that one day's shooting, four men were chosen to be a U.S. "Running Deer Team." Using their regular rifles, they took third place in a match of expert European running deer teams.[144] If anything more had been needed to demonstrate the remarkable shooting ability of American riflemen, that match provided it. But there was more!

The .22 caliber rifles picked up by us over the counter were not at all like the European well-made weapons for small bore shooting. Their rifles had every known refinement to insure accuracy—their sights were fitted with verniers for both vertical and lateral adjustment. Our rifles were the run of the mill, often spoken of as "floberts" made for American boys, and were equipped with old-time open sights that had no means of adjustment. It did not seem possible that our men, in a form of shooting new to them and with such relatively crude firearms, could win a single point against the perfectly equipped experts with whom they had to compete. Nevertheless, they did, and by the time all but one of the small bore matches had been completed, every man on our squad, except

An Admiral's Yarn

for one of the substitutes, even including the doctor and the team adjutant [Colonel William Libby], had won one or more of the prized "Olympic Medals."

The afternoon preceding the last of the small bore matches, the substitute [Frederick Hird], who had not yet won a medal, came to me with a long face and wanted to know what to do since he simply could not return to his home in Iowa without an Olympic Medal. There was only the one remaining rifle match, and the only advice I could give him was to tell him he must win first place. "But how can I?" said he. "That match is the most difficult to win of all the small bore matches. The entire target is smaller than a post card; there are the concentric circles on it, the inner one a bull's-eye that counts as ten, being smaller than a ten-cent piece, and each successive circle outside it counts one point less. To win that match, a man not only has to be a perfect shot but also must have a perfect rifle made for that kind of shooting. Perhaps I am a good enough shot to win such a match but never in the world could those .22 caliber guns of ours, with their fixed open sights, do it." "Well," I said, "that may be true for most people, Hird, but it is not so for you. If you will work to win in the way I know you alone can work, the match will be yours. So go to it and work like hell."

Next morning when the match started, there at his firing point was Hird with his over-the-counter rifle, a box of .22 caliber cartridges, and a tack hammer. As compared with that of forty or fifty other competitions, his equipment was a sorry sight. But even so, no one on the firing line seemed more business-like than Hird, as we stood back of the line to watch him shoot. What we saw was the most unusual and wonderful exhibition of shooting, wherein all his talent and energy went into every shot, even to the three sighting shots allowed each contestant that he might adjust his sights to perfection. But Hird had none of the ordinary means of sight adjustments, and when his first shot went far to one side of the bull's-eye, he picked up his tack hammer and calmly knocked his front sight a trifle to one side to correct it. Then he fired his other two sighters, stopping after each to make a few more tack hammer adjustments, where upon he fired his record string of twenty shots, each a bull's-eye except for one that was outside by a hair's breadth. He had made the remarkable score of 199 out of his possible 200, which won him the match and the coveted gold Olympic Medal. To win first place in any Olympic contest a man must fight all the way, but to win with the poor equipment and little training that Hird had, showed a brand of determination and courage seldom encountered in this world.[145]

The amazing shooting of the Americans drew attention to them whenever they competed, and starting with the military team match, we always had a

The Olympic Games

gallery. Among those ever following our team was a fine appearing young man to whom the other spectators showed such deference that I inquired as to his identity and learned that he was the Crown Prince of Sweden [later Gustav VI]. Not only did he show great interest in shooting, in which he was said to be rather expert, but also he seemed to enjoy talking to our men and "hobnobbing" with them in a free and easy manner that surprised me. In fact, with us, he did not act the Crown Prince at all but was rather a companionable individual, apparently as democratic as we Americans were.

He seemed particularly attracted to one of our riflemen, a typical "as good as anybody" American who at home was a sergeant in the National Guard of his state, and the two often sat together on the ground laughing and talking without restraint. As the sergeant was given to considerable loud joking and horseplay, his bearing and manner when with the Crown Prince was nothing short of startling to me; but as the Prince seemed to enjoy it and always sought him out, I could only watch with amusement, although with a bit of consternation too.

However, during one of the small bore matches, when the sergeant was not shooting and all was quiet along the firing line, I noted the Crown Price and he were seated together on the ground with a large clump of grass between them. As they talked, each would occasionally pluck a blade and chew it, a habit to which the sergeant was much addicted. Though their doing that seemed somewhat unconventional, I did not give particular heed to them and turned my back to watch the shooting. Suddenly from behind me came such loud guffaws and roars of laughter that I turned to look. What I saw surprised me, for the laughter came from the Crown Prince and the guffaws from the sergeant who was lying on his back with his heels kicking in the air! Shocked beyond words that an American sergeant would behave with such levity in the presence of the Crown Prince, I called him to me when they had separated. I asked how a fine soldier could so lose his dignity to behave as he did and wondered if he knew with whom he had been talking. In a loud voice, so that the Prince could hear, the sergeant said, "Of course I know exactly who he is, the Crown Prince of Sweden." Then he added, "You needn't worry about us, Captain, him and me is great friends." I had nothing more to say.

Whether or not the Crown Prince spoke to his father about our team, I do not know, but now and then I saw the King [Gustav V] himself watching us shoot, and then, as the last match drew to its end, the King's aide came to me and said, "His Majesty has noted the remarkable shooting of the American team and has sent me with his congratulations and compliments to ask if you will permit the team to give a demonstration of its shooting tomorrow morning for the Royal Artillery School." Of course I said we would be greatly pleased to do so

An Admiral's Yarn

and spent the next morning explaining and showing his young officers all we knew. However, that was not all, for the King came to the range with them and spent an hour with me, learning about our shooting. Inasmuch as the King had a thorough knowledge of rifle shooting, it was a pleasure to explain our methods to him—but the greatest honor was his recognition of the United States' supremacy in military marksmanship.

Another recognition of that supremacy came from the Russians, when the captain of their team asked me for a set of certified composite targets showing exactly where each shot fired by us, at each distance, had hit. All our men had picture records of their hits, and authentic composite records were easily prepared, but because I could not conceive why he wanted them, I asked. His reply was perhaps typical of foreign opinion, for he said, "On my return to Russia I must make a full report on the military team match, and I know that when I tell of the remarkable shooting by you Americans, no one will believe me. I will need the authenticated composite targets for proof."

The shooting part of the Olympic Games was completed the day before the *Finland* arrived in Stockholm. When the ship arrived, the rifle team returned on board where word of our success had preceded us. Hence, when we went to dinner that night, the entire U.S. Olympic Team was present to give us an ovation, for not only had we won the military match and the three points that a first place gives to a nation, but also we had won a total of thirteen points for our country out of a possible eighteen in the events we had entered. In fact, of the total points for all rifle shooting, even though we could not enter all contests, we had won more points for the United States than had been won by all the other countries of the world together. We had given the United States Olympic Team a splendid start.

Not all the Olympic contests are held in the stadium. Those such as shooting, swimming, diving, rowing, sailing, skating, skiing, football, etc., are held at other specially prepared places. But because the stadium was the assembly center for the meet as well as where all field, track, and gymnastic competitions were to take place, it was opened with a grand ceremonial parade in which all contestants took part, each marching as a member of his country's team, at the head of which was carried the country's flag. To the spectators as well as the competitors, that opening was an inspiring sight for the teams of the various countries, marching once around the stadium, lining up in a row of columns, each headed by its national flag, completely filling the stadium field. Then after a few words of welcome by the King of Sweden, the teams marched forward and the stadium events were started.

The Olympic Games

In the march around the stadium, our victorious rifle team in Rough Rider uniforms, was greeted with such applause as to dumbfound us. At first I thought it was given us for winning our event, but I soon learned differently, for as we passed an English speaking group, I heard them shouting, "Look! Look at the Americans! There goes Teddy Roosevelt almost in the lead." Then I remembered our doctor was marching with me at the head of our rough rider group. The applause was not for our victorious rifle team at all; it was a tribute to Theodore Roosevelt.

With our shooting completed, we riflemen were free to watch and enjoy the games from our "season seats" in the American section. We attended the stadium competitions morning and afternoon, and in the evenings we watched the aquatics. As the games were held in the early summer when, in that latitude, the sun is below the horizon for only a few minutes before and after midnight, it was always daylight, and because there were so many competitions, each contest was a series of "preliminaries" followed by "finals." Being acquainted with every man on our team, the games thus became one long strain of nervous excitement for us. It was like attending an Army-Navy football game that lasted twelve hours a day, every day, for three weeks! Fortunately for our peace of mind, the United States teams did most of the winning and stood at the top easily, but even so, the end of the games brought general relief.

The last great feature of the Olympic dream was the awarding of medals and the crowning of winners with laurel wreaths. That, too, took place in the stadium, where the flags of the competing countries were massed and into which the winners marched, no longer grouped in national teams but by competitive events. Perhaps that final act was not as spectacular as the opening one, but those who witnessed it saw before them the champions of the world in every amateur sport known at that time. Only once in every four years is there such a gathering. Assuredly, it is impressive.

With the winners assembled, the King of Sweden took his stand before them, and as their names were called, each advanced to be given his medal, to be crowned with the coveted laurel wreath, and to be congratulated. It may be that somewhere in life there is a greater individual thrill than being crowned an Olympic champion, but if so, not many in this world experience it.

When the games were over, every member of our team could have returned to the United States on the *Finland*, but as each one had been given a ticket for passage on any Red Star Liner within the next few months, many of us took advantage of the allowed delay to visit European cities. I myself joined a group to spend a carefully planned sightseeing week in Paris, and since we were all vigorous men, we covered the interesting points of that great city rather

An Admiral's Yarn

thoroughly. However, at the end of the week I was weary and more than delighted to return to my little family and my new work at the Naval Academy.

That academic year was a busy one in the Department of Navigation, for we changed it from one on theories of navigation to that of practice. Our first move was to make each recitation room a navigator's workroom, with all the books, charts, and paraphernalia found in a ship's "chart house," and which every midshipman was taught to use. We went over Bowditch's *Practical Navigation* carefully, and when we had written new chapters for it and brought its old ones up to the minute in modern navigation work, it was reprinted by the Navy Department and became our basic textbook. Although the old textbooks on the theories of navigation were retained, they were utilized only as reference books—now, instead of reciting daily on the deduction of navigational formulae, midshipmen were taught how to use them to obtain navigational fixes from astronomical observations. To practice them thoroughly in a navigator's work at sea, two two-hour periods each week were devoted to what was called "practical nav."

The course we put in effect that year was not one to make midshipmen good theorists in navigation, but it certainly taught them to be the proficient navigators required for the navy. More than that, once the confusing influence of theory no longer interfered with the practice of it, the midshipmen began to like navigation and ceased to worry about becoming "unsat" in it. Instead of from one-third to one-half a class making unsatisfactory marks on the annual "exams" in navigation, as was the case the year before, on a more thorough exam only two men in the entire class failed. I was elated with our progress and accomplishments.

As the year neared its end, I was again due for sea and made a formal request to be ordered as executive officer of a battleship, but the detail officer felt I had had more than my share of battleship duty and should take command of a destroyer. Soon came my orders to report to the USS *Cassin*, which had just been built in Bath, Maine, and was a fine, large destroyer which I was to command and put into commission. I was pleased.

XXVIII

In Destroyers

ARRIVING IN BATH about the end of June, I had six weeks there before the USS *Cassin* was completed.[146] At the same time, a sister destroyer, the *Cummings*,[147] was also being finished, and the officers of both ships, who did not have their families with them, joined in keeping "bachelor hall" in a large, old, colonial house that we were able to rent fully furnished.

It was summer, and we had a joyous time during the height of the season in southeastern Maine. Early in August, after work on the *Cassin* was finished, the new ship was delivered to the Navy Yard in Boston. Commissioned at once and quickly fitted out, *Cassin* joined the destroyer flotilla in Narragansett Bay about the first of September, 1913.

There we entered a new kind of naval life, for although all ships are similar, as are all horses, I was to change from the draft horse type of work done by the battleships to the race horse sort performed by the destroyers. It was akin to a shift from driving truck horses to the thrilling excitement of racehorse jockeying. Nor was the change merely in the kind of work, for just as race horses are livelier than draft horses, so destroyers with their great speed and slender lines are far more lively at sea than other ships. Their personnel must develop a set of "sea-legs" considerably stronger and more active than those required on slow-moving ships.

The quick twists, rolls, and pitches of speeding destroyers are such a physical strain to those on board that they are always waiting and hoping for a lessening of the activity. Hence, when the *Cassin* joined the flotilla, all eyes were on it to note the behavior of a new type of ship, a third larger than the old vessels.

An Admiral's Yarn

Naturally I too was interested as well as pleased to have a division of older boats steam along with us on our first run in a rough sea so that we might compare proficiencies and skills. When we reached port, the division commander remarked that though his ships had cavorted as usual in the seaway, the *Cassin* went along "as steady as a church." Only it really had not, for our carefully kept records showed the *Cassin's* movements to be just as fast, hard, large, and frequent as were those of the older destroyers.

In fact, every ship at sea rolls and tosses at certain times to a degree that is dependent mostly on the hull shape and the size of the seas. The larger the ship the larger the sea must be to affect it, but there is little difference between destroyers, whatever the class. As soon as a fresh wind creates a rough sea, all behave abominably, and for that reason, life at sea on a destroyer is perhaps the most trying challenge in a navy man's career.

That month with the flotilla gave me a fair insight into destroyer life as well as an understanding of what is needed to prepare destroyers for service. When the rest of the flotilla went to navy yards to prepare for a winter's cruise in the West Indies, the *Cassin*, which had just left a yard, was ordered to do a "shakedown cruise" in Florida waters. The *Cummings* and two other destroyers, the *Downes* and *Duncan*, also were to get ready for the flotilla and were directed to join the *Cassin* to form the "Sixth Division," under my command.[148] That Sixth Division was a fine command, and I was keen to have it show up well that winter.

The other ships were not ready to go south at the moment, so the *Cassin* proceeded alone, to be joined by them later where they came out for a "shakedown" period around Key West and the Dry Tortugas. Situated on the most western and remote of the larger Florida Keys, only ninety miles from Havana, Key West had a life all its own—American, southern, tropical, and Cuban. Linked to the mainland only by steamers and the railroad over the Florida Keys, its easygoing life was one we entered into fully when in port.

Proud of their isolation and individuality, Key Westers called themselves "Conches," after the shellfish of that area, a name they retain to this day.

Although we often went to Key West for mail, fuel, supplies, and liberty, our base for work was the Dry Tortugas, a ring of small coral keys and sandbanks about sixty miles farther west, within which is a large deep-water area suitable for anchorage and torpedo work. On Loggerhead Key, the small islet farthest to the westward, stood the great Tortugas lighthouse to guide the ships entering or leaving the Straits of Florida. While the entire Dry Tortugas group is a bird sanctuary, a low flat sand key on the southern side of the harbor, known locally as "Bird Key," fairly teemed with feathered life, and during the winter months was so filled with migratory birds that it drew many naturalists there to study them.

In Destroyers

But the outstanding features of the group were the abandoned Fort Jefferson and the naval coaling plant on the larger of the keys, on the southeastern side of the harbor.

Unless one actually sees them, it is almost impossible to believe that in the remote Tortugas, our country could have erected and then completely abandoned such costly affairs. Yet there stand Fort Jefferson and the coaling plant, monuments not to an error in judgment but to the tremendous changes in warfare that took place in the 19th century.

In the first half of that century, to protect its seaports, the United States spent about a billion dollars erecting massive stone and masonry forts—from Maine to the Rio Grande—covering the entrance channels to its important ports. When completed, those forts were the last word in harbor defense; but of them all, because it defended the harbor from which the entrance on the western side to the Florida Straits was controlled, Fort Jefferson was perhaps the costliest, as every brick, stone, and even the earth for it had to be carried there in ships. Huge and seemingly impregnable, the fort approximated half a mile in diameter; around it was a moat and huge seawall; and inside it were barracks, many buildings, and a large, earth-covered, parade ground. In addition, a deep channel had been cut through the reef to the eastward, the coral and sand from which had been used to enlarge an area alongside the fort where the navy had erected two coaling plants, and where several fine wharves had been built.

During the Civil War, and even as late as the war with Spain, "Dry Tortugas" was vitally important to the United States, though in neither war was it attacked. In the former, Fort Jefferson came to be a Federal prison where many war prisoners as well as the Jefferson Davis and the Lincoln assassination conspirators (except Booth) were confined. In the war with Spain, the great coaling plants supplied fuel for the U.S. naval ships fighting around Cuba. But the introduction of long-range guns and oil fuel changed all that and rendered the entire Dry Tortugas outfit so useless that when we went ashore there in 1913, we had it to ourselves except for the lightkeepers on Loggerhead Key and a custodian for the immense abandoned military plant, who lived with his wife in a small house within the old fort.

Deserted and isolated though it was, the Dry Tortugas area was ideal for training work, and we progressed rapidly. Without the fleshpots of a seaport town, one might think it would be a dull place for several hundred officers and men, but instead of feeling disconnected from life, we found ourselves (at no expense whatever) enjoying a winter outing in the Florida Keys for which other men had to pay hundreds of dollars. We worked hard during work hours, but for every moment of recreation time, we had no end of healthy and interesting

An Admiral's Yarn

outdoor pastimes right at our door. In the old fort's parade ground, we had a perfect baseball field; on the concrete floors of the old coaling plant we had splendid tennis courts; in the fort and around the seawall, we took wonderfully interesting walks; there was no end to boating, swimming, and bathing; on visits to the nearby reefs and Keys, we collected a vast number of beautiful sea life curios, and the fishing was such that few men have the opportunity to enjoy.

The Florida Keys have long been famous for wonderful fishing, but in all that vast area, the Dry Tortugas is perhaps the best. Depending on where and how we fished, we had no difficulty in catching immense barracuda, grouper, red snapper, Spanish mackerel, and kingfish and a dozen kinds of beautiful pan-fish. Tarpon were plentiful, though not having proper equipment and bait we never tried for them, being quite satisfied with the gaminess of fish easier to catch, which often weighed from twenty to forty pounds. The barracuda were particularly large and so voracious that they often stole our hooked mackerel and kingfish before we could land them. One day when I had worked for some time bringing a large kingfish to the boat, we saw an immense barracuda nip off the greater part of it, right alongside the boat. When I returned to the ship, I weighted the part the barracuda had failed to get and it weighed fourteen pounds. A fish that could bite off considerably more than that amount in one gulp had to be of substantial size.

Having spend some eight or ten weeks around Key West and the Dry Tortugas, the division went to Guantánamo Bay where we joined the destroyer flotilla and the entire U.S. Atlantic Fleet for a winter of training. We had prepared ourselves rather fully in the individual work of destroyers and even in operating as a division, so when we joined the flotilla, we were ready for the work that destroyers had been called upon to do up to that time.

But that year they were assigned a new type of work by the then flotilla commander, Captain W.S. Sims. The fleet had become proficient in gunnery and engineering, and the battleships were trained to maneuver as a unit in battle, but other types of ships had learned little of teamwork. Sims developed it that winter.[149]

Although enemy heavy ships have always been the main objective for both battleships and destroyers in war, it was the general naval practice in 1913 for the two types of vessels to work more or less independently. Although the battleships were fairly well trained in their task, the destroyers had yet to be prepared. The only way destroyers could get close enough to hit large ships with torpedoes was to slip up on them under cover of darkness. Hence, Sims began training the flotilla in what he called "night search and attack." This was a new type of operation that became possible only because our ships were equipped with

In Destroyers

radio. Radio brought an almost complete change to naval warfare, but at that time, use of it was still in its infancy—so much so that "night search and attack," as developed that winter, was just about the first step in a great revolution.

Although not entirely recognizable at that time, what Sims did in the winter of 1913 marked the very start of profound change in our fleet's war operations. A considerable amount of teamwork between battleships had been done previously, but what we did that winter not only developed teamwork in destroyers, but at the same time began teamwork between battleships and destroyers. That winter was the beginning of what our battle fleet has become today, a huge company of teams working together in one coordinated effort to destroy the enemy fleet.

It was an arduous winter. We worked night and day, sometimes at Guantánamo, sometimes in "Hungry Gulf," but mostly at sea. At last, however, it ended with the new destroyers being hurried north for their inspection preliminary to final acceptance. The rest of the fleet remained to rest for a week in Guantánamo. In all, eight destroyers went north for those final trials, four in my Sixth Division and four in the Seventh, which had been formed when additional, just completed ships, joined the flotilla in Cuba.

On the run north, we encountered a bit of rough weather. As senior officer of the group, I directed the Seventh Division to proceed independently to better meet weather conditions. The two divisions were in rough sea in the vicinity of Cape Hatteras about two o'clock one morning, when I received a radio message from the other division asking that my ships stand by them as a boiler explosion in one of its ships had killed or wounded several men and blown out one side of the ship abreast the boiler. Of course the Sixth Division rushed at best speed to assist, but by the time we reached the stricken ship, the *Aylwin*, it had been taken in tow by another destroyer, and the Seventh Division was slowly standing toward Hatteras lightship.[150]

Never before had I seen such a sight as that disclosed by our searchlights and the breaking when we drew near the *Aylwin*. It was so far down by the head that it seemed to be sinking. Utterly without lights or power, its personnel, all gathered on deck wearing life preservers, were ready to jump overboard should the ship go under. It was truly a weird sight that became even more so when I saw that a great piece of the outside hull had been torn away at the keel. It was blown so far out and upward that it appeared like a giant wing over a tremendous hole in the ship's side, through which the sea rolled in and out. From its appearance, the *Aylwin* seemed almost certain to break in two in the heavy sea then running, or sink if the inside bulkheads should give way. But it did neither, for miraculously, the wind dropped, the sea flattened, and we moved slowly

An Admiral's Yarn

toward Norfolk where we arrived late that night. The *Aylwin* was immediately placed in dry-dock.

After that, our final trials and inspections went off according to schedule, with only one occurrence worth recounting. It had to do with an enlisted man on the *Cassin*. His name was Carter. Carter, who was almost jet black, was cook for the officers' mess. He first came to my notice one day when, shortly after the commissioning of the ship, he greeted me at the galley door saying, "Captain, I guess you don't remember me, but I was your mess hall boy when you was a midshipman at the Academy. I'se been a cook in the navy for nearly fifteen years now, and I'se mighty glad to be working for you again. My name is Carter."

During all the time he had served in the *Cassin*, Carter had proved such an excellent cook and was so interested in his work that all the officers thought highly of him, especially since his record showed that in all the years he had served in the navy, he had never been "on the report." He seldom left the ship, never asked a favor, and proved steady and reliable. It is little wonder we officers were great believers in Carter.

One day during our final acceptance trails, the *Cassin* sailed into Hampton Roads to pick up supplies for another week at sea. Because it was already about five o'clock in the afternoon when we anchored, and we were to depart at seven the next morning, I announced there would no be liberty that night—the only men to go ashore would be stewards going for supplies. Shortly after that and just before the boat with the stewards was to shove off, the officer of the deck came to me and reported that Carter was at mast and wished to see me about going ashore that night. Had anyone but Carter wanted to request liberty that night, I probably would not have seen him, but since it was faithful old Carter, I went to the mast. There stood Carter dressed in his best shore-going clothes. When I neared him, he said, "Captain, I ain't never asked for nothing before, but it is so important for me to get ashore tonight, I begs you to let me go. I'll sure come back in the market boat at five o'clock tomorrow morning."

I felt I had to do something about it, so after thinking it over, I said to him, "Carter, you need not tell me why it is so important for you to go ashore, but when a man of your stand and reliability feels it is so necessary to go ashore, I will allow it. But remember, you must not fail to return in the market boat early tomorrow morning." "Yes sir, Captain," replied Carter, "I'll be in that boat and I thank you."

Before seven the following morning, the officer of the deck reported the *Cassin* ready to get underway and added, "The market boat has returned and is hoisted and all stewards are on board with their supplies, but Carter did not

In Destroyers

come back, although the boat waited an hour for him. So he is absent over leave and has missed the ship."

The next week at sea without a cook was not a happy one, and by the time the ship was in Hampton Roads again, we officers were in a bad humor and disgusted with Carter, whom I intended to have counter-martialled as soon as he returned. He did so in the first boat, but as it was then evening and the officer of the deck reported him almost in collapse over the enormity of his offense, I decided to wait until I held mast next day to take his case.

When I did so, there stood Carter waiting his turn with tears rolling down his face, the first time he had ever appeared before his captain for punishment. Seeing his distress, I made his the last case called. When his turn came, the ship's officers and the master-at-arms present at the hearing all drew long and solemn faces as I said to him, "Carter, you have betrayed the great trust I put in you when I granted you a very special favor. Now what have you to say about your treatment of me in not returning to the ship as you promised?" When I finished, Carter's tears increased and he could scarcely speak, but at last he managed through his tears to explain. "Captain," said he, "I didn't mean to treat you that way, deed I didn't. When you let me go ashore that night I sure thought I'd get back in that market boat, but, Captain, things began to happen as soon as I got ashore. I got married right away and the baby was born next morning, so I just couldn't come back to the ship."

Although doing so was difficult, those of us who heard Carter remained as solemn as owls. When at last I was able to speak, I said, "Carter, I have heard many excuses for being over leave, but never have I heard one like yours. I shall think about it and review your record again, for this is indeed a grave offense." A few days later I decided the excuse was worthy of a dismissal of the case against Carter but warned him never to overstay his leave again. "Deed, Sir, I won't," sobbed Carter, and as far a I know, he ever did.

The spring of 1914 proved an eventful one in several ways. I had been a member of the American Olympic Committee at the time of the 1912 games, but until I came north that spring, there had been no call for my services. The International Olympic Committee was to meet in Paris in June, and I was designated to attend it as one of the United States representatives. Inasmuch as the month of June had been set aside as an overhaul period for the fleet, and I could be absent during it, arrangements were made for me to go to Paris. I would be accompanied by my family, who was to remain several months in Europe after I returned. Alas, these plans never materialized, for in April a crisis in Mexico changed the U.S. Fleet from its peacetime schedule to a

213

An Admiral's Yarn

ready-for-emergency basis, requiring it to rush from Guantánamo Bay to Mexican waters to meet the situation.

To the destroyers then in the Chesapeake Bay undergoing final acceptance trials, not being with the fleet at that time was a great blow, especially when we read of the Vera Cruz incident, handled so well by the navy. We, of course, wished we had been there, but we were far away and seemingly not needed as well as having our own work to do. We gave up all hope of going to Mexico, and after establishing our families in Hampton Roads, we settled ourselves in to remain there for a month or two. I was, therefore, greatly surprised when shortly after the Vera Cruz affair I was aroused one night by an officer from the *Cassin*, bearing a radio message that had just reached the ship.[151] It stated that the merchant ship *Morro Castle*, with a large force of Marines on board, had just left New York for Mexico and it directed the *Cassin* to contact the ship off Hatteras the following afternoon and convoy it to Vera Cruz.[152]

Having been wakened from a sound sleep to receive it, that message was a veritable bombshell to my family. Not only did it send me on what they considered war service, but at the same time it ended our reunion after a six-month separation. It also removed every possibility of attending the Olympic Conference.

Fortunately the *Cassin* had taken on a full load of fuel and supplies that day, so as soon as I understood the order, I told the officer to return to the ship, send a boat for me at six o'clock the next morning, and have the *Cassin* ready to leave as soon as the liberty party returned at eight o'clock. I then went back to bed and promptly slept. While this was a bitter disappointment to me, it was part of a regular day's work in the navy. But to my family, it was indeed a catastrophe.

We met the *Morro Castle* off Hatteras and convoyed it to Vera Cruz where we found all the larger ships at anchor. But no destroyers were there, and as soon as the *Morro Castle* had been turned over to him, the admiral [Henry T. Mayo] ordered the *Cassin* to Tampico to join the destroyer flotilla in blockading that port to prevent the escape of three Mexican gunboats there. I found the flotilla anchored in a huge semicircle in the Gulf around the mouth of the Pánuco River. Having been assigned a berth, we anchored.

Although the destroyers off Tampico had to be continuously ready to get underway and to fight should the Mexican gunboats attempt to leave the river, there was little excitement in being there, and we suffered hardships. Perhaps the worst was from the heavy and incessant rolling. There was no protection from the huge Gulf of Mexico swells, and taking a position in the trough of them, the destroyers rolled terribly. Being accustomed to some rolling, it did not bother us at first, but as it went on, thirty-five degrees or more to each side, every six

In Destroyers

seconds, day and night, it ultimately became wearing beyond words—so much so that every ten days or so each destroyer would be sent to Lobos Keys, a group of reefs off the great oil port of Luxpam, to get a twenty-four hour rest. But the best break in the dreadful monotony came in being tasked to Galveston for mail and for a night at the pier there. Fortunately the *Cassin* was sent on several missions, one with a group of three army transports carrying troops dispatched from New Orleans; we were flag-boat for the destroyers, with orders to convoy them to Vera Cruz. Later, when permission had been given the three Mexican gunboats at Tampico to proceed to Puerto Mexico, to be laid up there, the *Cassin* once again was flagship for destroyers that accompanied them.

Our most interesting trip was when the *Cassin* was ordered to assist a stranded merchant ship. The *Atlantic*, a steamer on the run between New Orleans and Tampico, was returning from the former port when it ran ashore about a hundred miles from its destination. The ship usually carried a few passengers on its return trips, but on that occasion it had more than one hundred renegade aliens who had tried to escape to the United States from Mexico. They had been held up by the immigration authorities at New Orleans and were being returned to Tampico. Of course we knew nothing about the people we had to rescue, nor would that have made any difference. The *Cassin* was ordered to their assistance.

We found the *Atlantic* soon after sunrise the following morning, hard ashore on a long, sandy beach. As it was a ship several times the size of the *Cassin*, and aground for its full length with but little water under the stern and its bow deep in the sand, it was at once apparent we could not do anything except save those on board. They were in no immediate danger from the weather, but we realized that should the seas increase, the passengers would be swept off, and at best, rescuing them from the ship would be both difficult and dangerous. We anchored the *Cassin* as near the ship as possible and started the rescue.

It was quite a task taking off one hundred and five passengers in the heavy Gulf rollers breaking all around the *Atlantic*. Nerve and skill were required to keep the boats from floundering or being smashed, and only five or six passengers could be taken at one time. Late that afternoon the *Cassin* had them all on board and sped back to Tampico, where we arrived at midnight, too late to rid ourselves of our guests that night.

They were indeed a motley crowd, the very scum of the alien population of the Mexican oil fields around Tampico. There were no U.S. citizens or Mexicans among them, but almost every other nationality was represented—Chinese, Hindu, Greeks, Indians, Negroes, etc. The great majority were men, but there were many women, several with children. They were the gamblers and the

An Admiral's Yarn

keepers and inmates of dives, brothels, and baudy houses of Tampico, the very riffraff of a wide-open, oil-rush, waterfront city.

Caring for that crowd overnight in an already well-filled ship, with sleeping quarters and toilet facilities barely sufficient for the crew, was no delicate matter. We were further complicated by the need to protect the ship and ourselves against damage and looting. It is little wonder that we were thankful when daylight came and we received orders to put our guests ashore in Tampico after removing the weapons we found on the adults. I do not recall ever seeing a more vicious looking lot of weapons than we found on them—pistols of all kinds, daggers, dirks, and knives, and even black-jacks, all of which they tried to retain against their return to Tampico. When we had garnered them in, the *Cassin* steamed up the Pánuco River to a city pier and put the passengers ashore in the very face of Mexican troops whom we expected to fire on us, but fortunately they made no attempt to do so. When we finished that task we returned to our station.

After we had been in Mexican waters for about three months, the situation began to ease there as far as the fleet was concerned. The army and Marines had taken control on shore, and fewer ships were needed. Accordingly, the *Cassin* was sent home, long overdue for Navy Yard overhaul. As the crisis in Mexico seemed about over, many newspaper representatives took the opportunity to return home on the ships. One, a writer for *Collier's Weekly,* sailed on the *Cassin*.

Our return trip was about like any other on a destroyer, but to the *Collier's* reporter, it seemed sufficiently unique to warrant a write-up in which a little storm that we encountered figured conspicuously. It came as quite a surprise to us that the next issue of *Collier's* after our return, carried so many photographs and such an extensive account of the trip as to make it appear almost historic.

Nevertheless, it was pleasant to be on a peace basis once more and to enjoy the restfulness of the Boston Navy Yard. However, I was soon ordered to Washington to be examined for promotion to the rank of commander and then to assume command of the Reserve Destroyer Flotilla.

XXIX

Commanding a Destroyer Flotilla

THIS NEW DUTY WAS VERY INTERESTING, for although it would take me away from a certain amount of activity with the fleet, my command, which was increased to thirteen destroyers and a tender, was practically independent, and I became entirely responsible for the war preparation and training of an important part of the fleet. While the ships operating with half complements of officers and men could accomplish only as much as reduced personnel allowed, I realized that good results under such conditions would be very meaningful both to the navy and to me, so I went to work. It marked that important turn in life wherein one ceases to be a follower and becomes a leader. For me it meant that I would no longer work always under plans and orders of others, but would be doing the planning and ordering myself.

Since it was impossible to operate on the fleet's schedule, a special one was laid out for the flotilla, with the Navy Yard, Charleston, South Carolina, as its repair base. In general, the schedule called for four months of operation from a northern base, two months for repair and upkeep at Charleston, four months of work from a southern base, and then two more months at the Navy Yard. For the summer, the Block Island Sound-Narragansett Bay area was chosen, and for the winter, the Key West-Dry Tortugas area.

However, although training was the all-important matter of the moment in order to prepare my command for war, it was only a peacetime job for me, utterly unlike what I would be called upon to do in war. Hence, though my orders made me entirely responsible for preparing those under me for active

An Admiral's Yarn

service, it was nonetheless my responsibility to prepare myself for what might come my way.

From having worked with them for a year, I knew what to do for the destroyers, but I also gave much thought to preparing myself. Of all the efforts of man, the most tremendous and difficult are those of war, because it is not merely force against force but wits and force against the like, and it is the most kaleidoscopic of men's activities. From history we have gleaned a few general principles that must be observed—principles that students of warfare sometimes sum up in the words "get there first-est with the most-est." Other than such few generalities, we can be taught little about war other than learning through the experience of war operations.

To educate its command officers to conduct their forces in war, our country established the Naval War College. To most people, the name "College" seems something of a misnomer, since, while one may learn much about wars there and how to fight them, there is practically no standard teaching. By reading history and writings, we may learn why wars develop and the general principles that a commander of forces must observe to gain success. But what the nature of war will be, where and how it will be fought, and what will constitute a final decision, must be deduced. By conducting wars, campaigns, operations, and battles in miniature, with the goal in mind to win, we may learn much about moving the forces we command.

The conduct of war is an inexact science; one is never sure what the enemy will do. Furthermore, because technology advances so rapidly, what one learns today may be obsolete tomorrow. Uncertain as war operations may be, those in high command must know how to conduct them successfully, and studies at the Naval War College are designed to do just that. It makes possible an ongoing examination of the constantly changing practices of war.

Before one is fully prepared to take up high command in war, he must have served long enough in positions of low command to know fully the capabilities and limitations of the ships and weapons under him. Not every high-ranking officer is able to attend the War College. Therefore, to assist those unable to go there for early training, the college started [April 1914] what is called the "Correspondence Course," one that in no way takes the place of the regular course but which will partially prepare an officer for high command. He will not become well-practiced in war operations, but at least he will learn to "estimate the situation" and thereby draw up plans and issue orders for his force.

Although the correspondence course would not offer nearly as much preparation for high command as I felt I needed, it could do much to improve

Commanding a Destroyer Flotilla

me for war duties in the rank I then held and at the same time better prepare me for further study at a later date. Therefore, I enrolled.

That summer of 1914 marked a momentous period in the history of the world. About six weeks after I took command of the Reserve Flotilla, the nations of Europe became engulfed in war. Though we little thought that we too would become involved, those of us in the service nevertheless gave close attention to it and endeavored to have the navy prepared should the United States be dragged in. We hoped that by our preparing, the warring nations would be forewarned not to interfere in the preservation of our rights. Unfortunately, while the spending of only two billion dollars or less on our navy would have made other nations respect our power, the United States did almost nothing. Day by day, the warring nations encroached on our rights, until about three years later we too were drawn in. During those years the navy had done all it could to make itself ready. What a pity the entire United States had not done the same.

The next two years, though of vital importance to my command and to me personally, were not given to many exciting activities. We simply worked hard at our task, trying to be thorough in it while making as much use as possible of recreational facilities such as our bases provided. There were many: Narragansett Bay for summer; Dry Tortugas in winter; and Charleston in between. Always having a perfect climate in which to operate, and following a carefully prepared routine in which we were all intensely interested, we kept ourselves and our flotilla continuously ready for a call.

For my personal preparation, the conditions were splendid. Whenever the destroyers were on individual work, my time was free for the correspondence course for which I had the facilities and space of the flotilla commander's cabin. Thus I had an unusual combination, and because the war problems proved intensely interesting, it soon took the place of all my other recreations, such as chess, bridge, golf, and tennis. I gave every free moment to the course between breakfast at 7 a.m. and turning in at 11 p.m. As can be supposed, I learned a great deal about wars and how to conduct them, and that was an asset of continuing value.

It was nearly a year and a half before a truly unusual occurrence happened to the Reserve Flotilla. We had been called on a few times to operate with the fleet, and we showed up well enough in the maneuvers to prove that our training work was good. Perhaps more than satisfactory, for to our surprise, in the early spring in 1916, when I had been in command a bit over eighteen months, the flotilla was suddenly ordered to Santo Domingo to assist in quelling a severe uprising inimical to both the Dominican Republic and to the United States.[153]

An Admiral's Yarn

The use of destroyers for such a purpose was theretofore unheard of, and the use of destroyers with only a half complement was even more unexpected. Nevertheless, we felt highly honored to have been called on for the duty and set out without delay. Fortunately our ships were materially ready, and what we lacked in personnel we made up for with a will to succeed against all odds.

The destroyers went to Santo Domingo City direct and, arriving there before my flagship, the *Panther*,[154] were sent to various coastal towns by Admiral Caperton,[155] commanding our naval forces, to protect American interests. The *Panther* was obliged to stop at both Port au Prince and Cap-Haitien for a marine contingent for delivery to Santo Domingo City. Having done that, I was immediately ordered to Montecristi in the northwest corner of Santo Domingo with the *Panther*, about eighty Marines, and five of my destroyers to handle the situation there. The situation was the most serious in all Santo Domingo at that time. A group of several hundred armed outlaws had over-awed the entire province and were living on tribute and loot exacted from the inhabitants.

Arriving at Montecristi, we found its people in great distress and fear, surrounded by bandits that had preyed at will on them, taking nearly all their money and supplies. I wanted to land at once and clean out the outlaws, but since a similar condition existed throughout Santo Domingo, and it was still hoped that it would be corrected without our actual intervention, landing was delayed. Unfortunately, the situation not only failed to improve but became worse. The governor of the Montecristi province was forced to take refuge in Haiti; government disappeared; no raw food was allowed to enter the city, and its people were existing on seagull eggs; the demands of the brigands were fast bleeding the entire province to death; and the city of Montecristi was in danger of even having its fresh water cut off.

When at last almost every city and town in the Dominican Republic had become menaced by thieving groups—each group seemingly acting only for itself—an order came for us to land the following morning and take control in the Montecristi area. In the face of the bandit strength and talk, doing that seemed a tall order for our small number of men, particularly because the outlaws far outnumbered our force and had sent us word that they would fight if we landed, and that "one Dominican bandit could whip seven Yankees, anyhow." Nevertheless, we sent word ashore that we would land and take control early the next morning and that if any of our men were hurt or a shot fired as we moved in, our ships would blow up Montecristi, bandits and all.

That message probably had its effect, for when at sunrise the destroyers took up covering positions and Captain [Frederick M.] "Fritz" Wise with his eighty Marines moved ashore and took over the town, peace and quiet reigned supreme. But the situation was still precarious, for although the outlaws left the town when we entered, they took stations just outside and defiantly sent word they would retake the city when they wished and everything would be as before. Of course we knew they would never try to capture the town from our Marines, but they did hold the waterworks some miles outside the town, and we feared they might deprive the people of water.

In such a condition, and in spite of the fact that we had control in the city, the brigands had something of a whip hand and let us know they would fight any attempt to seize the waterworks. This was, of course, an unendurable state of affairs, and though there had not been bloodshed so far, we realized there soon might be when we attempted to take control of the water supply, as we had been directed to do.

Matters remained that way for about two days after our landing. We hoped that the brigands would recognize our power and surrender without fighting, but as they grew bolder and more threatening, and as the admiral gave emphasis to the necessity of our controlling the fresh water supply everywhere, it became evident that we must act. That evening, Captain Wise came on board to discuss the situation, and I told him the waterworks must be seized the following day.

Being a splendid Marine officer and not wishing bloodshed any more than I did, Wise could not but point out to the bandits what would happen if he moved to take the water supply, saying it could probably not be done without some people being killed. I sent some "blue jackets" ashore at sunrise the next morning to hold the town, and Captain Wise took about forty Marines and set out for the waterworks, hoping to take it without fighting.

It was shortly before dark that night when Wise returned to the ship to inform me that he had accomplished his mission and all was quiet on shore. Then he added, "In our fight, a few of the outlaws were killed when two or three hundred of them 'jumped' us at noon as we ate our lunch. But we surprised them with our readiness to meet them, and they turned tail and ran without even wounding a Marine. They were still running the last we saw of them. When all was quiet and serene, we went on to assume control of the waterworks and en route saw two or three bodies. We regretted that bloodshed had been necessary to accomplish our important mission."

With that seemingly small fracas, a sudden peace came to Montecristi—not a bandit appearing anywhere. Taking advantage of it, I rushed a destroyer to Cap-Haitien to bring back the governor who, within two days, had so reestablished normal civil government that leading citizens of the town hurried to inform me that not in twenty years had they known such quiet and safety. It amazed us that they were so certain that their troubles were over, for with several

An Admiral's Yarn

hundred outlaws in hiding, the trouble seemed as alarming as ever to us. However, we were told that the bandits were so thoroughly "licked" by Captain Wise that the band was broken for all time, and one can well imagine the relief after being preyed upon by the outlaws for years.

There being no further need for it, my flotilla was ordered to return to Key West to resume its schedule.

As the summer of 1916 drew to an end, so did my three years of sea duty, which, while not exciting, were nevertheless years as fruitful and interesting as I had ever known. During them, I had completed the long correspondence course, but at the same time I had well prepared myself to "estimate situations" by drawing up plans and orders. Thus, I felt I could meet most duties that a commander might expect in the near future, but not, I realized, for the far future—I knew my study of naval warfare had barely begun.

My orders to the Office of Chief of Naval Operations soon came, and I was greatly pleased.

XXX

War

IN OCTOBER 1916, I REPORTED to the Office of the Chief of Naval Operations,[156] responsible for the navy's war plans and readiness for war. Inasmuch as "Operations" is to the navy what the "General Staff" is to the army, the winter of 1916–1917, with war increasingly imminent, was a trying time, especially since it was impossible to predict what might happen should the United States be drawn into war.

Our war plans were utterly unlike those of a nation about to engage in a war entirely on its own. The World War had been going on for over two years. In a military sense, it was almost a stalemate on the western front, while at sea, although the Allied navies controlled on the surface and had cut the Central Powers off from all overseas supplies, the Germans, by their unrestricted submarine campaign, were fast depriving the Allies of their overseas supplies too.[157] Thus the war was nearing an impasse, with both sides worn to a frazzle and badly in need of various means of assistance. However, as neither dared announce their particular need, the United States had no way of knowing what role it was expected to assume until after it had joined with the Allies.

In April 1917, conditions had become so intolerable that war was declared on Germany. Even then it was some weeks before the Allies and we could reach an agreement on the best action for us to take to insure winning. They needed assistance from us to frustrate the German submarine campaign, though not from our main naval fighting strength. They needed our manpower to give their armies superiority on the western front; our help in finance, supplies, and military equipment; and substantial shipping to offset the terrible toll being

An Admiral's Yarn

exacted by the German submarines that were sinking the Allies' merchant ships. These desperate circumstances determined the role the United States had to assume, although for the navy, it was very different from a usual one in a war at sea. Nevertheless, our navy had to adjust itself to the circumstances and simply do it.

The British navy was in control of the surface of the sea. Therefore there was no call for the great fighting power of our fleet—though we were obliged to keep it fully manned and ready to fight should the British lose that control. Hence, even though our battle fleet would not be actually engaged in hostilities, it still had to be kept in readiness. Simultaneously, the navy had to prepare for and carry out a successful antisubmarine campaign in European waters and to safely transport huge armies and vast supplies to France.

The tasks of both the army and navy were difficult.[158] The former had to raise and operate armies and provide the military equipment and supplies needed by the Allies, while the latter had to create and put antisubmarine forces into operation and provide a transocean transportation service of tremendous proportions. Under such circumstances, our maximum assistance could not be extended immediately; but to show our good will, the War Department hurriedly sent General [John J.] Pershing and his staff to France to command our armies as soon as they arrived, and the Navy Department sent Admiral Sims to command our naval forces in Europe. Destroyers were sent at once to assist in the antisubmarine effort.

When it was decided to send armies and supplies to France, our naval operations became confronted with the serious and complex problem of transporting them safely. At the time, the navy did not have ships suitable for either troop or cargo transport. All such government ships were under the newly created Shipping Board, which, though it probably understood peacetime merchant shipping operations far better than the navy did, had little knowledge of wartime operation. Since troops and supplies would have to be carried to France in merchant ships rather than in combatant ships, the Shipping Board assumed it would control the transportation; whereas the navy, responsible for all ships at sea, knew that proper safeguard could be assured only by the navy's control of every detail. Although the lives of our soldiers and the important cargoes were far too valuable to trust to merchant shipping methods, which had previously proved utterly unsafe in the submarine-infested waters of the war zone, the Shipping Board of that time nevertheless believed the problem theirs rather than the navy's.

The first clash regarding control of our war zone shipping occurred almost as soon as war was declared and before General Pershing set sail for France. As soon as it was decided to send troops and supplies across, the navy immediately began to plan safe transport. Since we did not have ships suitable for the task, the first step was to obtain the sixteen large German passenger and cargo ships that had been interred in our ports early in the World War and later seized by our Treasury Department when we entered the hostilities. The Shipping Board expected those ships to be turned over to it for general shipping purposes, while the navy Department wanted them to meet important war needs. At the time, I was Assistant to the Aide for Materiel in Operations [Captain Josiah S. McKean], and the matter of acquiring ships for the navy, whether of combatant or other types, was the responsibility of our office. I was at once on a collision course with the Shipping Board, which sought to give the seized German ships to the merchant marine service rather than to the navy for overseas transportation.

Inasmuch as the country at large still had a more peacetime than wartime conception of what transportation problems would be in the war area, it is probable that the seized German ships would have been turned over to the Shipping Board had it not been that General Pershing and his staff were being assembled in Washington at just that time. On the staff was my boyhood friend and brother-in-law, Colonel John M. Palmer, who was staying at my home for his few days in Washington and with whom I discussed the problem of transporting our armies and military supplies to France. John understood the difficulties and dangers in sending General Pershing's great expeditionary armies across in merchant ships that were untrained and unversed in war operations at sea. He realized that unless the navy, which was trained for such work, took complete charge of the transportation, our country would face horrible disasters. So fearful was he that he asked me to give him a memorandum on the subject to hand to General Pershing, who was, of course, vitally concerned that our troops and supplies reach France safely.

I prepared the memorandum on the Sunday before General Pershing sailed, and as soon as the general had read it, he indicated to the War Department the necessity of the navy controlling the transport service to France. What in particular was done by the War Department, I never knew, but in a few days all the seized German ships were turned over to the navy, and they became the nucleus from which grew the enormous transportation service that worked so splendidly for the United States throughout the war.

"Operations" continued working on the navy's antisubmarine effort and immediately sent every available destroyer across to help. But we were not entirely sufficient to meet the emergency and therefore accumulated every yacht, tug, and other small vessel suitable for the work, and laid out a plan for building as many destroyers and 110-foot sub chasers as could be constructed.

An Admiral's Yarn

Thus began a huge expansion program for the navy, which, although it entailed no building of heavy ships, ultimately increased our naval strength from a 65,000-man navy of heavy fighting ships to a 600,000-man navy that could perform every type of operation called for by the World War.[159]

By July 1917, the general plan the navy would be obliged to follow in the war was fairly clear. At that time, I made up my mind that I might go to sea in the fall when I had completed one year's duty on shore. But it was not to be, for just as I made that decision, the Chief of Naval Operations sent word that the Chief of the Bureau of Navigation (which handles many matters, including the personnel of the navy) wanted me to take charge of the Officer Personnel Division. Admiral [William S.] Benson honored me by saying that, though he wished to retain me in his own office, Admiral [Leigh C.] Palmer, then Chief of the Bureau, needed me badly. My orders came the next day and I took over, armed with a memorandum of the naval plan and a list of the many vessels that would be added.[160]

I relieved [Captain Thomas Senn], who had been ordered to sea. He had worked hard to complete the stationing of officers in accordance with the navy's previously prepared mobilization plan, and when he turned over the office to me, he said, "There is little to do in this office immediately. The navy is completely mobilized in accordance with the plan, and every officer has been sent to his station for war." When I asked what plans had been made to detail officers for the multitudinous additional activities about to be started, he told me that no officers were left; everyone had been assigned in the mobilization plan.[161]

Having in my pocket the names of the sixteen large German ships that had to be manned almost immediately for transports, and knowing that we soon would be obliged to man many more ships of that type as well as hundreds of new destroyers, sub-chasers, converted yachts, tugs, etc., I was stunned by the knowledge that the supply of naval officers was exhausted and it was my job to provide the many thousands more required if the Navy's program for winning the war was to be effective.

This was the situation that confronted us when we entered the World War. Our great fighting fleet had to be kept constantly ready, and new naval forces, many times larger, had to be created to meet the submarine and transport problems of the time.

Perhaps of all the problems that I ever experienced, the officer problem of the World War was the most difficult to solve as well as the one most vital to our country, since upon its solution much of the navy's success depended. It would have been difficult enough for peacetime operation of ships, but to furnish officers who would be prepared not only for such duties but also for duties in

War

war was infinitely more difficult—our great naval efforts in the World War were to be so different from those usual to a navy, and the old laws and training methods had to be utilized in an entirely unanticipated way to accomplish this. An utter hodgepodge of laws and training facilities had to be combined to form an accurately working machine that would "grind out" officers as fast as needed for a navy multiplying rapidly in size and hastily acquiring new duties to be performed.

To create such a machine, a careful estimation of the situation had to be made, so I listed all the calls for officers that were then apparent. Realizing that this need would not only continue throughout the war but would also constantly increase, I was appalled. Making note of every law under which officers could be appointed and every facility we had for training them, I tried to combine laws and training facilities to turn out enough properly trained officers to meet the demand, but it seemed impossible. Day and night I worked on the problem and lost much sleep over it. Then one night while tossing and worrying, the idea for a solution occurred to me. I jumped out of bed and made a note of it lest I not remember the details in the morning, and then promptly went to sleep for my first night's rest in over a week.

As I look back, it should not have been so difficult to arrive at the solutions. The answer was, merely, rather than prepare every new officer for *every* rank and duty in the navy, we should use our previously highly trained officers for duties requiring all-around naval skill, high rank, and great responsibility, and use the additional temporary officers in lower ranks where a minimum of skill, knowledge, experience, and responsibility was required. Thus, by familiarizing officers of lower rank with a particular task of a higher ranking officer, and then requiring the lower ranking officer to take up that task when learned, we could develop officers trained for one duty only, to help replace officers who were trained in every line. This would enable us to release higher ranking regular officers from the fighting fleet for duties in the war zone. Such a plan, of course, meant that our battle fleet would ultimately lose most of its older and best trained officers, which would tend to weaken it. But, since we would not be called upon to fight as long as the British fleet remained undefeated, I felt the risk was warranted to meet the immediate and far more urgent demand. I therefore prepared the plan along that line.

It took many days to work out all the details, after which came the problem of "selling" the idea to the Bureau of Navigation, the Chief of Naval Operations, and the Navy Department. Fortunately my "estimate" proved the case to them. Success, however, would depend upon the fleet's acceptance of the understudy

An Admiral's Yarn

and agreement to carry out the idea. I was sent to the fleet to explain it and to learn the reaction of the fleet's officers.

That visit was outstanding in importance. At the time, nearly the entire U.S. Fleet was concentrated in Huntington Bay, Long Island. It was such a tremendous gathering of our country's naval power that a mere commander like myself could not but be awed by it. The fleet commander in chief [Henry Mayo][162] had been advised of my arrival and sent a boat to meet me. His greeting was far from cordial, and because I had known him since my Academy days, I was scarcely prepared for his gruff opening remark—"Laning, I know what you are here for. You want to take more officers from this fleet; and I tell you now, it can't be done. I have been ordered to keep the fleet ready to fight and you have not left me enough officers to do it. You might as well know right now that no more officers can be taken from me." Of course that remark was a terrible blow and I feared for my plan, which had to be explained to the admiral in any event. I then asked to be allowed to talk over my plan with him. "Of course you may," said he. "Take dinner with me and talk all you want."

That evening proved important to both the United States and its navy, for the admiral was not only enthusiastic over the "win the war" program planned for the navy but also of the place the fleet had in it, of officers that would be required, and of what had to be done to provide officers, etc. After I had explained the situation as well as I could, I said, "Admiral, merely keeping the fleet ready to fight will not be enough to win this war, for as long as the great British navy exists, our fighting fleet will not be called on. But, although our fleet will probably not have to fight, what the navy does toward winning the war, depends almost entirely on the battle fleet. If it can keep itself ready to fight on a few week's notice, and at the same time train the thousands of officers and tens of thousands of men needed to carry on our 'win the war' activities, the United States and our Allies will win. As I see it, winning the war is up to the fleet, whether it has to fight or not."

When I rose to leave him, the admiral rose too, put his hand on my shoulder and walked to the cabin door with me, saying as he did so, "Go to bed, Laning. Don't worry, and get some sleep, for the fleet will do its part. We will hold a conference on it tomorrow afternoon."

I will never forget that conference. The admiral kept me in his cabin [of the flagship *Pennsylvania*] until the attendees were assembled, and then, taking me by the arm, led me in. Never before had I seen such a gathering of high-ranking officers of the navy. Not only were all the flag officers of our great fleet there but also all the captains and executive officers. So much rank in one place rather staggered me, and as the attitude seemed as hostile as the admiral's had been when I reported to him, the sinking feeling returned to me. Nevertheless, the admiral marched me in, and when we stood before the gathering, he said, "Gentlemen, Laning has come from the Navy Department to explain something of the navy's plan for the war. When he reported to me last night, and before I knew those plans, I told him he could not get any more officers from this fleet. After he had talked with me for over three hours, I changed my mind. However, unless you officers come to that conclusion and will agree to work for Laning's plan, the navy can do little toward winning the war. I want to know if you think the fleet can do what is proposed. Laning, tell this conference what you told me last night."

I first called their attention to the fact that our navy had only a secondary part in the war and that the great task ahead was to overcome Germany's submarines and carry our troops and supplies to France safely. Merely keeping the fleet ready to fight would not bring real United States power into contact with the enemy, and such contact could not be made unless the plan being suggested was carried out. At any rate, I could feel the attitude changing as I talked, and when I closed by saying, "If the United States Navy does its part to win the war, it will be by carrying out the unusual tasks that this particular war calls on the navy to perform. Whether the navy does that or merely maintains a ready fleet depends on what you officers of the fleet are willing to do. I have explained the situation; now it is up to you."

No sooner had I said that than the second in command of the fleet jumped to his feet and said, "By God, my part of the fleet can do it." Immediately the other admirals and captains followed his lead. Never have I seen such unanimity or such intensity of purpose to make a plan work than was shown that day by the leaders of our fighting fleet. They were out to win the war.

Having sold the plan "lock, stock, and barrel" to the fleet, I hurried back to Washington to report the result and to put the plan into operation. This was not easy, because of the many laws to observe and the activities involved. However, the various difficulties were overcome, the various parts assembled, and our machine for grinding our officers started.

I will not try to describe the detail of the plan. It was too complicated. We sought officer candidates from everywhere—from not only the navy but outside of it, giving preference to men with education comparable to that received at the Naval Academy. These men were then given three month's of intensive instruction in naval subjects at schools established at the Naval Academy and elsewhere. They were then hurried to ships from training in actual service. Every ship in home waters was filled with them, and each took the training job seriously and with great energy.

An Admiral's Yarn

To this day, I continue to be amazed at what the fleet accomplished, for it not only kept itself ever ready for sea and to fight, but at the same time very quickly turned out officers fairly well qualified in a particular duty. Initially, all individuals considered eligible for duty as officers were accepted, and consequently, the growing number of personnel compelled continuous redistribution of grades and ranks. Promotion became very rapid, and we always kept our best prepared officers at the top. Each ship continuously reported, by name and duty, the qualified officers who could be detached, and my office soon became a clearing house for placement of officers. Before long we had all the officers we needed.

While our greatest difficulty with the early ships was filling officer requirements, it was the rush to get our great armies across the ocean that consumed our energies with later ships. Our first call was for officers needed on the seized German transports. Fortunately they would not be sent at once, as the Army and American industry needed time to train and equip the soldiers those ships would carry.[163] We had the transports ready as soon as the troops and supplies were ready, and once the transport service started, it grew and grew. I suspect that had we foreseen what it would become we might have given up in despair, but thanks to the training work of the fleet, the larger the transport service became, the better prepared we became to provide officers and men. The transport demand was not the only one we were required to meet successfully. There was also a need for officers for our hurriedly built sub-chasers and destroyers, of which there were several hundred. We also were called on to man yachts, tugs, and small craft of all kinds as well as cargo ships by the dozen, many built by the Shipping Board to meet the emergency. We provided officers for the ships that laid the great antisubmarine barrage across the North Sea as well as the railroad battery of heavy guns sent by the navy to the Western front. We prepared to man the antisubmarine "Eagle Boats" as fast as they were built and provided officers for seven old British battleships that were loaned for our transport service.[164]

Looking back, the plan used by the navy to provide additional officers for the World War worked perfectly. Not only did we supply efficient officers for every naval project that arose, but under the plan we could go on supplying them for years, should the war continue. But it did not, ending just about the time the Officer Personnel Division had reached its stride and seemed capable of providing officers forever.

Although my job in the department was important, I felt that in war a naval officer should be at sea. Hence, as soon as it was apparent that our officer plan was working satisfactorily and required only its administration, I again began to plan for sea duty. I knew I would not be entitled to a sea job of great importance such as the one I had on shore; but even so, I abhorred the idea of not meeting up with the enemy. Therefore, as soon as I knew the officer problem was well in hand, I asked permission to be sent to sea—but was not allowed to go. On the contrary, I was told not to ask again, for not only must I continue to run officer personnel for the time being, but when the chief of the Bureau went to sea, I would still be serving there.

One day a ray of hope that I might get near the hostilities appeared when the Chief of the Bureau said, "Laning, it may interest you to know that in seeking three officers to send to London for the planning division of the British Admiralty, Operations has asked me to permit you to be one of them." I was delighted and promptly said to the chief, "That group is to sail from New York tomorrow night and I can turn over this office immediately and join it." "Oh, no you can't," said he, "for you are not to go. I told Operations that our Navy Department needs you much more than the British Admiralty does, so you will stay here. But," he added, "I am telling you of the request only because I thought you might like to know about it." I simply cannot describe my bitter disappointment.

The war dragged on. When I had been in the department over a year, the Assistant Chief of the Bureau was allowed to go to sea and I was assigned to his job. Then, when the war was nearing its end, the Chief of the Bureau went to sea too, and I became Acting Chief, a duty that I performed for about five months.

One might think our personnel troubles would have ended with the end of the war, but they did not, for we were not able to return to our previous status. Our navy was vastly different from what it had been before. We were adding hundreds of new destroyers and submarines to it and had launched a building program of capital ships that would give the United States the greatest navy in the world. During the war, Congress had increased the authorized personnel strength from the 65,000 men allowed before the war to 135,000. But, even though this new number would not be sufficient to man the substantial increase in navy materiel, there were very powerful influences at work to force us back to 65,000 men. Because of this, the Bureau found itself in a quandary as to the number of personnel to recommend to Congress. Should we recommend that the navy again be made completely unprepared for war as it would be with 65,000 men? Should we suggest an authorized strength of only 135,000 men, which was certainly not sufficient to man the ships Congress was building, or should we prepare to man all the ships being built? Congress itself had not given a clue as to the navy it intended to keep in readiness; it had authorized the building of ships but without plans for manning them. This left the Bureau in

An Admiral's Yarn

the position of having to submit a plan for manning ships without knowing the strength of the navy that Congress would provide.

Under the circumstances, it was difficult to prepare a personnel plan, to say the least, but I was to be appointed Chief of Bureau and had to submit one. I knew of the powerful move being made to return the navy to its 65,000-man pre-war status, but I dared not base the plan on 65,000 men or even on the 135,000 already authorized, since the latter number would not be sufficient for the navy being built.

Realizing that the size of the navy our country should maintain in readiness was something Congress, not the Navy Department or an individual like myself, should decide on, I determined, if called on, to tell the Congressional Committee exactly the personnel required to man all the combatant ships that Congress had authorized and then leave the decision to Congress.[165] In the United States we did not then, and do not even now, measure naval strength by our readiness to fight but rather by the types and numbers of our ships, whether or not those ships are manned.

Since unmanned ships are of little use in war, I felt the responsibility of Congress to man them was just as great as its responsibility to build them and that it must be made fully cognizant of that. I decided to make the Congress aware of this during the hearings, if possible.

It was no easy matter to bring the situation home to the Naval Committee, for certain powerful influences were at work to prevent my doing so. The questions I was to be asked were to be answered only yes or no—answers that would make it appear that in the opinion of the personnel bureau, the navy should be allowed only 65,000 men. Fortunately I was able to avoid the traps set for me, and when a member of the committee insisted on hearing what I wanted to tell them, I was allowed to explain the whole matter and show that if the building plan were carried through, it would take over 200,000 men to man the ships—a considerably larger number than the 135,000 men certain high civil authorities wanted for the navy.

I think my report must have been fairly convincing, because several members of the committee rushed to me after it was over and said that their responsibility to naval personnel had been made clear to them and that, of course, the navy would get the men to man all the ships being provided. However, Congress failed to do this. The powerful 65,000-man "bloc" worked so hard to break down my report that Congress refused to authorize the 200,000. However, we were allowed to retain our 135,000 strength, which was better than 65,000.

In presenting the navy's actual personnel problem to the Congressional Committee, I fully realized I was making myself "persona non grata" with certain political powers, and as I had otherwise made myself unpopular because I insisted on the personnel bureau being conducted on naval standards rather than political ones, I knew I would not be made Chief of the Bureau of Navigation. The appointment of this man was no great shock to me, however, for I would not play politics to get advancement, and I longed to be at sea again after over two years on shore. I was asked by Admiral [Charles] Plunkett, recently ordered to command our then-huge destroyer force, to become his chief of staff, and I accepted at once. At that time I had the temporary rank of captain, but as soon as the peacetime naval strength had been established at 135,000, it created a vacancy for me as a permanent captain, to which rank I was appointed shortly after taking over my new duty.

XXXI

The First Transatlantic Flight

ABOUT THE FIRST OF APRIL 1919, I reported on the *Rochester*, Destroyer Force flagship, at the Navy Yard, Brooklyn,[166] for duty as Chief of Staff. At that time, one hundred fifty destroyers were in commission, and nearly all that had been in Europe during the war had now returned. Our East Coast ports and Navy yards were so crowded that we wondered how it could be possible to employ so many people during peacetime.

I did not wonder for long, because no sooner had I taken over the new duty than I was directed to prepare a plan for the Destroyer Force's participation in the U.S. Navy's attempt to fly the first airplane across the Atlantic. When I received the order, I thought the complete flight plan would be prepared in the Navy Department and that the destroyers' only participation would be to police the route and lend assistance if needed. However, I soon learned differently, for instead of merely having a part in an operation planned by the department, the Destroyer Force commander was to be in charge of the attempt, and instead of merely policing the route, he was to prepare all plans for the flight and then follow through on execution of them. Of course, aviators would ready the planes and fly them, but all other details were to be worked out by the Destroyer Force.

Trans-ocean flying in 1919 differed vastly from such flying today.[167] The equipment now used for long distance flying over the sea was almost unknown then. There were no radio direction finders, and flight courses were obtained from the magnetic compasses then available. Because it was nearly impossible for a plane flying over the sea to ascertain the exact effect of the air currents, its probable position on a long sea flight could only be estimated, and the

An Admiral's Yarn

calculation could be far from correct in both direction and distance covered. To add to the difficulty, navigating planes by celestial observation was new, and Lieutenant Commander (later Admiral) Byrd was only then developing the "bubble sextant" that made it possible to accurately calculate an airplane's altitude.[168]

Because planes could not accurately compute over-sea navigation, the Destroyer Force provided navigation marks for them. Many other requirements were also filled by the force, the most important being the distance that the plane's fuel capacity would allow. There were few planes in the world carrying sufficient fuel to fly from Newfoundland to Ireland, even if aided by a strong following wind all the way—and there were none that could fly the distance under adverse wind conditions.

Since there was no way to predict winds that would be encountered on a trans-ocean flight, it was evident that if airplanes were to fly across the North Atlantic, they could do so only by "hopping" from point to point within their flight range.

Even so, there were few planes with sufficient flying radius to make the successive hops—the only ones being the large NC type planes of the U.S. Navy. Four planes of that type had just been acquired, and it was decided to use them in the attempt; it fell to me to prepare the planes for the flight. The care and thought needed in overseas flight preparation in 1919 was indeed complicated and intense. Under existing conditions, distances, points of touching, weather and winds that might be encountered, navigational assistance, rescue, fuel, supplies, bases for the planes and personnel at ports, and many other matters had to be provided for. That I might cover all those points properly, I had to learn from the aviators and then base all my decisions on that knowledge.

It took several weeks to prepare an "estimate of the situation," conclude what should be done, and prepare orders to carry out the work; I was obliged to contact the Navy Department for all information necessary to complete the plan.

The first step was to learn precisely what the planes could do and then to suit the other elements of the flight to those limitations and capabilities. As the problem was utterly new, even to the aviators, and involved ramifications never before considered, the estimate I made was quite the longest and most complex I had ever prepared. Just as the estimate was long and complex, so were the decisions reached for carrying out the order. That order followed the form of our campaign orders in war, but only in form, since almost every task under the plan was new in both kind and purpose.

The First Transatlantic Flight

Nevertheless, though what needed to be done was very different from anything the Navy had attempted before, the order had to be completely foolproof; every man connected with the flight, whether at sea, in the air, or on the ground, must know exactly what was to be done and then do it.

I will not dwell on our order for the flight which covered the entire plan. It was widely published at the time and is doubtless easily available to anyone interested. The planes were to fly from New York to Trepassey Bay, Newfoundland; to Ponta Delgada, Azores; to Lisbon, Portugal; and to Plymouth, England. Ships to serve as bases for the planes were provided at each stopping place along the entire route. Destroyers were stationed every fifty miles to guide the planes and lend assistance if necessary, and battleships were stationed in various parts of the North Atlantic to gather and report weather data by radio. The route chosen was based partly on the length of the "hops," but particularly on the weather that years of observation had shown could be expected in the North Atlantic during the month of the scheduled flight. From that data, we determined that if we started the flight when good flying weather was assured for the first half of the distance to the Azores, the balance of the trip through the almost invariably good June weather near the islands and on to Lisbon would allow the planes to fly the entire trip with a minimum of weather-related trouble. Under the plan, weather risks seemed almost negligible.

There was a short delay in starting from Trepassey, because of ice, fog, and weather conditions there, but when permitted, the flight started. Four planes were scheduled, but one was unable to lift its heavy load of fuel, leaving only three to take off. When they did, the *Rochester*, carrying the Destroyer Force Commander in charge of the flight, left Ponta Delgada en route to Lisbon to be there when the planes arrived. As we proceeded toward that port, we were kept informed by radio as the planes passed each destroyer along the route. The flight went so well all during the night that we became rather confident that the three planes would reach Ponta Delgada. However, as the planes neared the Azores, we began to receive reports of bad weather from the destroyers—and in the very area where high winds and fog were almost unheard of. One by one, contact with checkpoints was lost in the thick weather, and by the time the *Rochester* reached Lisbon, all communications with the airplanes had ceased.

For the next few hours we were under a tremendous strain on the *Rochester*, and when sufficient time had elapsed for the planes to have reached some part of the Azores, we began to fear that not only had the flight failed, but infinitely worse, the six brave men in each of the planes may have been lost.

The first break in the horror we were suffering was some hours reaching us, but finally a message came saying that the plane commanded by Lieutenant

An Admiral's Yarn

(now Captain) P.N.L. Bellinger, having run into fog and rain when nearing the precipitous islands, had landed on the water rather than risk hitting a mountain in the fog, and in coming down on what appeared from aloft to be a smooth sea had found the water so rough that it carried away a wing of the airplane.[169] No land could be seen and the plane was badly wrecked. The aviators saw little chance of being saved, but at that point, fortunately, a tramp steamer, without radio, appeared, took our men aboard, and carried them to a nearby port.

The saving of "Pat" Bellinger's crew gave us heart, and we were rejoicing when a second message came reporting that NC-4, under Lieutenant A.C. Read, had arrived at Horta, plane and crew intact. Knowing he was among the islands, Read had also come down, fortunately in the lee of the one on which Horta is situated. By taxiing his plane Read had succeeded in taking it to the city under its own power, and when the weather cleared sufficiently, he flew it on to Ponta Delgada.

Two of the starting planes were now accounted for; but the third, commanded by Lieutenant J.H. Towers (now Rear Admiral at the Bureau of Aeronautics),[170] was still unreported and its whereabouts unknown. Quickly, all destroyers and other naval craft in the vicinity of the Azores were started on a systematic search. We did not know whether it was short of or beyond the islands or whether it had passed them to the right or left, and the search was like hunting for a needle in a haystack. Nevertheless, it continued.

Into the third day we were almost frantic over not having the slightest clue, when a radio message announced that a plane was in sight, on the water, approaching Ponta Delgada. It proved to be Towers' plane approaching its official destination.

In the thick weather, it had flown to the right of and well past the Azores. It landed, when its fuel gave out, striking heavy seas that carried away a pontoon on one side. Then, with the character of a true sea epic, in that rough water, with the men perched on the wing on the side of the good pontoon to keep the plane from turning over and sinking, Towers and his crew utilized the wind and the plane's rudder to make the plane sail backward, and they navigated to Ponta Delgada where, just as it entered the port, the plane turned over and sank.

The navigating skill and seamanship shown by Towers and his five men during the trying three days that it took to bring the crippled plane to Ponta Delgada should never be forgotten, for they are splendid examples of the ability and resourcefulness of our naval men. With nearly nothing to eat, with no fresh water other than that in the radiator of the plane, and fearful the plane would capsize and sink any instant, those men succeeded in bringing the plane to its

The First Transatlantic Flight

proper destination. The story of that adventure, found in the annals of naval history, is well worth reading.

With all the fliers safe in Ponta Delgada, completing the flight across the ocean became again the major task of Admiral Plunkett and his staff, so we set about to finish it with one plane intact. We established the line of ships from Ponta Delgada to Lisbon. "Putty" Read made his plane ready, and with the *Rochester* in Lisbon to receive it, NC-4 started the last leg of the flight to Europe.

With only one plane remaining out of the four that had left New York, those of us in charge of the flight watched with intensity the NC-4's progress from the Azores to Lisbon, as successive destroyers along the route reported it. To me, that day was the longest I have ever known; the plane left Ponta Delgada at dawn and did not reach Lisbon until the sun was going down. We felt very hopeful when the last sea station reported the plane passing, but the next hour dragged horribly as we strained our eyes for a glimpse of the plane coming up the Tagus River. When at last we sighted it on the horizon, we were still fearful that something might happen before it could land at Lisbon. On it came, slowly rounding into the wind and alighting on the water like a bird—the NC-4 completed the first successful air flight across the Atlantic Ocean.

That the first crossing would have an important place in world history is perhaps the reason why the U.S. Navy made such a tremendous and costly effort. When the *Rochester* arrived in Lisbon, we found that the eyes of the world were so focused on the crossing that all the great newspapers and press associations had rushed representatives to Lisbon from the Peace Conference in Paris to report the completion of the flight. Those representatives and the leading Portuguese officials were all on the *Rochester* to witness the plane's arrival and to welcome and congratulate Read and his crew on their great accomplishment.

As soon as the NC-4 was safely moored, boats brought the fliers to the *Rochester* where they were received with great acclaim. Portuguese officials and officers who had planned and supervised the flight gathered around them, and soon Portugal's Premier, representing the President, who was too ill to come on board himself, stepped forward and pinned on each one of us the most cherished of Portugal's decorations, the order of the Avis, which had originated during the Crusades.[171]

That night was a gay one in Lisbon, with all the people of the city joining in celebration of the historic event. Somewhat off the usual tourist path, Lisbon at that time was not well known to Americans, but we found it charming, interesting and hospitable, and especially suited for the celebration held that night.

An Admiral's Yarn

It almost surpassed Monte Carlo and other Riviera cities in attractions and gaiety—wine, women and song, gambling, and hilarity. All of its great clubs, created as they had been out of royal palaces when the revolution [1910] changed Portugal from a Kingdom to a Republic, were opened to welcome us, and a truly gala night was experienced.

Although NC-4 had flown successfully from the mainland of the United States to the mainland of Europe, the flight was not yet officially completed. The scheduled terminus was Plymouth, England, and so, even though the plane was across, we still had to continue the flight as planned. While NC-4 was making itself ready for that last hop, the *Rochester* hurried to Plymouth. We would have arrived there after NC-4 except for trouble the plane had en route, forcing it down at Vigo, Spain, where it remained overnight. Because of that delay, the *Rochester* reached Plymouth about ten o'clock in the morning and NC-4 arrived shortly after noon.

When it became evident that the *Rochester* would reach Plymouth first, we sent radio messages to the Lord Mayor [J.B. Brown] and to the admiral and general in command there, inviting them to the *Rochester* to meet the fliers when they arrived on board.

That gathering to welcome Read and his crew was unique. The first British official to arrive on board was the Lord Mayor, wearing the official robes of his office, followed by the town clerk in his robes, and then by a most attractive lady whom we all assumed to be the Lord Mayor's wife and to whom we were accordingly attentive. A few minutes later the British admiral and general arrived in full regalia to complete the official reception party.

In the interim, NC-4 was approaching the station with destroyers reporting its progress. When the plane reached Plymouth, we brought its personnel to the *Rochester* where they were once more officially received, this time at the very end of the first transatlantic flight. We had quite a bounteous luncheon for them and the official party. Then we all went ashore, landing at "Plymouth Rock," which marked the place from which the Pilgrim Fathers had embarked on the *Mayflower* and sailed centuries before to establish Plymouth Colony.

Having the Americans who made the first successful transatlantic flight step on English soil at the very spot from which their Pilgrim forefathers had left was a perfect ending for the historic crossing. The crowd assembled there was enormous—apparently all of Plymouth and the surrounding country were either at the landing place or along the route the party followed to the City Hall where the fliers were officially welcomed.

Plymouth is not New York City, and the crowd that lined the route was not like the one in later years [1927] that cheered Lindbergh in his ticker-tape

The First Transatlantic Flight

parade up Broadway to New York's City Hall after his successful solo flight across. But as demonstrations then went, the one in Plymouth was one that I marveled at and personally will never forget.

When luncheon was over, the official party, consisting of the aviators, the Lord Mayor's Party, the army and navy representatives of Great Britain, and Admiral Plunkett and his staff, went ashore in the admiral's barge, from which we stepped out onto England's "Plymouth Rock." An area for the party had been roped off, and cars stood ready to take us to City Hall. Quite naturally, the official British parties took the first cars to lead the parade and then came the cars for the aviators. Behind the aviators was a car for Admiral Plunkett, and following that were cars for the remainder of the party. The Lord Mayor, the British admiral and general, and the aviators all took their proper cars, but when the one for Admiral Plunkett drove up, the lady who had come to the *Rochester* with the Lord Mayor quickly stepped into it and directed the driver to keep right behind the aviators, thereby obliging Admiral Plunkett to take the next car. When the parade started, the lone lady in the car ahead of our admiral and next behind the aviators, became a cynosure for all eyes, since she seemed to belong to the aviators.

As the aviators passed, the crowd set up a tremendous cheering, which the aviators acknowledged with becoming sailor-man meekness. While the cheers were not for her at all, the lady following them seemed to take the enthusiasm to herself and stood up in her car, bowing right and left to the great throng. It was as perfect an example of "stealing the show" as I have ever seen, and I could not but admire the ability and astuteness of the lady in the way she did it. Believing she was the wife of the Lord Mayor, I thought to myself that under her guidance it was little wonder that he had been elected Mayor of Plymouth.

Slowly the parade made its way to City Hall, where a great reception was given the aviators, and, after which, we Americans returned to our ship.

Talking over the events of the day at dinner that night with Admiral Plunkett, I said to him, "Admiral, it is little wonder the Lord Mayor of Plymouth was elected, with a wife like his. From the way she stole the show, even from the aviators, I am sure she could elect any man to any office. But is it not strange, Admiral, that the woman is an American? I looked out for her on the ship while waiting for the plane and during lunch, and I noticed that she has exactly the charm and speech of our southern girls. Still, I must say, she did not show particular interest in the Lord Mayor. As a matter of fact, she often mimicked and made fun of him in that delightful southern drawl of hers." "Humph," said the admiral, "you took her to be the Lord Mayor's wife, did you? Well so did I for a time, until she accused me of not recognizing a girl I had once taken to a hop in

An Admiral's Yarn

Annapolis. Then looking at her closely I realized she was the young lady I hand known as Nancy Langhorne, now married to Waldorf Astor, son of Lord Astor."[172]

At that time, the original Lord Astor was still living, and his son Waldorf was the House of Commons member of Plymouth. Later, when Lord Astor died, the son fleeted up to the title and left the House of Commons to take his seat in the House of Lords. His wife, Nancy Langhorne Astor, then Lady Astor, was chosen to fill the vacancy he left in the House of Commons. She has been a member ever since, and judging from what I have read about her in the newspapers, she is a leading member. I am not surprised at that. Anyone who could turn the acclaim for that first transatlantic flight into an ovation for herself as she did, certainly has what it takes to be a good politician, and apparently she is quite as able in politics as she is a very charming woman.

Having succeeded in flying a plane from the United States to England, the navy officers felt our worries were over for the time being, and we had only to enjoy life until returning home to take up our regular duties once more.

There remained much to coordinate in the celebration—the British Government wished to show its appreciation and had arranged to give honor to the accomplishment in London, so the next day the aviators, Admiral Plunkett, and his staff went there.

Since the demonstrations in London were for the fliers rather than for the admiral and his staff, we avoided attending them as much as possible, leaving the aviators to be the official guests in London. The admiral arranged for himself and his staff to stop at the Savoy Hotel, which, because wartime regulations were still in force, was a sort of headquarters for high naval and military officers visiting London. At the Savoy we were given a wonderful suite at small cost, and then set out to see all that we could of London.

At that time, Admiral Knapp, who had relieved Admiral Sims as Commander, U.S. Naval Forces in Europe, was in Paris at the Peace Conference. Having learned that Admiral Plunkett and his staff would be in London with the fliers, he directed that his official automobile be turned over to us for the London visit. The Cadillac was a seven-passenger car equipped with a chauffeur who knew London well. It was a wonderful opportunity to see the city, especially since our uniforms opened nearly every door in London to us.

We set about sightseeing in a big way, but Admiral Plunkett wanted to get to Paris, possibly to take advantage of peace conditions to see where his naval railroad battery had operated in war, but more probably to be in Paris where the Peace Conference was. He arranged to go to France as soon as the splendid welcome in London would permit. He applied to the British Air Ministry for a plane to take him and his chief of staff from London to Paris the morning after our last London function, but during the night, before we were to leave London, such a storm broke that the Air Ministry was unwilling to risk flying the admiral to Paris. Inasmuch as the admiral was in a hurry, he decided to go by train and boat, at once, leaving me in London with the rest of his staff and turning over to us the official automobile of the Commander in Chief, U.S. Naval Forces in Europe.

XXXII

London and Paris

LIVING AT THE SAVOY HOTEL and having an official automobile at our service gave us a rare opportunity to see London. It helped also to be on official duty and in uniform at all times, because the uniform of the U.S. Navy was well known in London at the end of the war. Our appearance opened doors everywhere, inviting every possible attention and courtesy from British officials.

Under such auspicious conditions, we visited Hampton Court, Westminster Abbey, the Tower of London, the Parliament, and many other nationally supervised points of interest in London. But of all there was to see, I think the British Museum attracted us the most, and we decided to leave the hotel early one morning and devote an entire day to a visit there.

While we were eating breakfast that morning, the headwaiter hurried to me and said that I was wanted on the telephone by our naval headquarters. When I answered, an officer asked if we had planned to use the official car that morning. When I told him yes, and we intended to go to the British Museum in it at nine o'clock, he cried out, "Captain, don't you know that today is the King's birthday and he is to be honored, as of yore, by the 'trooping of the colors'?" I told the officer that having read the newspapers we knew of the King's birthday, but that we were weary of parades and had decided it would be a good time to visit the museum.

"Great heavens," said the officer, "don't you realize that the King's birthday is a gala day in the British Empire? This one is particularly so because it will be celebrated by the 'trooping of the colors'—the first since the war began—and it will also celebrate the end of the war." Then he added, "This trooping will be

An Admiral's Yarn

the most elaborate ever held, and because of the tremendous crowd expected, it will be held in Hyde Park. You will miss the opportunity of a lifetime if you do not see it. The King has but one birthday a year, and on that day only may the trooping of the colors be performed. Because this is the first in five years and celebrates the end of the war, it will be the greatest trooping of the century. Why bypass it for the British Museum?"

Realizing the truth in this conversation, I replied that of course we would attend the trooping and would be glad to provide transportation to it for as many as possible from headquarters.

When we left the Savoy, the seven-passenger car held eight officers in uniform, and of course the driver, for a total of nine people. As we neared Buckingham Palace on our way to the Park, we found such a huge throng waiting to see the Royal family as they left for Hyde Park that we thought we could go no farther in the car. However, as soon as the police saw an official automobile filled with U.S. naval officers, a way was opened to us through the crowds. When we neared Hyde Park we encountered a far greater crowd, so large in fact that the car could not enter, so we decided to walk to a point near the parade ground.

Out of the car we were little better off, for the dense masses of people lined up, dozens deep, along both sides of a road that paralleled the park's boundary and which we had to cross to be near the "trooping." While we were discussing our situation, a tall officer from headquarters, standing on something that made him visible to the police, held up his hand and called out to one of them, "I say, officer, how do we get to the reserved seats?" That query was sufficient. A way through the crowd was opened for us, and we were to follow that roadway right to our seats. The only thing we had wished to do was cross the road, and we were rather embarrassed to be directed to seats for which we did not have tickets.

Nevertheless, we started along, but as soon as we came to a curve in the road, out of sight of the accommodating police officers, we hurried to the other side of the road where the crowds opened to let us pass. Then, seeing the huge assemblage around the parade grounds, where both infantry and cavalry regiments were lined up, we headed in that direction.

As the prospects for actually seeing the "trooping" seemed nil, we held another quick consultation and decided not to waste any more time on it but to go to the British Museum. However, when we tried to retrace our footsteps and return to the car, we found ourselves still blocked by the great crowd. Once again our tall officer went into action and, over the heads of the huge assemblage, caught the eye of the British officer in charge of the troops on the roadway and cried out to him the "open sesame" he had used before, "How do we get to the

London and Paris

reserved seats?" The officer opened a passage through the crowd for us, and then the Army officer added, "This officer with me is going right to the reserved seats and will escort you there."

Once more we were in the embarrassing predicament of not having tickets for reserved seats and certainly did not want to be refused admission when we reached them. At that moment the police, the troops, and the great crowd galvanized to "attention" as a tremendous clatter of hoofs could be heard coming along the roadway. We officers, of course, stood at attention too, and looking at the approaching cavalcade, we saw it was the King and his party on their way to the "trooping."

They made a remarkable picture. Everyone was in full uniform and mounted on a beautifully equipped horse. Heading the cavalcade were King George and the Prince of Wales, (now Duke of Windsor) riding abreast. Next behind rode the King's brother, the Duke of Connaught. Behind him rode the highest officers of the World War, including many representing foreign nations, making the group perhaps the most imposing that could be assembled anywhere in the world.

When the party had passed us and we intended to return to our car, the British army officer, still looking out for us, said to me, "Captain, just follow the King's party with this officer and he will show you to your seats." Of course we did not wish to follow at all but were obliged to form in columns of two and, led by the British Army officer, marched down the roadway right behind the King and his followers.

I suppose the sea-minded British who knew sailors did not ride horseback thought nothing of seeing American naval officers on foot, apparently accompanying the King. In any event, as we passed, the crowd gave us a tremendous ovation, cheering so hard that we could not but continue on. Then suddenly we found ourselves passing from the roadway into a huge roped off parade ground, surrounded by an even denser crowd. Ahead we could see the lines of British troops and bands, mounted and unmounted, each organization in its special uniform. To our right was the royal pavilion in which were members of the Royal Family of Great Britain. On each side of the royal pavilion and a little forward of it were large roped-off areas which held the seats reserved for invited foreign diplomats, leading British officials, high-ranking naval and army officers, and members of the nobility.

Seeing that we were in the "holy of holies," where we had no right to be, and with the British army officer pointing out the reserved seat section, we were at a loss as to our next move. Automatically we drew together to discuss the best way to get out, but as we did so, a gentleman in a top hat and morning coat hurried to

An Admiral's Yarn

us from the royal pavilion and, after saying, "Gentlemen, please follow me," started toward a point between the roped off sections and rings in front of the royal box.

We followed him for a moment, but when we saw he was leading us from our already conspicuous place into the very center of the official party, we held back, hoping he would get so far ahead that we could beat a retreat without being missed. It was not to be, for as soon as he noticed our reluctance in following, he said, "Come right along, gentlemen. I assure you it is quite all right." Then, with the entire Royal Family watching us, he placed us in front of the pavilion.

I doubt if anyone was ever more embarrassed than we were. Our group, though not official, had been given the place of highest honor for the trooping of the colors. Leaving us there, the civilian then returned to the royal box. Then, when we saw him speak in a very cordial manner to Queens Alexandra and Mary, we became more perturbed then ever. I asked one of our officers from headquarters to ask a British naval officer in the roped off area near him if it was all right for us to remain in those seats. The British officer said, "My word, how in the world did you get there?" "Oh," replied our officer, "That gentleman in civilian clothes in the royal box, talking to the Queen, put us here." "Well," said the British officer, "if he did it, it is quite all right as he is the Master of the King's Household."

That statement relieved us somewhat, but scarcely had we heard it than the Master of the Household hurried back and, handing us each a program, said, "Gentlemen, the ladies of the Royal Family send you these programs with their compliments." At that we turned toward the royal box and bowed acknowledgment. The Queen and Royal Family returned bows and smiled broadly at us. The entire Royal Family, except the King and the Crown Prince, were in the box—the Queen, Queen Mother, and all the princes and princesses were being most gracious to us. While we stood there trying to place each one from the pictures we had seen, there was suddenly a great clatter of hoofs approaching. It was the King's cavalcade which, having completed its ceremonial inspection of the parading regiments, was taking position in front of the pavilion for the "Passing in Review."

Maintaining formation and order of rank, the King's party took position for the "March Past." I expected it would be well ahead of our group, but not so. The King and Prince of Wales took their station exactly abreast of us, with the remainder of the party formed behind them. As we Americans were in line, in order of rank from the right, when the King and Prince stopped, it made the reviewing party appear to consist of the King, the Crown Prince, and our line of American naval officers.

London and Paris

The Prince was next to the King on his left while I was next to and so close to the Prince that I could have touched him. Then with the King's party in position, the march started. Being abreast the King, and somewhat in front of the Duke of Connaught and the rest of the King's party, we saw the "trooping" exactly as the King himself did. Be that as it may, we saw the "trooping" amid great splendor and in a most unusual way.

The "trooping of the colors" probably originated hundreds of years ago for the amusement of a very young King and was far more spectacular and colorful than any other parade I have ever seen. As soon as the "March Past" was completed, the King's party departed, the King and Crown Prince dismounting near the royal box where the royal carriage waited to take them back to Buckingham Palace. As they left, we Americans faced the royal pavilion, bowing our appreciation to its occupants and once again receiving bows and smiles from the Queen and her party in return. Then, still flustered and greatly perturbed over what had happened, we made our way back to our car and went, at last, to the British Museum.

However, we were still greatly worried over the experience with the King's birthday party, and I was especially concerned over what our Admiral [Plunkett] and Ambassador [John W. Davis] might do when they heard that an unofficial group of U.S. naval officers had crashed the party. Therefore, we determined not to say anything about it to higher authority, and as none of the officers of the group ever heard of it again, I presume there was no aftermath.

Still, I could not but marvel over our wonderful treatment and felt that had such a crashing of an official function occurred in the United States, the uncredited foreigners would have been shown scant courtesy.

At a reception that evening at the Royal Air Club, we discussed with a British army officer our embarrassing situation during the "trooping of the colors" and how royally we had been received. He said he was not surprised, as both the United States and its navy were highly esteemed for their help during the war and also for having completed the first transatlantic flight. Hence, when a group of American naval officers in uniform asked the way to the reserved seats, British army and police officers could not but lead us to them. Then, when the Royal Family observed our entering the parade enclosure right behind the King's party, appearing lost, they knew at once that a mistake had been made and, whether ours or Great Britain's, it had to be corrected immediately. That is when they sent the "Master of the Household" to do the greatest possible honor to representatives of the United States. The clever handling of what might have become a delicate international situation was characteristic of the reigning Royal Family.

An Admiral's Yarn

The next day I took luncheon at the famous London restaurant of Dickens' day—"The Cheshire Cheese." I had just given my order for its famous kidney and beef pudding when a waiter rushed to me asking if I were Captain Laning and, if so, I was wanted on the telephone by our naval headquarters. I was informed that a dispatch had been received from the Chief of Naval Operations, who was then attending the Peace Conference in Paris, directing me to report to him as soon as possible and that, in accordance with the order, they had arranged transportation for me by the first train and cross-channel boat the next morning. The orders were a complete surprise and would deprive me of more sightseeing in London, but as Paris and the Peace Conference lured me too, I was not greatly perturbed.

The first "boat train" left London early in the morning, and I was on it, looking forward to a lonely and dull crossing. Just before the train started, a most attractive couple entered my car and took seats near me. The man was a complete stranger to me, but, the lady, although very heavily veiled, looked familiar and seemed to be expecting me to join them. I was reluctant to do so as I was not sure of her identity through that veil.

Reaching Dover, I hurried to board the channel steamer and then watched the other passengers come on board. At length the couple from my car came aboard and then I recognized the lady as Mrs. Astor. I hurried to greet her, and she introduced me to her husband, Waldorf Astor. We sat together for the crossing.

Waldorf Astor did not remain with us long, for seeing a man he knew looking over the rail, Mr. Astor joined him. When he left, Mrs. Astor remarked, "Is that not just like a politician? The man he has joined is Lord Northcliffe,[173] owner of our most powerful newspaper chain, and they will talk politics for a long time. We will enjoy the crossing without him." (I could not have had a more charming companion.) Mrs. Astor and I were discussing both Great Britain's and our after-the-war problems when a man Mrs. Astor knew joined us. He was introduced as Mr. Thomas Grasty, the internationally famous war correspondent of *The New York Times*, whose articles on the war and its aftermath I always read with great interest. As Mrs. Astor seemed as well posted on events as Thomas Grasty, and as I was fairly familiar with our American problems with which they were out of touch, we had a most interesting and enlightening talk—and Waldorf Astor and Lord Northcliffe joined us later.

The Astors and Lord Northcliffe left us at Boulonge, but Grasty and I continued on to Paris where we arrived in the late afternoon, and where I found Admiral Plunkett waiting at the station for me with the official car assigned to him during his stay in Paris. Surprised at being met, I asked the admiral immediately about my orders, and he said that the Chief of Naval Operations wished to talk with me about NC-4's flight, and he gladly arranged for my orders. He said that I was to occupy a suite with him at the Crillon Hotel, which our delegation to the Peace Conference had taken over, and that as soon as Admiral [William S.] Benson (our Chief of Operations) had finished interviewing me, I would join him in seeing Paris. Then he added, "Tonight, after we have had dinner, we will go to the opera."

Grand Opera, unfortunately, has never appealed to me and usually makes me sleepy, so, since I was fatigued after my early start and long day, I feared the worst. Nevertheless, we went to the opera, and although it was the delightful "La Boheme" and splendidly presented, I could not stay awake. Naturally the admiral, a true lover of Grand Opera, was disgusted, and on our way back to the hotel said, "Laning, you went to sleep on me tonight but you will stay awake for the show I am taking you to tomorrow night."

He was right, the show that second night was too typically Parisian to miss by going to sleep. It was put on to attract the thousands of English-speaking people passing through Paris on their way home after the war, and, all in uniform, they packed the theater—soldiers, nurses, and war workers of every kind. The show, called "Hello Paris," was a spectacular musical extravaganza of the type seen only in Paris.

I will not attempt to describe that show, but you may draw your own conclusions from the way it opened. The curtain rose on a scene in the "Bois," and as it went up, a "gendarme" could be seen strolling along swinging his club. Just then, three soldiers on leave from the war front met there—an "Anzac," a "Tommy," and a "Yank," all in Paris for the first time. As they started talking, a very attractive young woman entered the park, selected a shady spot, unfolded a little stool, seated herself, and began to knit. Naturally, the soldiers stared at her, and as they did the girl crossed her legs and displayed her very shapely "starboard" calf to the knee, encased in a vivid green stocking. The sight was too much for the soldiers, and as they gazed, the young woman crossed her legs again, exposing her "port" calf which instead of being in a bright green stocking, was encased in a bright red one. The soldiers were dumfounded, and as they discussed the subject, the girl pulled down her shirt. Thereupon a solider argument started regarding the color of her stockings. The debate soon became so vociferous that the gendarme rushed over to learn the trouble. When he did, he walked over to the young woman, lifted her skirt to the knees, and the shapely legs were clothed in neither red nor green stockings, but in brown ones. The astounded soldiers asked the gendarme how it was done. "Humph," said he, "this is nothing. Come with me, and when I have shown you Paris, you will

An Admiral's Yarn

understand." With that the gendarme took the soldiers to see Paris and the rest of the show was what they saw!! It was enough to keep anyone awake, and I ceased to wonder why the thousands of English-speaking strangers, passing through that fascinating city, remained to see "Hello Paris."

We left Paris the second morning after the show, taking the train to Brest where the *Rochester* awaited our arrival, and from there we started for home the following day. Our return was uneventful and ended in Narragansett Bay where our huge destroyer force was assembling to once more engage in peacetime training for war.

XXXIII

Destroyers after the War

IT MIGHT BE THOUGHT that after participating in the most colossal war the world had ever known, our navy, and especially the destroyers that had been so active in it, would be well-trained for another war. Such, however, was far from the fact. The U.S. Navy efficiently trained great numbers of men for war duty in combating submarines, in minelaying, in operating a huge overseas transport service, etc. But in the usual naval tasks of warfare, there had been little experience, except perhaps in the four battleships that had joined the British Grand Fleet long after the battle of Jutland.

The sea-fighting of the war, even after we entered, continued to be the task of the British navy, without much help from us. Hence, when the war came to an end, although highly efficient in its actual activities, our navy was decidedly out of training in the usual war operations. Not only had there been little experience in such operations during the year and a half we were in the war, but most of the great lessons learned from it were yet to be applied in our navy. Further, the United States and even the navy had developed erroneous ideas for operating in a war of our own; these plans were based on our own war problems rather than on those of the British and Allied navies in a European war. We found ourselves investing too much emphasis on antisubmarine warfare, troop transport and supply, and too little on naval fighting.

Utilizing our navy in a secondary role in a naval war peculiar to the geography of Europe was one thing, but on our own, in a war peculiar to the geography of the United States, would be quite another. The navy had to prepare for this probable eventuality, however, and it began intensive training

An Admiral's Yarn

that would never stop because of the continuous upgrades in naval equipment and improved combat.

When the World War ended, we had the largest destroyer force in the world, and since the war had given us many new ideas with regard to destroyer employment, preparing that huge force for a future war of our own became the immediate and all-important task of Admiral Plunkett and his staff.

The problem was immense and intricate, involving as it did the training of almost two hundred destroyers in each one of its manifold duties in war, while at the same time training all destroyers to operate in groups or as a unit to destroy the enemy. It was a considerable job to plan and oversee such a course of training for so many destroyers, most of which were new and practically untrained in the usual war duties of destroyers. But in reality, it was the lesser part of the task to be carried out by the admiral and his staff. The greater part was the development of destroyer teamwork in fighting maneuvers, which we had to devise if the United States was to make the most of the great force it had created.

Night search and attack and other surprise efforts of destroyers on which we had previously concentrated, while still of great importance in destroyer warfare, had become secondary to using destroyers in major battles. The Germans had demonstrated the value of such an attack with a small destroyer group at the battle of Jutland, which caused the vastly superior British battle line that had the German line "T'd" to turn away, thereby breaking off that engagement at the crucial moment and saving the German High Seas Fleet from destruction.[174] That one example of the power of destroyers in naval actions opened the eyes of the world to their possibilities. Hence, Admiral Plunkett's staff, in addition to many other matters pertaining to destroyer training, employment, tactics, and administration, had to make a particular study of using torpedo power in battle. It took much time, and from the late summer of 1919 until this very day, the U.S. Fleet continues developing uses and tactics for destroyers as well as training the entire fleet in their employment.

We started our training work as soon as the destroyer force assembled in Narragansett Bay after the transatlantic flight. Since many destroyers that returned from the war or the flight had to be repaired, and many newly built ships were joining immediately upon completion, the assembling of the huge force was not finished until nearly summer. Then arose the question of where to base them so that their training might continue without a break during the fall and winter months.

That was soon settled by orders to Pensacola Bay for the fall and Guantánamo Bay for the winter. From these bases we could train in every form of destroyer fighting that was then known, while also testing new ideas and methods as rapidly as we devised them. For the next ten months our staff was busy indeed.

I might write at length about that training period, for during that time we introduced many of the fighting ideas and methods that have since become standard practice in the U.S. Fleet. However, because such details are confidential as well as much too technical to be interesting, I will not dwell on them. Suffice it to say that as chief of staff, I spent every moment in the study of destroyer uses and tactics and became very familiar with the war operations of an entire fleet. The work was most interesting to say the least.

About the end of January 1920, there arose a matter of great import to the United States and particularly to its navy. Admiral Sims, who had commanded the U.S. naval forces operating in Europe during the war, chose that time to submit a letter to the Secretary of the Navy on "Certain Lessons in War." This letter, although possibly intended to make the navy more efficient in war, was seemingly an arraignment of the Navy Department for its conduct in the handling of some of the operations in the World War. The letter was made public and was sufficiently severe in stricture to start an after-the-war controversy similar in tone and bitterness to the so-called "Sampson-Schley Controversy" after the Spanish-American War.[175]

As happened in that case, the new controversy was largely developed by a press ever-seeking news items. Then too, since 1920 was a presidential election year, every newspaper with a political bias was quick to grasp anything that might supply political ammunition for the campaign. Republican papers sought to damn the Democrats by slamming President Wilson, his cabinet and supporters, while Democratic papers sought to retain the party's prestige by praising the Administration's work.

But, be all that as it may, Sims' letter started a tremendous controversy in the press. At its beginning, the navy as a whole was not party to it, but later, as a result of the publicity, it seemed to divide into two groups, one composed of the rank and file who believed Sims to be right, the other composed mainly of officers closely associated with the Navy Department during the war and who were against practically everything Sims said and recommended.

Working up to a maximum pitch by the newspapers, the so-called "Naval Controversy" soon became the news feature of the day. So bitter became the squabble between administration and anti-administration papers that the U.S. Senate, then Republican, decided to investigate the matter and appointed a committee for this purpose. That committee met in March 1920, and for the next several months, everything that took place before it was headlined daily in the press.

An Admiral's Yarn

It is not my intention to dwell on either the "Controversy" or the Senate investigation. A complete history of the facts is covered in the report of about six thousand printed pages. Having been in the Navy Department, in touch with its workings during the war, and having collected and retained a number of "not wanted documents" that I could turn over to the committee, I was one of the officers called by the committee to testify and my testimony gave considerable support to Sims' charges.

As often happens in Congressional investigations, that one gradually ended, assisted somewhat by political expediency. Even so, it lasted from March until the latter part of May 1920, during which time it furnished front-page material for politically minded newspapers. Both sides of the controversy were fully examined by the committee, and most of us in the navy thought it had obtained all the information needed from which to draw conclusions and make sound recommendations. But evidently it did not. The presidential campaign had started by the time the hearings were completed, and since Congress wished to adjourn for the campaign, on about May 20th, without finishing its report, the investigating committee was also adjourned to await the call of the chairman. Shortly thereafter, Congress adjourned the 66th Session.[176]

Whether the controversy influenced the presidential election of 1920 I do not know, but the election was won by the Republicans, and on March 4th, 1921, the new administration took over. I think the entire navy expected the change of administration to also bring a change in the senior officers of the Navy Department, but it did not, for they were retained in their posts. Since many of them had supported the Administration in the "controversy," little change took place in the Navy Department's attitude or policies. Some thought a change might be made when the committee finally issued a report. But when that happened about a year later, it merely covered testimony taken without recommending changes in laws or in naval administration to correct the faults found by Sims—no changes were made.[177]

Thus died the greatest naval controversy of my time. Although it turned out to be something of a "dud," I personally felt its consequences for a long time, because I became "persona non grata" with many high officers who had been retained in the Navy Department under the new administration. However, at that time, I was becoming engrossed in the conduct of naval warfare, strategy, and tactics, disliking the political atmosphere surrounding a government department, and much preferring fleet operation to administrative work on shore. For that reason I was serene in mind and worked blissfully to prepare our destroyers for war.

Destroyers after the War

Although no highly exciting incidents occurred during my second year as chief of staff of the Destroyer Force, many important matters besides those of training arose. One developed at the end of the winter's work in Cuba when it became evident that not all of our two hundred or so destroyers could be retained in a full commission status. The country could not afford the expense of such a large force and the personnel of the navy was not sufficient to fully man it—the number of new destroyers we had was disproportionate to the rest of the navy. Hence, even though the United States had started a huge building program that would give us the most powerful navy in the world, it was still inadvisable to retain in full commission all the destroyers built during the World War for our antisubmarine effort. Then, too, a large part of the fleet was being sent to the Pacific Coast, thereby changing the number of ships to be kept fully manned. The ships of the battle line and others belonging to the battle force were sent to the Pacific, while the lighter ships, useful in what was called the "Scouting Force," were kept in the Atlantic—most of them with "skeleton" crews.[178]

With the navy divided between two oceans and Admiral Plunkett retaining command of the destroyers in the Atlantic, nearly all of which were manned with one-third crews, conditions changed completely for our staff. We still had to train our destroyers in all war duties, but now with crews that were hardly large enough for mere material upkeep. These complications made our problem more difficult.

Fortunately, my two years' experience in the Reserve Flotilla now came to our support. The new problem was similar to my old one, the main difference being that we now had about eight times as many ships, each with only a one-third crew instead of the one-half I had previously worked with. Our first task was to find bases that would conveniently accommodate such a large number of ships and also provide sufficient, easily accessible sea room for the necessary war maneuvers.

To solve that problem we considered every harbor from Maine to Panama, but at last came to the conclusion that Narragansett Bay would be best in the summer months, and Charleston, South Carolina, during the rest of the year.

Our next step was to provide moorings for the destroyers—no small task with so many ships to be accommodated. However, by utilizing the buoys and anchors employed during the World War in connection with our antisubmarine nets for harbor entrances, we solved that problem too. We had Charleston Harbor ready for our huge force of undermanned destroyers by the time the force assumed its new status at the end of the summer's work in Narragansett Bay.

An Admiral's Yarn

That winter in Charleston was delightful and proved a great success. I will not bore you with details of our work there, but probably I should relate something about the life we led.

Charleston was not a large city, and the basing of so many ships in its harbor exercised a decided influence over the area. At times there were over a hundred destroyers, flagships, and tenders, which contained a total of about seven or eight thousand officers and men. Thus, the actual wage earners our force took to Charleston was over one-tenth the population of the city, and, with their families, the total contingent equaled nearly a fifth of the people living there. The ships purchased considerable quantities of supplies and provisions in the city, and the resulting increases in business were appreciated.

We were shown great hospitality in the social life of Charleston that winter, which we greatly enjoyed while we carried on, most successfully, our navy work with the destroyers.

With the onset of spring, we gave thought to moving our ships to our northern base to continue the training. The base had been prepared but there arose the problem of moving more than a hundred destroyers over the ocean on a trip of about seven hundred miles with crews only large enough to operate at sea for a few hours at a time.

At first it seemed that such a movement should not be attempted, but some of our young and highly energetic commanding officers were positive their ships could make it, and we issued orders for the trip.

When an order is undertaken in the navy, everyone concerned works with all his might to carry it out successfully. But if the order unduly jeopardizes a ship, that jeopardy must be reported at once. For that reason, as soon as the order was issued, a few of our more than a hundred commanding officers felt obliged to report the potential dangers to their particular ships while being operated by such small crews. Admiral Plunkett issued the order that any captain who doubted the ability of his destroyer to make the trip safely could hold his ship in Charleston for the summer.

We rather expected some of the destroyers would consider the trip too risky, but when the signal was given to get underway, every destroyer responded, even with its few men on a watch and watch basis. I must admit to a bit of worry over that trip lest some untoward happening should mar it, but nothing did. Exactly on time, in perfect formation, and in fine condition, the destroyers entered Narragansett Bay and secured to the buoys awaiting them.

By that time my tour of sea duty was about over. I was then a permanent captain and thereby allowed but two years on a cruise. I had given considerable thought to my next duty, and as I had developed an intense interest in naval strategy and tactics, I requested duty at the Naval War College as a student. The orders were issued shortly after that; and so, after twenty-six months as chief of staff of the Destroyer Force, I became a student of the Naval War College at Newport, Rhode Island.[179]

XXXIV

Naval War College Student

THOUGH THE NAVAL WAR COLLEGE has a vital place in our national defense, few civilians know anything of it. The college is on an island in Narragansett Bay in Newport, R.I., but because there is nothing spectacular to be seen there and the War College is not open to the public, even sightseers are given little more than a distant glance at it. Aside from those interested in naval features of our national defense, few people give any attention to the War College.[180]

Yet, in spite of that, the college does more toward the development of sound fighting ideas in the United States Navy than does any other agency. Most Americans seem to believe that naval fighting power is measured by the types and numbers of ships possessed, and little or no thought is given to the fact that unless men give life to ships, they are as inanimate as ore in the mountains. In any country, fighting ships are merely the tools of its navy. What is done with those tools depends on the skill with which they are handled. It is the aim of the Naval War College to develop in the higher officers of the navy the skills in the use of their ships and weapons that will permit them the utmost power should war befall us.

Another idea prevalent in the country is that four years of study at the Naval Academy fully prepares its graduates for practically everything pertaining to naval warfare. Nothing could be further from fact. At the Academy, young men of college age simply learn the ABC's of a profession that requires a lifetime to master. When a young man graduates, he is merely beginning the naval profession. What he later becomes depends, naturally, on his ability. Like great

An Admiral's Yarn

surgeons or doctors, our great war commanders become great through practicing their profession, not through intuition or inspiration. In the medical profession, however, doctors and surgeons have almost instant practice, whereas in both the navy and the army, professional practice is to be had only in the event of war—which we endeavor to avoid.

Every nation must develop vitally important war skills, or ultimately pay for not having done so. To develop war skills while not begin engaged in war is difficult. A man may spend a lifetime thinking of and studying war operations, and he may develop many ideas for winning. But unless they can be tested in practice, he will never know whether they will prevail against those of an opposing commander. The Naval War College curriculum was devised to provide such tests. In miniature, it pits naval forces against each other in every conceivable form of war operation. By constantly measuring results and applying losses as they occur, the miniature operations become almost exactly those of actual war.

By carrying out battles, campaigns, and even entire naval wars in miniature, the college develops in officers the skill and wit essential to operate successfully the navy's fighting tools that are so vital to our national defense.

The system used at the college is referred to as the "Applicatory System," because student officers train for high command in war by actually applying their knowledge of fighting to war situations; in war, no one condition is quite like another, and what might win in one case could bring complete disaster in another.[181] All that can be done for prospective high commanders is to give them an understanding of the principles of fighting that tend to succeed when followed, and then allow them to practice applying those principles.

Because the ability to fight skillfully, regardless of the situation, is achieved only through practice, the War College does not have lessons, recitations, or examinations, nor is there any formal attempt to measure the relative ability of students. Thus there is no competition in class standing; each student works solely to perfect himself in war strategy and tactics. Certain students do, of course, show up better than others as winners of conflicts, but no attempt is made to rate them in that ability. Each officer is strictly on his own and works to enhance his performance in the art of naval warfare.[182]

The student course is eleven months' long, and during that time an officer has no other duty than to study for high command in war and prepare himself for the greatest responsibility a man can have—that of winning for his country should he be chosen for high war command.

The game of war, even when played in miniature, is one of intense fascination, and its lure surpasses all other competitive games. In other games, the stake, if any, is small, and the reward of winning applies generally to an individual or to small groups of individuals. But in war, the ante is often the very existence of a country and its people, and the contestants are entire nations. The teams for contests in war often consist of many thousands or even millions of people who operate powerful weapons of destruction. A country's navy is a team made up of many teams. One large ship often requires a team of over a thousand men to operate it. Groups of one type of ship form "type" group teams, and "type" group teams are formed into fleet teams.

Little wonder there is fascination in practicing war with such teams. Still less should be any wonder that the officers who are to command and operate such teams in war must devote every minute of their eleven months at the War College to perfecting themselves for that task. But even so, they are not completely prepared for war when they finish the course. They may be well-versed in the principles to observe when fighting, but constant practice in operating fighting teams must ever continue to win the finals in war contests.

Until I became a student at the War College, I thought my previous work was as important as it was interesting, and of course for one in low command, it was, However, as soon as I realized (from the college course) what I would be responsible for if chosen for high command, the visualization I had of my life changed. Instead of dealing with only the relatively minor war duties for which officers in low command are responsible, I now might be responsible for the important war duties of a high command. Not for much longer would I be obliged only to carry out the plans and orders of someone else; I might be called on to do the planning and ordering, and since it was ever my ambition to be an able high commander in the navy, I bent every energy to prepare myself to make good in the role.

Looking at my future in that light, I worked feverishly on the War College course and in particular strove to improve myself in naval fighting through the war operations conducted in miniature. It proved worthwhile, for, about a month before my student course ended, I was sent for by the president of the college. Admiral Sims invited me to join the War College staff as head of the Department of Tactics; he told me that my work at the college had warranted this.

That invitation to be head of the Tactics Department hit me like a thunderbolt, for until that time, I had no idea that my work as a student warranted such recognition. I knew I had given all of my time, energy, and ability to the course and had been quite successful in winning miniature war games, but had never given thought to having even a minor position on the War College staff. I had given a little consideration to what duty I would like to have after

An Admiral's Yarn

completing the course and, desiring to continue my study of war, had decided to request assignment as a student at the Army War College. Should that request be granted, I would have two months between courses to spend with my little family, and I had planned to take them to visit my wife's sister, who had a delightful summer place in the pristine forests of western Oregon.

We had practically made up our family mind as to what we wanted to do after my graduation, so I was completely surprised when Admiral Sims asked me to joint the college staff. Since I was not entirely confident of my ability a make good on the job, was keen to continue my study of war by going to the Army War College, and realized that a two-month vacation in the woods of Oregon was quite essential to keeping physically fit, I felt compelled to explain the situation to the admiral. When I had done so, he said, "Laning, the college wants you, and if you will take the position I believe I can arrange everything else to your satisfaction. As the tactics work of the college course does not start until a month after the course opens, you can have your two months leave and still be back in time for it. When that course is ended, and you wish to attend the Army War College course, I think I can arrange it. Under those circumstances, will you accept the billet?" Quite naturally I said I would.

XXXV

A Vacation in the Oregon Woods

IMMEDIATELY AFTER GRADUATION the Laning family started for Oregon. The place we visited is an island on the Umpqua River. Owned by my wife's sister, it is not far from where the river flows into the sea, to the westward of Oregon's coastal mountains.

In 1922, when we were there, that part of Oregon was still a barely opened primeval forest. It was nearly devoid of roads, and only here and there, where lumbering operations had cleared off trees along streams, were there people or houses. The only means of reaching that area were by boat, by rough wagon roads across the mountains from the railroad village of Drain, and over a spur of the Southern Pacific Railroad which was constructed, I believe, during the World War to remove spruce timber used to build airplane propeller blades. Because of the poor connections with the outside world, entering this area was spoken of as "going in" and leaving as "going out."

We left our train at the village of Gardiner where the Gardiner Mill Company, largely owned by my brother-in-law and his family, had a sawmill for the huge logs that were floated down the Umpqua River and its tributaries. But the mill had burned, and the lumber operations of the area had almost ceased with the ending of the war. About the only business remaining in the small villages came from the fishing industry and from the small dairy farms along the streams where lumbering operations had cleared openings in the forest.

To make the situation more difficult, my sister-in-law's husband had recently died, and her two sons, after graduating from college, needed guidance for their future; there were several important opportunities open to them in both San

An Admiral's Yarn

Francisco and Oregon. My brother-in-law had envisioned a great future for the Umpqua area and had become heavily involved there. Not only did he have vast timber and other land holdings in it but he had also started several development projects. He had established a chain of banks in the villages, and since water was the easiest means of transportation, he had created what he called "The Umpqua Navigation Company" with a number of shallow-draft power boats that operated on all the streams (those with enough water to float them) in the largest cleared off space in the remarkably fertile valley of the Umpqua. He started a ranch and had selected a mile-long island in the river abreast of it for a summer home among the giant spruce trees. Out of logs, a house had been built which was named "Spruce Reach Cabin," and then, so that his and other remote cabins along the river might have contact with each other and the villages of Gardiner and Reedsport, he arrange a telephone line up the Umpqua Valley to all the cabins.

But for all of that, the country was scarcely tapped, and when we stepped off our little train shortly after dawn one morning, even though we were met by my wife's sister and her sons, we seemed to be entering an almost uninhabited world of great beauty and charm. We were given a tremendous welcome and then hurried to a small boat landing near the station where we boarded a fine cabin motor launch that immediately started up the river.

I will never forget that seven-mile run up the Umpqua to Spruce Reach Cabin. We seemed to go deeper and deeper into a dense forest that covered the river valley. The beautiful mountains enclosing it and the scenery were awe-inspiring—so close to nature and unspoiled by the world's progress. Only now and then could we see a cabin or any sign of human life. After an hour's run, we arrived at Spruce Reach Island and, leaving the launch at a log raft landing, we went to the cabin.

Both Spruce Reach Island and the cabin on it were in keeping with the primal forest surrounding it. The underbrush had been cleared away, leaving a land of giant spruces with a rambling, many-roomed cabin sprawled between the huge trees. While from the outside the appearance of the cabin seemed to be in keeping with the primitive surroundings, inside we found practically all the comforts of civilization, although most of the furniture and equipment had been made in the backwoods pattern. The cabin was heated by huge, log-burning fireplaces, and it was lighted by electricity from a motor-driven dynamo and storage battery; it had bathrooms with an endless supply of fresh water piped from a spring in the mountains four hundred feet above. Spruce Reach Cabin provided all the comforts of a city, in a remote area where all else was deep forest.

A Vacation in the Oregon Woods

Thoughts of war operations and sea life had no place there, so I banished them from my thoughts and thoroughly enjoyed life in the forest.

For relaxation, rest, and freedom from worries, Spruce Reach left nothing to be desired. Wonderful fishing and hunting were to be had nearby, and the beautiful Umpqua valley provided enchanting picnic places to which we were taken on many delightful jaunts, one of which, though, nearly caused my undoing. For this one, the launch took us some fifteen or twenty miles up the river to the mouth of "Little Mill Creek." At that point, the riverbank provided a splendid picnic place, while the creek fairly teemed with what my nephew called brook or mountain trout. The plan was to secure the launch to the riverbank at the mouth of the creek, where the ladies of our party and one nephew would remain to prepare the picnic supper, while the other nephew and I fished the lower two miles of the creek.

As the plan was an excellent one, I entered it with great zest, especially because I had never before fished a mountain stream for trout. Not knowing just how to equip myself for such fishing, I dressed as I would for sea fishing from a boat. I donned old clothes, the heaviest shoes I had, and an old green Austrian velour fedora that had a lone feather sticking up on one side. Though I probably looked the way I knew a fisherman to look, I noted my nephew looking askance when I appeared in that outfit. He asked if I had "corks" in my shoes and could get through the brush in such clothes. He was wearing woodsman's canvas clothes over a heavy khaki shirt, a cap and high, thick-soled, laced, watertight boots, heavily "corked." However, I said I could do without "corks" and go through the woods easily. Hence, when we reach the mouth of the creek, the two of us went some miles up that we might fish the stream coming down.

Going the two miles up that creek, I realized what struggling through the virgin forest of Oregon meant. The stream rushed down the mountain in a somewhat precipitous valley, and close to the creek, the woods and brush were denser than they were back on the rugged hillsides. Therefore, we climbed the hills. But even so, I made heavy weather of the passage, and it took me almost two hours to cover the two miles to the "starting to fish" point.

By that time I was fairly tired, but when we had worked back to the creek and found rocks and boulders sufficiently clear of trees and underbrush for me to cast, I went at it. The fishing was excellent and I quickly landed several fine trout, but working down that stream was slow, hard work for me. It would take me from five to ten minutes to get from one casting place to the next, and since we dared not stop long, I could make only a few casts before having to move on. It was therefore lucky for me that the fish were so plentiful.

An Admiral's Yarn

When I had gone farther downstream, I came to a waterfall about twelve feet high where the stream, after rushing through rocks and boulders, poured over a cliff into a large pool. Although I knew almost nothing about the habits of mountain trout, I thought there must be hundreds of them in that pool and decided to fish it.

Inasmuch as the trees and brush were too thick to permit casting from the side I was on, I crossed over at the crest of the falls as it looked easy enough at that point as the water rushed between a series of boulders that made fine stepping stones. True, the boulders were wet and moss-covered, but I thought my heavily soled shoes would prevent slipping and I made the hop—but landed on my right hip and then down the falls I shot, feet first! I do not know whether or not I hit a boulder at the bottom of the fall, but the first thing I knew, I was standing on my head in the icy pool. I struggled to reverse ends and was soon on my feet, gasping for breath in the icy cold water that came up to my arm pits, with my right leg seemingly out of commission. As I looked around, too paralyzed to move, I saw my green velour hat with the feather still sticking up as cocky as ever, floating near one side of the pool and my fishing rod floating near the other side. Meanwhile, lying across a fallen log, where he had collapsed from laughing, was my nephew. He had seen me shoot the falls into the pool, come up feet first while I stood on my head, and for a moment he feared I was badly hurt. However, when he saw me on my feet, my head above water, and the green hat floating with its feather up, it was too much for him and he exploded with laughter. Such is youth. Personally I did not see anything funny about the situation, for not only was I nearly freezing in the cold water, but the pain in my right leg was excruciating. I thought I could not get out of the pool, let alone ever use my leg again. However, I floundered to the bank and crawled up before collapsing. I laid there for some time, but my nephew assured me my leg was not broken and that I must get back to the launch. With his help, keeping to the bed of the creek, we started—but I will never forget my two-mile crawl down icy Little Mill Creek. Time and again I thought I could not make it, but we finally reached the launch where food and hot coffee were awaiting. Wrapped in blankets after the removal of my wet clothes, I relaxed a bit but was indeed thankful to reach the cabin where treating the badly injured leg began at once.

By morning that leg was a sight, for not only was it blue from hip to knee but ruptured blood vessels had turned almost the entire leg purple. To move it was agony, even in bed, and it was over a week before I could sit up, and still another week before I could limp around—a cruel way to spend a vacation with all out-of-doors beckoning me. During that time my nephews were planning what they called a *real* fishing trip, and as soon as I was able to go, we went first to the

A Vacation in the Oregon Woods

Mill Company's store in Gardiner to outfit me for it. When that was done, I looked woodsy. My green hat with its feather was too fantastic to give up, but below the hat I wore a khaki shirt, canvas trousers and coat, heavy woolen socks and high, watertight lumberman's boots into which the boys had driven long, sharp pointed corks that would prevent my slipping on logs and mossy rocks. It took me some days to accustom myself to the outfit, but the boys made me practice going through the woods near the cabin before we started on the "real fishing trip."

Leaving Spruce Reach at the crack of dawn one morning, the launch took us down the Umpqua to Reedsport, where we transferred to the Navigation Company's Smith River boat. This was an imposing flat bottom power affair of about ten feet beam and fifty feet in length. When we boarded it, we found there were several passengers who were going up the river, a small cargo of supplies, and a full cargo of empty ten-gallon milk cans. As soon as we were aboard, the boat started off.

Near its mouth, Smith River was a long, fairly wide bay, the shores of which were lined for several miles with immense booms of logs for the sawmill. As we went up the channel between them, we could see an occasional little boat landing, cabin, or shed; but where the bay and boom ended and the river narrowed, the valley seemed to close in and we found ourselves once again entering the great woods. Here and there along the river we saw small areas that had become farms, each having a log raft landing at the river bank. As it neared a landing, the boat would whistle, and when alongside, deposit the required number of empty milk cans, such supplies as had been ordered from the Mill Store, and the mail. Seldom was there anyone at the landing except those wishing to go farther up the river. The boat went twenty-two miles before the river became too full of shallows, rocks, and rapids to navigate.

As we progressed we delivered passengers and cargo along the way until we had left on board only those for the last landing, above which no one lived in the Smith River Valley. However, it was the most important landing, for in addition to being the entrance to a great unopened forest of the Upper Smith Valley, it was the landing of a seven-mile flat area that, having been completely de-forested, had become the largest dairy area of the region. There several families lived and, compared to other places along the river, it was something of a metropolis. The boat reached there every day just before noon, and after stopping for an hour, started on its return trip. During that stop, dinner was served, generally to fire or game wardens going up or leaving the valley, who were joined by several men of the neighborhood to discuss the news of the day.

An Admiral's Yarn

I thought that in such a remote spot my nephews and I would be complete strangers, but on the contrary, I found that everyone but myself knew the others well. The men who lived in the cabins had known my nephews from the day they were born and had watched them going in and out of the company's timberland so often that they called the boys by their nicknames. More hearty greetings and backslapping I had never seen, and when the boys told them we were on our way up Smith River to fish, they offered every kind of help.

From what I had seen of the country and the way men in it lived, I was greatly surprised after lunch to find an old, decrepit "Model T" car with a pack saddle in it waiting for us at the door of a cabin. As it was, of course, the only car in the valley, I naturally began to ask questions about it—how it ever got that far and where it would go when there were no roads. It had been taken up on the little boat and used for distributing and collecting milk cans and doing other chores for the small farms on the flat area. There was a so-called road through the cleared area, the remains of a trail the Mill Company had used in taking supplies from the boat landing to its logging camps. The "road" was just a succession of ruts which nothing except a decrepit "Model T" car would have attempted to negotiate.

Nevertheless, on that road we went some four miles through the cleared area until the upper end of the valley narrowed to cliffs and steep hills and the forest remained unopened. At that point we unloaded ourselves, our gear and the pack saddle. There were several mules and burros and also a cow grazing nearby. I wondered if the boys would be able to catch the mules which were so wild, but they soon had the pack saddle on one of them and piled our gear on top. The mules had been turned loose by the Mill Company when it stopped logging in that location and anyone going up Smith River was welcome to capture one to transport his pack.

Although we were only going fishing, that mule was of great service, for instead of having to carry our equipment up the valley on our backs, the mule could take all but about fifteen pounds or more from each one of us. It was not just fishing gear, but what three men would need for a week in the forest, miles beyond where even backwoodsmen lived. The paraphernalia was not that of a deep sea sailor, but the boys were greatly pleased with it as the three of us and the mule started up the valley.

We finally reached the fishing place by following a faint, rugged trail some seven miles farther along, and just as the sun was setting. At that point the trail was close to the river and mostly covered by beautiful giant ferns and heavy underbrush. There we unpacked and the boys told me to catch a mess of trout for our supper while they made camp.

I had about an hour of fishing before dusk came, and the boys called out that camp was ready. In that time I had landed seven beautiful trout, each weighing from one to two pounds. Then the boys cleaned and cooked the trout, and soon we were eating a supper of freshly caught fish, bacon, flapjacks, and coffee. It was a bully meal. Then, as it was getting dark, we turned in. We had neither tent nor overhead covering, but our sleeping bags were laid on piles of ferns and made a comfortable sleeping place. Through the trees the stars shone brightly, and the sound of the river's rapids soon lulled us to sleep.

It seemed as though I had only just closed my eyes when I was awakened by the boys moving around. On looking at my watch I found it was half past three and time to turn out—dawn was breaking and we had decided on early fishing.

That night in the woods brought me some realization of the hardships our forefathers endured to open up that wonderful country for us. Even with modern equipment such as we had, living in the woods seemed mighty difficult to a sailor, but for the early settlers with almost no equipment, in forests teeming with wild animals and Indians, it must have been appalling.

With our comforts and luxurious living, we Americans of today give little thought to what our forefathers suffered for us, but ever since that first night in the woods of Smith River, I think often of those early settlers and what today we might speak of as their "guts." we might do worse than to adopt for ourselves their standard of "intestinal fortitude."

We remained in the woods several days as planned, and they were full of new experiences for me. We fished mostly at sunrise or sunset, and even in those short hours caught more fish than we could use, so we explored the forest, which we had all to ourselves, for there were no people within miles.

Our return trip was simply a reversal of the trip "up," and when we reached Reedsport, we found the launch waiting to take us up the Umpqua River to Spruce Reach Cabin. It had been a glorious experience, and I will always be grateful to my nephews for making it possible.

A few days later we journeyed back to Newport, Rhode Island, so that I could take up my new duties.

U.S. Naval War College Staff and Graduating Class of May 1923. See page 469 for key.

XXXVI

On the War College Staff

THE WAR COLLEGE was just going into the second month of the course when I assumed charge of the Tactics Department.[183] During the first month, the students had devoted their time to reading and studying the causes, nature, and conduct of wars; in the second month, they began strategy and tactics. The course work covered the same ground that I had studied, except for the addition of a pamphlet on tactics titled "The Naval Battle," a not too long treatise on the team play of a modern fighting fleet, which had been culled, without my knowing it, from the thesis on tactics I had submitted at the end of my student year.[184]

At the time that I had taken the course, students were required to submit four theses on war subjects during the year,[185] and I used mine to make a rather complete resume of the general principles I would observe were I responsible for fighting operations. I wanted to be ready to win in battle, so I went into considerable detail on tactics. However, since my writing was intended only to crystalize sound ideas in my own mind, and was in no way intended for anyone else, you can imagine my surprise on returning from leave to find it had been published by the college as a guide for students in the conduct of naval battles. By that action, the college conveyed to me that I was no longer responsible merely for preparing myself for high command in battle but for training all officers who attended the college.

Until that tour of shore duty ended in two years, I remained Head of the Department of Tactics. I had learned much during my student year, but it was only a smattering to what I learned during my time on the college staff.

An Admiral's Yarn

Although my department was an intensely busy one, I was able to attend the weekly lectures and discussions of national and international affairs, enter the discussions of international law, study the strategic problems under consideration, and participate in all critiques of them. But of all the college work, what I considered the most interesting—as well as the most important—was that of training officers for battle command.[186]

Although preparing officers to conduct war has always been the primary purpose of the War College, a by-product of doing that had become of tremendous importance: the miniature war operations that are really researches that test and evaluate every detail of naval warfare. Because of that, the College gradually evolved into a guide for the entire navy.

Its influence may not be realized even by naval officers, but it is my opinion that much of our naval advancement in recent years has resulted from War College research.

Because of the importance of the college, both to the navy and to the entire United States, it appeared to me that its work in naval tactics should be progressive from year to year and that student officers of our class should take up tactical work at about the point where the preceding class left off. As a student, I had found it impossible to do that, since no record had been kept of the miniature battles of the preceding classes. It was largely because of that deficiency that I summarized in my thesis on tactics what my class had learned.

That summary was now being made a starting point for the new classes and, hence, "The Naval Battle" had become the connecting link for a progressive development of battle tactics.

Realizing that, it occurred to me that if we would correct, revise, and add the sound fighting ideas developed by successive classes to "The Naval Battle" pamphlet each year, we would have not only what would enable one class to start tactical work where its predecessor stopped, but also a pamphlet that would be a guide even for a fleet in battle. I therefore determined to use the pamphlet that way; in order that the principles enumerated in it would be based on recorded data, I started making full records and analyses of each miniature battle fought, confident the results would be well worth the effort.

Histories and analyses of battles from which sound principles of fighting can be deduced are essential in the study of tactics. However, because real naval battles are, fortunately, few and far between, not only are they too rare to provide sufficient information but the only records we have of them are from recollections of men participating in them rather than from exact data. For that reason, what we have concerning real battles is incomplete and often incorrect, frequently leading us to wrong deductions.

On the War College Staff

In miniature battles, which can be stopped instantly to permit accurate plotting of movements and measurement of the effects of gunfire, torpedoes, bombs, mines, etc., there are no uncertainties. Causes and effects are accurately determined.

When I was a student, we had but one modern naval battle to study—Jutland. That battle had been fought years before, and when I started to study it closely, I found the records too incomplete to permit more than a general conclusion. Hence, although we studied that battle thoroughly, we learned little from it. However great and important the battle of Jutland was, it could teach us only so much about naval fighting; it was almost as outmoded as the battle of Trafalgar. The characteristics of naval ships had changed greatly since then, and two startling new types had been added to fleets. We were in a new era of naval warfare, one quite different from the battle of Jutland days.[187]

The changes in characteristics so affected the capabilities and limitations of surface ships that radical changes were needed in the battle tactics of a fleet made up only of surface ships. The addition of underwater and air forces to fighting fleets brought about still greater changes. At the time the World War ended, neither submarines nor aircraft had taken part in a major naval battle, so no one knew much about their use.

Inasmuch as both are extremely powerful hitting types, it was essential that the U.S. Navy learn how to utilize them to best advantage and how to defend against them. It was therefore to a post-Jutland type of naval battle that the War College devoted its energies, paying particular attention to air and underwater forces of modern fleets.

As can be imagined, the changes in tactics necessitated by the makeup of naval fighting teams were very great. The fundamental principles of fighting that centuries of war had proved to be immutable were of course the same as ever; but in the application of those principles, almost everything was different. The changes in fighting methods would be great, and we went into them with zest, assembling all known data about the characteristics, capabilities, and limitations of each type of modern naval craft, and, having established rules based on them to govern our miniature battles, we went to work.

The task of making a complete record and analysis of every battle fought was enormous, for the ramifications in naval battles are innumerable. They result from the complicated operations of opposing fleets, the ships that fight not individually but in teams composed of many groups of ships. Of the half dozen or more types of ships in a modern fleet, only battleships operate together as a unit. Cruisers, destroyers, aircraft carriers, submarines, and aircraft operate in groups, each having a particular position and role in the team play of a battle.

An Admiral's Yarn

Since sea battles are between fleets, every part of which does its fighting while maneuvering at high speed, it is exceedingly difficult to picture actual battle for any particular instant, even though every part of each fleet knows exactly where it is and what it is doing at that instant. To visualize such a picture for an entire battle at sea seems, of course, impossible. Nevertheless we could and did make detailed records of our miniature battles, from which we deduced the corrections, additions, and changes to make in "The Naval Battle."

Doing that work took much time and application, but by it, I gained considerable knowledge of the new naval fighting, as did both the college staff and students. Still, it took a man from outside the college and navy to make us realized the extent of our learning.

Usually civilians are not permitted to watch the college war games, but one day while we were at work on the big game at the end of my first year on the staff, the president of the college, Admiral Sims, sent for me. He introduced me to Mr.—— of Harvard University, told me the gentleman was making a study of the research work being done in our colleges and universities, and was particularly interested in the work we were doing. He directed me to allow the gentleman to watch our battle and to explain to him our method of fighting.

Our visitor watched our fight closely for several days, and on departing said to me, "Captain, I am reluctant to leave this fascinating game, the most interesting I have ever seen. No wonder you navy men enjoy it. But I did not come here to see your war game but rather to study what you are doing in research work. I am making a study of such activities for Harvard University and so felt obliged to see what the Naval War College is doing. I want you to know that I am amazed at what I have found here. I thought the research conducted at our universities was about the last word on that work, but at the Naval War College I find the most thorough example of it. The work here not only teaches naval officers how to fight their fleets but also determines for the United States the line it should follow in its naval policy, naval building, and naval operations. The United States is indeed fortunate to have a research laboratory from which it derives such great knowledge."

That statement not only encouraged us but made us realize clearly the value of our teachings, and we worked even harder to perfect the new edition of our pamphlet on battle. No attempt was made to force the students to observe the principles and methods of fighting set forth in it. On the contrary, the idea was simply to make available what the college had learned, in a continuing effort to improve and give the United States the best battle navy in the world.

Not all officers agreed with the methods of fighting suggested in the pamphlet, and of course every officer sought to improve on them. During my

On the War College Staff

second year on the staff, a group of the cleverest tacticians among the students came to me and said that though the conclusions enumerated in the pamphlet seemed sound, they believed there were better methods and they intended to find them. As I was merely the analyst of the battles fought, had no vested interest in what seemed proved by them, and wished only to make the U.S. Fleet the best fighting fleet in the world, I was delighted with their attitude. Therefore, the group took up its self-imposed task with all the support I could give.

The group analyzed every idea in the pamphlet and thought up many new ones to try out against them, but strange as it may seem, the methods of "The Naval Battle" proved so sound that one by one the group members became convinced that if there were better ways to fight, they could not discover them. Nevertheless they could and did suggest a few improvements in the pamphlet.

That proof in the soundness of our ideas impressed me greatly, and I had considerable faith not only in the tactical employment of modern surface ships but in submarines and aircraft as well. Having proved their hitting power in the World War, submarines and aircraft were being proclaimed by the "Press" as having revolutionized naval warfare, and that it was essential that the United States Navy learn immediately the best ways to use them, and that it was for the War College to ascertain those ways.

It mattered not to the navy what type or types of craft—surface, sub-surface, or air—might dominate in war, only that the United States be better prepared to use them than anyone else. The college research therefore had to make certain what could be done with the new types and then determine how best to accomplish it.

Through research, the War College pioneered modern ways of fighting on the sea, and although I did not realize it at the time, I soon found that what we were learning was considered most important by both the fleet and the Navy Department. Although we made no direct recommendations to either, both began studying our pamphlets, which were based on our research work. I also noted that several officers in positions of responsibility in the fleet and the Navy Department often wrote personal letters to inquire about the work we were doing at the college on jobs for which they were responsible. One was from a friend holding an important post in the Navy Department's Bureau of Aeronautics [Rear Admiral William A. Moffett], which is largely responsible for the aircraft policies of the navy. He asked what our research seemed to prove.

Just as in the case of submarine and surface craft, the college had devoted much energy to aviation research—not to aircraft design but to the status of aircraft in modern sea warfare. Up to that time, naval aviation had developed airplanes, but how the planes would reach enemy ships and how they would

An Admiral's Yarn

operate was still unknown to the navy—while non-seagoers were shouting that airplanes would blast surface ships from the sea. So we thoroughly researched both offense and defense naval air activities, allowing the officers who were commanding miniature fleets a rather free hand in the use of aircraft. They were allowed planes of any type and as many as their ships would carry. The only restriction was that planes had to operate in accordance with the capabilities and limitations established by the knowledge and experience of aviators.

That freedom of action in aviation work brought forth an extraordinary number of ideas in the study of offense and defense. No sooner would officers on one side try something new in offense than the officers on the other side would work up a defense against it. With about fifty keen officers familiar with sea conditions in each of the opposing fleets, each trying to win for his side, everything that any of them could think of was tried out. From that welter of tests, certain points regarding aircraft and air fighting in sea operations began to establish themselves as facts. Gradually we came to know what aircraft could and could not do. With that knowledge we were able to decide on the proper aviation equipment for our miniature fleets and to know the principles of fighting that equipment should observe.

I wrote to my friend in Aeronautics, giving him the summary of our deductions, not thinking they would be of great help. You can imagine my surprise a few weeks later when I received a dispatch order to appear before the General Board of the Navy for a hearing on naval aviation. The General Board of the Navy recommends to Congress the naval policies and building program for our country, and I knew that in preparing its recommendations, the Board often called on the navy's experts for information on technical points. However, not being an aviator, I though some mistake had been made when the Board called on me to attend an aviation hearing. As soon as I reached the Navy Department, I hurried to my friend to learn what was up.

In reply to my query he said, "You know, Laning, the General Board is now at work on its recommendations to Congress, and a few days ago it called on this Bureau for aviation suggestions. Probably influenced by the insistence of the press that planes would blow up all surface ships, the Board had all but decided to recommend only one type of plane for the navy, a heavy bomber. It may be that if you had not written that letter to me, the Bureau would have concurred in the recommendation, but the letter opened our eyes. Until we received it, the officers of the Bureau could suggest only such aviation procedure as could be deduced through sitting here thinking. But the War College deductions were not of that kind, for instead of presenting untested visions, you have conclusions drawn from many visions, all thoroughly tested to determine the soundest ones.

The correctness of your deductions was so self-evident that, as soon as we read them, we decided to make them our recommendations to the General Board. When we did that, however, the Board thought them only aviators' flights of fancy, so we suggested they call on you to obtain the results of the War College research. All you have to do is give the Board your War College conclusions and explain how they were reached."

What my friend said did not completely reassure me, so when I appeared before the Board at ten o'clock, I still was not convinced I could give any worthwhile information. However, the longer the Board and the aviators before it quizzed me, the more important the results of our research appeared to be. We had started with the newspaper idea that airplanes could destroy ships, ports, and anything else on the earth's surface with their bombs and machine guns. From there we went on to find, from our miniature battles, that the bombers would encounter every form of defense the opponents could devise. From those defense activities, it quickly became apparent that not all planes carried by a fleet should be of the bombing type, but that an efficient air force had to have speedy fighting (or combat) planes too. Then again, from using planes for other essential purposes, we found that types other than fighters were required in sea work—scouting planes and observation planes. Now, since the total number of planes any fleet can have is the number it can carry in its ships, we had to apportion that total number among the several types we found to be necessary. By actual trial, we established for our tiny replicas of the navies of the world the air equipment that each should carry.

It was about equipment for our own fleet that the General Board wanted information, so I gave our conclusions as best I could without notes or preparation. As I told of our "step by step" progress, the members of the Board and the aviators present showed intense interest and asked innumerable questions. I think the Board was antagonistic toward me when the hearing started, but as it went on, the conclusions of the War College seemed axiomatic once the Board had a picture of our battles. At the end of the hearing, the President of the Board said to me, "Captain, what you have said has cleared up many points for us. The War College research seems to have developed such sound conclusions with respect to naval aviation that this Board will call on the college soon for its conclusions on other naval matters."

It was some weeks before I knew the extent to which our college deductions on aviation had been adopted by the General Board, and then I learned that its recommendations to Congress conformed exactly to the conclusions the college had drawn for its fleets. That recommendation further proved the value of our aviation research, but inasmuch as our researchers also covered

An Admiral's Yarn

underwater and surface craft operations, I reasoned that we had probably learned as much about other aspects of naval warfare as we had about aviation. To one whose great ambition was to be an able, high, naval commander, that belief was a great comfort.

Among the many points our researchers studied was the effect of the Treaty Limiting Armaments on the United States, which came into being while I was at the college.[188] You may recall that the conference leading to the treaty was suggested by the United States, as was the proposal to reduce the likelihood of war by so limiting and balancing naval armaments that although each of the great powers would have a navy sufficient for its defense, none would have one sufficiently strong to be certain of winning an aggressive war against another signatory power. The United States was at that time about to become the greatest naval power in the world, and everyone wished to avoid the terrific cost of competitive naval building. Therefore, the other nations were quick to accept our proposals.

To my mind, the treaty that resulted was probably the best initiative toward peace that the world had ever known, for, if the signatory powers lived up to its terms, rival navies would be so nearly balanced that none would have a winning advantage over another in war. However, it should be noted that the value of the Treaty was to be derived entirely from the balancing of naval strengths. Unless they were kept in balance, in accord with the terms of the treaty, the agreement would be worthless as a war preventative.

Until the terms of the treaty were known, the miniature navies of the War College continued to be replicas of the navies of the world. However, as the various changes in navies were made, our little navies were changed to emulate them. For most navies, these changes were usually small and were generally additions; but for the United States, the changes were great and resulted in reductions. The United States had to scrap most of the splendid new ships it was building to reduce its navy from the strongest in the world to what was allowed by the treaty.

To those who believed that having the strongest navy in the world was the surest way to prevent another country from attacking us, scrapping the best fighting ships in the world seemed a terrible calamity. However, if by suffering this loss, war between the United States and any of the great powers could be prevented, it was perhaps not too great a price to pay. As the terms of the treaty became known, the College changed its little navies to conform to them, and by the time the treaty was ratified, our researches were being based entirely on "Treaty Navies." We soon knew what the changes meant to the United States.

Shortly after the treaty's ratification, when I was in Washington, I encountered on the street the Chairman of the House Naval Affairs Committee [Thomas S. Butler, R-PA]. As I had previously had many contacts with him during the World War, he greeted me warmly. But I was surprised when he said, "Captain, you are just the man I want to talk to about this Disarmament Treaty. Can you meet me in the Naval Committee Room at the Capitol this afternoon?" I said I could, and when I arrived there, he drew me at once into his private office and demanded to be told whether or not the treaty was a success. As no one could answer that unless he knew the treaty was really preventing war, I had to admit I did not know. Then I added, "Of course you realize it cannot possibly be a success unless the powers signing it maintain their navies at exactly the strength assigned them by the treaty. That fact applies to the United States as well as to other countries. The treaty is not a disarmament treaty but is one to balance naval strengths by limiting armaments. Therefore, although we have to scrap ships of certain types to get down to our limit, we must actually build ships of other types."

As I said that, the Congressman appeared enraged, shook his fist at me and shouted, "That is just the way with you navy men. No sooner than we agree to disarm than you tell us we must keep armed. We cannot count on you for anything." With that, the "powwow" ended.

That gave me my first intimation of the danger to the United States in the treaty. All during the conference leading to it, the "press" and pacifists spoke of the conference as a "disarmament conference." When it ended in a treaty intended to prevent war by limiting and balancing naval armaments, the treaty was spoken of as the "disarmament treaty." Because of that wrong title, many unthinking people believed there would be no war if only the United States would disarm itself.

In this way, a mere misnomer caused great trouble for the United States as foreign countries, pacifists, and even some of our legislators playing politics advocated our practical disarmament. I have since seen misnomers create similar trouble—for instance when an embargo act that was meant to eliminate a possible cause of war became spoken of as the "neutrality act."[189] However, it did not prove as harmful as did referring to the treaty limiting naval armaments as a "disarmament treaty." That name so befuddled the country that, after scrapping our excess ships in certain classes, we refused to build up the classes in which we were insufficient. For years the country did no naval building, and as a result, the United States not only ceased to be the greatest naval power in the world but quickly went so far below the strength assigned to it that it was nearly reduced to third place.

An Admiral's Yarn

Our failure to do our part in keeping naval armaments in balance destroyed the strategy for making war improbable. Although the idea had originated with us and was a splendid one, it was the United States' failure to do its part that ruined us. When other countries realized we had permitted our navy to plunge from first place to a poor second, they refused to renew the treaty. Therefore, not only did rivalry in naval building return, but the United States was forced into far greater building programs to catch up. Not only was prevention of war by balancing naval armaments lost to the world, but our country was forced into enormous expenditures to regain its naval standing.

Of course we could only surmise these results as that tour of duty at the War College was drawing to a close. The knowledge I had gained there on naval fighting would be, I hoped, of use to the fleet were I to become chief of staff to a high command. But I realized that should I be given such an assignment at that time, it would probably finish me in the navy, since too much staff duty was frowned upon in the selection of officers for flag rank, and I was soon to be up for selection.

I never quite understood why staff duty was not considered important, since there is nothing else better that prepares an officer for high command than being an assistant to an officer in that position. Apparently the important thing with selection boards is whether an officer under consideration has commanded a capital ship. Although I might be of vastly more value to the navy at the moment in a chief of staff job, I knew that if I were to be of any value to it later on, I must qualify for selection. Accordingly I made a written request for command of a battleship and was informed I would be so assigned.

While waiting for the orders, I received a letter inviting me to become chief of staff to the vice admiral in command of battleships. As I was a great admirer of that admiral and would have dearly loved to assist him in operating the navy's battle line, about which I had learned so thoroughly, declining that invitation was not easy. Nevertheless, I felt obliged to say the only duty I could afford to accept was the battleship command promised me.

At that point, I understood one of Satan's temptations, for the admiral promptly sent word that if I would be his chief of staff for the one year more that he would command the battleships, he would see to my getting command of our best battleship at the end of that time. As the proffer was flattering and apparently met my requirements, I was rather prone to accept it but decided to think it over before doing so. After much thought, I declined the offer once more.

The orders I received assigned me to command the battleship *Pennsylvania*.

XXXVII

Commanding a Battleship

WHEN I JOINED, the *Pennsylvania* was at San Pedro, California, with the battle fleet. I had heard much of the vast harbor improvements there, of course, and expected to find considerable change from my middy days, but it was far greater than I had dreamed. In addition to a mile-long breakwater extending eastward from Point Fermin, a large, deep-water inner harbor had been constructed, and a city with paved streets, city blocks, and streetcar lines stood where only a fishing village had been.[190]

The changes were not confined to San Pedro. To the eastward, where there had been only miles of white beach and sand dunes, stood the city of Long Beach, famous for its Signal Hill and other oil fields. It was filled with fine houses, hotels, and even "skyscrapers," and it was teeming with activity. Nor were the changes only on shore. The Port of Los Angeles had become one of the leading seaports, full of busy merchant shipping, great seagoing passenger and cargo ships, oil tankers, lumber carriers, and even many fine yachts. So changed was the entire area that I could scarcely believe I was once again in San Pedro. But as I thought about it, I realized that equally changed, too, were the naval ships in the harbor.

While I had lived and grown up with naval changes, I nevertheless was a bit awed by the huge battleship I had been ordered to command, over thirty-three thousand tons of it. The old *Nebraska*, less than half the size, had seemed to me about the last word in battleships when I joined it fifteen years before, but as a matter of fact, it was only a step beyond the older *Oregon*. However, the *Pennsylvania* was many more steps beyond the *Nebraska*. It could smother an

An Admiral's Yarn

enemy ship with gunfire at several times the distance at which the *Nebraska* could make a few hits; it used oil instead of coal for fuel; it could steam much faster and farther; it carried radio, gyrocompasses, and even airplanes; and it required almost a hundred officers and over twelve hundred men to man it for battle. The *Pennsylvania* was one of the fifteen battleships that the United States was allowed to have. It had cost the country almost forty million dollars, and it had taken several years to build it. Merely to supervise such a plant was no small responsibility, but to operate for the purpose of securing safety, security, protection, and victory in war was an infinitely greater one. Small wonder the outlook appeared awesome.

I had, however, the good fortune when I assumed command to find that the crew of the *Pennsylvania* was a wonderfully trained and highly skilled fighting unit. It stood at the top of the battleship list in both gunnery and engineering, and from its masthead flew the "meatball," the most prized trophy a naval ship can win, indicating it had stood first in battle efficiency for the preceding year. One might suppose that in taking command of a ship so splendidly trained for fighting that many of the problems were over for me. In certain ways they were. On the other hand, the perfected fighting efficiency of the *Pennsylvania* was something of a handicap, since an officer's ability in command is measured almost entirely by the improvement he can make in his ship's fighting efficiency. It is far less difficult to improve that efficiency in a low-standing ship than in one at the very top, which the *Pennsylvania* then was.

Difficult as it always is to better the top score of a big competition, doing so in the navy's battle efficiency competitions is still more so because of the "handicaps" brought by success. They are much like golf handicaps and in the navy are determined by setting a standard for a ship based on its best scores. The higher the score, the higher the standard set for it in the next competition. Hence, a ship that scores a top rating for a year's excellence is assigned a top "standard," which, if equaled the following year (rather than surpassed), reduces the ship to an average score in that following year. In other words, a score at the top for one year must be followed by improvement to allow a top score again the following year.

Fortunately for me, the ship's crew at that time was not only the finest I had ever managed but also the "fightingest." Never considering the handicap too great to overcome, they sought to stay at the top. They almost did. They made the ship the runner-up in the next year's competition, and when that brought a further increase in handicap, they continued to keep it near the top. It was a remarkable display of the will to win.

Commanding a Battleship

However, I must mention that the afternoon of the day I assumed command, a great tragedy occurred that brought deep sorrow to all in the navy. I had been two hours on the bridge and in the conning tower, planning how to control the ship both in peace and in battle, when suddenly the communication officer rushed to me with a radio message that had just been intercepted. It was from the battleship *Mississippi* reporting an explosion in the forward turret; the ship was rushing to port for medical assistance. Looking to seaward, I could see the *Mississippi* and at once ordered our medical department into boats to go to its assistance.

Not knowing how great the explosion had been, I feared the ship might be seriously damaged and was greatly relieved to see it apparently intact as it came to anchor. But although the ship looked normal, a frightful catastrophe had occurred. A flareback from a turret gun had fired the powder charges being sent up for loading and had exploded them. The entire crew of the turret, except one or two men who had miraculously escaped, had been killed. Fifty-six officers and men had lost their lives, making the explosion the worst of its kind the navy had ever known.[191]

As is always the case in such tragedies, the public was greatly aroused and there was talk in the press of probable carelessness by the navy in its handling of high explosives. However, if the United States Navy is careless, I have never known it. In tragedies such as this, every precaution devised has always been taken; but just as with railroads, ships at sea, and even industrial plants, not every danger can be foreseen and guarded against. It is the unforeseeable accidents that show the navy the additional precautions it must take, and of course the *Mississippi* explosion did just that. The navy seeks to preserve not only the nation's fighting ships but its personnel as well.

Although our immediate concern was to ensure against further explosions, the fleet personnel were also overwhelmed with grief over their brother officers and men who, in serving their country, had suffered so tragically. But great as our grief was, we longed to honor them in the manner they so well deserved, and the most impressive funeral service I have ever known was arranged.

Every officer and man of the fleet wished to attend the services, and it had to be held on the fleet's athletic field to accommodate all of them. As junior battleship captain, I was placed in charge of the funeral cortege. Led by the massed bands of the fleet, with all officers in dress uniform, it was an inspiring spectacle as they entered the field to the music of the funeral dirge—but little thought was given to that, because the focus of everyone's aching heart was upon the fifty-six caskets, each covered with a flag and flowers, in rows across the football field. In the sideline stands were thousands of enlisted men of the fleet; at

An Admiral's Yarn

the ends were the thousands of civilians who came to honor the dead; in special stands were the families of the deceased, while around the entire circumference of the field stood rank after rank of mourning officers. The church service was short, but it brought home to every navy man present that "in the midst of life we are in death."

The service over, the cortege and the massed bands marched off the field. Perhaps in this world there is a more inspiring and heart-rending ceremony than a navy funeral, though not to navy men. We returned from that one with a sadness men rarely feel or ever forget.

A few days later, the battle fleet left San Pedro for its summer cruise, stopping at San Francisco for the Fourth of July week and then proceeding to the Puget Sound area. There was little unusual in the cruise, though we did enjoy the manifold hospitalities of the Puget Sound ports between the sea maneuvers that lasted a week at a time and were spent in training and practicing the fleet-in-war operations. It was interesting but not always enjoyable, as the weather was generally bad and fogs were frequent. Our mood was still somewhat downcast.

To my mind, of all the vicissitudes at sea, the most trying on captains is when the fleet encounters thick fog. Fog is a worry to the captain even when his ship is operating singly, but more so when his ship is one of many in close formation where even a slight change of speed or course by any ship may cause a collision. Responsibility for the safety of over a thousand lives and a forty-million-dollar ship is certain to bring worries to any captain in a fog, and they came to me that summer.

One of our worst fog areas is west and northwest of the Strait of Juan de Fuca, where our sea maneuvers were held that summer. Few days were entirely free of fog, and frequently it was continuous for several days. Not only did I remain on the bridge for five days but had to remain awake and alert for any emergency. None came, I am thankful to say, but when at last we returned to port, I had been sixty-two consecutive hours without any rest. I sometimes hear that eight hours should be a day's work for a man at sea, and certainly it would be a relief if that could be. However, I doubt if it ever will be, since the perils of the sea do not observe union hours. Sailors must meet them without respect to hours of work, be they stretches of eight hours, twenty-four hours, or even several days. I believe in unions and in union hours, but they do not work at sea.

Between training periods, we visited Puget Sound ports from Port Angeles to Tacoma and enjoyed their many hospitalities. Besides attending dinners, receptions, luncheons, and dances, we were taken on numerous trips about the surrounding country to view the scenic wonders. One such trip was up Mt. Rainier to Paradise Inn, at the foot of the great glacier, where we spent two days.

Commanding a Battleship

The Inn is about halfway up the fourteen-thousand-foot peak, and the road leading to it is as beautiful as it is spectacular. Above the inn, the mountain is covered by the glacier, and the great adventure is for visitors to climb to the mountain top. To reach there takes a day and a half of hard work, but the return passage is made less difficult as the climbers wear what the guides call "tin pants." Sitting in the pants, on the snow, you simply slide down the glacier to the inn.

Through large telescopes we watched a "climb up" and a "slide down," which were most interesting. The only other sport was horseback riding. Whether or not putting "sailors on horseback" was to work a time-honored joke on us, I never learned; but the first thing I knew, admirals and captains were on horses. We had a great time covering considerable distance along the foot of the glacier and even examining ice caves and all sorts of unusual formations.

By the end of September, the fleet was once more in southern California waters and starting another six months of strenuous gunnery training. During these months we spent one week of each month in port for ship overhaul and upkeep work, and two days at sea for fleet maneuvers. The remainder of the time was used to prepare for and engage in target practice, which covered every form of defense against an enemy. Ships fired singly at short range, battle range, and extreme range, and singly practiced with torpedoes, anti-aircraft, and anti-torpedo-boat batteries. Collectively, they fired at targets as they would in battle, until at last every part of the fleet's fighting paraphernalia was as ready for war as we could make it.

The shooting season ended with spring, and our major training effort was changed from gunnery to fleet operations at sea. In this practice, the entire fleet engages in a great war game for about two months. Each year the game is based on a particular naval problem. Those of 1925 were centered about the Hawaiian Islands and were designed not only to test the defenses there but to train both navy and army, the former in attacks on shore bases, the latter in defending against them. In addition to the war problem, the operations that year were to afford still other opportunities for training; the fleet was given orders to make a three-month cruise in the southern Pacific, visiting Samoa, Australia, and New Zealand.

The fleet assembled in San Francisco Bay in April and, as was to be expected, there was much ado over the upcoming war game and cruise. Not only was the United States interested in a cruise that would culminate in a great gesture of amity toward Australia and New Zealand, but there was even more excitement in those islands; Australia went to the extent of sending its only official

An Admiral's Yarn

representative in the United States to speed the fleet on its way, while San Francisco made every effort to honor the country's departing convoy.

Of the many parties that were tendered the fleet, the one that most impressed me was the luncheon the Australian Commissioner gave for the admirals and captains. While it differed little from other luncheons of international character, including the speeches, the one given by the Australian Commissioner was quite different and amazing, for after voicing Australia's welcome to the fleet, he added words to this effect: "Officers of the fleet, you should not allow yourselves to gauge Australia's welcome to the fleet by San Francisco's marvelous farewell. I concede the spontaneousness of that and realize that as a city San Francisco is most generous to the fleet. But last night as I walked down Market Street, I realized that something was missing when I saw groups of handsome, young sailors and groups of San Francisco's lovely girls parading Market Street, allowing only glances at each other. Your strict American custom demanded formal introductions, and without them, they could not meet one another."

"Thank Heaven, you will not find introductions necessary in Australia. When your young men encounter Australia's young ladies in Sydney or Melbourne, they will be taken right to their bosoms, and I mean that literally as well as figuratively. Permit me to suggest, gentlemen, that you advise your men accordingly."

Needless to say, the interest in the cruise was intensified to some extent after that speech, and it may be that all minds in the fleet were not on our war games when we stood out of the Golden Gate. But if such were the case, it was not apparent. The fleet worked its hardest on the battle problem for some six weeks and seemed to think of nothing else. A royal welcome awaited us everywhere we stopped along our way to Australia.

XXXVIII

We Visit the Antipodes

It was in july (wintertime in australia) when the fleet left Honolulu. To many of us the voyage was just another cruise during which training for war would continue throughout the day and night. Nevertheless, we could not help but enjoy the many experiences of that journey.

The Samoan Islands were along our route both going and returning, and the four thousand miles between Honolulu and Australia and New Zealand were mostly in tropical waters where the weather was perfect for drills. We made the most of it, but did not fail to observe the amenities, the most important occurring when "crossing the line," an event for which every ship made elaborate preparations.

I doubt if Father Neptune's minions ever had a busier day than when the great fleet crossed the equator on its way to Samoa. Every ship had to be visited, and each one of the thousands of men on board who had never before crossed the line had to be initiated and accepted into his realm by the "God of the Sea." Since the entire day of crossing was required for initiations, it was made a holiday for the fleet, and all thoughts turned from war maneuvers to Father Neptune. However, because the ceremony is an ancient one, the details of which are always carefully observed, I will not attempt to describe it here.

Where we crossed the equator, I fully realized how small the world had become because of radio. When I was a youngster, a ship at sea was entirely severed from the rest of the world. Later, ships could exchange wireless messages with shore stations that were nearby, and when the battleship fleet made its cruise around the world in 1908, we received the big league baseball scores and a

An Admiral's Yarn

few news items every night. But by 1925, radio was covering the world rather thoroughly. Not only were messages transmitted day and night, but news broadcasting was such that every ship of the fleet turned out a little newspaper each morning containing highlights of the world's news.

To sailors who had first experienced sea life in the old sailing ships before radio was even dreamed of, the changes were impressive, especially since radio was available for private telegrams as well as official messages and news broadcasts. I was a bit skeptical about private messages—however, as the 24th of July approached and with it my silver wedding anniversary. I was determined to send greetings to my wife.

At that time, we were in the middle of the Pacific Ocean, while my wife and daughter were in Paris, France. I knew of course that, given time, the message would reach them, but in the hope that they might receive it when they wakened on the 24th, I filed it the morning of the 23rd. To my utter amazement, less than three hours after I sent it, I received a reply not only thanking me for my message and extending anniversary greetings, but to my great comfort it told me that my little family in Paris was in fine health. Though separated ten thousand miles by sea and land, my family and I were only an hour or two apart by wireless. How small the world had become.

Radio bettered life at sea, which had been improved in many other ways too, one of which was in the care of the sick and wounded. When I joined the navy, every ship had its doctor—larger vessels often had more than one—and every man was given medical attention as good as he would have received at home in a city. The doctors also performed emergency operations, but a patient requiring hospitalization could receive it on shore only. During the Spanish War, the navy acquired several "hospital ships" and stationed them at fleet bases. Those ships marked a great advance in naval medical care and became a regular part of the fleet, accompanying it on cruises, providing us with a hospital in every port. That Australian cruise, however, was fraught with incidents that made us realize how much we under-valued our hospital ships. One such occurrence was on the *Pennsylvania*.

One afternoon while on our way to Samoa, the senior doctor of the ship rushed to me and reported that one of our most beloved officers had acute appendicitis and must be operated on at once. He said he could perform the operation on the *Pennsylvania*, but it could be done more quickly and with far greater prospects of success if the officer were transferred to the hospital ship. I therefore rushed a radio message to the commander in chief [Robert E. Coontz], requesting the hospital ship's aid. Almost immediately that ship, which was then leading the fleet, turned back, and the *Pennsylvania* was directed to

We Visit the Antipodes

leave formation and transfer the officer to it for treatment. Within an hour after the case was reported to me, the patient had been transferred and the *Pennsylvania* had rejoined the formation. In another hour the hospital ship reported the operation a success. That experience revealed to all of us how much the care of naval men at sea had improved.

For the remainder of the run to Australia, all went as usual. The fleet anchored for one day in the Samoan Islands on the southeastern side of Tutuila, and the *Pennsylvania* was sent into Pago Pago harbor for a few hours. The small harbor has room for but one battleship. Pago Pago, the capital of American Samoa, also is the site of our naval station. The harbor is fascinating; it appears to be the crater of an extinct volcano, part of whose outside wall had fallen into the sea, thus providing an entrance channel. The rest of the crater wall forms mountainous cliffs close around the anchorage, and centuries of rain have produced a dense growth of tropical trees that make the cliffs as beautiful as they are awe-inspiring. But, because every few hours there would be a heavy downpour followed by great heat, we were thankful to leave that pocket of far too much rain and steaming heat. As we stood out, the fleet got underway for the last of the run to Australia.

The ships of the fleet were divided into two parts for the visits to Australia and New Zealand. One went to Sydney and Auckland and the other, to which the *Pennsylvania* belonged, to Melbourne and Wellington. The city of Melbourne looked about the same as it did when I was there in the *Nebraska* eighteen years before, but, whereas all the ships had anchored out in the bay on the previous visit, they now were assigned berths at the recently completed piers. The one to which the *Pennsylvania*, two other battleships, and the fleet flagship *Seattle* were moored was enormous. Even with two ships on each side, it had room for two more. Because the huge pier could handle tens of thousands of visitors at a time and all types of transportation to it were available, we received a tremendous welcome as soon as the ships secured.

The commander in chief at the time was a close and very dear friend of mine who had been executive officer of the *Nebraska* on my previous visit to Australia. Because of our duties on the first visit, neither of us had partaken of the hospitalities then, so we both had much to learn and to enjoy on this, our second visit to Australia. The commander in chief was certain to be on every important invitation list, but to insure that I would be also, he informed me in Honolulu that he had directed his aide to schedule me for them too.

I cannot begin to do justice in relating the many delightful entertainments. They covered every day and night for the two weeks—official ones by the governor general, the Australian Parliament, and the city of Melbourne, and

An Admiral's Yarn

unofficial ones by various organizations and individuals. In addition, a number of one-day trips were made to nearby cities, one of which was a group of five hundred men of whom I was given charge to take to a health resort in the hills some sixty miles east of Melbourne.

That trip was delightful, and the town we visited outdid itself entertaining us. Unfortunately the weather was cold and, although southeastern Australia has a climate much like ours in southern California, artificial heat is often needed in mid-winter. However, the heat in the buildings usually came from one open fireplace which, while sufficiently warming the Australians, left us feeling uncomfortably cold.

Conversation often drifted to heat in houses, and while I was talking to a leading citizen of the town and his wife, they commented on the central heating system of America and wondered how in the world we endured it. They said they had been in a New York hotel one winter and almost "roasted." I cleared the point a trifle by saying that, even though the weather outside might be zero, Americans would open windows, something rarely done in Australia during the winter, and also would turn off the heat occasionally. Our hosts seemed not to realize that heaters could be adjusted, but even so, they did not care for central heating.

About a week later I entertained the hospitality committee of that town at a luncheon on the *Pennsylvania*. The weather was like a fine fall day and the guests seemed to enjoy themselves immensely. They arrived about eleven o'clock and were shown over the ship before luncheon. but when that was over, they remained right in my cabin until seven o'clock that evening. I finally asked if they would kindly excuse me because I was obliged to dress for the House of Parliament dinner. They soon departed, but before they left, the lady who had condemned American central heating said to me, "You know, Captain, we realize as well as you do that we should have left this ship hours ago, but we were all warm for the first time this winter and decided to make the most of it. Central heating is indeed delightful."

Of all the experiences that winter in Australia, the most interesting to me was a four-day train tour, which included a party of sixty higher fleet officers, taken around the state of Victoria. It was arranged to enable the outlying cities and towns of the state to participate in Australia's welcome to the fleet, and they responded with a great ovation. The train was the finest in Australia, used a few months previously for a tour of the state by the then Prince of Wales, later British King, and later the Duke of Windsor, on his visit to the Commonwealth. It was a fine train, comparable to those used in the United States for similar

We Visit the Antipodes

occasions, but because the state-owned railroads used different gauges, it was forced to remain within the state.

We lived in the train for four days—it had sleeping, dining, and "club" cars, one of which contained a wonderfully equipped bar, so it was quite an ideal arrangement except that it did not have central heating, and the weather was well below the freezing point. We were forced to wear overcoats, wrap ourselves in blankets, and ask constantly for the hot-water foot warmers provided by the train.

The schedule was a stiff one, and about the only good rest on the trip came the first night. We left Melbourne at about dark in order to reach a Murray River town on Victoria's northern boundary early the following day. From then on, a typical day's festivities would start with a two-hour forenoon visit in the town, a short run to another town for luncheon, a run to a third for an afternoon reception and tea, and then to a fourth where we would attend a dinner and grand ball. As the balls were generally all-night affairs, the train would wait until about 3 a.m., and at that, we would barely catch it. In spite of our schedule being strenuous we saw much of the state of Victoria.

We visited all of its principal towns and cities, including Bendigo, Ballarat, and Geelong. We were taken over Australia's mined-out gold fields, and we saw a few of the immense ranches, which they call "stations," for huge herds of cattle and sheep. In most respects the country did not appear greatly different from our own. The people lived much as we do and faced similar problems. Their automobiles were not quite as numerous, and all were American made. Advertising signs in Australia were about the same as in our country, for apparently most manufactured articles—from automobiles to sewing machines, typewriters, and patent medicines—came from the United States.

Although Australia's entertainment, business, luxuries, habits, and problems seemed about the same as our own, there was one different form of life we particularly wanted to see—the wild kangaroos. We had seen them in zoos and circuses but never in the wild. Since they are native to Australia, we had expected to see many of them jumping about in the vast open spaces where the train passed through. When we failed to see a single one the first two days of the trip, all hands watched eagerly for them. The people at one of the small stations brought a baby kangaroo to greet us, which only increased our desire to see wild ones en masse.

Then, when we were running between distant and far apart little towns in western Victoria, we suddenly came upon a herd of a dozen or more kangaroos jumping across a pasture, apparently frightened by the noise of the train, and we

An Admiral's Yarn

had an excellent view of them. The newspaper men with us evinced even greater excitement than we naval officers.

In discussing the trip after our return to Melbourne, a leading citizen told me he had followed the newspaper account of it with much interest. Then he added, "But those reporters with you must have been storytellers. I believed everything they wrote except their kangaroo story. That one was too much for me. Were they drunk when they wrote it, or what happened?"

I looked at him in amazement, for to us those kangaroos were merely what we expected to see. I asked the reason for his doubt, while stating that every naval officer as well as the newspaper men saw them exactly as described in the paper—the story was true. "Great Scot," said he, "there has not been a wild kangaroo in this part of Australia for years, and if that is a fact, I once again take off my hat to the Australians in entertaining visitors!"

Shortly after the tour, our stay in Australia ended. The usual functions marked its close, perhaps the most outstanding being the fleet's farewell "reception and ball," the largest affair of its kind that we could manage. The *Pennsylvania* had been designed as a fleet flagship, and being the best-equipped for entertaining, it was chosen to do the honors. We soon realized, however, that for all its size, the *Pennsylvania* would not hold all our invited guests, of whom there were legion. We wished to entertain everyone who had entertained us, and thousands of invitations were issued, not only to private individuals but to government and city officials as well as the entire membership of many organizations. We knew too that each of the invitations would bring whole families to the party, so we prepared for an enormous gathering.

Fortunately the great pier and the three other large ships secured to it enabled us to meet the situation. We arranged to receive our guests on the *Pennsylvania*, using the other three ships for dancing, and the pier for promenading. In that way we could care for thousands of guests—and we had them!

The invitations were for nine o'clock, but just as I was starting to dress for the ball shortly before eight o'clock, the orderly hurried to the cabin to report that guests were arriving. The early arrival greatly surprised me, just as it would, I knew, the other fleet officers. I therefore hustled into my evening uniform and rushed messengers and signals to the commander in chief and the other ships. How they did it I do not know, but before eight-thirty, all officers were at their stations and the ball went off like clockwork. At nine o'clock, all other guests being present, the Governor General, representative of Britain's King, came on board. At this point, something became clear to me. In Great Britain and its Colonies, I surmised, guests must arrive before the King or his representative appears. The wording in our invitations told Australians that the governor

We Visit the Antipodes

would arrive at nine o'clock; therefore, they were all on board to greet him well before that time. Thus we learned an important lesson in British royal etiquette.

A day or two after the ball, the fleet left Australia, with the division at Melbourne going to Wellington, New Zealand's capital. To reach there, we crossed the Tasman Sea, continuing on through Cook Strait between North and South Islands. Having read much concerning the rough weather of the Tasman Sea in winter, we expected what we found there. We were not, however, prepared for the scenic splendors of New Zealand that we saw from Cook Strait on that clear cool morning when we stood through the break in the great mountain chain that extends the length of New Zealand.

Wellington, on North Island, lies at the eastern entrance to the strait and has one of the most beautiful harbors I have ever seen. It is large, with high, steep hills surrounding it, some of which jut out toward the bay like huge fingers. In the city, the houses and buildings are of typically old English design, sprawling over the hills, the red roofs showing through the trees, creating a remarkable picture. The harbor apparently leaves nothing to be desired, but in actuality, it is not an ideal place for ships. Fierce squalls from the mountains rush across it so frequently that the city is spoken of as "Windy Wellington." We found it very deserving of this name.

New Zealand's entertainment of the fleet was similar to Australia's, and we were shown as many courtesies and attentions along the same lines. Nevertheless, the two peoples were very different, I thought, for while the Australians are quite outspoken like the Americans, New Zealanders have the more formal manner of Englishmen. However, after greetings were over, we found them very charming.

Aside from attending innumerable entertainments in Wellington, we were shown historical places of interest and many wonderful factories, including those producing woolen goods, etc. Never had we seen such blankets, steamer rugs, and fabrics as we saw being made there, and every man in the fleet purchased as much as he possibly could. Interesting though New Zealand's greatest industry is, our sightseeing activities were not confined to it. Especially intriguing to me was the visit to Parliament.

At one of the great banquets, I sat next to the "Speaker of the House," who invited several of us to attend one of the afternoon sessions of Parliament, which of course we did. The "Capitol" of New Zealand, or Parliament as they call it, is the large, handsome structure one would expect the "Capitol" of a great Commonwealth to be—but we were scarcely prepared for our reception there. No sooner was our party announced to the speaker than he hurried out to great and escort us into the "Chamber," where seated around the Speaker's table were

An Admiral's Yarn

the members of Parliament. Being the senior officer present, I was given a seat on the rostrum, and for nearly an hour we were treated as participants in the legislative activities of New Zealand.

Then came time for tea, and in apparent accord with an old English custom, the House took recess for it. Expecting the members to hurry to their restaurant, our party started to say goodbye, whereupon the speaker informed us that we were to have tea with them and we were conducted to a beautiful housekeeping apartment in the Capitol. In addition to that apartment for the speaker and his family, the building contained one for every member of Parliament. Thus we learned something new about governments. Some are far more liberal toward "public servants" than are others.

As many of the House members accompanied our party to tea, we soon found ourselves in a gathering of New Zealand's political leaders, all of whom seemed to be dominated by the Speaker's charming wife. Not only was she a perfect hostess for such an occasion, but she seemed to radiate a political wisdom much sought after by the men. When at last I could engage her in conversation, she told me much about New Zealand politics, on which she undoubtedly was an authority. Then she greatly surprised me by saying that she was the daughter of a Maori chief.

When New Zealand was discovered by the whites, it was inhabited by the Maoris, perhaps the finest people in all the Polynesian Islands. Though they lived in much the same way as other Polynesians, they were almost as light in coloring as northern Europeans and were of a fine physique and appearance. In their dealings they observed high standards of moral obligation. They were great warriors, willing to fight for their land, but they had none of the blood-thirstiness of savages and always fought fairly or not at all. Being a splendid people, they quickly won the hearts of the British who took the islands and who have since then looked to the natives with pride, accepting them as equals. Many intermarried, and when we went to New Zealand we found that many of its finest men and women, its leaders, boasted Maori blood. Our hostess was one of them and gave me a clear understanding of Maori character and life.

Scheduled for a few days later was a tour to Rotorua, which we were anxious to make, and it proved to be the outstanding event of our visit to Zealand. Our train left about mid-day from Wellington and carried us to a city where a fine, small hotel provided a late dinner for us, gave us an impromptu dance, and put us up overnight. After an early breakfast we were taken the remainder of the way to Rotorua in automobiles, stopping en route to see New Zealand's wonderful caves, which are said to be the largest and most spectacular in the world—although at that time the Carlsbad Caverns had not been opened. I

We Visit the Antipodes

know now that in size and in certain beauties, Carlsbad Caverns surpass them, but in its "Glow Worm Cave," New Zealand apparently had something entirely its own.

Glow Worm Cave, through which runs a subterranean stream, probably ranks among the world's finest, but what makes it so utterly unique is the myriad of glow worms that hang from the dome, outlining it in a pale blue ethereal light. As artificial light is not permitted in the cavern, its darkness is intense. Too dark for walking, we were taken through it in boats pulled along wires stretched over the stream, with not a sound to be heard. We seemed to be in another world, impressive and wonderful, but from which we were rather glad to emerge and then enter our automobiles for Rotorua.

Rotorua is in the heart of what New Zealand calls the "thermal regions," an immense national park filled with geysers, boiling springs, warm mineral springs, fiery pits, and red hot fumaroles. Except for sightseers and those who go there for medicinal baths, the area is a reservation for Maoris, where they may pursue their own way of life. The men carry on the agricultural work and industries of the area, while the women, particularly the unmarried ones, in addition to their household duties, act as guides for visitors. Besides its marvels of nature, Rotorua has the quiet charm of Maori life.

Our party from Melbourne reached the Rotorua railroad station at the same time a train from Auckland appeared with a contingent of officers from the part of the fleet that was based there. After the two groups joined, we marched into the native village at the entrance to the park where we were received in the ancient Maori manner, the like of which we had never before experienced.

The village is built around a large plaza. In the plaza were groups of children, old women, men, and girls. At the plaza entrance stood rows of the fiercest looking warriors that can be imagined. All were garbed in accordance with the old Maori ritual. In addition to their savage dress, the warriors were painted in a horrifying manner and carried long spears and huge war clubs. They made ugly faces at us, stuck out their tongues, and acted sufficiently ferocious to scare away any enemy. Gradually the warriors fell back to allow us to enter the plaza. Having thus been accepted by the Maoris, we were seated on one side of the plaza, while in front of us they exhibited their native dances, their skill in fighting, and cleverness in handling their peculiar weapons. It was a picturesque performance in which we were very interested and regretted when it was time for tea.

After that we were shown "medicinal baths," and most of us tried one. The one I was given was a sunken affair in a marble pit that had steps all around

An Admiral's Yarn

leading to the tub—quite enticing, I thought, but when I got into the horrible smelling water I started to collapse and an attendant pulled me out.

After a hasty supper, we were taken to the amusement hall, a small theater similar to those in our own little towns, where the Maoris put on a "musical show." In collaboration with the natives, it had been composed and staged by New Zealand's leading producers for the Prince of Wales' visit to Rotorua and was repeated for us. We did not expect much of a show when we entered the little theater, so were greatly surprised when it proved to be quite beautiful and delightful. Stage settings and acts were all based on Maori scenes and customs. Into the music and songs was woven the full Maori personality of handsome young men and beautiful girls. They seemed to be natural born actors, and they put on a most convincing exhibition.

After the performance there was a grand ball with all Rotoruans in attendance in native dress—quite a spectacular and unusual affair which we enjoyed until the "wee small hours."

After breakfast the next morning we were shown Rotorua's natural wonders. We had been told that the villagers would guide us, and we expected to find them waiting for us in their native garments. Imagine our surprise when instead of wonderfully bedecked natives, we were met by formally attired English ladies and gentlemen. It was hard to believe they were the hosts and hostesses of the night before. They conversed with us in beautiful English, proved to be highly educated and well informed, and were vastly pleased over having fooled us the night before. Little wonder I think highly of Maori acting ability.

They made that morning a memorable one, and the wonders of the "thermal regions" lost nothing by their exploitation of them. Each officer had a Maori maiden guide watching over him to see that he did not burn a foot off in a fumarole by walking into boiling mud or springs or from being drenched by a geyser. At noon that day we were taken to our trains for a return to Wellington and Auckland.

Our New Zealand visit was then almost over and farewell parties became the order. After a Grand Ball given on the *Pennsylvania*, we regretfully got under way and sailed for home ports.

XXXIX

We Return to the U.S.A.

GREATLY THOUGH WE ENJOYED OUR VISIT and interlude from training, we were happy to be returning to our own United States. Off Auckland, the two parts of the fleet reassembled, and from then on training at sea was again continuous.

The first break in it came at Samoa, where the fleet anchored off the island of Tutuila for a few days. On the way to Australia, we had visited the windward (southeastern) side of the island, but on the return trip we anchored in long lines close to the shore on the lee (northwestern) side. From there, Tutuila looked very different, for instead of high mountains rising abruptly from the rough waters of a rockbound coast, there is a long sandy beach behind which hills rise somewhat gradually into the mountains. The verdure and beauty of the island are the same on both sides, but because the lee probably provides easier living, its nooks and crannies are filled with small villages. Hidden away, they were not visible from our anchorage, but scarcely were our anchors down before huge canoes hurried from them to trade and barter with us.

The ways of Samoans may not be different from the natives of other islands in the South Pacific, but to us they were new and strange. The great canoes carried not only coconuts, fruits, and curios for trade but also about forty natives—men, women, and children. We learned later that each canoe was a native craft under the charge of the village chief who was responsible for the welfare of the inhabitants, and he had brought them to the ships with everything they had for trade. Unfortunately, some of the men had elephantiasis, but as a people, they were handsome and of splendid physique. What they had to barter, other than

An Admiral's Yarn

fruit was rather crude, for having no tools as we know them, their curios were mostly tapa cloth, miniature Samoan canoes, ferocious looking war clubs and fantastic fighting weapons, mats, and other articles of plaited reeds and palm leaves.

Apparently there was no trading competition between the canoes of the different villages, although when a ship dropped anchor, the canoes engaged in a race to it. The canoe to first reach a ship "claimed" that vessel for its village. Thereafter, no other canoe would approach that ship, and all of the ship's intercourse with shore was always through the inhabitants of that one village.

The village that gained charge of the *Pennsylvania* was about the same size as the others, but was somewhat more important because of an experience it had had with France. Many years before, when native tribes were supreme, a French man-of-war visiting Tutuila had permitted its officers to land in the village, where three of them were ambushed and killed by the wild Samoans. The French, of course, retaliated, but later, when the island became peaceful once more, France erected a small memorial cemetery in the village for the slain officers. It was enclosed by an iron fence; the tombs were substantial and suitably inscribed; and arrangements were made with the village to care for it. To impress Samoans with the importance of the trust, the village was presented with the gold-lace embroidered coat and cocked hat of an ambassador of France, to be worn by the village chief on important occasions. Evidently it served its purpose, for among the numerous villages, the one whose chief could sport such a coat and hat stood at the very top of his fellow man.

Having acquired the *Pennsylvania* for his village, the chief called formally on the Admiral [Coontz] and Captain [Laning] the morning after our arrival. On anchoring, we had seen him in native garb in his village canoe and expected him to appear in the same outfit when calling. But, although canoe, cargo, and the other occupants were as before, the chief was of vastly different appearance. Dressed otherwise as a native, he sported the ambassador's coat and cocked hat!

As he sat in his canoe, he looked rather imposing, but when he came over the side, where the admiral and I met him to extend formal greetings, he appeared much less so. Although he wore the usual native short pants and a shirt with tails out, his only other garments were the coat and cocked hat, neither of which fitted him. His huge feet and legs were bare, his great arms far too long for the coat, and because of their age, both coat and hat were badly worn and faded. On our great modern battleship, he looked grotesque—a fact that bothered him not at all.

Accompanied by the several lesser lights of his village and a native interpreter, he acted the chief and was treated as such. Neither to the Samoans nor to

We Return to the U.S.A.

ourselves was there anything ludicrous about the visit, and when it was time for his departure, he invited the admiral, captain, and ten of the ship's officers to visit his village. We accepted with alacrity. Soon after, we prepared our gifts, since gifts are the all-important feature of an official visit to a village. We took colored cloth, broken tools, old garments and numerous cans of salmon, the food prized above all others by Samoans.

The visit was one to remember. The coral reefs prevented our boat from reaching the beach, so the natives waded out, carried us ashore on their backs, and led us to the well-kept little cemetery. Then we were taken to the village of some fifteen or twenty huts sprawled over about ten acres of cleared jungle. The huts were all alike, thatch-covered domes set on about a dozen high posts arranged in a circle. The huts were utterly bare and, except when mats were hung from the roofs as screens, afforded no privacy. The floors were the hard, dry earth.

Outside each was a small rock oven, but otherwise, the natives seemed to possess absolutely nothing but the scanty clothing on their backs. If there were any living conveniences, they were not visible, and in that climate and those surroundings, it is probable that none were needed. I believe the natives cultivated a few yams and perhaps raised a few pigs, but otherwise they seemed to live on what grew wild. There was no evidence of their making curios.

The official welcome started in one of the huts. We officers and the leading men of the village sat on mats in a large circle, made speeches, and then partook of the native drink of welcome. The highly ceremonial drink was prepared in a large calabash in the center of the circle. It contained no alcohol and was made by soaking a native plant in the water of the calabash and then squeezing it out. While we thought the drink seemed insipid and utterly without effect, the whites on the island vociferously opposed its use by the natives in their welcoming ceremonies, claiming it caused "trouble." Each of us drank the half coconut shell of liquid passed to us by a Samoan warrior.

After the welcome speeches and drinking were completed, we were taken to another hut for a feast. A large circle of fresh palm leaves had been laid out on the floor, and food for each village dignitary and guest had been arranged in piles around its outer edge. In addition to the food, the place for the admiral boasted a bent pewter knife and fork and also a broken cup, the only eating utensils in the village! We drank from freshly opened green coconuts and used our hands to consume food. On the inside of the palm leaf circle, opposite each place on the outside, sat a woman of the village waving a green palm leaf. The women were not there to eat with us, so we thought their duty was to keep us cool by fanning

An Admiral's Yarn

us, but we soon learned they were there to fight off the millions of flies that swarmed about us.

As the measure of a Samoan feast is determined by the number and size of the yams served, this was probably a great affair, for at each place were six or eight huge yams. Also there were many pieces of roast pig and much fruit. We tried to eat a little of everything but found it difficult; the meat was overly tough and the yams enormous. Consequently, immense quantities of food remained when we rose from the feast, and the women started shrieking and grabbing for it. It was not that they were so hungry, but each one was supposed to gather in the leftovers for her family. It was a Samoan custom.

After the feast we were taken through and around the village. All of the inhabitants took part and we went to a hut overlooking a fair-sized open space where the natives gave what they called their "Siva-siva dance." The dance had many ramifications, since old men, young men, women, children, warriors, and maidens all dramatize different features of Samoan life. The last presentation was by unmarried girls, who, just as the sun went down, were apparently offering themselves to the guests in accordance with the old Samoan custom. At that point our admiral announced it was a time to return to the ship, which we did.

Naturally we gave a return party on the *Pennsylvania*, and the entire village came. The natives did not seem to care for our tables, chairs, or eating methods, but after piling their food on paper plates, they squatted about the deck to eat. Afterward they made a series of speeches and then gave another "Siva-siva" dance for the benefit of the *Pennsylvania*'s crew. We were careful, however, to send them ashore before sunset.

Although the battleships evidently impressed them greatly, the Samoans were most excited over our airplanes which, not having been flown in Australia or New Zealand, were sent up daily for drill at Tutuila. In one of the flowery orations that the native chiefs love to make, the oldest of them, who in his younger days had been a great warrior, brought his speech to a close by speaking of the aircraft. It was interpreted for us that he had recounted the legendary history of the island and spoke of the wonders that our American occupation had brought to it. Then he added, "We are not awed by your great ships that go on the water or under the water, but when we were told that you have ships that fly like birds we would not believe it. Now I have seen those ships that fly like birds and I am ready to die."

Remarkable as our mechanical devices must have seemed to Samoans, I suspect some of our everyday customs were equally amazing, especially our use of money for trade. I discovered that when I tendered money for curios, the natives did not want it and appeared not to know what it was. I tried to buy two

We Return to the U.S.A.

or three war clubs and a canoe, but when I offered money for them, they turned me down. Thinking they might not be satisfied with the amount offered, I kept raising my bid until it was seven dollars and a half, much more than the curios were worth. The more I offered the more disgusted they became. At that point, my Filipino mess boy came to me and suggested that I offer two enlisted men's undershirts (which I think cost sixty-five cents each). That worked like a charm, and not only did I get all the curios I had tried to buy but numerous sea-bean necklaces, carved coconut shells, tapa cloths and the like. All for two shirts!

Our next run was to Honolulu where we interrupted fleet training for a week to enjoy Hawaii before returning to our California bases for six months of intensive gunnery. The work was along the lines of the preceding winter, though aircraft were much more important now. Not only did our larger ships have full quotas of planes, but two huge aircraft carriers had also joined the fleet. Having battleships, cruisers, destroyers, and submarines as well as aircraft gave us a navy vastly different from the one I had joined as a boy. No longer was it merely a few antiquated ships operating singly here and there over the world. It had become an aggregation of powerful modern warships to be operated together as an immense fighting team, and it was probably as well trained for war as any in the world at that time.

To test its readiness, we had the annual war problem, that particular one concentrating on the defense of the Panama Canal against an enemy in the Pacific. After that main problem was completed, the fleet remained at Panama about six weeks to engage in minor ones, but the *Pennsylvania* did not remain there. Our time for Navy Yard overhaul had come, so when the big game was over, the ship made a high-speed run to Puget Sound.

The overhaul took nearly two months, and at its end, about the first of June, the *Pennsylvania* rejoined the fleet at San Pedro. Because I was then finishing my allowed two years in command of a battleship, I prepared for shore duty by requesting duty as a student at the Army War College—spending my time until then at the Naval War College. The request was granted, and when my two years in command were up, I relinquished the *Pennsylvania* to my successor.

Leaving a ship at the end of a cruise is always trying, but leaving the last ship an officer will ever command is a fearful strain on the heart strings. It marks his end in the navy unless he should be selected for flag rank, and I had arrived at that point. But sad as I was over the possible ending of my sea-going life, I was more distressed over leaving the *Pennsylvania* and the officers and men who, by their tireless teamwork, indefatigable energy, and never-ending loyalty and devotion, had kept the ship outstanding in spite of every handicap. Small wonder I broke down when the entire ship's company gathered on deck to bid me

An Admiral's Yarn

good-bye; when officers manned the boat to take me ashore; when the band played "Auld Lang Syne," and I was given a tremendous farewell cheer. I had hardly recovered my voice that night when the crew gave a great ball in my honor, and it was only after I had boarded the train the next day to start east that it lost its huskiness.

XL

Shore Duty Again

TRYING THOUGH IT WAS TO LEAVE THE *PENNSYLVANIA*, compensation lay ahead. My little family had toured Europe the last year of my cruise and was now in Newport waiting to greet me when I reported to the Naval War College. Since being together would mean personal happiness for us, my sadness over giving up command soon disappeared in the joyful anticipation of resuming family life after the longest separation we had known. Reunions had always been joyous for us, but of them all, this one meant the most, because it promised to keep the family together for a long time.

Our plan was a delightful one. We were to spend July and August in Newport while I worked at the War College, and then live in Washington all winter during my course at the Army War College.[192] The arrangement seemed perfect. I could continue my study of national defense, my family could enjoy Newport and Washington, and best of all, we would be together.

However, no sooner had I reported to the Naval War College than I was handed orders to proceed to Washington at once for temporary duty as senior member of a Joint Army and Navy Board to plan the underwater defense of our coasts and harbors. Those orders played havoc with our summer plans, but since the Board would probably complete its work before the Army War College course started, we still expected at least to carry out our winter plans. Because of the heat in summer in Washington, and the uncertainties of the temporary duty, my family remained in Newport.

It may seem that planning underwater defense for our coasts and harbors would be a simple matter, but take it from me, it is far from that. Underwater

An Admiral's Yarn

defense is an important part of the total defense system and must fit into it closely. Both navy and army have their parts to play, and with the divided responsibilities, planning becomes difficult.

Perhaps the most severely criticized aspect of national defense is the seeming friction between generals and admirals who are working together. Both groups have been condemned for failing to cooperate, when actually the fault was rarely theirs. The trouble generally arises from laws that delegate to each service responsibility for certain parts of the coastal defense, but make neither service responsible for the defense in its entirety. Thus the joint operations for defense have had two masters, neither of whom can assume each other's responsibilities.

Though much thought was given to joint action before our Board met, little actual progress was made in overcoming the conflict in responsibility that had been imposed by law. Our board consisted of experts on the underwater devices of the two services, but since navy devices had to be used even within entrances to harbors, and army devices had to be used well to seaward, we still faced the same conflict in authority with all joint actions, whether they be in the air, on the sea's surface, or under it. Nothing could be done until the board studied all plans and rules governing all joint coast defense activities. Under such circumstances, we had to go far beyond our orders by assuming what would be the general rules that should govern joint coast defense activities, and then plan an underwater system that conformed to them. It was a considerable undertaking, and we worked on it day and night. In one way, the weather helped us, for without doubt, the seven weeks we worked were the hottest I have ever known. For ten consecutive days the mercury went to 105° or over. However, instead of considering it too hot for work, we hustled all the more from eight in the morning until after midnight every day, including Sundays, to finish the job.

We first drew up what we considered to be adequate rules to govern joint action, and based on those rules, we planned for the underwater part of the defense. Naturally our report went far beyond what we were directed to do, and the Board felt quite satisfied with it, accepting fully our underwater plan.

As the Board's work neared an end, I began to look for a house in anticipation of my family moving to Washington. I was surprised indeed when I received word from the detail officer not to rent a house because I was to be ordered to command the Naval Training Station in San Diego, California.[193] Having recently left the West Coast, and looking forward to a tour of duty in the East, I could hardly believe my change of orders. Going back meant the destruction of our family plans. The news was upsetting because, not only would I be unable to continue my war studies, but the plans of my family for a winter in Washington, where our daughter was to make her debut, were completely wrecked.

Shore Duty Again

Command of the Training Station at San Diego is considered a "plum" in the naval service, not only because it is splendidly equipped, but because southern California is blessed with all the attractions of that type of climate, such as flowers and ease of living. We arrived to a warm welcome at the railroad station by a delegation of San Diegans, who took us to the commanding officer's quarters where we were made to feel at home.

I might write pages on that tour of duty—so different from any I had ever experienced. Having authority over one of San Diego's most prized naval assets, we immediately became a part of the community's social and civic life. Since I also supervised the training of nearly all the navy's recruits from west of the Mississippi River, we had a busy and interesting life.

Having entered the navy at a time when its recruits were mostly seagoing foreigners picked up on the waterfronts of our seaport cities, it was indeed revealing to see our naval recruits of 1926. All were young men a trifle over eighteen years of age; all had gone to our public schools; and all were American citizens. Though many had graduated from high school and some had been in college, their combined education averaged over two years of high school work. Nearly all of them joined the navy to prepare for the future and were sincere, hard workers.

We Americans are ever boastful of our young men and of what they can accomplish compared with others, but not long after I began training recruits, and when I found they could do almost anything and do it well, I became more boastful than anyone. I do not mean that they, as individuals, were "Jacks of all trades," but collectively they were. The specialties that recruits could select for study covered every branch of naval activity, allowing them to choose what they desired. Since the activities covered almost every line of human endeavors, small wonder young men sought to join the navy. Not only did they receive pay while learning the trade they wished to follow, but they could see the world while doing it.

To help young men perfect themselves in their specialties, the navy offered a number of educational courses covering all branches of public school work, many of college work, and various specialties of the navy—electricity, radio, gas engines, marine engines, ordnance, etc. All were available for the asking. However, one man who said he was preparing for the ministry requested a course in "Ancient Hebrew," and I believe a partial course was arranged for him.

Although our time was well occupied, Sundays and holidays were free, and we made the most of them. I purchased my first automobile and we spent many interesting hours seeing southern California, the mountains, deserts and seacoast. I took the opportunity to read many historical novels of the area and to

An Admiral's Yarn

visit the localities of the stories. It was fascinating to see where such stories as Charles Dana's *Two Years before the Mast* and Helen Hunt Jackson's *Ramona* had their origin.[194]

But not all our amusements were sightseeing or historical. There were other adventures, such as being taken to Hollywood for the preview of a Marine Corps movie featuring Lon Chaney, and being called on to fight overflowing rivers after a deluge of rain. Of them all, the most exciting was Charles A. Lindbergh's preparation for his famous transatlantic flight.

There was little interest in San Diego when a fair-haired aviator came there seeking an airplane for a flight across the Atlantic. Enterprising reporters wrote short news squibs about it for the local papers, but in the area of huge navy, army, and commercial air activities, Lindbergh's proposed flight attracted little public attention. However, our recruits were intensely interested in flying and spent much of their spare time at the commercial airfield and plant across the road from our station, where Lindbergh's plane was being built. They soon came to know all about the plane, and since Lindbergh himself was always friendly toward them, his flight quickly became theirs.

At last the plane was assembled, and tuning it began—much of which was done in the air over the station. The noise became terrific, though it did not seem to annoy the recruits. They looked on that plane and Lindbergh as their particular property and watched them by the hour. When the plane started eastward, they eagerly noted its progress; and when the flight across the Atlantic started, they could think of nothing else.

Although few of the several thousand experienced aviators of the neighborhood thought one lone man could fly a plane all the way across the Atlantic, the station's recruits were certain that Lindbergh could do it. Therefore, while the flight was in progress [20–21 May 1927], it was difficult to get them to think of anything else. When it ended successfully, they assumed the "I told you so" attitude and returned to work.

Our radio loud speakers were busy spreading the news of Lindbergh's triumphal ovations to the recruits, and I particularly recall his arrival in Washington, D.C., where President Coolidge and the entire capital welcomed him. What a great achievement and how small the world has become since then.

After a year at the Training Station, it began to appear that I would be under consideration for selection to the rank of rear admiral when the Board met in July, but at that time I gave little thought to being chosen. You can imagine my surprise, therefore, when, while at my desk one morning, I heard a loud cheer in my outer office and a clerk rushed in waving a telegram, shouting, "Captain, Captain! You've been made an admiral." Never will I forget the thrill of that

Shore Duty Again

moment! My boyhood ambition had been to be an admiral in the navy, and for thirty-six years I had worked steadily to become worthy of the rank. So, little wonder I was thrilled and excited over the news that I had made it.

I suspect my excitement transmitted itself to the entire Training Station. At any rate, they hurried to do me honor, and my last few weeks there were exciting with all sorts of entertainments to celebrate my promotion. And, as though that were not enough joy, I received a message from the commander in chief of the Battle Fleet asking me to be his chief of staff for the year he would be commanding it. That invitation filled my cup of joy to overflowing, for not only was I to be an admiral but also I was to assist in operating our country's Battle Fleet, the paramount naval duty in war and the one for which I had worked years to prepare myself.

Inspection visit to the Naval ROTC unit at the University of California-Berkeley (1927). **Left to right** Admiral Louis R. de Steigeur, USN, Commander in Chief, Battle Fleet; W. W. Campbell, President, California-Berkeley; Rear Admiral Harris Laning, USN, Chief of Staff, Battle Fleet; Colonel R. O. Van Horn, USA, in charge of Army ROTC Unit; Captain W. D. Puleston, USN, Assistant Chief of Staff, Battle Fleet; Captain Chester Nimitz, USN in charge of Naval ROTC unit.

XLI

At Sea as a Rear Admiral

ONE YEAR AFTER TAKING COMMAND of the San Diego Training Station, I became a rear admiral and Chief of Staff of the Battle Fleet. Having spent years preparing for such work, I was ready for it, and, as the Commander in Chief [L.R. de Steigner] and I generally agreed on most solutions to problems, we had an unusually happy year together, during which the battle fleet improved steadily in fighting efficiency.[195]

The battle fleet's general schedule followed the pattern of previous years—six months devoted to gunnery and tactical training at the regular base, three months to major war exercises and games at sea, and three months to minor exercises at San Francisco Bay or Puget Sound.

For the first six months my family took a house in Long Beach, California, which was during the "winter season." Unlike most parts of the world, southern California has two "seasons," both delightful, with very little difference in temperatures. Visitors flocked there in winter to avoid freezing weather, snow, and ice, and in summer to bask in the sunshine of a temperature that rarely rises to 90°. About the only difference in California seasons is that beaches are crowded in summer compared to fewer bathers during the winter.

Our house was on the bluff, at the foot of which lies the seven-mile beach for which Long Beach is famous. Our view was magnificent. To our right, facing the ocean, lay San Pedro harbor, full of ships, with mountain-like San Pedro Hill rising spectacularly behind it. To our left the sea and beaches reached beyond the horizon. In front, mountains rose in the sea to form the Santa Barbara Islands of which the nearest and most famous is Santa Catalina.

An Admiral's Yarn

For scenery and delightful climate, we were on the "Riviera;" for naval training work we had perhaps the most suitable base in the world.

It is difficult to conceive of a more perfect setting for the intense naval activity than we had that winter. However, we had more than a scenic setting and work to interest us, for in our free time there were innumerable things to do and see. Pasadena, Palm Springs, Los Angeles, Santa Monica, and Hollywood, and other world renowned spots were not far away. We could drive over Skyline Boulevard and visit Lake Arrowhead high in the mountains in less than a day; we were guests of Pasadena for its Rose Parade and Rose Bowl football game; we were guests of Hollywood, invited to see movies being made, and among other delightful experiences we visited Santa Barbara for the "Old Spanish Days Fiesta" that had replaced the Flower Carnival of former years. All in all it was a marvelous winter; but still, when spring came, we were not averse to carrying out the navy's great annual war games.

The games that year were centered on the Hawaiian Islands, and the major problem for the battle fleet was to transfer its bases from California to Honolulu without suffering seriously from the attacks of an "enemy" who was particularly strong in submarine activity. The operation was an excellent one, purposely made difficult for the battle fleet by limiting its time to complete the movement, thereby forcing it to pass through areas that would surely be covered by the "enemy." For the fleet, the problem was twofold, first to evade as many of the enemy forces as possible, and second to avoid being attacked by their submarines. Since we had worked all winter on the latter problem and believed we had the solution to it, evading the enemy became the all-important issue to us. If the fleet could accomplish that, it would be completely successful.

In war, of course, each side endeavors to foresee everything the other side can attempt, and then makes plans to defeat the other's efforts. Hence a vital factor in war is to surprise the enemy and counter its ability to meet the attack. The courses of action a naval force can take are generally controlled by factors, most of which—strength, hitting power, speed, etc.—are usually well known to the enemy. Hence, if an enemy is to be surprised at all, strategy or tactics are the tools to accomplish it. In this case, we were so restricted by the moderate speed of some of our ships that the only way we could create a strategic surprise was to find a way to increase our speed beyond anything the enemy force would think possible.

Though the battle fleet had many ships that could make fairly high speed, it also had a number of slow ships, such as submarines, supply, and repair ships. We had a dozen subs capable of only 10½ knots sustained speed, even on the surface, and a repair ship that could make only 9½ knots. The speed that a fleet can sail is

At Sea as a Rear Admiral

established by its slowest moving ships, and since the enemy knew our speed as well as we did, there seemed little likelihood, at first, of springing a surprise on him. Then it occurred to me that we might accomplish our objective if we could increase the speed of the slow ships by towing them. Accordingly, we arranged for battleships to tow the slow submarines and for our highest speed tanker to tow the 9 ½-knot repair ship.

We hoped the towing scheme would enable the fleet to make as much as 12½ knots per hour instead of 9½, which in the ten or twelve days permitted for the trip would give us six or eight hundred miles that we could utilize for a strategic surprise move. We found, however, that we could count on only a 12-knot speed by towing, but even that would allow us almost five hundred miles for a strategic move—so we decided to make a southerly detour to where we would find favorable trade winds and ocean currents to aid us.

The added speed, for which the opposing force failed to prepare, did the trick for us. It enabled us to slip around the southern end of the enemy scouting line without discovery and approach Honolulu from the southwest instead of from the expected northeast. In fact, when the battle fleet reached Honolulu, the "enemy" was still searching for us some four hundred miles to eastward. The surprise had worked perfectly.

The fleet remained in Hawaii for about six weeks, spending most of the time, when not at sea, in Honolulu. Around the islands there was no end of "sea room" for maneuvering, and since there were ships from other forces to act as an "enemy" for the battle fleet, we could train the entire United States Battle Fleet as a unit in the battle operations we had planned. The fleet was also kept busy with many other forms of training, principally in conjunction with the army's defense of Hawaii. Still we had some time for pleasures and made the most of it.

Because the fleet was to remain about six weeks in the islands, many officers' families had arranged to be in Honolulu for that time, and when we arrived, they were all set to greet us. The flagship was given a berth at a pier in Honolulu's inner harbor, and as soon as the ship reached it, the commander in chief's family and mine, heavily laden with Hawaiian leis, boarded and extend to us the usual Hawaiian welcome. The admiral, however, refused to be decorated, so all the leis were thrown over my head until I was fairly smothered with them—looking anything but the Chief of Staff of the Battle Fleet. Suddenly out of nowhere popped a dozen newspaper men with cameras to take our pictures, which to me at the time seemed quite a joke. I learned later, however, that the pictures were not a joke to them but were "news," and in about three weeks friends from all over the United States started sending me pictures of the leis episode, culled from the newspapers. They had been published in rotogravure supplements all

An Admiral's Yarn

over the country, and though the texts under them credited me with being Chief of Staff of the Battle Fleet, I cannot say I felt like one when I saw the pictures.

Soon after our arrival, social activity began as the Islanders showered us with hospitality. So busy were we in port that only while training at sea did we have any relaxation at all. Still, we enjoyed ourselves.

My family had a hotel cottage on the beach at Waikiki. I had sent my automobile to Honolulu with that of the commander in chief, so we were able to move at will about the island of Oahu. We were shown everything of interest including the ancient royal robes (made entirely of feathers), hula dances, native feasts, the Pali, Mount Tautulus, the Punch Bowl, and Diamond Head. Also, there were dinners, receptions, teas, and balls ad infinitum, all of which my family enjoyed with me.

When our duty in the islands ended, the fleet returned to the West Coast, and after another Fourth of July in San Francisco, we went to Puget Sound. While in Washington my family made another visit to Spruce Reach Cabin on the Umpqua River, where we were somewhat shocked to see the changes there. In the five years since our previous visit, several automobile roads had been constructed, and the great forests were being opened. Trout was still to be caught in the mountain streams, but otherwise the area appeared to have lost much of its old backwoods' flavor. Spruce Reach Cabin still remained the most delightful vacation spot I had ever known, but people visiting and settling in the neighborhood did deprive it of some of its charm.

When the fleet returned to San Pedro and a new commander in chief [William V. Pratt] took over, my tour as chief of staff ended and I was ordered to command Battleship Division Two. I rather disliked giving up the work with the battle fleet, but I had reached the point where I must exercise a flag command, and I could not but be proud of the one given to me. Young rear admirals of that day did not usually command a battleship division.

"Batdiv Two," as the command was called, belonged to what was then known as the Scouting Fleet, stationed in the Atlantic.[196] It was used in summer as a "practice squadron" for the Naval Academy, and when I took command, it had just returned to Annapolis with the midshipmen. Its battleships were the oldest in the navy, but they were still powerful fighting ships, one-fifth of the country's battleship strength, and very important. But, being in the scouting fleet instead of the battle fleet, and being composed of older ships, Batdiv Two had lost prestige, and some of its personnel were discouraged—a condition to be rectified immediately.

At Sea as a Rear Admiral

It so happened that the cruises of all the current captains of the ships expired just as I assumed command, and new captains took over. They were all able and energetic officers seeking to make good in their first big commands, and therefore were quick to join in rebuilding the prestige of their ships and the division. The tireless work and loyal efforts soon reaped results, and "Batdiv Two" started on its upward trend.

That fall and winter the division cruised from New England to Panama. With no opportunity to train after the midshipmen cruise, it was necessary to conduct several forms of target practice off the Virginia Capes in September and October. We did poorly, but after a Navy Yard overhaul, we went to the Caribbean for the winter where we started in earnest on the rehabilitation. We knew exactly what would make the division efficient in war and what would make it a "smart division." Our goals were "efficiency and smartness," and centered our efforts on attaining them.

We spent about two months at Guantánamo and then a month or two at the Canal. While at Panama, the itinerary for the midshipman practice cruise for the next summer was announced, and we learned that for the first time in years it would be in Europe. Inasmuch as all recent cruises had been along our Atlantic Coast, the division was delighted. When my wife and daughter, who were in Panama at the time, heard the news, they promptly announced they would go to Europe for the summer too.

I pondered. Within one year they had visited Hawaii, the Pacific Northwest, the Atlantic seaboard from New York to Hampton Roads, and were then in the Canal Zone. Adding a three-month tour of Europe to such travels seemed rather staggering, particularly since they could be with me in only two of the ports we were to visit. We discussed the issue pro and con for a week or two, my wife and daughter taking the affirmative and I a rather weak negative. How long the debate would have lasted if our daughter had not proposed that a vote be taken was unknown. Finally, she took charge and asked, "Daddy, how do you vote?" I replied, "I vote no." Turning to her mother she asked how she would vote, and to my amazement my wife voted "Yes." Thereupon our daughter shouted, "And I vote 'yes,' so the vote is two to one and off to Europe we go!" They went, and the result of the vote proved so happy that ever since then the family has regarded that method of deciding questions as most satisfactory, and I strongly recommend it.

When Batdiv Two returned north after the winter's work, it was beginning to "feel its oats." Its personnel had the exalted idea that they could do better work than most could; that even if their ships were old they could keep them cleaner, snappier, and better than new ones; and that within the limits of their somewhat

An Admiral's Yarn

outmoded gun batteries, they fought as well or better than any other ship. The navy spirit was again rampant in Batdiv Two.

People may wonder how it happened that three of our battleships had become reduced in fighting efficiency, but the cause is very clear. To keep a ship in fighting readiness, its crew must be permanently on board and practice daily as a fighting team. Unfortunately, that very obvious rule had not been observed for Batdiv Two. Each year when it was being used for the midshipmen's practice cruise, a considerable portion of the fighting crews of the ship would be removed in May and not replaced until September, after the cruise ended. The men retained on a ship were there to train the midshipmen but not to engage in team fighting. Thus for four months of each year, the ships were without fighting crews, and all effort was concentrated on teaching midshipmen the ways of life at sea. Small wonder that with fighting crews for only eight months of a year, the ships suffered in war efficiency.

Realizing that Batdiv Two could never maintain the navy fighting standard under such circumstances, we sought ways to retain and train the fighting crews, even with the midshipmen on board. Doing so seemed hopeless at first, but by consulting together and devising ways to gain additional space for midshipmen, we ultimately arranged matters in such a way that we could carry the midshipmen quotas in addition to holding nearly every man in a key position in the regular fighting complements. Therefore, on the cruise in 1929, each ship carried almost two crews, one of midshipmen for training and another for fighting the ship.

That two-crew system about doubled the work for the ship's officers, since both crews had to be trained daily. However, we arranged a schedule that would do that. We started our drills much earlier and continued with them much longer. Midshipmen gun crews were exercised first and then turned over to the Naval Academy officers who supervised their instruction in technical subjects. Thereupon the regular crews took up their battle training, and for the rest of the day midshipmen and regular crews underwent training simultaneously.

Strange to say, both midshipmen and regular crews seemed to enjoy working under such heavy pressure and soon started an unofficial competition between themselves in developing fighting efficiency. This, of course, made for cruise success, and the results proved far beyond our fondest hopes. When the cruise ended, each of our ships had a highly skilled regular fighting crew and well-trained midshipmen.

XLII

A Cruise to Europe

LEAVING ANNAPOLIS IMMEDIATELY after graduation day, the Practice Squadron started for Europe en route ports in Barcelona, Naples, Gibraltar, and Weymouth, England.

Standing out of the Chesapeake the weather was fine, but almost immediately the barometer began to drop and the predictions became bad. We knew we were in for a storm. It hit us the next day with a northeast wind that quickly rose to gale force and created a very heavy sea. Apparently our course across the Atlantic was the very track of the storm, for we went along in it for ten days before it finally passed ahead of us. During that time the ships took a terrific pounding, huge seas boarded them and did considerable damage. Boats were badly smashed and the midshipmen learned rather quickly what might be expected in a life at sea.

Of course they were horribly seasick, and I suspect many would have given up sea careers then and there had we not required them to go right on with routine work—seasick or not. Doing that may seem heartless, but men who follow the sea learn early that no matter what the weather is, their work must be done. At sailor may be considered incapacitated from other illnesses but never from seasickness. So the storm could really be considered a blessing in disguise for the midshipmen. From it they learned something of the responsibilities of sea life. At the same time, they developed their "sea legs"—some would never again have to worry over that type of sickness, and almost all the others knew they would adjust and recover quickly enough when it recurred.

However, one result of middy seasickness on previous cruises had been a great increase in appendicitis among those stricken, so a navy specialist was sent on this cruise to operate immediately should a case develop. I was hopeful he might be merely a passenger, but after about a week in that storm, one of the ships made a sudden call for his service. At that time the seas were enormous, and the ships were jumping around like so many corks. I hesitated to lower a boat to transfer the doctor, feeling, too, a doubt that he could successfully operate in such a storm. However, the doctor was willing to take the chance so the squadron hove to, and a boat with the doctor in it was lowered without being smashed. We were fearful every second that the boat would swamp in the tremendous seas, and more fearful it would smash up alongside the other ship. Our prayers were answered when the boat went under the ship's crane, which hoisted the doctor on board. The boat then returned to the flagship where our own crane hooked on and hoisted it on board. What had appeared to be the impossible had been accomplished without mishap; but the delicate appendicitis operation, to be performed aboard a heavily pounding ship, had yet to be accomplished.

I had long known that most of our naval surgeons were the peers of any in the world and quite as good sailors too. It was only about an hour after the specialist had boarded that the ship reported the operation completed successfully, and we could breathe easily once more. But our troubles with appendicitis were not over. That night a middy on the flagship developed an acute case, and early next morning he was operated on successfully. There was a third case, while we were in port, so it was easily handled.

Our first stop was Barcelona, Spain, where a great "World Industrial Exposition" was being held. Even without an exposition, Barcelona is well worth a visit, and pages might be written about Spain's great industrial city, its beauties, and places of interest in the country about it. Such descriptions are far beyond my ability to offer, but I will relate some of our experiences while there.

The first had to do with hotel accommodations, since my wife and daughter were to join me. I had written ahead to hotels and to my surprise was informed that two rooms with bath, without food, would cost me half again as much per day as the United States paid me for commanding a division of its battleships. That struck me as a rather steep price for merely a place to sleep, so I decided to seek a less expensive hotel. At the time I was in correspondence with the U.S. Consul-General at Barcelona [Nathaniel B. Stewart] in connection with the official features of our visit, and I told him of our hotel predicament and asked if he could have someone from his office meet my wife and daughter on arrival and find a more reasonably priced place for them to stay. Imagine my surprise when on reaching Barcelona the Consul's representative boarded the flagship

A Cruise to Europe

immediately and told me my family had arrived safely and were awaiting me at Barcelona's "swankiest" hotel, the one that had quoted the highest rates of all!

When I reached there I found we had been assigned a beautiful suite, were having a great fuss made over us by the entire ménage, and that the hotel was flying a large United States flag. Having some idea of what the cost would be, I was somewhat appalled to think of what I was in for until the Consul-General informed me that as commander of an American squadron on an official visit to the city, I was entitled to diplomatic courtesies. He said that every hotel in Barcelona wanted us as guests and the charges would be nominal. They were.

The consuls were as eager as I to uphold the prestige of our country, and they looked out for us well, extending to us all the courtesies that a member of a reigning family might expect.

Immediately the exchange of official calls had been completed, the hospitality of Barcelona opened in full with dinners, luncheons, receptions, and dances. I daresay our having so many handsome young midshipmen, all excellent dancers as well as being attractive, added considerably to the attentions shown us. Aside from social activities, there was the Exposition to see, trips to the monasteries of mountainous Catalonia and visits to the museums, churches, and cathedrals. But of all, Barcelona's night life taxed us most. It did not really begin until one or two in the morning, and then for two or three hours the whole city turned out to parade the "Avenue" and fill the cafes, restaurants, and clubs with strenuous gaiety. Each night was almost a "Carnival Night," but since our days had to be devoted to work, we needed relaxation.

Soon, too, I noted a peculiarity in the attentions shown us, which though multitudinous, were not of the official nature usually bestowed upon visiting ships of another country. Individuals and organizations outdid themselves to honor us, but except for exchanging "official calls," we were scarcely noticed by the Spanish government officials. Commenting on this to the Consul-General, I was surprised to learn that the laws we Americans made for our internal welfare often did considerable injury to other countries.

The cause of Spain's official coolness toward us that summer was a tariff bill which, while passed by one of the Houses of Congress, was not a law because adjournment had preempted it being taken up for vote by the other House. The bill, if enacted into law, would increase tariffs on certain imports. We had given little thought to it because it was still far from becoming a law. Spain was greatly upset over an anticipated increase in duty on items such as olives and their by-products, laces, etc.—increases which seemed of little importance to us, apparently. However, to Spain the increase meant that many thousands of its poorer families would lose the principal market for their products, so the

An Admiral's Yarn

Spanish government showed its displeasure over the bill through coolness toward us. Thus I came to understand the effects that tariffs can have on international relations.

But for all the official coolness and the strenuousness of the unofficial entertaining, we enjoyed Barcelona, and before leaving gave a great reception on the flagship in return for the many courtesies shown us. That reception was planned with great care, and to make sure no one was overlooked, the Consul-General worked with us on the invitation list. When it was completed, we found we had to issue over three hundred and fifty invitations—a goodly number of guests to care for on a ship anchored well outside the harbor in the open Mediterranean. However, when I suggested to the Consul-General that we were possibly inviting more people than we could care for properly, he laughed and said, "Don't worry, I know these Catalonians, and not one-half of those invited will venture that far from shore."

That relieved my mind, so I ordered all officers not on duty and three hundred middies to assist at the reception, make ready for five or six hundred guests, and ordered every powerboat in the squadron to carry guests to and from the ship.

It was well we had so many boats, for although the expected guests numbered fewer than four hundred, I think all who were invited came and brought their sisters, cousins, and aunts in addition to their daughters and nieces. The boats could scarcely handle the crowds and soon we had over fifteen hundred guests on board, of whom a thousand or more were young ladies the age of midshipmen. Realizing that three hundred midshipmen were far too few for so many girls, I made signal for all midshipmen still on the ships to come to the party at once, and soon our decks were crowded.

Since we were not sufficiently familiar with Spanish social customs, we soon found a great mass of middies on deck amidships, while along the ship's rail, with their duennas, were hundreds of girls waiting to dance with the middies. Our giant navigator of the flagship, Jack Shafroth, suggested a "Paul Jones," and he managed to succeed in arranging the girls and middies alternately in a huge circle that extend completely around the ship's deck. Then ordering "grand right and left," which of course the middies understood, it was not long before the girls and middies were at least shaking hands. Then, when he blew a whistle, they started waltzing. It seemed for a minute that we were set for a good party, but no sooner was the waltz over than the girls rushed back to their duennas. Once again we found ourselves in the original dilemma. We started another Paul Jones and passed word to the middies to keep the girls away from their chaperonesses when the waltz ended, and soon the party became a huge success.

A Cruise to Europe

True, the unexpected crowd quickly consumed all of our refreshments, but otherwise there were not any real flaws.

As stated in the invitations, the time for the reception was from four until seven o'clock, and most of the guests arrived promptly at four. Nevertheless, when seven o'clock came, not one made a move to leave the ship, for by then the dancing was at its height. When at eight o'clock there were still no departures, and it was time for us to prepare for dinners being given us on shore, I directed the band to play the national airs and so end the party. However, our guests did not respond. In fact one lady, whose husband had been the Spanish Minister to Washington, and who spoke English perfectly, rushed to me and said, "Admiral, why do you play the national airs now when we are all having such a good time?" When I told her we must send our guests safely ashore before dark and that we officers were due at dinners and other engagements ashore, she sniffed and said, "Well, we don't care to go home now. We are ready to dance all night and leave at dawn in the morning. Why is it when you Americans come to Barcelona, you do not observe our ways? If while you are here you would do everything three hours later than your American schedule, you would be on ours. You make the midshipmen return to the ships at midnight, which is just the time enjoyment is starting with us. Do learn to observe our ways when you visit us." Of course we could not oblige the lady, so the party ended. Two days later we went to Naples.

We found Naples quite different from Barcelona—not nearly as many entertainments and more things to see. However, the Italians were just as cool to us officially as the Spaniards had been, and except for the usual courtesy calls, paid little attention to us. Even the vice admiral in command of the local naval activities avoided us, his aide telling mine that the admiral had intended to honor us with a large dinner but had received word from Rome not to extend official courtesies. When I asked why the Italians were so against us, I was told that it was due to our proposed tariff on preserved cherries, from which practically all of the small farmers on the slopes of the Apennines derived their living. Perhaps there were other causes, too, but Italy was so displeased that it was boycotting both United States products and U.S. officials.

I had intended to visit Rome, and arrangements had been made for my family and me to have an audience with the Pope [Pius XI]. However, we did not make the trip (although my wife and daughter did so later) as our naval attaché informed me that even though I would be going to Rome unofficially for a papal audience, I would still be obliged to call officially on the King and on Mussolini. I felt it best not to go at all and remained in Naples, seeing many

An Admiral's Yarn

points of interest thereabouts, such as Vesuvius, Pompeii, Sorrento, and the famous Amalfi Drive, and also Capri with its famous Blue Grotto.

Fortunately the midshipmen were not so restricted as I, for they not only saw all the interesting places that we saw, but they also went to Rome. For that visit they were divided into two groups, each numbering about five hundred and each staying there two full days. Of course that was far too little time to see Rome, but one of the great tourist agencies handled the middies' trip and they probably saw as much in their visits as most tourists would see in a week. In addition, each party was given an audience with the Pope.

When the first party returned, our chaplain, who was a Catholic priest and had accompanied the midshipmen, immediately reported on the visit. Evidently it was a great success, and what most impressed him about it was, of course, the audience with the Holy Father, who was exceedingly gracious to the middies. So pleased were they by his cordial reception that when the audience ended and a middy called for three cheers for the Pope, the cheers were given so heartily that they resounded throughout the Vatican. I could not but shudder when told of the cheering, for I felt the Pope must have been greatly shocked by it. "Oh no, not at all" said the chaplain. "He liked it."

After the second midshipmen party made its visit, the chaplain reported it to be even more successful than the first, although I had cautioned against any such repeat of enthusiastic outburst. When I expressed the hope that the second group had been more decorous than the first and had not done any cheering in the presence of the Pope, the chaplain looked at me in disgust and said, "Admiral, you don't suppose the second party was going to be outdone by the first, do you? When their audience ended, the cheerleader called for the Naval Academy '4 N' with three 'Pope's' at the end. I wish you could have heard it." When I asked if the Pope had not been deeply shocked and angry over it, I was assured that he was delighted, especially when the cheer ended with "Pope! Pope!! Pope!!!" If he was not shocked, I was!

The next port after Naples was Gibraltar, which, being a British military and naval outpost, received us quite differently than ports previously visited. Not only was the squadron made very welcome, but we were once again in a naval-military atmosphere rather than one of international relationship. There were few sights to be seen there, and our stay was brief.

Our next port was Weymouth in southern England, where the British fairly overwhelmed us with courtesies. Weymouth is a well-known summer resort bordering on Portland Hill, the small but well-known naval station. Three British battleships had been sent there to welcome us, and every attention

A Cruise to Europe

possible was extended to us, not only by the navy but by the people of Great Britain.

Weymouth is an interesting city, formed by several old towns growing into each other: Weymouth, Melcombe Regis, and Wyhe Regis. The steep green hills of Dorset Heights rise behind it, and on one side, visible for twenty miles at sea, is a huge picture, inlaid of white rock, of a man on horseback standing toward the town. It represented King George III on his way to Weymouth where he spent his summers, and brought to mind the close association of Weymouth with the last king to govern the American Colonies. It made us realize that we might find much connected with the colonial history of the United States in that neighborhood.

The first fact of historical interest developed almost immediately when I returned the official call of the mayor of Weymouth and Melcombe Regis. The "City Hall" of Weymouth is across a small park from the head of the pier where the boat landing is, and I was taken directly to it on arrival. When the call was over, the mayor announced that he would walk back to my boat with me so that a photograph of us together might be taken at the "monument," which was close to where I had stepped ashore and could easily be seen from the head of the pier. As I surmised, it had to do with the pilgrimage, after the one by the *Mayflower*. The mayor related that at Plymouth there is the famous "Plymouth Rock" marking the spot where the Pilgrim Fathers boarded the *Mayflower* for their passage to America; but in Weymouth, the monument represented the "Salem Pilgrims," where they embarked eight years later to found the colony of Salem.[197] He continued, "I think it would be fitting for us to be photographed together in front of the monument that marks that spot." Strange that in my two consecutive visits to England I would, on the first visit, which was in connection with the first transatlantic air flight, step on English soil at the spot from which the Pilgrim Fathers had left England, and on my second visit, stand on the ground from which the Salem Pilgrims had departed for America.

Little do we realize how closely our colonial history is joined to southern England, which our visit to Weymouth impressed upon us. The automobile trips constantly led us to towns and localities connected with the founding of our country. Recalling and discussing these connections in a casual way as we went along, we were quite surprised when near the end of our visit the mayor said, "These little trips with you have opened my eyes historically. I was born and raised in this vicinity, but not until you Americans came here did I realize how little I knew of its importance in your country's early history. I may be showing history to you, but you are teaching it to me."

An Admiral's Yarn

There was more to those trips than history—we were seeing the attractions of rural England, its simple but fascinating homes, it flowers and splendidly kept gardens, its attractive tiny shops with the unusual signs and names, and its many inns where we longed to stop and enjoy the quaint quietness. When I called on the major, I had expressed a wish to see something of the countryside and particularly the great estates of the region. Therefore, I was not surprised on the first trip we made that the mayor announced we were to stop for tea at the largest and most beautiful estate in the south of England.

When we reached it, we were received by the family, and although they were most gracious, I could not but feel that instead of being invited to the estate as the mayor had made it seem, we had apparently forced ourselves upon the owners. Accordingly, when we returned to Weymouth, I directed my aide to ascertain the preliminaries of our visit to the estate and found that we had not been invited at all but that the mayor had merely telephoned that the "American admiral" wished to visit at four o'clock and, adhering to Britain's customary courtesy to foreign officials, the family had shown us every hospitality. However, having no wish to thrust myself on British noble families, I requested the mayor not to repeat such trips. There were enough other trips of interest, including one of two days in London.

But to me the outstanding effort of sincere hospitality demonstrated by the people of Weymouth was the mayor's official banquet given at the King George III Hotel. When the invitation came, we thought it just another large civic dinner, but when we entered the hotel I realized it was to be quite different. The fine appearing attendants in gold-braided, red velvet uniforms directed us not to an ordinary hotel reception room but to an oak-paneled drawing room with handsome furnishings. When the guests had assembled, a large double door at the end of the room opened and there stood two elderly men in red uniforms, each bearing an enormous brass mace. Thereupon, the mayor took my arm and announced that we would led the way to the dining room. When we reached the double doors, the mace bearers faced about, and marching ahead down the hall between two rows of the uniformed attendants, led us to the dining room where they took positions directly behind the chairs that the major and I were to occupy. That march to dinner was quite the most formal I had ever known, and even when the guests were seated, the formality continued for a time. Noting that the dining room was unlike that of the usual hotel, I commented on it to the mayor, who thereupon said to me, "No, this hotel is not like the modern hotel. This part of it was the summer residence of George III and has had few changes. In fact, this room has not been altered at all. Weymouth glories in its history and tries to follow the old traditions. For instance, we are proud of the maces that led

A Cruise to Europe

us into this room and never fail to use them on occasions of state. They were presented to Weymouth over seven hundred years ago and have been used ever since." When I asked if the elderly men carrying the maces had come with them, he said, not even smiling, "No, those men are newer and the finest looking of our retired police officers. They will stand there like ramrods until dismissed, which I will do now and end some of the formality."

It is probable that where I sat at that dinner was the approximate place occupied by George III during the days when the American colonies were not in accord with his administration. However, times had changed since George III. The United States had become a great country; it had almost forgotten the reign of George III; and instead of being hostile, Great Britain, possibly because of him, had become its ally in the World War.

Although it was rather a new experience for me to give an after-dinner speech in such an atmosphere, I did so.

After the usual farewell party on the flagship, the squadron left for home. The return passage was delightful, the weather clear, and the sea sufficiently rough to afford excellent training conditions. After the pleasures of Europe, all hands were apparently glad to be at work again, and the training went on almost continuously day and night. It was very thorough and the gunnery and other officers reported splendid results. Nevertheless, I was apprehensive of what might develop later in our target practice and fleet maneuvers. Would our training system continue to prove its efficiency?

The midshipmen target practices were held as soon as the ships had been fueled and provisioned after reaching Hampton Roads. They were surprisingly splendid; never before had middies made such scores. They even broke the best records of our ships' type of 14-inch turrets, no small feat in itself, and a particularly fine one for midshipmen. Hence, we were very proud of ourselves when we returned to Annapolis, but we became even more so when the Academy authorities informed us that, in their opinions, it was the most successful cruise midshipmen had ever experienced.

Getting our ships back to normal routine after the three months of practice cruise was not difficult under our new plan, and after a week for stabilization, we went out to fire the ships' own "short-range battle practice." Having seen the middies break the previous record for their type of turret, the regular crews were on their mettle and proceeded to outdo them, chalking up even better records. The morale had become very high, the ships were "spic and span," and because we had become particularly proficient in battle maneuvering, we no longer thought of ourselves as "has beens" but rather as fine examples for even new ships.

An Admiral's Yarn

After carrying out further training details and being docked and repaired at navy yards, the division was sent south with the scouting fleet for winter training. During most of it we based on Guantánamo for long-range battle practices off Gonaïves, Haiti, and anti-aircraft practices in the Caribbean. To break the monotony of the heavy shooting schedule, we were sent to Puerto Rican ports for a week, and from Mayagüez, Ponce, and San Juan we were shown over most of that remarkably beautiful and fertile island. Later, when the target practices had been completed, the scouting fleet was sent through the canal to join the battle fleet from California bases for several weeks of combined maneuvers in the Pacific and the Gulf of Panama. When the two fleets combined, Batdiv Two was given a place in the "battle line." It had never trained in battle maneuvers, and for that reason I was somewhat fearful of the showing we might make in such skilled company, although knowing what would be expected of the division were it put in the battle line, we had worked assiduously to develop precision in all battle movements. I quickly learned that our training work had been thorough. The division not only showed a complete understanding of battle tactics, but also it proved outstanding in the precision with which it maneuvered.

In addition to noting these facts, the commander in chief of the fleet also noted the excellent appearance of our ships, their efficient operation, and the "cockiness" of personnel that ever sought to do things better than anyone else. The tremendous improvement of Batdiv Two was remarked about throughout the fleet and was a considerable reward for our efforts. But the greatest reward came from the commander in chief himself, who characterized "Batdiv Two" as one of the smart, if not the smartest, divisions in the entire fleet. It could shoot, maneuver, and fight as well as the fleet's best. However, all this could not have been accomplished without the splendid cooperation of every man on board the ships.

That cruise lasted about five months, and not until early May 1930 did we return north to prepare for another practice cruise. By that time I had been on sea duty for almost three years and had commanded a battleship division for two of them. I knew I would be assigned shore duty that summer, and I requested duty as President of the Naval War College, for which I felt quite prepared, having concentrated on naval war operations for years. I had little hope of being so assigned, however, so you can imagine my delight to learn, when the slate for flag officer assignments was announced by radio the day before Batdiv Two reached New York, that I was to have the duty I wanted. I was slated to be President of the Naval War College.

XLIII

President of the Naval War College

IN JUNE 1930 I TOOK OVER MY NEW DUTY, and on July 14th the college year opened. Inasmuch as training for high naval command must keep abreast or even somewhat ahead of the changes in sea warfare brought about by new inventions and improved methods and equipment, the college courses are anything but static. They must reflect naval developments, actual and proposed, and employ them in miniature war operations for the students' application. It is through this training that officers are prepared for the conduit of wars for today and tomorrow.

Though not always credited with being "up-to-date" by taking advantage of new ideas in sea warfare, the United States Navy, thanks to its War College, probably has the most advanced officer personnel in the world. Although the college uses the fleet as it is actually built, or being built, for its games, the navies that oppose us are given every known improvement, whether or not the United States has adopted it.

Since our students operate the other navies as well as our own in the games, nothing new is overlooked, be it for the sea surface, under the sea, or in the air. Every form of attack and defense that hundreds of skilled officers can imagine are tested so that very little connected with fighting at sea is neglected. Nevertheless, in spite of that, I have often heard men, who are entirely uninformed concerning war at sea, express beliefs that certain weapons or types of ships will dominate all others and should replace the existing, when, as a matter of fact, what they advocate has generally been thoroughly tested at the college and perhaps been found wanting.

An Admiral's Yarn

For instance, the navy is frequently criticized because it does not accept as a fact the complete domination of the sea by air or underwater forces, and its officers are said to have some ulterior motive because they do not admit it.

Those critics fail to realize that naval officers, more than anyone else, want to win our wars at sea and care little as to the kind of weapon used, only that it be legal and bring victory. For that reason they try out every device, every method, and every suggestion, but advocate only those with satisfactory results. The writings and talks of columnists and others unacquainted with sea warfare or with the practical utilization of sea weapons cannot convince the navy to adopt unproven ideas. The navy tries every new, feasible, and worthwhile suggestion, hoping to find more certain ways to win a war. It does not however, accept neophyte suggestions.

Though the college devotes most of its time to practicing war operations, its students are required to study the policies of the various world powers to ascertain in what ways they may conflict with our own. Where friction appears possible, students study ways to best fight in support of our policies, should we go to war in defense of them. That takes much study and time, and coupled with practicing the actual fighting operations, the students fulfill a heavy schedule. Every detail of possible wars must be tested if students are to derive maximum benefit from the course. Because for the two or three years that an officer serves on the staff he must analyze and measure the results of fighting operations, perhaps he learns even more than the students.

It is evident that members of the college staff become unusually well-versed in naval warfare, from the "grand plans" for an entire war to the very details of fighting. That is as true for the president of the college as it is for staff members; but since the president's directives are meant to engage officers in activities that best prepare them for high command in war, I soon found myself an unusually busy person. Fortunately there was no need to drive the students. The college had only to point the way to these energetic, middle-aged officers who sought skills in naval fighting and who desired to perfect themselves in war operations. As does everyone in the Navy, the students immediately put all their energies to work on the task at hand.

Few activities in life are carried on with an intensity as great as that of the Naval War College. For that reason, the work is not only greatly important to the United States but also to every country with the potential to become our enemy in war. Potential enemies are constantly seeking confirmation about the courses at the War College, and there is little doubt they would give much to learn the planned strategy and tactics that our navy would use if war presented itself. Not only do they study all public utterances of college spokesmen in the

President of the Naval War College

hope of obtaining some hint to developments there, but their naval attachés make periodic official visits to the College for the purpose of gathering whatever information may be gleaned. These visits of foreign attachés probably net them little, since in appearance the college is supremely innocuous.

In the large, somewhat rambling building, with desk-filled rooms of staff officers and students, fairly good-sized but rather bare game rooms, and a library, there is little of the underlying purpose apparent. War games are not carried on for the viewing of visitors who see only officers working at desks. Game equipment is almost nil, and the tiny lead ships used in the games tell nothing of the characteristics of the ships they represent in battle. Since visitors to the college may inspect the interior without learning a thing about work being conducted there, attaché visits are infrequent and not too worrisome. But talk outside the college can be.

This concerned me, for no sooner had I become president than I found myself in considerable demand as a speaker. Gifted though I may be in that art, it was apparent that I was wanted not for my oratorical ability but rather because as President of the Naval War College, I was a student of international policies and how our navy would operate in war in support of United States policy. Such thoughts are of great interest to the citizens of our country, of course, but probably of even greater interest to the foreign governments with which we might go to war. For that reason, and because my position was that of a follower rather than a leader in national affairs, I dared not talk about them lest, inadvertently, I give away what might be national secrets. Accordingly, I resolved never to speak publicly on War College affairs.

Although that resolution caused me to decline most invitations to speak on Atlantic or Pacific problems requested by organizations, I still had much talking to do. Having the prestige of the War College behind me, and being the senior naval officer thereabouts, I think every patriotic, civic, or historical organization that met in the vicinity requested me to be present and give a talk—the Society of Cincinnati, Sons of the Revolution, D.A.R., G.A.R., Spanish War Veterans, American Legion, Chambers of Commerce, Rotary Clubs, and many others. Fortunately I was generally expected to talk about patriotism, civic affairs, or history. Hence, I succeeded in complying with such request, but they proved an onerous duty and took far too much valuable time. Also, even though not forewarned, I often would be called upon to "say a few words," so I had always to be prepared for an extemporaneous talk when I attended any gathering of that type.

One of my first speaking invitations came a few days after I assumed the presidency of the college. It was from the Episcopal cathedral in Providence,

An Admiral's Yarn

which asked me to deliver the sermon at its Armistice Sunday Memorial Service. You can imagine the surprise of a fighting sailor on being asked to deliver any sermon, let alone one in the cathedral of the presiding Bishop of the Episcopal Church of the United States.[198] So appalled was I that I felt more then comforted upon looking over my engagement book to find I had an appointment for that day. I therefore declined the invitation, and in doing so thought I was safe for all time. But I was badly mistaken, for no sooner had I declined for that Sunday three months ahead than I received another request to deliver the sermon on Armistice day the following year—fifteen months ahead and for which "I undoubtedly would be free." Believing something would surely come up in the meantime to prevent me from fulfilling the engagement, I accepted.

However, not a thing occurred to prevent it, and on Armistice Sunday 1931, I delivered the sermon. Knowing that I would be like "Alice in Wonderland" in a pulpit, the Dean of the Cathedral offered to help me with the sermon if I would send an advance copy to him. I decided neither to accept his kindness nor his proposal to wear a surplice at the service, which would have been in keeping with the attire of the Dean as well as Bishop Perry, the presiding bishop. I felt that, after all, I was merely a naval officer and should not hide the fact behind the vestments of the Church, so I delivered my sermon in the uniform of a fighting rear admiral.

The Episcopal service is impressive, and not only was the congregation large, but a considerable part of it was made up of patriotic organizations dressed in full regalia. While I had many qualms as I mounted the steps to the pulpit and looked down on those men in uniform, I soon gained my composure.

I believe that the pulpit of that church was by far the most ideal place for giving a talk. Realizing the importance of what is said from their pulpits, churches have made them highly efficient. Speaking is made easier than it is from a banquet table or even the usual lecture platform. Because of their position above the congregation, looking down, preachers are able to read prepared talks while appearing to speak extemporaneously. Doing that was a tremendous help to me, and in the pulpit I felt far more convincing than I had ever before felt.

I have often wished my grandmother, who wanted me to become a bishop, could have lived to attend that service. Hearing me talk from the pulpit of the presiding bishop of her church, at a service in which he participated, would perhaps have ameliorated her disappointment in my choice of profession. Nevertheless, I still felt my proper calling to be that of naval officer.

President of the Naval War College

Not all activities outside the War College were of a speech-making nature. Many were social, since my official position opened much of Newport's society life to us, and many were civic because I was the highest naval or military officer on duty in that locality. We became familiar with the Casino, the Reading Room, Bailey's Beach, the annual tennis tournaments, horse shows, flower shows, the Clambake Club, and in fact with all the centers of Newport's social life.

There were conventions, yacht races, and dedications of historical spots, as well as visits by high U.S. officials, foreign military or naval leaders, and contingents of our own and foreign fleets. In arranging to handle those important events, city officials of Newport always invited the local naval and military authorities to assist, and we took pleasure in doing so, as they generally were most interesting.

One of the most unusual events was the 1930 international yacht races for the America's Cup. I had hardly assumed my new duty when Newport's mayor invited me to join in preparation for the races. Although the City of Newport was not responsible for the races, the competing yachts and thousands of people would base in Newport for them, and great preparations needed to be made. I was on the committee to welcome Sir Thomas Lipton and his *Shamrock V,* and through that pleasant duty became associated with him.[199]

Newport harbor was very much alive when Sir Thomas, in his steam yacht, accompanied by *Shamrock V,* rounded Fort Adams. Hundreds of America's finest yachts, both sail and steam, were there to greet the contender, and the shoreline was packed with people. A shore battery opened up with a salute when *Shamrock V* headed in, and at the first gun, every yacht and vessel in the harbor dressed ship, rainbow fashion, and every whistle in Newport blew its loudest.

A more spectacular or noisier welcome could hardly be imagined, and Sir Thomas Lipton, who for the fifth time had brought a yacht to the United States to race for the Cup, was greatly moved by it. He could scarcely speak and his eyes were still wet with tears when our committee boarded his steam yacht to extend Newport's official welcome.

The races were sailed in accordance with schedule, and I witnessed most of them. However, as I had seen many previous Cup races, which though always a beautiful sight were not highly exciting, I paid more attention to the shore activities. This brought me constantly in the presence of Sir Thomas and his cohorts, and I did then become intensely interested in the outcome of the races. However, Sir Thomas, as usual, failed to win the Cup, though by that time he had made a place for himself in the hearts of the Newporters, who realized that the fine old gentleman was fast failing in health and probably would not enter a

An Admiral's Yarn

yacht race again. He died a few months later. I will ever cherish having known him.

The same holds true for the many other contacts with distinguished men who visited Newport during the next three years: British war admirals, French admirals and generals, and even our own General Pershing. Most of them were received officially by the City of Newport, although many others of importance came to address the War College classes and slipped in and out of the city practically unbeknownst to all but college associates. Some were world-renowned commentators on national and international affairs; some were famous students, analysts, and lecturers on Near or Far East problems; and some came from the Department of State to acquaint the college with the official attitude of our country in certain of its dealings with other nations.

The distinguished men who came, unheralded, to Newport to address our classes were indeed important to our work. Almost every Friday afternoon during the college year one of them would give an "up-to-the-minute" confidential talk on some aspect of world affairs in what we termed the "lecture course." This was, possibly, as complete a presentation of the international situation of the moment as could be made. Fortunately for the college, which had but little money to spend on them, the lectures were not expensive, usually costing little more than the expenses incurred by the visitors. They were patriotic citizens doing what they could for our national defense without monetary reward. If reward were theirs, it possibly came from the prestige of being a Naval War College lecturer. Hence, at small cost to the government, the officers who were being prepared to lead its navy in war gained much knowledge that would be extremely useful to them.

Perhaps though, I, as college president, gained the most from the lecturers, for many of them were lunch guests in my home, and the intimate contacts were not only tremendously interesting, but very educational concerning international relations.

Among the most famous of Newport's visitors were France's great military leader, Marshal Petain, and our General Pershing. In recognition of the sesquicentennial of the surrender at Yorktown and the part France played in bringing about that surrender, an official delegation headed by Marshal Petain had been sent from France. The celebration was quite elaborate, but Newporters were a bit chagrined not to have been invited to participate. One hundred fifty years ago the French forces had landed first in Newport and then had gone on to help win at Yorktown—Newport officials felt there should have been some recognition of the connection between Newport and the French forces. The City of Newport therefore invited the French delegation to visit it officially, and

President of the Naval War College

the invitation was accepted. Immediately after the Yorktown celebration, the French squadron brought the delegation to Newport, accompanied by General Pershing.

That visit helped to refresh our memories of the role that Rhode Island, Narragansett Bay, and particularly Newport played in the birth of our country. When Marshal Petain came to Newport, they were recalled in full, and I came to realize the historical importance of my surroundings.

Though Newport's sesquicentennial observance of the arrival of the French forces in the Colonies did not compare with the elaborate ceremonies at Yorktown that remembered the battle and surrender, it was illuminating. All of Newport and much of Rhode Island took part in it, and Marshal Petain was given a busy day, including a banquet at night where I was called upon to "say a few words." He also managed to visit the War College and made brief addresses to the students and staff.

It might appear that with so many outside diversions, the training of officers for high war command would be wanting, but it was so arranged that every forenoon and most afternoons were devoted entirely to it, with no interruptions permitted. Thus there was a vast amount of training that yielded consequences of inestimable value to our national defense.

During my first tour at the college, we had been told of the part that aviation would have in sea warfare, so we were able to advise what the navy's aviation policy should be. On this second tour, we found that the college could recommend policies for other types of naval craft too, thereby considerably increasing its value to the country.

That the college could contribute much to the plans for national defense had long been recognized, so much so that its president was ex-officio a member of the Navy's General Board. To my mind, that membership was of inestimable value, not only to the Board in drawing up naval policies but also to the college in preparing officers to conduct war. I therefore took great interest in the work of the Board and particularly strove to use my connection with it to aid both it and the college.

To illustrate how close the relationship is between the college and the General Board, I need but to recall to you that the aircraft policy of the navy was established with their close cooperation. That policy was only one of many that had to be determined, and not long after I took over the presidency, there arose the question of what submarine policy we should follow. The existing policy had become badly obscured because of an interpretation given to the popular slogan, "A Navy for Defense Only." For some reason a "navy for defense" was believed by many persons of national influence to be one suited only to preventing an invasion of our homeland. Apparently defense against anything but invasion was not contemplated, even though the country could be as effectively bled to death by cutting off distant arteries that sustained its economic life. A question that arose concerned the type of submarines the country should build. It was being strongly advocated that all our submarines be small, suitable only for use close along our coasts.

Naturally the War College gave considerable attention to the use of submarines in national defense, and it soon became apparent that subs restricted by size to only coastal operation would be of little help in protecting distant national interests. Furthermore, the cost to building numerous small subs would be above that for a sufficient number of the deep-sea submarines. The college reported to the Navy Department what it had learned—with some influence. At least, all the subs built since that time have the capabilities to go to any port where defense measures must be applied.

Because the "dividends" of the War College training courses were so valued by the navy, they became emphasized and the college was asked to heighten its research and experimentation. We replied that if we had officers for the purpose we could do so, but the college staff was already overworked merely carrying out training operations. The only way to develop further would be to establish a "research department" for that purpose.[200] Accordingly, officers were sent to the college to engage in this activity and, having only that work to do, quickly began to gather many worthwhile facts concerning details of sea warfare that theretofore had not materialized. We obtained data that told us the amounts of ammunition, fuel, and supplies that would be required in various kinds of distant operations; the probable amount of damage (not the kind that would occur) in such operations and for which repair facilities should be provided; where and what fleet base should be prepared for them; and other numerous vitally important details. In addition to training the officers for high command, the college became an almost perfect research laboratory for every detail of naval warfare.

Among the many recommendations made by the college was the one concerning so-called "light cruisers." Under the terms of the Washington Treaty Limiting Armaments, the United States was permitted to have a specified amount of cruiser tonnage, a certain portion of which could be used only for "light cruisers" carrying guns of six-inch caliber or less. The rest of the tonnage could be used for what is known as "heavy cruisers" with guns of not over eight-inch caliber, and the United States had already laid down its allowed quota for ships of that type. It had not, however, decided on its program of "light cruisers," and considerable discussion had arisen as to what the size and characteristics of such ships should be. Each of several types, all differing in size, armament, defense, etc., were being advocated, but which type would be the most effective for the United States could not be determined merely by argument.

The War College was directed to ascertain the relative merits of the several types through miniature fighting operations. The order came just before the Christmas holiday period, and because there was no other time open for research, the college staff devoted its holiday period to it. The conclusions reached were surprising but sufficiently irrefutable to decide the type of light cruisers the Untied States should build under the terms of the treaty. That type was adhered to for as long as the treaty limiting armaments remained in force.

The research activities of the War College were so valuable to the General Board, it was difficult to understand why, in later years, the President of the College was no longer a member of that Board.

During the winter of 1932, I was informed that in the spring I would accompany the fleet on the annual war problem as assistant to the chief umpire. I was delighted with the assignment since it would place me in a position to observe all that the fleet had accomplished from its greatest training activity and the latest forms of war operations at sea.

Taken at the headquarters of the U.S. Naval Training Station (now Founders Hall), Newport, R.I., on 27 May 1932 just after the review of the Regiment of Apprentice Seamen and just before the graduating exercises of the War College class of 1932. **Front row, left to right:** Rear Admiral Harris Laning, USN, President, Naval War College; Admiral W.V. Pratt, USN, Chief of Naval Operations and the only former Naval War College President, as of this publication date, to become CNO; Secretary of the Navy, Charles F. Adams; and Captain G.J. Rowcliff, USN, Commanding Officer Training Station, Newport. **Second row:** Commander T.A. Thomson, USN, Executive Officer, Training Station; Captain Adolphus Andrews, USN, Chief of Staff, Naval War College; Captain H.R. Stark, USN, Aide to Secretary of Navy; Lieutenant Commander C.W.A. Campbell, USN, Aide to Chief of Naval Operations. **Third row:** Lieutenant J.L. Holloway, USN, Aide to the President, Naval War College.

XLIV

Interlude at Sea

THE UMPIRE DUTY [FOR FLEET PROBLEM XIII] LASTED about two months [in 1932], and I enjoyed it thoroughly. when I joined the fleet at San Pedro, the commander in chief [Richard H. Leigh] took me into his quarters and mess, which gave me close contact with all fleet activities but without the responsibility for them. To one who had theretofore exercised important responsibility in maneuvers, being in their midst without such oversight was a delightful, interesting, and unique experience.

When the fleet arrived off Honolulu, it found itself in the midst of the famous *Massey* case, which was being headlined in most of our country's newspapers.[201] The trial of five natives accused of horribly assaulting the wife of a U.S. naval officer had just ended in a "hung jury," and bitter feelings over it had developed between the whites and the natives of Hawaii. The former felt there had been such a dreadful failure of justice that white women would no longer be safe in the islands, while the latter seemed jubilant that natives were not to be punished for the crime.

When we arrived, the situation was tense, especially between the native sympathizers and navy men. Fearing it might develop into rioting and fighting, shore leave for the navy had been canceled, and navy men were restricted to their ships or stations. Into that serious situation arrived the U.S. Fleet with about forty thousand more navy men, all wishful for liberty in delightful Hawaii after two weeks at sea.

Thus arose several complications. All Hawaii had prepared for the fleet's visit and especially for garnering the several million dollars that visiting sailors would

An Admiral's Yarn

spend. Therefore, while canceling shore liberty was a terrific blow to navy men, it was an even worse disappointment for the people of Honolulu, who had counted on a boom in business activities. The commander in chief had no desire to add fuel to the fire by sending thousands of men ashore each day, and Honolulu was in no position to stop a riot should one develop. It was a dilemma of the first order.

Whether it was due to a suggestion from Washington or by his own initiative I never knew, but shortly after we reached Pearl Harbor, the commander in chief started an investigation of the situation and asked me to attend. Of course I had no official connection with it, but when it was over, I had gained considerable knowledge of the *Massey* case.

Apparently the horror of the crime had given way to bitter feelings toward the courts for not having convicted men of native blood for their outrageous crimes. To me, an outsider, the clash appeared to be between a group that felt it stood for law and order and one that (though not opposed to law and order) had been led to the belief by the trial defense lawyers that the white element was using the guise of a court of law to seek control of the islands by sending natives to jail.

The clever lawyers responsible for developing that idea in the minds of the natives had been hired by Kanaka groups to provide the best possible defense for the accused men. Doing so was quite right, of course, but opposing this brilliant defense lawyer was a prosecuting attorney who was also an elected official—whose re-election was dependent upon native votes! Whether the prosecuting officer's presentation of his case was influenced by a desire not to antagonize voters, no one could say, but we were informed that the defense lawyer was able to "put it over" the prosecutor and cause the jury to "hang" in spite of seemed to be absolute proof of guilt.

We were told that the scheme used by the defense to "hang" the jury was to get considerable native representation on it and then take advantage of their ignorance of American law, causing them to misinterpret the meaning of "corroborative testimony." In Hawaii, as elsewhere, convictions on rape charges cannot stand on the testimony of only one person. For the protection of men who might be wrongly accused by a single blackmailing individual, corroborative testimony is required. The defense cleverly used that requirement to convince one or more members of the jury to believe that the essential "corroborative" testimony required must relate to actually witnessing the assault. Of course, since none of the attackers would turn state's evidence, that particular form of corroboration was impossible to obtain and for that reason the jury "hung."

Interlude at Sea

In fact, the corroborative evidence was plentiful. Mrs. Massey had neither seen nor heard of the defendants before the assault, but she so fully described her assailants that there was no doubt as to their identities. She gave many details about their automobile, even most of the figures of its license number, the places she was taken, and all details of the attack. That testimony alone was not sufficient to convict, but the prosecutor was able to corroborate it in many ways. He proved through the testimony of other witnesses that the men so fully described by the victim were seen before and after the attack in the car. Beads torn from the woman's dress were found in the car, and medical examination proved clearly the brutal attack. As far as I could tell, the prosecution made a case that would have convinced every member of the usual American jury. However, he appeared to have failed in one particular aspect. He had not made it clear to the Hawaiian jury how completely the victim's testimony had been "corroborated."

The apparent miscarriage of justice tended to increase the already considerable antagonism between the races. While the native group was satisfied with a "hung" jury, the white element thought another trial was essential. That justice might surely be meted out, the whites sought to obtain "corroborative evidence" of the attack itself. Hoping one of the attackers might turn state's evidence, the Chamber of Commerce offered $10,000 for the testimony of an eyewitness. Through that and other actions, the law-and-order group hoped to leave no doubt, in even the most ignorant mind, as to what had actually happened.

When the fleet arrived, both Honolulu and the U.S. Navy wanted the normal activities of a fleet visit to take place. But when even a slight argument between a navy man and a civilian might set off an explosion, this appeared to be impossible. Nevertheless, a way to clear the situation was found through making it plain to both navy men and civilians that the processes of law must be allowed to take their course, and pending that, all controversies must be avoided or shore liberty would cease at once. Inasmuch as such a stoppage would inflict hardships on everyone, a condition of truce quickly developed, and the tension gradually lessened. We were skeptical of what the outcome might be when the commander in chief lifted the liberty ban, but the truce proved to be effective for the entire visit of the fleet.

This is not to say that the *Massey* case was then over—it was far from that. Preparations went on for a second trial, and the hunt for additional corroborative evidence continued. During that time, the leader of the assault gang was abducted and shot by the complainant's family, which brought about a renewal of friction. However, I was no longer in Hawaii when the second

An Admiral's Yarn

flare-up occurred, so it has no place in this story. As it was, the fleet remained in the islands several weeks after the truce started, and except for newspapers, particularly those that came from the West Coast, no one would have guessed that affairs in Honolulu were at a near-explosive stage.

A few days after the lifting of the liberty ban, the fleet moved to Lahaina Roads, at the northwest corner of the island of Maui. Since I was not concerned with the fleet's work there, I took ten days leave to remain in Honolulu for a rest. In cognito, with not even the hotel knowing of my position in the navy, I slept, ate, and enjoyed the swimming. The commandant of the Naval Station [Yates Sterling, Jr.] placed a small automobile at my disposal. Whenever weather permitted, I used it to visit every part of Oahu, for the defense of which I had made as complete a study as possible from military maps and naval charts. By having that car, I visited every accessible part of the island and learned by personal investigation Oahu's weaknesses and strengths as the site of our country's most advanced and important Pacific naval base. Between doing that and relaxing about a dozen hours a day, I was greatly improved physically, so when the leave was over and I rejoined the fleet at Lahaina, I was a new man.

While I had visited Maui many times, the several days I spent on the island that spring, with no work to do, were unusual. Living with the commander in chief, I partook of all the entertainments given him. He was an enthusiastic automobile cruiser, and took me on drives that covered most of the island. On one trip, we went to the head of automobile navigation on huge Haleakala Crater, which rises directly from the sea to about twelve thousand feet. This extinct volcano's crater is said to be the largest in the world, miles across and almost two thousand feet deep—impossible to visit. When we arrived at the high spot of automobile traffic, some six or seven thousand feet up the mountain, we stopped for the night at a beautiful estate, the owner of which was a friend of the admiral's. From it we could see the whole of beautiful Maui, a magnificent sight which tourists came thousands of miles to see.

That night on the mountain was delightful, and we were shown the full hospitality of a great Hawaiian estate in its food, drink, and attention. Our quarters were in a charming guest bungalow, which was the coolest spot we had encountered in Hawaii. But how really cold it could be on that mountain I did not realize until morning, for from the time I turned out until I was dressed and warming myself before a big wood fire in the main house, I nearly shook apart shivering. I could not see that the cold had frozen anything thereabouts, but to me, the temperature that morning felt considerably below the freezing point. If you are ever to spend the night on one of the high mountains of tropical Hawaii,

Interlude at Sea

take my advice and have woolen clothes for the morning. (I had only the thinnest of tropical suits!)

After breakfast we spent the morning driving around the highest mountain roads, which were very beautiful and at times exciting, but when we returned to the house for luncheon, we were greatly upset to be met at the door with the announcement that there had been a death that morning, a few miles down the mountain, from bubonic plague. Hawaii is covered with sugar plantations, and rats, the carriers of plague-infected vermin, inhabit the cane fields. Even one case of plague causes intense apprehension in the islands, because it is so difficult to prevent an epidemic. With thousands of men on liberty in the island, the commander in chief was greatly perturbed over the situation and became more so when he learned the case had appeared near a school—the children of which were scheduled to visit his flagship the following day. It was time for prompt action and the admiral proceeded to take it.

His first step was to locate the principal of the school in order to cancel the visit of the children. We started down the mountain at a furious rate, and fortunately the principal was found quickly. After calling off the visit, the admiral drove the full length of Maui, at high speed, to Lahaina. Upon reaching there, he found all serene, since word of the plague case had not been received, but he immediately recalled all men then on liberty and stopped all communication with Maui.

It was remarkable how quickly and completely that great fleet was severed from all contact with shore. But isolated though the fleet was, the several days it remained at Lahaina were days of anxiety. The plague did not become epidemic due to the quick and effective action of Hawaii's health officials, who succeeded in preventing the spread of the disease on shore, and the admiral's prompt action, which prevented it from reaching the fleet. Hence, when the time came for our return trip to California, the plague threat had ceased.

When I arrived once more at the War College, I was scheduled for one more year as its President before having the opportunity for a last tour of sea duty before retiring from the navy. Having another year to devote to naval warfare in miniature, I worked harder than ever to prepare myself for my next command. Externally, that last year at the college was quite like the two that preceded it, but internally it provided the finishing touch to my study of naval warfare.

It is sometimes said in our country that high war commanders are chosen for "political pull" rather than for fitness. This may or may not be the case, but for all of my naval life I have wanted to achieve high command through competency, not political favor. And, while not an inkling of my next command was even

An Admiral's Yarn

rumored during all that winter, I knew I would be sent to sea when summer came.

About the middle of April a break came. As I left home one morning to go to my office, the garbage man was in the roadway with his wagon, and as usual we passed the morning hail. Then, to his "good morning," the garbage man added, "Congratulations on your being made a vice admiral." When I questioned him, he said he had read it in the little Newport paper along with the new command assignments, and that I was to command cruisers with the rank of vice admiral. When I reached the office, clerks coming from town verified the news, but it took me some moments to get over the jolt that the garbage man knew more about my future orders than I did.

I was greatly pleased over becoming a vice admiral and having a three-star admiral's flag, but even more so to command the "heavy cruisers"—the navy's newest and fastest large ships. For the three years I was president of the War College, we had continuously utilized those ships in miniature wars, so I felt well versed on their war operations. I did not have long to wait to utilize my knowledge, as I was directed to assume command on May 26th. I therefore had to leave the college soon after the slate was announced.

The change of duty, of course, affected my family's plans too, and they remained in Newport two weeks longer to pack our household goods, while I left by automobile almost at once. Ordinarily I would have made the transcontinental trip by rail, but as I wanted to take my automobile to the West Coast, I decided to go across the continent in it. An enlisted man ordered to my ship offered to drive the car from Newport to San Francisco, and we started off.

XLV

Vice Admiral

Although crossing the continent by automobile was not unusual in 1933, such trips were not as commonplace as they are today. There were fewer highways, and those that had been opened were not hard-surfaced from beginning to end. Furthermore, they were not equipped to meet the demands of automobile traffic. Therefore, our route had to be carefully planned and each day's stopover decided on before getting underway lest we unexpectedly reach the desert without gas, food, or a place to sleep. Hence, transcontinental navigation differed considerably from that at sea.

Nevertheless, we enjoyed the trip. Being well up on auto touring in the east, we experienced no difficulties as far as Kansas City, where I spent three days with my mother. However, from there on, matters were not so simple. Leaving Kansas City before six o'clock one morning, we found ourselves in western Kansas at noon, where we stopped for lunch. The roads were excellent, and we had averaged nearly fifty miles an hour. Therefore, we began to think that cross-country driving had few difficulties. However, we realized we might be quite mistaken when the blackest cloud I had ever seen appeared on the southwest horizon about one o'clock in the afternoon. From the way it looked, I though we were in for a terrific rainstorm or cyclone, but other symptoms did not support the case. The air was hot and dry, the little bit of wind was from behind us rather than in front, and almost before we knew it our freshly filled radiator started to boil over, obliging us to head into the wind every two or three miles to cool if off. I though there was something definitely wrong with our car.

An Admiral's Yarn

Although there were no cars going our way, those passing in the opposite direction seemed to have no difficulty at all.

All this time it was growing darker and the air becoming thicker with dust. Soon every car had its headlights on, and we were stopping at every store or gas station along the way to fill the radiator with water. While we were stopped at one, an old "Model T" drove up and the driver said, "This is the strangest thing I've ever seen. Until now, my Ford has run on gas, but today it is running on 'water.' I have to fill up every time I come to a house."

Between the heat and the awful dryness of the air filled with dust, we felt suffocated, but what bothered us most was the intense darkness. At two-thirty in the afternoon we could see absolutely nothing, and even in the rays of our headlights, the road was visible for less than twenty feet, so we crept along the edge of the pavement at slowest speed.

That utter blackness lasted nearly four hours until about five-thirty when it seemed a bit less intense, though even then our headlights would penetrate only about fifty feet. I had heard of dust storms that came from the so called "dust bowl," but until that experience, it never occurred to me that such quantities of earth could be carried by the atmosphere. Though we closed the car tightly, dust more than an eighth of an inch thick soon covered everything in it, while opposite each crack through which air could enter, the dust lay in snow-like drifts.

During the four hours of darkness, we crawled along for some fifteen miles. About six o'clock we found ourselves in a village with a crossroad leading north about thirty miles to the town of Colby, through which ran another highway to Denver. Suspecting that dust storms might follow what seafaring men know as the "law of storms," and that, like ships at sea, automobiles could navigate themselves out of a storm area, I decided to change our course from west to north at the crossroad, in hopes of running clear of the storm.

I happened to be right, for apparently we were on the northern flank of the storm and in this new direction we soon began to run out of it. The air gradually cleared and before long we could see the pavement without our headlights and could increase our speed, but we still found difficulty in breathing. At seven-thirty we reached Colby and decided to seek a hotel and call it a day.

In the six hours before we struck that storm, we had driven over three hundred miles, but in the next six hours, even with our best efforts, we had covered less than fifty.

I will not forget the car's appearance as I disembarked that night, for instead of the shining car in which we had left Kansas city that morning, it was the worst looking wreck I had ever seen. Dust had piled over it exactly as snow during a heavy fall. It looked unseaworthy for the fifteen hundred miles of desert and mountains that lay between us and San Francisco. However, you cannot always tell about automobiles by the way they look. We turned that one (a Pierce-Arrow) over to a garage to be cleaned up during the night, then we had baths and dinner and went to bed. In the night the wind shifted to north, the dust blew back toward the "bowl," and the morning dawned bright and clear. Far to the west the Rocky Mountains rose over the horizon. The country about was green with budding spring, and in front of the hotel stood our car, shinning and looking very fit for the trip ahead.

I wanted to continue west from Denver and cross the Rockies before heading for Salt Lake City, but we were told in Denver, under no circumstances attempt that route because of snow, but to travel via Cheyenne where the Lincoln Highway was clear. So we turned north again and arrived in Laramie that evening.

Our next day's run was on the high plateau and over the "Continental Divide" to Salt Lake City, so, after leaving Laramie, we found ourselves going higher and higher. We were not actually "climbing" mountains, but as we worked our way up valleys, we could see them rising high on both sides of the road, their tops covered with snow. There was no vegetation. Now and then we could see a few ranch houses or a tiny village, but for the most part, the country, though beautiful in the clear atmosphere, seemed barren and uninhabited. As we crossed the Continental Divide at snow level altitude, the view was magnificent and we had the highway to ourselves.

As we worked down to Salt Lake City, we found a change in the country. Towns became more frequent, there were more rivers, vegetation, and people, and we began to believe ourselves clear of the desert country. When we reached Salt Lake City, we seemed, once again, in a metropolis. As night was closing in, and hotels were available, we anchored there for the night, getting under way the next morning at five-thirty for the five hundred-and forty mile run to Reno, which proved to be quite different from our previous treks.

Although the country was beautiful and green as we left Salt Lake City, it did not continue that way. Great Salt Lake looked to have the charms of the ocean as we rounded its southern end, but as soon as we left it we entered the uninhabited Great Salt Lake Desert. I daresay the world contains other places just as desolate as that desert, but I doubt if many sailors ever see them. At first I thought we were crossing a great, frozen lake, for as far as the eye could see, the desert was as flat as water, covered with what looked like ice. That illusion became greater as we went along, and here and there we could see small hummocks or stakes that the highway construction workers had left. Each seemed to be supporting immense ice cakes, but when we neared them we found huge rocks of solid salt that sparkled in the sunlight like a fancy Christmas card.

At the highway, Salt Desert is some fifty miles across, and for all that distance the road runs west as straight as an arrow. It is built of earth thrown from each side, and stands two or three feet above the floor of the desert, absolutely level through its entire length. It was not paved but its surface was of a smooth, hard gravel on which cars could travel maximum speed. Inasmuch as the road was wide and devoid of traffic, we made standard speed of seventy miles per hour and covered the fifty miles across the dried up salt lake in less than forty minutes.

Strange to say, though going steadily at that high speed, we seemed to be moving leisurely, since the desert had no landmarks on which to gauge our speed. The apparently slow movement produced a peculiar effect, for as we looked across the dead level white salt, we became obsessed with a desire to ride on it and "really" travel. I suppose the same feeling comes to every automobilist on that road, and that is why there are signs all along it, and even road maps, that warn against venturing on the salt. Therefore, in spite of our longing, we stuck to the road, and almost before we knew it, we were climbing the hills that mark the western boundary of Great Salt Lake Valley. Although the level Great Salt Lake Desert was then behind us, we were still in desert country with hills and mountains all around us. Every twenty or thirty miles we could see a group of houses or gasoline stations, but otherwise not a sign of people, and the highway remained deserted.

Going over one of the high hills, we saw another automobile far ahead in the valley. The sight of a car was sufficiently unusual to attract attention, but we soon saw that this particular one was not moving, and we had learned from experience that any car stopped in the desert was in trouble. As we approached we found a large and dilapidated old roadster with two women in the front seat waving frantically and calling for help. That, of course, was quite startling, but when we saw that the rumble seat contained a young couple "spooning," we concluded there was not a real disaster. The woman driver cried out, "Can you beat this? Here we are in the middle of the desert without gas. Please give us some." We had filled our tank at the last station we had passed and had come only thirty miles since, so we promptly backed our tank against theirs to transfer gas. Then and there we learned something about motoring in the desert, for to our utter consternation, neither car had a tube with which to siphon gas out of a tank or even a container in which to carry it from one car to the other. Being unable to render assistance when it was needed was, of course, a disturbing situation for sailors, and we quickly made up our minds never to be in a desert again without proper equipment. All of which caused the people in the roadster

Vice Admiral

to become more excited than ever, and even the spooners joined in the lamentations.

The only answer seemed to be the nearest gas station. Our map showed one about twelve miles distant, and I suggested taking the young man in the rumble seat with us to bring back a can of gas. He strongly objected, but when I told him we would have him back quickly, he consented to go. The three of us sat on our front seat, and soon we were traveling seventy miles an hour toward the gas station. Suddenly he cried out, "Great Scot, the speedometer shows seventy miles an hour and we can't be going that fast. What on earth is the matter?" When we told him it was our usual speed in the desert, he was amazed that there was so little motion. He exclaimed, "In that car of ours, when we run it up to thirty-five it throws us almost through the top."

The remainder of our run, after delivering the young man to his car, was uneventful. Exactly twelve hours after leaving Salt Lake City we arrived at the Reno Hotel. Our odometer registered that in twelve hours we had covered five hundred and fifty miles, even doing our "Boy Scout" deed, stopping twice for gas, and once for lunch. Deserts have drawbacks, but automobiles can certainly make speed on them.

We found Reno an attractive city, and after dinner I took a walk through the business section, which differed greatly from most I had seen. Everywhere there were evidences of its predominant activities—gambling and divorce. But as important as the divorce business appeared to be, Reno was filled with diversions of every kind for those seeking them. I thought I had learned about "wide open" towns in my middy days, but, for its size, Reno outclassed them all in gambling dens, nightclubs, dance halls, and gilded palaces of gay life. However, being anything but divorce bent, those places held no charm for me, and after looking at them from the outside for an hour, I returned to my hotel and turned in.

As navy craft always report arrival in port by dispatch, I sent a telegram to my wife in Newport telling her of having reached Reno, and I was surprised to find an answer when I returned from my walk. It read: "Reno very dangerous for married men. Suggest you leave at once. All well here." Both of us having a keen sense of humor, and inasmuch as we had been married over thirty years and I had always found my wife right in everything, I decided not to tarry in Reno but to get underway for San Francisco as soon as I had some sleep and breakfast.

At seven the next morning I went out to board my car, and for the first time failed to find it ready and waiting. Not knowing where the driver had put up for the night, and being fearful of the effect that a wide open desert town might have on a sailor, I worried quite a bit for the next fifteen minutes before the car

An Admiral's Yarn

appeared. When it arrived, I was even more worried. My seaman driver, who never drank or smoked, was a sight to behold. His eyes were red and swollen, and he was almost asleep at the wheel. To my query as to what was wrong, he answered, "Admiral, let's get out of this town as fast as we can. It's no place for sailors. I decided to take a look at Reno before I went to bed last night and I've been looking ever since." Then he added, "I have not had a drink but I took in every 'hell spot' in this place. I thought a sailor might show a desert town a thing or two about gambling, but I have changed my mind. It not only took all my money but it kept me up all night even after all that hard driving yesterday. I need rest but I need more to get away from Reno, so let's be off to San Francisco."

The run to the West Coast was delightful, though we had to stop often for strong coffee to keep the driver awake. Soon after starting, we were standing up the eastern slope of the High Sierras, and when we gained the top, all vestige of desert disappeared. The great mountains were covered with melting snow, down every valley tumbled a stream of water, and the highway led through great forests of huge trees. It is hard to imagine the difference between the desert and that gorgeous western slope of the Sierras with fertile California lying before you. After we left that awe-inspiring scenery at the top of the forest-covered mountains, we came to the old "gold diggins," where picks, shovels, and manpower long ago had given way to the giant hydraulic machines that melted mountains down to bare clay cliffs, showing that vast despoiled area which the lure of gold had produced and which had been the ruin of one of the great beauty spots of nature.

With our speed, we were not long among the ugly clay banks but soon reached Sacramento and the fertile farms of central California. Pressing on, we were ferried across Carquinez Strait at Benicia and, following the eastern shore of San Francisco Bay, stood on to Oakland where another ferry carried us across the bay to our destination.

I had wired the *Chicago*, my flagship, the anticipated hour of arrival at its boat landing. On reaching there, I found my flag lieutenant with the barge and a working party to transfer us to the ship. He had arranged for the care of the car, and it was turned over to the working party to unload while we went directly to the ship. We had enjoyed our auto cruise across the continent, but it had made us long more than ever to be afloat once more with the navy, and the U.S.S. *Chicago* looked mighty good to us.

Next morning I formally assumed my new command and rank. The navy has a prescribed procedure for such functions, which we carried out to the letter—officers and men in dress uniform, all hands on the quarter-deck, band and marine guard paraded, and the orders read aloud. Having read mine so all

Vice Admiral

could hear, I announced that I assumed command and directed the *Chicago* to break my flag. At that instant a three-star admiral's flag flew out from the masthead and a fifteen-gun salute was fired. I had become vice admiral.

XLVI

In Heavy Cruisers

AT THE TIME I BECAME "COMMANDER CRUISERS," the heavy cruiser group was not yet a complete unit. Ten ships of the type had been commissioned, but five more still under construction were to join later.[202] Since all were of a type new to our navy and their employment in war not yet fully determined, my task was a complex one. I was responsible for war employment as well as training in a class of ships, born of the Washington Treaty, to replace some of our all-powerful capital ships.

Do not imagine that up to that time this country had not given thought to heavy cruisers or considered them unimportant. However, until the Washington Treaty limited the signatory nations in the size and number of capital ships they could possess, the United States had developed its navy on the basis that hard-fighting battleships and battle cruisers were more important than ships of lighter displacement. Therefore, heavy cruisers were considered unnecessary to us before the treaty. Also, since the country had interpreted the treaty to be one of disarmament, and in so doing had ceased naval building for years, it was almost 1931 before heavy cruisers appeared in the fleet. However, by 1933 the importance of the type under Washington Treaty conditions had become evident, and my responsibility was to ascertain for the United States the utmost that could be expected from the heavy cruisers in time of war. What might constitute that utmost was something of a moot question because of the changes in sea fighting brought about by a treaty that limited and balanced naval strengths and took from us our superiority in striking power.

An Admiral's Yarn

Before the restrictions in naval buildings, our plan was to have more and stronger fighting ships than other nations, using them to obliterate enemy ships. This plan was sound policy for our rich country when it was not bound by restrictions on ship types. We could build enough capital ships to increase armor and armament by making some sacrifices, even in speed to some extent. The American way of naval fighting had become "to bore in" and take such punishment as an enemy might inflict, if by so doing we were afforded the opportunity to destroy him with our superior ships.

"The wade in and fight anything" idea that flowed so naturally from the building policy prior to the Washington Treaty had become almost a fetish with us. For that reason, when the treaty took away the superior hitting ability and its advantages to us, we continued to feel the "fetish." Even though balancing the strengths of the navies had so equalized them that no one nation had a fighting advantage over another, and even though we had not maintained our navy at the strength set for it by the treaty, we still wished to fight as though we had superior striking power. Therefore, when we were given heavy cruisers with eight-inch guns that could shoot ten or fifteen miles with nearly the accuracy of capital ships' guns, it was thought that they too could wade in and fight anything.

It seemed that only by doing so could the U.S. Navy live up to its fighting traditions. The intent to fight that way was still prevalent in the fleet when I joined the cruisers, exactly as it had been the governing influence in student operations at the War College when I had become President. However, at the college it soon became evident that fighting capital ships with heavy cruisers usually resulted in the cruisers being sunk without their inflicting much damage to the battleships. Having found that a heavy cruiser was subject to large-caliber shellfire while closing the enemy battleships, and that once the enemy had been brought within range of the cruiser's eight-inch guns the cruiser was under far more devastating fourteen- and sixteen-inch fire, the students saw the danger in attempting to close with the powerful ships. Therefore, a new procedure for operating cruisers gradually developed.

Inasmuch as efficient cruiser operation is of far more importance in war than the small amount of damage the cruisers could inflict on capital ships, the War College sought to develop a suitable technique for them. It had gone far in doing so when I took over the cruisers, but the technique had not been introduced into the fleet, and it became my duty to install it.

Doing so was no simple matter, but I selected a staff of War College officers familiar with the changed technique, and the work progressed rapidly. Within a year we had a "doctrine" for heavy cruiser work in war with which all ships had been familiarized, and thereafter we had only to perfect ourselves in teamwork—for which the fleet schedule provided ample opportunity.

To a student of naval warfare, our course to prepare the heavy cruisers might be interesting, but it is very technical and has no place in this yarn. Suffice to say the training went on steadily, and the unusual experiences that happened to me on that cruise were mostly outside routine work.

In addition to commanding all heavy cruisers, I had direct command of one division (four ships) of them. When I joined the division, it was in San Francisco for Memorial Day exercises, and as soon as they were finished we returned to our training base at San Pedro. A month later the Scouting Force (of which the cruisers were a part) went north for a summer in the Puget Sound area; but inasmuch as the cruise was merely a repetition of former ones, I will not dwell on it here. It was very much like its predecessors except that much of the speech-making at banquets and luncheons fell on me. For that reason, although I otherwise had a fine summer, I was not sorry to return to San Pedro where we could carry on our work without so many folderols on the side.

But folderols and other out-of-routine events continued to crop up, some of them sufficiently unusual to be worth mentioning. One was in connection with an "inspection" visit by members of the Naval Affairs Committee of the House of Representatives, who, accompanied by wives and other members of their families, came to the coast in a navy transport.[203] As might be expected, an official visit by members of that committee to the bases of the great United States fleet, for which it recommended appropriations, created considerable excitement in southern California. No opportunity was missed either to aid in the inspection or to entertain the men conducting it. They were given receptions, banquets, and luncheons, which included nearly all the higher officers of the fleet.

Being vitally concerned with fleet appropriations, we officers were delighted to be included in the hospitalities, and although they often interfered with our routine work, each was something new and worth recalling. Of them all, the one that stood out was an all-day entertainment in Hollywood, sponsored by the moving picture industry.

Hollywood and its great industry were not new to the fleet, but what they did for the Congressional Committee possibly surpassed any previous effort along that line. Ordinarily, visitors to Hollywood are lucky to be shown over the "lot" of one of the great companies. But "all lots" were to open the committee, had there been time to visit them, which of course there was not. We were rushed from one movie high spot to another, the principal event being a mammoth luncheon. As I remember, it was held in one of Warner Brothers' huge studio

An Admiral's Yarn

buildings that had been cleared of its usual picture settings and converted into a "set" for the luncheon with that perfection of detail for which movie sets are famous. I do not know how many people were seated at the luncheon, but from my experience, I suspect that over a thousand people attended. At the head table alone, on the great dais around one end of the enormous studio, were seated nearly one hundred men—the heads of the movie organizations, who were our hosts, members of Congress, the twenty admirals of the fleet who were honored guests, and the speakers of the day. At the table before us sat nearly every man and woman then famous in the movies, may of whom were introduced while luncheon was being served.

I sat next to a man who apparently knew them all and pointed out the celebrities to me. Some I had met at smaller gatherings, but most of them I had seen only on the screen. Nevertheless, by the time luncheon was over, I had met them all personally and especially enjoyed Will Rogers, who sat at the head of the table and later made a speech.

Participating in the Congressional entertainments in addition to carrying out routine work was a bit strenuous, so most of us officers were relieved when the committee's visit was over. But even when it was, other extraneous activities continued to occur. In accord with the usual custom, the fleet split up for Navy Day, October 27th, each port on the coast being assigned a ship or a larger fleet unit according to its size. My own Division was assigned to San Francisco, so shortly before Navy Day, we proceeded there.

Ordinarily we knew what to expect on a little trip to San Francisco, but we certainly were not expecting what happened on that one. The Division left San Pedro about noon one day to reach San Francisco the next evening. The first afternoon and night were fine, and dawn found us about twenty miles off Point Sur with one hundred and fifty miles to go. Everything seemed propitious at that time, and having been on the bridge most of the night, I was thankful to turn the ships over to their skippers at 7 a.m. to carry out specified exercise singly, while I went below for breakfast.

Just as I was finishing, about eight o'clock, the *Chicago* sounded its fog whistles and slowed speed. A few moments later I felt the engines stop and heard the ship sound the "stopped signal." I hurried to the bridge. There I found all quiet, the ship stopped with it powerful whistle sounding the two required blasts. There was a slight fog. The visibility ahead and in some directions extended for miles, although in other directions there were patches of fog. My signalman on watch said he heard a steamer's whistle coming from it, so the *Chicago* had stopped. As I stood looking, the fog patch drifted away and disclosed the whistling steamer, probably two miles away, standing on a course parallel to our own and in no way dangerous to us. Finding he was clear of the steamer whose whistle he had heard and seeing that all was clear ahead for several miles, the captain [Herbert Emory Kays] ordered the engines started and we began moving ahead slowly.

However, toward our course and well away on our port bow was another small patch of white fog which our ship would evidently miss, but because of its peculiar whiteness, all hands were watching it. Suddenly, out of it appeared a large steamer with a big "bone in its teeth," heading across our course at very high speed.

As the steamer was then a mile or more away and the atmosphere beautifully clear except for the small fog patches, we had no idea it might in any way endanger the *Chicago* which, under the "rules of the road," was required to maintain course and speed that the other ship might maneuver freely to avoid colliding. But the other ship came on and on, holding a course that would surely bring on a collision if continued, and so our captain rang for full speed astern, sounded the collision siren, and sounded the whistle to indicate his movements.

From what I saw as I stood there watching, the other ship apparently had no suspicion of the *Chicago*'s nearness until the siren and whistle were heard. Even then it made no change in its course to avoid colliding, though as it neared I did note a slight diminution in bow wave.

It appeared certain the oncoming ship would ram us near the crew space abaft our engine room, but the backing power of the *Chicago* was great, and as it took effect, the apparent point of impact slowly drew forward. It passed the engine rooms, fire rooms, wardroom, the bridge where I stood, and even the forward turret. Had there been fifteen or twenty seconds more time, the *Chicago* would have drawn clear of the other ship's track. On and on came the fourteen-thousand-ton freighter, still making about twelve knots, and struck the *Chicago* slightly forward of the forward turret at an angle of about 60°.

From where I was, I looked down on the freighter driving its way into my flagship. I saw its great bow crush through the ship to the centerline, where it struck the forward barbette and then stopped. I saw the *Chicago*'s heavy steel plates and frames buckle under the terrific impact and roll up as if made of paper. And I saw the stem and bow of the freighter, a ship's strongest part, crumple and telescope back for a distance of fifteen or twenty feet.

Never having been in a bad collision, I braced myself for the impact, expecting to be thrown down by it. However, it was less of a jolt than I expected, for the buckling of plates and the "slewing" around of the *Chicago* gradually absorbed the impact until both ships were moving in the same direction, the crushed bow of the freighter half-way through the *Chicago*. For a moment I

An Admiral's Yarn

thought the two ships might cling together, but then the freighter started backing and pulled itself clear.

When I saw the section missing, I wondered how the *Chicago* could proceed but was thankful to note the calmness of the crew as they went about "saving ship." The instant of the collision I radioed my other ships to stand by and soon received word that though they were in a fog patch, they would be alongside in a few minutes. That knowledge was a comfort, for in the havoc it could not be ascertained at once what bulkheads were gone, how badly the ship was flooded, or how effectively the crew had established watertight integrity. The crew's work had been perfect, and soon the captain sent me word that the only water in the ship was in the stove-in compartments and that he would soon know the full extent of the damage to the bulkheads.

The damage to the *Chicago* was great but confined to the compartments containing officers' quarters and the ship's storeroom. Casualties to personnel, therefore, were fewer than feared. One officer had been crushed in his room, another was so badly injured that he died later, and a third officer lost his foot.[204] Though deeply depressed over what had happened to our shipmates, we took some comfort in the fact that the casualties would have been far greater had the ship been hit farther aft—for instance, at a crew's compartment or the officers' mess room, where practically all hands were at breakfast.

Still, our troubles were not over, especially my own, for the badly injured *Chicago* was in a fog a hundred and fifty miles from port, and radio warnings of bad weather were constant. The first of my ships, after contacting the freighter and being informed that it did not need assistance, joined the *Chicago*. Afterwards the other cruisers joined us, so the Division was assembled and ready for eventualities. As rapidly as inspections were completed, the captain reported results and in half an hour informed me that the bulkheads would hold if the ship steamed ahead slowly. Thereupon I signaled the Division to make five knots and form column with the *Chicago* leading. In that formation the other ships could render assistance immediately if needed.

Each hour or less after proceeding, the captain notified me of the condition of our bulkheads and I gradually increased the speed. In an hour or two we were going ahead at fifteen knots in an effort to reach San Francisco Bay shortly after dark to avoid having to stay at sea all night in a predicted gale. The fog cleared as we started ahead, but when we were making fifteen knots the captain sent word that it was inadvisable to increase the speed.

To one seeing it from starboard, the Division looked as snappy and immaculate as ever, but from the other side, the *Chicago*, with a huge section gone was a sorry sight.

In Heavy Cruisers

We crossed San Francisco bay at nine that night and an hour later anchored off California City where a tug with the inevitable news gatherers came alongside immediately. We told them the story of the collision and for two hours they made flashbulb photographs of the damage. The next day, front pages of newspapers the country over were devoted to the thrilling yarn.

When the tide turned, the *Chicago* made its way to the Mare Island Navy Yard where it was placed in dry dock, ending our worries for the ship's safety.

As always in the navy when an accident occurs, a court of inquiry was convened at once to investigate the collision and to report the damages. As was to be expected, the court placed the entire blame on the freighter, reporting half a million dollars damage to the *Chicago*. Since the ship would require two months of repair work, I directed another of my cruisers, the *Chester*, to come to Mare Island and transfer my flag and equipment to it. Then we proceeded to San Francisco where we carried out our Navy Day task as directed.

When the blame for the collision was officially placed on the freighter, the United States promptly libeled the ship and sued its owners for the cost of repairs and for compensation to injured personnel. As the freighter had been insured by Lloyds, that great company fought the suit "tooth and nail," but with little effect. The United States won its case completely, contrary to the usual result in collisions. Almost invariably both ships are held partly to blame, and the amount of reparation is based on the allocation of blame. It should be a comfort to Americans to know that in the case of the *Chicago* collision, the courts placed the entire blame on the freighter.

Navy Day over, we returned to San Pedro and took up a winter's schedule that had few interruptions. There were the usual warm, gusty winds known as Santa Anas, and a ten-day holiday at Christmas. Otherwise, for the most part, our time was devoted to gunnery exercises and to training for war. We made great progress in both.

One event that is vivid in my memory is the Rose Festival in Pasadena, held on New Year's Day. Occurring in mid-winter when much of our country is covered with ice and snow, the magnificent display of blooming California flowers invariably attracts nationwide attention. But to navy men and other seafarers who attended the Rose Festival of 1934, it will ever hold a treasured memory.

In planning the annual event, Pasadena always establishes a "theme," and each float in the great parade presents a picture—made entirely of freshly gathered flowers—that illustrates the theme. One would scarcely think the many blossoms needed to create even one of the gorgeous pictures could be

An Admiral's Yarn

assembled, but nearly one hundred such floats were in the parade, and each one was remarkably complete in detail and beautiful in coloring.

The "theme" chosen for the 1934 parade was "Tales of the Seven Seas," so each float depicted some "saga of the sea"—a story of the Spanish Main, a whaling adventure of Moby Dick, a cruise of a Viking ship, sea battles ancient and modern, the voyage of Christopher Columbus, and, among others too numerous to mention, "Little America" as established by Admiral Richard E. Byrd in his successful attempt to reach the South Pole. To add to the interest for sailors, the parade was reviewed by the country's leading World War naval figure, Admiral William S. Sims, who was well attended by all the admirals of the existing fleet.

I had attended other Rose Festivals, once as a guest of Pasadena, so they were not new to me, but never before was I so closely associated with one. A goodly portion of the leading hotel had been taken by the city for its guests, the admirals, and their families, and we were treated royally for three days at the hotel as well as at many social functions connected with the festival.

While all went off beautifully for official guests, Pasadena and the million people who wished to attend the festival had a somewhat more difficult time, since the worst storm I had ever seen in California took that occasion to visit. Not only did fierce winds blow, but there was a deluge of rain—thirteen inches of it in forty-eight hours!

If you are familiar with southern California, you will understand what so much rain in such a short time will do to it. The area is mountainous and hilly, and water runs off quickly. While rivers, creeks, and drains were sufficient for the ordinary rains of the region, they were utterly inadequate in a downpour of what equaled an entire year's precipitation in less than forty-eight hours. Streets became rivers, and every depression where water could accumulate became a lake. Right up until nearly time for the Rose Parade to begin, we thought the floats were going to float on a sea background and that the delicate flowers that made the pictures would be washed away. Then, miraculously, the rain stopped and, the gorgeous floats that had been so carefully created undercover came out and went over the route in perfect condition. The huge crowd that watched the parade had their reward, for the flowers and floats were magnificent. However, the improved weather did not last long, and later, when about ninety thousand people waded through mud and pools to the Rose Bowl to see America's annual football classic, it started to rain again shortly after the kickoff and flooded out most of the spectators, including my family. As the game marked the end of the festival, we made our way through the downpour to our station in Long Beach.

In Heavy Cruisers

The Pasadena Rose Festival is well worth seeing. There is not anything quite like it any place in the world. Let me hope, though, that when you attend you will be greeted by fair skies.

The New Year's events over, we once more concentrated on training, but in connection with it, something new appeared. It was decided that the annual war problem of the fleet would deal with the defense of the Panama Canal, passing through it and operating in the Caribbean, ending with a great fleet review by the President off New York and followed by several months of visits in Atlantic ports. Needless to say, everyone in the fleet was greatly intrigued by such a program, and for the next three months we worked harder than ever to perfect ourselves for war work and to be ready for inspection by the President of the United States as well as millions of people on the East Coast who had not seen the fleet for almost fifteen years.

USS *Chicago* (CA-29), arriving in Philadelphia for the 4th of July celebration in 1934, served as Vice Admiral Harris Laning's flagship from May 1933 to April 1935, when he was Commander, Cruisers, Scouting Fleet and additionally, Commander, Cruisers, U.S. Fleet and Cruiser Division Five.

XLVII

We Change Oceans

THE FLEET'S WAR GAME OF 1934 began in early April when we left California, bound southward. The run to Panama is long, and since our advance was limited to about two hundred miles per day, the fleet had ample time for war exercises en route. Every fleet element in both offense and defense was practiced, so we not only were busy but progressed far in developing our team play for war. The last exercise before entering Panama was to attack the canal with all the forces of the fleet—surface, sub-surface, and air—opposed by the canal's army and navy defense forces.[205]

Americans are greatly interested in the practice games of their armed forces—so much so that for years press associations and leading newspapers were allowed to send special correspondents with the fleet to provide eyewitness reports. Because of the variety of operations in the 1934 games, which extended from California through the canal and ended with a review of the fleet by the President off the coast of New York, we had an unusual number of correspondents with us. Since there was intense interest, too, in canal defense, other correspondents were in the zone to witness the attack from shore. All reports had to be carefully censored before release lest confidential information be divulged, but otherwise the correspondents endured few restrictions. They were welcomed into the ships officers' messes and soon became almost integral with the ships' personnel. With the war game so fully covered by the press, the attention of the entire United States was focused on the fleet and the canal by the time we reached Panama.

For days, radio invitations to official functions had been pouring in from zone and Panama officials, and when we arrived in port from our cruise, where

An Admiral's Yarn

practically all our time had been given to war operations, we found ourselves dedicating that much time and more to the social side of international relations. For the ranking officers who were in need of rest but were obliged to attend the functions, the prospects were not alluring.

Since the cruise, as scheduled, required the fleet to operate from ports on the Atlantic coast all summer long, many officers' families planned to spend that season in the east too. My own family decided to go there by steamer, leaving San Pedro on one of the beautiful Grace Line ships about the time the fleet did, stopping in Panama for a month to be there with the fleet. Therefore, when I arrived, I gathered up my "gold-laced" uniforms for official functions and rushed ashore to join them.

Seven o'clock the next morning found me at the boat landing, returning to the ship, and to my surprise, I found it in great commotion. Officers and men were rushing to the ships which were then "standing" through the canal. When I asked my coxswain about it, he said he did not know except that the ships had recalled every one and were starting through the canal. When I arrived on board, the captain of my flagship told me that the fleet started transiting the canal at 2 a.m. and that orders were on board for the *Chicago* to start through at 2 o'clock that afternoon. Beyond those facts, he knew little.

Needless to say, I was startled by what he told me. It meant not only a cancellation of the Republic of Panama's official entertainment but that we must rush the fleet through the Canal. What could it mean? Was the move discourteous to Panama, or had an emergency arisen necessitating quick action? No one seemed to know. The commander in chief had issued the order and the movement started.

Having a few hours before the *Chicago* sailed, I rushed ashore to recover my uniforms and notify my family that my stay in Panama City was over. On my return to the ship, I was met at the gangway by the press correspondent on the *Chicago,* who begged me to tell him what was up. When I replied that I knew no more than he did, he would not believe me and hurriedly began questioning my staff and other ship's officers to find a leak in the news somewhere. But there was none, since they knew no more than I did. The correspondent came to me again saying he was done for, that his press association would decide he had failed completely for not reporting on the occurrence when he was in the very midst of it. He complained that even the ship's radio was closed to him. When I explained that radio silence had been ordered for the fleet he became desperate. There were still two hours before the *Chicago* would leave, so he called a water-taxi alongside and rushed ashore, remaining there for an hour. When he

We Change Oceans

returned, he was smiling like the cat that swallowed the canary and announced he had put one over on the navy by sending his report by cable.

Happy over having beaten us, you should have seen his face when just as the *Chicago* got underway it received a message from the cable office informing the correspondent that his message could not be transmitted immediately, but would be sent when the ban on cables had been lifted. That information was not pleasant for him, but he realized the other correspondents must be experiencing the same dilemma.

By that time, the people of the United States had a mystery on their hands. In a blaze of headlines, the press had made them aware of the fleet's arrival in Panama and of the great reception to be tendered it there. Then came sudden silence. Neither Panama nor Washington divulged what was occurring, and curiosity became rampant.

Had it been a publicity stunt, the country's loss of contact with the fleet and the canal would have proved the most successful one ever. Not anything of the kind was intended. The fleet had reached the canal in a war game that would take it into the Caribbean; what better opportunity would there ever be to test the ability of the canal to quickly transfer the fleet from one ocean to the other in an emergency. Neither the canal nor the fleet was expecting it. Both had been lulled into a quiet state of mind by the week of entertainment in Panama and by the leisurely plan of transit prepared by the canal. Suddenly, in the dead of night, came an order for the fleet to transit the canal at once. If you have not been through the Panama Canal, you may think it is simply a channel through which ships can steam, almost at will, from one ocean to the other—but it is not that type of waterway. A ship goes but a short distance into the canal at ocean level, then is raised by locks to the artificial lake over the backbone of the isthmus, and is lowered at the other end to ocean level. It takes an army of men to operate the canal, and since only trained canal pilots can conduct ships through it, the unexpected order to rush the fleet through gave the canal force a much more difficult task than even the navy had. To the navy, unexpected orders are almost routine, and it is generally ready to meet them. But to expect and require the canal to change suddenly from the peacetime handling of merchant ships to wartime operations of a fleet in rapid transit is something else again.

I have ever admired the efficiency of the Panama Canal, but the way it met that unexpected call opened my eyes. It went from peacetime operation to emergency war operation at once, and ships began to move through the canal with clocklike regularity. The frequency of passage, of course, depended on the time required by a lock to handle a ship, which seemed to be about fifteen minutes. In that time, a ship, often over thirty-five thousand tons, would be

An Admiral's Yarn

pulled into a lock, the gate closed, the ship raised or lowered to the next level, another gate opened, and the ship pulled into the next lock where the process would be repeated while the first lock made ready for another ship. The operation called for infinite precision, and though requiring the teamwork of hundreds of men, we heard no sound other than an occasional mouth whistle.

So perfect was the coordination between the several locks and pilots, that ships moved along steadily about fifteen minutes apart. Perhaps somewhere there is a more perfect man-operated machine than the Panama Canal, but I doubt it. What can be more perfect than perfection?

Because of the canal's length, the many operations necessary to bring a ship through it, and the restrictions on speed in cuts (where the waterway had been dug through mountains), about eight hours is required for a transit. However, the flow of ships was so continuous that scarcely thirty hours after the movement from the Pacific started, the United States Fleet was quietly at anchor in Cristobal harbor on the western end of the Caribbean.

By that time, both fleet and canal were well aware of the absorbing mystery that gripped the United States, for though neither could transmit messages, both heard all news broadcasts. Our morning news sheets were full of them, and what to us was merely an unexpected naval exercise had drawn the attention of the entire Untied States. For the remainder of the summer it held the spotlight.

We stayed at Cristobal for the length of time the fleet was scheduled to be in Panama City, but being no longer in the country's capital, there were few functions for us to attend. Our families crossed the isthmus to join us, so we had a delightful rest in the cooling trade winds of the Caribbean while making ready for our Atlantic maneuvers.

While these first great exercises in the area since the "World War" came all too soon, they were also most interesting. They took us back to old haunts—the West Indies, the Greater and Lesser Antilles, Cuba, Haiti, Puerto Rico, Jamaica, Guantánamo Bay, and even "Hungry Gulf"—all of which elicited pleasant memories.

The exercises in the Caribbean covered many of the war operations that might be expected in that area and were followed by a period of repairs, cleaning, and painting in preparation for the President's review and our visit in New York. Leaving Guantánamo, the fleet headed for the reviewing point a few miles from Ambrose Lightship off New York. All went well until the morning of the review, when a thick fog almost ruined our plans. The cruiser carrying the President had so much difficulty getting out of New York harbor that the fleet, in formation to parade past him, had to maneuver for two hours until the President was in position. Had the visibility been even fair, the delay would not

We Change Oceans

have bothered us, but to hold that miles-long fleet in review formation in a dense fog in the main traffic lane to the world's greatest seaport was a real test in fleet control. However, the fleet was equal to it, and the instant we were advised that the President was ready, the parade started exactly as though there had been a fog, and fortunately the visibility increased to several miles.

Our long column was headed by the giant aircraft carriers *Saratoga* and *Lexington*, while next came my heavy cruisers. The fleet could see enough of its ships to maintain exact formation, but in the remaining haze we could not see the President's ship until almost upon it. Then suddenly it loomed up in the exact position as planned. Until then I had been concerned about the review in the open sea in such poor visibility, but when I saw that the fleet would pass the President exactly as planned, my mind became at rest. I knew that, barring another closing in of fog, the spectacle would be perfect.

It was. As each ship approached the President with "rail manned" and crew "paraded," it fired the President's salute of twenty-one guns. Then, as it passed, the ship's band played the national air with all hands saluting. For two hours the parade of ships continued, and then behind the last ship came the fleet's air force in mass formation, providing a noisy and fitting finale to a magnificent spectacle.

We had feared that in the fog no one would see the review except those in the fleet or reviewing party, and the great steamship companies that had prepared to carry over two-hundred thousand people to witness the parade would be deeply disappointed. Imagine our surprise on nearing the reviewing ship to see assembled there a great fleet of passenger ships packed with sightseers.

Until that moment I little realized New York's intense interest in our visit. Great though the crowd was that greeted the fleet at sea, it was small compared with that along the shore as we stood up New York Bay and North River. People were everywhere—in windows, on roofs, and in every vantage point from the Narrows to the George Washington Bridge. It gave us the feeling of being in a vast stadium fifteen miles long, filled with human beings. Then and there we realized the extent of Americans' interest in their navy.

Knowing the sun would set before the fleet would be anchored in North River, the exchange of courtesy calls between city and fleet officials had been scheduled for the next morning. Promptly at ten o'clock, Mayor Fiorello La Guardia, accompanied by New York's official reception committee, called on the commander in chief, and an hour later the flag officers of the fleet, in dress uniforms and cocked hats, assembled at the 72nd Street landing to return the call. There we were met by a large police escort and a dozen open automobiles to take us to City Hall.

An Admiral's Yarn

It is about five miles from 72nd Street to the Battery, and as New York's West Side Highway was then under construction, our cavalcade used the regular city streets. However, doing so seemed not to bother city police and chauffeurs, so with sirens shrieking we went at fifty miles an hour, and I must admit that holding on to our cocked hats with both hands detracted from our efforts to present a dignified appearance.

When that wild ride was over, we found ourselves at City Pier and the boat landing at the Battery where a parade was forming—the Police Band leading and "motor cops" surrounding it. Almost before we knew it, we were moving up Broadway in the same way that "heroes" returning from abroad are escorted to City Hall. Having read of those triumphal processions, I had long wished to see one, and here, unexpectedly, I found myself a part of one with paper snow, confetti, and ticker tape being showered upon us from the great office buildings that make lower Broadway a canyon. It was a spectacular beginning to one of New York's greatest displays of hospitality.

It would take volumes to describe the city's festivities—morning and evening papers devoted pages to them—yet entertaining personnel was only a part of the attention given the fleet. New Yorkers and people from nearby cities fairly filled Riverside Drive and the Palisades for a look at the fleet lying so quietly in North River. Hundreds of thousands filled the ships every day, and the interest continued for our entire stay in North River.

We were well worn from the continuous official ceremonies and hospitality extended during our visit and hoped to be able to rest when we left New York, but it was not to be. Though divided into groups to visit several Middle Atlantic ports, attention remained focused on the fleet. I had command of a group of cruisers and destroyers sent to Philadelphia, and although it was not a large force, its welcome to the "City of Brotherly Love" was on the same colossal scale as the one in New York.

I sensed it as we stood up Delaware River where, from Wilmington on, immense crowds filled every vantage point to watch the ships pass. Arriving at Philadelphia, each ship was taken to the city pier that had been prepared for it and for handling the throngs that would visit. Near my gangway stood the official limousine and police escort assigned me by the city for the duration of the visit. I was taken at once to Philadelphia's most delightful hotel where the city had provided a large suite for my family and me.

Our arrival in Philadelphia on a Saturday evening gave us an opportunity to rest the following day and prepare for the week ahead, which included the Fourth of July celebration. The festivities began on Monday morning when the major and I exchanged official calls. They continued for a week, beginning at ten o'clock each morning and lasting nearly all night. My family and I rushed from one function to another, and at many I was called on for a speech—a trying task for a sailor.

On the Fourth of July I delivered a broadcast address during the Independence Hall ceremonies and attended divine services in Old Christ Church, where my family and I sat in the pew that had been occupied by George Washington when he was President. During the week we visited many other historical shrines, including Independence Hall, Congress Hall, the Liberty Bell, Valley Forge, Betsy Ross House, and others perhaps less well known. Between these visits were luncheons, receptions, dinners, banquets, and balls, so that for eighteen hours out of each twenty-four, it was rush, rush, rush. We were whisked from place to place in the city's official car, surrounded by a police detachment with shrieking sirens, and we had less privacy than goldfish. I asked the chief of police if the sirens could not be dispensed with, but the Mayor would not permit it and said, "Admiral, for a long time Philadelphia has not been able to honor the fleet that the nation depends on for security and independence, and I want our people to realize the importance of the U.S. Navy. You are its symbol, and for that reason I am having as much attention drawn to you as possible. Aside from that, Philadelphia has its share of radicals opposed to our government. We must continue the police escort and the sirens."

Being accustomed to long hours with little sleep, we sailors might have given little thought to the physical strain had the weather been reasonably cool, but it was not, and the intense humidity added greatly to the discomfort of our visit the entire time we were in Philadelphia. However, we did appreciate the great welcome that had been extended to us and the hospitality shown not only to the officers of the fleet but to all personnel. Our week in the "City of Brotherly Love" will remain a treasured memory.

After leaving, we headed for sea and anchored off Cape Henlopen, where we had a twenty-four hour wait before joining the rest of the fleet for a week of war exercises, which were strenuous and took pace in bad weather. Later the fleet was divided between Narragansett Bay and Provincetown for a period of individual ship training. My cruisers went to the latter, where we remained about three weeks and saw much of interesting Cape Cod.

I had not expected to attract much attention there, but not only did everyone on the Cape for the summer take a lively interest in us, but daily excursions from Boston brought so many visitors that Provincetown became a carnival city for the duration of our stay. Still, we carried out our scheduled work, and we enjoyed ourselves in the Cape's usual delightful summer weather.

An Admiral's Yarn

After that training period, the fleet was again subdivided and ships were sent to many New England ports. My flagship, the *Chicago*, went to Marblehead, where for a week it was the center of excitement for the surrounding area, and we were shown all the points of historical interest in the vicinity.

With the New England visits finished, the fleet assembled at Hampton Roads for another week of war training, but unfortunately the *Chicago* could not join it. While in Marblehead, we had discovered parts of our fire mains so eaten by electrolysis that immediate replacement was required. The ship was rushed to the New York Navy Yard, and I began seeking another flagship.

It so happened the cruiser *Houston* had just returned from a trip to the Pacific with the President, and being immediately available, I requested a transfer to it. A day or so after the *Chicago* reached Brooklyn, the *Houston* came in, the transfer was made, and we joined the fleet in time to participate in a maneuver that extended from the Chesapeake through the Florida Straits. At its end, the fleet was once again subdivided, this time to visit ports south of Cape Hatteras.

The *Chicago* had been scheduled for New Orleans, but my new flagship was assigned to the city for which it was named—Houston, Texas. The change of port was not unwelcome, since it would take me to an area about which I had heard much but had never seen.

Unless one visits Houston in a ship, one does not realize what people can do to create a seaport where there is no sea. In that respect Houston seems unique.

I had seen Galveston and its Bay and thought highly of them, particularly of the energy and foresight that had made Galveston the fine city that it is. Also, I had read much of Houston and how by dredging a fifty-mile canal and digging a harbor it had made a great seaport in the plains of Texas. Still, I was not quite prepared for what I saw. The twenty-mile channel across shallow Galveston Bay did not end at the shoreline but continued across the prairie for thirty miles to Houston harbor. As long as we were in the broad Galveston Bay with water around the ship for miles, I thought little of being in a dredged channel. However, once the Bay was behind, a different feeling arose, for from the bridge the *Houston* seemed to be standing straight across a prairie that ended only at the horizon. I had cruised through a sand desert in the Suez Canal, had become reasonably accustomed to ships passing through mountains in the Panama Canal as well as their being hoisted up and down hill by locks—but to stand through farmland in an oceangoing ship was a new experience indeed.

Reaching Houston's harbor we found it small, busy, and completely surrounded by piers crowded with ships taking cargoes of cotton, grain, and oil, for which Houston is a great shipping center. There was no loafing and the ships

We Change Oceans

were loaded with amazing speed, after which they departed immediately to make way for others.

Houston's man-made harbor may be small compared with those nature provided elsewhere, but it makes up in speed of operation for all it lacks in size. Its activity is that of Houston itself, which, from being a small town a few years ago, is today a rapidly expanding bustling city of over three-hundred thousand souls.

Half-way measures seemed to have no place there, either in business, building, or hospitality. In particular, Houston is devoted to the cruiser that bears its name, and from the time we arrived, attentions were showered upon us. Not only did all Houston visit the ship, but excursionists came from hundreds of miles. The week in Houston was a gala period, and we thoroughly enjoyed it, especially our visits to historical places where we were presented with histories of Texas and books about Sam Houston. We left the city knowing much more about the earlier days of Texas.

After leaving Houston we went to Guantánamo, where the fleet was assembling for its return to the Pacific. The never to be forgotten summer was over, and once more tactical training and gunnery work became paramount. Our westward trip was devoted to it, and when November found the fleet again at California bases, it was prepared to go on with winter training exactly as though it had been at the bases all summer.

Little out of the ordinary occurred that winter as we continued to perfect our team play of war. In January I began to think what might happen to me when summer came, since in May I would complete two years at sea as a vice admiral, the length of cruise that is usually allowed flag officers. It was certain I would not be left at sea as a vice admiral in command of the cruisers, and I was hopeful the years I had devoted to preparing myself for the navy's highest commands would be rewarded. To a considerable extent they were, for although I was not made commander in chief of the fleet, I was given command of the Battle Force with the rank of admiral and the responsibility of winning in battle for the United States should war beset us.

Admiral Harris Laning, USN, in the flag plot of the USS *California*, with his Chief of Staff, Captain R.S. Holmes, USN, plotting war game movements. (Associated Press Photo, 4 May 1935)

XLVIII

Four-Star Admiral

ON 1 APRIL 1935, with all the pomp prescribed for the ceremony, I took command of the Battle Force. After reading my orders aloud and announcing my assumption of command, I directed the captain of my flagship, the *California*, to break my flag.[206] The four-star flag of an admiral then flew out from the masthead, and as it did, the *California* fired a salute of seventeen guns. The moment was tense for me, marking as it did the attainment of my life's ambition—rank of admiral in the navy.

My first complex task in the new rank ensued with the annual war problem that began a few weeks after I hoisted my flag. It was an extensive exercise, its main operation covering the northern Pacific from Hawaii on the east to just beyond Midway Island on the west. It was also an unfamiliar type of operation. The enemy, which had considerable strength in surface ships and particular strengths in aircraft and submarines, was occupying Midway Island. It was the job of my force—superior in heavy ships but inferior in other types—to retake the island. This was a situation that would test the defensive power of aircraft and submarines opposing heavy surface ships.[207]

My command was the battle force minus three battleships and one large aircraft carrier assigned to the enemy. In addition, the enemy had all the heavy cruisers (except three which were assigned to my force), many destroyers, all submarines, the harbor-based aircraft of Hawaii, and a large force of marines. Under the distribution, my force would be superior in hitting power if I could bring it to Midway intact, but the process of reaching there would subject us to all the attrition an enemy strong in scouting ships, bombing aircraft, and

An Admiral's Yarn

submarines could inflict in a 1,300 mile passage from Hawaii at slow speed. Considering the damage that heavy bombers and submarines were reputedly able to inflict on battleships, the situation did not look very bright for the battle force.

The commander in chief had said the problem was designed to make the force suffer heavily from air and submarine attack all the way from Hawaii, so it seemed little of my force would be afloat to recapture Midway, should any of it reach there.

On the face of it, the problem for the battle force was not encouraging to contemplate. It seemed hardly possible the enemy could fail to locate us and deliver attacks incessantly from the moment we left Hawaii. However, in war situations, a high commander must often fight with the odds decidedly against him, and the measure of his ability is often reflected by the outcome. Hence, though the set-up was anything but favorable for my force, it was my task to win in spite of it.

The Hawaiian archipelago extends some thirteen hundred miles west-northwest from Hawaii, with Midway at its western end. From an atlas map, it appears simply as a chain of widely separated small islands, but as shown on navigational charts, the archipelago is actually a long stretch of shoals and reefs which, if they show above the sea at all, are little more than uninhabited sandbanks. Since there are no navigational marks along the chain, ships usually pass well to the northward or southward, but seaplanes find considerable directional value in the sand patches as well as occasional areas where safe landings can be made. Thus the chain, though it handicaps ship operations, is an aid to air operations—another point unfavorable to the battle force!

With the enemy having so many advantages, "estimating the situation" and "preparing plans" for my force was unusually difficult. There was little we could do to destroy his aircraft or submarines, so to be successful we must evade them.

We hoped to weaken his air strength by a surprise night attack on the long-range bombers that we knew were in "Midway Lagoon" when the war opened, but the vital element remained evasion. In fact, we made the surprise air attack, although our available air force was puny and not equipped for the work. The only planes we had within a thousand miles of Midway were the scouting planes of the three heavy cruisers—which were four to each cruiser. They were equipped with machine guns to fight enemy planes in the air but otherwise had no hitting power at all. Still, it was so important to reduce the enemy's air strength that we decided the possible gain was well worth the risk of a theretofore untried night air attack on the enemy's long-range planes. Having been in command of the heavy cruisers for two years, responsible for their training, I had little doubt their aircraft could successfully carry out the unusual task.

That attack was one of consummate gall on the part of the battle force and of even more consummate nerve and skill on the part of the aviators that made it. Knowing the moon would be nearly full, we counted on its light to enable the attack. When the sun went down, our cruisers were over a hundred miles from Midway, much too far for planes to fly at night and find a group of small, low sandbanks ringing the atoll. Accordingly, at dusk the cruisers started for Midway at high speed and reached a point, about ten miles from the island, where it could be seen in the moonlight. At that point they catapulted their planes and, turning to a prearranged course, steamed directly away from Midway at top speed, leaving the planes to attack and then return to the cruisers.

The details of the attack were told to me afterwards by the aviators. Apparently it delivered all the surprise we had hoped for. Knowing we had but three cruisers near the strongly defended Midway area, the enemy, seemingly, was not prepared to fight a night air attack twelve hours after war had been declared. Perhaps they were as ready as was possible under the conditions at Midway, but if so, the objective of the attack—the bombing force—was wide open to it. The shore defenses surrounding the lagoon were ready, but apparently the lagoon itself was not poised for attack by air. There, moored in long lines, lay the entire force of giant enemy seaplanes. Had our attack group been larger or better equipped, it doubtless could have done great damage to the huge unprotected planes lying quietly in the lagoon. As it was, they probably crippled many seriously, though their small caliber machine guns could only make holes that efficient mechanics could certainly repair.

The attack on the bombers continued until the ammunition of the attacking planes was theoretically exhausted. For as long as the ammunition held out, the planes stood back and forth close above the lines of anchored bombers and sprayed them with their machine guns. They then withdrew and followed after the cruisers, joining them at dawn to be taken aboard. The cruisers continued standing away from Midway at high speed, lest they be located and bombed by the enemy, but neither enemy ships nor enemy aircraft found them. The surprise attack had been accomplished with perfect success, and although we could not determine the damage it did, a message broadcast the next morning by our cruisers informed us that the battle force had struck a considerable blow at the heart of the enemy without our being damaged in any way. The knowledge was cheering, and as the cruisers were then free to create a previously planned diversion northeast of Midway, we began to feel greatly encouraged over the situation.

An Admiral's Yarn

At the time the mock war opened, my entire force, except the three cruisers near Midway, was in Pearl Harbor ready to sail. It got underway immediately, and at exactly noon stood out of its base in the face of an enemy concentration of submarines that gave it a busy afternoon. Fortunately, the army defense of Hawaii was available to help us, and as its aircraft forced enemy subs to keep submerged, the battle force suffered little in getting to sea and forming for the advance on Midway.

That afternoon and evening was a period of vital importance to us, since we were to lay a plan for outwitting and evading the enemy. We knew that although they might not be able to attack us, enemy submarines would certainly report our movements, and we hoped to deceive them by standing southward from the harbor entrance to form up and then ostentatiously turning the fleet to a northwest course as if to pass through Kauai Channel west of Oahu and gain the northern side of the archipelago. By late afternoon we had passed the submarines, and our air force concentrated on keeping them submerged until dark to prevent them from reporting our movements. Then, when darkness fell, we increased our speed, and at nine o'clock, an hour before the moon rose, the entire battle force suddenly changed course to southwest to reach the southward of the archipelago.

After the abrupt change of course and the route in darkness, we had no way of knowing whether or not the enemy had observed us. So when the moon rose, we became not only vigilant for enemy contacts but especially alert for intercepted enemy radio messages or detected signals emanating from nearby that might be reporting the movement. However, none were heard and at dawn we were some two hundred miles from where we appeared to be going at dark. All that day we waited for enemy scouting ships or planes to discover us, but when darkness came again and no contact had been made, our great worry was over, for by the time it would be light again, the enemy would have a considerable search problem on his hands.

By then we might be anywhere from five hundred miles north of the archipelago where our early movements indicated we would be, or five hundred miles south of it where we actually were. The enemy's task had become equivalent to hunting for a needle in a haystack.

In the next several days our force held a due west course drawing farther to southward of the northwesterly trending archipelago. We expected to be discovered at any moment, especially when, having searched to northward of the chain of islands, the enemy would realize we must be south of them.

We could tell by the radio activity that his force was becoming a bit desperate over not locating us, but as the messages seemed to be emanating from points far to the northward, we felt fairly secure. They were usually in enemy code that we were unable to break, but now and then we would catch a rush message in plain language reporting a contact where we had no ships at all. In spite of the reassurance given by the enemy's radio, we still felt certain that we would be discovered before reaching the longitude of Midway. We were not, and when we had reached that longitude we turned north at dusk one evening to head directly for the island.

Dawn the next morning found us only three hundred miles from Midway, heading for it on course north. Every minute we expected to be "picked up" by enemy scouts and attacked by submarines and heavy bombers. Although we heard the enemy's radio constantly, we remained unseen until just before sunset when a scouting plane located and reported us. We were then two hundred miles from Midway, and it was too late in the day for the enemy subs to gain attack positions before dusk.

Nevertheless, as soon as our position was reported, a force of heavy bombers set out to attack us. Fortunately darkness came before they could see us, and although we saw the big bombers plainly against the bright sky background, they could not see us against the dark water.

We were therefore safe for the night from air, but enemy destroyers and submarines would certainly attack with torpedoes unless we could fool them. Accordingly, when it was completely dark, the battle force changed course ninety degrees to the left for about three hours and then turned back to head for Midway. I dare say those course changes bothered the enemy considerably, for no attack reached us until about 2 a.m., when a few destroyers found us. Their doing so gave our position away, so when dawn came and we were closing Midway to deliver our attack, the enemy met us with all his forces in concentration.

Though the situation still left my force considerable fighting to do before capturing Midway, we had nevertheless accomplished our main task and were starting the attack at nearly full strength. We had gained the tactical advantage of hitting power superiority at the critical point and were deployed to take advantage of it.

It is never possible to measure results in sham battles at sea, and the outcome in that one was certain to be guesswork. But as matters turned out, the result was even less determinable than usual, for the big fight had barely started when the commander in chief suddenly sent us a radio flash discontinuing the battle and directing radio silence. As a flash of that nature could mean but one thing—a disaster—the entire fleet awaited instructions. We had no idea what had

An Admiral's Yarn

occurred, but we held ourselves ready to meet the emergency whatever it might be.

We were not long in learning. One of the "enemy" giant bombers had crashed into the sea with six officers and men, and the fleet's task thereby changed instantly from fighting the final battle in a mock campaign to rescuing real aviators. Unfortunately no ships were sufficiently near the crash to see it or lend assistance. We knew only that the big plane reported itself falling and then there was silence.

Locating the exact spot of an unwitnessed plane crash at sea is difficult, since water shows no trace of the crash except through floating survivors or bits of wreckage. It therefore became necessary for the fleet to go over the possible area very carefully. For ten hours we searched so thoroughly that every bit of floating material in the area was recovered. With its crew of brave men, the plane had gone to the bottom of the sea.

The sun went down that night on a saddened fleet that had known for hours that further search was futile. As darkness closed in, the commander in chief reluctantly stopped the search, and after assembling the fleet, started our return to Hawaii. The trip was without incident, and in about six days we were once more in Honolulu, where we were shown the customary hospitalities while preparing for our return to southern California.

There was nothing unusual in that passage. Although we had been engaged in war exercises for the previous two months, we continued them on our way home so that by the time we were again at fleet bases, we were ready for a rest. However, there was little time to relax. The summer schedule was at hand with the fleet going to San Francisco for Fourth of July week and then on to Puget Sound.

That was my last summer in the northwest. Exactly forty years after I had gone there as a middy, I returned as a full admiral in command of the battle force. The change in me personally was great, but no greater than to the northwest where development and improvements were amazing. From a distance, Mt. Rainier, Mt. Baker, and Mt. Olympus seemed unchanged, but when I drove over the beautiful highways to them I found myself in immense national parks with paved roadways leading to every scenic wonder. Cities stood where only towns and villages had been, while factories and farms covered what, in my youth, had been dense forest.

I had made a trip in my earlier years to the wild virgin forests of Oregon, but they were no longer wild. Automobiles and people were everywhere, and news from the outside world was as frequent and complete as in New York City.

One day I motored up Smith River Valley and in two hours had reached the point where less than fifteen years before men were seldom seen and game and trout abounded. But now the situation was quite reversed. We found a two-hundred-man C.C.C. [Civilian Conservation Corps] camp where formerly there had been no men at all, and Smith River utterly denuded of fish. The country was as beautiful as ever, but it had lost its charm for me.

Summer over, the fleet returned to southern California and began its winter schedule. The work was as continuous, as interesting, and as important as ever, but I was then completing six years at sea as a flag officer. Accordingly, in January 1936, I wrote to a friend in Washington, at work on the high command slate, that if my services at sea were not needed I would like to become Commandant of New York Naval District when that officer retired for age, in April.

Shortly after that I received orders detaching me from the battle force exactly one year after taking command, allowing me one month's leave and directing me to assume duty as Commandant of the Third Naval District and the New York Navy Yard on May first. It was a shock to know my seagoing was soon to end, but I was not greatly depressed since, after all, it was merely age catching up with me. As I had passed my sixty-second birthday anniversary, had been in the navy about forty-five years, and had almost completed twenty-five years of duty at sea, what else could I expect?

The last two months of sea life passed quickly, and then came the day to relinquish command. Remembering how I felt when I left the *Pennsylvania*, I expected the day that I gave up sea life forever to be a sad one. To some extent it was. But there was something different in this situation. Whereas I still had my goal in life to pursue when I left the *Pennsylvania*, that had now been attained and surpassed. As I gave up the battle force, not only were my years of preparing for high command in war ending, but my great responsibilities were finishing too. The sadness of giving up my last command was ameliorated by my relief to transfer the burden to younger shoulders.

I must confess to husky voice and tearful eyes when my four-star admiral flag came down.[208] Nevertheless, when my wife and daughter met me at the boat landing, both voice and eyes returned to normal in their rejoicing that cruises, separations, and tremendous responsibilities were now in the past. We found much happiness in the thought of a future together, for we were an unusually devoted family.

Admiral William D. Leahy, USN, (**right center**) relieving Admiral Harris Laning, USN, (**left center**) as Commander, Battle Force, U.S. Fleet, on board the battleship USS *California* on 30 March 1936. In this ceremony, Laning passes to Leahy a force consisting of fourteen battleships in four divisions, eight cruisers in two divisions, the Navy's only four aircraft carriers, and forty-three other vessels including a destroyer flotilla and a light cruiser. Overall, the force was manned by 2,762 officers and 30,370 enlisted men.

XLIX

A Transcontinental Cruise

WHEN WE KNEW SEAGOING WOULD SOON BE OVER FOR ME, my family began to make plans for life ashore. We had toured most of our coastal states as well as many foreign countries. This brought us to the conclusion that there were more places left in the United States that we wished to see than in all the rest of the world together. Our plans for the future, therefore, were based largely on seeing our own country.

I still had a short tour of shore duty before retiring, leaving little we could do to immediately gratify our wish to travel. However, I had a month's leave before having to report for shore duty, so my wife and I determined to make a leisurely automobile trip to New York. In our many traversings of the country, we had become familiar with sights along the transcontinental rail routes, so we planned our motor trip to places not visible from trains. The first visit was to Boulder Dam.[209]

Our daughter had started east by rail the night before, and my wife and I got underway the next morning. Spring had come and southern California was gorgeous with flowers. But we were quite familiar with the country west of the mountain range, so we hurried across it and over Cajon Pass into the Mojave Desert. All went well until we were in the desert, whereupon entering we found a strong westerly wind driving across it, carrying dense clouds of sand.

When we reached Barstow and stopped for gas, we were inclined to remain there awhile, even though sand and dust were as heavy in the town as on the highway. While we were getting gas, a car came in from eastward looking so strange that we stared in amazement. Not only was it devoid of paint, but its glass

An Admiral's Yarn

windows seemed to be frosted. Being accustomed to queer looking cars on highways, I assumed it to be just another old desert car—until the man driving it climbed out to look it over.

When he did so, his face became one of utter horror. He asked me if we had come from westward and if I though he could make it to Los Angeles. As we had just traveled the road, I told him I though he could, whereupon he exclaimed, "I've been driving automobiles for years, but this is my first experience in a desert. My wife and I are on our honeymoon, driving this brand new car. We spent last night in Las Vegas, and when we left this morning our car was without a blemish. Just look at it now—all blemish."

The car looked the part and I became apprehensive about leaving Barstow until the sandstorm was over. However, the station attendant, while not encouraging, said that since strong westerly winds often blew sand that way for days, we might just as well go on. The he added, "Don't let that eastern dude scare you. Being in the desert for the first time he tried to buck a forty-mile-an-hour sandstorm at sixty miles an hour. He 'sand blasted' the paint off his car himself. If he had been satisfied to slow down his car, it would not have been damaged. However, it will be different with you, since you will be going with the wind and sand, no matter how fast you go. My advice is to go on to Las Vegas at best speed."

Although skeptical, we took his advice and continued on across the desert. The flying sand was thicker than ever, but it merely dropped on the speeding car like dust. At times visibility was too reduced to travel fast, but on we went for about a hundred miles, when we had to go over the mountain pass at Ivanpah Lake. As we neared the top of the pass, we found ourselves above the flying sand, and as we went down the eastern slope, the air was so delightful that we stopped to eat sandwiches and drink ice water and soda pop while the car cooled off.

All was well until we tried to start the engine, which refused to work. It had been given a careful check-over the day before, and our driver was an excellent mechanic, so we worried that it was serious and feared we would be stalled in a desert where only one car had been seen since we left Barstow. Fortunately we were headed down the mountain, and, having assured himself that the engine was all right mechanically, the driver proposed coasting down the grade. Coasting down a mountain toward a desert in a heavy automobile is no pastime for a sailor, and I was a bit dubious about it. But inasmuch as it was better than spending a night on a desert mountain, I told him to try it.

I have no idea what trick he used to start the flow of gas again, but when we had coasted a mile or so, the engine began to run and we made it to Las Vegas, Nevada, sixty miles away. We took advantage of the clear air and splendid

A Transcontinental Cruise

highway to make high speed, but I must confess to a nervous tension all during the run lest the gas stop again on an upgrade.

By the time we drove into a Las Vegas gas station, I felt our troubles were over, but they were not. Although the station attendants and men from a nearby garage found our gas line clear from tank to engine, the latter once more refused to start. We therefore "manhandled" the car a couple of blocks to a garage, where by dint of persuasion on the boss who had a brother in the navy, they agreed to work all night, if necessary, to correct the trouble. It turned out to be sand in the carburetor, of course, but I had no idea until then what a job it would be to rectify it. It seemed so complicated as those mechanics went about it that I feared we would be obliged to spend a day or two in Las Vegas. But the men worked with such knowledge and skill that in less than four hours the engine was running smoothly and we were underway for Boulder City where we had reserved rooms for the night.

It was a great surprise when, driving through the desert, we suddenly came out on the enormous lake created by the dam. I had informed the supervising engineer of our visit to the dam, and he had sent word to come to the Administration Building in Boulder City so that one of his assistants could show us over it. Accordingly, at nine o'clock next morning, we were taken to the project by an engineer. Merely to see the lake that had been created in the desert was astonishing enough—but when we were told the lake extended seventy miles up the Colorado River gorge, and was seven hundred feet deep at the dam, we realized as never before what man can do.

As inspiring as the lake was, the feeling was dwarfed at the sight of the dam that created it. Driving out on the roadway atop the arched structure and looking over the lake, one felt it was like any great dam; but turning in the opposite direction and seeing the huge gorge that the dam had closed left one spellbound. Nearly eight hundred feet below us lay the bed of the Colorado River. Spouting from the cliff on one side were three giant geysers, the Colorado River flowing around the dam site through the tunnels, while the dam was under construction.

Perhaps the world contains a greater engineering feat, and while I have seen many, none impressed me as did Boulder Dam, when I stood atop it looking first at the lake it created and then at the great gorge it closed. The sight is well worth traveling thousands of miles to see.

Remarkable as the view is from the top of Boulder Dam, one must visit its base to realize what a wonderful achievement it is. A giant elevator takes one down to the bottom of a gigantic canyon to the power plant with its enormous turbines. Closed at one end by the man-made dam, it is held open at the other by

An Admiral's Yarn

the tremendous forces of nature. Perhaps nowhere else can one see the awesome power of nature consisting with the nearly as great power of mere man. It is amazing what man can do in this world of ours.

From Boulder Dam we went to the Grand Canyon in Arizona via some fifty more miles of desert before reaching a main east-west highway. Once on it, the worst of the desert seemed behind us. The country remained arid and thinly populated as we gradually climbed to the high plateau where winter snows had been and where desert flowers and other vegetation began to appear between mountain ranges. At length we reached the timber line, and from there on into Grand Canyon National Park the country was gorgeous, snow on the hilltops, snowdrifts near the highway, snow flowers blooming profusely, and great evergreen forests all about. The altitude was nearly six thousand feet and the air so clear, cool and invigorating that the change from the desert regions was delightful and greatly appreciated.

An hour or two before sunset, we reached the park entrance where all visitors must register. Imagine my surprise when the ranger who looked at my registration card suddenly exclaimed, "Oh, you are Admiral Laning. I've been watching for you all day." Although I was traveling "incog," I replied in the affirmative and asked how in the world he knew I was coming to Grand Canyon. He said, "That was easy. A navy captain who had been on your staff arrived early this morning and asked if you had reached here. I told the park superintendent you were coming and he gave orders to let him know when you arrived so that he could place all the park at your disposal." With that we drove on to our hotel where the captain and his wife were waiting for us. They had investigated the most interesting point we should see, and at once suggested that with the sun about to set, we should hurry to a certain place overlooking the canyon to witness the marvelous changes in color at that time. We were treated to the gorgeous spectacle of sunset across the Grand Canyon.

After dinner that night the park superintendent came to see me, and I realized that to experience all the canyon's glories, which he so eagerly described, would necessitate a much longer visit than we had planned. The superintendent hoped to show us the canyon from top to bottom. However, having looked at the bottom, and noting the thousands of feet of cliff to be negotiated to reach it, I regretfully decided it was no trip for a sailor. In any event, we had to be on our way the following day. The superintendent kindly charted a morning cruise for us along the south rim, which was awe-inspiring and beautiful, and he also advised us to see the canyon at sunrise. So, we walked out of the hotel about five o'clock the next morning to watch the morning's rays brighten the walls and pinnacles of the Grand Canyon.

A Transcontinental Cruise

You may think of April as balmy in the Arizona high plateau, and you would be correct as far as mid-day temperatures are concerned. However, it was anything but balmy when we departed—in fact all of the outdoor surfaces were frozen tightly! Although we believed we had seen the greatest of nature's spectacles at sunset, we found the sunrise equally gorgeous and very different. The actual colorings obviously were the same; but whereas at sunset they lead to a fade-out of the picture, at sunrise they go from blackness to the wonderful majesty of the Grand Canyon. One can hardly say which effect is the more beautiful, since each defies comparison. But having seen the canyon at both sunrise and sunset, I found its immensity and colorings in mid-day an anti-climax. When noon came we were willing to move on.

For the next several days our stops were at less spectacular spots. We went to Prescott, Phoenix, and Tucson, then across the Dragoon Mountains to Tombstone, Arizona, which, judging from its numerous tombstones, is the most properly named town we encountered. Over the mountains and down a beautiful canyon lies Bisbee and the enormous copper mines for which it is famous.

After Douglas, Arizona, and El Paso, Texas, we went to Carlsbad, New Mexico, to inspect the Carlsbad Caverns, which, within my time, had become one of our most remarkable national monuments. One might think of them as merely caves, but having seen some of the other famous caves of the world, particularly those of New Zealand, I am certain Carlsbad Caverns is one of the greatest wonders of our time. Going down a prosaic looking caved-in hole on a desert hillside, one is not prepared for the overwhelming beauties soon to be encountered.

The story of Carlsbad Caverns—their discovery, exploration, and exploitation—is a romance all its own, but even today the story is not complete. There are still vast caverns yet to be explored. Only a portion of those on one of the three known levels has been opened to visitors, and they surpass imagination. That level is eight hundred feet below the surface and lighted by electricity, but so numerous and vast are the others that visitors go through the lighted caves in carefully counted groups, surrounded by Cavern Rangers lest someone go adrift in the black darkness. The trip through the opened chain of caverns takes about five hours to complete and has to be made on foot. Visitors usually start down the "hole in the desert" hill at ten in the morning and return to the surface at three in the afternoon.

Noon finds the party in an enormous cavern where a light lunch is served before entering the last of the awe-inspiring caverns, after which an elevator carries the visitors nine hundred feet to the surface.

An Admiral's Yarn

The five hours in Carlsbad Caverns was not only one of our most unique experiences but probably, in its way, the most spectacular. One cannot dream the myriad of fantastic shapes created by the infinitesimal rock deposits, all from water dropping slowly for millions of years. They run from seemingly delicate lacework to immense mounds, icicles, and gigantic columns of every color of the rainbow; and in the artificial illumination, they sparkle like so many diamonds. Yet though drops of water created those grandeurs, to sightseers the caverns are as dry as a bone. Year in and year out the temperature remains at 50°, and though a visitor may find dust on his shoes when returning to the surface, there is never any moisture.

Having seen one of the most remarkable spectacles of our trip, we left the caverns with a resolve to return someday for a more comprehensive visit.

Our route then took us south to Pecos, Texas, where we again struck a main east-west highway, and thence to Fort Worth, a run which, though of about four hundred miles, crossed only a part of central Texas. Not until we made that run did we realize the vastness of Texas, its endless resources, and its development. All were so far beyond our imaginings that we became more wedded than ever to the idea of cruising about our country on land. Seeing the world via water is interesting and exciting, but seeing the United States via highways is even more so.

At Fort Worth we turned northward, and after visiting Tulsa and Oklahoma City, and Joplin, Missouri, we made our way to Kansas City where we stopped to spend a week with my mother before driving on to my "old home town," Petersburg, Illinois.

I had written a relative that we would be there for a day or two and had accepted an invitation to a dinner my fellow townsmen wished to give in my honor. Nevertheless, I was not prepared for the greeting I received.

Having been but sixteen when I left home forty-five years before, and having returned for only occasional visits in that time, it seemed hardly possible that Petersburg would still look upon me as one of its citizens. The night before reaching there we stopped in Jacksonville [Illinois]. We left at about eight in the morning for the thirty-mile drive to Petersburg. It was through country I had known well as a boy, but although the route was the same, paved highways replaced the former dirt roads and we traveled sixty miles an hour instead of the five or six in horse and buggy days. The old road along the Sangamon River to New Salem had become the important highway linking Petersburg and Lincoln's old home with Springfield, but thirty minutes away now, by car.

It was indeed a different road from the one I had known, but with the changes I still did not lose my bearings and, too, I had kept abreast of the numerous

A Transcontinental Cruise

improvements. Not only had New Salem been made an important historical park, but its restoration to the days of Lincoln was complete. It was difficult to hurry on past the entrance to the park to arrive in Petersburg on time.

Driving into Petersburg, I was surprised to find flags flying everywhere. And when we arrived at my aunt's house, I asked what sort of celebration was going on. She looked at me in disgust saying, "Goodness, man! Don't you know? Petersburg is celebrating the return home of its native son, Admiral Laning. You may think yourself still a boy around here, but to the town you are one of our great admirals. Please remember that."

A few minutes later a delegation of citizens came to pay the town's respects, and among the oldest were several boyhood schoolmates. Not until I saw them surrounded by the younger men who were taking their places in town leadership did I fully realize that I too had reached the "has been" status.

That afternoon we went to New Salem and were shown over the restored village by the curator, another boyhood friend.

The contour of the land and the woods were the same as when I had wandered over them as a boy, and I could even spot one or two of the old trees that I thought Lincoln had studied under. But although the village with its restored log cabins looked about as we boys had imagined it, the impressive sight was beyond our dreams. No wonder that thousands visit New Salem each year. It shows, as do few other shrines, from where a man may start and yet leave a name in history to last through the ages.

Later that day I visited my father's grave and once more looked at Ann Rutledge's, so close beside it.

I toured Petersburg's "public square," which had scarcely changed since I was a boy, but except for the oldest men, there were few I remembered. However, as my arrival had been published, I was given a most hearty welcome.

The town looked about the same as it did when I was a lad, but there was something missing. I know now that it was my youth.

It was with very deep appreciation that in my boyhood home I was made to feel, in the eyes of those who lived there, that I had made good. A man may attain great responsibilities and be received with acclaim wherever he goes, but to me, doing so is far short of appearing successful to boyhood friends. Because of that, I look back on that visit to Petersburg as the high point in my life.

After that homecoming, the remainder of our springtime cross-country drive to New York seemed commonplace. We enjoyed it and saw many places we had long wished to see, but after the earlier thrills, where we had experienced too many wonders in too short a time, we were delighted to arrive at the

An Admiral's Yarn

commandant's house at the Brooklyn Navy Yard, where we were destined to remain for the next year and a half.

L

Commanding a Naval District and Navy Yard

WHEN I ASSUMED DUTIES IN NEW YORK, I found I had two commands, both of importance. As Commandant of the Third Naval District, composed of New York, Connecticut, and northern New Jersey, I was coordinating head for all naval activities in our country's most important seaport and industrial area, with headquarters in downtown Manhattan. As Commandant of the Navy Yard, I was head of one of the navy's greatest industrial plants, with offices in the Brooklyn Navy Yard.

In war, each of these commands is a full-time job for an energetic officer, but in peacetime, without war activities to conduct, my principal duty was to maintain efficiency in work while keeping the commands ready to move into war status on a moment's notice. Inasmuch as both commands maintain skeleton organizations for war operations during peacetime, the dual duty was not overly strenuous. Each was one of coordinating previously organized activities, which, though complex and technical, were individually supervised by experts. Therefore, I had little to do with details and could devote my time to supervising the District and the Yard as separate entities, which together were quite sufficient to cause me to observe strict office hours.

This was not a hardship for one trained to the twenty-four-hour-day of sea life and sea-fighting. As a matter of fact, being without responsibility for lives and ships at sea was a considerable relief.

However, the duty had its drawbacks. I was ranking officer in our country's most densely populated area and as such was expected to represent the navy at nearly all important civic, patriotic, and historical functions in the District. Mere

An Admiral's Yarn

attendance was not sufficient; almost invariably I was expected to make a speech. Had I accepted the innumerable invitations, I could not have kept office hours during the day and would have been busy most nights too.

When I realized that even though I canceled considerable speechmaking, I would still have to be on "display" most of the time from noon until after midnight each day, I was forced to draw the line. All purely official functions, of which there were many in the great seaport, had to be meticulously observed. But as such functions were activities for which I had been trained, and rarely required speechmaking, there was little cause for worry. However, other functions did require speaking, and I had to consider them carefully. Some merely wanted a speechmaker, some sought an admiral in uniform as a sort of "table decoration," while others wished to add a touch of official recognition to a gathering.

To avoid having my official position abused and also prevent over-taxing myself on activities extraneous to my duty, I was obliged to restrict outside requests. However, as Commandant of the Navy Yard, one of the city's greatest industrial plants, I was pleased to represent the navy at the multitudinous official functions of Greater New York.

An invitation from the Mayor [Fiorello La Guardia] to do so was invariably accepted, but when it came to attending the meetings of patriotic, military, or business organizations, I had to decline unless they were of state-wide or nation-wide importance. Though the restrictions keep me from being utterly swamped with attendance at hundreds of local activities, I still found it rather rough going.

Fortunately there were compensations. Many of the functions were intensely interesting and of historical importance, and I will relate some to show the variety of happenings in a naval officer's life.

There were the usual official naval functions for foreign men-of-war visiting New York—during my time as commandant, there were British, French, Japanese, Swedish, Canadian, and Danish as well as visitors from other countries. But while the exchange of naval courtesies was invariably the same, the city's activities were somewhat varied, depending on the length of the visit, and as a city representative as well as a naval official, I had little rest when a foreign warship sailed into New York harbor.

My unique experiences in New York had little to do with the navy. Taking advantage of holidays, leave periods, etc., my family and I made several automobile tours through most of the area of my command. We covered Long Island, Hudson River Valley, the Adirondacks, the shores of Lake George and Lake Champlain, and much of Connecticut and New Jersey. In addition, these areas featured many places of historical interest, and after seeing them, I was better prepared to understand the history and romance of our nation's early life. More than ever I was convinced there are more interesting places to see in the United States than in most other parts of the world.

We did not have to leave Greater New York to find points of interest, for there are hundreds right in the city limits, and most were known to us from previous visits. One event that particularly remains in my memory was the fiftieth anniversary celebration of the [1886] dedication of the Statute of Liberty.

Although only a school boy in Illinois at the time of the dedication, I always felt a proprietary interest in the Statue of Liberty. I was therefore determined to see it on my first trip to New York, which occurred when I was seventeen and so full of energy that I climbed through it from top to bottom. I even went to the light in the raised arm, which long since has been closed to visitors.

Having had this interest in the statue for the fifty years of its existence, and having felt its significance every time I passed it "standing" in and out of New York harbor, observance of the dedication anniversary meant much to me. Accordingly, when I received an invitation to participate in the ceremonies, I was delighted, especially so since the President of the United States and important officials of this nation, France, and other countries would participate.

The celebration was inspiring. Before actual exercises began, the guests were taken over to Bedloe's Island and were told its history. They saw the old forts upon which the foundation for the statue had been erected, and in one of the forts was shown a motion picture reproduction of the convention where the United States Constitution had been adopted. I can imagine no better preliminary to the commemoration exercises, which were held in front of the huge statue. Around it were gathered representatives of historical organizations bearing flags and banners and wearing uniforms and costumes of the time when the Republic was established and our national liberty came into being.

In that setting, President Franklin Roosevelt spoke by radio with the President of France (who was in Paris at that time) as well as in person with the French Ambassador and other world personages. Their exchange recalled to Americans the greatness of our country and the meaning of the statue before which we were gathered. As a boy I had known the statue as Bartholdi's emblem of our United States—"Liberty Enlightening the World."

That night at a great banquet held in one of New York's largest hotels, I represented the navy and was seated with the dignitaries on the dais. I did not know the gentleman on my right until in the course of conversation he asked when I would retire from active service and what I would do afterward. I told him my retirement would come in about a year, and when it did, my wife and I

An Admiral's Yarn

hoped to spend a year touring the United States in an automobile, stopping here and there to fish and visit all our national parks. "Well," he said, "perhaps I can help you on your park visits. I am Head of the National Part Service and as such am attending this celebration because Bedloe's Island and the Statue of Liberty have been made a National Park within my jurisdiction. When I return to Washington I will send you literature on all our parks and a letter of introduction to the park superintendents. From the literature you will learn what to look for, while the letter will open all our parks to you."

I hardly thought he would remember that talk, but a few days later, descriptive pamphlets covering all the national parks arrived and also a letter introducing me to the park superintendents. I retain them still in the hope of using them some day. However, the letter of introduction goes further than merely asking each park superintendent to aid me in seeing the sights. It speaks of me as a fisherman and requests them to show me the best fishing a park affords! Poor though I be with rod and reel, I look forward to the rare treat ahead.

Many but not all events that I participated in while at the New York Navy Yard were commemorative. On Memorial Day, Fourth of July, and other anniversaries, I was asked to "receive" the parades, but most celebrations had to do with happenings of "today." I took part in the official opening of Tri-Borough Bridge, the groundbreaking for the Midtown Tunnel under the East River, the receptions for distinguished foreign representatives entering the United States through New York, the banquet on the *Queen Mary* the night of that giant ship's arrival, and in dozens of functions of similar nature.

Still there were others. At the Navy Yard, we had our own ceremonies for laying of keels and the launching and commissioning of ships. During opera season, we had a box for certain nights sent by a member of the Metropolitan Opera Association. In the horse racing season we had club privileges at one of the great tracks and could enjoy the delights of the fall and spring race meets whenever we had time. Even without office hours, I never lacked for something to do in New York. The difficulty was in finding time for the things we particularly wanted to do.

One form of activity out of the usual was attending commencement exercises, making graduation addresses, and delivering diplomas. Doing so for the Submarine School at New London and the Merchant Marine School of New York State went with my line of work, but certain others did not; among those were the graduating exercises of my pre-Naval Academy school at Peekskill.

Although I had left that school forty-six years previously, I retained a great fondness for it. Not having had an opportunity to visit it during my varied career, I eagerly accepted an invitation to deliver a graduation address. I cannot claim that the experience fitted me to address young men about to enter college or business positions, but nevertheless I felt the same sort of pleasure in addressing them as I had felt upon returning to my boyhood town as an admiral. A few months later I became a trustee of the Peekskill Military Academy and later its cadets had my portrait painted to hang with other Academy trustees.

Time flew in New York, and my sixty-fourth birthday anniversary with consequent retirement for age approached with horrifying rapidity. Although there is nothing unexpected in retiring for age, and officers have learned to look on doing so with considerable equanimity, one's actual retirement is nevertheless a shock. To pass, in one moment, from a position of great responsibility to one having so little in comparison is a blow indeed, even though I had prepared for it for many years. I was dazed as I turned over my last active command, saw my flag come down, heard the final gun salute, and bade farewell to the fighting navy I loved and in which I had served for over forty-six years.

I had been depressed when I had given up my last ship and when the four-star flag that marked my last sea command came down, but on neither occasion did I suffer as I did when I left what had so long been my very life.

Fortunately I was not to be completely severed from the navy just then. Many years before, when I was a lieutenant, my wife and I had discussed the retirement and had talked over plans for those future days. We had decided we would be delighted if I were ordered as Governor of the Naval Home at Philadelphia.

You can imagine our happiness when I received the orders (a few weeks before my retirement) from the Navy Department that if I wished the duty, I would be made Governor of the Naval Home. I lost no time in accepting it, and the very day my name went on the retired list of the Navy, I became Governor of the Naval Home—another dream had come true.

Launching the light cruiser USS *Honolulu* (CL-48) at Brooklyn Navy Yard (26 August 1937. **Front row, left to right**: Hester Laning; Mayor of New York, Fiorello La Guardia; Helen Poindexter, the ship's sponsor and daughter of E.G. Poindexter, the governor of Hawaii; Mrs. E.G. Poindexter; and Rear Admiral Harris Laning, USN.

LI

The Naval Home

THE NAVY IS CONCERNED with many activities, but possibly none so little known to the public at large, or even to the navy itself, as the U.S. Naval Home at Philadelphia.

It was established in 1820 "to provide an honorable and comfortable home during life for old, disabled, and decrepit officers and men of the Navy and Marine Corps who may be entitled under the law to the benefits of the institution and who shall be known as beneficiaries."

The home is not a disciplinary institution but is intended to provide a retreat for the beneficiaries, where they may pass their remaining years in contentment and happiness. It is the duty of all connected with the home to contribute their utmost to this end, and the only such discipline enforced is that which may be necessary to secure the highest good for the beneficiaries—individually and collectively. Under the supervision of the Navy Department, the home is subject to laws that Congress may pass from time to time.

While officers of the Navy or Marine Corps may be admitted to the home by permission of the Secretary of the Navy, few request it. Practically all beneficiaries are former enlisted men. To be eligible, a man must have been discharged from service under honorable conditions, must have served in the armed forces of the United States until incapacitated for further service by disability incurred in the line of duty, or must be on the retired list. Additionally, he must be unable to earn a living by manual labor because of physical disability.

Under such rules for admission, all beneficiaries are either elderly or have serious physical defects. For that reason, the home is unlike any other naval

An Admiral's Yarn

activity. Its operation resembles somewhat a hospital, though the beneficiaries are in no sense patients undergoing hospital treatment. They are, however, under fairly constant medical observation and are sent to the hospital immediately when advisable.

It is difficult to imagine a more dramatic change in work then that which transpired with my transfer from an active naval command to governorship of the Naval Home. War operations that had been my constant work for over forty-five years simply faded away. But the change had a compensation. In all the years I had commanded men, it had ever been a conviction of mine that men would follow a leader better through devotion to him than they would through fear. Requiring much from the men under me, I always sought to keep them happy, contented, and satisfied in their daily life. Hence, when I became governor of the home, I found I could continue that course for the very men who had served actively in the navy when I did.

For years I had thought that commanding the Battle Force and being a four-star admiral marked the high spot of life for me, and of course it did as far as my active naval career was concerned. However, I cannot say it also marked the high spot in my entire life, for there is something wonderfully satisfying in making the "old salts and leathernecks" of the Naval Home happy.

As I write this, the home has some two hundred and forty beneficiaries, and quarters for as many more are nearing completion. Since each has his own room, is clothed, subsisted, and looked out for in every way, the governor has a large family to care for, not merely as to actual living but even recreation, amusement, medical, and dental care.

Fortunately, I enjoy the care of the big family. Once it was my ambition to win battles for my country during war, but age has precluded that, and my ambition today is to bring contentment and happiness to the veterans of the Navy and Marine Corps in their remaining years. In the eyes of younger men, this ambition may not loom large. Nevertheless, in the eyes of a one-time admiral, it is the most alluring one he has ever had. At least it is not connected with fighting and killing.

Looking backward, there is little I would change in my life. Looking forward to my remaining years, I am content to enjoy them in the bosom of my family, dangling a grandchild on my knee. Separations, war, and unpredictable movings are over, and I am grateful for the many blessings that have been bestowed upon my family and me during the years.

When I was seventeen it was my ambition to be an admiral in the navy. Through hardships, my ambition never wavered, and it would not today. Could I live my life over, I would choose the navy for it.

USS *Laning*

Destroyer Escort 159

Commissioned at Navy Yard, Norfolk, Virginia

1 August 1943

christened by

Mrs. Harris Laning

DE 159, USS **Laning**, *served thirty-two years*

The keel of the destroyer escort USS *Laning* (DE 159) was laid on 23 April 1943 at the Norfolk Navy Yard. On the 4th of July, Admiral Laning's widow, Mrs. Mabel C. Laning, was the ship's sponsor at the launching ceremony. The *Buckley*-class destroyer escort was commissioned on 1 August 1943.

During World War II, the *Laning* escorted numerous convoys to the Mediterranean until November 1944, when the ship was converted into a high-speed transport (APD 55) at the Philadelphia Navy Yard. Sailing to the Pacific in 1945, *Laning* was modified further in San Francisco to operate as an underwater demolition team flagship. The ship reached Okinawa when the war ended; occupation duties in Korea and China kept the *Laning* busy for two months, then she returned to the U.S. East Coast, decommissioning in Green Cove Springs, Florida, on 28 June 1946. *Laning* earned one battle star during the war.

On 6 April 1951 the *Laning* was recommissioned in the Atlantic Fleet. From 1955 through 13 September 1957, the ship was assigned to the Third Naval District (New York) as a Naval Reserve training vessel. After decommissioning at Norfolk, *Laning* remained in inactive status, reclassified as LPR 55 in accordance with general amphibious redesignations occurring on 1 January 1969.

The ex-USS *Laning* was stricken from the Naval Vessel Register and sold for scrapping to the Trebor Marine Corporation of Camden, New Jersey, on 3 December 1975.

Rear Admiral Harris Laning, USN extends best wishes to his successor, Rear Admiral Clark H. Woodward, USN, during ceremonies installing Woodward as commandant of the Third Naval District at the Brooklyn Navy Shipyard, New York City, 1 October 1937. (ACME photo)

Appendix I

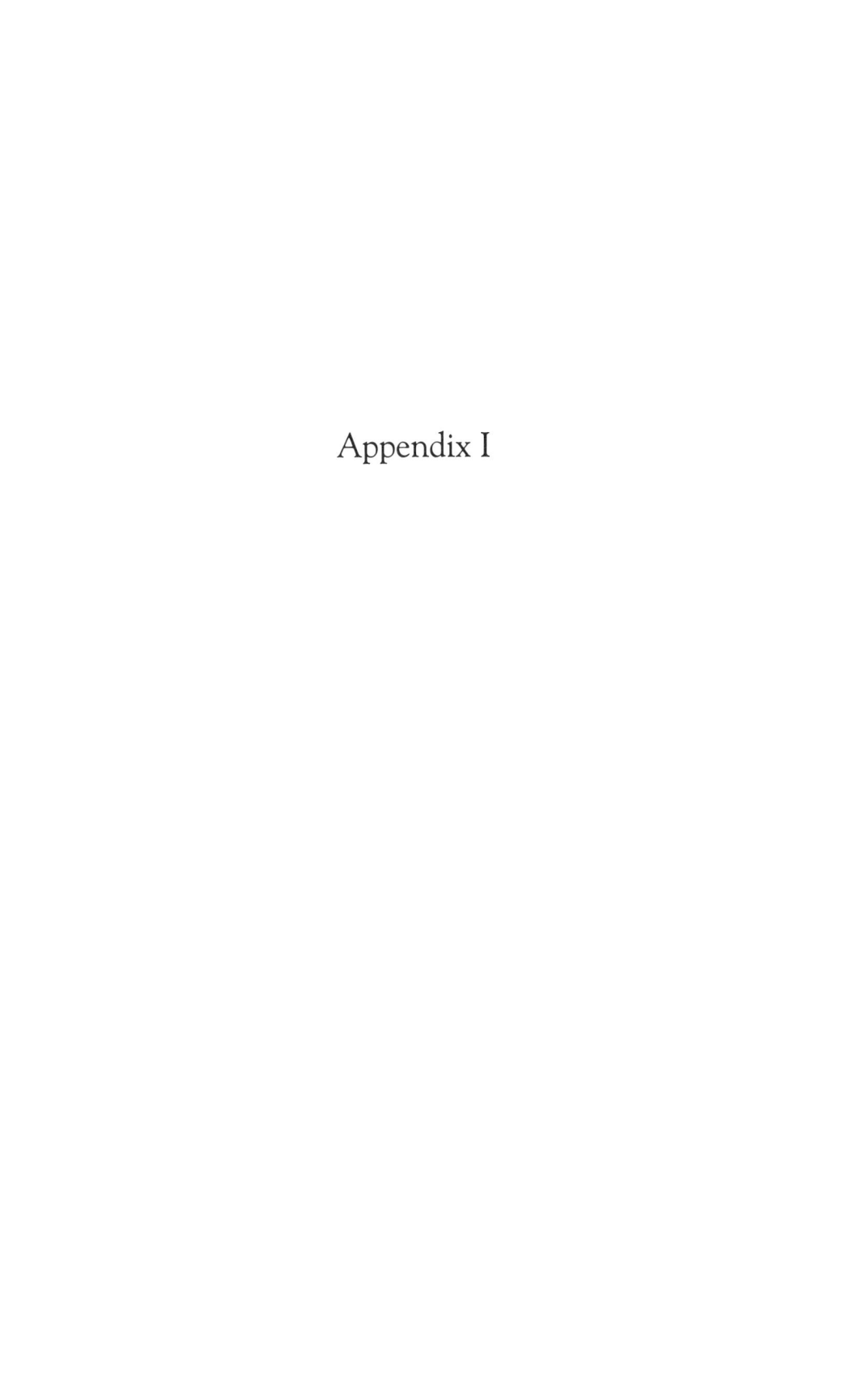

Opening Address

*Delivered before the Naval War College
staff and classes of 1931*

by

*Rear Admiral Harris Laning, United States Navy
President of the Naval War College
Newport, Rhode Island*

2 July 1930

It is a pleasure to welcome to the Naval War College its classes of 1931. The entire staff joins with me in the hope that all members of the classes will find their time at the college to be both enjoyable and profitable.

Many officers coming to the college course do so with the feeling that they are being let in for a year of hard work not unlike what they experienced in their academy days and hence look on coming here as "going back to school." However, while anyone who completes the college course is certain to study a great deal, work hard, and learn much, nevertheless the college has little that resembles the ordinary institution of learning. We call it the Naval War College, but in reality this institution is more of a laboratory than a college. Here we study only enough to learn the sound principles on which successful warfare is based, the greater part of the time being devoted to actual operations and experiments carried out in chart maneuvers or on the game board. It is through such war games, conducted in miniature, that we can see the whole picture, that the student learns how to apply to actual war situations the principles he has learned through this study.

In addition to affording students the opportunity to perfect themselves in the practical application of the principles of war, this institution is also a research laboratory of very high measure. Here we can try out, test, and weigh almost any idea that has to do with naval war operations. The rules governing our game work are based on the actualities we have found at sea, and if the rules are correct, the results of the game work are just what we may expect during sea operations. For this reason, not only can students see their ideas given a thorough test, but also the college is in a better position than any other part of the Navy to

An Admiral's Yarn

reach sound decisions as to the type and characteristics of the ships we should have as well as to how to organize, employ, and operate those ships in war.

With the War College offering the opportunities it does, it must be evident that taking the course cannot but be of immense value and intense interest to every officer who comes to the class and who desires to succeed in his profession. In fact, the course seems to me to be essential to any officer who may be attached to a high command in war, for it is impossible, except by war operations in miniature, to bring a complete picture of the naval team play in war before the individual, or to train the individual in using his wits against another's in naval operations.

The college, therefore, is not a theoretical institution but an intensely practical one. However, the extent to which a student profits from taking the course depends entirely on the student himself. If he comes here only with the idea of getting credit for having taken the course, he probably will not make a great deal out of it. On the other hand, if he comes with the idea of getting from the course everything he can that will make him better for the more important jobs in our services, he is almost certain to go far.

There are many officers who feel they are completely successful as officers if they attain a certain rank or get certain important assignments. Not all of us weigh in our own minds our personal fitness for the ranks or jobs we aspire to. While most of us will seemingly get along passing well in almost any job during peacetime, even without the special training that can be had at the college, it might be that in war, those of us without that training would find ourselves unprepared to carry through successfully the tasks that are ours. Certainly no officer in this class can desire to go to a job which he may be inadequately prepared to carry through successfully in war, and for that reason, each of you here should be glad of this opportunity to prepare thoroughly for war duty in any assignment you desire or that you may be called to during war.

While we all believe that a proper navy will tend to prevent war, we must not overlook the fact that such a proper navy is more than mere material. It also must be thoroughly skilled in the conduct of war operations. Too often we think more about the material that is supplied to us by acts of Congress than we do about skill in utilizing that material—for which skill we officers alone are responsible. But no matter how good our material may be, unless we handle it with skill, it will get us nowhere. On the other hand, even poor material can be partly compensated for by skillful use. And in connection with this thought, your attention is especially called to the fact that with naval armaments limited and equalized by treaty, skill—and skill alone—will be the decisive factor of our naval campaigns in the future.

Appendix I

You who are entering the class at this time, when naval teams are apparently about to become standardized as regards material strength, are very fortunate. At no other place can we learn as we can here the team play of our standardized navy to assure its success in war. Hence, if at the college we can carry through what we hope to do, those of us here should, at the end of the year, have a better idea than anyone else about how best to use our standardized naval team should war come about. Thus we should have a considerable advantage over many of our brothers in service.

That skill in war is the great essential for our Navy must be evident to everyone, but to make it skillful in war, much must be done during peace. Too many officers are prone during peace to take things as they find them. During peacetime, they do not devote the thought and energy they should to developing either their service or themselves for that perfection in team play so essential in war. They accept whatever is found in our War, Tactical, and Fleet instructions as final, whether or not what is there is good or bad or whether or not new material or new conditions call for changes. That is not a correct attitude to take, since the responsibility for the efficiency of our fighting services rests not on a certain few officers but on each and every one of us. It is the duty of every officer to bear his share of that responsibility and not leave it for someone else. First, each must know thoroughly the Navy as it is provided for us and understand how that Navy should play its game to succeed. And then, each must do what he can to point out any defects in organization or operation, suggest ways to correct those defects, and try in every way to make the Navy the most perfect and highly skilled naval team in the world.

It isn't so much what an officer gets in the War College course that counts as what he does afterward with what he gets. If he keeps what he gets here under his hat and does nothing with it to improve and perfect the work of our armed forces, his taking the course will lose most of its value. He will probably perform better the work assigned him, but that is not enough. Unless he also endeavors to use his knowledge for the improvement of his service as a whole, he will be failing in his full duty—and certainly not one of us here will willingly do that.

We therefore hope that the classes, in taking this course, will keep in mind two of the great benefits that can be derived—first the benefit that will accrue to each one personally from the knowledge and training for war that he receives, and second, the benefits that he can give to his service as a whole by using his knowledge and training to make that service better. The good you get from the course will be measured by these two things and especially by the latter. This applies to all students, whether from the line of the Navy, the Staff Corps, the Army, or the Marine Corps.

An Admiral's Yarn

As must be expected, the course as carried out has generally to do with fighting operations on the sea, and on its face would seem to be of more moment to student officers belonging to the Navy line than it is to other members of the class. However, a little thought will show there is great benefit for all—for not until each student knows how the Navy will operate and fight in war can that student be in a position to determine how his particular department or branch of the service can best cooperate and coordinate in the work for which the Navy exists. The background for everything connected with the Navy is the fighting that the Navy may be called on to do, and not until there is an understanding of that fighting can members of the Navy Staff Corps properly coordinate the work of their corps to meet the fundamental needs of the Navy, or can members of other services cause those services to cooperate efficiently with the Navy.

That the course will be a bit difficult for students not of the Navy line is probable, and to the end of simplifying matters for such students, we place each of them in a room with an experienced Navy line officer who can advise and help them with the technicalities with which they are not familiar. In addition to the help they get from their roommates, we want such students, and in fact all students, to feel free at all times to ask for help and advice from the staff. We want each one of you to get every possible advantage from the course and will consider it a privilege to be of assistance to you in making the course a pleasure for you to take.

Although the course as laid out will require much work from every student, the college uses no coercion on students to drive them to it. What the student does and what he gets out of the course is up to his own conscience and himself. There is no grading of students and no comparison of individual ability other than what must go in on the regular reports of fitness. That you will find the work intensely interesting we have no doubt, but always bear in mind that what you get out of it and what you do with what you get, we must leave to you.

Appendix II

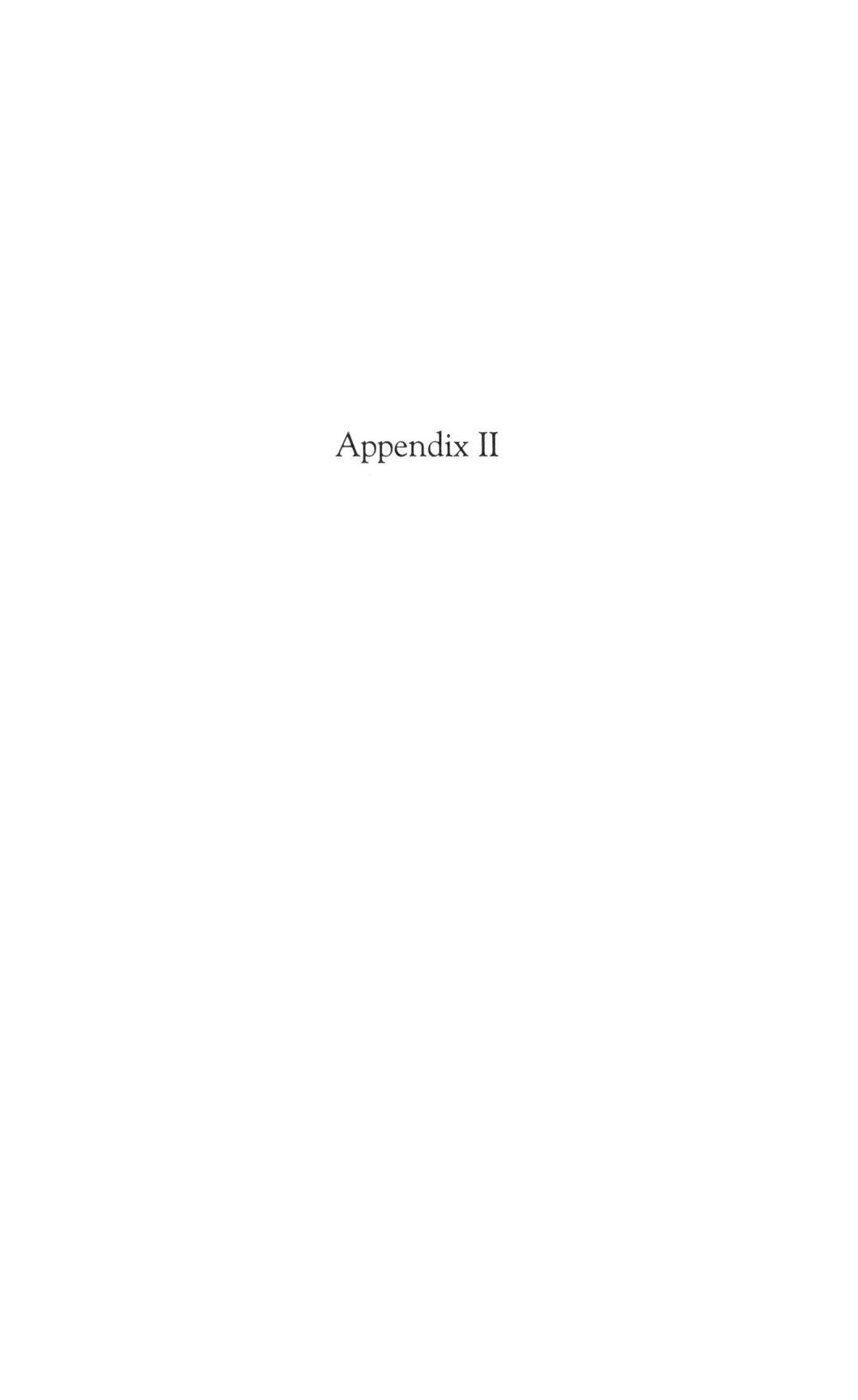

THE NAVAL BATTLE

by

Rear Admiral Harris Laning, USN
President, Naval War College

Revised to May 1933

Naval War College
Newport, R.I.
May 1933

CONFIDENTIAL

Not to pass out of the custody of officers of the U.S. Naval or Military Services. When no longer required this pamphlet should be returned to the Publication Section, Room N-11, Naval War College, Newport, R.I.

The Naval Battle

Introduction · 409
I Analysis of Tactical Dispositions and Operations in Battle 411
   Procedure Followed in the Analysis · · · · · · · · · · 411
      (1) Variations in sea tactics limited · · · · · · · · · 412
      (2) The weapons of the sea · · · · · · · · · · · · · · 412
      (3) Types of ships found in battle · · · · · · · · · · 413
      (4) Coordination of effort between types in battle · · · 414
   The Role of Each Type in the Coordinated Effort · · 415
      Battleships · 415
      Battle Cruisers · · · · · · · · · · · · · · · · · · · 417
      Destroyers · 419
      Light Cruisers · · · · · · · · · · · · · · · · · · · 419
      Submarines · 420
      Aircraft · 421
      Anti-Submarine Craft · · · · · · · · · · · · · · · · 423
      (5) The Advance, Approach, and Deployment · · · · · 423
      The Advance · 424
      Linking Up · 427
      Types of Cruising Dispositions · · · · · · · · · · · 428
      (6) Tactical Scouting · · · · · · · · · · · · · · · · 428
      (7) Concentration, Approach, and Deployment · · · · 431
II Tactical Principles · · · · · · · · · · · · · · · · · · · 436
      The Basic Principle · · · · · · · · · · · · · · · · 437
      The Objective · · · · · · · · · · · · · · · · · · · 438
      Offensive versus Defensive Tactics · · · · · · · · · 440
   Conditions and Elements that Influence Tactics · · · 440
      The Weather Gauge, Gas, and Spray · · · · · · · · 441
      Roll and Pitch · · · · · · · · · · · · · · · · · · · 441
      Sun Glare, Silhouette, Light · · · · · · · · · · · · 442
      Surprise · 442
      Time · 443
      Smoke and Smoke Tactics · · · · · · · · · · · · · · 443
      Preparation before Battle · · · · · · · · · · · · · 444
      The "Follow-up" · · · · · · · · · · · · · · · · · · 445
      Your Next Step · · · · · · · · · · · · · · · · · · · 446

Introduction

Just as the supreme effort of a state must be put forth in war if the state is to win, so in battle must be put forth the supreme effort of the men and material engaged in it. Were the mere assembling of men and material all that is necessary to bring a state to its greatest strength in war and war's battles, the task for those who are responsible for the conduct of war would be comparatively simple. But such is not the case. For those who conduct war, the assemblage of men and material is barely the starting point, for unless both are used to the maximum of their power they are practically certain not to win against even a smaller but well handled force. From this it follows that those to whom the handling of forces in war is entrusted are in duty bound to so handle them that those forces will exert their maximum power all during the campaign but especially exert it in the battles that are the campaign's crucial and decisive points.

We all know that even tremendous power may be dissipated and utterly wasted if exerted piece-meal and haphazard, when, were it exerted in concentration, it could easily accomplish what we want. It is exactly that way with forces in battle. Utilized each to its maximum strength, and the strength of all applied in a supreme and coordinated effort, such forces can win; but operating without coordination, no matter what their individual strengths may be, the forces can easily fail. Therefore, to get the maximum from our fleet in battle we must make our battle fleet a battle team—a team so perfected in the application of its concentrated power that it will overwhelm an opposing battle team in any contest it enters.

To keep any team always ready to win its contests requires constant effort, and this is especially true of the greatest of all teams, a naval battle team. Take the familiar instance of football teams. Although football contests are always between forces equal as regards numbers and general make-up, and which are greatly restricted as to what they can do by rules that change only slightly from year to year, nevertheless the tactics found sufficient to win in one year are rarely sufficient to win in the next. Even under the restrictions of football, the team that wins year after year is the team that progresses. With that situation so plainly evident in just a tiny team of fixed strength and restricted as to what it can do, it is still more evident in our infinitely greater battle team where the units are thousands of men on dozens of mechanisms, and where there are no restrictions as to what the units may do.

An Admiral's Yarn

Increasingly complicated by a vastly greater number of units and not restricted by rules as to operation, the naval battle team also has other things that work constantly to change its style of play. New weapons, more and newer players, and improved uses of old material are constantly interjected into the team and whole plan of battle as well as the team work of battle must take them into account. Hence no matter how nearly perfect we may make the team work of a naval battle team of today, that team work and style of play will surely be inadequate tomorrow. To keep our battle team up to date thus becomes a never ending task, involving continuous study and development, and continuous progress.

It is toward the end of making our country's largest and most vital team—its naval battle team—the most nearly perfect team of its kind in the world that we try to make the War College course in tactics a progressive course. The College endeavors by means of this pamphlet, which is revised frequently, to give each class, at the very start of the course, a sound <u>general</u> conception of the naval battle as our Navy would fight it today. By giving it that conception each new class starts where the last class at the College left off and goes onward from that point. Thus on leaving the College students will be up to the moment in the major tactical development of the day, and, taking their ideas to sea with them, will be better prepared to keep the fleet as perfected in team fighting as is possible for that particular time.

The conception of the naval battle as given in this paper is the general plan for battle as set forth in out War Instructions, which plan, while approximating the general plan and ideas followed by both fleets at Jutland, takes into account the new ideas, the improved weapons, and the new uses of old weapons developed since that battle. It shows what at present seems to be the best <u>general</u> utilization of each weapon and each type of ship when operating as a part of the naval battle team.

The general term applied to the courses of action taken in battle is <u>tactics</u>, which term covers all of the operations of a naval force from the time it approaches another to engage until it is again out of touch. In a major engagement these courses of action divide themselves into two classes: first, those having to do with the broad <u>general</u> plan under which the battle as a whole is to be conducted, which courses are covered by the term major tactics; and second, those having to do with the several parts of the fleet as each part carries out the task assigned it under the general plan, which courses are covered by the term <u>minor</u> tactics. Major tactics decides on the role in battle of each subdivision of the battle force, places <u>each</u> subdivision in position to carry out its role, and indicates the manner in which the several subdivisions are to cooperate with each other in breaking up the enemy strength and destroying it; minor tactics covers the operations of a subdivision in carrying out the role assigned to it.

Appendix II

Minor tactics has many branches, such as battleship tactics, destroyer tactics, submarine tactics, air tactics, etc., each developed to make use of the peculiarities of the type to which it applies. At the War College it is assumed that student officers taking the senior course are as familiar with minor tactics as they are with the other fundamentals of a naval officer's education such as navigation, gunnery, engineering, etc., so that in the Senior Course minor tactics are dealt with only incidentally. Unfortunately, the assumption that student officers are generally familiar with the minor tactics of every type of craft is entirely unwarranted since the minor tactics for some of our types are not fully developed and very few officers are familiar even with what has been developed for types on which they have not served. It was largely for the purpose of developing a more thorough knowledge of minor tactics that the War College Junior Course was established and the War College Correspondence Course was recently revised, and it is hoped that by causing all officers to concentrate on the study of minor tactics in these courses our minor tactics will soon be not only well developed but also well known by every officer in the fleet and before coming to the college.

The conception of the naval battle, as given in this paper, will not go into the field of minor tactics but will confine itself to the major tactics that cover the work of a <u>battle</u> <u>force</u> operating as a team. Although minor tactics will not be dwelt on any further than to state some <u>general</u> principles that govern them as well as major tactics, one must not overlook the importance of such tactics. Sound major tactics makes the winning of battles possible, but only sound minor tactics wins them. The one is under the province of the high commander, the other under the subordinate commanders. However, a subordinate commander can make but little progress with his minor tactics unless he understands exactly what his force is expected to accomplish in battle, and the purpose of this paper is to develop such an understanding. It will analyze battle tactics from the viewpoint of the high commander, which having been done, opens the way for subordinate commanders to analyze and develop the minor tactics that will enable their forces to do successfully the things major tactics expects them to do.

I. Analysis of Tactical Dispositions and Operations in Battle
Procedure Followed in the Analysis

The operations of a fleet in battle have four distinct phases: *first*, the advance toward and development of the enemy force; *second*, the concentration of the battle groups and their deployment to engage; *third*, the engagement; and *fourth*, the "follow up." The critical phase of battle being the engagement, the key to all battle tactics lies in that phase. Hence in order to analyze and develop the sound

An Admiral's Yarn

tactics required in battle we must begin with the engagement phase to determine the tactics to employ in it, knowing which we will be in a position to determine the tactics to employ in the preceding phases to bring about the tactical situations we find to be required if we are to succeed in the fighting phase. When we have done those things we can proceed to the "follow up" stage, which, if a victory is to be complete, must be carried through even more thoroughly than any other phase of the battle. But, as stated, the key to the whole battle lies in the engagement phase, and before one can proceed to a full understanding of the tactics to be employed in it, one must have a thorough grasp of the principles that govern that phase.

(1) Variations in sea tactics limited.

As compared with land battles the possible combinations of forces and movements in sea battles are somewhat limited. The forces on either side are practically restricted to those created before the war opens, and each commander has a fair idea of the types he may meet. The terrain of battle, the sea, offers few peculiarities that can be taken advantage of by either side. The great uncertainties in a modern sea battle come from the freedom and rapidity of movement inherent in sea forces and from variations in the employment of the several forces and types engaged; yet even the movements and the special employment of the forces and types in sea battles are more easily detected than in land battles and are restricted by the known speed and maneuvering ability of ships. For these reasons it is possible to establish a much more definite *general* plan to be followed in a *naval* engagement with a particular enemy than it is to establish such a plan for land battles in each of which forces, terrain, and positions have more influence on the tactics to be employed than have movements and the special employment of forces. Therefore let us look into what such a general plan should be for a modern fleet, bearing in mind of course that while the basic idea will be the same in all major battles against a particular enemy, the detailed movements and operations of the several forces will differ in each battle since each <u>part</u> of the fleet team, though carrying out its mission as called for by the basic or general plan, will, in carrying out that mission, have to operate not only in conformity with any <u>special</u> task assigned it in the general plan but also in conformity with the particular opposition it meets in doing so.

(2) The weapons of the sea.

The weapons of modern navies are *guns, torpedoes, bombs* and *mines*, all used to destroy enemy fighting craft in order that one's own craft may remain afloat and thereby have control of the sea. While under favorable circumstances any one of the weapons is sufficiently destructive to prove decisive, nevertheless, owing to the development of the defense against it, unaided, not one is capable of winning a decision against a combination of all. Aided by the gun other weapons can be made to exert a decisive effect, or aided by other weapons the gun can be made decisive. But because of its protection against destruction, and because of its great range of accuracy, rapidity of firing, hitting power, and ammunition supply, the gun can do the greatest damage of any weapon and for that reason tactical effort in modern sea battles is still *centered* around the main gun action, and the other weapons are made to come into the engagement to aid the gun or to take advantage of situations created by it. Only by combining the effort of the several weapons can each be made to exercise its maximum influence in destroying the enemy, and the end and aim of tactics is to bring about such coordination of effort of one's own weapons that by their *concentration* they will destroy the ships carrying those of the enemy.

(3) Types of ships found in battle.

Naval weapons are carried on ships of various types, the types being more or less standard in all navies. As a general rule each type has been developed to utilize one of the weapons as its primary weapon, and though it may carry other weapons they are of secondary importance—the ships of a type being operated in battle in a way to make their primary weapon most effective. Thus though capital ships may carry both guns and torpedoes the gun is their primary weapon and capital ships are always operated in battle to make their guns most effective. While destroyers carry both torpedoes and light guns, the torpedo is their primary weapon and the movements of destroyers in battle are to the end of getting their torpedoes home against enemy heavy ships. Light cruisers that carry intermediate guns and have torpedoes have a dual role, the torpedo being the primary weapon against the capital ships and the gun primary against light ships. Anti-submarine craft may carry both depth bombs and torpedoes, the depth bomb being primary when operating against submarines, the torpedo when operating against heavy ships. Submarines carry only torpedoes and their function is to get them home with maximum effect on the enemy. Bombs and aerial torpedoes are launched from aircraft, which latter must be carried to the scene of the engagement in carriers. The weapon of the aircraft carrier is the airplane, and carriers are operated to the end of getting their planes to a position from which they can be sent out to play their part in the battle.

In addition to having the paraphernalia necessary to make its primary weapon effective, each type of ship has been given such other characteristics as will best enable it to make use of that weapon. These characteristics are

An Admiral's Yarn

expressed in size, protection, speed, maneuvering ability, submergence, etc. Thus we find in modern battle fleets types of ships as follows:

(1) *Battleships*, of great size, medium speed, heavy armor, many heavy guns, and several airplanes;

(2) *Battle cruisers*, of size equal to battleships, high speed, little armor, heavy guns, and several airplanes;

(3) *Destroyers*, of small size, high speed, many torpedoes, no armor, and with small guns;

(4) *Cruisers*, of medium size, high speed, light armor, intermediate guns, probably some torpedoes, and observation planes;

(5) *Anti-submarine craft*, often destroyers that carry depth charges;

(6) *Submarines*, of medium surface speed and long surface radius, low submerged speed and short submerged radius, carrying torpedoes; and

(7) *Aircraft carriers*, with characteristics similar to battle cruisers or light cruisers but carrying intermediate guns, and airplanes, instead of heavy guns.

(4) Coordination of effort between types in battle.

With so many weapons carried on such different types of ships it is apparent that if we are to get the maximum effect of all weapons and make our blow the sum total of the blows of all, there must be perfect coordination between the types carrying them. The gun being the only weapon of past years, and in the present continuing to be the most powerful weapon, sea battles have revolved for centuries around the ships carrying heavy guns. As other weapons came into being each endeavored and still endeavors to wrest supremacy from the gun, and hence in battle the efforts of each type of ship are directly or indirectly against the ships that carry the heavy guns. However, as each new weapon came to threaten the gun-carrying ship, steps were taken to counter it, and it is upon these attacks and counters that battle tactics are based. We have, as the dominating phase in battle, the gun fight between heavy ships, which fight establishes the main line of battle. Then we have the attacks on the battle line by vessels carrying torpedoes, the idea of which is to make the enemy heavy ships either accept the torpedo menace or else pay a price either in gunfire or in position, in maneuvering to avoid it. Against such attack we have the counter made by fast light cruisers which by their speed and superior gun power can prevent surface torpedo craft from obtaining the position to deliver their attack. Again we have the attacks of submarines which are directed against the heavy ships and which are countered by anti-submarine craft carrying depth bombs.

Appendix II

Finally we have air attacks which can be countered only by guns or air forces, but which can be prevented if enemy aircraft carriers are damaged in such a way that they cannot launch their planes.

The Role of Each Type in the Coordinated Effort

From the foregoing, it appears that what we call tactics is in reality the movements or actions necessary to insure getting home the attacks of one's own weapons while preventing the enemy from getting home his attacks. The central and dominating part of the fleet in battle, and around which the entire action will revolve, being always the *battle line*, the approach and deployment for battle always must be such as will not only establish one's heavy ship line to the best advantage for engaging that of the enemy but also such as will place the ships carrying other weapons where they can deliver their attacks in coordination with the main gun attack, or/and where they can prevent the enemy delivering similar attacks. Therefore as the foundation for our tactical ideas, let us get clearly in our minds the general procedure each type of ship should follow in battle. To do this, let us start with the center of the engagement, the fight between the heavy ships, and then take up the operations that radiate about it as other types join the issue and attempt to exert the deciding influence on it.

Battleships

Necessities of design give heavy ships their maximum hitting power when firing on or near the beam, hence in sea battles heavy ships naturally take a formation approximating column and endeavor to hold the enemy about abeam and under the fire of all heavy guns. The most advantageous position one battle line can gain over another is the "capping" or "T" position by which that line is in a position to fire its full broadside against the enemy while the enemy can reply with only the end-on fire of his nearest ships. The position equally favorable to each of two engaged battle lines is when they are abeam of each other. The "T" position being so overwhelmingly advantageous, each battle line endeavors to obtain it for itself, or to approximate it as nearly as possible, while preventing the enemy from doing anything of the kind; and for this reason we have as the fundamental principle of battleship tactics that of *always* keeping one's own line normal to the bearing of the center of the enemy's line. Both before and during the gun fight between heavy ships this principle must be observed and it is because all competent commanders do observe it that even at the opening of an engagement between heavy ships we almost invariably find two lines on approximately parallel courses and almost abeam of each other. We

An Admiral's Yarn

therefore start from this position of the battle lines in evolving the theory of modern battle tactics.

Although the heavy ship engagement usually starts under nearly equal conditions as between the opposing battle lines, due to their being parallel and about abeam of each other, each line naturally attempts to gain the most advantageous position, that of the "T." Now the position where the opposing lines are most nearly equal gradually changes to where one has the maximum advantage as one column draws ahead of and across the end of the other column to the "T" position. The battle line that draws ahead of the other and keeps itself perpendicular to a line from its center ship to the nearest enemy ship while doing so, not only has its full broadside bearing on the enemy line but also, and at the same time, reduces the number of enemy guns that can be brought to bear or kept within range. But to obtain a "T" or "cap," or even approximate it, one battle line must have a decidedly greater speed than the other, and the other must hold its course. To prevent a cap, even when a column has less speed, it is only necessary to "swing the line" sufficiently to keep the enemy always abeam. This "swinging the line" may be accomplished in either of two ways—by a head of column movement that changes the course of the column to the right or left by the necessary amount to bring the enemy abeam, or by a "redeployment" of the line (see *Maneuvers of the Battle Line*) to bring the enemy on the beam bearing.

In using the first of these methods, a head of column movement, grave danger exists since it takes considerable time to complete the maneuver and, in order to keep the other line abeam or nearly so, the change in direction of the head of the column may be abrupt and through many degrees of arc, thereby creating a bend, or "knuckle," at the turning point. A battle line so bent is in a bad position, for ships at the knuckle or ahead of it are laid open to a concentration of gunfire easily controlled, while those in the rear may be out of range or have but few guns that will bear.

In using the second method, i.e., "swinging the line" by a "redeployment," gunfire may be somewhat interfered with by the several turns and movements the individual ships must go through, while at the same time the signals and movements connected with the maneuver are hard to make especially when both battle lines are firing heavily. Nevertheless, using this second method to keep the enemy line abeam is usually preferable since the maneuver can be completed much more quickly than a column movement, thereby permitting one's own battle line to be ready in less time to carry out future maneuvers, while at the same time it will disconcert the enemy's gunfire much more than one's own because one will know beforehand when and what turns are to be

Appendix II

made, and can make the set up on his own fire control instruments to cover them, whereas the enemy will require time to ascertain the changes and make his fire control corrections.

So valuable is bending an enemy battle line, or forcing it into complicated and possibly wild maneuvers while under heavy gunfire, that all battle line commanders seek to force one or the other of these conditions on the enemy line and thereby gain an advantage in gunfire that will be decisive. However, in these days, it is hardly possible for one battle line to have sufficient speed to force a properly handled enemy line into a knuckle or even into difficult maneuvers in redeploying, and since some such decisive advantage must be gained other craft are brought into play to produce it. The types used for such purpose are heavily gunned and fast battle cruisers, and vessels that carry torpedoes. By the proper use of these types their weapons can be brought to bear on an enemy line, forcing it into possibly wild maneuvers to avoid the menace or to accept the menace and the damage to ships it imposes. In either case, the advantage gained may prove decisive; hence battle tactics, to be sound, must be such as to give one that advantage while denying it to the enemy. Let us see how forces not of the battle line should be used to gain the advantage for ourselves while at the same time preventing similar enemy forces from doing that same thing to us.

Battle Cruisers

Battle cruisers, like battleships, have guns for their primary weapon. Their high speed enables them to do what battleships cannot do, i.e., obtain or approximate the capping position. However, weak in heavy armor and having but few guns, they dare not engage battleships ship for ship, but must by their speed attain a position from which they can bring their full broadsides to bear while the enemy, unless he maneuvers his line, can return the fire with but few guns. Hence, in battle, battle cruisers have their greatest value as "fast wings," fighting from advantageous positions against either end of the enemy line, but preferably against its head, and causing the enemy line to suffer either from the cruisers' guns or from those of the other heavy ships as the line maneuvers to parry the battle cruiser attack. It is this that determines the disposition and employment of battle cruisers in a general engagement, and we therefore, wherever practicable, use them as fast wings, with missions to attack the enemy battle line from advantageous positions and destroy its ships by gunfire or force them to maneuver so the battleships can do so.

From the advantageous position battle cruisers can take at the ends of a battle line, they are able to play a dual role in an engagement. Not only are they placed

An Admiral's Yarn

well to attack the enemy heavy ships but from these positions their great speed and gun power enable them to protect the ends of their own column from all kinds of attacks by enemy light fast surface craft.

Prior to the time of the treaties limiting armaments, a fleet that had battle cruisers without having to sacrifice battleship tonnage to get them had many advantages. Not only was such a fleet able to use battle cruisers to strike hard at the enemy line at its weakest point—its flanks—but at the same time it had a most powerful support for its own light forces on the flanks of its battle line, and a most powerful defense against enemy light force attacks from the flank. One should always remember, however, that for all their strength battle cruisers could fill their dual role successfully *only* when in gun support of their own battle line. Worked, as regards gun range, in perfect coordination with a battle line approximately equal to that of the enemy, they could do much to the enemy line while at the same time protecting their own, and in this was their great value. But to use them successfully, and to have them always sufficiently supported by their battle line to prevent their destruction through lack of gun support, required the closest coordination in gun range between the cruisers and the battle line, and it is in the difficulty of so coordinating the ranges of dispersed forces that the weakness of battle cruisers lies. This point must be remembered always, and especially now when capital ship tonnage is limited, for should there be a failure in mutual gun support between a battle line and its detached wing, even if the wing is a fast one of battle cruisers, both the battle line and the detached wing open themselves to destruction in detail. One of the groups will get within range when the other is out of it, or will get to a short range when the other is at extreme range, and when this happens a concentration of gunfire on the near group will quickly destroy it.

It is the impracticability of coordinating in battle the movements and gun ranges of two widely separated groups of capital ships that has caused navies, limited in capital ship strength by treaty, to cease to build battle cruisers. The price paid for them in battleship strength is far above any possible gain they might give us in battle. However, although we ourselves have no battle cruisers and therefore have no worries as to our using them in battle, other countries still have them; hence we must reckon with them in our battle operations. But we will suffer little damage from them in battle if we keep our own battle line in concentration, for doing so will enable us to remain at least equal to our enemy in the battle line if he operates his battle cruisers in his own battle line, and will give us an almost certain opportunity to destroy his capital ship strength in detail if he separates his battleship and battle cruiser groups.

Appendix II

Destroyers

In the same way that battle cruisers, through their speed, can gain a position favorable for attacking a battle line with heavy guns and force it into a knuckle or cause it to maneuver when under heavy fire, lighter craft of high speed can gain a similar position from which, by attacking with torpedoes, they too can force the same disadvantages on an engaged enemy. Since the positions least open to enemy gunfire are those on the flanks of his line, such positions are comparatively safe not only for vulnerable battle cruisers but also for the still more vulnerable destroyers. Therefore, destroyers sent in on the bow, or forward of the beam, of an enemy battleship line to fire long range torpedoes have excellent opportunities to compel an engaged battle line to maneuver under fire or accept the menace of their weapons. This fact gives us the key to the employment of destroyers in battle, and it becomes a principle of battle tactics to so employ them. Like battle cruisers, their stations, except those of the anti-submarine screen, on deploying are on the engaged bow of their battle line (in order that they may strike at the enemy line from ahead if the enemy continues on his course), or astern, or on the engaged quarter, that they may strike in case he turns about.

Thus are the positions of the ships that have heavy guns and torpedoes as their major weapons of attack determined for us, and in the opening stages of modern battles they probably will be found about as follows: opposing battleships will be in parallel columns and about abeam of each other while the major part of the battle cruisers and destroyers will be ahead and on the bow of their battleship line, the remainder in the rear on its engaged quarter. From these positions, and all advancing simultaneously, each type will endeavor to hit the enemy heavy ships with the full power of its weapons, overcoming such resistance as may be met in reaching the position to deliver their attacks.

Light Cruisers

In a normal naval engagement, other things being equal, the force that can get home quickest the simultaneous attack of its several weapons or types of ships has every prospect of winning the engagement, and to prevent the enemy getting home such a simultaneous attack each side counters the various parts that go to make it up. Such counters, however, are not always carried out by ships of the same type as the attackers. The counter to heavy ship attacks is generally made by heavy ships, but the counter to the attacks of destroyers is made by ships of the cruiser type, by battle cruisers from their positions as fast wings, and by heavy or light cruisers which have the speed of destroyers but very much heavier batteries. Hence, interposed between the enemy's cruisers and destroyers and our battle line and destroyers, we place cruisers, whose mission it is to cover and clear the way for their own destroyers and light craft in their attacks at the same time that they prevent attacks on their own heavy ships by enemy destroyers and light craft. With this disposition and use of the cruiser type also before us, we have the broad general plan for the deployment stations and use of battleships, battle cruisers, destroyers, and cruisers in battle.

Submarines

In addition to the offensive types so far discussed as operating entirely on the surface and against surface craft, and which, as we have seen, work in close coordination with each other, we find in battle two other offensive types previously mentioned, submarines and aircraft. These types, though capable of delivering powerful attacks, cannot carry out their roles in battle with anything like as much synchronization as is possible between the surface types. Though the submarine is a more recent addition to battle fleets than the surface types already discussed, its weapon—the torpedo—is not new. Like the torpedoes of surface craft, those of submarines, to be effective, must be launched from favorable positions, but owing to the limitations imposed on submarines by their low submerged speed and their inability to observe, gaining that position is most difficult. Their great strength lies in the element of surprise contained in their attack, but their success is largely dependent on their original position as the battle opens and on the movements of the enemy thereafter. Hence only the broadest principles can be laid down for their use in battle. All that can be done is to so place them in the disposition for advance that as many as possible will be in or near the area that the enemy battle line must occupy to be within gun range of our own, and then afterward to so maneuver our own battle line as to hold or draw the enemy battle line near the submarines so they can attack. *That* they must do at every opportunity with a view to destroying the enemy heavy ships or throwing them into such confusion that gunfire can destroy them.

When successful, a submarine attack exacts a heavy toll, usually at small cost, and so, though successful attack by submarines cannot be counted on in battle to the extent we can count on the attacks of surface craft, nevertheless submarines always offer the possibility of obtaining a decisive advantage. The mere suspicion that submarines are in a certain area may be sufficient to interfere with the enemy's plan either by keeping his heavy ships out of the area or by forcing them into maneuvers they do not wish to make.

Appendix II

Aircraft

Of the many weapons or types found in the up-to-date naval battle, aircraft stand out as peculiarly affecting battle operations. Because of the newness of aircraft in actual war operations at sea their capabilities and limitations are not as well established as are the capabilities and limitations of other types. However, much study has been made of aircraft operations in peace-time maneuvers and through those studies we have obtained a fair understanding of the manner in which they probably will be used. But before going into the manner of using them in battle, it is advisable to have some understanding of what our studies have shown aircraft can be relied upon to do. It appears they can accomplish the following:

First: Locate and keep touch with practically all types of enemy craft, reporting their strength, dispositions, and movements. This includes such things as
  (a) Tactical scouting and protective scouting against all surface types, and
  (b) the detection of submarines and torpedoes.

Second: Spot gunfire, thereby increasing both effective range and accuracy.

Third: Attack enemy ships with bombs containing high explosive or chemicals, or with torpedoes.

Fourth: Lay smoke screens.

Fifth: Engage other aircraft, and

Sixth: Possibly supply an auxiliary means of communication by radio, or as direct messengers, should the ordinary lines fail.

From the above list of things that aircraft can do it is evident that the influence of aircraft on the naval battle may begin when the opposing fleets are still several hundred miles apart and will continue even after all other types have passed far out of sight contact. By the information aircraft can gain before, during, and after battle, they can provide what is necessary to enable all types of craft to be maneuvered intelligently to gain decisive tactical advantages. By spotting for gunfire they may give a decisive advantage in such fire. By attacks with chemical bombs, the gas from which temporarily disables personnel, they may place vital units hors de combat for a period sufficiently long to give one side a decisive advantage in gun or torpedo fire. By the use of torpedoes or explosive bombs they may inflict lasting damage to vital units or even destroy them; and smoke screens made by aircraft often can be better and more quickly placed than those by destroyers, and may be even more efficacious.

An Admiral's Yarn

Great as will be the influence of aircraft on the trend of a naval battle, it is apparent that to get full results the aircraft effort must be closely coordinated with the efforts of the other types. Only by direct attack on enemy ships can aircraft by themselves accomplish much, and though such attacks may prove deadly and possibly have a decisive value, nevertheless, because of the limited number of carriers allowed by treaty, air attack usually cannot be made in sufficient numbers to gain as much for their fleet as can be gained by other aircraft efforts in which the influence is indirect, as, for instance, information work, spotting gunfire, laying smoke screens, etc. But that aircraft may do the things open to them their carriers must be so placed, both before and during battle, that they can launch their planes freely and in safety, and for this reason carriers must be well protected and kept out of the area of gunfire. Hence in battle, carriers are usually stationed well away from the battle line on its disengaged side as the battle opens. Also there must be for the battle a very definite and well understood "air plan" conforming to and furthering the general plan established for the surface craft.

In order to carry out any worthwhile air plan, and particularly to protect one's own fleet against enemy air attacks, the first effort in an air plan should be to insure, as nearly as possible, control of the air in the vital areas. Such control often has to be fought for, and for that reason we usually find the first step in any air plan is the getting up of sufficient combat planes to dominate the air at least in the vicinity of one's own fleet. It has been found, however, that aircraft alone, no matter what the type, can not insure complete control of the air over a fleet or protect it against all enemy air attacks. Apparently the only way to insure protection to a fleet is to so damage in time the enemy's carriers that planes cannot take off from them; and for that reason great effort must be made to attack and injure enemy carriers at the earliest possible moment.

Once one is in position to make full use of his aircraft hitting power, one should lose no time in taking advantage of it to attack enemy fighting ships, to lay smoke screens either to blanket the enemy's gunfire or cover the attacks of one's own forces, and to destroy all remaining enemy planes. However, in attacking enemy ships or in laying smoke screens to cover attacks by our own forces, sound judgment must be used. The objective for either effort must be selected with wisdom and must be that part of the enemy fleet we most desire to put out of action. Also, in attacking from the air, careful consideration must be given to the weapon used by the planes, and the one selected should be a suitable one. For instance, if the attacks are made before the objective is under gunfire, one should use bombs or torpedoes that do lasting damage. When the objective is under fire it may be advisable to have some planes use chemical or smoke

Appendix II

bombs, for the increased effectiveness that comes to one's own gun, torpedo, and bomb attacks from a wise use of chemicals or smoke that renders a part of the enemy force helpless for even a short time may far exceed any damage a like number of aircraft can possibly do with torpedoes or explosive bombs. These and many other things must be considered in preparing the air part of a battle plan; only by considering them can we arrange to gain from air forces all the assistance of which they are capable.

But however great the air effort may be in other directions, one must never lose sight of the necessity of watching the enemy from the air. Aircraft are the eyes of the fleet in battle, and without such eyes, because of the enormous area covered by huge modern fleets in battle, a fleet may easily become as a blind man. For that reason, both long before and all during battle we must have observation planes out in sufficient numbers and so stationed as to see and report all enemy movements. As a corollary to this part of the air effort, the air plan should provide means for denying the enemy similar information by fighting off his planes. In the air, as on the surface, one must gain information for one's self and deny it to the enemy.

Anti-Submarine Craft

All the types of craft found in the naval battle of today have now been discussed except the purely defensive anti-submarine type. Ships of this type merely keep in positions to protect the more important ships from submarine attack; as long as they maintain such positions they have no great offensive role to play in battle. But in protecting important ships against submarine attacks, anti-submarine craft, when in position, are able to play another very important defensive role, for should the ships they are protecting suffer too much from gunfire, the anti-submarine craft are in excellent position to cover them with smoke and thereby reduce the damage being done. While such defensive operations will not of themselves win a battle, they may prevent one's losing it and thereby make winning possible, and for that reason a fleet must be ready to use them whenever advisable or necessary.

(5) The Advance, Approach, and Deployment.

With the idea in our minds of the general role each type has to play in the engagement phase of battle and of its approximate station as that phase opens, we are now in a position to determine the dispositions and tactics to employ in the advance, approach, and deployment. To do this we again start with the battleships, taking up the other types in turn, just as was done to determine the dispositions and procedure in the fighting phase.

An Admiral's Yarn

The Advance

To win in battle with as little loss as possible, it is necessary to bring the maximum gun hitting strength of the heavy ships to bear on the enemy at the earliest possible instant after the firing starts, and because of that fact battleships must, during the advance of a fleet, be kept concentrated and ready for quick deployment. Unfortunately for a fleet commander, there can be no certain knowledge beforehand as to what will be the bearing of the enemy battle line from one's own line when contact is made, and for this reason, in the advance and approach, heavy ships cannot be placed in a battle formation while seeking the enemy but must take some other formation from which they can deploy quickly for engaging on such course as happens to be normal to the bearing of the enemy battle line when that line is approaching gun range.

Without going into details as to why, it has been found that the best cruising formation for battleships, from which quick deployment can be made in any direction and in any order of divisions, is some form of a "line of division columns," and heavy ships are always kept in such a formation, with its general line of bearing normal to the expected bearing of the enemy when sighted, whenever there is any possibility of meeting him. It is impracticable in this paper to discuss these cruising formations of the battle line or the deployments therefrom, and it is unnecessary to do so since they are all indicated in the official publication *Formations and Maneuvers of the Battle Line*. For the purposes of this paper it can be accepted that battleships must be in such a formation whenever battle is even a possibility, and that from the formation they can deploy quickly on any course and in almost any order of divisions. Bearing this in mind, we will pass on to the disposition of the other types of ships during the advance.

The fundamentals of a sound disposition for the advance of a battle fleet are:
First, that it be suitable for offensive operations;
Second, that it provide for the quick and accurate deployment of the entire fleet no matter what may be the bearing of the enemy when contact is made;
Third, that it insure time for deployment after contact has been made, no matter what the visibility may be;
Fourth, that it permit rapid maneuvering of the entire fleet during the advance but more especially after scouting contact has been made and tactical advantages in position are being sought; and
Fifth, that it insure the safety of the units in the disposition and provide an overwhelming defense against surprise attacks of every kind, including those of destroyers, aircraft, and submarines.

Appendix II

If a fleet had an unlimited number of ships of the types other than heavy, it would not be difficult during an advance of the fleet to provide both for information and security and still have a complete "battle team" in concentration and ready for quick movement and deployment for battle. As things are, however, a battle force has to do much if not all of its own tactical scouting and screening, and the task of providing for both, while at the same time permitting flexibility of movement for the force, yet holding all types ready to take their position and play their roles in a general engagement, is very difficult. Not only must all types be in correct position and ready to engage as the heavy ships come within range of each other, but immediately prior to that time they must be in an easily maneuvered disposition that will enable them to locate the enemy, prevent surprise attacks of all kinds, and deny the enemy information. Assuming that the heavy ships will be in concentration and in a formation from which they can deploy quickly for battle, what, in the advance, should be the disposition of the other types found in a battle force?

The ships nearest the battleships will, of course, be those of the anti-submarine type. Beyond them there must be ships for protective screening, and, still further beyond, ships for searching and contact scouting. These necessities largely determine the disposition of the outlying ships during the advance of a battle force to meet an enemy, and in the several outlying lines of ships that result from meeting the necessities we find we must use ships of all the types at our disposal, excepting only battleships and aircraft carriers. Further, when the enemy has battle cruisers and we have not, or is greatly superior to us in light cruisers, even battleships may have to be placed in these outer lines.

Though many dispositions can be laid out, each of which will provide the necessities for the advance and still leave the fleet ready for quick concentration and deployment for battle, nevertheless any one of them, to be effective, will have attributes about as follows:

First: Around the disposition, and well beyond all other forces, and covering them especially on the front and flanks, a force of submarines;

Second: Inside the submarines, one or more lines of destroyers to act as a protective screen, give timely information of enemy forces, and to force down any submarines coming into the disposition;

Third: Within supporting distance inside of the destroyer line (or lines), a strong line of cruisers to support the outer lines (note: The actual distances of the second and third lines from the center are direct functions of the visibility and therefore cannot be definitely laid down in a paper of this nature);

An Admiral's Yarn

Fourth: Between the cruiser line and the main body, a protective screening line of destroyers, concentrated, as far as their numbers and the area to be covered permits, in sections of divisions, and ready for further concentration before deployment takes place;
Fifth: Inside the several screening lines, the battleships in a quick deployment formation;
Sixth: Near the battleships, the aircraft carriers;
Seventh: Around all heavy ships, wherever placed, an anti-submarine screen.

Any disposition used in advancing into waters where enemy forces may be encountered must be strong in defense as well as in offense, for unless it is strong in defense, *especially against surprise raiding attacks*, the strength of even a powerful battle force may be seriously impaired before it can force a general engagement. This fact is sometimes lost sight of, and in developing a disposition for the advance, students frequently base it solely on its efficiency for deploying without taking into account what may and probably will happen before an engagement starts if there is not sufficient defense against surprise raids by aircraft or submarines, or even by fast cruisers and destroyers. No matter how much on the offensive an advancing force may be, it must not overlook the vital necessity of having a thorough defense against raids. In fact, the more offensive an operation is, and the deeper it penetrates into the enemy's area, the more likely it is to be subjected to surprise attacks, and to overlook the defensive necessities of a disposition just because it is to be used in an offensive operation is to make one of the most dangerous mistakes a naval commander can make.

If in laying out a disposition for the advance there were nothing more to it than giving it the ability, first, to destroy enemy raiding forces that attack during the advance and, second, to deploy and fight a general engagement when the enemy's heavy forces are met, the problem of our cruising dispositions would be much simplified. However, in addition to providing both for an overwhelming defense against raids and for quick deployment and fighting, a disposition for the advance must be able quickly to change both the direction of its advance and the direction of its axis. Let us investigate these several requirements, taking up first the matter of quick deployment.

In our discussion of the employment of types of ships in battle, we deduced the approximate station of each type at the time the major ship action opens. Also we have seen how, for the purposes of security and information, the types must be dispersed in a cruising disposition just prior to that time. (For diagrams of Cruising Dispositions see *Tentative Fleet Dispositions and Battle Plans, U.S. Fleet, 1930* and the War College pamphlet *Example Fighting Instructions for a Battle Force*

Appendix II

using a Circular Disposition.) Now the deployment of a fleet changes it from a "disposition for the advance" to a "battle disposition," and as can be readily seen the problem in deploying becomes one of time and distance. Evidently the disposition used for the advance must be such that when contact is made with an enemy battle force there will be sufficient time, before the opposing battle lines get within gun range, for the outlying forces in the disposition to concentrate and cover the distance to their stations for deploying and opening the engagement. Providing for even that would be less difficult were we always sure of a smooth sea and could count on all types making their maximum speed. What makes the quick deployment requirement difficult to meet is the effect the wind and sea may have, for the outlying craft in a cruising disposition are generally small and light and the speed they can make is often reduced several knots by even a moderate wind and sea. Therefore a disposition for the advance must be such that, even with their speed reduced by adverse sea or weather conditions, the light craft in it will still have time to concentrate and reach their deployment stations by the time the major ship action opens.

In addition to permitting rapid concentration of its many subdivisions and their quick deployment for battle, the "disposition for the advance" must also be such as will permit the quick maneuvering of the entire force whenever necessity warrants and especially when seeking an advantageous position over an enemy force just prior to engaging. Hence to be properly efficient our dispositions must be able to make changes of course quickly and without confusion, during either daylight or darkness, must not weaken its strong defensive properties while so doing, and must retain at all times its ability to deploy quickly and accurately.

Linking Up

While every sound cruising disposition must have all the above-named qualities, there is yet another point that must be looked for in them. Because of the very great area it covers when in a cruising disposition, no part of a huge modern fleet is visible to all the other parts, nor can enemy ships outside of or even on the edge of the disposition be seen by more than a few ships in it. Yet the units of the fleet must maintain their stations at all times when the fleet is cruising or maneuvering itself into a position favorable for deploying for battle, must concentrate and gain their positions for deployment when engagement is imminent, and then must fall on the enemy quickly with all the hitting power they have. To do all these things requires considerable precision both as regards

An Admiral's Yarn

keeping position while cruising or advancing to engage, and as regards movements while concentrating and taking battle stations.

That all contacts made can be reported and plotted with the accuracy necessary to enable subordinate commanders to bring their forces into concentration and to their deployment stations with rapidity and precision, all ships in a cruising disposition must know at all times their exact location with reference to the battleship force. Therefore all ships must keep positions accurately with reference to that force, and to facilitate their doing so, ships for "linking up" positions by visibility must be provided in all cruising dispositions. Keeping stations accurately through "linking up" ships, and aided by frequent reports as to the "reference position" of the battle line, a fleet is ready to concentrate and deploy its forces promptly and accurately.

So vital to successful deployment is the accurate linking of all other forces to that of the battle line that the utmost attention must be paid to it. Great as may be the disasters arising from an improper arrangement of forces in a disposition for the advance, almost as great disaster can result when the fleet's parts are not sufficiently linked to the position of the battleship force as to make possible their quick and accurate concentration and deployment.

Types of Cruising Dispositions

To meet the necessities when advancing a fleet or force into waters where the enemy may be met, two general types of cruising dispositions have been provided for our Navy, one type <u>axial</u> with rectangular coordinates, the other <u>circular</u>. Both of these types, each in several modifications based on the purpose for which it is to be used, are described in the publication *Tentative Fleet Dispositions and Battle Plans, U.S. Fleet, 1930*. Each type has advantages and disadvantages, and the one to use, in any particular situation together with the special modification of it, can be determined only by weighing all the factors that govern in it. Having weighed them we can then select the cruising disposition best suited to the need.

(6) Tactical Scouting.

It will be noted from our official publications that the cruising dispositions laid down usually utilize all the ships we will probably use as a Battle Force in war but make no special mention of the ships that probably will compose the Scouting Force. This should not be taken to indicate that our Scouting Force will not cooperate with the Battle Force to give the latter security and information, but only that in doing so its dispersion may become so great that it

Appendix II

cannot be relied on to take part in the battle or even to do the tactical scouting preliminary to battle. All we can surely count on from the Scouting Force in war is that it will scout and screen *strategically* and will keep the Battle Force informed as to whether or not the enemy is near. Having that information the Battle Force must depend on itself for such other information as it needs to engage successfully, and it is to the end of gaining such information that our cruising dispositions are given their rather far flung outer screens. Should the Scouting Force drop back on the Battle Force as the latter nears the enemy, so much the better for us; but we dare not count on its doing so and must provide accordingly.

While the cruising dispositions laid down for our Navy are so devised that water-borne craft, surface or submarine, will probably give us reasonably early information of the nearness of the enemy and will generally prevent our main body being surprised, it is evident that an enemy only eighty or ninety miles from the main body might not be discovered by them. Were a Battle Force merely on the defensive and awaiting attack it might be sufficient only to know the enemy is within such a distance, though with earlier information even a fleet on the defensive would be benefited by having more time to maneuver for a favorable position as regards wind, sea spray, light, etc. However, to a Battle Force on the offensive and seeking the enemy, it is essential that it know if the enemy fleet is within two or three hundred miles. So, in addition to the far distant strategic scouting done by the Scouting Force, a Battle Force requires tactical scouting of far greater range than is provided by the outlying surface craft in our cruising dispositions. Such tactical scouting, in ordinary weather, can be done by aircraft; hence, having adopted a somewhat concentrated cruising disposition for the Battle Force in cruising or advancing toward the enemy, we must also provide means for air tactical scouting that will let us know of any enemy forces within several hundred miles of us.

The question of air tactical scouting is far from being solved. Until the engagement phase opens it must be done by planes that can return to their ships when their search is completed, which planes from light cruisers or other combatant type ships not fitted with flying-on decks cannot do with certainty. Therefore planes on combatant ships should be held on their ships until just before those ships start to engage, at which time they should be launched and take up the duty of spotting and supply information. Until battle is joined, all air activities, and especially tactical scouting activities, should be carried out by planes from ships with landing decks and only when engagement is certain, or some other extremity demands it, should planes be launched from other ships. But once the main engagement opens, all tactical scouting and spotting should

An Admiral's Yarn

be done by planes from ships other than those with landing decks in order that the latter may drop such tasks and use their planes for offensive purposes.

Having given carriers such stations in our cruising dispositions as will enable them to carry out air operations as above outlined, the question then before us is how they may provide suitable tactical scouting prior to the time battle becomes certain and the aircraft from combatant ships become responsible for supplying information.

If carriers had unlimited numbers of long-range planes and air pilots, air tactical scouting prior to battle would not bother us greatly. But the numbers both of pilots and of long-range planes are limited. Casualties are not infrequent even in scouting flights where no contacts are made. Continuous air scouting for many successive days is often impracticable and even frequent flights exact a considerable toll in damaged or lost planes. Hence there should be practically no air scouting except when there is a possibility that the enemy is near, and even when he may be near the number of scouting flights and the number of planes in each flight must be a minimum.

In view of these things and holding the idea that among our Scouting Force, secret agents, and, other elements of our information service we will at least know when there is a *possibility* of our Battle Force being near the enemy, it is suggested, that we confine the Battle Force's air tactical scouting to that time. The one best scouting plan to be followed in that time has not as yet become evident, but when devising a plan, the following should govern.

First: Searches must be thorough and cover all the area in which the enemy can be.

Second: Use the minimum number of planes commensurate with thorough search.

Third: The plan of search should be such as to call for not more than two changes of course by any one plane between its leaving and its return to the disposition.

Fourth: The plan of search for a fleet seeking out the enemy may differ greatly from the plan of search for a fleet on the defensive, so in drawing up a tactical scouting plan one must base it on his scouting needs.

Fifth: Usually at least two flights per day is the least number that will suffice—one made at the earliest possible time after there is sufficient light, the other made as late in the afternoon as is commensurate with getting planes back before dark. The morning flight should cover all the area from within which surface contact with the enemy is possible before the afternoon flight; the evening

Appendix II

flight should cover as much as possible of the area from which attacks could get home during the night.

Having in our minds the dispositions suitable for a Battle Force when cruising or seeking the enemy, and understanding how that Force will locate any enemy near enough to be engaged, we are now ready to take up the steps preliminary to engaging.

(7) Concentration, Approach, and Deployment.

When the outlying portions of opposing fleets—be they air, surface, or sub-surface craft—make contact with each other, they endeavor to locate all the enemy forces in the vicinity, and, when the heavy forces have been located and reported, the fleet, after maneuvering to gain the best possible position as regards wind, sea, light, etc., must then deploy. Let us not forget that success in battle depends on many other elements than the mere arrangement of one's own forces with reference to themselves and to the enemy after deployment. Important as is the disposition of one's own forces for battle, these other elements must be given attention long before deploying. Under the weather conditions must the fleet seek the weather gauge or can it be content with the lee gauge? What bearing from the enemy is best to gain the advantages of sun and light? What bearing from the enemy will give a battle course least handicapped by wind, sea, and spray and at the same time not cause our aircraft carriers to run into dangerous situations when heading into the wind to launch and receive planes? Can we interpose between the enemy and his base? Each of these points or a combination of them and others can easily become a decisive factor in a battle, so much so that before closing the enemy a battle force must often maneuver to gain the position that will give it their advantages and avoid their disadvantages. When a battle force commander has the power to do so and other things being equal, he must maneuver his fleet to obtain the deployment course that will give to himself the major portion of the advantages and the fewest disadvantages as regards wind, sea, light, etc. Having acquired as many of the advantages as possible and practicable, he is then ready to close and fight.

As previously stated the concentration of forces and their approach and deployment are vital features of battle. Just as decisive advantages from wind, sea, light, etc., may be gained or lost by the position a fleet has with reference to the enemy and by the direction in which deployment is made, so also decisive advantages as regards the arrangement of one's forces as the engagement opens may be gained or lost in reaching action stations. Each part of the fleet must know its station and be in it when the main engagement opens, but owing to the dispersion of outlying forces while cruising, and to the pressure put on them by

An Admiral's Yarn

enemy forces once contact is made, their reaching such stations is not always easy. The easiest part in deploying to fight falls to the battleships and their anti-submarine screen, for (concentrated and protected as such ships are) their operations are simple. With other forces it is very different. The cruisers, far distant from their fighting positions, widely separated and probably being pressed by the enemy, not only have to assemble before it is time to deploy but after assembling may have to reach stations on the extensions of the battleship line before that line engages. Even more difficult feats may have to be accomplished by destroyers, while the submarines must attain positions that will be close to the enemy line after its deployment.

So complicated is the concentration of light forces and their accurate deployment that a very definite plan must be followed by all parts of a fleet between the time the outlying forces make contact and the main gun action opens. Usually the process consists of three distinct steps—first, a concentration of forces; second, their arrangement into what is called the "approach dispositions" and, third, the deployment from the approach disposition that brings all forces to their engagement stations.

The general rule for deployment in our Navy is that two-thirds of the light forces shall be at engagement stations opposite the van of the enemy battle line and one-third opposite its rear when the deployment is complete. Since shortness of time for deploying and avoidance of confusion in doing so both require that forces nearest these positions while cruising go to them on deploying, it follows that for deployment we must divide the light forces into three equal groups and make it clear to each group whether it is to be on the right or left flank of the battle line as the battle opens. This is provided for automatically in most of the cruising dispositions prescribed for us; but when for any cause the automatic feature for the deployment of light forces fails to work, or whenever the Force Commander so desires, the groups can be easily directed by signal when to take stations. The stations to be taken by the light forces are of course dependent on the direction the enemy battle line will bear from our own when the engagement opens. The bearing of the enemy battle line from our own is known as the "general bearing" line, which line plays a very important part both before and all during battle. It becomes the "fleet axis" both for the approach disposition and the deployment disposition.

That all forces may know what the "general bearing line" is, not only for approach and deployment purposes but also that they may be ready for emergencies, the Battle Force Commander, from the time the enemy battle line is located, uses every effort to keep his force constantly informed by signal of the approximate bearing of that line. If the direction of the "general bearing line"

Appendix II

changes due to the relative movements of the two fleets, the new "general bearing line" or "fleet axis" must be indicated by a signal, for only when all forces know the direction from our battle line in which the enemy strength lies can they be ready to meet surprises or have any idea of what will be the battle course on which they will have to reach deployment stations.

Remembering that a battle line when properly deployed is always on a line of bearing normal to the bearing of the enemy battle line, knowledge of the bearing of the enemy's line (i.e., the "general bearing line") shortly before deployment is all that is necessary to enable forces to know the general direction the deployment course will take. Naturally the battle will be opened with the fleet deployed on one or the other of the two courses *normal* to the "general bearing line." Hence, once we know approximately what the "general bearing line" of the enemy will be when the action opens we can at once start the concentration of our forces for deployment—and we should start it immediately for all forces on that side of our cruising disposition *away* from the enemy bearing.

The necessity of starting early the concentration of forces preliminary to deployment is not always realized. Again, when it is realized, commanders often make the mistake of concentrating all forces early and at a time when a concentration of certain forces is most dangerous and undesirable. Ordinarily one should not concentrate the light forces between his own and the enemy's main body until the latest possible moment, for not only should those forces retain their positions as long as possible for information purposes and for screening against enemy surface craft, but also they are needed in those positions to prevent or help defend against air submarine attacks. Furthermore it usually takes very much less time to concentrate forces that lie toward the enemy fleet than those that lie away from it, since the former have only to drop back on the battle line, whereas the latter usually have to catch up with it when it is going only a few knots slower than themselves. Hence, just as soon as we are sure of what the approximate bearing of the enemy battle line will be when our own closes it to maximum gun range, all light forces on the side of our disposition away from the enemy must start their concentrations. Concentrations may be started at any time by a signal but should start automatically without special signal as soon as pressure is felt if, in sending out his intentions as regards engagement, the Battle Force Commander indicates the approximate course on which he intends to fight.

One can diagram in a general way how concentrations may be effected by the outlying units in a circular disposition, these concentrations being by type groups in each sector. The result would show the approximate arrangement and

An Admiral's Yarn

position of all forces in a circular disposition when those from the side of the disposition away from the enemy have concentrated and reached their positions for deployment on the flanks of their battle line—the flank a sector group goes to being the one that lies within, or nearest to, its own sector. Thus we see what the first step is in going from a circular cruising disposition to a deployment. This same step is necessary in any disposition.

It often takes considerable time to complete this first step toward deployment and especially so when the disposition is standing directly toward the enemy at the fleet's best speed and forces on the side of the disposition away from the enemy have a considerable distance to gain. To reduce the time required to complete this step, a Battle Force Commander should keep his fleet speed as low as possible during this phase of the situation. This point is frequently lost sight of and, by standing directly toward the enemy battle line at best speed as soon as that line is located, fleets sometimes close to fighting ranges long before the concentrations of light forces have been completed. This is especially true of fleets in any disposition other than an axial one with all forces ahead, and this fact is one of the strongest arguments for such formations. However, it is not always necessary to go full speed toward the enemy as soon as he is sighted; and even when it is necessary, concentrations can usually be completed in ample time *if there is no delay in starting them.* And, anyhow there is no sound disposition for cruising so fool-proof that it will neutralize the errors of its commander, and one of the errors most frequently made by commanders is in failing to start soon enough the concentrations that take long to complete. The very instant a Battle Force Commander is sure of what the approximate "general bearing line" will be when the major action starts, he should order the concentration, at deployment stations, of all forces on that side of his disposition that is <u>away</u> from the enemy. And at that same time he should place his battleships in such a battleship cruising formation as will permit their quick and simple deployment on either of the two courses normal to the general bearing line.

Even though ordered to concentrate promptly, all of the forces on the side of a cruising disposition *away* from the enemy will usually not reach the positions assigned them before the forces on the side toward the enemy are in contact with and under the pressure of the enemy forces. For this reason it is not often that the ideal disposition will be fully attained. However, even though only partially attained, it will have served its purpose, and when pressure from the enemy becomes such that the forces toward him have to concentrate, those on the side away will be near enough to their deployment stations to reach them by the time those nearer the enemy can reach theirs.

Appendix II

The forces on the side of a disposition *toward* the enemy can of course be ordered to concentrate whenever the Battle Force Commander wishes but usually he will not order them to concentrate. On the contrary they should retain their stations until enemy pressure forces them to seek support, which they do by falling back towards the battle line and concentrating, then taking stations to support the main body.

The arrangement of forces envisioned between initial sighting of the enemy and battle line deployment is the "approach disposition." It is a disposition from which deployment can be made very quickly and is taken in order that the decision as to the direction of deployment (i.e., to the right or left) can be postponed to the last instant.

There is a tendency among inexperienced tacticians to rush into this approach disposition as soon as an enemy is located without waiting to see whether or not the "general bearing line" changes its direction as the fleets near each other. Besides doing away with a fleet's defensive screening at a time when it is most needed, the early assumption of the "approach disposition" is most unwise since if the "general bearing line" changes much while in the disposition, the disposition must be re-oriented to keep its axis pointed toward the enemy. The re-orienting of a battle force while in the approach disposition requires not only a series of complicated maneuvers by each part of the force but often takes so long that deployment becomes necessary before the re-orientation is completed. For that reason taking the approach disposition should be delayed as long as possible and done only when the enemy pressure becomes felt by the outlying forces and deployment is imminent.

From the standard approach disposition, deployment can be made quickly either to the right or left, the center group of light forces going to the flank directed by the Battle Force Commander, or to the flank that will be the van when deployment is completed, or to a position to interpose between the enemy light forces and our Battle Line. But as with concentration and with taking the approach disposition, deployment should always be made as late as is commensurate with being fully deployed when gunfire opens.

The matter of delaying deployment until the latest practicable is most important for several reasons. First of all, too early a deployment may require a re-orientation of one's forces before the main bodies close to gun range, which for the far-flung flank forces means long maneuvers at high speed to complete, and always with the danger that the engagement will open before the flank forces are again in position. Also, too early deployment will leave the choice to the enemy as to whether the engagement shall take place with the opposing forces on the same course or on opposite courses, and will leave to him the ability to put the major part of our light forces in his rear while the major part of his own light forces are on our bow. Furthermore, once committed to a deployment course, a commander will find that changing it is usually very difficult, and by deploying too soon he may find the movement of the enemy will prevent his engaging as he wants to or in accordance with his desired plan. All these, as well as other things, make it advisable to delay deployment until just reaching extreme gun range; good commanders never lose sight of that fact.

In the approach disposition, when the signal for deployment is executed two of the three groups of light forces will already be at or near their stations on the flanks of the battle line while the third group will have only a short distance to go to reach the flank to which assigned thus bringing about the disposition for battle we have already deduced as being desirable. With battle cruisers not present, one flank, probably the van, will have in it an attacking force made up of two-thirds of the destroyers supported by two-thirds of the light cruisers, while the rear will be covered by one-third of these types. This disposition of the light fast forces completes the main deployment but of course does not cover the deployment of the submarines or carrier-based air forces.

As for the submarines, from their position outside of all in the disposition for advance, once contact is made with the enemy they proceed at once to place themselves where they can best attack his heavy ships, acting on their own initiative from that time on to get their torpedoes home in the best way to further the general battle plan.

As regards air forces, the consideration they get in deployment is the same as we give to other forces. We place their carriers in such favorable positions that the planes on them can be operated to carry out their part in the battle plan. These positions are usually on the disengaged side of the battle line and, being near and in rear of the battleships when cruising, the carriers can reach them easily and quickly once deployment is ordered. From those positions the carriers operate as necessary to enable their planes to carry out the air plan.

II. Tactical Principles.

We have now discussed in a *general way* the procedure and operation of a battle force from the time the force enters enemy waters until it is in general engagement. It is impossible to lay down for the operation of a battle force or fleet, as a whole or as to its parts, in engagement anything more definite than the battle plan in general. However, when the force or fleet as a whole and in each part is familiar with the plan, and when the commander of the force and the commanders of each part are thoroughly indoctrinated with it, are imbued with initiative, and have the will to win, the force will operate as a team to produce

Appendix II

the desired results even though definite details can not be laid down to guide the individual forces in doing it. The possible combinations standing in the way of any subordinate commander as he tries to carry out his part in the general scheme are infinite in number and variety and for that reason no commander can be given a one sure and certain method of procedure that will cause him to arrive at the desired result no matter what happens. The recorded experiences in battle, however, have shown that certain principles, when followed, tend to bring success and when not followed tend to produce failure or disaster. Therefore, let us discuss the more important of these principles to the end of applying them, so far as they fit, to our tactics.

The Basic Principle

The fundamental principle of engagement tactics, axiomatic on its face, but proved by history and confirmed on the game board, is expressed in the phrase "Superiority of force at the point of contact." By this is meant one's tactics should be such as to isolate for the time being from the full support of the remainder of the fleet such portion of the enemy's fleet as one is engaging, while at the same time a superior part of one's own Force is brought to bear on the isolated portion.

It should not be gathered from this that superiority of force at the point of contact can be obtained only through causing an enemy to divide his fleet and then throwing one's own fleet against a part, though that is one way of obtaining the superiority referred to. An able commander will not usually divide his fleet but, for all that, a fleet not divided regarding distance between its parts can still be put in such a situation that there is not full support between its parts or even between all the units in one certain part. For instance, a capped battle line, a line maneuvering under fire, or a line, part of which is blanketed by smoke, has not mutual support throughout itself, and concentration on a portion of it at that time is one method of carrying out the basic principle. Similarly, the falling upon a fast wing when it is out of gun support by its battle line, or the bringing of a full line to bear on an enemy line only part of which is in range, answers the requirements. It is impossible to indicate the innumerable ways in which superiority of force at the point of contact can be gained. Some of them—for instance, the blanketing off of a portion of the enemy line with smoke—may be provided for in the general plan adopted for a battle. Other ways of getting it develop in the deployment and at various times throughout the engagement. Hence, commanders must be constantly on the alert not only to create such situations or take advantage of them when they occur but also to prevent the enemy from doing so.

The deployment stations herein deduced, and which are standard for our fleet for opening an engagement, tend to put a fleet in such concentration that when the fighting starts it is ready to exert its greatest strength against any and all points of contact, and this is as it should be, both for offense and defense. Because of this fact the general method of deployment is basic and is always followed no matter what <u>special</u> plan the fleet commander may put into effect for the battle. Like a football team, the battle team, when deployed, is lined up for a play. What special play, if any, is to be used in the fight is indicated by the fleet commander and that play must be carried out. But how the fleet and its parts move once the play is started is of course in the hands of the subordinate commanders, and if such commanders wish to have success they must have a clear conception of what constitutes proper points of contact and what they must do with the superior force they bring to them.

While the "point of contact" in the expression quoted above of course refers to any point where opposing forces are engaged, such points may be divided into two classes: one, the *main point*, where superiority has a decisive effect on the battle as a whole; the other, the *secondary points*, through which certain parts of the fleet pass in their attempts to reach the main point and influence the main decision. Whether the point of contact of any part of a fleet at any particular instant is *main* or *secondary*, the principle to be followed by a commander is always the same—his tactics must be such as to develop a superiority there for his own force. But having developed a superiority, it must be used in one way at a main point of contact and quite another at a secondary point, and again there will be secondary points of contact that may have considerable influence on the battle and others that will have little or none.

The Objective

It is evident that if one is to gain success in battle the important points of contact must be something more than mere haphazard points where parts of opposing fleets happen to come together. Of course the *main* point of contact is determined by the *main objective* in the battle, but the only important secondary points are those immediate objectives forced on parts of a fleet by the counters they meet in trying to reach the main objective. Hence, it is vital in battle that commanders at every instant have not only a clear conception of what the main objective is and what the immediate objective may be to enable them to reach the main, but also they must clearly understand what constitutes gaining an

Appendix II

immediate objective to the extent of permitting them to drop it and proceed toward the main. Thus, after the basic principle of "superiority of force at the point of contact," we have as a first secondary principle "the efforts of a fleet as a whole or as to its parts must be directed toward the objective and that objective must be the proper one for the instant and for the force concerned."

That the objective of a fleet as a whole is the enemy fleet is, of course, self-evident, but the immediate objective of any part of one fleet is not just any part of the enemy fleet that happens to come near. On the contrary, it is only such part of that fleet as lies in the way of reaching the main objective. To gain an understanding of the immediate objective of his force at any given instant in battle, a commander has but to look upon the battle as a whole. Remembering that the foundation around which the battle play of any fleet is built is its heavy battle line and that when the enemy's battle line is broken or destroyed his whole fighting structure will crumble, it is evident that the main or primary objective of all parts of a fleet in battle is the opposing battleship line. Every part of the fleet that can hit that line a blow must do so at the earliest possible moment and must keep hitting it with its full strength as long as the line exists and blows can be struck against it. However, in their attempts to strike that line, the various forces meet counters to their attacks and, when they do, they must destroy or evade the countering forces to such extent as will permit their proceeding to the main objective. Thus, countering forces frequently become the immediate objective of an attacking force and because of the necessity for clearing them from their path, subdivisions of a fleet often lose sight of the main objective and become so engrossed in an immediate minor objective as to fail to return to their real mission at the earliest opportunity.

The tendency of outlying forces to follow a temporary, minor, or useless objective too far must be overcome at all costs, for, unless it is, one's strength can be utterly expended on fighting minor forces without in the least influencing the general trend of the battle. Subdivisions of a fleet must fight their way through any opposition tending to hold them from the main objective, but they must never do so at the expense of the main objective. Destroyers that can attack the main objective should never stop their attack to enter a melee with other destroyers or light forces trying to hold them off; cruisers covering a destroyer attack should never stop to engage enemy light forces that cannot break up the attack unless such light forces are threatening their own capital ships; battle cruisers should not forsake a grip on the enemy battle line to drive off cruisers unless such cruisers threaten to break up the systematic attacks being made on the enemy line.

An Admiral's Yarn

These just stated minor principles are but a few examples of the many that have arisen from forces losing sight of their primary objective in battle, but they are sufficient to press home the idea that losing sight of it may cost a commander his opportunity to deliver the decisive blow. To prevent such occurrences, all commanders in a fleet must always know what the primary objective is and keep before them the fact that nothing they do will count for much if it draws them from that objective before it has been gained. When, as always happens in battle, an enemy force stands in the way of reaching the primary objective, that enemy force may for the time become the immediate objective, but rarely for long. As soon as the way to the primary objective again becomes open, the immediate objective has been gained and no time should be lost in dropping it and going on to the key of the enemy strength, his battleship line. If in his battle tactics each subordinate commander keeps this idea to the fore he will at least do his maximum toward bringing victory, for success in battle hinges on knowing the objective—the right objective for the instant—and going for it.

Offensive versus Defensive Tactics

There is usually only one successful way of going for the objective in battle, and that is the offensive way. In a sea battle, unless a fleet is forced to a defensive attitude by the necessity of protecting something, as, for instance, a convoy of supply or repair ships, defensive tactics will never bring a decisive victory. When guarding a convoy, even though the dispositions may be defensive, victory may be obtained by using offensive tactics from them. Therefore, a commander of a fleet or any part of a fleet, as soon as his objective of the instant becomes evident, must go for it and gain it in the offensive way. So going, the commander seizes the initiative and, putting his enemy on the defensive by compelling him to conform to his movements, he takes the first step that will ultimately enable him to gain "superiority at the point of contact." Let us not forget that though defensive tactics sometimes prevent defeat, only by offensive tactics can a decisive victory be gained.

Conditions and Elements That Influence Tactics

While reference already has been made to some of them, there are certain things that influence tactics in such a vital way that close attention must be paid to them from the time of earliest contact to the closing moments of battle. These points and the bearing they have on tactics will now be discussed: the weather gauge, gas, and spray; roll and pitch; light, sun-glare, silhouette; surprise; time; smoke and smoke tactics; and preparation before battle. Knowing how these

Appendix II

things may affect results in battle, a commander must at all times take cognizance of them in his tactics and give their advantages and disadvantages due consideration in every move he makes.

The Weather Gauge, Gas, and Spray

It is a generally accepted rule that the weather gauge gives one the advantage in a modern sea battle, and looking on the fleet as a whole this is probably true. But it is not always true for any single part of the fleet. The advantage to a fleet as a whole comes from the fact that, having the weather gauge, its torpedo craft close for attack <u>with</u> the wind and sea rather than against them, thus retaining their speed, while at the same time the fleet can make effective use of smoke screens not only to cover its own attacks but also to protect any of its threatened parts. Also a fleet having the weather gauge has a decided advantage in operating the aircraft from its carriers since carriers must steam *directly into the wind* to launch or take on planes. A leeward position for carriers in battle greatly restricts their operation since heading into the wind tends to run them into such enemy gunfire as to jeopardize the carriers and all their aircraft operations. We thus see how the weather gauge offers possibly decisive advantages both for offense and defense.

But these are not always its only advantages. If the wind is strong, spray, both from the sea and from shells that fall short, blows toward the leeward ships and materially slows the rate of fire especially of ships not fitted with directors. This may become a disadvantage of no small importance. On the other hand, ships having the weather gauge often suffer greatly from the interference of their own gun and funnel gases, sometimes to such an extent that they lose much of their gunfire while the enemy retains all of his. Hence, while the battle force commander will almost invariably seek the weather gauge for the action as a whole, or will at least avoid the lee gauge, minor commanders when they have a choice as to course and direction must weigh the spray against the gas penalty and select the course that will be the better for them.

Roll and Pitch

Another element resulting from weather conditions, and which may have a very considerable effect on the results of battle, is ship motion. Superiority in gun hitting being practically the deciding factor in battle, all tactics are based on it, and roll and pitch seriously interfere with hitting. He who can keep his ships on courses that will give them the minimum roll and pitch will at least not lose hits on that account. In any event, unit commanders should not accept roll and pitch handicaps without trying to impose equal handicaps on the enemy.

Sun Glare, Silhouette, Light

Before the day of telescope sights and colored lenses, another element interfering with gun pointing and spotting was sun glare, and, until recent years, sound tactics required one to obtain and keep the "sun gauge," especially if the sun were low. In recent years, and more particularly in the late war, the sun gauge has been found to be sometimes distinctly disadvantageous, for not only have colored lenses partly nullified the glare when the sun shines, but also, because of the great ranges used, ships with the lighter horizon behind them when the sun is obscured make much better targets than those having the darker background. It is believed that the decisive results of Coronel and the superior fire of the Germans over the British battle cruiser fleet in the early stages of Jutland were both due to the silhouette of the British ships even before the sun had set. Hence, an effort to impose sun glare on the enemy, which at best may have but little effect, is of doubtful value, while the danger of silhouetting one's own ships if the sun becomes obscured may prove decisive. Therefore, unless the weather is clear and the sun very bright, the sun gauge should be avoided rather than sought even though it may be possible to nullify the effects of silhouette by throwing a smoke screen behind ships having the sun gauge.

Surprise

In tactics, as in strategy, no one thing has more far-reaching effect than the element of surprise. A commander whose battle plan or tactics contain some element of surprise stands to make great gains thereby, since catching an enemy when unready to ward off a blow makes it possible to inflict great damage that often may be carried through to decisive victory. So great is the danger from a surprise attack that the safety of a fleet demands at all times a disposition that will make a major tactical surprise impossible, and such dispositions have already been discussed in this paper. In spite of these dispositions, however, in war each fleet always endeavors to get some of the advantages of a major tactical surprise by coming up on the enemy fleet in a way not expected, even though a complete tactical surprise rarely occurs. However, the possibilities of surprise do not end with surprises in major tactics, for a surprise at any state of the battle, even if brought about by a comparatively minor force, may be sufficient to give a decisive turn to the whole battle.

Appendix II

Any sudden maneuver that enables a commander to hit the enemy a heavy blow when that blow has not been anticipated has the nature of a surprise and this should be remembered by all minor commanders. Destroyers attacking from a smoke screen, a submarine attack, a sudden closing of the range, an unexpected concentration of fire, a sudden cutting off a part of the enemy's gunfire by a smoke curtain, and heavy air attacks are all examples of minor tactical surprises that may bring tremendous results. And just as it is strong in offense, a tactical surprise has great possibilities for defense, as was shown by the Germans in their "ships right about" maneuver in the battle of Jutland.

There is no possibility of indicating the infinite number of ways in which the element of surprise can be injected into battle tactics. It often results from changes in visibility conditions, unavoidable or created intentionally, but more generally it is obtained by taking quick advantage of some situation brought about by the maneuvers of battle. All that can be laid down about it is first, that the fleet commander must seek to inject surprise into his general battle plan and then, after the battle has opened he and each of his subordinate commanders must take advantage of every opportunity to strike a blow that has not been anticipated.

Time

In battle, once a fleet begins to reduce the relative strength of an enemy, that enemy's loss of remaining strength multiplies rapidly. Hence, other things being equal, the fleet that can hit hard *first* has made a long stride toward winning the battle. Time, therefore, becomes a most vital element and makes it imperative that every force strike at the main objective at the earliest possible instant after the battle lines become heavily engaged. It is not sufficient that a force knows what to strike and how to strike it. It must also strike in the absolute minimum of time and with its utmost strength. Any commander who fails to keep the time factor in mind and, after the main gun action opens, delays his attack on the main objective beyond the earliest possible minute it can be delivered, is risking the success of the whole battle. In tactics, as in strategy, "*Time is everything.*"

Smoke and Smoke Tactics

The introduction of steam-driven ships affected tactics in many ways, some of which have been touched on in this paper in an indirect way. While the broad fundamental tactical principles enunciated long ago remain as sound as ever, new motive power has caused many changes in minor tactics, the results of added maneuvering ability, speed, etc. But one of the more recent developments arising from mechanical driving devices has come from their making smoke. We

An Admiral's Yarn

have already mentioned the effect on tactics of gun and funnel gases because of their interference with gunfire, and smoke in its commonest form is a funnel gas. But smoke has another bearing on tactics in that it can be made a mantle of invisibility; because certain ship types can make smoke at will, this attribute has come to play an important part in naval tactics.

To a force driven to defensive measures, ability to make and hide itself in or behind a screen of smoke is of tremendous value. Possibly no other defensive measure can so quickly and successfully save a force from punishment as a smoke screen properly thrown between it and a force firing on it. Similarly, a force that can advance under the cover of a smoke screen has a splendid opportunity of doing so with the maximum immunity. Again it is frequently possible, especially with smoke-laying airplanes, to cut off the support one part of an enemy fleet is giving another by putting a smoke screen in front of that part and blanketing it. As a defense against air attacks, the value of smoke has not yet been determined, but it is possible that smoke can be made a great handicap to air attacks. These and other uses of smoke in battle show its enormous tactical possibilities, and special devices for making it having been developed for aircraft as well as surface craft, and may be developed even for submarines, all commanders must make special study of the use of smoke, and their tactics must be such as to take advantage of it to the fullest extent for both offense and defense.

But great as are the possibilities of success arising from the proper use of purposely made smoke in battle, there are grave dangers arising from using it carelessly, for smoke moves with the wind and once launched there is no controlling it. If carelessly laid, a smoke screen may put out of action a part of one's own fleet at a time when the hitting power of that part is absolutely essential to safety or success, and hence, though commanders must know and use smoke tactics, they must use them with discretion, lest they be hoist by their own petard. But, as has been the case with other things bearing on tactics, we can give no definite fixed rules concerning the use of smoke. When to make it and when not, and how to use it when made, can be determined only on the field of battle where the multitude of factors operating at the instant can be taken into consideration. But knowing the possibilities smoke has for good and evil, it is apparent that any commander who may go into battle must make a study of smoke and must use it, as far as it may be advantageous to do so, in all his tactics.

Preparation Before Battle

The several points we have just discussed as having a decided bearing on the tactics to be employed are points that must be considered in and applied during the various phases connected with the naval battle. There are many other things

Appendix II

upon which success in battle depends but which, though given their actual test in battle, must be provided for long before it. In fact, no battle tactics can succeed unless these things are fully developed beforehand, and because they are so vital to the success of battle tactics we cannot omit to mention them as being the things a commander must look out for before he enters battle.

The points particularly referred to are perfection in ship handling, excellence in gunnery, by which is meant accuracy and rapidity in the use of all weapons, readiness of the material to stand up under all strain, knowledge of the general plan and the part each unit is to play in it, and last but not least, such a will to win that nothing short of complete victory will be accepted. Only when a fleet has these things is it ready to enter battle; but, after entering, it can win only by employing sound tactics which, to a large extent, are based on the principles herein deduced or discussed.

The "Follow-Up"

Having been thoroughly prepared for battle, and employing sound tactics in it, a fleet has every prospect of gaining its primary objective, the breaking up of the enemy battle line. When that has been done, the decisive point of the engagement has been reached. But having reached it, what remains to be done to turn the advantage gained into a decisive victory?

As soon as any fleet finds the center of its strength breaking, it cannot but realize that to continue on as it is then going means only greater disaster. When this point has been reached the fleet naturally will attempt to withdraw from the action, and, when it does, the final phase of the battle opens. If a weakening fleet can withdraw successfully, the battle, even though lost, may not be decisively lost, and though the other side has won a victory it will not be a decisive victory. It is therefore apparent that though the decisive point in battle comes in the engagement phase, the *decisiveness* depends on the follow-up stage. Hence, commanders must devote as much attention to the "follow-up" as to any other phase of battle, employing tactics in it that will save their fleet if being defeated, or, if winning, that will complete the destruction of the enemy.

As to what tactics the retreating and following fleets should employ in this phase of battle, nothing definite can be stated. The one fleet attempts to conceal itself and avoid action as much as possible while seeking a safe refuge, while the other attempts to come up with it and defeat it as a whole or in detail. In general, both sides endeavor to follow the tactical principles already laid down whenever contact is made, but the one does so by fighting rear guard actions in a defensive manner, while the other constantly attacks.

An Admiral's Yarn

In this phase, history seems to indicate that a following fleet has the more difficult role to carry out successfully. Aided by the inevitable smoke of battle, as well as by smoke screens purposely made, strengthened by the initiative in attack that to a certain extent goes with retiring tactics, especially in the use of destroyers, submarines, and mine-laying craft, and often covered by the darkness of night, a retreating fleet has usually been able to get away. However, it seems probable that such a result comes less from the strength of retreat than from the fact that winning fleets have not prepared themselves as they could and should have done for carrying out this phase of battle.

Possibly the greatest impediment to success lies in the fact that the Battle Force Commander usually places himself in a battleship in the battle line, and going through the battle suddenly finds himself without the communication facilities necessary for reorganizing his fleet for the change in operation. But whatever the cause may be, certain it is that modern battles between large fleets seldom result in decisive victory, since when one fleet decides to withdraw from battle the other is either unable or incompetent to "follow-up" successfully. In view of the vital effect this stage of a sea battle may have on the result of the war as a whole, much more attention must be paid to it in the future than it has received in the past. It requires a plan just as the engagement phase does, though the tactical principles governing it merely continue from the preceding stages.

Though but briefly outlined, you have now before you a mental picture of a Naval Battle. We hope that through this presentation first of our general battle plan and second of the tactical principles to be followed in carrying it out, you are now impressed by these facts: first, that if any subdivision of our battle team fails in the task assigned to it, the battle may not only not be won, but may be disastrously lost; second, that to perform its task successfully, each subdivision of our battle team must in itself be a team highly skilled and trained in the work peculiar to its type; third, that only by perfect coordination and teamwork between the type teams is there any reason to hope for a victory in battle for the *fleet team*; and fourth, that we officers have a tremendous work before us to prepare ourselves, our type teams, and our fleet team to be always invincible in battle.

Your Next Step

It is hoped that having studied this paper to this point the student now has a good general understanding of a "Naval Battle" as our fleet of today would fight it. With such a general understanding, the student is now ready to go more into

Appendix II

the details of handling a battle fleet as a whole, and to the end of having a full knowledge of those details should now study:

(1) The *War Instruction*: (Navy Department publication),
(2) The *General Tactical Instructions* (Navy Department publication),
(3) The *Tentative Fleet Dispositions and Battle Plans, U.S. Fleet, 1930* (U.S. Fleet publication), and
(4) *Example Fighting Instructions for a Battle Force using the Circular Cruising Disposition* (War College pamphlet).

A thorough knowledge and understanding of what is set forth in these publications is prerequisite to properly handling our battle force and is the logical sequel to this preliminary paper on "The Naval Battle." When the above publications also have been digested—but not until they have been—the student can proceed logically to a study of the minor tactics that necessarily follow the major tactical ideas and conceptions he has already learned. This further study will take him through such publications as:

(1) *Formations and Maneuvers of the Battle Line* or *Battleship Tactical Instructions*,
(2) *Cruiser Tactics and Doctrine*,
(3) *Tactical Employment of Destroyers* and *Formations and Maneuvers of Destroyers*,
(4) *Submarine Tactical Instructions*,
(5) *Aircraft Tactical Instructions*,
(6) *General Signal Book*,
(7) *Contact and Tactical Report Code*.

A thorough knowledge of these will complete his study of up-to-date naval tactics so far as it can be completed by a study of current official publications. However, although a student may, from that study, have a fine general knowledge of present day naval tactics, that knowledge alone will not necessarily make him a fine tactician. Only by practice in war games in miniature and at sea will he become that. Hence, after the studies outlined above must come *practice* of which the efficient tactician can never get too much.

Endnotes

Introduction

1. Quotation of Henry L. Stimson (Secretary of War 1911–13 and 1940–45 and Secretary of State 1929–33) from his memoir, *On Active Service in Peace and War*, written with McGeorge Bundy (New York: Harper & Brothers, 1947), p. 506.

2. See, among other works, Mark Russell Shulman, *Navalism and the Emergence of American Sea Power, 1882–1893* (Annapolis: Naval Institute Press, 1995); Kenneth J. Hagan, *This People's Navy: The Making of American Sea Power* (New York: Free Press, 1991); Michael Vlahos, *The Blue Sword: The Naval War College and the American Mission, 1919–1941* (Newport, R.I.: Naval War College Press, 1980); and Robert L. O'Connell, *Sacred Vessels: The Cult of the Battleship and the Rise of the U.S. Navy* (Boulder: Westview, 1991).

3. Peter Karsten, *The Naval Aristocracy: The Golden Age of Annapolis and the Emergence of American Navalism* (New York: Free Press 1972), pp. 9, 12, 16–18, 26, 31, 75. The fathers of 5 percent of the candidates were bankers. According to Karsten, 40.1 percent of Naval Academy midshipmen in the years 1885–1895 were Episcopalian, compared with the approximately 2 percent national average. Laning followed his brother-in-law into the military; John McAuley Palmer went on to a successful career in the United States Army and to considerable renown as a writer on military affairs. For Laning's reading list before entering the Naval Academy, see *Yarn*, p. 5. For a comprehensive and insightful biography of the fascinating Palmer, see I.B. Holley, Jr., *General John M. Palmer, Citizen Soldiers and the Army of a Democracy* (Westport: Greenwood Press, 1980).

4. Vlahos, *Blue Sword*, p. 71.

5. See Craig Cameron, *American Samurai: The Influence of Myth and Imagination on the Conduct of Battle in the First Marine Division, 1941–1951* (New York: Cambridge Univ. Press, 1994), especially chapter III, "Images of the Japanese 'Other' Defined: Guadalcanal and Beyond"; and John W. Dower, *War without Mercy: Race and Power in the Pacific War* (New York: Pantheon, 1986), p. 36 *et passim*. For the best one-volume history, see Ronald Spector, *Eagle Against the Sun: The American War with Japan* (New York: Free Press, 1984).

6. The source of the quotation is International News Service report, 31 March 1936, upon Laning's relinquishing his command of the U.S. Battle Force to "Edward [sic] D. Leahy," available in Naval War College Archives, Manuscript Collection 115, Series VI, folio 8.

7. The American officer-memoir writers followed a long Anglo-American tradition. See most notably: Daniel Ammen, *The Old Navy and the New* (Philadelphia: Lippincott, 1891); Bradley A. Fiske, *From Midshipman to Rear Admiral* (New York: Century, 1919); Hugh Rodman, *Years of a Kentucky Admiral* (Indianapolis: Bobbs-Merrill, 1928); and Winfield Scott Schley, *Forty-Five Years under the Flag* (New York: D. Appleton, 1904). The unfortunate exception is that of Stephen B. Luce—the leading reformer of the "New Navy." Robley D. Evans and Alfred Thayer Mahan each published two: Evans, *Sailor's Log* (New York: D. Appleton, 1901) and *Admiral's Log* (New York: D. Appleton, 1908); Mahan, *From Sail to Steam: Recollections of a Naval Life* (New York: Harper, 1907) and *The Harvest Within: Thoughts on the Life of a Christian* (New York: Harper, 1909).

8. *An Admiral's Yarn* has been cited in several pu ished works including: Karsten, *Naval Aristocracy*; Vlahos, *Blue Sword*; John Hattendorf et al., *Sailors and Scholars: The Centennial History of the U.S. Naval War College* (Newport, R.I.: Naval War College Press, 1984); and Shulman, *Navalism*. Gerald C. Wheeler published a portion of it in the *Naval War College Review*, March 1969, under the title "The War College Years of Admiral Harris Laning," pp. 69–87.

9. See David Alan Rosenberg, "Beyond Toddlerhood: Thoughts on the Future of U.S. Naval history," in John B. Hattendorf, editor, *UBI SUMUS? The State of Naval and Maritime History*

An Admiral's Yarn

(Newport, R.I.: Naval War College Press, 1994). Rosenberg calls for increased attention to be paid to the support system, noting that "the shaft is just as much a part of the naval establishment as the spearhead, and the shaft may well have determined the nature and effectiveness of the tip that was sent into harm's way" (p. 417). This is certainly the case for Laning's role in the World War I buildup.

10. Laning's classmates at the Naval War College during 1922–1923 included future admirals Chester Nimitz, Harold Stark, and Thomas Hart. Laning stayed on for two years as Head of the Department of Tactics. His presidency there lasted from 1930 until 1933. See his opening presidential address of 2 July 1930 in which Laning presented an updated version of the thesis he had written as a student only a few years earlier. "The Tactics Department of the War College and the Relation Between It and the Fleet" (NWC Archives, Record Group 16, "Addresses," Box 1) is reproduced in the appendix to this volume.

11. Cited in Hattendorf et al., *Sailors and Scholars*, p. 127.

12. Laning, *Tactics*, NWC thesis, 22 February 1922, p. 7.

13. Laning, "The Naval Battle" (May 1933), Naval War College Archives, RG 64/1836, p. 18. See reference to Sims in *Yarn* as well as in Elting E. Morison, *Admiral Sims and the Modern American Navy* (Boston: Houghton Mifflin, 1942).

14. John Tetsuro Sumida, "'The Best Laid Plans': The Development of British Battle-Fleet Tactics, 1919–1942," *International History Review*, November 1992, pp. 661–880, especially p. 687.

15. Robert S. Jordan, "Introduction" to John B. Hattendorf and Robert S. Jordan, eds., *Maritime Strategy and the Balance of Power* (New York: St. Martin's Press, 1989), p. 7 *et passim*.

16. Origins of this Anglophilia can be found in two prosopographies: Christopher McKee, "Learning to Be a Navy," in *A Gentlemanly and Honorable Profession: The Creation of the U.S. Naval Officer Corps, 1794–1815* (Annapolis: Naval Institute Press, 1991), especially chapter XIX, pp. 210–5; and Karsten, *Naval Aristocracy*, pp. 1, 107–14.

17. *Yarn*, p. 105.

18. *Ibid.*, p. 109.

19. *Ibid.*

20. Hawaii was a republic under the domination of white planters in the years following the U.S. Navy-assisted revolution of 1893. American annexation of Hawaii came with the war of 1898.

21. *Yarn.*, p. 63.

22. *Ibid.*, p. 65.

23. *Ibid.*

24. *Ibid.* Indeed, Laning frequently attributed good in a strange society to European influences. Of the natives of Guam, whom he encountered in 1898, he remarked, "Their faces are those of intellectual men, the forehead usually being high. This good appearance of the people may be do [sic] to the white blood which they all have." "Journal of Cruise of U.S.S. *Monadnock*," 4 August 1898, p. 24 in Naval War College Archives, Manuscript Collection 115, Series II, box 1.

25. *Yarn*, p. 66.

26. *Ibid.*

27. Laning, "Journal of Cruise of U.S.S. *Monadnock*," 4 August 1898, p. 24.

28. The *Chicago* was one of the controversial (9,300 tons) 8-inch-gunned heavy cruisers built at Mare Island and commissioned in 1931. These cruisers could fire only three rounds per gun per minute and were thus not very useful at times of poor visibility (especially at night or in bad weather, but also during a smoky battle) or against fast moving targets, which were difficult to hit on so few shots. Thought not to be useful for defending the fleet, the 8-inch-gunned cruisers were expected to be assigned to distant cruising where, in war, they could either protect sea lines of

Endnotes

communication or carry out independent raids. *Conway's All the World's Fighting Ships, 1922-1945* (New York: Conway Maritime Press, 1980), p. 112.

29. *Yarn*, p. 357. Interestingly, this is Laning's only use of the word "yarn" in the entire narrative entitled *An Admiral's Yarn*.

30. *Yarn*, p. 357.

31. *Ibid.*, p. 277. See also pp. 327–328.

32. Fiske, cited in P. Coletta, *Admiral Bradley A. Fiske and the American Navy* (Lawrence: Univ. of Kansas Press, 1979), p. 189.

33. Hattendorf et al., *Sailors and Scholars*, p. 143.

34. The Destroyer Force—Its Mission in the Fleet and the Organization to Enable It to Best Fulfill its Mission, XTYV, (1919–80), 15 June 1919, p. 2, in Naval War College Archives, Record Group 8, Intelligence and Technical Archives. Vlahos, *Blue Sword*, p. 93 refers to Laning as a protégé of the insurgent Sims, but more likely Laning was a solid professional who managed to navigate the shoals between conservatives like CNO William S. Benson and the "Simian" insurgents. Sims quoted in Hattendorf et al., *Sailors and Scholars*, p. 88.

35. David MacIsaac, "Voices from the Central Blue: The Air Power Theorists," in Peter Paret, ed., *Makers of Modern Strategy from Machiavelli to the Nuclear Age* (New Jersey: Princeton Univ. Press, 1986), p. 632. Another good primer is Robin Higham, *Air Power: A Concise History* (New York: St. Martin's, 1973). See also Charles Melhorn, *Two-Block Fox* (Annapolis: Naval Institute Press, 1974), especially p. 90. For Mitchell, see MacIsaac, pp. 630–1, as well as Alfred F. Hurley, *Billy Mitchell: Crusader for Air Power* (Bloomington: Indiana Univ. Press, 1975), who refers to him as an "originator" to de-emphasize his genius in favor of his ability to bring together doctrine, people, and machines.

36. "The Destroyer Force," 15 June 1919, p. 2.

37. *Yarn*, p. 275.

38. International law agreed with Laning. In 1922, the Washington Conference outlawed unrestricted submarine warfare—an interdiction continued by the subsequent London Treaty. The conference dictates had been sketched out by navalists, each of whom had a stake in sustaining the battle fleet-oriented navies. See O'Connell, in "Requiem: The Washington Conference" in *Sacred Vessels*.

39. *Yarn*, p. 275. Compare this with Edward L. Beach's comment, "The minds of the men in control were not attuned to the changes being wrought by advancing technology. Mahan's nearly mystical pronouncements had taken the place of reality for men who truly did not understand but were comfortable in not understanding" as cited in Hagan, *This People's Navy*, p. 275.

40. Paul M. Kennedy, "The Relevance of the Prewar British and American Maritime Strategies to the First World War and its Aftermath, 1898–1920," in Hattendorf and Jordan, *Maritime Strategy*, p. 167.

41. *Op. cit.*, p. 173, or see Edward Beach, *The United States Navy: a 200-Year History* (Boston: Houghton Mifflin Co., 1986), p. 435: "As is not unusual in man's development, improvement of the battle line continued to be pursued by its devotees long after time and events had passed it by."

42. *Boston Evening Transcript*, 5 November 1923.

43. *Ibid.*, Laning also made this point in public in a 19 March 1924 speech "The Navy in National Defense," before the Providence City Club. He said, "That aircraft alone can drive every other type of ship from the sea, as claimed by certain air radicals, is of course ridiculous." NWC Archives, Record Group 4, Publications, 1400/3-24, p. 18.

44. John Keegan, *The Price of Admiralty: The Evolution of Naval Warfare* (New York: Viking Press, 1988), p. 161.

An Admiral's Yarn

45. George Grafton Wilson, editor, *International Law Situations with Solutions and Notes* (with introduction by Admiral Harris Laning) (Washington: U.S. Govt. Print. Off., 1929), pp. 98–104.

46. NWC Archives, RG 16: Harris Laning, Opening Address, 1 July 1932, p. 3, and J. Hattendorf et al., *Sailors and Scholars*, p. 142.

47. Keegan, *Price of Admiralty*, p. 162. See also William T. Larkin, *U.S. Navy Aircraft, 1921–1941* (Concord, Calif.: Aviation History Publications, 1961); and Nathan Miller, *The U.S. Navy: An Illustrated History* (New York and Annapolis: American Heritage and the Naval Institute Press, 1977), p. 285.

48. Testimony on House Bill 6661, NWC Archives, RG 8, "Military and Technical Intelligence," file XYTB, Accession 1931-120, p. 7 (does not appear on Laning collection register). For Moffett, see Edward Arpee's descriptive *From Frigates to Flat-Tops: The Story of the Life and Achievements of Rear Admiral William Adger Moffett, USN, "The Father of Naval Aviation," October 31, 1869-April 4, 1933* (Lake Forest, Ill.: Lakeside Press, 1953); and see William F. Trimble, *Admiral William A. Moffett, Architect of Naval Aviation* (Washington: Smithsonian Institution Press, 1994).

49. "Military and Technical Intelligence," p. 7.

50. Moffett, "Are We Ready," pp. 222–35.

51. "The Naval Battle," NWC RG4/1836, May 1933.

52. Hattendorf et al., *Sailors and Scholars*, p. 143.

53. This is a trend well-documented in Hagan, *This People's Navy*. See also David Alan Rosenberg, "Process: The Realities of Formulating Modern Naval Strategy," in James Goldrick and John B. Hattendorf, eds., *Mahan Is Not Enough: The Proceedings of a Conference on the Works of Sir Julian Corbett and Admiral Sir Herbert Richmond* (Newport, R.I.: Naval War College Press, 1993), especially pp. 150–5, which discusses many factors that shape naval strategy, including foremost: "*the nature of training and education programs, career patterns and professional . . . operational, technical and staff backgrounds of individual naval officers in significant (national or fleet) positions of leadership . . . [and] the procurement costs, capabilities, operating patterns, and sustainment requirements of naval weapons systems.*" Laning's *An Admiral's Yarn* provides insight into each of these crucial factors and thus goes far towards explaining the over-reliance upon battleships in the United States Navy up to December 1941.

54. Spector's, *Eagle Against the Sun* was the most important volume for bringing out the extent to which the Americans were able to use submarines to defeat the Japanese.

Chapter I

55. The Sangamon river rises near Bloomington, flows near Champaign, Decatur, Springfield, and Petersburg, before emptying into the Illinois.

56. Petersburg (named for Peter Cartwright, an original settler) was founded in the eighteen-teens and is still the principal city in Menard County.

57. A variation of hockey played by schoolboys with a curved stick and a ball or block of wood (also the stick that is used).

58. The New Salem Park, including Offutt's Store, was indeed restored as it would have been during Lincoln's youth. The mill and dam were again restored in 1992. Lincoln did do some of the surveying but did not lay out the town. All this information comes from Mr. Lester Ott (born 1911), who served as town librarian until 1992.

59. By "Henderson," Laning probably means William Henry Herndon and his famous biography, *Herndon's Life of Lincoln* (Springfield: Herndon's Lincoln Publishing Company, 1888) in three volumes.

Endnotes

60. See Willis J. Abbot, *Blue Jackets of 61* (New York: Dodd, Mead & Co., 1887); Elbridge Street Brooks, *The Story of the American Sailor in active service on merchant vessel and man-of-war* (Boston: D. Lothrop, 1888); J.F. Cooper, *Sea Tales* (Laning probably means *The Pilot: A Tale of the Sea* (New York: D. Appleton, 1819), the cover of which had the words "Sea Tales" on the Porter & Coates edition [Philadelphia, n.d.]); Frederick Marryat, *Mr. Midshipman Easy* (Boston: Marsh, 1836); George Francis Train, *Young American Abroad in Europe, Asia, and Australia* (London S. Low, Son, & Co., 1857) with American edition under title, *An American merchant in Europe, Asia, and Australia*; and any of following: Oliver Optic, *The Yankee Middy; or The Adventures of a Naval Officer* (New York: Hurst [1865?]; Harry Hazel, *The Yankee Middy, or the Two Frigates* (New York: H. Long, 1853); or Ward Edwards, *A Yankee Middy, or Hero of the Blockade* (New York: Novelist, 1886).

61. In 1870 there were four Academy graduates from Illinois. The editor was unable to ascertain which was Laning's uncle.

Chapter II

62. John McAuley Palmer (1870–1955) graduated from West Point in 1892, having been appointed at large from Illinois. Although posted in the infantry, Palmer served widely throughout his Army career, including on special topographical duty in Arizona (1896–1897), as Professor of Military Science and Tactics at the University of Chicago (1897–1898), and as a member of the technical staff at the Washington Conference on Limitations of Armaments (1921–1922) as well as active infantry service in Cuba (1899), China (1900 and 1913–1914), the Philippines (1914-1915), and France (1918), for which he was awarded the Distinguished Service Medal. Directly after World War I, he urged Congress to institute a universal military training program. Palmer retired as a brigadier general in 1926 and continued to write military history.

63. A strong-flavored tobacco with tough and gummy fiber raised in St. James parish, Louisiana, cured in its own juices, and used chiefly in smoking mixtures.

64. In 1900 the Navy acquired the 115.8-acre Iona Island, which is on the west bank of the Hudson, nine miles south of West Point. Iona Island provided ammunition to the merchant and naval fleets during World War I. It continued to grow in importance into the Second World War. See Paolo E. Coletta, editor, and K. Jack Bauer, associate editor, *United States Navy and Marine Corps Bases, Domestic* (Westport: Greenwood Press, 1985), p. 370.

65. This match was heralded as "a test of athletic strength between the two Academies." On the way to West Point, the navy team decided it needed a mascot, as Yale had its "Handsome Dan" the bulldog. The first candidate to appear was taken, and the Naval Academy adopted a tough old goat for good luck. See Walter Arnold, "Naval Academy Athletics, from 1845 to 1945," *U.S. Naval Institute Proceedings*, October 1945, vol. 71, no. 512.

66. William McKendree Springer (1836–1903), an Illinois Democrat, served in Congress from 1874 to 1894. From 1895 to 1899, Springer was judge of the U.S. Court for the Northern Indian Territory and Chief Justice for the Court of Appeals of the Territory.

Chapter III

67. The *Santee* was originally a sailing frigate of forty-four guns, 1,726 tons, laid down in 1820 and completed in 1861. The *Santee* served as a school ship at Annapolis after the Civil War.

68. The *Constellation* was a large sailing frigate of 1,265 tons.

69. A "bilger" is one required to resign from the Naval Academy because of failure in studies.

An Admiral's Yarn

Chapter IV

70. For a complete and more modern account, see Jack Sweetman, *The United States Naval Academy: An Illustrated History* (Annapolis: Naval Institute Press, 1979). For ephemera, see the yearbook, published annually since 1894, *Lucky Bag*.
71. A party with dancing.
72. The editor has not been able to ascertain which of the officers in charge was called "Frenchy."
73. The Commandant of Cadets was Commander C.M. Chester and the Superintendent of the Naval Academy was Captain R.I. Phythian.
74. The USS *Philadelphia* was authorized in 1887 and commissioned in 1890, a cruiser of 4,324 tons. She was housed over in 1904 and served from then until 1912, and again in 1916–1924 as a receiving ship. From 1912 to 1916, the *Philadelphia* was a prison ship.

Chapter V

75. The struggle between line officers and engineers for power, rank, and recognition had been bitterly waged since the introduction of steam engines in the 1820s. It was not resolved until 1899 when the two lines were set equal and merged.
76. Foods that are salt-treated for preservation.
77. A box used by sailors to hold small articles of gear, such as thread, needles, and tape.
78. Restrictions of non-U.S. nationals were generally unheeded. For a social history, see Frederick S. Harrod, *Manning the New Navy: The Development of a Modern Naval Enlisted Force, 1899–1940* (Westport: Greenwood Press, 1978).

Chapter VI

79. The USS *Pennsylvania* (BB–38), 31,400 tons, was launched on 16 March 1915 and commissioned on 12 June 1916. She joined the Pacific Fleet in California on 26 September 1922 and was decommissioned on 29 August 1946 after being towed to Kawajalein Lagoon in the Marshall Islands.
80. The fish, indeed named for Lester Beardslee, is also called a blueback trout.
81. The Puget Sound Naval Shipyard is on the western shore of the Sound, some fifteen miles west of Seattle, and was founded in 1891 at the urging of Lt. A.B. Wyckoff. Captain Alfred Thayer Mahan headed the commission which eventually selected the site. The 1890 Naval Appropriation bill had provided $210,000 to purchase the land and to construct a dry dock. Construction started in 1892 and continued into 1896 at an eventual cost of $610,000. The dry dock's sides were constructed of native timber, and the inlet of limestone blocks.

Chapter VII

82. The population of Los Angeles in the 1890 census was 50,395 and in 1900 was 102,249.
83. Although there had been intermittent naval basing activities in the Los Angeles area since 1846, no major bases were established there until after the First World War. San Pedro became the principal port for the U.S. battle force as the U.S. Navy turned its attention to Japan. In 1938, a naval air facility was built at Terminal island, San Pedro, which became U.S. Naval Base, Terminal

Endnotes

Island, San Pedro, during the war. The base was closed after the war but reopened during the Korean crisis.

84. The Hotel del Coronado was built in 1888 and was quickly hailed as one of the great hotels of the world. Its main building has been supplemented and, with renovations, provides world-class lodging.

85. In 1895 four ladies (with the given names of Zulette, Lena, Agnes, and Caroline) founded this women's rowing club at San Diego. In 1932 Zlacs moved to Pacific Beach where it remains as California's only all-female rowing club.

86. On 7 July 1846, United States Navy Commodore John D. Sloat landed a force at Monterey, Mexico and proclaimed California to be part of the United states by virtue of conquest. On 23 July the ailing Sloat was replaced by Commodore Robert F. Stockton, who declared himself to be governor of the newest U.S. territory. Soon after the war with Mexico ended and Sloat's conquest was confirmed by the Treaty of Guadalupe-Hidalgo, gold was discovered in the Sierra Nevadas, leading to a massive influx of American settlers. Two years later, California became a state (1850). See K. Jack Bauer, *The Mexican War, 1846–1848* (New York: Macmillan, 1974).

87. The USS *Independence* was authorized in 1813 and commissioned a ship of the line in 1815, on a revised 1799 design. She was razeed [upper deck was cut away] in 1846 and served as a receiving ship at Mare Island from 1857 until she was sold in 1914.

Chapter VIII

88. The *Oregon*, third ship of the *Indiana* class, was authorized in 1890 and commissioned in 1896. At 10,288 tons (11,688 full load), *Oregon* was capable of 15 knots.

89. The *Marion* was a *Swatara*-class steam sloop commissioned in 1876 at 1,900 tons, with compound engines and one screw, as well as a set of bark-rigging. She served as a training vessel from 1898 until she was sold in 1907.

Chapter IX

90. European-Americans had been settling in Hawaii ever since Captain James Cook first visited the Sandwich Islands. By the late nineteenth century, Americans in Hawaii controlled the plantation economy. In 1893, they overthrew Queen Liliuokalani and formed the Republic of Hawaii with the help of the United States Navy's cruiser *Boston*. U.S. President Grover Cleveland rejected Hawaii's petition for admission to the union. His successor, William McKinley, endorsed it during the war with Spain (1898), and in 1959 Hawaii became a state. In 1897, Laning and the crew of the *Marion* were visiting a republic of Polynesians and Asians dominated by a white minority. Sugar and fresh fruit were the main export.

91. Ensign Clarence England, U.S. Navy.

92. The population of Honolulu in 1890 was 22,907 and in 1900 was 39,306, according to the United States Census of 1900, Abstract.

93. Nuuanu Pali, a cliff and mountain pass at the head of Nuuanu Valley, six miles from Honolulu.

94. As a youth, Burton Holmes (1870–1958) travelled with his family and later photographed and made slides of his extensive travels. He enlisted artists to tint his slides and eventually made the first travel films. Holmes thus created the idea and coined the term "travelogue." In his adventures, which brought him to Europe fifty-six times, he traversed the globe six times and covered two million miles.

An Admiral's Yarn

95. The United States Weather Bureau was founded in 1890 when the Weather Service of the Army Signal Corp was transferred to the Department of Agriculture by Congress (26 Stat. 653).

96. The Executive Officer of the *Marion* was Lieutenant Commander James K. Cogswell.

Chapter X

97. The USS *Mohican* was a 1900-ton steam sloop with compound engines and a set of bark rigging. Although laid down in 1872, she was not completed until 1885 due to corruption and changing plans. She served until 1920.

98. The apprentice system was started by Rear Admiral Stephen B. Luce in 1875. By the early 1880s, the program was training 750 fourteen and fifteen-year-old boys to become sailors—although few continued in the service, even in the depression-era nineties.

99. The USS *Maine* was a 6,315-ton battleship authorized in 1886 and commissioned in 1895—by which time she was designated a "battleship second-rate." She was visiting a tempestuous Havana to protect American interests during a revolution against the corrupt and brutal Spanish rule. At the time of the explosion (which left 266 dead), most Americans believed it to be an act of Spanish treachery, and it proved to be the trigger for war. Later investigations have shown that the explosion originated from within the ship's coal bunkers.

100. Major James A. Connally, member of Congress, arranged for the ensign's transfer from the *Mohican* to the *Monadnock*, according to Laning's "Journal of Cruise of U.S.S. *Monadnock*" (3 July 1898) p. 2.

101. The USS *Monadnock* was an iron-hulled monitor laid down in 1875 as a "rebuilding" of a Civil War vessel of similar design. Its construction, and that of its three classmates, was put on hold from 1877 to 1882, but then restarted. The ship's pieces were shipped from Brooklyn to Mare Island where they were assembled. The monitor was commissioned in 1896. At 3,990 tons, with two triple-expansion engines, four ten-inch guns and nine-inch armor, *Monadnock* was a formidable coastal defense ship. With an extremely low freeboard and virtually no habitable quarters for her complement of 171, she was hell at sea. The *Monadnock* served until 1921.

Chapter XI

102. On 1 May 1898, the United States opened effective hostilities against Spain when Commodore George Dewey's Asiatic Squadron sank the inferior Spanish fleet at Manila Bay. For weeks, however, the Americans could not locate the Spanish squadron of Admiral Marivel de la Cámara, which had departed Spain either to reinforce Admiral Pascual Cervera y Topete in Cuba or to fight Dewey. On 9 July Cámara was recalled to defend Spain.

103. The USS *Charleston* was authorized in 1885 as a "semi-armored" cruiser of 3,730 tons, with 3-inch shielded, ten 6-inch and two 8-inch guns. Two horizontal compound engines produced eighteen knots. The ship was wrecked on Camiguin Island in the Philippines in late 1899.

Chapter XII

104. Because of the fluid ships' complements at this point, there are several possible identities for "Dickey," but the editor has not been able to ascertain it for sure.

Endnotes

Chapter XIII

105. Henry Ware Lawton (1843–1900) joined the 9th Indiana Volunteers in 1861, rising from sergeant to captain, taking part in twenty battles, and receiving the Medal of Honor in the course of the Civil War. In 1866 he was appointed lieutenant in the regular army (41st Infantry—Colored), taking part in the Indian Wars and rising through the ranks. In 1898 he was the brigadier general in charge of the U.S. volunteers in Cuba, and then military governor of Santiago. Lawton took charge of the regular army forces in Manila and was killed during the suppression of the Philippines. "Citizens of America" raised $98,000 for his widow.

Chapter XIV

106. The *Panay* was a small gunboat of 162 tons, capable of 8 knots, launched by the Spanish in 1885 to patrol Philippine waters. She carried one six-pdr. and 2 four-pdrs. The boat's successor-namesake was attacked by Japanese fighters in China in December, 1937. The captured gunboats ranged from *Callao, Panpanga* and *Samar*, all built in 1888, weighing 243 tons and capable of a little more than 10 knots, to the *Eclano* built in 1885, weighing 620 tons, and capable of 11 knots.

107. The USS *Wheeling* was authorized in 1895 at 990 tons with six 4-inch guns. She had two vertical triple-expansion engines and two screws and was capable of 12 knots. Commissioned in 1897, the *Wheeling* served until 1946.

108. The USS *Concord* was authorized in 1885 as a gunboat of 1,700 tons and commissioned in 1889. With two triple-expansion engines and two screws, she was capable of sixteen knots. Having six 6-inch and six 5-inch guns, she was the lightest seaworthy fighting ship in the fleet. She was struck in 1915.

Chapter XV

109. A small boat found in Pacific water.
110. A long, single-edged, heavy knife.
111. A long, straight-bladed dagger.
112. Emilio Aguinaldo was born to a Chinese-Philippine family in 1869, and as a young man was a political leader who, by 1896, led the Philippine independence movement. In 1897 he was bought off and exiled by the Spanish, only to be returned the next year by Americans hoping to over-throw Spanish rule. When the United States annexed the Philippine Islands as part of the December 1898 Paris Peace, Aguinaldo again started revolution against the colonial power. When he was finally captured in 1901 through an army ruse, the Philippine Insurrection was declared over. Aguinaldo lived to declare the creation of a Philippine Republic in 1946 and to have his sword returned by the American ambassador in 1960.
113. The USS *Castine* was authorized in 1889 at 1,177 tons as a gunboat and commissioned in 1894. With two vertical expansion engines, she was capable of 15.5 knots. She had eight 4-inch guns and two 6-pdrs. serving as a gunboat until 1907 and then for two years as a training ship. In her final decade, she was employed as a submarine tender.

Chapter XVI

114. The two ensigns assigned to the *Monadnock* were Fred Payne and James P. Morten—each acting as lieutenants junior grade. Giving the similar spelling, Payne seems the likely candidate.

An Admiral's Yarn

115. In the spring of 1898, the *Monadnock* was given two assistant surgeons in the rank of lieutenant junior grade: Eugene Grow and Frederick Benton.
116. The *Isla de Cuba* was launched in the Spanish navy in 1886 as a small cruiser. Raised from Manila Bay and reconditioned in Hong Kong, the *Cuba*, 1,030 tons, capable of 13 knots, for a dozen years served as a gunboat. In 1900 it carried four 4-inch guns and three 14-inch torpedo tubes.

Chapter XVII

117. The senior officers, other than the captain, included Commander Fernando Gilmore, Lt. Chester Knepper and Lt.(j.g) John Morris.
118. On 24 July 1900 Laning married Mabel Claire Nixon, daughter of Thomas Nixon—a Santa Barbara architect.
119. See George Ade, (1866-1944) *Fables in Slang* (New York: Grosset & Dunlap, 1899) illustrated by Clyde J. Newman.
120. Officers of the *Bennington* included Ensign William Reynolds and Lieutenant John A. Bell.
121. The *Solace* was an ambulance ship of 4,700 tons under Commander Herbert Winslow, with Lt. William V. Pratt among his officers. The China Relief Expedition was a multi-lateral great power intervention to put down the Boxer Rebellion—a millennialist and nationalist struggle to free China of colonial influence in 1900. It also precipitated U.S. Secretary of State John Hay's proclamation of an "Open Door" policy which would not allow any nation unilaterally to close the door to world trade in China.

Chapter XVIII

122. Richard Wainwright (1849–1926) entered the navy in 1864, taking his commission in 1868. As Executive Officer of the *Maine*, he assumed charge of its wreck before being given command of the *Gloucester*. His place in history was secured when he took the *Gloucester* under heavy fire to destroy the *Pluton* and the *Furor* (3 July 1898). Advanced ten numbers (and soon after promoted to commander) for eminent and conspicuous conduct in battle, Wainwright was given command of the Naval Academy. He was promoted to captain in 1903, later serving as the first Aide for Operations (1909–1911).
123. The *Chesapeake* (renamed *Severn* in 1905), a three-masted, sheathed bark with auxiliary steam power, was commissioned in 1900 and became a station and practice ship at the Naval Academy.

Chapter XIX

124. The *Dolphin*, a dispatch vessel of 1,486 tons, was authorized among the ABCD's of the "New Navy" in 1883 and commissioned in 1885. A comfortable ship, the *Dolphin* was the Secretary of the Navy's launch, used for entertaining guests of the navy.
125. Moody (1853–1917) was Theodore Roosevelt's choice to succeed John D. Long as Secretary of the Navy in May 1902. He served until elevated to the position of U.S. Attorney General in July 1904.
126. Hale (1836–1918) was a Republican from Maine who dominated naval affairs committees in the House (1869–1879) and Senate (1881–1911).

Endnotes

127. Penrose (1860–1921), like Hale, was an anti-Progressive Republican and a Senator from Pennsylvania (1897–1921).

128. Cannon (1836–1926), a Republican from Ohio, served in the House (1873–1891, 1893–1913, 1915–1923) and led it as Chair of the Appropriations Committee or as Speaker throughout the first decade of the twentieth century. He lost influence in a split with the Progressive Republicans.

129. Alfred Thayer Mahan (1840–1914) graduated from the Naval Academy in 1861 and served with minor distinction, rising to the rank of captain. In the mid–1880s, Mahan wrote *The Influence of Sea Power upon History, 1660–1783* while preparing his lectures on history for the new Naval War College, of which he was the second president. Mahan published this work in 1890 (Boston: Little, Brown & Co.,) and soon became the world's preeminent navalist philosopher and historian, with numerous publications and widespread influence in the years succeeding. His lessons centered on a blue water fleet concentrated to control the seas and to bring decisive victories and greatness to its nation.

130. William Sowden Sims (1858–1936), who graduated from the Naval Academy in 1880, was a controversial leader of the "Young Turks," who introduced modern technology and methodology to the New Navy. He served as an eager naval attaché in Europe, introduced the "Morris Tube" for sighting guns, and has been called the "Father of Target Practice." Sims commanded U.S. Naval Forces in European waters in 1918–1919 and soon after caused a great stir by criticizing Navy Secretary Josephus Daniels for his allegedly inept prosecution of the war effort. Sims served as President of the Naval War College, 1921–1922, and published *Victory at Sea* in collaboration with Burton J. Hendrick (Garden City: Doubleday, Page & Co., 1920), which received a Pulitzer Prize.

Chapter XXI

131. Paul Morton served as Roosevelt's second of five Secretaries of the Navy, from 1 July 1904 to 30 June 1905, at which point he was succeeded by Charles Bonaparte. Laning appears to have confused the various secretaries or dates, as the passage otherwise recounts the summer of 1903.

132. There were two other officers on the *Dolphin* at this point: Lieutenants Frank Brumby and Newton S. McCully. The latter eventually attained flag rank. McCully soon left for a tour as a special representative of the Office of Naval Intelligence to cover the Russo-Japanese War. See *The McCully Report: The Russo-Japanese War, 1904–1905*, edited by Richard Von Doenhoff (Annapolis: Naval Institute Press, 1977).

133. Bonaparte served from 1 July 1905 to 16 December 1906. See note 131 on Laning's confusion.

134. The *Mayflower* was a luxurious steam yacht (2,690 tons) built in 1896 and brought into service against Spain. From 1904 to 1929, the *Mayflower* served as the presidential yacht.

Chapter XXII

135. Riflery instructors at the Naval Academy in 1905 included Lieutenants A. Buchanan and P. Babin.

Chapter XXIV

136. USNA 1871, Nicholson retired as a rear admiral in 1914 and died in 1939.

An Admiral's Yarn

137. The USS *Nebraska* was authorized in 1899 to reflect lessons from the Spanish War about the ability to steam great distances and the usefulness of a secondary battery. Commissioned at 14,948 tons and capable of 19 knots, the *Nebraska* had four 12-inch and eight 8-inch guns as well as numerous smaller arms. At 441 feet and carrying a complement of over 800, she was considerably larger and more expensive than any previous American battleship.

138. In a show of strength to impress and the Japanese the Europeans, President Theodore Roosevelt sent the Great White Fleet on a cruise around the world between late 1907 and 1909.

Chapter XXV

139. On 28 December 1908, an earthquake destroyed Messina and killed 85,000 people.

Chapter XXVI

140. Nathaniel Bowditch (1773-1838) first published his perennial best-seller, *The New American practical navigator: being an epitome of navigation; containing all the tables necessary to be used with the nautical almanac, . . . illustrated by proper rules and examples: the whole exemplified in a journal kept from Boston to Madeira, . . .* (Newburyport: Edmund M. Blunt for Cushing and Appleton, Salem) in 1802. Published privately until 1867, it was then printed by the U.S. Naval Observatory in successive editions.

141. Robert M. Thompson (1849–1930) graduated from Annapolis in 1868, resigning his commission three years later to become a lawyer and industrialist. Always a navy booster, Thompson founded the Naval Academy Athletic Association and the Naval Academy Alumni Association of New York. He was President of the Navy League in 1917 when it openly attacked Secretary of the Navy Josephus Daniels for allegedly undermining American preparedness. As well as Thompson Field, he donated (with his brother) the Thompson Cup which goes to the annual winner of the Army-Navy football game. He also served as chair of the U.S. Olympic Committee for the 1912 Stockholm and 1924 Paris Olympiads.

Chapter XXVII

142. In the Military Rifle Team event of 29 June, the Americans scored 1,687 points to Great Britain's 1,602 and 1,570 for third-place Sweden.

143. In both the 300-meter and 600-meter Individual Military Rifle competitions, Americans took silver in fields of twelve nations.

144. According to David Wallechinsky, *The Complete Book of the Olympics* (New York: Viking, 1988), the American team placed second in this event; p. 418.

145. According to the Wallechinsky volume, Laning's memory is faulty here. On 4 July 1912, Frederick Hird won the Small Bore Rifle, Prone event with 194 points, with British competitors making 193 and 192 points respectively. The next day he was part of the Miniature Rifles Team which took bronze medals in both the 25-meter and 50-meter events. On the final day of rifle competition, 11 July, Hird finished eighth in the Small Bore Rifles competition.

Chapter XXVIII

146. The *Cassin* was a destroyer of the second line, weighing approximately 1,000 tons, capable of 29 knots, and commissioned in 1913.

Endnotes

147. USS *Cummings*, another "thousand-tonner" destroyer designed with a larger steaming radius and guns as well as with more torpedo tubes, was laid down in 1912 and served the navy until 1923 when it was transferred to the Coast Guard.

148. *Downes* and *Duncan* were the last two of four *Cassin*-class destroyers. *Downes* was loaned to the Coast Guard from 1924 to 1931, but both remained on the navy list until 1934 and 1935 respectively.

149. For more on Sims, see above chapter as well as E.E. Morison, *Admiral Sims and the Modern American Navy* (Boston: Houghton Mifflin, 1942).

150. *Aylwin*-class destroyers (four in number) were virtually identical to the *Cassins*—laid down in 1912 and commissioned in 1914. *Aylwin* survived until struck in 1935.

151. Vera Cruz Affair—In April 1914, the *Dolphin* was part of the forces that had for several months been blockading European shipments of war materials for Victoriano Huerta, whom Woodrow Wilson refused to recognize as president of Mexico. On the 9th, some crew members landed at Tampico to resupply and were arrested for violating martial law. Although the sailors were released promptly with an apology, the U.S. admiral, Henry T. Mayo, demanded that the port commander fire a 21-gun salute and hoist the American flag, threatening an intervention should he refuse. Under orders from Wilson and with the support of Congress, the Americans bombarded Vera Cruz and occupied the city on 21 April, bringing the two nations close to war. Mediation by Argentina, Brazil, and Chile proposed that Huerta retire and that Mexico's constitution change, although the U.S. would not be paid an indemnity for the occupation costs. Although rejected by Huerta, these events soon led to his retirement, leaving Venustiano Carranza as president with Wilson's support. U.S. occupation of Vera Cruz ended 23 November, but Mexico's revolution continued, drawing another American invasion in 1916–1917 before most matters were settled in the spring of 1917. See Jack Sweetman, *The Landing at Vera Cruz, 1914: The First Complete Chronicle of a Strange Encounter in April, 1914, when the United States Navy Captured and Occupied the City of Vera Cruz, Mexico* (Annapolis: Naval Institute Press, 1968).

152. The *Morro Castle* was a screw steamer of 6,004 tons gross, measuring 400 by 50 feet, and built in 1900. She served the New York and Cuba Mail Steam Ship Company out of New York.

Chapter XXIX

153. In 1912, Dominicans started to fight a U.S.-imposed customs receivership. A full-blown rebellion in the spring of 1916 brought a U.S. invasion, which forced the collapse of the government of the Dominican Republic and imposed an occupation regime that lasted until 1924, secured by the Marine Corps and martial law.

154. The *Panther* (originally the *Austin*) was an iron-hulled armed merchant ship weighing 4,260 tons, capable of 13 knots, and commissioned in the U.S. Navy during the war with Spain.

155. William Banks Caperton (1855–1941) graduated from the Naval Academy in 1875 and rose through the ranks, serving in many positions including as a surveyor, engineer, navigator for the famous 1898 run of the *Oregon*, and then presiding over the invasion of Haiti in 1915. The next year he also commanded the navy's efforts in Santo Domingo. In the years following, Caperton commanded the Pacific Fleet and retired as a full admiral in 1919.

Chapter XXX

156. William Shepard Benson (1855–1932) graduated from the Naval Academy in 1877 and served most notably on the Greely Relief Expedition (1884), on the *Dolphin* for its world cruise (1888–1889), and three tours at the Naval Academy—the last of which as commandant. Benson

An Admiral's Yarn

was Chief of Staff for the Pacific Fleet (1909–1910) and commanded the *Utah* in 1911. In 1915, Navy Secretary Josephus Daniels elevated Captain Benson over all admirals and four senior captains to the new position of Chief of Naval Operations. As expected, Benson served competently and without controversy until the fall of the Central Powers and his retirement on 25 September 1919. See Mary Klachko with David Trask, *Admiral William Shepard Benson: First Chief of Naval Operations* (Annapolis: Naval Institute Press, 1987). The new office of the CNO oversaw all operations and plans, taking these roles from various bureaus and boards. The burden of planning had previously been shared by the Office of Naval Intelligence, the Naval War College, and the General Board.

157. The war opened in August 1914 with Britain immediately declaring Germany to be blockaded. With the German High Seas Fleet bottled up, the Royal Navy had "command of the seas." Instead, however, of conceding the common highway to the British, the German submarine fleet started its own counterblockade. Because the British merchant ships were illegally armed and sinking the fragile U-boats, Germany ceased to warn Allied ships that they were about to be sunk. In May 1915, the British liner *Lusitania* was sunk with contraband and over a hundred American citizens on board. The Wilson administration's outrage forced the Germans to renounce unrestricted submarine warfare. The military and domestic crises of 1917 encouraged the Germans to announce unrestricted submarine warfare again in January 1917. By March, several American merchant ships had been sunk, and the nation was further outraged by the release of the Zimmermann Telegram, which proposed a German alliance with Mexico. In April, President Wilson asked Congress to declare war.

For a more sustained account, see Paul Kennedy, "Stalemate and Strain," chapter 9 in *The Rise and Fall of British Naval Mastery* (London: Macmillan, 1983) or Barbara , *The Zimmermann Telegram* (New York: Macmillan, 1958). For excellent accounts of America's entry into the war from different perspectives, see Walter Millis, *Road to War: America 1914–1917* (Boston: Houghton Mifflin Co., 1935) and John W. Coogan, *The End of Neutrality: The United States, Britain, and Maritime Rights, 1899-1915* (Ithaca: Cornell University Press, 1981).

158. For the Navy, see: *Annual Report of the Secretary of Navy* (Washington: U.S. Government Printing Office, 1918, 1919); William S. Sims, *Victory At Sea* (New York: Doubleday, 1920; reprinted with introduction by David Trask (Annapolis: Naval Institute Press, 1984); Paul Halpern, *A Naval History of World War I* (Annapolis: Naval Institute Press, 1994) and Robert Love, ed., *The Chiefs of Naval Operations* (Annapolis: Naval Institute Press, 1980).

159. For a detailed account of the 1916–1918 buildup, see Robert Love, *A History of the U.S. Navy*, volume I (Harrisburg: Stackpole Press, 1992).

160. Leigh Carlyle Palmer (1873–1955) graduated from the Naval Academy in 1896 and served as Chief of the Bureau of Navigation in late 1916, and as Chief of Staff to Commander Division 9, Battle Force 2, Atlantic Fleet during the American participation in World War I. As such, Palmer took part in the German surrender and was awarded the Distinguished Service Medal.

161. For transport services see: Albert Gleaves, *A History of the Transport Service: Adventures and Experiences of United States Transports and Cruisers in the World* War (New York: Doran, 1921); Lewis P. Clephane, *History of Naval Overseas Transportation Service in World War I* (Washington: U.S. Government Printing Office, 1969 edition of 1920 volume), which contains selections from the Naval Records and Library Manuscript Collections.

162. See Henry Thomas Mayo, "The Atlantic Fleet in the Great War," in Edward M. House and Charles Seymour, editors, *What Really Happened at Paris: The Story of the Peace Conference, 1918–1919* (London: Hodder & Toughton, 1921), pp. 348–369 and appendix XV, pp. 490–491.

163. See Clephane, *History of the Naval Overseas Transportations Service in World War I.*

Endnotes

164. Each of these roles is described briefly in Mayo, "Atlantic Fleet" cited above, as well as in Josephus Daniels [Secretary of Navy, 1913–1921], *Our Navy at War* (New York: Doran, 1922); William S. Sims [Commander U.S. Naval Forces in European Waters] with Burton Hendrick, with introduction and notes by David Trask, *Victory at Sea* (Annapolis: Naval Institute Press, 1984), reprint of 1920 Doubleday original.

The Navy established the North Sea Mine Barrage between Scotland and Norway, which covered an area 250 miles long and 15 to 35 across. By the armistice, a joint USN-RN task force had planted some 70,000 of these mines which could be triggered by contact with their 70-foot antenna. The effort proved moderately successful, sinking between four and eight U-boats and complicating operations for the others. See, Allan R. Millett and Peter Maslowski, *For the Common Defense* (New York: Free Press, 1984), p. 341.

For the Eagle boats and the close relatives, the "110-Foot Boats" see, *Jane's Fighting Ships of World War I* with a foreword by John Moore (New York: Military Press, 1990 edition of London: Jane's Publishing Co., 1919 original), pp. 151–152.

165. The House Naval Affairs Committee was chaired by Lemuel Padgett (D-Tenn). For hearings, see: House Naval Affairs Committee, Public Hearing H211-11 (December 17–18, 1918).

Chapter XXXI

166. The *Rochester* was originally the *New York*, authorized in 1888 and commissioned in 1893. Launched at 8,150 tons and 384 feet in length, with six 8-inch and twelve 4-inch guns, capable of 20 knots, and partially protected by four inches of belt and reinforced turrets, she was the armored cruiser that served as William Sampson's flagship at Santiago in 1898. She was rebuilt in 1905–09 with new turrets for 8-inch guns. She was renamed *Saratoga* in 1911 and *Rochester* in 1917, being decommissioned at Olongapo Naval Station in 1933 and scuttled in Subic Bay in 1942.

167. Compare the account in Richard K. Smith, *First Across! The U.S. Navy's Transatlantic Flight of 1919* (Annapolis: Naval Institute Press, 1973). Smith has the following to say: "The planning for the task force to support the transatlantic flight was put in the hands of Captain Harris Laning, a brilliant staff officer who had been Assistant Chief of the Bureau of Navigation during the war," p. 50.

168. Richard E. Byrd (1888–1957) spent most of his career pushing back the frontiers of aviation in various roles: on the first dirigible flight across Atlantic (1921); as commander of the aviation unit of the Navy-MacMillan Polar Expedition (1925); in the first overflight of the North Pole (1926); leading four expeditions (1929, 1933-35, 1939, and 1946-1947) to Antarctica. The "bubble sextant" allowed navigators to find longitude and latitude by combining the technology of a sextant with that of a level. Although not theoretically complex, its use was complicated.

169. See also Paolo E. Coletta, *Patrick N.L. Bellinger and U.S. Navy Aviation* (Lanham, Md.: Univ. Press of America, 1987).

170. Towers (1885–1955) retired as an admiral in 1947. For an excellent biography, see Clark G. Reynolds, *Admiral John H. Towers: The Struggle for Naval Air Supremacy* (Annapolis: Naval Institute Press, 1991).

171. The crew was received by President Canto y Castro, a former admiral and an avid aviation fan.

172. Major Waldorf Astor was the son of Viscount Astor; Nancy Astor was later the first woman elected to the British Parliament.

An Admiral's Yarn

Chapter XXXII

173. Alfred Charles William Harmsworth, Lord Northcliffe (1865–1922), a newspaper magnate, owned and ran the following London papers: *Evening News, Daily Mirror, Daily Mail* and, finally, *The Times*. In 1918 he was the government's director of British propaganda in enemy countries.

Chapter XXXIII

174. When the commander in chief of the German High Seas Fleet (Admiral Reinhard Scheer) realized that he could not destroy the British Fleet, he ordered his line to turn away from the British in order to flee. Each German ship having a different turning radius made this an extremely dangerous maneuver, but one less so than having the ships turn in succession (on a specific point) which would have allowed the Royal Navy to get the proper range and sink the German line in sequence.

For an extended discussion of the most widely replayed battle in naval history, see Arthur J. Marder, *Jutland and After*, volume III of *From the Dreadnought to Scapa Flow: The Royal Navy in the Fisher Era*, 1904–1919 (New York: Oxford Univ. Press, 1966), especially pp. 110–122 and chart 10, or N.J. Campbell, *The Fighting at Jutland* (London: Conway's, 1988).

175. During the one-sided Battle of Santiago (3 July 1898) Admiral William Sampson, Commander-in-Chief of the U.S. North Atlantic Squadron, had briefly steamed away from the fleet for a meeting with his army equivalent when the Spanish made their desperate effort to flee Santiago Harbor. Commodore Winfield Scott Schley was, consequently, the ranking officer *in situ* during the brief and successful engagement. After the war these officers became involved in a vituperative struggle for the glory of the day, with charges of cowardice and incompetence soiling the reputation of each. A court of inquiry (1902) eventually vindicated the less popular and dying Sampson. For a brief discussion, see Hagan, *This People's Navy*, pp. 223–227. For more, see *Record of Proceedings of a Court of Inquiry in the Case of Rear Admiral Winfield S. Schley, U.S. Navy* (Washington: U.S. Government Printing Office, 1902).

176. For hearings, see: Senate Committee on Naval Affairs (66-2) public hearing S. 185–Pt.2 (March-April 1920). Testimony was provided by all the leaders of the service.

177. See Elting Morison's account, keeping in mind that Morison married one of Sims' daughters: *Admiral Sims and the Modern American Navy* (Boston: Houghton Mifflin Co., 1942), pp. 433–469.

178. The fleets shifted in June 1921. Prior to that, the disposition was as follows: The Atlantic Fleet had two battleship squadrons each, with two divisions of four ships (save for one of three), for a total of 15 battleships. It also had two destroyer squadrons, number 3 and 1. Destroyer Squadron 3 had three flotillas each, with three divisions of six ships, for a total of 54 destroyers. Destroyer Squadron 1 had 38 ships, either in reserve or building. The Pacific Fleet also had two battleship squadrons, each of these with two divisions of 3–4, for a total of 14 battleships. The Pacific Fleet also had two destroyer squadrons, numbers 4 and 2. Destroyer Squadron 4 had three flotillas of three divisions of 5–6 ships each, for a total of 53 destroyers. Destroyer Squadron 2 had 38 ships of reduced commission.

After the realignment, the Battle Fleet was stationed in the Pacific and the Scouting Fleet in the Atlantic. By 1923, when the numbers had settled down, they were as follows: the Battle Fleet had three divisions of the best (most modern, fastest, and most highly armed) battleships, for a total of eleven. The Scouting Force had two divisions of older battleships totaling six in number.

Endnotes

Additionally, it had two divisions of destroyers, each with 18 ships. The information cited is from the *Navy Directory* (Washington: U.S. Government Printing Office, 1920 and 1923).

179. The class of 1922 convened with forty-five students on 30 June 1921.

Chapter XXXIV

180. The Naval War College was founded in 1884 to provide officers with a forum for post-graduate study of tactics and strategy. The first President was Stephen B. Luce, who wrote, "No less a task is proposed than to apply modern scientific methods to the study and raise naval warfare from the empirical stage to the dignity of a science." See: Ronald Spector, *Professors of War* (Newport: Naval War College Press, 1977); John B. Hattendorf, B. Mitchell Simpson, III, and John R. Wadleigh, *Sailors and Scholars: The Centennial History of the U.S. Naval War College* (Newport: Naval War College Press, 1984); and Shulman, *Navalism*.

181. The Applicatory System, better known by the officers as the "estimate of the situation," consisted of a three-stage exercise: 1) analyzing a situation and determining a plan; 2) generating orders; 3) acting on same. It was introduced via the Army War College between 1909 and 1912 and would remain a staple of the Naval War College education. See Hattendorf et al., *Sailors and Scholars*, pp. 69–72 ff.

182. This was the practice until grading and academic standards were introduced in 1972. The college was accredited to award the master of arts degree in 1991.

Chapter XXXVI

183. The class of 1923 began on 3 July 1922 with fifty students, including Chester W. Nimitz, Harold Stark, and Thomas Hart.

184. "The Naval Battle" (3/1/24) is housed in Record Group 4, as is the 1933 revision, "The Naval Battle."

185. See the Naval War College, Naval Historical Collection, Record Group 4, boxes 16–19, for strategic, tactical, screening, and scouting problems undertaken by the classes of 1922–1924. Record Group 4 contains student and faculty publications.

186. Lectures were presented approximately twice weekly and ranged widely. Policy and international relations lectures included those by William V. Pratt and George Grafton Wilson on the Washington Conference, Dr. Lathrop Stoddard on "Present Race Conflicts in World Affairs," and Professor E. Huntington on "The Relation of Geography to the character of people in the Far East." There were as well lectures by officers on logistics, communication, and also coordination with the army. See P.B. Whelpley, editor, *Outline History of the United States Naval War College, 1884 to date* (unpublished in the Naval War College Historical Collection, updated through 1937). For Harvard Law Professor Wilson's lectures, see the annual series *International Law Discussions* and *Notes* (Naval War College, annual). Laning's lectures in this period include: "Major Tactics at Jutland," "The Battle of the Marianas," and "The Battle of Emerald Bank."

187. For more see: Vlahos, *The Blue Sword* and John T. Hanley, "On Wargaming: A Critique of Strategic Operational Gaming" (Ph.D. dissertation, Yale University, Department of Operations Research/Management Science, 1991.)

188. For the Washington Conference, see William R. Braisted, *The United States Navy in the Pacific, 1909–1922* (Austin: Univ. of Texas Press, 1971); Thomas H. Buckley, *The United States and the Washington Conference* (Knoxville: Univ. of Tennessee Press, 1970); Thomas C. Hone, "The Effectiveness of the 'Washington Treaty' Navy," *Naval War College Review*, vol. 32, no. 6 (November–December 1979); and Robert H. Van Meter, "The Washington Conference of

An Admiral's Yarn

1921–1922: A New Look," *Pacific Historical Review*, vol. 46, no. 4 (November 1977). For an extensive discussion, see Emily O. Goldman, *Sunken Treaties: Naval Arms Control between the Wars* (University Park: Pennsylvania State Univ. Press, 1994).

189. The Neutrality Act of 1935 was passed to place an arms embargo on all belligerents, with the 1936 Act adding loans to the original list of embargoed goods. The 1937 act insisted that all trade with belligerents be "cash and carry" and also prohibited Americans from passage on ships of belligerent nations. Each of these laws was passed to avoid the entanglements alleged to have dragged the United States into the First World War.

Chapter XXXVII

190. According to Bauer and Coletta, *United States Navy and Marine Corps Bases, Domestic*, there was hardly anything at San Pedro in the 1920s. There was a submarine repair base, and in 1922 it was used to house destroyers. However, Frank Uhlig's introduction (p. xv) said that the area was growing at this time, confirming Laning's report.

191. In 1844 the USS *Princeton's* great "Peacemaker" gun exploded during a demonstration for dignitaries, killing the Secretaries of State and Navy, a senator who was the father of future first lady Julia Gardner Tyler, as well as a diplomat, a commodore, a servant, and two crew members. Sixty years later, a turret explosion on the battleship *Missouri* killed five officers and thirty-one crew. In 1987, a similar explosion on the battleship *Iowa* killed forty-seven.

Chapter XL

192. As part of the reforms spawned by Secretary of war Elihu Root after the poorly organized 1898 war effort against Spain, the Army War College opened at Fort Leavenworth in 1902. After two years it moved to Washington, D.C. where it remained for nearly half a century at the Washington Barracks. In 1950 it moved back to Fort Leavenworth and the next year to Carlisle Barracks, Penna., where it remains today. See Harry P. Ball, *Of Responsible Command: A History of the U.S. Army War College* (Carlisle Barracks: Alumni Association of the U.S. Army War College, 1983).

193. In June 1923, after six years of planning, the U.S. Naval Training Station, San Diego, was opened on the bay near Balboa Park. At that point, the NTS had facilities to train 1,500 men, either as new recruits or for sixteen-week "boot camp" courses in four fleet schools: Preliminary Radio, Yeomanry, Bugler and Band. In World War II, the facility trained 40,000 people at a time, was redesignated the Naval Training Center, San Diego, and nicknamed "The Cradle of the Navy."

194. Charles Dana, *Two Year's Before the Mast, a personal narrative of life at sea* (New York: A.L. Burt Co., 1840) and Helen Maria Fiske Hunt Jackson, *Ramona: A Story* (Boston: Roberts Brothers, 1884).

Chapter XLI

195. As Chief of Staff, Laning had Captain William D. Puleston as his assistant and Commander H. Kent Hewitt as an aide. The former would soon retire and make his fame as a historian, writing: *Mahan: The Life and Work of Captain Alfred Thayer Mahan* (New Haven: Yale University Press, 1939); *Annapolis: Gangway to Quarterdeck* (New York: D. Appleton-Century, 1942); *The Influence of Sea Power in World War II* (New Haven: Yale Univ. Press, 1947); *The*

Endnotes

Influence of Force in Foreign Relations (New York: Van Nostrand, 1955). Hewitt would remain in the service, eventually rising to the rank of vice admiral, commanding the navy's side of the amphibious landings in North Africa, Sicily, Italy and finally southern France in the Second World War.

196. The Commander in Chief of the Scouting Fleet was Vice Admiral Montgomery M. Taylor. Laning succeeded Rear Admiral G. W. Laws, and his staff included: Lt. M.B. Byington (Aide and Flag Secretary), Lt. J.L. Holloway (Aide and Flag Lieutenant) and Lt. A. J. Detzer (Aide and Division Radio Officer). Battleship Division Two's ships and the captains (outgoing/incoming) were: *Arkansas* [flagship] (A. Bronson/H. Ellis); *Utah* (C.R. Train/W.L. Littlefield); *Florida* (P.F. Boyd/W.R. Sayles); *Oklahoma* (T.A. Kearney/J.F. Hellweg); *Nevada* (H.H. Royall).

Chapter XLII

197. In 1628, John Endicott and others sailed from Weymouth, landing at Naumkeag (now Salem, Mass.) to establish a colony there. Endicott served as governor of Massachusetts for the following two years.

Chapter XLIII

198. After the split of the American Episcopalians from the Church of England during the Revolution, a practice began of the American bishops selecting one, *primus inter pares*, to preside over the new establishment.

199. Lipton (1850–1931) made his first million pounds in a string of grocery shops by 1880 and then became a serious yachtsman, racing successive *Shamrocks* in the America's Cup at Newport, but never winning.

200. The new research department, headed by Captain Wilbur R. Van Auken, kept records and studied all the games played at the War College, later taking on questions of armaments and effectiveness as well as those of grand strategy. It eventually became the Center for Advanced Warfare Studies.

Chapter XLIV

201. The *Massey* case deserves another perspective, such as that provided by Gavan Daws, *Shoal of Time: A History of the Hawaiian Island* (New York: Macmillan, 1968).

Chapter XLVI

202. Two ships of the *Pensacola* class, six of the *Northampton* class, and two of the *Indianapolis* class, built beginning in 1926, were in service by mid-1933. Four of the *Astoria* class were nearing completion; the fifth had been ordered but not yet begun; and the last of the class would be ordered in August 1933. A great many more heavy cruisers, beginning with the transitional *Wichita*, would follow.

203. The House Naval Affairs Committee of the 73rd Congress, 1st session, was comprised of the following Democrats and Republicans, listed by party, then seniority, along with home state. Democrats: Carl Vinson (GA), P.H. Drewry (VA), S.W. Gambrill (MD), J.J. Delaney (NY), F.C. Kniffen (OH), J.O. Fernandez (LA), P.J. Boland (PA), L.W. Schuetz (IL), W.H. Sutpin (NY), J.B. Shannon (MO), W.J. Sears (FL), J.J. McGrath (CA), C.W. Darden (VA), W.D. McFarland (TX), J.H. Burke (CA), M.A. Zioncheck (WA), J.M. O'Connell (RI), L.L. McCardless (HI). Republicans:

An Admiral's Yarn

Fred A. Britten (IL), G.P. Darrow (PA), A.P. Andrew (MA), N.L. Strong (PA), C.D. Millard (NY), G. Burnham (CA), W.L. Higgins (CT), R.R. Eltse (CA).

204. The *Chicago* collided with the S.S. *Silver Palm* of the British Kerr Line (London) on 24 October 1933, some 130 miles south of San Francisco. Chief Pay Clerk John W. Troy and Marine Lieutenant F.S. Chapelle died. Machinist Joseph Ohlens was seriously injured. For one account, see the *New York Times* (25 October 1933).

Chapter XLVII

205. Fleet Problem XV (1934) was the first to involve the entire fleet in a canal transit. See *Annual Report of the Secretary of the Navy, 1934* (Washington: U.S. Government Printing Office, 1934), pp. 10–11.

Chapter XLVIII

206. The *California* was a 32,300-ton battleship (BB44) laid down in 1916 and commissioned in 1921 with twelve 14-inch main guns and an armor belt of 13.5 inches. She was capable of 21 knots and was refitted (1942–1944) after being sunk at Pearl Harbor. *California* earned seven battle stars in World War II.

207. Fleet Problem XVI (1935) centered on Pearl Harbor, and it was the first in which the report of the Secretary of Navy mentions submarines and airplanes: *Annual Report of the Secretary of Navy, 1935* (Washington: U.S. Government Printing Office, 1935), p. 11.

208. Having served a year as Commander, Battle Force, Laning passed the baton to William D. Leahy in April 1936, at which point he reverted to the rank of rear admiral (upper half), the senior rank that a naval officer than could permanently hold.

Chapter XLIX

209. On 30 April 1947, a joint resolution of Congress decreed the name of the dam to be Hoover Dam.

Key for photograph (on page 272) of Naval War College staff and graduating class of May 1923.

Front row: Captain C.S. Kempff, Captain L.R. Sargent, Colonel T.F. Dwyer (CAC), Colonel L.M. Gulick (USMC), Colonel E. D. Scott (FA), Captain W.D. Brotherton, Captain Harris Laning, Captain D.W. Blamer, Rear Admiral W.S. Sims, Captain R.R. Belknap, Colonel W.N. McKelvy (USMC), Captain H.B. Price, Colonel J.F. Madden, (INF), Captain Ralph Earle, Captain T.C. Hart, Captain Willis McDowell.

Second row: Lt. Comdr. T.G. Crapster (USCG), Comdr. Ralph Whitman (CEC), Comdr. R.R. Adams, Comdr. R.F. Dillen, Comdr. R.P. Craft, Comdr. H.A. Baldridge, Captain A.G. Howe, Captain Allen Buchanan, Lt. Comdr. C.E. Van Hook, Colonel A.S. Williams, Comdr. I.C. Johnson, Captain C.P. Nelson, Captain E. S. Jackson, Comdr. Leigh Noyes, Comdr. A.C. Read, Captain W.N. Jeffers.

Third row: Comdr. W. B. Howe, Comdr. W.O. Spears, Captain C.M. Woodward, Captain J.G. Church, Comdr. A.L. Bristol, Comdr. H.R. Stark, Comdr. R.C. MacFall, Comdr. J.T. Bowers, Comdr. W. A. Hall, Comdr. J.A. Randall (MC), Lt. Comdr. W.K. Kilpatrick, Lt. Colonel G.T. Bowman (CAV), Comdr. J.V. Ogan, Lt. Comdr. P.W. Lauriat (USCG), Comdr. J. W. Lewis.

Fourth row: Comdr. S.A. Taffinder, Captain H.C. Curl (MC), Comdr. W.B. Woodson, Comdr. W.C. Stiles, Lt. Colonel T.H. Brown (USMC), Captain W.C. Watts, Comdr. C. W. Nimitz, Comdr. L.B. Anderson, Comdr. R.T. Hanson (CC), Comdr. A.W. Sears, Comdr. D.W. Nesbit (SC), Comdr. D.C. Crowell (SC), Comdr. J.B. Gay.

Omissions: Colonel M.J. Lenihan and Captain F.J. Horne.

Lt (junior grade). Harris Laning, USN, reported for duty as gunnery officer on board the *Dolphin* on 23 July 1902 at Newport, R.I. He detached from the *Dolphin* in Spetember 1905 with orders to report for duty at the Naval Academy at the end of October.

From 1905 to 1907, Lieutenant (junior grade) Harris Laning, USN, served as an inspector in Ordnance and Gunnery at the U.S. Naval Academy, responsible for training cadets in small arms shooting. At the same time, he was captain of the Navy Rifle Team, depicted here competing for the National Trophy. In 1912, as a lieutenant commander, he served as captain of the United States team at the Olympic Games in Stockholm, Sweden.

Harris Laning on a fishing expedition on the Umpqua River in Oregon (1926).

The Commander in Chief, U.S. Fleet and his flag officers, 1934, on board the battleship USS *Pennsylvania*. Seated **front row, left to right**, Vice Admiral Harris Laning, USN, Commander, Cruisers, Scouting Force; Admiral Joseph M. Reeves, USN, Commander, Battle Force, U.S. Fleet; Admiral David F. Sellers, USN, Commander in Chief, U.S. Fleet; Vice Admiral Frank Brumby, USN, Commander, Scouting Force; Vice Admiral Walton Sexton, USN, Commander Battleships, Battle Force.

Philadelphia (July 1934). Vice Admiral and Mrs. Harris Laning; their daughter, Hester; and Secretary of the Navy and Mrs. Claude A. Swanson. A month after the Presidential Fleet Review in New York City, Vice Admiral Laning, as Commander, Cruisers, Scouting Force, brought a squadron of six cruisers to Philadelphia, where he gave the principal address at the Independence Day celebration.

Commander in Chief, U.S. Fleet and his flag officers. **Left to right**, Vice Admiral Thomas T. Craven, USN, Commander, Battleships, Battle Force; Admiral Harris Laning, USN, Commander, Battle Force, U.S. Fleet; Admiral Joseph M. Reeves, USN, Commander in Chief, U.S. Fleet; Vice Admiral Arthur Hepburn, USN, Commander, Scouting Force, U.S. Fleet (who served as Commander in Chief, U.S. Fleet after Admiral Reeves); and Vice Admiral Henry V. Butler, USN, Commander, Aircraft, Battle Force, U.S. Fleet, 1935.

Admiral Harris Laning, USN, (right foreground) commanded the Battle Force in 1935-1936. At the change of command ceremony on 30 March 1936, on board the USS *California*, William D. Leahy (walking next to Admiral Laning) had just been promoted to four stars, having previously served, while vice admiral, as Commander, Battleships, Battle Force. Leahy served in the position for only nine months before becoming Chief of Naval Operations.

Admiral Harris Laning, USN, Commander, Battle Force, U.S. Fleet, 1935-1936.

Admiral Harris Laning, USN, wearing the ribbons for the Navy Cross, Spanish Campaign Medal, the Philippine Campaigns Medal, the Mexican Service Medal, the Dominican Campaign Medal, the China Relief Expeditionary Medal, World War I Victory Medal, and Portugal's Military Order of Aviz.

Admiral Harris Laning, USN, commanding the Battle Force, U.S. Fleet, standing at the stern of his flagship, the battleship *California*. Steaming astern in column open order are the *New York* (nearest), *Oklahoma*, and two of the *New Mexico* class.